Strategic Environmental Assessment

A Sourcebook and Reference Guide to International Experience

Strategic Environmental Assessment

A Sourcebook and Reference Guide to International Experience

Barry Dalal-Clayton and Barry Sadler

London • Sterling, VA

First published by Earthscan in the UK and USA in 2005

ISBN: 1-84407-179-0 paperback
1-84407-178-2 hardback

Typesetting by MapSet Ltd, Gateshead, UK
Printed and bound in the UK by Cromwell Press, Trowbridge
Cover design by Yvonne Booth

For a full list of publications please contact:

Earthscan
8–12 Camden High Street
London, NW1 0JH, UK
Tel: +44 (0)20 7387 8558
Fax: +44 (0)20 7387 8998
Email: earthinfo@earthscan.co.uk
Web: **www.earthscan.co.uk**

22883 Quicksilver Drive, Sterling, VA 20166-2012, USA

Earthscan is an imprint of James and James (Science Publishers) Ltd and publishes in
association with the International Institute for Environment and Development

A catalogue record for this book is available from the British Library

Library of Congress Cataloging-in-Publication Data has been applied for

The views expressed in this resource book are those of the compilers and should not be
taken to represent those of the Organisation for Economic Co-operation and
Development or the United Nations Environment Programme.

Printed on elemental chlorine free paper

Contents

List of Figures, Tables and Boxes

FIGURES

TABLES

BOXES

Preface

Strategic environmental assessment (SEA) of policies, plans and programmes is a rapidly evolving field. New approaches and areas of application are emerging all the time – particularly in the fields of development cooperation and international trade. Despite much recent progress, there is still much to do to make SEA effective and more widely applied.

This review has been prepared in response to these trends and to support recent initiatives to address SEA frameworks and tools that can be applied by international agencies in their work. For example, the Network on Environment and Development Cooperation (ENVIRONET) of the Organisation for Economic Co-operation and Development's Development Assistance Committee (OECD/DAC) has established a task team on the role, scope and contribution of SEA in support of development cooperation. A major objective of this review of international experience is to provide a baseline and reference guide for developing SEA briefing papers, guidance and other outputs under the ENVIRONET work programme.

This review also intends to support a United Nations Environment Programme (UNEP) programme, initiated in 2003, on integrated assessment and planning (IAP) for sustainable development. The programme aims to develop a generic framework for such planning and involves pilot applications and policy experimentation in a number of countries. It builds on earlier UNEP work on an integrated approach to environmental impact assessment (EIA) and SEA and on integrated assessment of trade policies. We anticipate that the IAP framework will become a reference point for a shift towards applying what UNEP initially called 'strategic integrated assessment' or what others call sustainability impact assessment or sustainability appraisal. This 'frontier' end of the SEA spectrum is also a focus for the DAC ENVIRONET Task Team on SEA.

Both the UNEP and OECD/DAC initiatives respond to the changes taking place in the agenda for international development and, in particular, the increasing shift away from individual projects towards policy-based lending and sector-level programming. This transition has placed a new emphasis on approaches and tools for SEA, broadly interpreted. It is an 'upstream' continuation of a larger, decade-long process of mainstreaming environmental and social considerations into development cooperation. Recently there has been a call for more proactive, integrated approaches, notably in the Plan of Implementation of the World Summit on Sustainable Development (WSSD). A review of international experience with SEA is timely to help examine its role and potential in relation to these developments. In this book we cover SEA practice in developed countries, developing countries, countries in transition and development cooperation agencies. The aim has been to draw together information about SEA approaches and cases that illustrate current practice and lessons from experience. This provides baseline material for the work programme of the ENVIRONET Task Team and the UNEP IAP initiative. We hope this will also be of wider interest and help to SEA practitioners and observers. As far as we know, such a broad review has not been attempted so far.

It is apparent that the role and methods of SEA are unclear in some quarters. It is also perceived to be, amongst other things, too difficult, too time-consuming and too costly. In other circumstances various methods have been used to assess environmental dimensions and integrate these in the development of strategies, policies, plans and programmes. But these approaches have not been called SEA and those involved do not necessarily recognize them as a form of SEA.

We take a broad pragmatic view of SEA as comprising a diverse family of approaches that also includes *'para-SEA'* processes – a term we use for processes which do not meet formal definitions of SEA or their specification in law or policy but which have some of their characteristics and elements. The concern is to look at SEA and 'para-SEA' from three perspectives:

1   What is in place in developing and transitional countries, whether applied domestically or in relation to development assistance and lending?
2   How well do these processes and approaches work, especially from the standpoint of addressing the environmental and resource management agenda agreed at the WSSD?
3   Which options and measures could strengthen SEA application in the formulation of policies, plans, programmes, legislation and other higher-level proposals?

The first chapter sets SEA in its international context, whilst Chapter 2 discusses terms, principles, benefits and the evolution of SEA. Chapters 3–6 represent the core of the book and deal with SEA experience and practice in different regions/areas of application. Their structure varies, however. Chapters 3 (developed countries) and 6 (developing countries) are set out on a country-by-country basis. Chapter 4 (development cooperation) is organized into two main sections dealing with multilateral development agencies and bilateral aid agencies. Chapter 5 (countries in transition) is presented in a more thematic manner. This is partly a reflection of different experiences in applying SEA. In the Central and Eastern Europe region and the newly independent states, there has been a focus on regional learning, much helped by the EIA and SEA programme work of the Regional Environmental Center for Central and Eastern Europe (REC), which has enabled sharing and distillation that we have been able to draw upon. Finally, in Chapter 7, we present our conclusions and recommendations and consider future directions and challenges for SEA.

The review presented in this book is intended to provide a sourcebook and reference guide to key trends and issues of SEA, and to the different approaches being used in particular countries and by a range of agencies. Inevitably, the coverage is uneven and varies in extent, depth and tone, reflecting available information and contributions. This book cannot claim to be complete or comprehensive. SEA is a fast-moving field where information quickly becomes dated. As far as possible, we have tried to present the latest position but, inevitably, by the time this review is published, things will have progressed again.

Barry Dalal-Clayton and Barry Sadler
London, UK; and Victoria, BC, Canada
October 2004

Acknowledgements

This book builds on an earlier draft (Dalal-Clayton and Sadler, 1998a), summarized in Dalal-Clayton and Sadler (1998b), which was prepared with financial assistance provided by the Directorate General for International Cooperation (DGIS) of The Netherlands Ministry of Foreign Affairs. A large number of people provided information, suggested contacts or made available case material for the first draft, and grateful thanks are particularly due to the following individuals for information, case materials and comments:

Ron Bisset (Cordah Consultants); Elizabeth Brito (IADB, Washington); Aleg Cherp (Central European University, Budapest); Andriy Demydenko (UNDP Aral Sea Basin Capacity Development Project); Jiri Dusik (Regional Environmental Center for Central and Eastern Europe); Gilberto Gallopin (Stockholm Environment Institute); Jan Joost Kessler (AIDEnvironment, The Netherlands); Nenad Mikulik (State Department of Environment and Nature Protection, Croatia); Parvaiz Naim (IUCN-Pakistan); Nick Robins (IIED); Anna Spencely; Keith Wiseman (Cape Metropolitan Council, South Africa); Professor Chris Wood (EIA Centre, University of Manchester); and Hans van Zijst (Ministry of Housing, Spatial Planning and the Environment, The Netherlands).

Financial support for the updated and completely revised report upon which this book is based was provided by the Royal Norwegian Ministry of Foreign Affairs (MFA) and the United Nations Environment Programme (UNEP). We are particularly grateful to Inger-Marie Bjonness (MFA) for her support and encouragement, to Knut Opsal (NORAD) for technical advice and discussion on the scope of the work and to Hussein Abaza (UNEP) for his support and encouragement.

We are grateful to the following for their contributions:

Kulsum Ahmed and Jean Roger Mercier (World Bank) for helpful comments on SEA experience at the World Bank and edits on the manuscript;
Koassi d'Almeida (University of Quebec) for drafting text on SEA in francophone countries;
Pierre Andre, University of Montreal, for comments on the section on SEA in France;
David Annandale, Murdoch University, Australia, for documents and information on SEA application by multilateral development banks;
Kerstin Arbter (Arbter SEA Consulting and Research) and Ralf Aschemann (Austrian Institute for the Development of Environmental Assessment), for information on SEA application in Austria;

Gideon Asfaw (Project Manager, Nile Transboundary Environmental Action Project) for reviewing the Nile Basin Initiative case study;

Ralf Aschemann (Austrian Institute for the Development of Environmental Assessment) for reviewing the section on Austria;

John Ashe (Consultant) for information on SEA in Australia;

Michelle Audoin (CSIR, South Africa) for comments and SEA materials;

Leyli Bektashi (University of Manchester) for information on SEA in the Russian Federation, Azerbaijan and Slovakia;

Elizabeth Brito (Inter-American Development Bank) for information on SEA in Latin America;

Susie Brownlie (South Africa) for information on spatial development frameworks;

Aleg Cherp (Central European University, Budapest) for contributions to Chapter 5;

Eben Chonguica (Southern Africa Regional Office of the World Conservation Union) for checking the section on Zimbabwe;

Ray Clark (US) for information on SEA in the US;

Peter Croal (CIDA) for suggested text on the role of donors in promoting SEA in developing countries;

Holger Dalkmann (Wuppertal Institute) for reviewing the section on SEA use in Germany;

Jenny Dixon (Department of Planning, University of Auckland) for information on the Resource Management Act and SEA in New Zealand;

Sean Doolan, Jon Hobbs, Claire Ireland, Angus Mackay, Jean Paul Penrose and John Warburton (UK Department for International Development) for information on SEAs supported by DFID;

Jiri Dusik (Regional Environmental Center for Central and Eastern Europe) for contributions to Chapter 5;

Gerard Early (Department of the Environment and Heritage, Canberra) for information on SEA in Australia;

Paulo Eglar (Brazilian Academy of Sciences);

Kerstin Ehrhardt (German Federal Ministry of the Environment) for comments on SEA in Germany;

Anders Ekbom (University of Göteborg, Sweden) for editing the section on Sida;

Thomas Fischer (University of Liverpool, UK) for contributing text on SEA in Germany, and for helpful comments on the first draft of the report on which this book is based;

Dora Fu (Sustainable Development Unit, Hong Kong) for information on the Computer-aided Sustainability Evaluation Tool;

Richard Fuggle (University of Cape Town) for comments on SEA in South Africa;

Petrie van Gent (Netherlands Commission for EIA) for editing the section on The Netherlands;

Clive George (University of Manchester) for information on sustainability impact assessment of WTO multilateral trade negotiations;

Linda Ghanime (United Nations Development Programme) for reviewing the section on SEA use by UNDP;

Helene Gichenje (Canadian International Development Agency) for edits to the section on CIDA;

Domingos Gove (Centre for Sustainable Development for Coastal Zones, Mozambique) for information on SEA in Mozambique and Case Study 6.2;

Kogi Govender (CSIR Environmentek, South Africa) for comments on the manuscript and information on SEA in Mozambique;

Fabien Harel for providing information on SEA use in France;

Liichiro Hayashi (Mitsubishi Research Institute) for information on SEA in Japan;

Stuart Heather-Clark (CSIR Environmentek, South Africa) for a case study of SEA of the Port of Cape Town;

Mikael Hildén (Finnish Environment Institute) for reviewing the section on Finland;

Astrid Hillers (World Bank) for information on the Nile Basin Initiative;

David Howlett (DFID/UNDP) for information on SEA in Tanzania;

Emma Kambewa for information on EA in Malawi;

Kagiso Keatimilwe (CSIR Environmentek, South Africa) for contributing to the section on Botswana;

Jan Joost Kessler (AIDEnvironment, The Netherlands) for drafting text on the SEAN methodology and for comments on the draft text;

Bothepa Kgabung (University of Botswana) for contributing to the section on Botswana;

Sue Lane and Robin Carter (South Africa) for an SEA case study (6.9);

Young-Joon Lee (Korea Environment Institute) for information on the PES system in Korea;

Themb'a Mahlaba (University of Swaziland) for information on SEA in Swaziland;

Matt McIntyre (South Pacific Regional Environment Programme, Samoa) for information on SEA in the South Pacific;

Joseph Milewski (IADB) for information on SEA experience at the Inter-American Development Bank;

Julian Mlangeni for information on SEA in Swaziland;

Bore Moptsamai for information on SEA in Lesotho;

Mushibeyi Muliya (Department of Roads, Zambia) for information on SEA in Zambia;

Felicidade Munguambe (Ministry for Coordination of Environmental Affairs, Mozambique) for information on SEA in Mozambique;

Professor Raphael Mwalyosi (Institute of Resource Assessment, University of Dar es Salaam) for information on SEA in Tanzania and case studies;

Peter Nelson (Land Use Consultants, Bristol, UK) for information on SEA of the Ghana PRSP and on the sustainability test;

Maria Partidário (New University of Lisbon) for providing a review of experience with SEA in Portugese- and Spanish-speaking countries;

Stephanie Pfahl (Adelphi-consult) for suggested text on the integrative function of SEA;

Nigel Rossouw (CSIR Environmentek, South Africa) for updating the section on SEA in South Africa;

Urszula Rzeszot (Institute of Environmental Assessment, Warsaw) for Case Study 5.2;

Steve Smith (Scott Wilson Kirkpatrick consultants, UK) for revising the section on SEA in the UK;

Aboulaye Sene for information on SEA in Sénégal;

Eugene Shannon (African Development Bank) for information on ADB activities on SEA;

Bill Sheate (Imperial College, University of London) for permission to quote work that he and colleagues led on SEA in the European Union;

Peter Tarr and Gudrun Denker (Southern African Institute for Environmental Assessment) for organizing a regional workshop on SEA in Southern Africa, and for contributing text and case studies on SEA in Namibia;

Dewi Utami (Asian Development Bank) for information on SEA experience at ADB;

Rob Verheem (EIA Commission, The Netherlands) for information on SEA in The Netherlands and for Box 3.18;

Bryony Walmsley (WSP Walmsley consultants, South Africa) for Case Study 6.8;

Martin Ward (New Zealand) for comments on the text;

Mike Warren, Dirk Versfeld, Obed Baloyi and Gavin Quibell (Department of Water Affairs and Forestry, South Africa) for information on SEA for water use;

Edward Zulu (National Environment Council, Zambia) for information on SEA in Zambia.

The following provided information on SEA in Spanish- and Portugese-speaking countries:

Olivia Bina (Cambridge University, UK);

Miguel Carballo (Guatemala);

Maria João Coelho (New University of Lisbon);

Juan Carlos Garcia de Brigard (Colombia);

Fernando Garrote Garcia (Universidad Politecnica de Madrid, Spain);

Lídia Biazzi Lu (Tetraplan, Brazil);

Joseph Maria Mallarach (Higher-Education Studies in Olot, Catalunya, Spain);

Claudia Perazza (Inter-American Development Bank);

Rosa Maria Arce Ruiz (Madrid University, Spain);

Arcindo dos Santos (Inter-American Development Bank);

Izabella Teixeira (Federal University of Rio de Janeiro, Brazil); and

Custódio Voabil (Ministry of Environment and SEACAM, Mozambique).

Grateful thanks must also be extended to the participants of two regional SEA workshops that fed into the preparation of this book: first, a workshop was held in Windhoek, Namibia (13–16 May 2003) hosted by the Southern Africa Institute for Environmental Assessment (SAIEA); and second, a workshop was held in Szentendere, Hungary (28–30 April 2003) hosted by the Regional Environmental Center for Central and Eastern Europe (REC). Specific individual contributions from these workshops are acknowledged earlier in this section.

We would like to acknowledge the contributions of the members of the OECD/DAC ENVIRONET Task Team on SEA (see Box A) and the Steering Group of the UNEP Initiative on Integrated Assessment and Planning (see Box B).

Finally, we are very grateful to Rob Verheem (EIA Commission, The Netherlands) and to Professor Chris Wood (University of Manchester) for reviewing and critiquing the final manuscript. If we have inadvertently failed to acknowledge anyone who has helped us in this work, we are sincerely sorry. Needless to say, all errors of omission and commission are our responsibility.

Box A OECD/DAC ENVIRONET Task Team on SEA (as of October 2004)

a ENVIRONET members

Chairperson:	Jon Hobbs (DFID)
Vice Chairperson:	Linda Ghanime (UNDP)
Kulsum Ahmed	World Bank
Tomas Andersson	Sida
Steve Bass	DFID
Inger-Marie Bjonness	Ministry of Foreign Affairs, Norway
Georg Caspary	OECD
Miriam Ciscar	AECS, Spain
Etienne Coyette	EC-DG Environment
Naïg Cozannet	Agence Française de Développement
Arnold Jacques de Dixmude	Ministry of Foreign Affairs, Belgium
Anders Ekbom	University of Göteborg/Sida
Jouko Eskelinen	Ministry of Foreign Affairs, Finland
Joseph Gamperl	KfW, Germany
Helene Gichenje	CIDA
Jill Hanna	EC-DG Environment
Kaoru Kanoyashi	Japan
Laura Lee	UNDP
Simon Le-Grand	EC-DG Environment
Tamara Levine	CIDA
Harald Lossack	GTZ, Germany
Jean Roger Mercier	World Bank
Matti Nummelin	Ministry of Foreign Affairs, Finland
Remi Paris	OECD
Stephan Paulus	GTZ, Germany
Merete Pedersen	DANIDA
Jan Riemer	DANIDA
Jan-Peter Schemmel	GTZ, Germany
Ellen Shipley	DFAT, Australia
Daniel Slunge	University of Göteborg/Sida
Kojma Takeharu	Japan
Elsbeth Tarp	DANIDA
Rob van den Boom	DGIS, The Netherlands
Francoise Villete	EC-DG Environment
Bob Weir	CIDA

b Other members

Hussein Abaza	UNEP
Charles Arden-Clarke	UNEP
Elizabeth Brito	IADB
Peter Croal	SAIEA, Namibia/CIDA
Jiri Dusik	Regional Environmental Center for Central and Eastern Europe, Hungary

David Hanrahan	World Bank
David Howlett	UNDP, Tanzania
James Leaton	WWF, UK
Andrew McCoubray	DFID, Kenya
Richard McNally	DFID, UK
Jean-Paul Penrose	DFID, UK
Elizabeth Smith	EBRD
Peter Tarr	SAIEA, Namibia
Alex Weaver	CSIR, South Africa
Gregory Woodsworth	UNDP

c SEA specialists

David Annandale	Murdoch University, Australia
John Horberry	ERM Consultants, UK
Peter Nelson	Land Use Consultants, UK
Barry Sadler	Consultant, Canada
Steve Smith	Scott Wilson Consultants, UK
Rob Verheem	EIA Commission, The Netherlands

d Technical Secretariat

Barry Dalal-Clayton	International Institute for Environment and Development, London

Task Team website: www.seataskteam.net

BOX B STEERING GROUP OF UNEP INITIATIVE ON INTEGRATED ASSESSMENT AND PLANNING

Hussein Abaza	UNEP, Switzerland
Nurul Amin	Asian Institute of Technology, Thailand
Laurent Bardon	European Commission, Brussels
Ron Bisset	BMT Cordah Environmental Management Consultants, Scotland
Dieudonné Bitondo	Association Cameronnaire pour l'Evaluation Environmentale
Nick Bonvoisin	United Nations Economic Commission for Europe, Switzerland
Elizabeth Brito	Inter-American Development Bank, US
Nuria Castells	United Nations Conference on Trade and Development
Mark Curtis	McGill University, Canada
Barry Dalal-Clayton	IIED, London
Carlos Dora	World Health Organization, Switzerland
Jiri Dusik	Regional Environmental Center for Central and Eastern Europe, Hungary
Thomas B. Fischer	University of Liverpool, UK
Henk B. M. Hilderink	GLEAM (RIVM), The Netherlands
Jan Joost Kessler	AIDEnvironment, The Netherlands
Marina V. Khotuleva	Ecoline EA Centre, Russia
Colin Kirkpatrick	University of Manchester, UK
Kin Che Lam	Chinese University of Hong Kong
Nicolas Lucas	Millennium Ecosystem Assessment, US
Patrick Mendis	WWF International, Switzerland
Jean-Roger Mercier	World Bank, Washington, US
Konrad von Moltke	International Institute for Sustainable Development, US
Rachid Nafti	CITET, Tunisia
Sarah Richardson	Maeander Enterprises, Canada
Barry Sadler	Consultant, Canada
Abdoulaye Sene	Universite Cheikh Anta Diop de Dakar, Sénégal
Salah el Serafy	Consultant, US
Fuali Sheng	Conservation International, US
Mathew Stilwell	Legal Counsel
Robert The	World Trade Organization, Switzerland
Eliécer Vargas	Centro Agronomico Tropical de Investigación y Ensenanza (CATIE), Costa Rica
Rob Verheem	EIA Commission, The Netherlands
Zhijia Wang	UNEP, Nairobi
Claudia S. de Windt	Inter-American Forum on Environmental Law (FIDA), US
Gregory Woodsworth	UNDP, Kenya
Suh Sung Yoon	Korean Environment Institute

List of Acronyms and Abbreviations

ABE	Agence Béninoise pour l'Environnement (Bénin Environment Agency)
ADB	Asian Development Bank
AEE	assessment of environmental effects
AfDB	African Development Bank
ALARP	as low as reasonably practicable
AMDAL	*analisis mengenai dampak lingkungan* (EIA approach)
ANSEA	analytical strategic environmental assessment
APEIS	Asia-Pacific Environmental Innovation Strategy
ASE	*analyses stratégique de l'environnement* (strategic environmental analyses)
BATNEEC	best available technology not entailing excessive cost
BET	business effects test
BMU	German Federal Ministry for Environment
BMVWP	Ministry of Transport, Building and Housing (Germany)
BNDES	National Development Bank
BOMEDCO	Border Metropolitan Development Corporation, South Africa
BPA	Bonneville Power Administration, US
BPEO	best practicable environmental option
B-T	biodiversity-tourism
CAMP	Catchment Management and Poverty Alleviation (DFID programme)
CAP	country assistance plan
CAR	comprehensive, adequate and representative
CAS	country assistance strategy
CBA	cost–benefit analysis
CBD	Convention on Biological Diversity
CBO	community-based organization
CCA	common country assessment
CCI	cross-cutting issues
CCLIP	Conditional Credit Line for Investment Projects
CDR	Council for Development and Reconstruction, Lebanon
CDS-ZC	Centre for Sustainable Development for Coastal Zones, Mozambique
CEA	country environmental analysis/assessment cumulative environmental assessment
CEAA	Canadian Environmental Assessment Agency

CEC	Commission of the European Community
CEE	Central and Eastern Europe
CEEPA	The Centre for Environmental Economics and Policy in Africa, University of Pretoria, South Africa
CENR	country environmental review
CEO	chief executive officer
CEP	Copperbelt Environmental Project, Zambia
CEPEL	Centre of Research for Electric Energy, Brazil
CEQ	Council on Environmental Quality, US
CGIAR	Consultative Group of International Agriculture Centres
CH_4	methane
CIDA	Canadian International Development Agency
CIT	countries in transition
CITET	Tunis International Centre for Environmental Technologies
CLEIAA	Capacity Learning for EIA in Africa
CMA	catchment management agency
CMS	catchment management strategy
CO	carbon monoxide
CO_2	carbon dioxide
CONAMA	Comisión Nacional del Medio Ambiente, Chile
CONDES	National Council for Sustainable Development, Mozambique
CONNEPP	consultative national environmental policy process
COSS	country operational strategy studies
CP	country programme
CPC	Communist Party of China
CPD	country programme document
CPERs	*contrats de plan état–régions* (state–regions planning contracts)
CRA	comprehensive regional assessment
CSIR	Council for Scientific and Industrial Research, South Africa
CSP	country strategy plan/programme
DAC	Development Assistance Committee (of the OECD)
DANCED	Danish Development Agency (now part of DANIDA)
DANIDA	Danish International Development Agency
DDA	Doha Development Agenda
DEA	Department of Environmental Affairs, Namibia
DEAP	district environmental action plan
DEAT	Department of Environmental Affairs and Tourism, South Africa
DEFRA	Department for Environment, Food and Rural Affairs, UK
DENR	Department of Environment and Natural Resources, Dominican Republic
DETR	Department of Environment, Transport and the Regions, UK
DFAIT	Department of Foreign Affairs and International Trade, Canada
DFID	Department for International Development, UK

DGIS	Directorate General for International Cooperation, The Netherlands Ministry of Foreign Affairs
DMC	developing member country (of the Asian Development Bank)
DMEE	Danish Ministry of Energy and Environment
DoE	Department of Environment, UK
DoIR	Department of Industry and Resources, Australia
DPCA-I	Provincial Directorate for Coordination of Environmental Affairs of Inhambane, Mozambique
DPL	development policy lending
DSS	decision support system
DTI	Department of Trade and Industry, UK
DWAF	Department of Water Affairs and Forestry, South Africa
EA	environmental assessment
EAC	Environmental Audit Committee, UK
EAP	environmental action plan
	Environmental Action Programme for Central and Eastern Europe
EBRD	European Bank for Reconstruction and Development
EC	European Commission
	European Community
E-c-E	economic-cum-environmental (planning)
ECMT	European Conference of Ministers of Transport
ECO ASIA	Environment Congress for Asia and the Pacific
ECON	Norwegian Centre for Economic Analysis
ECZ	Environmental Council of Zambia
EEA	European Environment Agency
EER	energy and environment review
EIA	environmental impact assessment
EIA^3	environmental, economic and equity impact assessments
EIS	environmental impact statement
EMA	Environmental Management Act, Malawi
EMG	environmental management guideline
EMP	environmental management plan/programme
ENVIRONET	Network on Environment and Development Cooperation
EO	environmental overview
EP	energy policy
EPA	Environmental Protection Agency, Ghana/US
	Environmental Protection Authority, Western Australia
EPBC	Environmental Protection and Biodiversity Conservation
EP-CR	Energy Policy of the Czech Republic
EPIP	Environmental Protection (Impact of Proposals)
ES	ecosystem services
ESE	environmental, social and economic
ESFM	ecologically sustainable forest management
ESMAP	Energy Sector Management Assistance Programme (of the World Bank)

ESW	economic and sector work
E-test	environmental test (The Netherlands)
ETOA	environmental threats and opportunities assessment
ETP	Provincial Technical Team, Mozambique
EU	European Union
EWI	Ecosystem Well-being Index
FAO	Food and Agriculture Organization (of the United Nations)
FCT	feasibility and compliance test
FEARO	Federal Environmental Assessment Review Office, Canada
FEDER	Fonds Européen de Developpement Régional
FTIP	Federal Transport Infrastructure Plan, Germany
FY	fiscal year
GDP	gross domestic product
GEF	Global Environment Facility
GEMP	generic environmental management programme
GEO	Global Environmental Outlook (project)
GIS	geographical information system
GJ	giga joules
GM	'green minister'
GMA	game management area
GMP	general management plan
GMS	Greater Mekong Sub-region
GPRS	Ghana Poverty Reduction Strategy
GSA	General Services Agency, US
GWD	Great Western Development (Strategy), China
HIA	health impact assessment
HWI	Human Well-being Index
IA	integrated assessment
IADB	Inter-American Development Bank
IAIA	International Association for Impact Assessment
IAP	integrated assessment and planning
IBRD	International Bank for Reconstruction and Development
ICARM	integrated coastal area and river basin management
ICCON	International Consortium for Cooperation on the Nile
ICMP	integrated corridor management plan
IDASA	Institute for Democracy in South Africa
IDP	integrated development plan
IDPM	Institute for Development Policy and Management
IDZ	industrial development zone
IEA	integrated ecosystem assessment
IEE	initial environmental examination
IEM	integrated environmental management
IGBP	International Geosphere Biosphere Programme
IHDP	International Human Dimensions Programme on Global Environmental Change
IIED	International Institute for Environment and Development

IMF	International Monetary Fund
IMSSA	Independent Mediation Services of South Africa
INS	Immigration and Naturalization Service, US
IPA	integrated policy appraisal
IPAT	integrated programming and assessment tool
IPCC	Intergovernmental Panel on Climate Change
IPP	independent power plant
I-PRSP	interim poverty reduction strategy paper
IPTs	*instrumentos de planificación territorial* (land use planning instruments)
ISPP	integrated spatial development planning process
ITA	integrated trade assessment
IUCN	World Conservation Union
IUCN-ROSA	World Conservation Union – Regional Office for Southern Africa
JSA	joint staff assessment
LCA	life cycle analysis
LDD	local development document
LDF	local development framework
LFA	logical framework analysis
LHDA	Lesotho Highlands Development Authority
LHWP	Lesotho Highlands Water Project
LUP	land use plan
MA	Millennium Ecosystem Assessment
MAC	management advisory committee
MAWRD	Ministry of Agriculture, Water and Rural Development, Namibia
MDB	multilateral development bank
MDGs	Millennium Development Goals
MDMA	Marine Diamond Mines Association, South Africa
MDP	municipality development plan
MECIE	*Mise en Comptabilité des Investissements avec l'Environnement*
MET	Ministry of Environment and Tourism, Namibia
METAP	Mediterranean Environmental Technical Assistance Programme
MFA	Ministry of Foreign Affairs
MFMR	Ministry of Fisheries and Marine Resources, Namibia
MFPED	Ministry of Finance Planning and Economic Development, Uganda
MICOA	Ministry for Coordination of Environmental Affairs, Mozambique
MLD	Ministry for Local Development, Nepal
MMSD	Mining, Minerals and Sustainable Development project
MNR	Ministry of Natural Resources, Russian Federation
MoE	Ministry of Environment, France/Slovakia

MoPE	Ministry of Population and Environment, Nepal
MRC	Mekong River Commission
MZP	management zone plan
NBI	Nile Basin Initiative
NDP	national development plan
NDPC	National Development Planning Commission
NDSS	negotiation and decision support system
NEAP	national environmental action plan
NEMA	National Environmental Management Act, South Africa
	National Environment Management Authority, Uganda
NEMC	National Environmental Management Council, Tanzania
NEP	National Environment Plan, Austria
NEPA	National Environmental Policy Act, US
NEPAD	New Economic Partnership for African Development
NEPP	National Environmental Policy Plan, The Netherlands
NEQS	national environmental quality standard
NFPS	national forest policy statement
NGO	non-governmental organization
NH_3	ammonia
NI	Northern Ireland
Nile-COM	Nile Basin Initiative Commission
Nile-SEC	Nile Basin Initiative Secretariat
Nile-TAC	Nile Basin Initiative Technical Advisory Committee
NIS	newly independent states (of the former Soviet Union)
NLS	national-level screening
NOx	nitrogen oxides
NPA	National Ports Authority, South Africa
NPC	National Planning Commission, Nepal
NPCS	National Planning Commission Secretariat
NSDS	national sustainable development strategy
NT	New Territories, Hong Kong
NTC	National Tourism Council
NWA	National Water Act, South Africa
NWBM	National Water Balance Model, South Africa
NWRS	National Water Resource Strategy, South Africa
NZAID	Government of New Zealand
OAS	Organization of American States
OD	operational directive
ODPM	Office of the Deputy Prime Minister, UK
OECD	Organisation for Economic Co-operation and Development
OKACOM	Okavango River Basin Commission, Botswana
OP/BP	operational policy/bank procedure (World Bank)
OVOS	assessment of environmental impacts (Soviet Union process)
PA	policy appraisal
	protected area
PAC	*plan d'action communautaire* (community action plan)

PAE	Policy Appraisal and the Environment, UK
PAP/RAC	Priority Actions Programme Activity Centre (of the Mediterranean Action Plan)
PCB	polychlorinated biphenols
PCP	planning and compulsory purchase
PDR	People's Democratic Republic
PEA	programmatic environmental assessment
PEAP	Poverty Eradication Action Plan, Uganda
PEIA	preliminary environmental impact assessment
PEIS	programmatic environmental impact statement
PER	prior environmental review
	public environmental expert review
PES	preliminary environmental scan
PIA	policy impact assessment
PICs	Pacific Island Countries
PMA	Plan for Modernization of Agriculture, Uganda
PMO	Prime Minister's Office
POE	point of entry
PPA	participatory poverty assessment
PPEA	participatory poverty and environment assessment
PPP	policies, plans and programmes
PRC	People's Republic of China
PRS	poverty reduction strategy
PRSP	poverty reduction strategy paper
PRSP-PR	poverty reduction strategy paper progress report
PSAL	private sector adjustment loan
PSD	programme support document
PSDU	Poverty Reduction and Sustainable Development Unit
PSIA	poverty and social impact analysis
PSIP	private sector investment programme
PST-II	Second Transport Sector Programme, Sénégal
PUMA	Planning and Urban Management Act, Samoa
RAC	Resource Assessment Commission
RDEIA	regional development environmental impact assessment
RDPs	regional and rural development plans
REA	regional environmental assessment
REC	Regional Environmental Center for Central and Eastern Europe
REDSO	Regional Economic Development Services Office (of USAID)
REF	Regional Economic Forum, KwaZulu-Natal
RFA	regional forest agreement
RIA	regulatory impact assessment
RIAS	regulatory impact analysis statement
RISPO	research on innovative and strategic policy options
RIVM	National Institute for Public Health and the Environment, The Netherlands
RMA	Resource Management Act, New Zealand

RMC	regional member country (of the African Development Bank)
RRCAP	Regional Resource Centre for Asia and the Pacific
RTZ	Rio Tinto Zinc
RUL	Rössing Uranium Limited
SA	sustainability appraisal/assessment
SADC	Southern African Development Community
SAIEA	Southern African Institute for Environmental Assessment
SAL	structural adjustment loan
SAP	strategic action plan
SAPO	South African Port Operations
SAR	Special Administrative Region
SCDP	Sustainable Community Development Programme, Nepal
SCEP	State Committee of Environmental Protection, Russian Federation
SCOPE	Scientific Committee on Problems of the Environment, France
SDAN	Sustainable Development Agenda for Nepal
SDF	spatial development framework
SDI	spatial development initiative
SDU	Sustainable Development Unit, UK
SEA	sectoral environmental analysis/assessment
	strategic effects assessment
	strategic environmental assessment
SEACAM	Secretariat for Eastern African Coastal Area Management, Mozambique
SEAN	Strategic Environmental Analysis
SEF	strategic environmental framework
SEIA	strategic environmental impact assessment, The Netherlands
SEP	strategic environmental planning
SEPA	State Environmental Protection Administration, China
SER	state environmental review (also known as 'state ecological expertise') (Soviet Union process)
SFRA	stream flow reduction activity
SHD	sustainable human development
SIA	social/strategic/sustainability/impact assessment
Sida	Swedish International Development Cooperation Agency
SIDS	small island developing states
SNV	Netherlands Development Organisation
SO	strategic objective/overview
SO_2	sulphur dioxide
SOE	state of the environment
SOER	state of the environment report(ing)
SOP	sectoral operational programme
SPREP	South Pacific Regional Environment Programme
SRU	Solidarité et Renouvellement Urbain
SVP	Shared Vision Programme (of the Nile Basin Initiative)
SWAP	sector-wide approach
SWOT	strengths, weaknesses, opportunities and threats

TA	technical assistance
TANAPA	Tanzania National Parks
TBT	Tofo, Barra, Tofinho and Rocha (Beaches area), Mozambique
TCG	The Clark Group, US
TDP	tourism development plan
TDS	territorial development strategy
TEA	transboundary environmental assessment (project of the Nile Basin Initiative)
TEN	Trans-European Transport Net
TerKSOP	territorial integrated scheme for nature protection, Soviet Union
TOR	terms of reference
TRAC	target for resources assignment from the core
TRIPS	trade-related aspects of intellectual property rights
UDP	unitary development plan
UK	United Kingdom
UN	United Nations
UNCED	UN Conference on Environment and Development
UNCTAD	UN Commission on Trade and Development
UNDAF	UN Development Assistance Framework
UNDESA	UN Department for Environmental and Social Affairs
UNDP	UN Development Programme
UNECE	UN Economic Commission for Europe
UNEP	UN Environment Programme
UNEP-WCMC	UNEP-World Conservation Monitoring Centre, UK
UNESCO	UN Educational, Scientific and Cultural Organization
UPPAP	Uganda Participatory Poverty Assessment Project
US	United States
USAID	United States Agency for International Development
WB	World Bank
WBCSD	World Business Council for Sustainable Development
WCD	World Commission on Dams
WCED	World Commission on Environment and Development
WEHAB	water, energy, health, agriculture and biodiversity
WMA	water management area
WMP	waste management plan
WRAP	Water Resources Action Plan, Zambia
WRI	World Resources Institute
WSSD	World Summit on Sustainable Development (Johannesburg, 2002)
WTO	World Trade Organization
WWF	World Wide Fund for Nature
WWF-SPP	World Wide Fund for Nature – South Pacific Programme
ZAMSIF	Zambia Social Investment Programme
ZCCM	Zambia Consolidated Copper Mines

Chapter 1

SEA in International Perspective

The term 'strategic environmental assessment' (SEA) is now widely used to refer to a systematic process of analysing the environmental effects of policies, plans and programmes. Often, this process is equated with a formal procedure based on environmental impact assessment (EIA), as exemplified by the European SEA Directive (Directive 2001/42/EC), which came into force in July 2004 across the European Union (EU). However, for the purposes of this review, we consider the field of SEA to be much broader and to encompass a range of policy tools and strategic approaches as well as formal EIA-based procedures and near-equivalent forms of environmental appraisal. The boundaries of the field are mapped generically by reference to the function of SEA as a means of integrating environmental considerations into development policy-making and planning (which also are broadly considered).

Within this frame of reference, different types of SEA can be recognized, although some are at an early stage of development (Figure 1.1). These include forms of 'para-SEA', a term we use for processes that do not meet formal definitions of SEA or their specification in law or policy but which have some of their characteristics and elements. At present, few developing countries have established formal arrangements for SEA of policies, plans or programmes, but a growing number apply SEA-type processes and elements of SEA. There is also increasing use of a family of para-SEA tools to 'mainstream the environment' in international lending and development. Here, a more strategic agenda is emerging, characterized by a greater focus on policy and programme delivery.

Depending on the jurisdiction or circumstances, SEA may also consider social and economic effects. Their inclusion as a matter of principle is widely supported in the literature on the field and, increasingly, SEA is seen as an entry point or stepping stone to integrated assessment or sustainability appraisal. A holistic, cross-sectoral approach to the implementation of sustainable development is promoted throughout the Plan of Implementation agreed at the World Summit on Sustainable Development (WSSD), although what this approach entails is not spelled out. But there are numerous statements and recommendations on the development and use of policy tools and measures to strengthen development decision-making at all levels. These include explicit reference to EIA and integrated assessment and implicit

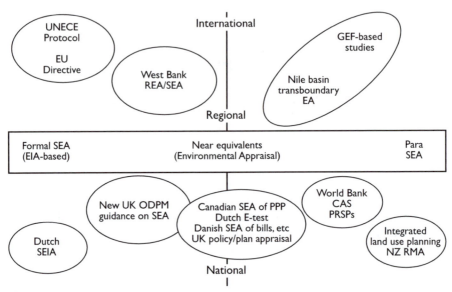

Notes:
Formal: prescribed in international or national EIA-type instruments
Near-equivalent: of environmental appraisal of policies/laws: and broader SEA-type processes/methods
Para-SEA: don't meet formal specifications or strict definitions; but share some characteristics or
elements and have some overall purpose

Figure 1.1 *Typology of SEA approaches*

reference to SEA, for example in the context of strengthening methodologies in support of policy and strategy (see Box 1.1).

In this context, national sustainable development strategies (NSDS) are of particular interest. All countries are requested to prepare them by 2005 under the 2002 WSSD Plan of Implementation (www.un.org/esa/sustdev/documents/ WSSD_POI_PD). They are in place already in some countries and in preparation in others. SEA and NSDS are related and mutually supportive instruments. First, the process of strategy preparation includes para-SEA elements such as evaluation of the state of the environment and identification of the critical trends and issues that require policy responses. Second, the NSDS provides a key framework for giving effect to SEA and more integrative approaches and particular attention is given to this relationship in this review (see OECD/DAC, 2001; and OECD/UNDP, 2002).

There is now considerable international interest in SEA with differing opinions and increasing debate about its nature and scope. Frequent conferences and workshops are held on the subject, and the literature on SEA is growing exponentially. An emerging theme of international debate concerns the applicability of SEA in developing countries, particularly with regard to the development and implementation of strategies for sustainable development and for poverty reduction. There is increasing demand for information and training on SEA. This outstrips supply despite the growing number and range of guidance materials and capacity-building programmes.

Box 1.1 References to EIA and integrated assessment in the WSSD Plan of Implementation

EIA

Para 19 Encourage relevant authorities at all levels to take sustainable development considerations into account in decision-making, including on national and local development planning, investment in infrastructure, business development and public procurement. This would include actions at all levels to:

(e) *Use environmental impact assessment procedures.*

Para 36 Improve the scientific understanding and assessment of marine and coastal ecosystems as a fundamental basis for sound decision-making, through actions at all levels to:

(c) Build capacity in marine science, information and management, through, inter alia, promoting the *use of environmental impact assessments* and environmental evaluation and reporting techniques, for projects or activities that are potentially harmful to the coastal and marine environments and their living and non-living resources.

Para 62 Achieving sustainable development includes actions at all levels to:

(h) Provide financial and technical support to strengthen the capacity of African countries to undertake environmental legislative policy and institutional reform for sustainable development and to *undertake environmental impact assessments* and, as appropriate, to negotiate and implement multilateral environment agreements.

Para 135 Develop and *promote the wider application of environmental impact assessments*, inter alia, as a national instrument, as appropriate, to provide essential decision-support information on projects that could cause significant adverse effects to the environment.

Integrated assessment

Para 15 [Re: accelerating the shift towards sustainable consumption and production ... all countries should take action ... at all levels to]:

(a) Identify specific activities, tools, policies, measures and monitoring and *assessment mechanisms*, including, where appropriate, life-cycle analysis and national indicators for measuring progress, bearing in mind that standards applied by some countries may be inappropriate and of unwarranted economic and social cost to other countries, in particular developing countries.

Para 40 [Re: implementation of an integrated approach to increasing food production ... action should be taken] at all levels to:

(b) Develop and implement integrated land management and water-use plans that are based on sustainable use of renewable resources and on *integrated assessments of socioeconomic and environmental potentials*, and strengthen the capacity of governments, local authorities and communities to monitor and manage the quantity and quality of land and water resources.

Para 136 *Promote and further develop methodologies at policy, strategy and project levels for sustainable development decision-making* at the local and national levels, and where relevant at the regional level. In this regard, emphasize that the choice of the appropriate methodology to be used in countries should be adequate to their country-specific conditions and circumstances, should be on a voluntary basis and should conform to their development priority needs.

SEA is not referred to specifically in the WSSD Plan of Implementation, but it is implied, for example in Sub-section 136.

Source: Plan of Implementation, World Summit on Sustainable Development, final version, 24 March 2003 (www.un.org/esa/sustdev/documents/WSSD_POI_PD)

Many see this relationship simply as one of transferring the current approach to SEA from the North to the South. This occurs, for example, through the application of World Bank procedures and practices by borrowing and client countries and the design and delivery of training and capacity-building programmes. The revised edition of the UN Environment Programme (UNEP) environmental impact assessment (EIA) training resource manual indicates that these programmes are still supply-motivated rather than needs-based (Sadler and McCabe, 2002). This calls into question whether SEA, as currently conceived and promoted, is necessarily an appropriate model for developing countries to adopt and adapt to their context and circumstances. There are arguments for and against this course of action. But, currently, this debate lacks a broader context and a larger range of alternatives that might be entertained.

This issue has become more pressing with the introduction of international legal frameworks for SEA, particularly the European SEA Directive (2001/42/EC) and the SEA Protocol to the UN Economic Commission for Europe (UNECE) Convention on EIA in a Transboundary Context (agreed at Kiev in 2003). Both instruments prescribe an EIA-based procedure for SEA that draws heavily on the earlier European EIA Directive (1997/00/EC). Many observers expect the SEA Directive and the SEA Protocol to become international reference standards, certainly within the sphere of influence of the EU and its aid and assistance activities. The SEA Protocol is based on the Directive and will be open to signatory countries beyond the UNECE region. Over time, it may become a global instrument or a catalyst for other regions to establish their own multilateral framework.

Against this background, the rationale for undertaking a critical review and reappraisal of international experience with SEA comes into sharp focus. This review makes particular reference to the application of SEA in developing countries, where experience remains relatively limited and there are many challenges, and to countries in transition, where there is a richer vein of recent experience and much innovation in application. In this context, the concern is to gain a better understanding of the opportunities that SEA offers and the constraints on its implementation. We take a pragmatic approach and examine: the application of SEA tools and processes; how well they work in meeting their objectives – including protecting the environment; and what improvements can be made to assure sustainability and to integrate these considerations into economic development and poverty alleviation strategies. Earlier exercises along these lines have been undertaken in the Central and Eastern Europe region (Mikulic et al, 1998; Dusik et al, 2001), and for individual countries such as Samoa (Strachan, 1997).[1]

A more general stock-taking of international experience with SEA now seems appropriate, given the trends described in this chapter and in light of the apparent momentum to 'transport' SEA from the North to the South. There is growing enthusiasm on the part of many EIA practitioners in developing countries to adopt this approach. Yet their experience with conventional EIA is sobering. There is growing evidence that this process does not work well in many developing countries – see, for example, Mwalyosi and Hughes (1998) who review EIA experience in Tanzania. In most cases, the reasons are not so much technical, as issues of lack of political and institutional will, limited skills and capacity, bureaucratic resistance, antagonism from vested interests, corruption, compartmentalized or sectoral organizational structures and lack of clear environmental goals and objectives.

Undoubtedly, these structural problems will loom large as constraints to the introduction of SEA. In addition, there are many issues regarding the use of SEA in industrial countries that remain unresolved. These include continued opposition by national and international development agencies to the systematic application of SEA, particularly at the highest levels of policy- and law-making. A major issue in the negotiation of both the European SEA Directive (2001/42/EC) and the SEA Protocol to the UNECE Convention on EIA in a Transboundary Context (2003) was the scope of SEA application, particularly in relation to policy and legislation. These aspects are omitted from the Directive and included in the Protocol as non-binding. Yet this issue is far from settled and questions concerning the role of SEA in policy-making are likely to resurface once the Directive is implemented.

In the next chapter, we examine these challenges in relation to the emergence and evolution of SEA practice.

---

1   The results indicated that with respect to the information requirements, there is good potential for undertaking SEA in the short to medium term in Samoa. However, institutional capacities are limited and policy implementation effects are likely to influence the effectiveness of SEA.

Chapter 2

Surveying the Field of SEA

During the last decade, a number of reviews of strategic environmental assessment (SEA) experience have provided perspectives and background on this evolving field. Some of the key references and findings are described in this chapter. These are both incomplete and continually updated by papers on SEA in conference proceedings and journals. In the last five years in particular, the literature on SEA has expanded rapidly. But much of this simply represents the restatement and recycling of basic premises and themes on SEA. It is much less concerned with new insights or methodological advances. In many respects, SEA practice has run ahead of theory in applying the ideas and tools in a policy or planning context.

Not all of this is necessarily called or seen as SEA. Nevertheless, it forms part of a broad and expanding field. For example, during the last decade there has been considerable experimentation and innovation in development planning, urban and rural planning, the development and implementation of national sustainable development strategies and the preparation of poverty reduction strategies. All of these fields have their own literature base[1] with much to offer SEA theory and practice (and vice versa). Yet impact assessment practitioners and development planners and policy analysts appear to occupy different universes. They rarely interact and use different terminology for approaches and processes that have much in common and could benefit from sharing experience and lessons.

2.1 OVERVIEW OF THE SEA LITERATURE AND KEY REFERENCES

Forms of SEA have been in place since environmental impact assessment (EIA) was first introduced in 1969 and, arguably, for an even longer time in land and resource planning practice. For example, the preparation of generic and programmatic environmental impact statements (EIS) has been an integral element of the implementation of the US National Environmental Policy Act (NEPA). Other SEA-type approaches reflect an extension of EIA trends, beginning in the late 1970s and 1980s. These include area-wide and regional

---

1   For overviews, see Dalal-Clayton and Dent (2002); Dalal-Clayton et al (2003); OECD/DAC (2001); UNDESA (2002b); and OECD/UNDP (2002).

assessments, and landscape-level or synoptic methodologies for cumulative effects assessment. Various sources provide references to the early application of environmental assessment to policy (e.g. Sadler, 1986; Wathern, 1988; Jacobs and Sadler, 1989; Bregha et al, 1990). Other work carried out through the then Canadian Environmental Assessment Research Council provided the basis for Canada's process of policy and programme assessment. This was established by Cabinet Directive in 1990 as a parallel system to the project-based EIA procedure.

During the1990s, SEA was introduced as a separate process from EIA in a number of other countries. Several perspectives and reviews of SEA were published in 1992, notably a United Nations Economic Commission for Europe report (UNECE, 1992) on principles and procedures that were agreed amongst a range of participating countries. Other studies also endorsed the need for SEA, compared its similarities and differences to EIA and elaborated the potential scope of procedure and practice (Wood and Djeddour, 1992; Therivel et al, 1992). The latter also discussed possible methodologies for undertaking SEA. A special issue of the journal *Project Appraisal* (7 (3), September 1992) examined the (then) status of SEA in the US, Australia, New Zealand and The Netherlands, and in relation to land use planning, the water environment and transport sector. In the overview paper in this volume, Lee and Walsh (1992) examined the reasons for the growth of interest in SEA, focusing on the limitations of project-level EIA. Subsequently, this theme has been returned to by many authors.

In the mid-1990s, the status and effectiveness of SEA processes in leading countries and international agencies were critically evaluated by Sadler and Verheem (1996), as part of the International Study of the Effectiveness of Environmental Assessment (Sadler, 1996). Their analysis was based on a portfolio of 52 case studies and institutional profiles of SEA systems established by leading countries and international agencies. A separate volume was prepared on SEA at the policy level (de Boer and Sadler, 1996). Other than SEA experience at the World Bank, both volumes focused almost exclusively on developed countries (and this emphasis is continued in new updates now in preparation).

Therivel and Partidário (1996) review international SEA guidance and regulations and discuss models and methodologies. They provide a further ten case studies – one from a developing country (Nepal) – grouped under three categories (sectoral SEAs, SEAs of land use plans, and SEAs of policies). Several volumes of collected papers review progress in SEA process and practice internationally. These include the *Handbook of Environmental Impact Assessment* (Petts, 1999). It includes updates on SEA generally and on particular themes. One of these focuses attention on policy environmental assessment as a separate approach (Bailey and Dixon, 1999). A special issue of *Impact Assessment and Project Appraisal* takes stock of 'SEA at a cross-roads' (Thissen, 2000). Ten papers review the methodological and institutional issues associated with moving from concepts to practice. Other overviews of SEA theory and practice are available in a collection of papers edited by Partidário and Clark (1999). All of these materials focus primarily on the situation in developed countries.

The application of SEA in particular sectors is receiving growing attention (e.g. Goodland, 1997; Pinfield, 1992; Sheate, 1995).[2] Fischer (2002) provides a systematic analysis of SEA in transport and spatial/land use planning based on 80 assessments in the UK, The Netherlands and Germany. He introduces three main SEA types, with distinct methodological requirements: policy-SEA, plan-SEA and programme-SEA. He also suggests that only a tiered system using all three types is able to meet the requirements formulated in the SEA literature. Transport and land use planning are the two sectors that are generally considered as having the greatest SEA experience. Fischer goes beyond the analysis of procedures, methods and techniques, and also considers the underlying political and planning systems. He found that most authorities believed it was possible to integrate SEA in the processes of developing policies, plans and programmes (PPP); and where such integration had occurred, SEA had performed well. But authorities also thought that SEA would probably delay PPP preparation.

The Second Environmental Assessment Review prepared by the World Bank (1996a) covers the period from 1993 to 1995. It contains perspectives and cases from developing countries. But it only briefly considers Bank-specific forms of SEA such as sectoral and regional environmental assessment (EA). These are viewed as 'special issues' to be reviewed in depth in the future. The report presents key findings relating to the potential of these instruments, particularly for focusing project-level EA. It also reports that experience with sectoral EA during this period varied. In general, it was narrowly focused on sub-programme components. Regional EA was rarely applied, although some sector assessments incorporated a spatial dimension as part of the analysis.

The Third Review of the World Bank's experience with EA covers the fiscal years 1996 to 2000. Progress in the use of sectoral and regional EA was again reported as a 'special issue'. Key findings (Green and Raphael, 2002, p121) were that:

- numerous sectoral EAs had been carried out in the Bank's regions;
- experience with regional EA remains limited, although certain approaches have similar characteristics (e.g. coastal zone and watershed management frameworks); and
- other SEA-type processes form part of new lending instruments, 'most of which did not exist at the time the second EA report was prepared'.

---

2   In October 1999, an international conference on SEA for transport was held in Warsaw as a joint initiative of the Organisation for Economic Co-operation and Development (OECD) and the European Conference of Ministers of Transport (ECMT). Sessions focused on: the role and potential of SEA; SEA approaches; Poland and Central and Eastern Europe; and perspectives from financing institutions (see: www.oecd.org/cem/topics/env/envdocs/SEA99.htm).

The Bank has decided to gradually broaden the use of SEA across a variety of sectors and operations. Its new Environment Strategy identifies SEA as a key implementation tool (World Bank, 2002b). As part of the preparatory process, the Bank commissioned a report on the international state of the art in using SEA as a tool for developmental planning, policy-making and decision-making (Kjørven and Lindhjem, 2002). The report reviews Bank experience of using SEA, presents eight case studies and discusses available options for mainstreaming SEAs. In 2002, the Bank also launched a three-year structured learning programme on SEA that focuses on the application of SEA approaches to Bank and client operations, on the relationship with other Bank instruments and on ways in which use of SEA can add value to the outcomes. As part of the programme, a dedicated part of the Bank's website (www.worldbank.org/environment – click on 'analytical and advisory assistance') provides a wealth of material on the broad use and definition of SEA.

Also of interest is a report (funded by the aid agencies of Canada and The Netherlands) presented to the Working Party on Development Assistance and Environment of the OECD Development Assistance Committee (DAC). This reviews SEA provision and practice in development cooperation agencies in the mid-1990s (CIDA/DGIS, 1997) (see Box 4.15). It provides a benchmark against which recent developments in that area (see Chapter 4) can be reviewed.

There is increasing interest in SEA is developing countries, but domestic applications are still at an embryonic stage. A notable exception is South Africa – an atypical developing country – where SEA thinking is particularly advanced. The Council for Scientific and Industrial Research (CSIR) has taken the lead on methodology development and testing an approach geared to national needs (see Chapter 6, Section 6.1.1). Principles for SEA have also been developed in South Africa and have been adopted, with minor modification, by the Canadian International Development Agency (Appendix 6). An SEA primer (CSIR, 1996) and draft protocol (CSIR, 1997a) identify the need for, and necessary components of, an agreed approach to SEA in South Africa. However, they have not been sanctioned by, and are not promoted by, government, which is still considering its approach to SEA.

2.2 TERMS AND DEFINITIONS

The term 'SEA' reportedly was first used in a draft report to the Commission of the European Communities (Wood and Djeddour, 1989[3]). It is widely used by the impact assessment community, but there are numerous related terms and institutionalized labels, especially for what we call para-SEA processes in this report (see Figure 1.1). In addition, SEA is not necessarily an official title

---

3   The final report was submitted to the CEC in 1990 and formed the basis of a published conference paper (Wood and Djeddour, 1990) which itself was reworked as a journal paper (Wood and Djeddour, 1992).

in many countries, particularly those with EIA systems that apply to PPP, or in the so-called European SEA Directive (Directive 2001/42/EC on the assessment of the effects of certain plans and programmes on the environment). The separate designation of SEA at the level of PPP reflects the limited coverage of EIA in the first two decades of its implementation (see Section 2.1).

Initial understanding of the concept of SEA was based firmly on EIA principles and process, although it was recognized that procedure and methodology would need to be adapted. Subsequently, the range of interpretations of SEA has grown much wider and, arguably, now extends beyond its EIA foundations. As Bina (2003, Chapter 2) notes, this 'diversity in SEA practice (approaches and tools) indicates a rebellion against the straightjacket of being conceptualised as a narrow impact assessment instrument'. The growing diversity reflects the range of types and contexts covered by policy, plan and programme decision-making. There is continuing discussion of what is strategic in SEA, particularly as a general designation for all types of decisions above and prior to the project level.

In general, SEA is currently understood to be a process for identifying and addressing the environmental (and also, increasingly, the associated social and economic) dimensions, effects and consequences of PPP and other high-level initiatives. This approach should take place before decisions are made, when major alternatives are open. Preferably it should make a contribution to their formulation and development rather than focusing only on the impact(s) of their implementation. SEA is a relatively new and a rapidly evolving approach (Dalal-Clayton and Sadler, 1998b) and there is no consensus or international agreement yet on its boundaries or precise characteristics.

Various definitions of SEA have been proposed as practitioners and academics have staked claims in this new territory. Amongst them, several are widely quoted in the literature or deserve attention because of their institutional weight (Box 2.1). These definitions also illustrate how interpretation of the concept of SEA is evolving. Early definitions saw SEA as a tool derived from EIA, extending its process and procedure upstream from the project to the strategic level, and focusing on the environmental impacts of programmes that are already proposed. More recent definitions – and the international trend – take a broader, more complex and varied perspective. They see SEA as including the social (and sometimes the economic) dimension. They also promote SEA not just as a means to 'upstream' impact assessment, but also as a diagnostic tool to help integrate environmental and social (and even economic) considerations during the formulation of policies and development plans and programmes.[4] In other words, SEA is seen as a key tool for sustainable development. Following a similar line of analysis, Bina (2003) notes three main trends in the evolution of SEA conceptions (Box 2.2). Policy-makers have reservations about the value added by SEA. So it is

---

4   Kirkpatrick and Lee (1997) examine the different ways in which such integration might be achieved in practice in the development planning process, using a variety of country case studies.

Box 2.1 Some definitions of SEA

SEA is a systematic process for evaluating the environmental consequences of proposed policy, plan or programme initiatives in order to ensure they are fully included and appropriately addressed at the earliest appropriate stage of decision-making on par with economic and social considerations.

Sadler and Verheem, (1996, p27)

The formalised, systematic and comprehensive process of evaluating the environmental effects of a policy, plan or programme and its alternatives, including the preparation of a written report on the findings of that evaluation, and using the findings in publicly accountable decision-making.

Therivel et al, (1992), and Therivel and Partidário, (1996)

SEA is a process directed at providing the authority responsible for policy development (the 'proponent') (during policy formulation) and the decision-maker (at the point of policy approval) with a holistic understanding of the environmental and social implications of the policy proposal, expanding the focus well beyond the issues that were the original driving force for new policy.

Brown and Therivel (2000, p184)

and more recently (although not strictly a definition), after reviewing international experience and its own practice in SEA, the World Bank assigns the following purpose to SEA:

A participatory approach for upstreaming environmental and social issues to influence development planning, decision-making and implementation processes at the strategic level.

Mercier (2004)

Box 2.2 Trends in the evolution of SEA conceptions

Bina (2003) observes three key trends in the development of SEA:

- the shift away from the traditional 'object' of assessment (draft PPPs) towards a more encompassing view of the policy process and its political dimension, with special attention to decision-making;
- the growing focus on the promotion of sustainable development, with the implicit need to combine hard and soft sciences, and develop dialogical assessment processes; and
- the reduced emphasis on the positivist dimension of the assessment of impacts within the overall SEA process, accompanied by an increased attention to SEA's contribution to, and integration in, the 'formulation' process of strategic initiatives.

necessary to be able to say clearly what it is and what it is useful for. At present there is anything but clarity. Instead, there is an expanding plethora of different acronyms, descriptions and interpretations of SEA and SEA-type approaches in use internationally (see Box 2.3). This reflects the fact that SEA is seen as a means to an end, a multi-lane route to addressing the environment and promoting sustainable development.

As in other areas of endeavour, there is sometimes a tendency for the owners or champions of particular branded approaches to promote those approaches exclusively. Sometimes they ignore, dismiss or even discredit other approaches (particularly when territorial turf or influence is perceived to be threatened). Where this happens, it restricts progress and experience gained through different approaches. Learning (e.g. what approaches or methods work well or less well) is not shared or absorbed, and general practice does not advance.

A number of reports have noted that 'lack of knowledge and standardised terminology, both as regards SEA and PPP, often confuses discussion on the issue' (Environment Australia, 1997). David Hanrahan (2003) of the World Bank has aptly summarized the situation: 'the terminology of SEA is like a menagerie – numerous creatures of varying interest and relevance to different partners' (see Figure 2.1). Some of these are integrated within particular policy and planning instruments, for example the World Bank's country assistance strategies (CAS) and structural adjustment loans (SALs). Others are applied separately, either covering environmental considerations only or sometimes including social or economic factors as well.

In this review, we do not offer a competing definition. Rather, our aim is to provide a review of experience and actual practice. We hope this might facilitate international debate and lead to further international clarification and agreement on the scope and limits of SEA, or perhaps of particular types of SEA.

Any broad definition of the current and growing 'family' of SEA approaches will need to remain generic and flexible. For the purposes of this review, we have interpreted SEA in this way. But to understand evolving experience and practice, we have found it useful to distinguish three broad categories:

- **formal SEA procedures** as prescribed in international or supra-national instruments (notably the SEA Protocol to the Convention on EIA in a Transboundary Context (1991) and the European Directive on SEA (2001/42/EC)), or under legal and policy frameworks established by certain countries and international organizations, such as the World Bank;
- other **near-equivalent processes** of environmental appraisal of policies and laws; and
- a broader range of SEA-type processes, methods and applications which we refer to as '**para-SEA**' – a shorthand term for approaches that do not meet formal specifications or strict definitions of SEA but have some of their characteristics or elements and the same overall purpose. This

Box 2.3 Examples of commonly used acronyms for SEA-type approaches

ANSEA   **Analytical strategic environmental assessment:** an analytical framework for evaluating decision-making processes, developed by a consortium of European institutions to assist in implementing the European SEA Directive (see Appendix 13).

CEA   **Country environmental analysis:** recently introduced by the World Bank to evaluate systematically the environmental priorities of development in client countries, the environmental implications of key policies, and countries' capacity to address their priorities.

EER   **Energy and environment review:** used by the World Bank for upstream analytical work on environmental issues related to the energy sector.

IA   **Integrated assessment:** a term usually used for a structured process to assess complex issues and provide integrated insights to decision-makers early in decision-making processes.

IEM   **Integrated environmental management:** an approach developed in South Africa as a code of practice to ensure that environmental considerations are fully integrated into all stages of the development process in order to achieve a desirable balance between conservation and development.

ITA   **Integrated trade assessment:** an approach used by the UN Environment Programme (UNEP) to assess the economic, environmental and social impacts of trade measures and the links between them.

PA   **Policy appraisal:** the assessment of the impacts of policies (sometimes focused on just the environmental dimensions, but increasingly also on social and economic issues).

PSIA   **Poverty and social impact analysis:** an approach developed by the World Bank to provide improved analysis to support poverty reduction strategy papers (PRSPs) and other processes. It draws from a menu of economic and social tools and quantitative and qualitative techniques. PSIA is used to mean analysis of the distributional impact of policy reforms on the well-being or welfare of different stakeholder groups, with particular focus on the poor and vulnerable.

REA   **Regional environmental assessment:** a form of EA that adopts a spatial or area-wide approach to development planning.

SA   **Sustainability appraisal:** a generic term for assessment approaches based on the broad integration of environmental, social and economic (ESE) dimensions of PPP.

SEA   **Strategic environmental assessment:** an umbrella term for the assessment of the environmental (and increasingly also the social and economic) impacts/dimensions of PPP.

Strategic effects assessment: used in The Netherlands to embrace broad effects and avoid undue emphasis on just environmental impacts.

Sectoral environmental assessment: a form of EA that addresses sector-wide issues.

SEAN   **Strategic Environmental Analysis:** a tool developed by AIDEnvironment and SNV (Netherlands Development Organisation) to enable environmental issues and options to be fully integrated into PPP design and priority setting; follows a ten-step participatory approach.

SEF   **Strategic environmental framework:** an approach developed for the Asian Development Bank to guide decision-making in certain sectors in the Greater Mekong Sub-region; uses a combination of analytical, participatory and policy processes and assessment methodologies.

SIA   **Strategic impact assessment:** used by some instead of SEA to denote an approach that includes not just environmental but also social and economic dimensions. Also an acronym for sustainability impact assessment (the same as SA) and social impact assessment.

SO   **Strategic overview:** a question-based approach developed by the UN Development Programme (UNDP) to help the design of aid programmes, focusing on baseline conditions, impacts and opportunities.

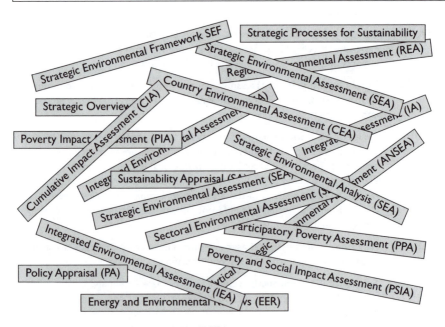

Source: Adapted from Box 2.3 by Jon Hobbs (DFID)

Figure 2.1 *The menagerie of SEA terminology*

BOX 2.4 SOME PRINCIPLES FOR SEA

(A) General – an SEA process should:

- fit the purpose and be customized for application at the policy level or at the level of plans and programmes;
- have integrity, so that it is applied in accordance with the objectives and provisions established for it; and be effective in meeting those objectives;
- be focused on delivering information necessary to the decisions to be made, and address the significant and key issues;
- be driven by sustainable development principles (taking into account environmental, social and economic considerations); and therefore;
- be integrated with parallel analyses of economic and social dimensions and issues, and with other planning and assessment instruments and processes;
- relate to project EIA where appropriate – perhaps through tiering mechanisms;
- be transparent and open;
- be practical, easy to implement, oriented to problem-solving and cost-effective;
- introduce new perspectives and creativity (it should 'provide bonuses, not be a burden'); and
- be a learning process (thus it is essential to start 'doing SEA' to gain experience).

(B) SEA steps – an SEA process should ensure the following:

- *Screening*: Responsible agencies carry out an appropriate assessment of all strategic decisions with significant environmental consequences.
- *Timing*: Results of the assessment are available sufficiently early for use in the preparation of the strategic decision.
- *Environmental scoping*: All relevant information is provided to judge whether: (i) an initiative should proceed; and (ii) objectives could be achieved in a more environmentally friendly way (i.e. through alternative initiatives or approaches).
- *Other factors*: Sufficient information is available on other factors, including socioeconomic considerations, either parallel to or integrated in the assessment.
- *Review*: The quality of the process and information is safeguarded by an effective review mechanism.
- *Participation*: Sufficient information on the views of all legitimate stakeholders (including the public affected) is available early enough to be used effectively in the preparation of the strategic decision.
- *Documentation*: Results are identifiable, understandable and available to all parties affected by the decision.
- *Decision-making and accountability*: It is clear to all stakeholders and all parties affected how the results were taken into account in decision-making.
- *Post-decision*: Sufficient information on the actual impacts of implementing the decision is gained to judge whether the decision should be amended.

Sources: Dalal-Clayton and Sadler (1998b), adapted from Sadler (1998b) and Tonk and Verheem (1998)

Box 2.5 Performance criteria for SEA

A good-quality SEA process informs planners, decision-makers and the affected public on the sustainability of strategic decisions, facilitates the search for the best alternative, and ensures a democratic decision-making process. This enhances the credibility of decisions and leads to more cost- and time-effective EA at the project level. For this purpose, a good-quality SEA process is:

integrated:

- ensures an appropriate environmental assessment of all strategic decisions relevant for the achievement of sustainable development;
- addresses the interrelationships of biophysical, social and economic aspects; and
- is tiered to policies in relevant sectors and (transboundary) regions and, where appropriate, to project EIA and decision-making.

sustainability-led:

- facilitates identification of development options and alternative proposals that are more sustainable.*

focused:

- provides sufficient, reliable and usable information for development planning and decision-making;
- concentrates on key issues of sustainable development;
- is customized to the characteristics of the decision-making process; and
- is cost- and time-effective.

accountable:

- is the responsibility of the leading agencies for the strategic decision to be taken;
- is carried out with professionalism, rigour, fairness, impartiality and balance;
- is subject to independent checks and verification; and
- documents and justifies how sustainability issues were taken into account in decision-making.

participative:

- informs and involves interested and affected public and government bodies throughout the decision-making process;
- explicitly addresses their inputs and concerns in documentation and decision-making; and
- has a clear, easily understood information requirement and ensures sufficient access to all relevant information.

iterative:

- ensures availability of the assessment results early enough to influence the decision-making process and inspire future planning; and
- provides sufficient information on the actual impacts of implementing a strategic decision, to judge whether this decision should be amended and to provide a basis for future decisions.

Note: * In other words, it contributes to the overall sustainable development strategy as laid down in Rio in 1992 and defined in the specific policies or value of a country
Source: IAIA (2002); criteria developed by Rob Verheem and members of the SEA section

involves the assessment of environmental concerns (sometimes together with social and economic issues) to enable these issues to be taken into account in decision-making and in the preparation and implementation of PPP.

2.3 SEA PRINCIPLES

A significant increase in the use of SEA might follow if progress can be reached in three areas: reaching consensus on its scope and aims; agreeing guiding principles on SEA for potential users; and developing a typology of the different forms that SEA can takes (we make a preliminary attempt in Figure 1.1). Kjørven and Lindhjem (2002, p9) observe that this would 'allow for variety in implementation forms, depending on the context'. A first approximation to SEA principles is offered by Sadler and Verheem (1996) and Dalal-Clayton and Sadler (1998b) (Box 2.4). Performance criteria for SEA have also been developed by the International Association for Impact Assessment (IAIA, 2002; see Box 2.5). The latter elaborate on the principles but concentrate primarily on procedural aspects of an effective or good-quality SEA.

For many developing countries, reference may be made to the SEA principles and guidelines prepared for South Africa (see Chapter 6, Section 6.1.1). Here, the priorities are sustainable land development and meeting basic needs of the majority of the population that lives at or near the poverty level. In the South African model, SEA is intended to be integrated flexibly within the planning processes, and applied iteratively to focus on the environmental potentials and constraints on development (DEAT, 2000).[5] This approach approximates to what is known as regional assessment in other countries. At the World Bank, such regional assessment provides a mechanism for pre-clearance of development programmes and policy options that apply to a particular area or natural unit such as a coastal zone. It provides a spatial framework for proactive environmental management. This is particularly important for 'impact zoning' to safeguard valued critical ecosystem components and to minimize impacts by setting limits on air or water pollution loads.

Thus, SEA is a decision-aiding tool rather than a decision-making process, and it needs to be flexibly applied to policy and planning cycles. Other commentators have argued that SEA needs to be more sensitive to the real characteristics of decision-making (e.g. Nilsson and Dalkmann, 2001). From this perspective, SEA encompasses assessments of both broad policy initiatives and more concrete programmes and plans that have physical and spatial dimensions. It can also be applied throughout the process to shape options

---

5   In practice, the Department of Environmental Affairs and Tourism (DEAT) has not actively promoted the SEA guidelines and most of the 50+ SEAs conducted to date in South Africa have followed different approaches, each shaped by local decision-making and planning contexts (Nigel Rossouw, personal communication).

and to assess the impact of implementing a preferred course of action. Bina (2003) examines the raison d'être of SEA and calls for its 're-conceptualisation'. She proposes a framework that 'emphasises the need to interpret and operationalise SEA at the level of organisations (such as ministries or multi-lateral development agencies), not of economic sectors alone ... [centralizing on] the interactions of the context, the nature of strategic objectives, the framing of "environmental", the purpose of SEA, and the assessment's approach and tools'.

The interrelationship of policies, plans and programmes is important. It is frequently idealized as a hierarchical or tiered process of decision-making (illustrated by Figure 2.2). But the reality is often quite different. This is particularly the case at the level of policy-making, which does not necessarily follow a logical sequence of discrete, technical steps. Often, it is a more complex, iterative process in which the range of choice is gradually narrowed and most options are foreclosed by the project phase. This fact has a critical bearing on practical applications of SEA (Sadler, 1998a).

In addition, terms such as 'policies', 'plans' and 'programmes' (PPP: the 3 P's) mean different things in different countries and their use is dependent on the political and institutional context. In this book, we use these terms in a generic sense. 'Policies' are taken to be broad statements of intent that reflect and focus the political agenda of a government and initiate a decision cycle. They are given substance and effect in plans and programmes. This involves identifying options to achieve policy objectives and setting out how, when and where specific actions will be carried out (Sadler and Verheem, 1996).

However defined, policies and programmes encompass a range of strategic proposals, all of which are likely to have environmental, social or economic consequences. Sadler and Verheem (1996) propose a 'pre-screening' check for SEA to establish the proposals that raise environmental concerns (Box 2.6). This procedure is simple and straightforward and therefore can be adapted to different decision-making contexts, including those in developing countries. It is undertaken by reference to:

- the policy area or sector covered – in general, all policy areas which concern or lead to changes in the use of land and natural resources, the production of raw materials, chemicals and other hazardous products and/or the generation of pollutants, wastes and residuals, are potential candidates for SEA; and
- the type of environmental effects that can be anticipated – typically, when moving from the policy to the project stage of the decision cycle, environmental considerations correspondingly shift from indirect to direct effects (although this rule of thumb does not always apply).

Logically, the scope and form of SEA should correspond broadly with the level of generality of decision-making and the type of environmental effects that are identified (see Box 2.5). Typically, direct effects can be correlated with projects and with plans and programmes that initiate and locate specific activities.

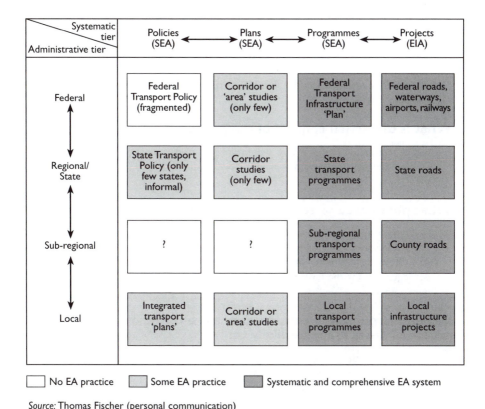

Systematic tier / Administrative tier	Policies (SEA)	Plans (SEA)	Programmes (SEA)	Projects (EIA)
Federal	Federal Transport Policy (fragmented)	Corridor or 'area' studies (only few)	Federal Transport Infrastructure 'Plan'	Federal roads, waterways, airports, railways
Regional/ State	State Transport Policy (only few states, informal)	Corridor studies (only few)	State transport programmes	State roads
Sub-regional	?	?	Sub-regional transport programmes	County roads
Local	Integrated transport 'plans'	Corridor or 'area' studies	Local transport programmes	Local infrastructure projects

☐ No EA practice   ▨ Some EA practice   ▨ Systematic and comprehensive EA system

Source: Thomas Fischer (personal communication)

Figure 2.2 *EA practice within the tiered transport planning system in Germany*

Indirect effects are associated more with policies, strategies and legislation – particularly those that are not easily separable into discrete actions but have an environmental dimension, for example, by influencing attitudes and consumer behaviour towards transport or waste recycling (Sadler and Verheem, 1996).

2.4 RATIONALE, BENEFITS, CAPACITY REQUIREMENTS AND PRECONDITIONS FOR SEA

From an 'environmental quality' or sustainability perspective, there is a range of benefits of introducing SEA. It can and should (Dalal-Clayton and Sadler, 1995; Sadler and Baxter, 1997):

• promote integrated environment and development decision-making (i.e. promote sustainability in decision-making);
• facilitate the design of environmentally sustainable policies and plans;

BOX 2.6 A PRE-SCREENING PROCEDURE FOR DETERMINING SEA REQUIREMENTS

The following questions can be used to make a quick judgement about SEA requirements:

What is the actual content of the proposal?

- Is it concerned only or primarily with broad general direction(s)?
- Does it address or specifically include operational measures (projects, activities, etc.)?

What policy area or sector is targeted in the proposal?

- Is it one known to have or likely to cause environmental effects (e.g. energy, transportation, housing, agriculture)?
- Are there components which are likely to have cumulative or long-term consequences for the environment (e.g. trade, industrial diversification, technology development)?

What environmental considerations are raised by the proposal? Does it appear likely to:

- initiate actions that will have direct or evident environmental impacts?
- raise broad environmental implications and/or issues that should be addressed?
- have marginal or no environmental consequences?

Source: Sadler and Verheem (1996)

- provide for consideration of a larger range of alternatives than is normally possible in project EA;
- take account, where possible, of cumulative effects (particularly by focusing on the consequences of sectoral or regional-level developments) and global change;
- enhance institutional efficiency (particularly where EIA-related skills, operational funds and institutional capacities are limited) by obviating the need for unnecessary project-level EIAs;
- increase the influence of certain ministries and increase coordination across sectors;
- strengthen and streamline project EA by:
  - the incorporation of environmental goals and principles into policies, plans and programmes that shape individual projects
  - prior identification of impacts and information requirements
  - clearance of strategic issues and information requirements
  - reducing time and effort taken to conduct reviews; and
- provide a mechanism for public engagement in discussions relevant to sustainability at a strategic level.

Politicians might see the benefits more in terms of (Rob Verheem, personal communication):

- more credibility in the eyes of their voters, leading to better commitment to their plans and policies, thus leading to easier implementation;
- better policies and plans – because, if better alternatives exist, SEA helps in finding them; and
- fewer costly mistakes – because of a better insight into the accumulated impact of a large number of smaller projects or potential conflicts between agencies.

These benefits apply to developing countries as well as industrial countries. But for SEA to function effectively, a certain level of institutional maturity is necessary. At a minimum, this should allow for environmental considerations to be taken into account and to influence decision-making. Appropriate skills are needed for this purpose, notably within government departments and agencies, in the private sector (e.g. industry, environmental consulting companies) and amongst academics and non-governmental organizations (NGOs). Where these are not in place, adequate capacity will need to be developed.

In broad terms, the rationale for the SEA of PPP falls into three main categories: strengthening project EIA; addressing cumulative and large-scale effects; and advancing the sustainability agenda.

Strengthening project EIA

EIA practice is constrained by certain limitations and weaknesses. These include structural weaknesses centred on the relatively late stage at which EIA is usually applied in decision-making. By this point, high-level questions about whether, where and what type of development should take place have been decided, often with little or no environmental analysis. Project-by-project EIA is also an ineffective means of examining these issues. It is far more preferable to use SEA or an equivalent approach to incorporate environmental considerations and alternatives directly into PPP design. This can also help to focus and streamline project EIAs, making them more consequential and reducing the time and effort involved in their preparation. For developing countries, SEA may yield significant other benefits. For example, it can rule out certain kinds of development at the policy level and reduce the need for many project-level EIAs. This, in turn, can relieve pressure where institutional and/or skills capacity is limited.

Addressing cumulative and large-scale effects

Recently, considerable efforts have been made to extend EIA-based frameworks to encompass certain types of cumulative effects. These deal reasonably well with the ancillary impacts of large-scale projects (e.g. dams, transport infrastructure) and the incremental effects of numerous, small-scale actions of a similar type (e.g. road realignment and improvement). However, more pervasive cumulative effects and large-scale environmental change (the end result of multiple actions and stresses that cut across policy and ecological boundaries) can be addressed best by SEA of PPP. World Bank sector and regional assessments, widely applied in developing countries already, are described in Chapter 4.

Advancing the sustainability agenda

When applied systematically, SEA can become a vector for moving from traditional to sustainability-based planning and decision-making, as called for by the Brundtland Commission (WCED, 1987) and Agenda 21 (UNCED, 1992). Conventionally, the emphasis has been on tackling the environmental symptoms or effects of development in the 'downstream' part of the decision cycle. In contrast, the sustainability approach focuses on the sources or causes of environmental deterioration. These lie in the 'upstream' part of the decision cycle, in the economic, fiscal and trade policies that guide the overall course of development. SEA provides a means for incorporating environmental objectives and considerations in economic decisions.[6] This approach is fully consistent with the perspective of developing countries, for example as expressed at the 1992 UN Conference on Environment and Development (UNCED) in Rio de Janeiro and in the Plan of Implementation agreed at the 2002 World Summit on Sustainable Development (WSSD) in Johannesburg.

In practice, the extent to which the benefits of SEA are achieved will depend on a number of factors. Based on recent experience, the following appear to be particularly important (Sadler, 1997):

- the provisions made for SEA should be clear and transparent, whether based on a legal versus framework;
- the prior record of implementation and acceptance by decision-makers;
- the degree to which overall strategies of sustainable development are in place; and
- the scope and level(s) of application – the broadest range of benefits are gained from SEA systems that include reviews of policies as well as plans and programmes.

General benefits of SEA

There is a burgeoning interest in SEA, not least from developing countries. This is because it meets the need for more integrated and balanced decision-making, and because of its potential to relieve the burden of assessment at the project level. This demand cannot be ignored and is likely to continue to grow. SEA enables decision-makers to develop policies and strategies that are based on a sound analysis and understanding of their sustainability implications. It is proactive, enabling decision-makers to avoid the costs and missed

---

6   Indeed, SEA is now being seen by some donors as an important tool to help frame the way that direct budgetary support is provided/targeted (an increasing trend in development cooperation).

opportunities that, all too often, are associated with inadequate information and limited choices. When applied as a flexible, consultative, transparent and iterative process, SEA helps to identify best practicable options for achieving positive outcomes and minimizing adverse effects in accordance with sustainability principles.

SEA should be applied at the highest level possible in planning or decision-making, for example to development policies, plans and strategies. In this way it can focus on the 'source' of environmental impacts rather addressing their symptoms later on. The results of the SEA can then cascade down the decision-making hierarchy and streamline subsequent, lower-level decisions. In this way, SEA can overcome a major limitation of project-level EIA – it operates only at the lower (downstream) end of the decision-making process.

When used systematically at a high level, SEA facilitates early integration of ESE concerns. It can also identify specific measures to mitigate any potentially adverse effects of implementing PPP and can establish a framework for subsequent project-level EIA. In the context of development cooperation, such a framework can include requirements for institution strengthening and capacity-building related to environmental management.

The WSSD in Johannesburg highlighted that many of the pressing challenges of sustainable development are interrelated, and that ESE aspects need to be addressed together at global, national and local levels. SEA can be used, with other tools, to establish a coherent policy response to the WSSD agenda. But the approach may differ depending on country and institutional contexts. Integrated assessment could be undertaken within an SEA, or SEA could provide the environmental contribution to integrated decision-making.

Considerable experience has been gained in applying SEA to development proposals in major sectors, such as energy and transportation, and as part of regional and land use plans. In addition, SEA has been extended to address a range of international development and trade initiatives. For example, at the World Bank, SEA is part of the Environment Strategy for 'mainstreaming' (integrating environment across sectors) and 'upstreaming' (focusing on policy).

Other policy and institutional benefits can also be realized through the use of SEA. These include long-term changes in the culture of decision-making. Examples include those changes arising when environmental values become part of the mandates and actions of sector agencies, or when public participation in SEA fosters greater openness, transparency and accountability. SEA also helps to *strengthen and streamline project EIA*, particularly when the results of the one approach can be tiered to the conduct of the other. There are opportunities for time- and cost-saving, particularly when SEAs of policies and plans initiate or set a framework for specific projects that are subject to EIA.

Some examples of SEA benefits in developing and transitional countries

A briefing paper prepared by UNDP and the Regional Environmental Centre for Central and Eastern Europe (REC) for the Fifth Pan-European Ministerial

Box 2.7 Benefits of SEA in transitional countries

A UNDP/REC workshop on SEA of Regional Development Plans in Central and Eastern Europe (December 2001, Slovenia) and other studies were carried out as part of the Sofia Initiative on EIA. These showed that SEA can help decision-makers to:

- achieve environmentally sound and sustainable development;
- strengthen PPP – policy-, plan- and programme-making processes;
- save time and money by avoiding costly mistakes; and
- improve good governance and build public trust and confidence in decision-making.

Achieving environmentally sound and sustainable development

The use of SEA enables the different objectives pursued by various administrative levels and sectors to be reconciled. In Central and Eastern Europe (CEE), SEA has supported evaluation of the full range of options and alternatives against these overall objectives. This has helped the design of environmentally sustainable implementation plans for preferred strategic options. For example:

> The SEA for the first National Development Plan of Poland provided us with useful recommendations for improved consideration of environmental issues. The SEA has a wider applicability and can also be used in elaboration of other documents. We will be able to use the lessons learned and methodology developed in the future.
>
> (Piotr Zuber, Ministry of Economy, Labour and Social Policy, Poland)

Strengthening PPP

SEA also helps to reconcile different goals and objectives. In this way, it supports a gradual shift of decision-making towards a focus on genuine sustainable development. Moreover, SEA assists in the coordination between environmental authorities and proponents of PPP. It helps to streamline decision-making systems by reducing the complexity of environmental issues at the different stages of planning hierarchies. For example:

> SEA helped us to improve the quality of the Hungarian Regional Operational Programme. Proponents of this programme often did not take into account natural resources, which form the basis of any economic activity. The SEA team identified the main relevant environmental issues and helped us to consider this information throughout the entire planning process. SEA also facilitated our cooperation with the Ministry of Environment, other sectoral ministries and regional authorities during environmental optimising of the programme.
>
> (Ágnes Somfai, Prime Minister's Office, Hungary)

Saving time and money

SEA gives an early warning of unsustainable or environmentally damaging options. So it saves time and money as problematic options are disregarded before resources are spent on their development and costly mitigation or remediation measures are avoided. SEA also enables planners to effectively gather and analyse input from relevant stakeholders.

Ultimately, this makes decision-making more effective and less time-consuming. For example:

> *Thorough application of SEA will help us in avoiding large-scale health problems that occur when environmentally problematic strategic decisions are made.*
>
> (Mojca Gruntar-Cinc, Ministry of Health, Slovenia)

Improving good governance and public trust in decision-making

SEA increases the overall transparency of strategic decision-making, helping to create public trust in the process. By allowing decision-makers to consider opinions of key stakeholders early in the planning process, SEA reduces the risk of deadlock during decision-making. And it may help to mobilize the support of key stakeholders for policy and plan implementation. For example:

> *SEA was very useful in elaboration of the Czech National Development Plan. It had benefits that went beyond its original purpose of ensuring full consideration of sustainable development during the planning process. SEA helped us to improve openness of the entire programming process and established a 'bridge' between the planning team and the public. This turned out to be a very positive feature that we later very much appreciated.*
>
> (Tomas Nejdl, Ministry of Regional Development, the Czech Republic)

Source: UNDP/REC (2003), prepared by Jiri Dusik, Thomas Fischer and Barry Sadler, with inputs from Andrej Steiner (UNDP) and Nick Bonvoisin (UNECE)

Conference, 'Environment for Europe' (Kiev, May 2003), discusses the role and practice of SEA in countries in transition (Dusik et al, 2003). It is based on recent experience and identifies the numerous benefits that have been or can be gained from the application of SEA in Eastern Europe, the Caucasus and Central Asia. SEA leads to better environmental protection and management and promotes sustainable development. It also strengthens policy-, plan- and programme-making processes, thereby providing a number of immediate and longer-term benefits for development agencies, planning authorities and governments. SEA improves the efficiency of planning processes and governance. Further explanation and examples of these benefits are given in Box 2.7.

In developing countries, SEA can make a critical contribution to improved transparency in decision-making, coordination amongst agencies and, over the longer term, good governance. For example, in a study of the potential of SEA in Nepal, ERM (2002) notes:

> *Implementation of SEA at local government levels would also require the support of the Ministry for Local Development (MLD). The profile of both MLD and the Ministry of Population and Environment (MoPE) is currently rather weak. MoPE's role, for example, is perceived as being more reactive than proactive.*

This perception could be a risk to the effectiveness of SEA. However, SEA could provide an opportunity for MoPE and MLD to increase their 'visibility' in more strategic, proactive planning and decision-making. For MoPE, this could enhance the image of environmental protection and management and its own proactive influence on sector ministries. For MLD, the introduction of SEA at local planning levels could enable it to increase coordination with other sector ministries, thereby enhancing its profile and status.

But to have such an effect, it is important that SEA is not promoted as an environmentalists' 'toy' and that ownership remains with the lead authority, with the weaker agencies in a strong consultation role.

2.5 OPPORTUNITIES AND CONSTRAINTS

In the wake of WSSD, there are many opportunities for introducing and mainstreaming SEA in domestic policy-making, decision-making and planning systems, as well as in development assistance and the work of lending and donor agencies. The policy and institutional benefits have already been described. They apply particularly to strengthening environment ministries. These are often weak in developing countries. However, there is a larger task outstanding. Many of those who must implement and use the results of SEA still remain to be convinced of its value. Some people have pointed to the challenges of using SEA, particularly in situations where issues and priorities are constantly changing, or where it has exacerbated inter-institutional conflicts, for example between water utility and environmental protection agencies (Sanchez-Triana and Quintero, 2003). As a next step, these benefits need to be better communicated to development agencies and policy-makers and their advisors in developing and transitional countries. A good example is the statement on SEA prepared by UNDP and the Regional Environmental Center for Central and Eastern Europe for the Kiev Ministerial Conference (UNDP/REC, 2003).

SEA offers good opportunities to integrate social, economic and environmental considerations in decision-making and to make the latter more transparent, accountable and effective (Table 2.1). For developing countries, the introduction and implementation of SEA support 'good governance', give visibility to more strategic, proactive planning and decision-making and *demonstrate* commitment to environmentally sustainable development. For environment ministries, this can enhance their role and proactive influence on sector ministries responsible for development and poverty reduction. For development ministries, the introduction of SEA at all levels can increase inter-sector coordination and policy and planning integration. This will be particularly important in the design and implementation of poverty reduction strategies that simultaneously aim to improve health, build infrastructure and provide food security.

Table 2.1 *SEA: constraints and opportunities to overcome them*

Constraints	Opportunities
• little interest by many government agencies in subjecting policy and planning proposals to assessment, reinforced by fear of losing control, power and influence by opening up such processes	• SEA is a transparent, participatory process that helps to realize good governance; it promotes inter-institutional relations in order to define priorities; and it supports informed, balanced decision-making, reinforces accountability and builds public trust and confidence
• limited appreciation of the potential utility of upstream assessment among senior staff (in both governments and donor agencies), and doubts about the robustness of results	• The efforts of the DAC and others to clarify the role and utility of SEA should improve understanding of how, when and where SEA can help senior staff achieve their responsibilities
• lack of resources for perceived 'non-essential' studies at early stages in the preparation of assistance programmes	• Investment up-front in an SEA can save time and the later expense of fixing the consequences of poor decisions
• perception that SEA will add significant costs and increase the work load of hard-pressed agencies	• It is likely that SEA costs will decrease over time as it is institutionalized (just as EIA costs reduced as it became routine)
• concern that SEA will increase the time frame for decision-making or delay development	• when applied appropriately and early, the SEA process is integrated within the decision-making process
• absence of clear guidance and known, tried-and-tested methods	• SEA principles, methods and guidance are in use internationally and can be drawn upon
• unclear lines of accountability and responsibility for undertaking SEA	• international legal instruments for SEA and practical experience with how to operate national systems can be built on
• lack of practitioners with expertise in SEA approaches in both donor agencies and in recipient countries	• Investment in SEA awareness-raising and training can build skills and competencies
• need to train and take on additional staff for this purpose	• Training can pay major dividends by improving decision-making, eliminating wasted time spent on fixing later problems and promoting more sustainable development.

In capitalizing on these opportunities, a number of constraints also need to be addressed. Some of these are listed in Table 2.1. The capacity of developing and transitional countries to introduce and implement SEA varies. In many cases, it will require assistance with policy, legal and institutional reforms to establish the basic preconditions. Even if SEA arrangements are in place or pending, it will be necessary to raise awareness and train practitioners. In China, the new EIA law requires SEA of plans and programmes. The potential needs and demands for training are huge. It is estimated that 100,000 trained SEA practitioners will be needed for the new law to become fully operational.

2.6 EVOLUTION AND TRENDS IN SEA

The evolution of SEA can be considered from two broad perspectives. In one, the impetus has come from policy analysis and planning and increasingly is driven by sustainable development concerns. The other approach has been driven by concern about the limitations and narrow, project-specific focus of EIA and the lack of coverage of higher-level decisions (which set the context and framework for project EIA). However, these lines of approach are overlapping as well as convergent. For example, both emphasize the importance of addressing environmental concerns and sustainability as substantive aims. Both seek to achieve their integration into the mainstream of policy- and plan-making through systematic analysis and transparent, open procedures. This emphasis on mainstreaming may also be seen as a third, mid-level approach through which SEA has evolved (Sadler, 2001a).

2.6.1 SEA in the context of EIA history

The history of SEA is best recounted in relation to the mainstream of EIA history, dating from the founding US NEPA (1969). Section 102 of NEPA contains the procedural requirements, including the provision for a detailed statement to accompany 'proposals for *legislation and other major federal actions* significantly affecting the ... environment' (emphasis added). One of the architects of NEPA has stated that this provision was to be an action-forcing measure, intended to reform and redirect federal policy-making (Caldwell, 1998). In practice, however, policy and other strategic decisions were excluded from review, other than for programmatic activities that could be grouped together (as specified in the NEPA Regulations).

From this standpoint, SEA can be seen as a second-generation process – one that moves EIA principles 'upstream' in the decision-making process. Although still at a relatively early stage, the evolution and take up of SEA has been rapid in the past few years and further changes are pending (see Appendix 1). In broad outline, the evolution of SEA can be divided into three main phases (Sadler, 2001a):

- the *formative stage* (1970–1989) when the legal and policy precedents for SEA were laid down but had limited application (largely in the US);
- the *formalization stage* (1990–2001) when different provision and forms of SEA were instituted by a number of countries and international agencies; and
- the *expansion stage* (2001 onward) when international legal and policy developments promise to catalyse wider adoption and use of SEA, particularly in Europe but also elsewhere.

2.6.2 The status of SEA systems

Currently, SEA systems are in place in more than 25 countries and jurisdictions.[7] With certain exceptions, these are member states of the UNECE region, which includes Europe and North America. However, an increasing number of developing countries are gaining experience of SEA as a result of regional and sectoral EA procedures established by the World Bank. These processes operate under different arrangements. Their scope of application, collectively, encompasses policy, legislation, plans, programmes and other strategies across a range of different sectors. So far, however, few, if any, countries have SEA systems that are comprehensive in their coverage (i.e. they apply to all strategic proposals with potentially important environmental effects), and not all of them apply to the highest levels of decision-making, typically defined by policy or legislation. The application of SEA to plans and programmes is more commonplace, with a particular focus on the energy, transport, waste and water sectors and on spatial or land use plans.

The legal and institutional bases of SEA systems also vary. This reflects differences in procedures between the application when SEA is applied to policies and to plans and programmes. Some countries make statutory provision for SEA under EIA or planning law. In these systems, EIA requirements and procedures usually are followed and apply particularly to SEA for plans and programmes. Other countries have established SEA through administrative order, Cabinet directive or policy guidelines. In these systems, SEA is applied as a separate or modified process from EIA, as in Canada, Denmark, Hong Kong, The Netherlands and the UK (which has a comparable process of policy appraisal). All these countries use a less formal, minimum procedure for SEA of policy or legal acts.

Current SEA processes vary considerably. Chapters 3–6 cover SEA experience in developed countries, development cooperation, countries in transition, and developing countries, respectively. They describe how SEA may be formal or informal, comprehensive or more limited in scope, and closely linked with or unrelated to other policy or planning instruments. In general, three broad approaches to SEA have been adopted to date (see Chapter 3 for further information):

- It has been introduced as a relatively separate, distinct process – typically as an extension of EIA.
- It has been established as a two-tier system (e.g. in The Netherlands) with formal SEAs required for specific sectoral plans and programmes and an environmental 'test' applied to legislation.

---

7 Countries and provincial or state jurisdictions with legal or administrative provisions that establish a formal SEA procedure include: Australia, Bulgaria, Canada, China (national and Hong Kong Special Administrative Region), the Czech Republic, Denmark, Finland, The Netherlands, Norway, Poland, Slovakia, the UK and US (federal and California).

- It has been incorporated into more integrated forms of environmental policy appraisal (e.g. in the UK) and regional and land use planning (e.g. in Sweden). Recently, there has been growing recognition of the importance of integrating EA with other policy and planning instruments.

Several countries in transition have established comparable SEA approaches, as described in Chapter 5. The Czech Republic and Slovakia, in particular, have considerable SEA experience at the level of PPP. To date, few developing countries have SEA arrangements in place and many lack some of the enabling conditions for this. SEA experience in the developing countries is reviewed in Chapter 6. However, there are a number of supportive trends and developments. Notably various international organizations have taken steps to promote the transition. These initiatives are summarized in Box 2.8 and analysed in Chapter 4.

2.6.3 International legal instruments

The number of countries with SEA systems is likely to increase now that EC Directive 2001/42/EC has come into force in member states and accession countries (in July 2004). It also promises to lead to a greater standardization of approach to SEA of specified plans and programmes that set the framework for the consent of projects subject to EIA. This process is modelled on the EIA Directive (97/11/EC) and applies a number of its procedural elements. These include the preparation of an environmental report, the information to be included in the statement, consideration of alternatives, arrangements for public consultation and factors to be considered in decision-making. The requirements and arrangements set out in the SEA Directive are described further in Chapter 3 (Section 3.2).

The SEA Directive will have international, as well as Europe-wide ramifications. First, other transitional countries and possibly some newly independent states (NIS) can be expected to introduce SEA arrangements that are aligned directly with the EU framework. Second, the provisions of the Directive have strongly influenced the SEA Protocol to the UNECE Convention on EIA in a Transboundary Context.

After a two-year negotiation, the SEA Protocol was formally adopted at Kiev, May 2003. Once ratified, the Protocol will be legally binding on signatories with regard to plans and programmes, and discretionary with regard to policy and legislation. It also places emphasis on the consideration of human health, going beyond existing arrangements in the UNECE region and internationally. The Protocol was drafted with the participation of CEE countries and many NIS, including those from Central Asia. It is reported that the Protocol will be opened to signatories from outside the UNECE region, thereby influencing the development of SEA processes internationally.

BOX 2.8 SOME INITIATIVES TOWARDS SEA IN DEVELOPMENT COOPERATION

- In 1978, the US Council for Environmental Quality (CEQ) issued regulations for the National Environmental Policy Act (NEPA). These apply to the United States Agency for International Development (USAID) and specify requirements for 'programmatic assessments'.
- In 1989, the World Bank (WB) adopted Operational Directive (OD) 4.00. This made provision for environmental assessment, including the preparation of sectoral or regional assessments. This was updated in 1991 as OD 4.01 and converted in 1999 into Operational Policy/Bank Procedure (OP/BP) 4.01, which formed part of the WB's environment and social safeguard compliance system. Recently, the Bank has introduced the discretionary use of other SEA-type processes for policy-based lending. A new OP/BP 8.60, approved in August 2004, recognizes the need for 'upstream analysis of social and environmental conditions and risks', and mentions SEA as one, among several, tools to carry out such an analysis (www.worldbank.org/sea).
- Article 2 (7) of the 1991 UNECE Convention on EIA in a Transboundary Context states that Parties 'shall endeavour to apply the principles of EIA to policies, plans and programmes'. The SEA Protocol to the Convention was finalized at the European Environment Ministers conference at Kiev (May 2003) and is now open for ratification by signatory countries (see www.unece.org/env).
- In 1991, the OECD/Development Assistance Committee (DAC) adopted a principle calling for specific arrangements for analysing and monitoring environmental impacts of programme assistance. An exploratory study of the role and scope of SEA in development assistance was carried out for the OECD/DAC by the Canadian International Development Agency (CIDA/DGIS, 1997). Currently, an OECD/DAC ENVIRONET Task Team is undertaking a programme of work on SEA (see Box 7.1).

A number of international assistance agencies of individual countries have promoted, developed or applied SEA tools or are in the process of doing so. Examples include:

- *Swedish International Development Cooperation Agency* (Sida) has used SEA guidelines in the preparation of country strategies that focus on the relationship of poverty, the environment and sustainable development (Sida, 2002a).
- *UK Department for International Development* (DFID) has experimented with SEA of draft transport policy in Tanzania, used various analytical tools in Uganda, which correspond to para-SEA, and helped the Nepal National Planning Commission to assess the feasibility of and requirements for introducing SEA.
- *Canadian International Development Agency* (CIDA) is currently preparing a handbook on SEA for use by Cabinet liaison staff, environmental specialists, programme and project analysts, and policy-makers. The draft handbook sets out principles for SEA, their implications for CIDA and the key actions that need to be taken.

Also certain UN agencies have promoted, developed or applied SEA tools. These include:

- UNDP's *environmental overview* (EO) was trialled in the mid-1990s and then proposed to be adapted as 'strategic overview'. But it is not currently practised by UNDP (see UNDP, 1992; Brown, 1997b; Chapter 4, and Section 4.1.5). EO is an example of para-SEA; it applies similar principles and has assisted in the design of other strategic tools including integrated programming and assessment (IPAT) and revised environmental management guidelines (EMG).
- UNEP's reference manual on integrated assessment of trade-related policies outlines a framework, toolbox and guidance for analysing the economic, environmental and social impacts of trade liberalization and identifying measures to mitigate adverse effects and enhancing positive effects (UNEP, 2002a).

2.6.4 Evolution of para-SEA, including global and integrative approaches

The SEA Directive and the SEA Protocol are legal instruments that promote a standardized approach, at least at the level of plans and programmes. They are paralleled by an increasing variety of approaches and applications of SEA. This suggests that the original distinction between policies, plans and programmes was perhaps too simplistic and artificial and did not relate or correlate with real decision-making procedures. There are now examples of SEA undertaken for a wider range of needs and objectives (Bina, 1999):

*   to select from a large number of projects that may be linked to existing inventories or past plans or programmes, and were not subject to a systematic assessment of their environmental implications;
*   to assess the cumulative impacts of a plan or programme;
*   to identify priority areas and types of projects for funding;
*   to identify priority areas and types of projects that will require more detailed evaluation before being approved;
*   to promote multi-modality in PPP for a sector;
*   to choose between (or propose a combination of) structural and non-structural alternatives (e.g. new or upgraded infrastructure, demand management strategies); and
*   to help define the key elements of a sustainable policy for a sector.

Looking at the big picture, a number of periodic global and continental environmental assessments have been undertaken. These have sought to provide a baseline for better decisions and policies, and can perhaps be regarded as mega-SEAs, for example:

*   *Global Environmental Outlook 2000*; *Global Environmental Outlook 3* (UNEP, 1999, 2002b) (Box 2.9);
*   *World Resources Report* (WRI/UNDP/UNEP/World Bank, 2000); and
*   *Europe's Environment: The Third Assessment* (EEA, 2003).

The latest addition to this family is the Millennium Ecosystem Assessment (MA) – an international, multi-agency initiative (2001–2005). It consists of a global assessment as well as assessments of conditions and change in ecosystems in individual communities, nations and regions. Its goal is to improve the management of the world's natural and managed ecosystems by helping to meet the needs of decision-makers and the public for peer-reviewed, policy-relevant scientific information on the condition of ecosystems, consequences of ecosystem change and options for response (see Appendix 4 for details).

Equally, the processes in many countries to prepare state-of-the-environment reports (Box 2.10) can be considered as a form of para-SEA, particularly where they are more than mere descriptions of conditions and

---

Box 2.9 The Global Environment Outlook project

The Global Environment Outlook (GEO) project was launched in 1995 by UNEP with two main components:

- a participatory and cross-sectoral global environmental assessment process, incorporating regional views and perceptions. It involves studies by a coordinated network of collaborating centres (multidisciplinary institutes with a regional outlook that work at the interface of science and policy) around the world, and associated centres. Advice and support are provided by expert working groups on modelling, scenarios, policy and data.
- GEO outputs in printed and electronic formats.

To date, three GEO reports have been published (1997, 2000 and 2003). *GEO-4* is scheduled for 2007.

GEO-2 (2000) reports on a comprehensive integrated assessment of the global environment at the turn of the millennium (UNEP, 1999). The report draws from a participatory process involving the work of experts from more than 100 countries. It also provides a vision for the 21st century and documents many policy successes in the recent past. It stresses the need for more comprehensive, integrated policy-making, especially given the increasingly cross-cutting nature of environmental issues. The 2000 report offers a more forward-looking perspective, setting out a range of environmental scenarios and their possible consequences.

GEO-3 (2003) provides an overview of the main environmental developments over the past three decades, and how social, economic and other factors have contributed to the changes that have occurred.

For further information, see: www.unep.org/geo.

---

include analysis of constraints and opportunities and influence planning and policy decisions. A recent example is a study prepared by UNEP on the environment in the Occupied Palestinian Territories. It aimed to help facilitate future negotiations and action related to environmental protection. The report (UNEP, 2003a) covers a number of areas identified as the most vital for the environment in the region: water quality and quantity; solid waste; waste water; hazardous waste; biodiversity; land use and land use change; and environmental administration. Similarly, the processes to prepare national conservation strategies and national environmental action plans during the 1980s and 1990s display many characteristics of SEA where they provide analysis and seek to mainstream environmental considerations in decision-making.

In recent years, a number of major studies and processes have focused on particular sectors. These can be viewed as large-scale SEAs, or even sustainability assessments. Examples include:

BOX 2.10 STATE OF THE ENVIRONMENT REPORTING

State of the environment reporting (SOER) is a general term used to describe the compilation and review of data collected over a period of time, usually two to five years. Reports generally provide a comprehensive review of the status and trends of different natural resources and ecological processes (air, soil, water, etc.). These are often correlated in some way with pressures arising from public issues (child health, noise, employment, training, etc.) for the particular time period, and note policy responses. SOERs collate existing data from different monitoring systems and programmes. They provide analysis of this data to clarify trends in relation to some base line. Geographical information system-generated data may be used for graphic representation.

Early SOERs in the 1970s and 1980s tended to be purely descriptive. More recently, many have had a broader sustainable development perspective, examining the relations between the environment and economic policies.

Sometimes, stakeholder institutions and the public are involved. In the County of Lancashire, UK, more than 70 organizations formed an 'environment forum' to jointly collect and analyse environmental data for the 'Lancashire Environmental Audit'. Such network-based approaches to SOER can increase access to data and information that is not normally made public. In addition, it facilitates the interpretation of data by knowledgeable stakeholders during the process of data selection and analysis.

UNEP/GRID-Arendal, the UNEP Regional Resource Centre for Asia and the Pacific (RRCAP), the European Environment Agency (EEA), and the World Resources Institute (WRI/IIED/IUCN, 1996) maintain databases of SOERs around the world. Among the key guidance documents for SOERs are the checklists prepared by the EEA which aim to harmonize approaches to SOERs in the European Union (EEA, 1998). These checklists cover 14 key environmental issues, from climate change to biodiversity, organized around four questions: What is happening? Why is it happening? Are the changes significant? How effective are the responses? UNEP/GRID-Arendal (1998) has prepared a brief guidance book on how to structure an SOER and how to place the report on the internet. UNEP has published a sourcebook on methods and approaches for SOERs (Rump, 1996).

Sources: OECD/UNDP (2002); Segnestam et al (2003)

- An independent study of the pulp and paper sector was commissioned following the Rio Earth Summit by the World Business Council for Sustainable Development (WBCSD). It was undertaken by the International Institute for Environment and Development. This study reviewed, inter alia, the economic, social and environmental impacts of the paper cycle, examining the concepts of sustainable practice at different stages of the cycle and the implications for current practice (IIED, 1996).
- The report of the World Commission on Dams assessed the performance of large dams. It reviewed their development effectiveness and assessed alternatives for water resources and energy development. It also developed internationally acceptable criteria, guidelines and standards, where appropriate, for the planning, design, appraisal, construction, operation, monitoring and decommissioning of dams (WCD, 2000).

- The Mining, Minerals and Sustainable Development (MMSD) project (2000–2002) was coordinated by IIED under commission from WBCSD and on behalf of a group of the world's major mining companies. This initiative provided an in-depth review of the mining and minerals sector from the perspective of sustainable development. Arguably, it can be considered a global-scale sustainability assessment of this sector (IIED/WBCSD, 2002).

Finally, throughout the Plan of Implementation agreed at the WSSD, the importance of taking a 'holistic and inter-sector approach' to implement sustainable development is stressed. In keeping with the Millennium Development Goals (MDGs), particular attention is given to poverty reduction. The challenge now is to sharpen tools and strategies to effectively address the root causes of poverty and their linkages with environment and development. Promoted by the World Bank and donors, PRSPs are being developed in many developing countries as the main strategic mechanism to develop across-the-board, pro-poor policies to alleviate hunger, reduce child mortality and provide basic infrastructure.

There is much that SEA can contribute here, especially if it is integrated with other strategic tools and processes. For example, SEA can be used to ensure that environmental opportunities and constraints are reflected in PRSPs, and in the management of natural resources under this agenda. Furthermore, SEA provides a powerful approach to support analysis, integration and synergy across the so-called WEHAB sectors (water, energy, health, agriculture and biodiversity). They were major themes in structuring the WSSD Plan of Implementation. These and other aspects related to international development assistance and cooperation are discussed in Chapter 4.

Chapter 3

SEA Experience in Developed Countries

Until recently, only a relatively small number of developed countries and state jurisdictions had made formal provision for strategic environmental assessment (SEA) of policy, plans and programmes. But this group has almost doubled in size following the recent entering into legal force of the SEA Directive (2001/42/EC) which requires European Union (EU) member states to transpose its requirements into domestic law. Some member states are introducing SEA for the first time (e.g. Austria, Greece and Portugal). Others have extended the scope or amended the arrangements of existing SEA systems (e.g. France, The Netherlands and the UK). Earlier experience suggests that it will take some time for these new SEA processes to be fully implemented, and even longer before the quality of practice and contribution to decision-making emerge into a coherent pattern.

This chapter focuses primarily on SEA experience in countries with well-established, operational systems, which were instituted during the 1990s or earlier in the case of the US (see Chapter 2). These SEA frameworks pre-date the EU SEA Directive and, in many cases, the decision to enter into its negotiation taken in 1996. As such, they illustrate the range and types of institutional arrangements and applications that are in place internationally and are generally accepted as leading examples of SEA innovation and development. Experience gained under these SEA systems has featured prominently in framing current notions of good practice. However, it also should be recognized that other jurisdictions have comparable levels of SEA experience including certain international organizations and countries in transition (their experience is reviewed in detail in Chapters 4 and 5, respectively).

This review of SEA experience in developed countries is organized in three parts. Section 3.1 provides a comparative analysis of the different SEA frameworks and institutional arrangements that are in force and attempts to delineate the main elements of their anatomy and approach. Section 3.2 examines SEA experience in the European Union, while the individualized processes and experience of individual developed countries are presented in Section 3.3. Specific guidance on the use of tools and procedures for carrying out the steps and activities of the SEA process can be found in Appendix 11.

3.1 BRIEF OVERVIEW OF SEA INSTITUTIONAL ARRANGEMENTS IN DEVELOPED COUNTRIES

Prior to the introduction of the EU SEA Directive in 2001, approximately 20 countries or jurisdictions are estimated to have had operating SEA systems in place.[1] Their mandate, institutional arrangements and scope of application vary, in some cases significantly. Table 3.1 summarizes the main characteristics of the SEA frameworks of selected countries. Of particular note are SEA systems that apply to or include coverage of policy and legal acts or which differ procedurally from the regime imposed by the EU SEA Directive, for example Australia, Canada, New Zealand, the US and certain European countries. Other than SEA of plans and programmes in EU member states, the systems listed in Table 3.1 are likely to continue to function in their present form.

A number of key features characterize the SEA arrangements in the countries reviewed:

(1) Provision for SEA is established through both legal and administrative means.

In each case, a mix of specific instruments is employed. Non-statutory provision for SEA has been made by separate administrative order or policy directive (e.g. Canada) or by guidelines on policy appraisal and plan evaluation (e.g. the UK). Statutory provision for SEA is made through environmental impact assessment (EIA)-specific (e.g. Finland), general environmental (e.g. the US) or resource management laws (e.g. New Zealand). The EU SEA Directive is a framework law that establishes a minimum common procedure for certain official plans and programmes, although it is not the first Community legislation in this area. Under Article 6(3) of Directive 92/43/EEC, plans likely to significantly affect a special protection area or a special conservation area must be subject to 'appropriate assessment' (Feldmann et al, 2001) – which the SEA Directive now defines.

There is an ongoing discussion about the appropriate basis for SEA systems, particularly with reference to proposed policies and legal acts. At this level, the arguments for flexibility of non-statutory arrangements are stronger than at the level of plans and programmes. In principle, executive instructions, such as those issued by the Prime Minister's Office in Denmark or the Cabinet in Canada, establish a duty to comply (but see also Point 3 later in this section). In practice, however, administrative instruments lack the powers to ensure that agencies fulfil their responsibilities or to enforce consistency in SEA application. This is especially the case with regard to advisory guidelines, such as those issued in the UK. Given that the EU SEA Directive (2001/42/EC) does not cover policy, there is no reason, prima facie, to expect changes to the separate SEA systems at this level now implemented by individual EU member states (e.g. Denmark, Finland, The Netherlands and the UK).

---

1   See Note 7, Chapter 2, for examples.

Table 3.1 SEA institutional frameworks and their scope of application in selected countries

Country/organization	Provision	Scope and relationship to decision-making	Elements of process and procedure
Australia	Environment Protection and Biodiversity Conservation Act (1999).	Section 146 provides for ministerial discretion to assess effects of actions under a policy, plan or programme. Sections 147–154 provide for specific application to fisheries management.	SEA activated by an agreement with proponent; Section 146(2) describes its content and basic procedure.
Canada	Cabinet Directive 1990 (amended 1999).	Policy, plan and programme proposals submitted to Cabinet or issued under ministerial authority.	Informal, two-stage procedure; guidelines encourage flexible application.
Denmark	Prime Minister's Office circular (1993, amended 1995 and 1998).	Bills and other government proposals sent to Parliament or on which Parliament must be consulted.	Minimum procedure; guidelines encourage flexible application.
Finland	Act on Environmental Impact Assessment Procedure (1994) Guidelines on EIA of Legislative Proposals (1998).	Policies, plans and programmes (will be amended to comply with SEA Directive). Laws, decrees and resolutions.	Formal procedure consistent with SEA Directive (2001/42/EC). Minimum procedure, flexible application.
The Netherlands	Environmental Impact Assessment Decree (1987, amended 1994) Cabinet Order (1995).	Listed plans and programmes (will be amended to comply with SEA Directive). Draft regulations and other policy intentions sent to Cabinet (Environmental test).	EIA procedure applied in full under Decree; may not apply in new legislation Minimum procedure, coordinated with business and regulatory tests.
New Zealand	Resource Management Act (RMA; 1991, various amendments).	Except for Section 32, generic rather than specific provision for SEA of policy and plans.	No definable procedure, other than Section 32, which refers to evaluation of the objectives and policies in meeting the purposes of the Act.

UK	Better Policy Making: A Guide to Regulatory Impact Assessment (2003). The Environmental Assessment of Plans and Programmes Regulations 2004 (for England; separate regulations exist for Scotland, Wales and Northern Ireland)	All substantial policies and proposals developed by central government departments and agencies which will have an impact on the public and private sectors. Plans and programmes as stipulated in the 'SEA Directive'.	Sets out a standard format for undertaking Regulatory Impact Assessment (RIA) Transposes the requirements of the SEA Directive into national law
	Strategic Environmental Assessment: Guidance for Planning Authorities (2003).	Spatial and land use plans developed by English Local Planning Authorities (separate guidance being developed in Wales and Scotland). Guidance for applying SEA to transport plans and programmes is also being prepared.	Advice on applying the SEA Directive and wider sustainability appraisal.
US	National Environmental Policy Act (1969) and Regulations (1978)	Legislation and programmes or actions that can be grouped geographically, generically or by technology.	NEPA process applies; specific guidance on preparing generic and programmatic environmental impact statements.
European Community	Council Directive on the assessment of certain plans and programmes (2001/42/EC); entered into force on 21 July 2004.	Plans and programmes in defined sectors and areas that set a framework for consent of projects subject to (EIA) Directive 85/337/EEC or which require an assessment subject to (Habitat) Directive 92/43/EEC.	Framework law based on EIA Directive; specifies common procedure to be adopted by member states.
United Nations Economic Commission for Europe (UNECE)	SEA Protocol (2003) to the Convention on EIA in a Transboundary Context (1991).	Mandatory application to plans and programmes; discretionary application to policy and legislation (Article 13).	Based on EC Council Directive for plans and programmes; no reference to procedure for policy or legislation.

Source: Sadler (2003b)

(2) The scope of coverage and application of SEA remains partial and limited in relation to levels and types of strategic decision-making that are likely to have a potentially significant impact on the environment.

Despite the pioneering intent of the 1969 National Environmental Policy Act (NEPA) in the US, which applies to 'all major federal actions' likely to have a significant effect on the environment, progress toward full inclusion of strategic decisions has been slow with different emphases among current SEA systems. Some countries have established SEA arrangements that apply uniformly, but not universally, to policy, plans and programmes (e.g. Canada, Finland, Hong Kong Special Administrative Region). For example, in Canada, the SEA process applies to strategic proposals submitted to Cabinet or authorized by individual ministers of state and can include draft legislation (although regulatory impact assessment also can be used to satisfy this requirement). In Finland, Denmark and Norway, the environmental effects of draft laws, regulations and other proposals submitted to Parliament are subject to SEA in a separate process from that applied to policies or plans. A similar approach is followed in The Netherlands except that the environmental test (E-test) of regulations is linked to executive or Cabinet decision-making. Finally, since 1991, the UK has maintained dual processes of environmental appraisal of policy and plans at the central and local government levels, although both systems are undergoing considerable modification (see below).

A new regime for SEA of plans and programmes will emerge in EU member states with the transposition of the EU SEA Directive into national legislation – either by integrating the requirements into existing procedures or incorporating them into new procedures (as described in Article 4.2 of the Directive). The plans and programmes that are subject to an assessment are described in Article 2(a). The scope of application of SEA is defined in Article 3, notably by reference to plans and programmes that are prepared for listed sectors and activities and which set the framework for consent of projects subject to the EIA Directive. Further discussion of the scope of activities that fall within the SEA Directive can be found in Section 3.2. For comparative purposes, the most notable point is that the basic approach corresponds to that taken in The Netherlands EIA Decree (which itself will need to undergo certain amendments to comply fully with the Directive). It may be contrasted with the approach taken in NEPA Regulations, which, inter alia, specify the use of programmatic EIA for activities that can be grouped geographically, generically or by stage of technology.

(3) SEA is implemented through a self-assessment process undertaken by the 'proponent' of the proposed policy, plan or programme.

In this context, the proponent is the government agency responsible for preparing or authorizing the proposed action. Generally, this process will be carried out in accordance with existing statutory and policy obligations of the agency and in conformity with specific requirements set out in the SEA provision and supplementary regulations or guidance. However, such an alignment appears to be far from complete in the implementation of the SEA processes of many countries, with inconsistencies in compliance evident across statutory and non-statutory arrangements. Even under NEPA, which explicitly obligated federal agencies to identify deficiencies that prohibited full compliance with the purposes and provisions of the Act (Section 103), application at the policy level has been circumvented and is now constrained by case law. Under the EU SEA Directive, the obligation is placed on member states to determine the detailed arrangements and accountabilities to implement the requirements and to ensure compliance with them (Article 13).

Although it provides a key means of instilling accountability amongst government agencies for their policies and plans, self-assessment can be effective only in association with appropriate measures for quality assurance and control. These measures are based on the steps and elements built into the SEA process (see below) and on the overseeing role of specialist and administrative bodies. Typically, the responsibility for SEA administration (including process development, guidance and monitoring compliance) is vested in the Ministry of Environment or an equivalent special purpose body (e.g. the Canadian Environmental Assessment Agency, the US Council on Environmental Quality). Some countries have also established a provision for independent review of the quality of SEA reports at the level of individual applications and of the effectiveness of process implementation at the systems level. In The Netherlands, the EIA Commission has performed this first role for specified plans and programmes, although it appears likely to have a more limited function under pending legislation to transpose the EU SEA Directive into a national instrument. In addition, advice on the application of The Netherlands' E-test of draft regulations (which is separately administered) is provided by the Joint Support Centre established by the environment, economic and justice ministries. At the systems level in Canada, the Parliamentary Commissioner for the Environment and Sustainable Development has undertaken audits of the SEA performance of federal agencies (see Section 3.3.3).

(4) With varying degrees of modification, SEA process and procedural elements correspond to those in place in EIA systems.

In broad, comparative terms, there are important differences between SEA processes and procedures applied to policy or legislation on the one hand, and to plans and programmes on the other. But, in some systems, the same legally prescribed elements of procedure apply to all proposals, from project-specific ones to those concerning plans and programmes (e.g. NEPA; see also Chapter 5). At the level of plans and programmes, SEA processes are usually based on EIA steps and elements, such as screening, impact identification and report preparation. For policy-level application of SEA, EIA procedures are still recognizable but often in minimum form, although not all SEA systems conform unambiguously with this model (see below).

In many ways, the EU SEA Directive establishes a new procedural benchmark for SEA of plans and programmes, not only within the EU but also internationally. It is modelled very closely on the EIA Directive (97/11/EC) and thus mandates a transparent and open process (e.g. certain articles of the SEA Directive relate to public consultation and information on the decision made). SEA is equated with the preparation of an environmental report and the information to be provided (see below) and the process is oriented to identifying and offsetting effects of implementing a plan or programme. It is open to question whether this procedural model is appropriate to meeting the basic objectives of the SEA Directive, in other words, to provide for a high level of environmental protection and to contribute to the integration of environmental considerations into plan preparation. The test will be in the way this process is transposed into national systems and implemented by member states. But the concern is that the provisions of the Directive are likely to entrench the approach to the SEA of plans and programmes at a relatively late stage in the decision-making process. We shall see.

EIA steps or elements have been amended and combined in certain SEA processes that apply to policy and legislative proposals. This is the case particularly in SEA processes that apply only at this level, as exemplified by the Danish, Dutch and Finnish systems. In The Netherlands, for example, the E-test has been reorganized into two main phases: a quick scan and, if necessary, a more detailed appraisal of proposed legislation. A similar procedure is followed in Canada for policies, plans or programmes, although the assessment phase may also include further steps. In New Zealand, under the Resource Management Act, SEA is generic rather than a separate procedure and is threaded into policy- and plan-making (e.g. preparation of regional policy statements). A more distinguishable form of policy evaluation or options appraisal is triggered under Section 32 (e.g. with regard to proposed national environmental standards). These process elements are described more fully in the national reviews in Section 3.3.

(5) The preparation of a report or statement on the environmental effects of a proposal is widely acknowledged to be one of the cornerstones of the SEA process.

This element was enshrined in the pioneering NEPA statute and the subsequent regulations, which describe the preparation of an environmental impact statement (EIS) as an 'action-forcing device to insure the policies and goals of the Act are infused into the actions of the Federal Government' (CEQ, 1986, p10). The parts dealing with EIS preparation include requirements related to: page limits (even for proposals of 'unusual scope'); plain language writing; issuing draft, final and, if necessary, supplemental statements; and following a standard format including for the preparation of a programmatic EIS. At this level, agencies also are encouraged to tier any subsequent project EIS to the findings of a programmatic statement, concentrating only on issues specific to the subsequent proposal. Tiering also helps to meet general-purpose NEPA requirements, including reducing delay and excessive paperwork.

The production of a report occupies a central position in the EU SEA Directive, which stipulates that 'environmental assessment shall mean the preparation of an environmental statement' (Article 2(b)). The types of information to be included in an environmental report are described in Annex 1 of the Directive (see Box 3.5). The report must also include information that may reasonably be required, taking into account 'current knowledge and methods of assessment, the contents and level of detail in the plan or programme, its stage in the decision-making process and the extent to which certain matters are more appropriately assessed at other levels' (Article 5(2)). Finally, there is a requirement to consult with authorities (to be designated by member states 'when deciding on the scope and level of detail of the information to be included' (Article 6(3)).

In the EU SEA Directive, as in some other SEA regulations, there is no formal requirement for a *separate* report on environmental effects – one of the procedural 'sacred cows' of the prescriptive literature. Rather 'environmental report shall mean the part of the plan or programme documentation containing the information required' (Article 2(c)). Until recently, similar provisions were included in the Canadian *Guidelines for Implementing the Cabinet Directive on SEA* which state that 'separate reporting is not required' but should be 'integrated into existing mechanisms to the fullest extent possible' (CEAA, 2000). Additional requirements now apply (see below). Under the Danish Circular, a statement on environment impacts is included in the observations on the bills and other government proposals submitted to Parliament and subjected to SEA (DMEE, 1995a). In the UK process for the environmental appraisal of policy, the preparation and publication of a report or statement is left to the discretion of departments (DETR, 1998, 7.1).

(6) New international legal instruments have been established that apply partly or primarily to SEA procedure and practice.

In addition to the EU SEA Directive (defined strictly, this is supra-national in its scope), two UNECE legal instruments have been adopted that bind signatory countries to a particular approach to SEA. They also have potential application outside the UNECE region. These comprise:

- *The Aarhus Convention on Access to Information, Public Participation and Access to Justice in Environmental Matters* (1998). Inter alia, the Convention establishes obligations on Parties with regard to the aspects of strategic decision-making. Article 7 covers public participation with regard to plans, programmes and policies. It does not specifically require SEA but this process is widely recognized as one the means of giving expression to its provisions (Stec and Casey-Lefkowitz, 2000). Similarly, SEA also may be seen as an 'implementing' mechanism for Article 8, which deals with the preparation of laws and 'normative instruments'. Equally importantly, the provisions of Articles 7 and 8 set international standards for public participation, which apply, inter alia, to Parties with SEA processes that operate on these levels. These standards are also reflected in the SEA Protocol (Box 3.1).

• *The SEA Protocol to the Convention on EIA in a Transboundary Context* (2003). This is a self-standing, international legal instrument that will be binding on Parties and promises to be influential beyond the boundaries of the UNECE region (see Box 3.1). The Protocol was drafted and finalized with the participation of a wide range of countries, including EU member states and then accession countries, other transitional countries of Central and Eastern Europe and the newly independent states of the former Soviet Union. It is intended to provide for a high level of protection for the environment and human health. It provides for the mandatory application of SEA to plans and programmes (excluding budget and fiscal ones). In this regard, the Protocol closely follows the provisions of the EU SEA Directive, for example with regard to screening, scoping, the information to be included in an environmental report, public participation and decision-making. Only one article specifically applies to transboundary consultations. Article 14 of the SEA Protocol extends it beyond the scope of the EU SEA Directive, providing for discretionary application of SEA to policies and legislation. While, initially, this provision is unlikely to be implemented widely, over time it may establish 'soft law' precedents for the Parties.

(7) There are several different but overlapping institutional models or types of procedural approach for SEA.

The various models and approaches listed in Table 3.2 are also reflected in Table 3.1. They are grouped to correspond with the generic typology of SEA types introduced in Chapter 1 – formal, near-equivalent and para-SEA – to which we also add integrated approaches.

3.2 SEA EXPERIENCE IN THE EU

The EU encompasses a single market made up of a significant proportion of the developed countries, including four members of the G8 group, and is a major force internationally in its own right. Specifically, the EU's legal and policy framework on the environment and sustainable development has Europe-wide and global dimensions, as well as having direct application to member states and accession countries. The adoption of the EU SEA Directive should be seen in this larger context and in relation to other legal and policy instruments for achieving the same purpose.

In the preamble to the Directive, for example, key references are made to the 'environmental' Articles (6 and 174) of the Consolidated EU Treaty, the Fifth Environment Action Programme (Toward Sustainability) – now replaced by the Sixth Programme to 2010 – and the Convention on Biological Diversity. Article 1 of the Directive sets out two broad objectives: 'to provide for a high

BOX 3.1 PROTOCOL ON STRATEGIC ENVIRONMENTAL ASSESSMENT (SEA) TO THE UNECE CONVENTION ON EIA IN A TRANSBOUNDARY CONTEXT

After a two-year process of negotiation, the Protocol on Strategic Environmental Assessment (SEA) to the UNECE Convention on EIA in a Transboundary Context was adopted formally and signed by 35 countries at the Ministerial Conference 'Environment for Europe' in Kiev, Ukraine, on 23 May 2003. It has not yet come into legal force (it requires ratification by at least 16 countries), but this is expected to occur soon. Moreover, there are a large number of potential Parties to the SEA Protocol, including the countries of Central Asia.

The SEA Protocol is about far more than transboundary impacts. It is a comprehensive legal instrument that follows the broad thrust of the SEA Directive and extends elements of this framework beyond the boundaries of the EU. Also, the Protocol will be open to all members of the UN. This means that, eventually, it could have wider uptake in other regions. However, it is likely that this process will be uneven, even within the UNECE region, since Canada and the US were not party to the negotiation process and are unlikely to ratify the Protocol.

Articles 4–12 (inclusive) of the Protocol set out mandatory procedures for applying SEA to plans and programmes. There is also a provision relating to non-mandatory application to policies and legal acts. However, this provision is self-standing and no implementing procedures are set out. Nevertheless, in the future, this provision could be interpreted as a 'soft law' precedent that establishes obligations on the Parties.

The Protocol also provides for the public to be informed about plans and programmes subject to SEA, to comment, to have their comments taken into account in decision-making and to be told of the reasons for the final decision. These provisions build on relevant articles in the UNECE Convention on Access to Information, Public Participation in Decision-making and Access to Justice in Environmental Matters, which applies to strategic decision-making.

Besides requiring assessment of the typical environmental effects of plans and programmes, the Protocol places a special emphasis on considering human health, going beyond existing European legislation. This reflects the involvement of the World Health Organization in the negotiations as well as the political commitments made at the 1999 London Ministerial Conference on Environment and Health.

level of protection of the environment and to contribute to the integration of environmental considerations into the preparation and adoption of plans and programmes with a view to promoting sustainable development'. Other than possibly in their order of listing, no priority is implied between these dual objectives, which typically are assumed to be complementary. However, Sheate et al (2001) provide a trenchant analysis of the evolution of EU policy for environmental integration and sustainable development. They argue that there is a potential divergence of these two fundamental principles, which is manifested, inter alia, in the recent adoption of the SEA Directive and the EC Communication on impact assessment for policy-making (COM (2002) 276 final). In that context, the stated objective of the SEA Directive 'to provide a

Table 3.2 *SEA models and approaches*

Institutional model or procedural approach	Description
Formal	
EIA-based	SEA is modelled closely on or applied under and in accordance with the requirements of EIA legislation (e.g. US, EU SEA Directive).
EIA-modified	SEA is carried out as a separate or parallel process to EIA, often as an administrative procedure with modified elements and characteristics (e.g. Canada, Denmark).
Dual or two-track systems	Examples include: • the Dutch E-test of regulations and SEA of plans and programmes, previously as specified under the EIA Decree and now being aligned with the EU SEA Directive; • Finnish EIA-based process for policies, plans and programmes and SEA of bills and other government proposals.
Near-equivalent	
Environmental appraisal	SEA is not applied formally but is covered by a near-equivalent overall process of environmental appraisal of policy or plans (e.g. in the UK, this approach is being phased, respectively, into integrated policy appraisal at the central government level, and into SEA of plans and programmes at the local authority level in accordance with the EU SEA Directive).
Regional assessment.	SEA applied to regional or sector development strategies for a particular geographic area (e.g. in Australia under the Regional Forests Policy, and as recently introduced in Canada under reforms to the Environmental Assessment Act).
Sustainability appraisal	SEA elements are part of or linked to integrated assessment of the environmental, economic and social effects of resource policy or regional plans (e.g. assessments carried out by the former Resource Assessment Commission, Australia and for UK regional plans as described below).
Integrated	
Procedural integration	No separate SEA procedure; this function is integrated into policy or planning process (e.g. as in the New Zealand Resource Management Act).
Substantive integration	No separate SEA procedure; this function is replaced by integrated assessment (e.g. EC impact assessment for policy-making, and as carried out by the former Australian Resource Assessment Commission).
Integrated assessment and planning	No separate SEA procedure; this function is replaced by a system that is procedural and substantively integrated, in other words integrated assessment is structurally integrated into the planning system (e.g. UK regional planning system).
Para-SEA	
Elements of SEA	Approaches or procedures that have some but not all of the features or characteristics of SEA and have the same overall purpose. Examples include a variety of progressive land use planning approaches and assessments undertaken within sustainability-based development strategy processes.

high level of protection' may be interpreted as establishing a basis for strong environmental integration in accordance with Article 6 of the EU Treaty;[2] especially when allied with the reference in the preamble to Article 174, which, inter alia, provides that Community policy on the environment is to be based on the precautionary principle.[3] In contrast, the EC internal procedure for impact assessment arguably calls for a weaker version of environmental integration, in other words in which the level of protection is lower (see Sheate, 2003).

3.2.1 EU legal and policy frameworks

The distinction made by Sheate (2003), mentioned earlier, is a matter of emphasis and interpretation. There is both convergence and ambivalence in the relevant EU policy documents, especially in the *Sixth Environment Action Programme 2001–2010*, and also in the *European Union Strategy for Sustainable Development* (2002). Both documents add a much-needed environmental dimension to the so-called Lisbon process of economic and social reform, which called for the EU 'to become the most competitive and dynamic knowledge-based economy in the world capable of sustainable growth'. In both agendas, there are a number of common themes and elements, encompassing (see Box 3.2):

- major environmental challenges to sustainable development for Europe;
- priority areas for environmental policy development and action; and
- the need for improved policy coherence and consistency to deliver on new goals and targets.

Specifically, the EU Sustainable Development Strategy calls for 'a new policy agenda' and 'a new approach to policy-making' (CEC, 2001, p24). This means, inter alia, that 'careful assessment of the full effects of a policy proposal must include estimates of its economic, environmental and social impacts inside and outside the EU'. Within the EU, there is an important distinction between the application of SEA and related instruments by institutions of the Commission and by member states. In the former case, under the EU Treaty, the EC must integrate environmental protection requirements into the definition and implementation of its own policies and activities, particularly in order to promote sustainable development (Box 3.3).

---

2 As stated in the preamble to the Directive: 'Article 6 of the Treaty provides that environmental protection requirements are to be integrated into the definition of Community policies and activities, in particular with a view to promoting sustainable development'.

3 As stated in the preamble to the Directive: 'Article 174 of the Treaty provides that Community policy on the environment is to contribute to, inter alia, the preservation, protection and improvement of the quality of the environment, the protection of human health and the prudent and rational utilisation of natural resources and that it is to be based on the precautionary principle'.

BOX 3.2 THE EU ENVIRONMENT ACTION PROGRAMME AND STRATEGY FOR SUSTAINABLE DEVELOPMENT

Section 1.2 of the Sixth Environment Action Programme underlines the environmental basis of sustainable development as follows:

> *A prudent use of the world's natural resources and the protection of the global eco-system are a condition for sustainable development, together with economic prosperity and a balanced social development... This Programme identifies the environmental issues that have to be addressed if sustainable development is to come about – climate change, the over-use of renewable and non-renewable natural resources, the loss of bio-diversity, and the accumulation of persistent toxic chemicals in the environment. It sets out the environmental objectives and targets that need to be met and describes how the instruments of Community environmental policy will be used to tackle these issues while pointing to the need for further action in other policy fields... This requires the integration of environmental protection requirements into other policy areas and a need for the Community to examine its current systems of governance and find ways of changing them to ensure consistency between our social, economic and environmental objectives and between the ways of meeting them.*

According to the Communication setting out the EU Strategy for Sustainable Development (CEC, 2001, p23), it *'should focus on a small number of problems which pose severe or irreversible threats* to the future well being of European Society' (original emphasis) . The issue areas encompass environmental, economic and social dimensions and comprise: global warming; loss of biodiversity and natural resource management; public health risks from antibiotic-resistant strains, hazardous chemicals and food safety; poverty and social exclusion; ageing of the population and its economic repercussions; and transport congestion, urban structure and regional imbalances. To meet these problems, the Commission proposes an EU strategy in three parts:

1   A set of *cross-cutting proposals and recommendations* to improve policy and make sustainable development happen. This means making sure that different policies reinforce each other.
2   A set of *headline objectives and specific measures* at EU level to tackle the issues which pose the biggest challenges to sustainable development in Europe.
3   Steps to *implement the strategy* and *review its progress* (original emphases).

Sources: CEC (2001, 2002)

As part of the integration agenda outlined in the EU Strategy for Sustainable Development, the Communication from the Commission on Impact Assessment (COM (2002) 276 final) has laid down the procedure to be applied to its own policy proposals. While representing an important step forward, the approach has been criticized as a potentially weak form of environmental integration (Sheate, 2003; see Box 3.4).

BOX 3.3 INTEGRATION OF THE ENVIRONMENT IN EUROPEAN COMMISSION POLICY-MAKING

The European Commission has established a number of internal administrative processes to promote the integration of environment considerations. Horizontal measures include reporting, green house-keeping and environmental appraisal of the Commission's policy proposals (the so-called 'Green Stars' system for legislative proposals that may have a significant impact on the environment). In practice, the implementation of such measures has proved difficult. In 1999, the Commission concluded that these measures were insufficient and reviewed other options for integration of the environment as its contribution to the Cardiff process on improving environmental integration (agreed at the European Council meeting in Cardiff in 1998) and the implementation of Article 6 of the Amsterdam Treaty (Cologne Report to the European Council, June 1999).

In outlining its strategic objectives for 2000–2005, the Commission noted that the degradation of the environment is taking place at an accelerating rate and that the continuation of current development patterns is unsustainable. The Commission itself is responding on a number of different fronts to integrate the environment into its major policy areas and to promote sustainable development. The Sixth Environmental Action Programme (6EAP, 2001) sets out environmental objectives and targets in a ten-year perspective for EU policy and identifies the means to achieve them. Closely linked is the EU Strategy for Sustainable Development (CEC, 2001), which requires the integration of social, economic and environmental considerations in policy-making. Other practical measures taken include the review of the Green Stars system and improvements to policy assessment, supported by guidance on tools and methods inspired by SEA. The Commission also launched a study to investigate in more detail how SEA and the integration of the environment into strategic decision-making are interrelated (see Sheate et al, 2001).

Source: Adapted from Feldmann et al (2001)

3.2.2 New areas of application

In 1999, the European Commission commissioned the Institute for Development Policy and Management (IDPM) at the University of Manchester, UK to undertake an independent assessment of the impact that World Trade Organization (WTO) multilateral trade negotiations may have on sustainable development. The main objectives are to develop a methodology for sustainability impact assessment (SIA) and to use it to make a broad qualitative assessment of the impact upon sustainability of the WTO trade negotiations. The work (ongoing) is being conducted through a number of phases (Appendix 9). Recently, the EC has adopted the SIA approach with the intention of applying it to all its policy proposals.

3.2.3 The EU SEA Directive in perspective

Under the Directive, 'environmental assessments' are to be carried out for a specified list of plans and programmes (as discussed later in this section).

BOX 3.4 IMPACT ASSESSMENT IN EUROPEAN COMMISSION POLICY-MAKING

In its Communication on Impact Assessment (COM (2002) 276 final), the European Commission sets out an impact assessment procedure that is to be integrated into its Strategic Policy and Programme/Activity Based Management programming cycle. This procedure is organized into two stages:

- preliminary assessment, resulting in a short statement and focusing on the identification of the issue/objectives and desired outcome, main policy options available and need for further assessment; and
- extended impact assessment, where necessary, including detailed analysis, consultation with interested parties and summary of the results in a report.

The Communication also includes checklists and key questions that need to be answered when conducting the assessment.

Sheate (2003) describes this procedure and observes that it seems 'on the face of it to be a positive move, but focuses very much on quantification – and where possible monetary quantification – of impacts, and explicitly recognises that trade-offs will be made' (COM (2002) 276 final, Annex 2, p16, para. 4.2).

The Commission has established a number of principles to guide it in assessing impacts:

> *The economic, social and environmental impacts identified for the proposed option should be analysed and presented in a format that facilitates a better understanding of* the trade-offs between competing economic, social and environmental objectives. *To show the different impacts, make comparisons easier and identify trade-offs and win–win situations in a transparent way*, it is desirable to quantify the impacts in physical and, where appropriate, monetary terms (in addition to a qualitative appraisal). *Impacts that cannot be expressed in quantitative or monetary terms should not, however, be seen as less important as they may contain aspects that are significant for the policy decision. Nor can final results always be expressed in one single figure reflecting the net benefit or cost of the option under consideration.*
>
> (emphasis added by Sheate, 2003)

There is no explicit requirement for public participation in this process; only consultation with interested parties and relevant experts as part of the extended impact assessment (not the preliminary assessment). 'Therefore, there is a risk that trade-offs will be made without sufficient scrutiny and transparency. This reflects very much a weak interpretation of sustainable development and contrasts with that in the Sixth Environmental Action Plan. But it is more consistent with that of the Sustainable Development Strategy, which provides the impetus for its development' (Sheate, 2003).

Policies are exempt but this is likely to be an issue in implementation of the Directive since many of these plans and programmes are not likely to be policy-neutral. In this respect, the Directive is also at odds with the EU's external strategy for sustainable development (CEC, 2002) which gives priority to 'ensur[ing] that an impact assessment is carried out for all major policy proposals, analysing their economic, social and environmental consequences in accordance with the conclusions of the Göteborg European Council, June 2001'. By comparison to the European Commission's internal EIA assessment procedure, the EU SEA Directive provides a potentially stronger basis for ensuring that environmental protection is an integral part of certain plans and programmes that are adopted by member states. The foundations of the Directive rest on two core pillars.

First, the Directive is reasonably encompassing in its coverage and scope of application, although there are legal question marks about the type of plans and programmes that will be subject to its requirements in different member states.

The certain plans and programmes referred to in the formal title of the Directive include those 'which are subject to preparation and/or adoption by an authority at national, regional or local level' (Article 2(a))[4] and 'are likely to have significant environmental effects' (Article 3.1). The scope of application is limited in Article 3.2 to plans and programmes that are prepared for 'agriculture, forestry, fisheries, energy, industry, transport, waste management, water management, telecommunications, tourism, town and country planning or land use and which set the framework for future development of projects listed in Annexes I and II to [EIA] Directive 85/337/EEC, or which, in view of the likely effects on sites, have been determined to require an assessment pursuant to Article 6 or 7 of [Habitat] Directive 92/43/EEC'.

Article 3.8 defines the plans and programmes that are not subject to the Directive; it excludes proposals that address financial or budgetary and (solely) national defence and civil emergency matters. In addition, the SEA Directive does not apply to plans and programmes co-financed under the current programming period for structural funds or rural development provided for in Regulations (EC) No 1260/1999 and (EC) No 1257/1999, respectively (Article 3.9). The Commission is required to report on the relationship between the Directive and the Regulations well ahead of the expiry of the programming period with a view to ensuring a coherent approach to their subsequent relationship (Article 12(4)).

Second, the requirements of the Directive incorporate a number of procedural 'safeguards' for appropriate implementation by member states, although, inevitably, much will depend on the discretion exercised by member states in their transposition and implementation.

---

4 Article 2(a) defines plans and programmes to mean those:
- 'which are subject to the preparation and/or adoption by an authority at national, regional or local level or which are prepared by an authority for adoption, through a legislative procedure by Parliament or Government, and
- which are required by legislative, regulatory or administrative provisions'.

In this regard, as noted earlier, a key requirement centres on the preparation of an environmental report and the specification of the detailed information to be provided in the statement. The information must include, inter alia, relevant aspects of the current state of the environment, environmental protection objectives that are relevant to the plan or programme, the likely significant effects on the environment and the measures to mitigate these, and an outline of the reasons for selecting the alternatives dealt with (see Box 3.5).

Although others may see matters differently, the last requirement, which lies at the heart of the creative application of SEA, is narrowly framed and unlikely to encourage real generation and consideration of alternatives. There are minimum procedures for statutory authorities (referred to in Article 6.3) and for the public to be consulted, and the member states are to make detailed arrangements for this purpose (Article 6.5). Both the information included in the environmental statement (Article 5) and the results of the views expressed by the statutory authorities and the public (Article 6) – including any transboundary consultations (Article 7) – must be taken into account during the preparation of plans and programmes and before their adoption (Article 8). A statement must be made summarizing how these aspects have been taken into account, which encourages transparency.

Finally, member states must 'monitor the significant effects of the implementation of plans and programmes, in order, inter alia, to identify unforeseen effects at an early stage and to be able to undertake appropriate remedial measures' (Article 10). Moreover, they are required to ensure that 'environmental reports are of sufficient quality to meet the requirements of the Directive' and to communicate to the Commission the measures taken in that regard (Article 12.2). Before 21 July 2006, the Commission must submit a first report to the European Parliament and Council on the application and effectiveness of the SEA Directive (Article 12). Collectively, these obligations represent a potentially important mechanism for quality assurance and control of SEA implementation. However, in practice, much will depend on the attitudes and actions of member states.

3.2.4 Towards implementation

The SEA Directive is widely regarded as a milestone in the evolution of the SEA field, but there will be considerable challenges associated with its implementation. Two initiatives may provide some pointers to the way forward.

First, a review by Sheate et al (2001) looked at a range of assessment-type mechanisms that have been used to promote environmental integration in the EU. It placed SEA in the broader strategic context of processes, institutions, arrangements and instruments and looked at integration practice in all member states. Drawing from this review, Appendix 10 summarizes key examples of strategic approaches in ten selected EU member states, and also the status of SEA at the time of finalization of the SEA Directive in 2001. These examples

---

**BOX 3.5 INFORMATION TO BE PROVIDED IN AN
ENVIRONMENT REPORT (AS SPECIFIED IN ANNEX 1 OF THE
EU SEA DIRECTIVE)**

- an outline of the contents, main objectives of the plan or programme and relationship with other relevant plans and programmes;
- the relevant aspects of the current state of the environment and the likely evolution thereof without implementation of the plan or programme;
- the environmental characteristics of areas likely to be significantly affected;
- any existing environmental problems which are relevant to the plan or programme including, in particular, those relating to any areas of a particular environmental importance;
- the environmental protection objectives, established at international, Community or member state level, which are relevant to the plan or programme and the way those objectives and any environmental considerations have been taken into account during its preparation;
- the likely significant effects on the environment, including on issues such as biodiversity, population, human health, fauna, flora, soil, water, air, climatic factors, material assets, cultural heritage including architectural and archaeological heritage, landscape and the interrelationship between the above factors;
- the measures envisaged to prevent, reduce and as fully as possible offset any significant adverse effects on the environment of implementing the plan or programme;
- an outline of the reasons for selecting the alternatives dealt with, and a description of how the assessment was undertaken including any difficulties (such as technical deficiencies or lack of know-how) encountered in compiling the required information;
- a description of the measures envisaged concerning monitoring; and
- a non-technical summary of the information provided under the above headings.

Source: Official Journal of the European Communities (21.7.2001, L197/36)

---

illustrate the larger framework and potential for SEA integration in the EU.

Second, the theoretical and methodological basis for the SEA Directive has been examined through a collaborative research programme (analytical strategic environmental assessment, ANSEA), although its practical application remains in question. ANSEA was funded by the EU Fifth Framework Research Programme and was an ambitious attempt to establish a framework for assisting the implementation of the SEA Directive (Appendix 13).

As suggested earlier in this chapter, the real test of the SEA Directive will lie in its implementation, a point that is often overlooked in the rush to judgement on its procedural pros and cons. In the interim, we offer two broad observations.

First, the SEA Directive is not the first or only Community piece of legislation to establish obligations on member states to carry out a systematic assessment of the environmental effects of plans and programmes. Such a requirement also applies through Council Directive 79/409/EEC on the conservation of wild birds, Directive 92/43/EEC on the conservation of natural habitats and Directive 2000/60/EC establishing a framework for Community action on water policy. Where an obligation to carry out an assessment arises simultaneously from the SEA Directive and other community legislation, member states may provide for coordinated or joint procedures in order to avoid duplication (Article 11.2). To date, however, SEA experience associated with these other instruments appears to be limited, and it is probably safe to say that implementation of the SEA Directive will be more extensive and it will be the cornerstone for meeting the requirements of Community legislation. Over time, we also expect it to reshape the way plans and programmes are made in Europe and, ideally, to infuse the environment into all aspects of their preparation and implementation. However, we accept that this will be a tall order and a long-term goal.

Second, it is important to remember that the SEA Directive was more than a decade in the making, from the time serious discussion began within the Commission to its coming into force in 2004. This process was far longer if we date it from the initial commitment to prepare a Directive in 1987 when the stated intention was to include policies. There was considerable debate on various drafts and five years elapsed from the release of the Draft Directive on SEA in 1997 to its finalization in 2001. Furthermore, there was considerable opposition from various member states until the negotiation process ended. Member states had to be in compliance before 21 July 2004 and only plans and programmes that are formally initiated after that date will be subject to the requirements of the Directive. Plans and programmes commenced before then have a 24-month period for completion, after which the Directive applies retroactively 'unless member states decide on a case-by-case basis that this is not feasible' (Article 13.3). In short, it is unlikely that the first batch of SEAs will be rolled out until 2005 and possibly it will be much longer before the SEA systems of the member states are fully operational.

3.3 NATIONAL EXPERIENCE WITH SEA

3.3.1 Australia[5]

The Australia Environment Protection and Biodiversity Conservation Act (the EPBC Act, 1999) replaced a number of federal statutes including the Environment Protection (Impact of Proposals) Act (the EPIP Act, 1974). EIA provision and procedure constitute an important part of the new Act and provide for a strengthened role for the Federal Government in matters of national environmental significance such as world and national heritage places, nationally threatened plants and animals, migratory species and internationally important wetlands (see Early, 2004). Part 10 of the EPBC Act provides for SEA of policies, plans and programmes, triggered by agreement with the

---

5   With contributions by Gerard Early, Department of the Environment and Heritage, Canberra; and John Ashe (Consultant).

Federal Minister for the Environment. In addition, it requires strategic assessment of all fisheries managed by the Federal Government and all fisheries involved in the export industry (paragraphs 147–154).

Marsden (2002) has evaluated the provisions of paragraphs 146 and 147 against principles of international best practice in SEA, as defined by Sadler and Verheem (1996), and identifies a number of procedural shortcomings. These include the relatively restricted scope of application of the Act – it excludes matters of national environmental significance (such as forests – see below), which, arguably, should be included. In his view, paragraph 146 also leaves too much discretion to the Minister and thereby lacks much of the certainty and transparency that a legal framework should bring. With regard to paragraph 147, as applied specifically to fisheries management, Marsden (2002) finds a closer correspondence with principles of international best practice and concludes that the SEA of the Heard Island and McDonald Islands Fishery represents a positive introduction to the implementation of the requirements of paragraphs 147–154. So far, a major SEA of Australia's offshore oil and gas exploration is being undertaken and some 90 strategic assessments of fisheries are complete or underway.

Under the National Forest Policy Statement (NFPS),[6] endorsed by the Federal Government and all states and territories, there is provision for the conduct of comprehensive regional assessment (CRA), which has many of the characteristics of SEA (Ashe, 2002). This process is a basis for the conclusion of regional forest agreements (RFAs), which the Federal and State Governments pursued from the mid-1990s as a means of resolving jurisdictional and fundamental conflicts over land use and management. CRA is undertaken through two parallel streams of assessment. One comprises an environmental and heritage assessment relating to the national estate and world heritage, indigenous heritage, endangered species, biodiversity, old growth and wilderness values and to ecologically sustainable forest management. The other comprises economic and social assessment of resource use and development opportunities and the consequences of exploiting them. To date, CRA has been applied to 11 regional forest agreements (Box 3.6).

An earlier SEA-equivalent process was introduced under the Australian Resource Assessment Commission (RAC) Act 1989, which established an independent body to conduct inquiries on resource policy issues referred to it by the Prime Minister. Section 7 of the Act requires the Commission to take an integrated approach and to have regard to considerations of efficiency, equity and ecological integrity (i.e. to explicitly address sustainability). The first inquiry on the future use and management of Australia's forest and timber resources (1989–1992) was part of the policy development process that led to

---

6   Commonwealth of Australia, *National Forest Policy Statement: A New Focus for Australia's Forests* (1992). The NFPS sets out policies and objectives for Australia's public and private forests. It identifies 11 broad national goals for land use, which are to be pursued within a regional planning framework that integrates environmental and commercial objectives.

Box 3.6 The Central Highlands RFA/CRA process, Australia

Regional forest agreements (RFAs) centre on regions in which commercial timber production is a major forest use, with boundaries determined by political and economic rather than bio-geographic criteria. This process is an attempt to find a lasting solution to the fundamental conflict between conservation and wood production in Australian forests and to settle jurisdictional disputes arising from intervention by the Commonwealth in state management of these lands. An integral component of the RFA process is a wide-ranging programme of environmental, economic and social assessments known as comprehensive regional assessments (CRAs).

With certain variation as to detail, the RFA process comprises four phases: scoping, assessment, integration and agreement. This process and the role of CRA, in particular, are illustrated by the Central Highlands RFA in Victoria, located north and east of Melbourne, the region comprises 1.1 million hectares, with public lands occupying 56 per cent of this area.

In January 1996, an interim agreement was signed to provide for the protection of forests that might be required for a 'comprehensive, adequate and representative (CAR) reserve system pending completion of the RFA'. A scoping agreement set out the arrangements for conduct of the RFA and, in broad terms, the matters to be assessed.

During the next 17 months, a CRA of the environmental, cultural, economic and social issues in the region was carried out. This included assessments relating to biodiversity, old-growth forest, wilderness, national estate, world heritage and ecologically sustainable forest management (ESFM). A CRA report was issued for public consultation in July 1997. The report may be compared in scope and scale to a conventional EIS. It drew heavily on existing studies and was accompanied by technical reports.

Following the public consultation phase, the process entered the 'integration' phase, initiated by the release, in September 1997, of the Central Highlands RFA Directions Report. This set out proposals for the CAR reserve system, ESFM in the region and forestry industry issues. The report was released for an eight-week period and provided the basis for negotiations between the Commonwealth and Victoria Governments. The Central Highlands RFA was signed in March 1998 and is to remain in force for 20 years, with provision for amendment by mutual agreement, for dispute resolution and for five-yearly reviews. Principal elements of the Agreement include:

- confirmation by the Commonwealth that its obligations under the Australian Heritage Commission Act 1975, the Environment Protection (Impact of Proposals) Act 1974 and the Endangered Species Act 1992 have been met;
- provisions concerning world heritage nomination of areas in the region;
- establishment of a CAR reserve system for the region; and
- Commonwealth accreditation of Victoria's ESFM system and processes, and industry development initiatives.

Under the Agreement, the conservation reserve system for the region increased by 116,000 ha (64 per cent) and nearly half the public land in the region is now in national parks or other reserves. The CAR reserve system meets the nationally agreed criteria for biodiversity, old growth and wilderness. Benefits for industry include certainty of access to forest resources and financial incentive for industry development. Social benefits include prospects for the creation of 300 new jobs.

Sources: Ashe (2001, 2002)

Box 3.7: Forest and Timber Inquiry, Australia

The Forest and Timber Inquiry conducted by the Australian Resource Assessment Commission was completed in 1992. Although now more than ten years old, the Inquiry remains one of the reference points for integrated, strategic environmental and sustainability assessment. Its mandate was to identify and evaluate policy options for the use and management of Australian forest and timber resources. The Inquiry combined industry and government submissions, public hearings and independent technical analysis. Major study components included:

- resource capability, tenure and use inventories;
- evaluation of forest management strategies and institutional arrangements;
- wood supply and demand projections;
- review of the environmental effects of logging, including soil productivity, aquatic systems, flora and fauna, nutrient recycling, and carbon sequestering;
- survey of social values of forests and attitudes to management;
- identification of five strategies of forest use and management, from maximization of timber production to no further logging of native species; and
- clarification of the choices and trade-offs at stake (although the Inquiry did not provide specific advice to the Government).

Source: Resource Assessment Commission (1992); summarized in Sadler and Verheem (1996)

---

the RFA and CRA process (Box 3.6 above). The RAC approach also had an evident influence on this process and is referenced internationally because of its scope and comprehensiveness (see Box 3.7). The Commission as a standing body was disbanded in 1993 after conducting only three inquiries, although the legislation remains on the statute books.

At the state level, recent changes to the Western Australia Environmental Protection Act (1986, amended 2003) enable the Environmental Protection Authority (EPA) to formally assess 'strategic proposals' likely to have a significant effect on the environment (www.epa.wa.gov.au). Previously, paragraph 16(e) of the Act, which gives the EPA an advisory function, was used to undertake informal strategic assessments on a range of proposals; for example, approximately 40 were completed between the beginning of 1995 and mid-2001 (Malcolm, 2002). The latest amendment to the Act allows proponents to refer their strategic proposals voluntarily. In subjecting them to SEA, the advantage to the proponent is that future 'derived proposals' will not require further assessment (referral of environmentally significant projects is compulsory under the Act).

During 2002 and 2003, an integrated, strategic-level assessment of the Gorgon Gas Development off the Pilbara Coast of Western Australia was undertaken by the State Government, which considered social, economic and environmental issues, as well as the strategic implications of the proposal for Western Australia. In the absence of a formal SEA or sustainability assessment process at the time, a unique process was developed for the Gorgon case. It was managed through a whole-of-government approach with a high degree of interaction between relevant agencies at both chief executive officer (CEO), and officer level. The process was modelled on the EIA process used in Western Australia. Scoping guidelines were prepared and the proponent subsequently provided an environmental, social and economic review document (ChevronTexaco Australia Pty Ltd, 2003), which was made publicly available. The proponent was required to respond to issues raised in the public submissions. In addition, three other assessment documents were prepared and submitted for Cabinet consideration:

- an environmental review undertaken by the Western Australian Environmental Protection Authority (EPA, 2003);
- advice on biodiversity conservation values by the Conservation Commission of Western Australia (2003) which is the vesting authority for Barrow Island; and
- advice on social, economic and strategic considerations to the Department of Industry and Resources (DoIR) (Allen Consulting Group Pty Ltd, 2003).

These documents also were made publicly available along with a separate summary/overview document (Government of Western Australia, 2003). Once public submissions were received, the chief executives of the relevant government agencies briefed the Cabinet on the proposal.

In September 2003, the Cabinet decided to grant the Gorgon Joint Venture access to Barrow Island for the purposes of gas processing. Currently the proponent is undertaking a formal EIA process (under Part IV of the Environmental Protection Act 1986) which will detail the environmental impacts and mitigation strategies associated with constructing the gas processing plant on Barrow Island. A detailed analysis of the Gorgon case study is in progress (Pope et al, submitted) which examines the project in light of the three concepts of sustainability assessment put forward by Pope et al (2004).

A number of other Australian states also take a strategic approach to development proposals and variously incorporate elements of SEA. For example, in New South Wales, the formulation of regional and local plans must take into account environmental studies of land likely to be affected. In Victoria, planning authorities must take account of significant effects that a development scheme may have on the environment and, according to Harvey (2002), ad hoc forms of SEA of plans are exemplified in the approach to site nomination and zoning for coastal marinas. A similar approach can be recognized in South Australia although, here, informal SEA takes place within coastal planning to integrate environmental criteria into the marina site selection process (Harvey, 2002). There are a number of other planning and policy-making processes at the state and federal levels that are analogous to SEA but have yet to be evaluated from this perspective (Marsden and Dovers, 2002).

3.3.2 Austria[7]

To date, SEA has been required formally in only a few cases. However there has been progress in that direction at the federal and provincial levels. First, a range of policy and planning mechanisms for integrating environmental issues into decision-making have been developed (see Appendix 10). Second, there are various initiatives underway to transpose and implement the EU SEA Directive, including amending existing and enacting new legislation:

- The Federal Government has amended the Water Management Act (Federal Law Gazette I 82, 2003; 29 Aug 2003).
- Salzburg province has amended its Spatial Planning Act (Law Gazette of Salzburg Province, No. 13/2004, 27 Feb 2004).
- The provinces of Lower Austria and Styria have drafted similar amendments.[8]
- Carinthia province has drafted a 'Carinthian Environmental Planning Act', covering all plans and programmes in its competences to which the Directive applies.

In addition, SEA pilot studies have been undertaken covering different geographical areas and planning sectors (Box 3.8). All of these applications have improved the planning process, for example through considering alternatives, analysing environmental consequences and documenting the likely environmental effects. Some of the pilots, particularly the most recent ones, also contributed to the adoption of better quality plans and programmes in which environmental concerns were taken into account in decision-making. Not all of the measures recommended have been implemented and the effectiveness of SEA remains to be seen. Although some of these pilots are still being evaluated, the Viennese waste management plan shows the most progress in implementing proposed measures (Box 3.9). In this case, a round table process was used to facilitate effective stakeholder involvement (Box 3.10). For more details on the pilot studies see Aschemann (2004).

SEA activities in Austria also include reviews of international and national approaches and experience, for example in relation to policies and legislation, plans and programmes that will be subject to the EU SEA Directive and

---

7   With contributions by Kerstin Arbter, Arbter SEA Consulting and Research; and Ralf Aschemann, Austrian Institute for the Development of Environmental Assessment.

8   Mining, water management and forestry are the responsibility of the Federal Government whereas spatial planning and nature conservation are under the jurisdiction of the nine provinces. The main actors involved in SEA activities in Austria are:

- the Federal Ministry of Agriculture and Forestry, Environment and Water Management (MoE), and the Federal Ministry of Transport, Innovation and Technology; and
- the relevant departments of the nine administrations of the provincial governments.

BOX 3.8 PILOT APPLICATIONS OF SEA IN AUSTRIA

1995	Local energy plan for Graz city
1997	Land-use plan of Weiz (Styrian municipality with 9300 inhabitants)
1997	Regional programme of Tennengau (an association of 13 municipalities in Salzburg province)
1997	Danube corridor demonstration study (part of the Trans-European Transport Net, TEN)
1998	Regional development plan for the Danube area in Lower Austria
1999	Vienna waste management plan
2001	Urban and transport development in northeast Vienna (part of the city and surrounding municipalities)
2003	Waste management plan for Salzburg province.

BOX 3.9 PILOT SEA FOR VIENNA'S WASTE MANAGEMENT PLAN

In recent years, Vienna has experienced growing volumes of waste, higher standards for waste disposal in landfill legislation, and bottlenecks in the city's waste treatment facilities. In response, the Environmental Commission of Vienna (a kind of environmental ombudsman) called for an SEA to help in preparing a waste management plan that would resolve these problems by 2010. The waste management authority decided to engage a wide range of stakeholders in the SEA process.

The Commission required that ecological, economic and social aspects be taken into account from the outset. They key issues were:

- Which waste minimization and waste recycling and treatment measures will solve the root problem?
- Does Vienna need additional waste treatment facilities to cope with the waste generated until 2010?
- Which treatment technologies are best suited to the specific local circumstances?
- How can the capacity of the existing facilities be optimized?
- What treatment capacities should newly built facilities comprise?

The SEA commenced in 1999 and adopted a participatory 'round table' stakeholder team approach (Box 3.10). A political decision on the plan was taken by the City Council in December 2001, following the recommendations of the 'round table' team. By 2003, some of the proposed measures had already been implemented: establishment of a strategy group for waste avoidance; selection of sites for the recommended new incineration plant and the new fermentation plant; and initiation of project EIAs for these two new installations.

---

screening procedure and criteria (see www.lebensministerium.at/umwelt). In addition, SEA training workshops and meetings have been organized, and SEA working groups meet regularly (e.g. a federal group on SEA and transport,

---

Box 3.10 Use of the SEA round table approach in Austria

The SEA team for the Vienna waste management plan (Box 3.9) adopted a round table approach. The team included representatives of local/national planning, environmental and other authorities, external waste management experts (planners) and interested environmental non-governmental organizations (NGOs). In this approach, team members act as equal partners throughout the process, from defining objectives to preparing the report, and share responsibility for the results. The team tries to reach consensus on a plan/programme that integrates the environmental aspects, combining elements of SEA and mediation. In this study, consensus was reached on nearly all aspects of the proposed waste management plan.

The model was developed further for SEA of urban and transport development in the northeast of Vienna. Besides environmental NGOs, Chambers of Commerce, Labour and Agriculture and Forestry, and politicians were represented in the SEA team. Also the participation of the broader public was strengthened and an SEA website was launched (www.wien.at/stadtentwicklung/supernow) – which received some 4000 hits. In addition, several public forums on SEA were organized (with about 1000 participants) and continuous media information was provided. This model has been used again for the most recent Austrian SEA for the waste management plan of Salzburg.

The SEA round table approach goes beyond the requirements of the EU SEA Directive. It means more proactive participation than mere consultation and provision of information, and provides possibilities to contribute to the whole SEA process and to influence its results. The experiences to date have been promising, providing opportunities to reconcile the interests concerned and to strengthen the implementation of a final plan when supported by all interest groups concerned.

---

and a provincial group on SEA implementation). A handbook has been prepared illustrating different aspects of the diverse Austrian SEA activities (Arbter et al, 2000). Finally, the Ministry of Environment has commissioned a study to explore the potential of sustainability impact assessment at the level of policies and legislation.

3.3.3 Canada

In Canada, SEA as a formal procedure is undertaken primarily at the federal level, although elements of this approach can be recognized in the EIA systems of certain of the provinces and territories. The federal SEA process was established by Cabinet Directive (1990), making it the first of the new generation of SEA systems that evolved in the 1990s (see Section 2.6.2). It was established as a non-statutory procedure, separate from EIA legislation, and intended to be applied flexibly and pragmatically to integrate environmental considerations into policy and programme proposals submitted to Cabinet or considered by ministers on their own authority. This is the highest level of political decision-making in Canada and, at the time, the application of SEA represented a major innovation. It was perceived as a challenge with respect to

Cabinet secrecy and ministerial discretion – key conventions of Westminster-style parliamentary democracy.

Early procedural guidance on SEA in Canada was contained in *The Environmental Assessment Process for Policy and Programme Proposals* (FEARO, 1993) – the so-called 'Blue Book'. It comprised a basic and non-prescriptive outline of the scope of coverage, the responsibilities of federal officials and the requirements for documentation and disclosure. For Cabinet submissions, the SEA was part of the formal procedure of preparation of a memorandum setting out the proposal and the issues for consideration. Tellingly, the 'Blue Book' noted that public consultation, which normally would be expected to become a key component of SEA, was difficult in the policy context 'because of the need for Cabinet confidentiality'.

In the initial phase, SEA implementation was ad hoc and uneven and limited by insufficient awareness on the part of the federal departments and agencies responsible for subjecting proposals to this process. Key principles were discretion and flexibility, in other words agencies were encouraged to develop and use approaches and procedures suited to circumstances. During this period, SEA implementation was subject to nominal oversight and occasional review by the Federal Environmental Assessment Review Office (FEARO) – later the Canadian Environmental Assessment Agency (the Agency or CEAA). For example, a survey by LeBlanc and Fischer (1996) found an inconsistent pattern of SEA application, with some federal agencies failing to comply with the Cabinet Directive and others meeting only the bare minimum requirements.

Subsequently, the Commissioner of the Environment and Sustainable Development (1998, 1999) audited the SEA practices and performance of federal agencies. This review indicated that aspects of SEA practice remained inadequate and unsatisfactory across many branches of the Government of Canada. Under the Auditor General Act, the Commissioner has wide powers to oversee and hold the Government to account for its policies and activities to protect the environment and to implement sustainable development. The findings of the SEA audits thus registered much higher on the scale of political attention than the earlier procedural review of the Agency, which has a relatively low-key role in SEA implementation (compared to its functions under the Canadian Environmental Assessment Act).

A revised Cabinet Directive on SEA (Government of Canada, 1999) was issued to strengthen the role of SEA in policy, plan and programme decision-making. It clarifies the obligations of federal departments and agencies in this regard and links SEA to their requirement to prepare and implement sustainable development strategies (introduced in 1997). Updated guidelines for implementing the SEA process were prepared by the Canadian Environmental Assessment Agency (CEAA, 2000) and include principles and advice on issues of application (see Box 3.11). The guidelines are presented as flexible (applicable to a variety of policy settings), practical (not necessarily requiring specialist skills) and systematic (based on logical, transparent analysis and on current, proven good practices within federal departments and

---

BOX 3.11 AIMS, PRINCIPLES AND ROLES FOR IMPLEMENTING SEA IN CANADA

The guidelines state that SEA will help federal departments and agencies to:

- optimize positive environmental effects and minimize negative environmental effects;
- consider potential cumulative environmental effects of proposals;
- implement sustainable development strategies;
- save time and money by identifying potential environmental liabilities and concerns;
- streamline project-level EA by eliminating the need to address some issues at this stage;
- promote accountability and credibility amongst stakeholders and the public; and
- contribute to broader government policy and commitments.

When implementing SEA, departments should be guided by seven principles:

- early integration – beginning in the conceptual stages of policy or plan formulation;
- examination of alternatives – evaluating and comparing their environmental effects;
- flexibility – agencies have discretion in determining how to conduct an SEA;
- self-assessment – each agency is responsible for SEA process application and decision-making;
- appropriate scope of application – SEA should be commensurate with the level of anticipated effects;
- accountability – SEA should be part of an open and accountable decision-making process; and
- use of existing mechanisms – to analyse effects, involve the public and report the results.

The main decision-makers are the Cabinet (collective responsibility) and ministers (individual responsibility for their department or agency). In addition, the Minister of the Environment has an advisory role with regard to environmentally appropriate courses of action. Other major participants in the SEA process are:

- line departments – officials are responsible for ensuring an appropriate SEA is completed;
- Environment Canada – provides expert scientific and technical advice to other agencies;
- Canadian Environmental Assessment Agency – provides guidance and training on SEA implementation; and
- Commissioner of the Environment and Sustainable Development – may subject SEA compliance and performance by government agencies to periodic audit.

Source: Canadian Environmental Assessment Agency (2000). The guidelines document is available on the Agency's website (www.ceaa-acee.gc.ca/0011/0002/dir_e.htm#guidelines).

---

agencies). Some federal departments have prepared their own policy statements on SEA (e.g. Transport Canada, 2001).

The SEA process covers policies, plans and programmes but there is no definition or differentiation of these levels of decision-making. Rather, SEA is triggered when proposals are submitted to an individual minister or to Cabinet for approval and these may result in important environmental effects (positive or negative). In addition, departments are encouraged to subject other initiatives to SEA 'as circumstances warrant'. There are, however, certain special cases when SEA does not apply, such as national emergencies or issues requiring urgent response, where the normal consideration by Cabinet is shortened. Also excluded from SEA are projects that are subject to the Canadian Environmental Assessment Act. Also, for proposed regulations, the preparation of a regulatory impact analysis statement (RIAS)[9] is deemed to satisfy SEA requirements, although, if an SEA has been conducted, the findings should be included.

Canadian guidelines emphasize that SEA is '*not an add-on process but one linked with the ongoing economic and social analyses on the proposal*' (CEAA, 2000, original quote italized for emphasis in original document). The guidance also notes that there is no single 'best' methodology for conducting an SEA of a policy or plan proposal. Instead, departments and agencies are encouraged to 'apply appropriate frameworks or techniques, and to develop approaches tailored to their particular needs and circumstances'. A general two-stage process is outlined, comprising a preliminary scan to determine if there are potentially important environmental considerations and followed, in such cases, by analysis of the environmental effects. The analysis should address their scope and nature, the need for mitigation, the residual effects and the need for follow-up measures. It also 'should identify for decision-makers, where appropriate, concerns about the environmental effects among those likely to be most affected and among other stakeholders and members of the public' (CEAA, 2000).

The guidelines describe sources of information on public concerns, such as including economic and social analyses of the proposal, direct consultation and use of expertise within and outside of government. Public involvement in the SEA process should be commensurate with that for the development of the proposal itself. According to the guidelines, 'separate reporting of assessments is not required' but may be chosen 'for some proposals, such as those involving significant adverse effects or serious public concerns' (CEAA, 2000). However, with effect from 1 January 2004, federal departments and agencies are required to prepare a public statement of environmental effects when a detailed SEA of a proposal has been conducted. The statement is intended to assure stakeholders and the public that environmental factors have been appropriately considered in cases of policy and planning decisions with potentially significant environmental effects. In all cases, the findings of the SEA are to be incorporated into memoranda to Cabinet and other forms of documentation for decision-making.

---

9   A RIAS is prepared for federal proposals to amend regulations or introduce new ones and also applies to statutes establishing new regulatory programmes. It is the means of demonstrating that the benefits of regulations are greater than their costs, and represent the best alternative when they address health, social, economic or environmental risks. The preparation of a RIAS is required under an administrative policy directive.

The current pattern and status of SEA practice is difficult to determine objectively. First, there is no central registry of assessments underway or completed at the strategic level as there is for project-level proposals under CEAA. Second, an audit of the implementation of the 1999 Cabinet Directive by the Commissioner of the Environment and Sustainable Development is currently being undertaken, and is expected to be released in October 2004. What stands out from disparate sources is increasing evidence of more visible and better quality SEA practice than before. Recent examples include:

- SEA is ongoing in support of a several trade negotiations, beginning with a pilot ex post review (in 1999) of the 1994 Uruguay Round of Multilateral Negotiations and the development of a generic framework for the conduct of SEA (Box 3.12).
- A series of SEAs were conducted under the Canada – Nova Scotia Offshore Petroleum Board. The latest assessment of Eastern Sable Island Bank, Western Banquereau Bank, the Gully Trough and the Eastern Scotian Slope (August 2002) was the first to cover lands not currently under licence to petroleum companies or included in a call for bids (see: www.cnsopb.ns.ca/Whatsnew/SEA0816.html).
- The SEA of the federal policy moratorium on offshore oil and gas development on the west coast of Canada has been in place since 1972 and was renewed in 1989 as a result of the Exxon Valdez oil spill off the Alaskan coast. This process is referred to as an 'extended SEA' (Natural Resources Canada, 2004) and, for the first time, it is being undertaken as a public review by an independent panel. As such, it can be expected to set an important precedent.

3.3.4 Denmark

In 1993, SEA was established by Administrative Order of the Prime Minister's Office for bills and other governmental proposals submitted to the Danish Parliament. Other government proposals in a Danish context may be broadly understood as corresponding to national policies or general plans (Elling, 1996, 1997; Elling and Neilsen, 1998). The Administrative Order was introduced to support the trend toward integration of environmental considerations in decision-making processes. It requires all ministries to prepare a statement on the environmental consequences for proposals that are likely to have significant environmental effects. An assessment of these effects should be made by the proponent ministry 'when administratively feasible and when the data are available' and so as to 'maintain the applicable legislation process' (DMEE, 1995a).

This last referenced work (first issued in Danish in 1993) provides basic guidance on procedures for SEA. It remains in force, although subsequent amendments have been made to the Administrative Order (in 1995 and 1998) to strengthen its scope and application. The 1993 Administrative Order provided for a flexible process and Danish policy was to 'keep it simple to

Box 3.12 Generic framework for ex ante SEA for trade negotiations, Canada

In November 1999, the Canadian Department of Foreign Affairs and International Trade (DFAIT) released a retrospective analysis of the 1994 Canadian Environmental Review of the Uruguay Round of Multilateral Trade Negotiations and began work on an SEA framework for WTO negotiations. This approach was then broadened to establish a generic framework for SEA that could be applied to bilateral, regional or multilateral trade negotiations. This framework is to be applied flexibly and adapted on a case-by-case basis according to the policy context.

Rationale and objectives: SEA is presented as an instrument that can help 'sensitize' trade negotiators to environmental considerations and lead toward greater coherence of trade and environmental policy. The primary aim of SEA in this context is to provide information necessary to integrate environmental considerations into the decision-making process from the earliest stage (and to document for the public how this has been done). A caveat is that the preferred way to mitigate adverse effects is recognized as appropriate domestic policy rather than prescriptive measures within trade agreements. In addition, this approach may identify opportunities for capacity-building for environmental protection.

Challenges: The framework recognizes that assessing the environmental impacts of trade negotiations is a complex and demanding task with a number of significant challenges:

*   Methodologies for SEA of policy issues including trade negotiations are still evolving.
*   Experience in their application is lacking since, to date, Canada has conducted ex post reviews of trade agreements rather than ex- ante assessments of trade negotiations.
*   Because trade negotiation is a dynamic process, the SEA process may have to focus on a 'moving target' as new and unanticipated issues arise.
*   Environmental impacts of trade agreements are difficult to identify and isolate from other factors external to trade (and quantitative data are limited).

Four-step SEA process: The main stages and elements comprise:

*   notice of intent to conduct an SEA issued when a trade negotiation is announced (with comments invited from key stakeholders on environmental matters);
*   an initial SEA to scope out the main issues likely to result from the proposed negotiation;
*   preparation of a draft SEA to identify and inform negotiators of the main environmental concerns; and
*   preparation of a final SEA report to document the anticipated environmental impacts (identifying any notable divergence from the draft SEA) and recommend any follow-up and monitoring actions.

Analytical framework: Because of the dynamic quality of trade negotiations, analysis may be required at various times in the SEA process. The methodology comprises four analytical stages:

*   identification of the economic effects of the trade negotiation and its relevance to Canada;

- identification of the likely environmental impacts of such changes (adverse and positive), noting their consistency with Canada's existing commitments under multilateral environmental agreements;
- evaluation of the significance of the potential environmental impacts (using criteria similar to those used in the application of the Canadian Environmental Assessment Act); and
- identification of the options for policies or to mitigate adverse effects and enhance positive effects, including regulatory institutions and measures and abandoning or altering a negotiation position.

Public input and stakeholder engagement: The framework identifies the form and stages at which public input will be sought. The scope and timing of public input will vary, depending on the type of agreement assessed. Given the confidentiality of trade negotiations, any re-evaluations of the draft SEA report will not be made public although advice will be sought from key stakeholders including environmental NGOs.

Ongoing strategic environmental assessments:

- Initial Environmental Assessment of the Canada–Singapore Free Trade Negotiations;
- Initial Environmental Assessment of the Canada-CA-4 Free Trade Negotiations;
- Environmental Assessment of Negotiations at the World Trade Organization; and
- Environmental Assessment of Free Trade Area of the Americas Negotiations.

Source: DFAIT (2001); for updates on ongoing assessments, see www.dfait-maeci.gc.ca/tna-nac/social-e.asp#environmental

start', developing procedure and methodology gradually and building on the lessons of practice (Elling, 1996; Johansen, 1996). The environmental effects to be addressed in SEA are broadly defined in the Administrative Order (e.g. safety and health, flora and fauna, soil, water, air, climate, landscape) and further described in guidelines. A checklist is provided to help determine the need for and scope of SEA, modelled on that for EIA of projects,[10] and the guidance notes that the principles and elements from this level can apply to strategic actions.

From the guidance on recommended Danish procedure, Elling (1996) identified four stages in the SEA of bills or other proposals, although he also notes that, in practice, the first two steps merge together:

1 *Screening* – the checklist (footnote 10) is used at the 'heading level' to identify proposals that are likely to have a potentially significant

---

10 The main topics listed in the checklist are: water including surface water and groundwater; air; climate; surface of the earth, soil and percolations; flora and fauna including impact on habitats and biological diversity; landscape and land use; other resources including use of renewable and non-renewable resources; waste; historical buildings and monuments; the population's health and welfare; and safety in connection with production, handling or transport of substances harmful to the environment.

environmental impact and require further assessment. In addition, according to Johansen (1996), the Ministry of Environment also carries out preliminary screening of the legislative calendar to flag bills that might be environmentally important.

2   *Scoping* – the checklist is used at the 'sub-heading level' of specific questions to identify the nature and scope of the major or cumulative environmental effects of a bill or policy. In the guidance, reference is also made to the fact that the effects of national actions occur on different geographic scales – primarily local and regional, but in some cases extending to the global level.

3   *Assessment* – an analysis of the effects that are identified as potentially significant is carried out by the responsible ministry and having regard to the data and administrative considerations noted earlier. Danish procedural guidance states that it is not possible to give an overall description of when environmental effects are considered to be significant; rather, it includes a list of factors for this purpose. For example, does the impact in question conflict or make it difficult to comply with environmental objectives or policies?

4   *Report* – a description of the environmental effects is included as a separate section in the commentary, which is attached to the bill or other government proposal when it is submitted to Parliament.[11] It should be an easily understood, non-technical statement that is publicly accessible, together with other background assessment.

More detailed, advisory guidance on the content and features of SEA of bills and other government proposals was issued in 1994 (in Danish) by the Danish Ministry of Energy and Environment (DMEE, 1995b, English version). This document is organized into three main sections (see Box 3.13):

- step-by-step guidance on what SEA should ideally include (aspects of which clearly reflect the influence of the EIA Directive and thus anticipate the European SEA Directive);
- case examples of eight assessments of bills and other government proposals to illustrate the application of the recommended methodology and checklist; and
- an outline of the environmentally related national plans (detailed in Annex 2 to the document) that can be used in connection with the checklist (Annex 1 of the document) to assess proposals against relevant objectives.

SEA practice in the first phase of implementation was closely monitored (Elling, 1996; Johansen, 1996). Approximately one-eighth of all bills or other government proposals submitted to Parliament were found likely to have

---

11 If the responsible ministry has determined that a proposal will have no significant effect on the environment, this opinion should also be stated in the commentary accompanying the bill or other government proposal.

Box 3.13 Danish guidance on SEA of bills and other proposals: examples and experience

Although now more than ten years old, the publication on *Strategic Environmental Assessment of Bills and Other Proposals: Examples and Experience* (Danish Ministry of Energy and Environment (DMEE), 1995b) is reportedly still current. New guidance on SEA was prepared in 2002 but never published due to a change of government (Elling, personal communication). Danish guidance is also of some interest internationally since it addresses the implementation of SEA within the first system to be directed solely at the legislative process. This document is organized into three main parts.

First, there is information on what SEA should ideally include. A six-step procedure is outlined:

*   formulating the problem and describing the purpose of the proposal and the alternatives considered;
*   identifying the relevant environmental effects (completing the checklist);
*   describing the extent of the likely environmental effects (in relation to the null hypothesis, time and space aspects, and levels of uncertainty);
*   identifying measures to avoid environmental harm and for monitoring or follow-up programmes; and
*   assessing and weighing the environmental effects in relation to policy objectives;
*   statement and summary of the main findings.

Second, there is a review of a series of statements on proposals, comprising six actual examples (five bills and one resolution) that were subject to the SEA process and two constructed examples of standing acts or orders. All of the examples have some form of environmental objectives or orientations. For example, five of the previous assessments relate to the protection of nature or species, energy efficiency, banning pesticides containing certain harmful ingredients and the periodic inspection of motor vehicles for safety and emissions control. The sixth case was an authorization bill for three by-pass routes (which cites certain environmental benefits from reducing the burden of urban traffic). Generally, the documentation in cases that are aimed at environmental improvements is more detailed than for the normal run of legislation. It is also perhaps atypical in emphasizing positive environmental effects.

Third, an outline is given of Denmark's most important national action plans in relation to the environment (in Annex 2). Reference is also made to international conventions and agreements to which Denmark is signatory, key environmental protection and planning acts and instruments and state of the environment reports and similar documents. The purpose is to indicate relevant objectives and targets of environmental policy when conducting SEA using the checklist identified in earlier guidance (reproduced in the document as Annex 1). Examples cited include:

*   action plan on cleaner technology, which aims to reduce total consumption of natural resources and direct pollution from production and consumption of products;
*   action plan on the aquatic environment, which sets quantified targets for reducing nitrate and phosphate discharge to water bodies;
*   Transport 2005 and Energy 2000 and follow-up, which include objectives relating to air quality and greenhouse gas emissions; and
*   strategies for biodiversity, natural forests and sustainable forest management, which are central to the conservation of flora and fauna and genetic resources.

Source: (DMEE, 1995b)

significant impacts on the environment and had a description of the impacts in the attached documentation. The large majority either had no reference to environmental impacts or stated that there were none in the attached documentation. When reviewing these figures, Elling (1996) reminds non-Danish reviewers that the majority of bills or government proposals concern administrative or procedural rules that have little or no environmental impact. However, both Elling (1996) and Johansen (1996) also note that the scope and quality of the assessments actually carried out vary considerably and only in very few instances were environmental impacts described in a thorough way.

Government guidance documents cited earlier (DMEE, 1995a, b) also called for improvements in these areas. Since then, no major changes have occurred, although the proportion of bills with a description of likely impacts in the attached documentation has increased and now represents about one-fifth of all bills submitted (Elling, personal communication, 2004). A recent study of the contribution that SEA makes to the reading of bills in the Danish Parliament yielded some interesting conclusions (Elling, 2000b). When fully qualified assessments of the likely environmental impacts are appended to the documentation of bills, they result in a more effective political process, defined by Elling (2000b) as one that is meaningful, understandable and focused on political priorities, including environmental ones, which become more transparent in the final decision.

Generally, the most comprehensive assessments are carried out for bills and proposals that are intended to protect or improve the environment. In other types of assessment, the environmental effects are described more briefly and in general terms (DMEE, 1995b). The examples listed in Box 3.14 are used to illustrate SEA good practice in application of the impact checklist against policy objectives for the environment set out in national legislation and action plans. An in-depth analysis of SEA application by Elling and Neilsen (1998) is instructive for understanding how this process works in the context of Danish Parliamentary decision-making and for relating this experience to internationally recognized elements of the approach. For example, they show that consideration of alternatives and involvement of the public can be accommodated within the Danish SEA system even though there is no requirement to do so (see Case Study 3.1).

Before the transposition of the Directive, there was no formal provision for SEA at other levels in Denmark, although EIA practice had a number of related features. Most notably, it is integrated into the land use planning system and (with certain exceptions) assessment and approval of specific projects take place within the context of regional development plans. This system was also widely recognized as an ideal mechanism for implementation of SEA along the lines of experience in the UK and other countries (Elling and Neilsen, 1996). In the late 1990s, the Ministry of Energy and Environment asked the county authorities to undertake SEA in conjunction with revising their regional development plans, which implement national policy directives and establish the guidelines for land use and infrastructure outside the urban zones (Elling, 1998a). A series of trial runs was undertaken, beginning with the Northern

---

BOX 3.14 PILOT SEA IN NORTH JUTLAND, DENMARK

Between 1995 and 1997, the Planning Administration in North Jutland, the Danish Ministry of Environment and Energy (DMEE) and the EIA Centre at Roskilde University collaborated on a pilot project financed by the former Ad Hoc Group for EIA under the Nordic Council of Ministers and the DMEE. The pilot project was a component of a research project to develop methods for SEA of regional plans and to test them through case studies.

The pilot project involved an assessment as part of the revision of the 1993 North Jutland Plan. Elling (1999) reports the conclusions of different actors, based on interviews:

- Planners said that whilst the SEA produced no new knowledge, the planning process became more clear.
- Politicians felt they got better information as a basis for choices.
- NGOs' experience was that they should participate early in the process, preferably during scoping.

Overall, it was concluded that a better regional plan had been produced.

The Planning Department has tried to carry SEA a step further in the newest regional land use plan revision. The NGOs have been involved at an earlier stage. The county used existing groupings like the Green Panel, the Ground Water Committee, and the Cultural Heritage Committee, where different NGOs are represented. Also the findings of the SEA process were integrated in the plan itself and not placed in an appendix as in 1997. NGO groups have shown a major commitment to SEA and interest also appears to be increasing among the general public and elected county council politicians.

Source: Elling (2000a)

Jutland regional plan (Box 3.14) and using this as a starting model for integrating SEA into the planning process (Elling, 1998b, 2000a).

Further SEA pilots have been carried out on an experimental basis for some years at the regional level (Elling, personal communication) and, to a lesser extent, at the municipal level in Denmark (Hvidtfelt and Kørnøv, 2001, 2003). The aim has been to achieve more sustainable spatial plans and to prepare for the EU SEA Directive on SEA. It is expected that SEA at the regional level will become mandatory for the next round of land use plans in 2005. At the time of writing, Denmark is introducing legislation to comply with the EU SEA Directive and make SEA of land use plans obligatory at the national, regional and municipal levels (Act No 316 was adopted by the Danish Parliament on 5 May 2004).

3.3.5 Finland[12]

Before the implementation of the SEA Directive, Finland had established two systems for SEA. First, a general requirement to assess the environmental impact of policies, plans and programmes is imposed on responsible authorities under the EIA Act. In addition, there is detailed provision for SEA of land use plans under the Building and Planning Act (1999) and brief reference to the assessment of environmental impact in the Act on Regional Development (1993). Secondly, the environmental impact of legislative proposals is subject to assessment under a decision-in-principle of the Finnish Government (11 June 1998). A general comparison of the two systems is given in Box 3.15.

BOX 3.15 FINNISH EXPERIENCE WITH THE ASSESSMENT OF BILLS COMPARED WITH THE ASSESSMENT OF POLICIES, PLANS AND PROGRAMMES

In Finland, all bills submitted to the Parliament are required to include, whenever relevant, separate sub-chapters on environmental, economic and administrative effects. This is a clear checkpoint to determine whether or not an assessment has been completed. Except for land use plans, the assessment of policies, plans and programmes lacks a comparable procedure. In this regard, SEA of bills is a more formalized process, although research indicates that often the procedural check is merely a formality. So far, no bill has been returned from Parliament because of a lack of proper assessment. Recently, however, there has been criticism of the quality of bills and their assessment (Ervasti et al, 2000).

Another difference between of the assessment of bills and of policies, plans and programmes concerns their format and content. The format of bills is strictly controlled and largely standardized, whereas policies, plans and programmes come in many forms. The standardized format of bills limits the presentation of assessment results. The bill and its justification, including the assessment, represent a synthesis of the preparatory work that precedes the bill itself. This work is frequently carried out by ministerial working groups or, on more sensitive issues, by committees or commissions, which include 'interested' organizations. The result is often an extensive report. If the assessment is taken seriously, it should be part of this report. The work of ministerial working groups, commissions and committees resemble more closely the preparatory work for policies, plans and programmes. The time constraints are usually less demanding and often, in their letter of appointment, they are asked to consider alternatives.

Frequently, there are links between the preparation of bills and policy documents. Policy documents may identify the need for more detailed legislative work. The National Climate Strategy is a case in point. Many of the measures envisaged in the Strategy will require amendments to existing legislation or new laws. In these cases, SEA of policy can support the preparation of the legislative proposals. It can be argued that this is the real test of its usefulness and use. However, since a bill is practically always a modification of an original proposal of a working group or commission (due, amongst other things, to intervening hearing procedures), the assessment needs to be adjusted accordingly.

Source: Hildén (2003b)

---

12   With contribution by Mikael Hildén, Finnish Environment Institute.

Chapter 5 of the Finnish Act on EIA Procedure (468/1994) relates to general investigation duty and states (Section 24) that policies, plans and programmes 'that may have a significant impact effect on the environment shall be investigated and assessed "to a sufficient degree"'. This provision requires all spheres of government to assess their own actions at this level. A subsequent Decree on EIA Procedure (268/1999) sets out the functions of various Finnish environmental authorities at the project level, but does not specifically address the role of the responsible authority with regard to policy, plan or programme. The Council of State issued guidelines for this purpose (Finnish Ministry of the Environment, 1998a).

After ten years, Finnish experience with SEA of policies, plans and programmes is relatively extensive. It is evaluated in Hildén and Jalonen (2003) as part of review of wider Nordic experience with SEA of plans and programmes (Hilding-Rydevik, 2003). SEA practice is reported by Soverii (personal communication) to be particularly well developed for land use plans, reflecting the detailed procedure laid down in the Building and Planning Act (1999), and in the transport sector (Jansson, 2000, provides an overview; and a case study is given in Kaljonen, 2000). However, SEA is by no means confined to these areas and examples of good practice are reported in other sectors: energy, resource management, and environment and nature protection (Hildén and Jalonen, 2003). In addition, there have been applications at the policy level, for example an SEA of national land use objectives and another of guidelines for road management and development to 2015.

This aspect of Finnish experience is of wider interest internationally because it highlights one of the challenges likely to be encountered in determining the scope of the SEA Directive at the member state level, as discussed in Hildén and Jalonen (2003). Although policies are explicitly excluded from the European Directive, the dividing line between policies and plans/programmes is unclear. In some cases, Finnish policies are linked to plans and programmes in such a way that they may be subject to assessment de facto, for example policy documents that contain explicit reference to consent procedures. According to Hildén (2003b), these include the National Climate Strategy, which is primarily a policy paper but contains an explicit prohibition on building new coal-fired power plants, and the National Forestry Programme which (despite its name) comprises guiding general policies (see also Hildén et al, 2000). This analysis also raises questions about whether it may be useful to retain the broader requirements of the Finnish EIA Act to assess policies, plans and programmes.

A separate SEA process applies to the preparation of bills and other proposals, such as government resolutions and ministry decisions. This system was established in 1998 in response to the Government's programme to improve law-drafting. It requires all statutes to be appropriately assessed and monitored for their overall environmental impact. Guidelines for EIA of legislative proposals were issued by the Council of State (Finnish Ministry of the Environment, 1998b) and are intended to complement other guidelines relating to economic and business impacts. Specifically, they are intended 'to promote and support comprehensive expert assessment of the environmental impact of all new legislation' and 'shall apply immediately'. Each ministry is responsible for assessing its own legislation but, if necessary, may undertake a cooperative approach with other branches of the administration.

The Finnish guidelines are of interest internationally with respect to several principles and measures (although, as indicated in Box 3.15, SEA practice may not always meet them):

- establishing the need for EIA by reference to the different functions of legislation and their potential environmental impacts;[13]
- inclusion of a checklist to address the effects of a new law and a flow diagram illustrating the progression of EIA at different stages of the legislative process (Appendices 1 and 2 of the guidelines);
- stipulation that 'the various alternatives and their environmental impact shall be examined broadly and methodically' including the zero alternative;
- obligations related to early communication with groups of citizens and parties who may be affected by the law and the authorities responsible for implementing it;
- requirement to present the information on the positive and adverse effects of the law in the government bill 'concisely but comprehensively'; and
- plan to monitor environmental impact of a law after it enters into force.

At the time of writing, an SEA bill (HE 243/2004) has been submitted to Parliament and will probably be approved in 2005. The proposed legislation retains the general requirements for the assessment of policies, plans and programmes of the Finnish EIA Act of 1994, but adds a formal procedure for the assessment of certain plans and programmes identified in the SEA Directive. In this context, the working group has listed more than 200 different types of assessments of plans and programmes potentially subject to SEA. Most of them cover land use plans, regional waste management plans and regional development plans. An integral part of the working group's proposal is an assessment of the likely effects of implementing the course of action, including consideration of the main alternatives. The bill aiming at an act on SEA will be debated by Parliament in autumn 2004 (Hildén and Jalonen, 2004).

---

13 Finnish guidelines state: 'A law will probably have environmental impact if one or more questions on the checklist answers in the positive. A law will probably have environmental impact if it: influences land use, guides activities that have environmental impact [or] guides activities that involve environmental risk. A law may have environmental impact if it: governs income transfer, such as subsidies, taxes and fees [or] changes the structures or operation of administration' (Finnish Ministry of the Environment, 1998b, p5).

3.3.6 France[14]

The law of 10 July 1976 on protection of the natural environment (enacted by an inter-ministerial decree of 12 October 1977) made EIA compulsory for projects and stated that planning documents (i.e. master and land use plans) 'must take into account environmental considerations'. For a number of reasons, including the reluctance of the Ministry of Planning and Public Works and lack of expertise, planning documents were not assessed on environmental grounds. In 1983, a government decree modified the Planning Code for Local Land Use Plans to require a preliminary report on the environment and the potential effects of planned actions upon it. A less clear requirement was that spatial master plans should describe 'the state of the environment and the measures taken to preserve it'.

These requirements represented elements of progress towards integrating environmental concerns into the strategic level of decision-making. However, they were largely ineffective, as evidenced by several laws suits in the administrative courts citing lack of substance. In practice, planners paid only lip-service to environmental considerations and judicial checks were insufficient to cope with non-compliance and administrative inactivity.

Even at the project level, environmental and land-related considerations were not necessarily well integrated into the EIA process, given the deficiencies of a screening procedure that relied on strict listing based on financial and technical importance and resulted in numerous[15] EIAs being produced each year and many smaller projects subjected to mini EIAs (*notice d'impact*).

Other early SEA-type developments included the following (Falque, 1995):

- In 1990, the Assemblée Nationale (Parliament) introduced a new procedure in order to assess the environmental impact of draft legislative proposals, although it does not appear that it was ever implemented due to a lack of political will.
- In 1992, Electricité de France, in conjunction with the Ministry of the Environment, decided to establish a form of programmatic impact assessment for each of its regional electricity transportation networks.
- In 1993, a new EIA decree required proponents of projects linked to a single institutional decision (e.g. a general road programme split up for financial reasons) to carry out an EIA of the whole programme. This prevented deliberate splitting of projects in order to escape the need for an EIA report, and provided an opportunity to assess cumulative effects.

In 1993, the Ministry of Environment also took a first step towards legislating a form of SEA by issuing a circular (30 September) to regional prefects (chief administrators) on the environmental assessment of state–regions planning

---

14 With contributions by Max Falque, Fabien Harel, Koassi d'Almeida and Pierre André.
15 Approximately 5000 EIAs each year, too many for a comprehensive check.

contracts (*contrats de plan état–régions* or CPERs).[16] This document set out
the principal environmental issues and indicators (Bertrand, 2001) and was
followed by an inter-ministerial circular (9 December 1993), which officially
instituted a regional assessment system for CPER at three levels:

- *The political decision-making level/policy-making level*: here, the
  committee piloting the assessment of the CPER (*comité de pilotage*) defines
  the nature of the assessment to be conducted, approves the composition of
  the technical body which will produce the assessment, approves the terms
  of references proposed by the technical body, and receives the conclusions
  of the assessment and decides on the follow-up.
- *Technical bodies*: for each programme or group of programmes to be
  evaluated, a specific technical body should be constituted to play the role
  of proponent (*maitre d'ouvrage*). It should include civil servants and
  experts with specific knowledge relevant to the matters concerned. The
  task of this body is to define terms of reference, to conduct the assessment,
  and to report their conclusions to the *comité de pilotage*.
- *The operational implementation level*: the individuals who actually carry
  out the assessment. They may or may not be part of the public
  administration (private research consultancies, consulting firms or research
  laboratories).

Three types of environmental assessment are provided for in the context of
CPER (André et al, 2004; Lerond et al, 2003; Larrue and Lerond, 1998):

- an ex ante assessment – a prior environmental assessment, to prepare for a
  decision, based on the precautionary principle;
- an accompanying assessment allowing for periodic review of the
  environmental effects of decisions following implementation; and
- an ex post assessment, offering the opportunity to take stock of the
  environmental consequences of implementing a plan or programme, and
  serving as a guide for future projects.

For ex post evaluation, the Ministry of Regional Development and the
Environment has proposed a six-step outline procedure capturing the main
principles (Larrue and Lerond, 1998) (Figure 3.1).

A new circular (25 August 2000) redefined the modalities regarding the
assessment for CPER (Lerond et al, 2003). Its aim was to take into account
the European Community and infra-regional assessment procedures. This
circular also considers the relationship between CPER and existing assessment
procedures and specifies the content of the assessment.

The new French law on land use plans (Solidarité et Renouvellement
Urbain, SRU, 13 December 2000) has also led to some progress toward SEA,
specifically:

---

16 *Contrats de plans* are general agreements between the central government and each
   regional government on co-funding certain facilities.

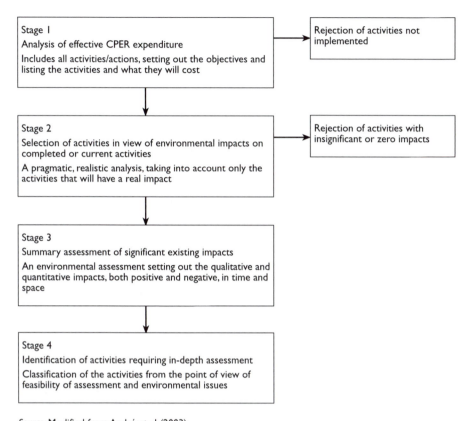

Stage 1	
Analysis of effective CPER expenditure	Rejection of activities not implemented
Includes all activities/actions, setting out the objectives and listing the activities and what they will cost	

Stage 2	
Selection of activities in view of environmental impacts on completed or current activities	Rejection of activities with insignificant or zero impacts
A pragmatic, realistic analysis, taking into account only the activities that will have a real impact	

Stage 3
Summary assessment of significant existing impacts
An environmental assessment setting out the qualitative and quantitative impacts, both positive and negative, in time and space

Stage 4
Identification of activities requiring in-depth assessment
Classification of the activities from the point of view of feasibility of assessment and environmental issues

Source: Modified from André et al (2003)

Figure 3.1 *Stages in the environmental assessment process proposed for evaluating state–regions planning contracts (CPERs) in France*

- local urbanization plans must now have a forward-looking focus that integrates sustainable development concerns and spatial planning, consistent with territorial coherence schemes (master plans);
- diagnosis and strategic planning must take account of the interactions between sectoral decisions; and
- the requirements of the EU SEA Directive are mentioned in the formal advice of the Conseil Général des Ponts et Chaussées (highways) on the so-called '*Rapport Chassande*' (20 June 2000).

In 2000, France adopted an environmental code which seemed to harmonize previous laws (www.legifrance.gouv.fr) and requested that environmental assessments be undertaken for projects, programmes and plans, and particularly for planning documents (Sections 122–1 and 122–4 of the code). More recently, a number of steps have been taken in preparing to implement the EU SEA Directive on SEA. For example, several pilot SEAs have been undertaken to develop methodologies and capabilities for implementing the

European SEA Directive, particularly in the areas of transportation and regional planning. SEA-type approaches have been integrated into transport plans at the national and urban level and the French Ministry for Management of Land and Environment has published guidance on the major environmental effects associated with transport at the strategic level (Michel and Monier, 2001). This document is likely to be of wider interest (see Box 3.16). At the regional level, the preparation of spatial planning documents became a legal requirement in 1995 for particular areas of national concern, such as for transport or nature conservation or because of their economic importance (e.g. mountain regions, estuaries). Based on experience with the Paris–Brussels corridor, the Ministry of Public Works, Transport and Housing has undertaken an exploratory study of SEA methodology and criteria to be applied to multi-modal studies.

The agricultural, energy and industrial sectors are likely to be important areas for France with regard to the plans and programmes listed in the Directive (Article 2(a)) but, so far, there has been no experimentation with SEA in these sectors. Other requirements of the Directive for which France reportedly is not well prepared include addressing the information to be provided in the environmental report. These specifically include (Harel et al, 2003):

- the relevant aspects of the environment including likely changes without plan or programme implementation (Annex 1(b)); and
- the likely significant effects on the environment and particularly the requirement to include secondary, cumulative and synergistic effects (Annex 1(f)).

The Ministry of Environment proposed to adopt the approach used in the UK for *environmental appraisals of development plans* in order to provide coherence between decisions. This SEA procedure follows four main steps:

- environmental diagnosis (an environmental profile describing the state of the environment and listing political objectives at different scales – international conventions and protocols, European policies, national objectives, regional objectives, etc.);
- compatibility analysis (using a matrix) between the focus of the strategic action and the main reference objectives;
- assessment of the importance of the potential impacts of the whole plan; and
- evaluation (ex post) of interactions between measures.

Ordonnance No 2004–489 was issued on 3 June 2004 introducing the EU SEA Directive in the French Environmental Law.

Box 3.16 French guidance on SEA of transport plans and programmes

Recent French guidance focuses on four larger-scale environmental effects associated with transport at the strategic level:

Safeguarding biodiversity: The guidance proposes a method for measuring the effect (negative impacts) of the fragmentation of major infrastructure networks on ecosystems. Key aspects include:

*   identifying the main land-unit areas that are separated by the existing transport networks;
*   determining the proportion of land-unit areas showing a significant nature conservation interest;
*   classifying the land-unit areas in relation to their nature conservation interest; and
*   evaluating the induced land quality through the land-splitting effect of transport plans and programmes.

Preservation of tranquil zones: Noise is one of the most tangible and direct effects related to the use of transport infrastructure. Because noise levels depend upon local environmental and meteorological conditions as well as the traffic levels, forecasting is much less straightforward at national or regional scales. A proposed methodology for this purpose is:

*   Identify quiet zones, defined as areas where noise emissions from existing transport infrastructure are less than LAeq 6 am–10 pm = 45 dB(A).
*   Map and classify quiet zones according to their importance.
*   Assess the impacts of transport plans and programmes by overlaying networks and quiet areas.

Protection of surface water and groundwater: Both the construction and use of transport infrastructure can affect water quality as a result of air pollution from exhaust emissions, fuel spills and pollutants associated with the transport of hazardous materials. Indicators to identify the quality of surface water areas and the fragility of groundwater resources in the vicinity of new infrastructure are proposed, but have yet to be tested.

Preservation of air quality: Concern with air quality relates to two major air pollutants:

*   Nitrogen oxides (NO_x): produced by diesel motor vehicles at much higher rates than petrol vehicles. Their contribution to ozone formation typifies global and local impacts of transportation on air quality.
*   Carbon dioxide (CO_2): transportation is a major contributor to emissions of CO_2, the most important greenhouse gas.

A third indicator, not directly related to pollutant emissions, is energy consumption. Reductions in fuel use slow down climate change, acidification and photochemical smog effects.

Source: Harel (2003)

3.3.7 Germany[17]

There has been extensive use of SEA-type approaches in Germany in a number of sectors, both domestically and in development cooperation, but, to date, there is no official legislation prescribing the application of SEA.

Requirements for environmental assessment at strategic levels of decision-making were first introduced in 1972, aimed at legislative procedures (Cupei, 1994). In 1975, 'principles for the environmental assessment of public measures by the Federal Government' were formulated for draft legislation and draft governmental regulations and activities that concern the environment. However, in practice, these were seldom applied (Cupei, 1994). New SEA legislation is being drafted together with an amendment to the building sector law.

Currently, SEA-type assessment is most widely applied in spatial/land use and transport planning. Over the past few years, there have been a number of SEA-related research projects, undertaken mainly by the Federal Environment Agency, particularly in the areas of federal transport planning and regional planning.

Spatial/land use planning
Essential elements of SEA can be found in formal spatial/land use plans, landscape plans and programmes prepared at all administrative levels of decision-making for the last 20 years. In the past, they served mainly as state of the environment reports, proactively setting objectives for environmentally sustainable land use. But, more recently, in certain states (*Länder*), local land use plans have also started to deal explicitly with the potential impacts of those changes and developments they propose through landscape plans. In this context, Fischer (2002) suggests that they probably meet the requirements of the EU SEA Directive to a greater extent than statutory and formally applied assessment types currently practised in other European countries. This is mainly due to the way in which baseline data are collected and presented, environmental objectives are set, professional consultation and participation are conducted, impacts are appraised and potential mitigation and compensation measures are set. But a particular shortcoming is that these local land use plans give insufficient consideration to different development alternatives.

There is increasing experience of assessment at the regional level with a number of authors examining the extent to which SEA Directive requirements are met in current regional planning practice. But here, current shortcomings include not only insufficient consideration of alternatives but also lack of public participation (Siemoneit and Fischer, 2002; UVP, 2003). One positive example of an SEA-type assessment is the regional management approach in the '*Westpfalz*' region (Weik, 2004) in which different individual and institutional actors cooperate in a participatory manner. Despite their different interests and

---

17 With contributions by Thomas Fischer, University of Liverpool; and Holger Dalkman, Wuppertal Institute.

problems, they follow the same defined objectives. In this case, regional management offers a suitable alternative to traditional regional planning.

In addition to landscape plans and programmes, since 1975, more than 200 local communities have introduced EIA in their local land use planning procedures (Hodek and Kleinschmidt, 1998), although the focus is on possible projects arising from such plans. Nevertheless, this fulfils one of the requirements of the SEA Directive – the consideration of environmental impacts at the level of local land use plans.

Transport planning

In Germany, a full SEA is not required for any of the relevant decision-making processes in the transport sector, but SEA-type assessments (or certain elements of an SEA) are applied at all administrative levels of decision-making in transport planning (see Figure 2.2). Whilst assessment practice is rather widespread at the programme level, little is currently undertaken at policy and plan levels. At all three levels, shortcomings include a lack of public participation and insufficient transparency. However, through the introduction of the EU SEA Directive, not only will the adaptation of certain ideas and elements of SEA become necessary, but also a modification of the present decision-making processes. These modifications, for example, will have to provide adequate opportunities for the general public to participate.

Some significant steps have already been taken in preparing to implement the SEA Directive. In this regard, the transport sector is often regarded as one of the good practice examples in Germany. During formulation of the new Federal Transport Infrastructure Plan (FTIP), the Federal Ministry for Transport, Building and Housing (Schaefer et al, 2003) undertook project-based, cost–benefit analyses, an estimation of the CO_2 impacts of the FTIP, an environmental and nature conversation appraisal, an ecological risk and Habitat Directive assessment as well as spatial impact assessments. All of these assessments were considered in the relevant decision-making processes. The German FTIP was also used as an SEA case study for several research projects (such as ANSEA – see Appendix 13) and studies (see Lee and Hughes, 1995; Fischer, 2002; Dalkmann and Bongardt, 2004; Wende et al, 2004). However, whilst the FTIP is subject to review every five years, to date a full SEA has not been required. Issues such as the net effects of transport measures (e.g. habitat fragmentation) or alternative transport modes are not currently considered in planning practice in Germany.

The Ministry of Transport, Building and Housing (BMVWP) and the Ministry for Environment (BMU) are currently discussing whether the FTIP will be regarded as a policy or a plan when the EU SEA Directive is implemented (UBA, 2003). The Ministry for Transport considers itself responsible for preparing only policies, not plans or programmes; so that the SEA Directive would not be seen as applicable. However, there is strong consensus in Germany's SEA 'community' that the FTIP is actually a programme, and that SEA is necessary.

Corridor or 'area' transport studies are still undertaken only sporadically – examples include the SEA of the Danube corridor between the Vilshofen and Straubing (EC, 2002) and the study of the northeast area between Hamburg, Hanover and Berlin (MWSVLSA, 1995). Furthermore, current practice in project EIA routinely considers different spatial options within defined transport corridors. However, these are usually uni-modal, rather than multi-modal.

At the *Länder* level, there are some interesting examples of applying elements of SEA, for example in *Bundesländer* Brandenburg and North-Rhine-Westfalia. In the preparation procedure of the new road infrastructure plan for the *Land* Brandenburg, several essential SEA elements were integrated, for example formulation of environmental development objectives, an environmental report, assessment of development alternatives, implementation of the findings into planning and decision-making processes, consultation, participation and monitoring (Bockemuehl, 2003).

In North-Rhine-Westphalia, transport planning has been carried out in an integrated manner since 2000. According to a law on integrated transport planning, from May 2000, transport planning has to be supported by the formulation of environmental development objectives as well as by analyses of the current situation, future scenarios and development alternatives (www.igvp.nrw.de).

Other practice
There is also some SEA experience in other sectors in Germany, for example for wind farms (Kleinschmidt and Wagner, 1996) and waste and water management (UVP, 2003). Since 1987, a pilot project in Bavaria has been assessing the environmental impact of agricultural practices. Furthermore, SEA is required for all development cooperation projects of the Federal Ministry of Research and Technology (Hodek and Kleinschmidt, 1998).

3.3.8 The Netherlands

As indicated in Table 3.2, The Netherlands has a dual or two-tier SEA system (for a comparison see Verheem and Tonk, 2000). The two processes are distinct in concept and approach, implemented separately and independently of each other, and both have been subject to evaluation recently with major changes made or pending. The environmental or E-test of laws and regulations was introduced in 1995 by decision of the Cabinet (Official Gazette 1995, No 15) and reformed in 2002. The EIA Decree (1987, as amended) applies to specified plans and programmes as well as projects and the same procedure is followed at both levels. At the time of writing, this process is being revised in light of the requirements of the European SEA Directive and the proposed changes are the focus of major debate in The Netherlands (Husmann, 2004; Verheem, 2004).

The E-test for draft legislation

The E-test is one of four instruments that are used in The Netherlands to assess the potential effects of draft laws and regulations. It is applied in conjunction with tests of business effects, feasibility and enforcement and all follow a general procedure laid down in the Instructions for Regulations (No 256, 1995).[18] The E-test is a qualitative appraisal, based on minimum steps and incorporates limited checks and balances. It is carried out using a short questionnaire and guidance from the Ministry of Housing, Spatial Planning and the Environment (VROM, 1996). Specifically, draft legislation is tested for its consequences for energy consumption and mobility, for use of renewable and non-renewable resources, for waste and emissions to air, soil and water and for use of available physical space. The results of any application of the E-test must be included with other relevant information in the explanatory memorandum attached to draft legislation.

As originally envisaged, the E-test was to cover all policy and regulatory proposals with potentially significant effects on the environment and sustainable development (de Vries, 1996). However, the Ministry of Environment focused on draft legislation in the initial phase of implementation, although de Vries (1998) also reported that attention was given to 'policy documents that set out the proposed structure of new legislation'. This process was introduced in a low-key, flexible manner with a mix of incentives and penalties designed to encourage cooperation whilst ensuring relevant effects were addressed (de Vries and Tonk, 1997). Key principles and characteristics of this approach are summarized in Box 3.17. These remain in force today, although the procedure now followed differs in certain respects from that in place from c1996–2002.

In practice, only about 10 per cent of draft regulations proposed annually were found to have environmental effects that warranted attention (de Vries, 1998). Under the initial E-test procedure, these were listed in advance by an interdepartmental working committee, which also determined the particular questions to be answered. When assessing them, the responsible ministry could draw on the assistance of a 'help desk' in the Joint Support Centre for Draft Regulations,[19] which also reviewed the quality of the information prior to its submission to Cabinet (Verheem and Tonk, 2000). The enabling role of the Joint Support Centre in providing information and advice is widely cited and credited in most accounts of the E-test referenced here. Modest progress also

---

18   The other instruments comprise: the business effects test (BET) to identify the consequences for economic sectors; the feasibility and compliance test (FCT) to identify the consequences for implementing and upholding the legislation; and the cost–benefit analysis (CBA) to identify the economic consequences for society. The E-test is applied in conjunction with the BET and FCT, and CBA is undertaken when the side-effects have been established.

19   The Joint Support Centre is maintained by three ministries: Economic Affairs, the Environment, and Justice. It is staffed by departmental representatives who work together to facilitate the application of the legislative tests (described in the previous note) and provide specialized advice as needed (e.g. on the E-test).

appears to have been made in documenting effects; for example, de Vries (1998) observes that explanatory notes 'now often contain one or two paragraphs' detailing environmental effects (compared with the previous one-line statement of no or acceptable impact).

A review of the first five years of experience with the E-test procedure was undertaken in 2001. It evaluated the content and quality of the information in the light of other developments in The Netherlands including interest in sustainability assessment and the pending transposition of the SEA Directive. The main conclusion was that the E-test procedure resulted in the preparation of environmental information that had little or no substantive influence on legislation or its adoption. Such a candid and critical conclusion appears, prima facie, to undermine the rationale and purpose of the process, although some positive instrumental aspects were identified. These have provided a basis for reorganizing the process and amending the arrangements for the E-test as part of a broader consolidation of legislative tests (van Dreumel, 2003). Specific improvements include:

- The E-test is now implemented in two phases: a 'quick scan' of proposed legislation and an appraisal of significant effects when warranted (Box 3.17).
- The appraisal process and the preparation of an explanatory memorandum are guided by a written agreement, equivalent to terms of reference and subject to comment from the Ministries of the Environment and Justice.
- The proposed Legislation Desk (formerly the Joint Support Centre) has a stronger role in reviewing the quality of information in the explanatory note.
- The effectiveness of the new approach was due to be evaluated at the end of 2004.

Finally, the E-test review and reform took place against a wider background of preparing for the introduction of the SEA Directive and an emerging interest in sustainability appraisal (Klassen, 2002). Currently, around 30 overlapping policy and legislative tests and appraisals are applied across The Netherlands Government (de Jong and Noteboom, 2001). A single sustainability test is seen as an attractive option to focus and streamline these tests and to improve their effectiveness and impact on law- and policy-making. In this case, van Dreumel (2003) notes that the scope of environmental appraisal will need to be broadened to encompass other policy documents and strategic proposals, and this course of action should be taken in parallel with new legislation to comply with the SEA Directive. Such a common framework had not emerged at the time of writing – in large measure for reasons described below.

SEA of specified plans and programmes

Under the EIA Decree (1987), specified plans and programmes are subject to the procedure laid down in the EIA Act (1987). These include national plans for waste management, electricity generation and water supply and regional

BOX 3.17 THE NETHERLANDS' ENVIRONMENTAL TEST OF DRAFT REGULATIONS

Provision and mandate: Known as the E-test, this instrument assesses the potential environmental consequences of draft regulations sent to the Council of Ministers (Cabinet). It was established in 1994 as part of a wider Cabinet project to improve the quality of legislation and regulation and reduce their administrative and financial burden. The specific aim of the E-test is to integrate environmental considerations in the introduction of bills, general administrative orders or ministerial decrees and orders. In addition, departments can also test 'other policy intentions, such as plans and notes' (VROM, 1996).

Principles of implementation: The E-test only applies to 'draft regulations that have substantial consequences for the environment'. It was deliberately introduced in a low-key manner and experimentally in the first year; and, thereafter, implemented flexibly in accordance with a number of underlying principles (de Vries, 1996):

*   The initiating ministry is responsible for applying the E-test.
*   The use of the E-test should not delay decision-making.
*   The scope and detail of application is geared to significance of issues.
*   The test has minimum content and procedural requirements.
*   There is efficient integration with the existing decision-making process.
*   The test has a user- or customer-focused approach with a help desk maintained by a Joint Support Centre.

Procedure: Between 1996 and 2001, the minimum procedural requirements for implementation of the E-test corresponded to three main stages in the SEA process: (i) screening and scoping; (ii) impact analysis and documentation; and (iii) review and submission (Verheem and Tonk, 2000). A new E-test procedure was approved by the Council of Ministers in October 2002 and became obligatory on 1 March 2003. It has been consolidated into two main phases (van Dreumel, 2003):

*   *Quick scan*: Used by the responsible ministry to substantiate the need for draft legislation, to identify potential significant effects and propose the tests to be carried out.
*   *Appraisal and documentation*: E-test (and other appraisals) carried out in accordance with a written agreement on the information to be included in the explanatory memorandum, which is reviewed by the Proposed Legislation Desk and Ministry of Justice and directed for comment to the Ministry of Environment.

Experience to 2001: A five-year review of E-test experience in 2001 indicated that the instrument was applied on a pro-forma basis and had a negligible effect on decision-making. The E-test procedure was widely criticized as 'unnecessary ballast', particularly for laws that had a lot of regulations, and its positive aspects were considered to be largely instrumental. In that regard, the E-test needs to move beyond simply providing information in an explanatory memorandum and aim to integrate and internalize the results in laws and regulations. This will require, inter alia, the Joint Support Centre to take a more independent and critical approach to the content and quality of the information (Klassen, 2002; van Dreumel, 2003). Various changes have been made to the E-test procedure and practice to address these issues (as above).

Lessons for SEA practice: A wider implication of the relative ineffectiveness of the E-test of draft legislation concerns the nature and stage of decision-making. Environmental appraisal should apply to other policy documents and strategic proposals prior to and separate from the legislative process. In the specific case of The Netherlands, the E-test evaluation pointed towards combining various policy tests into sustainability appraisal (within the framework of the National Strategy for Sustainable Development and with due regard to the Dutch transposition of Directive 2001/41/EC.

land use plans for the location of major new housing, industrial or recreational areas. Dutch policy and planning processes for this purpose are highly structured and facilitate the tiered application of SEA and EIA (as described in Case Study 3.2). This takes place against established policy objectives and facilitates a 'distance to target' approach to sustainable development, for example as recommended in the National Environmental Policy Plan (NEPP). Now in its fourth version (VROM, 2001), the NEPP provides an important reference framework for SEA of plans and programmes (see Sadler and Verheem, 1996).

As for projects, so-called strategic EIA (SEIA) for specified plans and programmes follows a mandatory process, including examination of alternatives, public involvement in the scoping and review phases and review of the quality of the information by the independent EIA Commission. This process is described in detail in ten Holder and Verheem (1996). It closely matches the planning procedure, which facilitates integration, and they have similar characteristics such as (Verheem and Tonk, 2000):

- early notification and involvement of the public;
- integration of information into SEA and plan preparation throughout the process;
- consultation with other government agencies and advice from independent experts;
- identification of the best alternative (from an environmental perspective in the SEIA);
- reasons for decision and justification of the adopted plan; and
- monitoring and follow-up to plan implementation.

There have been a number of reviews of overall and case experience with SEIA in The Netherlands at different periods in its evolution, including those cited above. Of particular importance are the five-year evaluations of the effectiveness of the Dutch EIA system. Although no distinction is made between project and strategic applications, the latest review underlined the value added by this overall process to decision-making. During the past 15 years, the EIA Commission (2003) reports that approximately 50 SEAs have been completed (90 if EIAs for rural development plans are included) and experience indicates the general positive evaluation of process effectiveness applies equally at this level (Rob Verheem, personal communication).

Specific examples of SEA applications in The Netherlands that illustrate elements of good practice include (Rob Verheem, personal communication):

- *SEA of the National Structure Plan for Surface Minerals*, which identified the elements of the decision most relevant to the environment and its alternatives. The advice of the EIA Commission focused on alternatives for the use of the scarcest raw materials and the decision on locations for the extraction of construction sands.
- *SEA of the Space for Rivers' Policy Plan*, which provided information on the combined environmental consequences of many measures in the Plan, such as the lowering of the endyked floodplain,[20] excavating side channels and re-routing dykes.
- *SEA for the Delta Metropolis* (the urban region of the west of The Netherlands), which established a basis for sound decision-making on whether to build a magnetic levitation railway or a high-speed railway and identified the best locations for new housing and industrial areas in relation to the infrastructure decision.
- *The SEA of the National Waste Management Plan*, which compared alternative technologies for waste processing, including the best option from an environmental perspective. It also developed a method to assess the environmental effects of waste treatment processes that can be used in subsequent EIA of projects, for example quantitative life cycle assessments (see Case Study 3.2).
- *The SEA of the Policy Rules on Active Soil Management*, which contributed to the development of guidance on dealing with polluted sludge in future river-widening projects along the Meuse and Rhine rivers.

Given the acknowledged strengths of the SEIA process, the transposition of the SEA Directive into national legislation will be of wider interest. In particular, there appear to be differences of opinion between the Ministry of the Environment and the EIA Commission. The Ministry recognizes the SEIA

---

20 In the Dutch approach to flood prevention, dykes are not built directly adjacent to river channels. Instead they are set back, creating a floodplain between the channel and the dyke. At low water levels, the river flows in its natural bed and floodplains effectively are meadows (cows graze on them). At high water levels (e.g. in winter), water inundates the floodplain up to the dykes. In other words, the floodplains increase the capacity of the river when needed. To date, the capacity of the floodplains has been sufficient. But because of the increasing river water levels, it has become necessary to lower the floodplains by excavation. This is positive from the perspectives of both safety (less flooding) and mining (sand and clay production), but negative from an ecological perspective (loss of natural value of the existing floodplains). Hence SEA is needed to find the best and least costly alternatives.

process has made a substantial contribution to more 'environment-inclusive' decision-making; but it considers that mission to be nearly completed and argues that requirements should not now go beyond what is required by the European EIA Directive – in effect, downsizing the mandatory procedure by some 60 per cent (Husmann, 2004). By contrast, the argument of the EIA Commission is to simplify SEA where possible, but to keep the core values in place for sector and spatial plans (Verheem, 2004). The outcome of this debate will be of wider interest internationally given the past leadership role of The Netherlands in EIA and SEA (e.g. as described by Wood, 1996). For a personal view on the issues at stake, see Box 3.18.

3.3.9 New Zealand[21]

In New Zealand, SEA is not formally instituted as a separate, dedicated procedure. Rather, its characteristics are reflected in a number of laws and policies. The Resource Management Act (RMA), 1991, is the major environmental statute and emphasizes an integrated approach to policy, planning and assessment of issues concerning the use of land and resources (see Table 3.2). SEA principles and features in this framework are widely recognized, but are somewhat differently characterized by international and New Zealand commentators (e.g. Dixon, 1994, 2002; Gow, 1996, 1998; Sadler and Verheem, 1996; Veart, 1997; Ward et al, 2002). They can be seen, arguably, both as generally 'threaded into' RMA policy and planning functions and as specifically represented in certain requirements of the Act (Sadler, 2001b). In addition, diverse other SEA-type processes operate beyond the remit of the RMA. These require a relatively broad account to be made of the policy and institutional framework for environmental protection and sustainable development.

The RMA was not intended to provide a general mandate for SEA. But this potential has been perceived and promoted since its implementation (Dixon, 2002). SEA process and practice under this legislative framework are more diffuse or ad hoc than in many of the countries described in this section. But it displays environmental and sustainability dimensions that are of interest internationally. From this perspective, the RMA has three defining cornerstones (Sadler, 2001b):

- a single purpose of promoting sustainable resource management and a supporting objective of safeguarding the capacity of critical life support systems;
- a tiered hierarchy of policies and plans that incorporates an effects-based approach – this corresponds to, and includes elements of, SEA and sets a framework for EIA of actions and approval of resource consent;[22] and

---

21 With contribution by Jenny Dixon.
22 There is no reference to SEA or EIA as such in the RMA; rather specific provisions are made for the assessment of environmental effects (AEE) in Section 88 and the Fourth Schedule of the Act. As defined in regulations and implemented, AEE in New Zealand corresponds to EIA as understood and applied internationally (for a comparison see Sadler, 2001b).

BOX 3.18 THE CHALLENGE OF IMPLEMENTING THE EU SEA DIRECTIVE IN THE NETHERLANDS: A PERSONAL REFLECTION[23]

Rob Verheem

As with all European countries, The Netherlands is now struggling with implementing the new EU SEA Directive. Unlike many other countries, however, The Netherlands is in the interesting situation that it already has two SEA systems, which have been in place for some time. Strategic EIA is mandatory for certain spatial and sectoral plans. It has been shown to be highly effective in safeguarding the proper consideration of environmental issues in decision-making but is unpopular with decision-makers as too heavy a burden. The 'E-test' applies to new legislation with significant environmental consequences. It has been shown to be insufficiently effective in strengthening the role of environmental goals in law-making but is very popular with most decision-makers because of its minimum approach.

This leads to an interesting dilemma in the current discussion on how to best implement the SEA Directive. Should we aim for a minimum approach, for example by simply implementing the SEA Directive as it is without adding extra safeguards? This may be liked by decision-makers but runs the risk of ineffectiveness. Or should we keep the current strategic EIA process because it is effective, but run the risk of being unpopular with decision-makers because we do more than 'Europe' requires? Or can we keep the effectiveness and still get rid of unnecessary rules and requirements?

In practice, the discussion is not as complex as it seems. When compared to Directive 2001/42/EC, the current strategic EIA process is not very much different. The most important additions are:

* publication of a starting note, so that everybody knows early in plan preparation that something is going on, and can start preparing to get involved;
* public participation on the required content of the environmental report;
* mandatory independent expert advice on the scope and the quality of the report; and
* obligation to explain the best alternative from an environmental perspective.

The question, therefore, is whether or not to keep all or some of these four requirements.

The current proposal of the Ministry of Environment is to adopt a new instrument, because SEIA is regarded as too unpopular and the E-test does not seem to work. The new instrument is given a new name (although in English it would translate as 'strategic

23 In The Netherlands the same process is followed for projects and plans and programmes. The evaluation took place of the effectiveness of this process. In reporting the results no distinction was made as to effectiveness at project and plan level. The results were that in 50 per cent of all cases the final decision was different than it would have been without EIA; in 70 per cent of the cases people had become more environmentally minded and in 80 per cent of the cases one or both of these effects took place.

environmental assessment'). More importantly, the Ministry considers that SEIA practice has now advanced in The Netherlands to the point where most of the four 'extra' obligatory requirements can be removed, recognizing that responsible government bodies will include them as and where necessary. The only exceptions are the early announcement of plan preparation and independent review by the EIA Commission if a plan or programme will affect an area protected under the EC Habitat or Birds Directive.

Not all parties agree with this proposal. The EIA Commission, for example, considers the Ministry's approach to be correct for the majority of plans and programmes but not for complex, controversial cases that involve choice of location, technology or use of resources. Such plans directly affect interests and lead to much debate and protest. Political pressure could then possibly lead to sub-optimal choices that could weaken the quality and the credibility of the finally adopted plan. As an alternative, a short list of these plans and programmes should be prepared and existing requirements should stay mandatory for them.

The current proposal is now in the political arena. At the time of writing, the outcome is hard to predict, but it is clear that, to some extent, the discussion has a 'religious or ideological character'. Do we have (or not have) sufficient faith in the environmental awareness or commitment of planners and decision-makers? If so, does this apply uniformly or are there limits to what we may expect when faced with short-term, economic advantages and long-term environmental disadvantages? And what kind of SEA will help us to then act sustainably?

- specific requirements that are analogous to the SEA approaches in other countries (see below).

Taken together, these three elements appear to give the RMA the same intent and scope as SEA processes undertaken elsewhere, in other words to anticipate and address adverse and positive effects on the environment and integrate these considerations into policy and plan formulation. However, many New Zealand practitioners take a more cautious and narrower view of the SEA profile of the RMA. They see the Act as an implicit mandate that provides 'possibilities' to use this approach and 'opportunities for policy learning' (Dixon, 2002; Ericksen et al, 2001).

Key points of reference for delineating the role of SEA in this regime include (Ward et al, 2002) (see also Box 3.19):

- the preparation of national environmental standards and national and regional policy statements that give strategic direction to regional and district-level planning; and
- the requirement (Section 32 of the Act) to consider alternatives and analyse benefits and costs as part of policy or plan-making. This can be interpreted as an SEA-equivalent instrument, especially when combined with the monitoring provisions of Section 35.

In practice, as a strategic framework for sustainable resource management, the RMA remains incomplete and less integrated than might be expected after

Box 3.19 SEA dimensions of the New Zealand Resource Management Act (RMA)

Three dimensions of the RMA embody or reflect the key characteristics of SEA as applied internationally (Sadler, 2001b):

- general principles, functions and duties that have the single purpose of promoting sustainable resource management – this approximates to, but is not exactly the same as, environmental sustainability;
- an effects-based framework and approach to policy-making, planning and approval of resource consents that, at the higher levels, corresponds to or incorporates elements of SEA and, at the lower level, is synonymous with EIA; and
- specified requirements for analysis of policies and plans that are analogous to an SEA of a policy, plan or strategic document (particularly as required by Section 32 of the Act).

Mandate for sustainable resource management: The sustainability mandate of the RMA is set out in broad, encompassing terms in the statement of purpose in Section 5. Some people consider that this is not sufficiently clear because it allows an overly wide interpretation by regional and district planners that results in unfocused plans (Ericksen et al, 2001). Yet there is little doubt that the mandate itself remains 'entirely appropriate'. It is frequently referenced in international literature as a statement of purpose and philosophy as follows (Section 5):

> *The purpose of this Act is to promote the sustainable management of natural and physical resources. In this Act, 'sustainable management' means managing the use, development and protection of natural and physical resources in a way, or at a rate, which enables people and communities to provide for their social, economic and cultural well-being and for their health and safety while:*

(a) sustaining the potential of natural and physical resources (excluding minerals) to meet the reasonably foreseeable needs of future generations;
(b) safeguarding the life supporting capacity of air, water, soil and ecosystems; and
(c) avoiding, remedying or mitigating any adverse effects of activities on the environment.

Effects-based approach and framework: The RMA provides for an environmentally focused, effects-based approach (Sections 5 (b) (c) above) that is given strategic expression through a tiered hierarchy of policies and plans comprising:

- national environmental standards and national policy statements;
- regional policy statements and plans; and
- district plans that govern the granting of resource consents.

The central government has discretion to prepare national environmental standards (Section 43 and 44) and national policy statements (Section 24), except for the National Coastal Policy Statement (1994), which is mandatory under Section 57. But when completed, such instruments must be implemented by agencies and authorities with formal responsibilities under the RMA. No standards or statements were issued during the first 12 years of RMA implementation, apparently because of the cumbersome and time-consuming process to be followed and the reluctance of previous governments to do so. This has been widely criticized as compromising the coherence of the integrated approach that lies at the heart of the RMA (Ericksen et al, 2001). But, recently, the government has released, inter alia, proposed National Environmental Standards for Air Quality and a National Policy Statement on Indigenous Biodiversity.

In contrast, the preparation of regional policy statements is a mandatory duty for regional and unitary (major urban) councils. All of them have completed regional policy statements that provide the framework for integrated planning and resource management. Except for mandatory regional coastal plans, regional plans may be prepared on topics considered to be appropriate (e.g. air, water and land, dairy discharges, and erosion and sediment control in the Auckland region). Finally, every territorial authority is required (by Section 31) to prepare a district plan that 'cannot be inconsistent' with regional policies or any regional plans that have been prepared. District plans are focused primarily on land use. They include rules for zoning (e.g. for industrial, commercial or residential housing) or to designate land for specific uses that can have significant effects on the environment (e.g. landfills).

SEA equivalent instrument: Section 32 of the RMA prescribes the duties of a minister or local authority to evaluate the objectives and policies of any proposed standards, policy statement or plans and to prepare a report on the findings.

An evaluation must examine (Section 32 (3)):

(a)   the extent to which each objective is the most appropriate way to achieve the purpose of this Act; and
(b)   whether, having regard to their efficiency and effectiveness, the policies, rules or other methods are the most appropriate for achieving the objectives.

An evaluation must take into account (Section 32 (4)):

(a)   the benefits and costs of policies, rules or other methods; and
(b)   the risk of acting or not acting if there is uncertain or insufficient information about the subject matter of the policies, rules or other methods.

There are two main aspects to the test of appropriateness according to a recent Section 32 analysis undertaken by the Ministry for the Environment (2004):

•   weighing up alternative objectives to determine which one will provide environmental outcomes that will best meet the purpose of the Act; and
•   being satisfied that the objective chosen can best be achieved through the Act, rather than through some other mechanism.

more than 12 years of implementation. Two key observations can be made. First, few national environmental standards and policy statements (which are discretionary) have been drafted, and then only recently. Second, regional policy statements (which are mandatory) have been rated as being of generally inferior quality and insufficient to promote good plan-making (Ericksen et al, 2001).

Inevitably, these weaknesses raise questions about the extent to which a tiered approach to policy and plan preparation is really in place; and about what value is added at each stage of devolved responsibility, from the national level downward. Ultimately, there is a heavy reliance on 78 territorial authorities to develop district or land use plans that achieve RMA objectives and principles. These plans must be supported by an assessment of the state of the environment. Ericksen et al (2001) report that there is scope for considerable improvement in this component and the overall interpretation of the RMA mandate by local authorities.

Section 32 of the RMA requires an evaluation to be carried out of the appropriateness, effectiveness and efficiency of the objectives and policies of any proposed standards, policy statements or plans. As indicated in Box 3.19, a number of features of a Section 32 analysis underline its near equivalence with SEA, particularly if combined with the monitoring provisions of Section 35: consideration of alternatives; analysis of the benefits and costs of proposed policies, rules or other methods; and preparation of a report. Bailey and Dixon (1999) characterize such analysis as a form of policy environmental assessment. Fookes (2000) reports that, in practice, the prevailing view amongst practitioners is that Section 32 reports contain little that indicates any systematic analysis.[24] In particular, with occasional exceptions, they lack rigour in evaluating options and issues, despite government guidance on these matters (New Zealand Ministry for the Environment, 2000). Recent amendments to the Act and 32 case examples of analyses of national environmental standards and policy statements suggest that improvements are being made on this front (Martin Ward, personal communication).

Beyond the RMA, SEA is not formally applied to policy- and plan-making, although elements of this approach can be found in a variety of arrangements and instruments that require environmental matters to be addressed strategically. Notable examples include the following (see also Dixon, 2002; Ward et al, 2002; Sadler et al, 2004):

*   *The Government's policy framework for environment and sustainable development* comprises a suite of strategies, action plans and new initiatives. Collectively, these fashion a mandate for SEA, broadly interpreted as a form of appraisal or integrated methodology (Dalziel and Ward, 2004). At their core is the Government's Sustainable Development for New Zealand Programme of Action. This focuses on four areas: water, energy, sustainable cities, and child and youth development. It also sets out principles for taking account of the social, economic, environmental and cultural consequences of the Government's policy decisions (see

---

24 Fookes (2000) explains the basis for this view as follows: 'In their Section 32 reports some councils seem to have described procedure as opposed to presenting a formal test of preferred options against alternatives. Sometimes these documents also double as an extended explanation of the meaning of selected objectives, policies and methods, rather than an analysis of them.'

Department of Prime Minister and Cabinet, 2003). Other related instruments are the Biodiversity Strategy, Climate Change Programme, Energy Efficiency and Conservation Strategy, and the Health Strategy. The latter is accompanied by guidance on health impact assessment (HIA) as a policy tool (Public Health Advisory Committee, 2003).

• *A number of inquiries carried out by the Parliamentary Commissioner for the Environment* (and the Select Committee of Parliament[25]) may be interpreted as SEA-type approaches or examples of para-SEA.

Under the Environment Act (1986), the Parliamentary Commissioner for the Environment functions as an independent ombudsman with wide powers of investigation in respect of environmental policies and administration (including RMA performance). Recent reviews have focused on bio-security risks, hazardous waste, urban water issues and progress toward sustainable development with particular reference to New Zealand's environmental management performance. The latter draws on many previous reports (see Parliamentary Commissioner for the Environment, 2002).

• *Certain ad hoc regional and sector planning exercises* appear to meet or approximate to international understanding of SEA. But they do not represent any systematic implementation of statutory or administrative responsibilities.

At the regional level, a widely cited case is the approach taken in the Auckland Regional Growth Strategy 2050. This was developed as a voluntary and cooperative initiative amongst several local authorities through a special purpose body (see Box 3.20). It was undertaken to address pressures of urban sprawl and divided planning responsibilities, and corresponds closely to SEA principles and methodology (Fookes, 2002).

At the sector level, the Land Transport Management Act (2003) and New Zealand Transport Strategy (2002) have introduced new environmental and social objectives, and requirements for taking them into account in planning and decision-making. Para-SEA approaches are

---

25 An example of this is the Parliamentary Transport and Environment Select Committee inquiry into the environmental effects of road transport in 1998, in the light of some major transport policy decisions that were pending in relation to possible changes to the ownership (public to private) and extensive user charging. In an interim report, the Committee, inter alia, concluded that 'environmental sustainability has been largely removed from consideration of the road reform process'. It went on to note that many aspects of the management of environmental effects of road transport lay outside the RMA, were not addressed in strategic planning by government agencies and the absence of an integrated legislative and policy framework for this purpose presented risks to the environment. This example is described further in Ward et al (2002).

BOX 3.20 AUCKLAND'S REGIONAL GROWTH STRATEGY 2050 AS AN SEA APPLICATION

Approximately one-third of New Zealanders live in the Greater Auckland Region. It is the major growth pole of the country with a population of more than 1 million. The political and administrative geography of the region is relatively complex by New Zealand standards. In accordance with the provisions of the Resource Management Act, four city and three district councils are responsible for controlling land use; and the Auckland Regional Council is responsible for preparing a regional policy statement to guide planning and management of the natural and physical resources of the area. However, there is no single agency responsible for coordinating land and infrastructure development in a rapidly growing metropolis where environmental and social impacts from urban sprawl and traffic pressures continue to intensify.

In the late 1990s, the Auckland Regional Growth Forum was established as a special purpose, collaborative body to address these issues and the policy vacuum underlying them. This initiative of the Auckland Regional Council enjoyed strong support and contributions from the seven local authorities. A particular emphasis was given to developing a long-term vision and growth strategy for the region to 2050 (a period during which time the population is projected to double). The strategy was developed over three to four years and incorporated both a strong technical basis and extensive public consultation. For example:

*   reports were prepared on the following topics: regional planning overview; national and physical resource constraints; transport capacities; physical infrastructure; social infrastructure; growth management techniques; employment location; intensification; and rural issues; and
*   public consultation was undertaken in two main phases: the first stage involved preliminary consultation with stakeholder groups and the wider public which helped to establish the draft strategy; this was then released for a second round of consultation, which included stakeholder and open meetings, formal submissions and public hearings.

Options for accommodating future growth were assessed by reference to preferred outcomes:

*   safe, healthy communities;
*   diversity of employment and business opportunities;
*   housing choices;
*   high amenity of urban environments;
*   the protection and maintenance of the character of the region's natural environments;
*   sustainable use and protection of the region's resources (including infrastructure); and
*   efficient access to activities and appropriate social infrastructure for all.

Although no reference is made to SEA, Fookes (2002) analysed the strategy process and methodology in relation to this approach and found a close fit. The Auckland Regional Growth Strategy 2050 is being implemented through various statutory and non-statutory arrangements by the local councils involved. Monitoring and adaptation is a key element of this process (Dixon, 2002). In addition to the councils, Infrastructure Auckland is a key implementation agency. It was established with the principal function of making grants to transport and storm-water projects in the region. The multi-criteria analysis of potential projects applied by the agency is reported to be one of the most advanced examples of its kind in New Zealand.

See also Auckland Regional Growth Forum (1999a, b) and, for updates: www.ia.co.nz/index2.html.

Source: Ward et al (2002)

evident in the procedural steps and content requirements for strategies prepared by regional land transport committees;[26] and also in the integrated methodology for evaluating investment and funding allocation proposals submitted to Transfund New Zealand for the fiscal year 2004–2005 (Sadler et al, 2004).

Looking ahead, it is not clear whether SEA (as understood internationally) will evolve in New Zealand from the variants identified under and beyond the RMA. As already noted, RMA implementation has been much slower than anticipated, particularly with respect to national policies and standards. These are critical if the promise of the RMA is to be fulfilled (Dalziel and Ward, 2004). Certain national environmental standards and a national policy statement on indigenous biodiversity are now being drafted. But it is recognized that the Government still has much to do (Jenny Dixon, personal communication).

The first round of RMA-based plans is still incomplete and it will take some time before the next round begins. At the same time, a new generation of long-term, strategic community plans are being prepared under the Local Government Act (2002). The relationship between the two sets of plans remains unclear. Equally, the potential role of SEA principles and practice in the preparation of plans at both levels has yet to be defined. In the RMA context, Dixon (2002) notes that much will depend on the extent to which planners and decision-makers adopt SEA principles and methods voluntarily (as opposed to introducing new legal and administrative arrangements).

Outside the remit of the RMA, there is considerable scope for SEA as both a formal and informal procedure in a number of areas. A more systematic approach could be taken at several levels: by central government in policy-making; at the local and regional level for land transport planning; and for local-level strategic planning under the Local Government Act (2002). But progress is likely to take time. In the near future, it is likely that SEA process and practice in New Zealand will continue to be distinctive and diverse – much like its ecology (Sadler, 2003b).

---

26 In the last round, the three metropolitan regional land transport strategies (Auckland, Christchurch and Wellington) all used relatively simple evaluation techniques to assess different sets of scenarios against transport planning targets or objectives and performance criteria. For example, the 'scorecard' or 'planning balance sheet' approach was used in developing the Canterbury regional land transport strategies. Although described as an evaluation matrix, it is little more than a checklist. Most indications are that this approach will have to become more systematic in the new round of strategy-making and should benefit from the use of formal SEA (see Sadler et al, 2004).

3.3.10 Norway[27]

The formal provision for SEA of policy and legislation in Norway is given in the Instructions for Consequence Assessment, Submission and Review Procedures in Connection with Official Studies, Regulations, Propositions and Reports to the Storting. These Instructions were issued by Royal Decree on 18 February 2000 and came into force on 1 March 2000 (replacing the previous Instructions issued on 16 December 1994).

Both policy and legislative proposals are subject to strategic assessment under the Instructions. The process followed is far more flexible than the EIA procedure. All potential impacts of an initiative are addressed, including financial, social, regional, gender equality and environmental issues.

As for EIA, responsibility for assessments undertaken under the Instructions lies with the line ministry/sector concerned. The Ministry of the Environment has a support and advisory role and has issued Guidelines on Environmental Assessment in Accordance with the Instructions for Official Studies and Reports.

Currently, there are no specific, formal requirements for SEA of onshore plans and programmes, but Norway will implement the EU SEA Directive. Legislation requires environmental assessment before opening an area for petroleum-related activities. In addition, the licensees are required to undertake regional EIAs within smaller areas if the authorities decide it is necessary. Environmental assessment has also been an integral part of preparing sector programmes such as the national transport plan and the national plan for hydroelectric power (Box 3.21), which are presented as white papers to the Parliament.

In preparing for the introduction of formal requirements for SEA of plans and programmes, the Ministry of the Environment has initiated several pilot projects to gain experience of how SEA might best be undertaken at the municipal and regional levels (see Box 3.22).

3.3.11 UK[28]

Prior to the entry into force of the EU SEA Directive on 21 July 2004, the UK had no statutory provisions for SEA. Nevertheless, several types of SEA process had emerged during the 1990s including appraisals of national policies, 'environmental appraisals' (and latterly 'sustainability appraisals') of local and regional development plans, and ad hoc SEAs carried out in specific sectors (e.g. transport and water). Examples of the latter include the strategic environmental appraisal of the Strategic Defence Review (Ministry of Defence, 2000) and the SEA for offshore oil and gas licensing and wind energy generation for the Department of Trade and Industry (DTI, 2001).

Good practice guidance has been prepared for both English local authorities and central government departments and local authorities (see

---

27 With contribution by Terje Lind, Ministry of Environment, Norway.
28 With contribution by Steve Smith, Scott Wilson Kirkpatrick consultants, UK.

BOX 3.21 ENVIRONMENTAL ASSESSMENT FOR HYDROELECTRIC POWER PLANS IN NORWAY

Norway's strategy for balancing the use and conservation of river systems involves plans and management systems as well as legislation. Elements of particular importance in the decision-making framework include the licensing procedures, the Protection Plan for Water Resources, and the Master Plan for Water Resources.

The first *Protection Plan* was adopted in 1973 and the most recent plan was adopted in 1993. The watercourses included in the plan are protected from hydropower development as well as other types of intervention. The aim of the current revision is to add watercourses to the Plan. The Plan is drawn up with close cooperation between the energy and water authorities, and the environmental authorities. It is based on an evaluation of the 'protection' interests related to the respective watercourses: cultural heritage, nature conservation, fish, wildlife, outdoor recreation and pollution control, as well as agriculture, forestry and reindeer husbandry. All interested parties, including local authorities and local and national NGOs, received the evaluation reports and were able to express their opinions in a broad hearing process.

The *Master Plan for Water Resources* is based on detailed reports (feasibility studies) made for about 400 potential hydropower projects (above 1MW) in the country. Each report contains an evaluation of the impact of the project on the different types of interests in the catchment area: hydropower potential, nature conservation (geology, landscapes, botany and zoology), outdoor recreation (aesthetic experience, walking, rafting etc.), fish (salmon, trout, science, fishing), wildlife (mammals, birds, hunting), water supply, water quality (protection against pollution), cultural heritage, agriculture and forestry (potential), reindeer husbandry (one-third of the projects are in *Sami* districts), flood protection and erosion control, transportation, ice and water temperature, climate (changes in the local climate due to more open water in winter) and regional economy. For some projects, many alternatives were studied. Each report was subjected to a hearing process and also, subsequently, the 'main report' (Master Plan) submitted in the autumn of 1984. The first generation of the Master Plan was approved by the Parliament in 1986. Since then it has been revised twice, most recently in 1993. It is currently being revised again.

Boxes 3.23 and 3.24, respectively). This guidance forms part of the Government's approach to ensuring that development is sustainable, for example as set out in the first and second UK Strategies for Sustainable Development (HMSO, 1994; Stationery Office, 1999). So far, policy appraisal has been applied narrowly and inconsistently and will not be directly affected by the EU SEA Directive. But development plan evaluation must be brought in line with the SEA Directive (see below).

Government guidance on undertaking SEA for spatial and land use plans (ODPM, 2003), advocates a five-stage approach to SEA (and SA) (see Figure 3.2 and Table 3.3). Further draft generic practical guidance on SEA for non-planning authorities, prepared by the Office of the Deputy Prime Minister (ODPM) together with the Scottish Executive, the Welsh Assembly Government and the Northern Ireland Department of the Environment, was published in July 2004 with a three-month consultation period provided for

---

BOX 3.22 SEA IN LAND USE PLANNING: EXPERIENCES FROM FIVE PILOT PROJECTS IN NORWAY

The Ministry of the Environment has initiated several SEA pilot projects. The aim has been to test how SEA (both the process and documentation) can best be implemented for land use planning in different settings and circumstances – for different municipality sizes and different planning processes.

The SEA pilot projects are built on three of the formal procedural requirements in the planning process:

- the *notice phase* (a more structured process in relation to the public as well as identifying issues relevant to the plan);
- the *circulation* of the draft plan to the public and to relevant governmental authorities (with more thorough information about the impacts of the plan as well as plans to abate them and for follow-up); and
- the *publication* of the adopted plan (with information on, for example, how the impacts will be abated and monitored).

The pilot projects show that the SEA elements can be integrated into different stages of land use planning under different planning situations. It has been found especially useful to strengthen the early phase of planning by providing a precise prescription for the process and documentation. In addition, the following considerations have proved to be important:

- a focused knowledge base, to ensure that the assessment of relevant impacts is integrated in the planning process;
- participation by public organizations;
- cooperation with relevant governmental bodies;
- political discussions and considerations; and
- documentation as the basis for communication and to steer the planning exercise.

---

comments. The guidance includes sections on the background and context of the SEA Directive, consultation, SEA and sustainable development, and the steps in the SEA process (ODPM, 2004).

The Government's Statutory Instrument 2004 No 1633 sets out regulations transposing the EU SEA Directive into law in England (available at: www.legislation.hmso.gov.uk, then follow statutory instruments).

Transposition of the SEA Directive into national law has been dealt with separately in Scotland, Northern Ireland (NI) and Wales. In line with the Partnership Agreement – *A Partnership for a Better Scotland* (Scottish Labour Party and Scottish Liberal Democrats, undated), – Scottish ministers aim to achieve and surpass the objectives set out in the EU SEA Directive. This involves a two-stage process. The Scottish Parliament has adopted a set of regulations implementing the SEA Directive; however, these will be revoked by a comprehensive bill on SEA, which will apply it to a wider range of public sector strategies, plans and programmes than the Directive requires (Sheate et al, 2004). Similarly *Sustainability Appraisal of Unitary Development Plans in*

Box 3.23 UK guidance on SEA for national policies

The Government's White Paper on the Environment, *This Common Inheritance* (DoE, 1990), emphasized the importance of incorporating environmental considerations into policy development. Commitments made in the White Paper resulted in the publication of *Policy Appraisal and the Environment* in 1991 (DoE, 1991). This guide was aimed at central government agencies and emphasized the use of cost–benefit techniques as a basis for taking environmental effects into account in policy development. A companion study provided advice on good practice. It indicated that progress was uneven and slower than anticipated with considerable variation in implementation of policy appraisal. It brought into question the extent to which the government-wide commitment to address the potential environmental impact of its own proposals was being met. A subsequent study drew similar conclusions and confirmed there was scope for further improvement (DETR, 1997). Updated guidance was prepared on this basis (DETR, 1998).

The policy appraisal process involved several basic steps (DoE, 1991; DETR, 1997):

- *list the objectives* of the proposal and *summarize the policy issue*, identifying possible trade-offs and constraints;
- *specify the range of options* for achieving the objectives, including the 'do nothing' option;
- *identify and list all impacts* on the environment and consider mitigation measures to offset them;
- *assess the significance* of the impacts in relation to other costs and benefits;
- use an appropriate method to *value costs and benefits*, including those based on monetary values, ranking or physical quantities;
- *state the preferred option* with reasons for doing so; and
- *monitor and evaluate the results*, making appropriate arrangements for doing so as early as possible.

More recently, the emphasis has switched from environmental to 'integrated policy appraisal'. The *Modernising Government* White Paper of 1999 committed Government 'to produce and deliver an integrated system of impact and appraisal tools in support of sustainable development covering impacts on business, the environment, health and the needs of particular groups in society' (UK Government, 1999). In response, an approach to integrated policy appraisal (IPA) was developed by several government departments to help policy-makers assess the full range of social, economic and environmental impacts of their initiatives. IPA was designed to act as a 'gateway' to other appraisal methodologies, reducing work by identifying which appraisals needed to be done for a specific policy proposal.

Following a series of pilot studies, the IPA tool has now been incorporated into the existing system of regulatory impact assessment (RIA). As part of RIA, policy-makers must explicitly identify the economic, social and environmental costs and benefits of their proposals. This is intended to provide a unified approach, bringing together within one tool the two complementary aims of better policy-making and sustainable development. From 1 April 2004, the RIA system was extended to cover all substantial policies and proposals, which will have an impact on the public and private sectors. In order to ensure that RIAs are properly completed, a number of quality checks have been put in place in addition to ministerial sign-off.

RIAs are placed in the public domain and are a key part of the consultation process:

- RIAs accompany letters seeking collective agreement to proposals so that ministers, in their responses, are able to comment on the analysis presented in the RIA.
- From 2003/2004, the National Audit Office has a new role in reviewing the quality of a sample of RIAs.
- From 2004, departmental reports will require statements on what is being done to support better regulation and to improve the quality of RIAs.
- The Cabinet Office Regulatory Impact Unit is working with departments to enhance the quality of analysis in RIAs and the Department for Environment, Food and Rural Affairs (DEFRA) and other departments will be involved in efforts to improve the assessment of social and environmental costs and benefits.

To supplement the RIA regime, DEFRA is preparing detailed guidance 'designed to make it as easy as possible for policy makers to spot the environmental impacts of their policy options during the policy-making process'.

For further information see: http://www.sustainable-development.gov.uk/sdig/integrating/index.htm.

BOX 3.24 UK GUIDANCE ON SEA OF DEVELOPMENT PLANS

Initial guidance on the role of SEA in the preparation of development plans was issued in *Policy Planning Guidance Note 12:2, Development Plans and Regional Planning Guidance* (DoE, 1992). This required planning authorities to consider the environmental implications of their development plans. In response, a number of local authorities began to carry out 'environmental appraisals' of their development plans and the Department of Environment prepared *Environmental Appraisal of Development Plans: A Good Practice Guide* (DoE, 1993). In comparison to the conventional model of SEA, 'environmental appraisal' of development plans has been described in various ways. Examples include 'a less systematic' but 'more integral and iterative process' (Sadler and Verheem, 1996), 'less comprehensive and onerous' (Therivel, 1998), 'less detailed' (Russell, 1999) and simply 'informal' (Glasson and Gosling, 2001). Therivel (1998) argued that many of the SEAs carried out in the UK – particularly the environmental appraisals of development plans – were only partial SEAs since they did not describe the baseline environment, consider alternatives, or make rigorous, quantitative predictions and offered little in the way of (concrete) mitigation measures. But she went on to argue that the majority of these nonetheless fulfilled the aims of SEA – including improved decision-making and greater awareness of environmental issues amongst decision-makers. Sadler and Verheem (1996) emphasized their sustainability dimensions and scales – a linkage that the Government has sought to maintain in preparing guidance pursuant to the SEA Directive.

During the mid-1990s, many local authorities expanded their environmental appraisal to encompass economic and social concerns; indeed, Therivel (1998) reported that approximately one-third of respondents to a 1997 questionnaire on appraisal practice characterized their appraisals as 'sustainability appraisals'. The trend toward sustainability appraisal (SA) culminated in the publication of a revised PPG12 in 1999. This required local authorities to carry out a full environmental appraisal of their development plans, but encouraged them to extend this to cover other sustainable development objectives. At the regional level, the former Department of Environment, Transport and the Regions published a *Good Practice Guide on Sustainability Appraisal of Regional Planning Guidance* (DETR, 2000). Recent research by the EIA Centre at the University of Manchester has demonstrated an increasing use of SA (Short et al, 2003). It shows that development plans have become more environmentally sound in the majority of cases. In just over half of the plans examined, some changes also occurred as a result of applying SA (mainly changes in wording of policies and reprioritization of proposed allocation sites within the plans).

The voluntary system of environmental/sustainability appraisal of local and regional plans is set to change considerably in light of the EU SEA Directive and the new Planning and Compulsory Purchase (PCP) Act, 2004. In particular, *The Strategic Environmental Assessment Directive: Guidance for Planning Authorities* (ODPM, 2003) indicates how the requirements of the SEA Directive are to be incorporated into the wider SA process. The PCP Act introduced fundamental changes to the planning system, replacing the system of unitary development plans, structure plans and local plans in England with a single level of planning: the local development framework (LDF). Significantly, the constituent parts of an LDF – local development documents (LDDs) – must undergo *statutory* SA. For the first time, SEA and SA will both be statutory requirements for local authority development plans. The Government advocates a unified approach to SEA/SA and has commissioned guidance (to be published by the end of 2004) on undertaking SA of LDDs, which fully incorporates the legal requirements of the SEA Directive.

Wales: A Good Practice Guide, issued by the National Assembly for Wales (2002) was superseded by interim guidance on the implications of the SEA Directive for unitary development plan (UDP) preparation. This in turn will be replaced by guidance on a combined approach to SEA/SA. In the UK at least, SEA is increasingly incorporated into a wider approach to sustainability appraisal or integrated assessment.

Further guidance on SEA in the UK includes:

- The Environment Agency is developing good practice guidance for SEA to assist external organizations in carrying out SEA (www.environment-agency.gov.uk).
- The Department of Transport has commissioned guidance on SEA of local transport plans (www.webtag.org.uk, click on documents).
- Guidance on SEA and biodiversity has been published by the Countryside Council for Wales, English Nature, the Environment Agency and the Royal Society for the Protection of Birds (2004). It explains how biodiversity implications can be considered in SEA on a step-by-step basis in the UK (www.rspb.org.uk/policy/planningpolicy/s_e_a.asp).

3.3.12 US

The National Environmental Policy Act (NEPA, 1969) applies to 'proposals for legislation and other major federal actions significantly affecting the ...

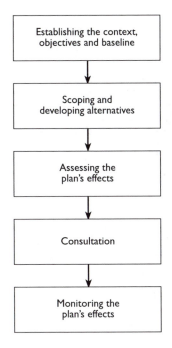

Source: ODPM (2003)

Figure 3.2 *Five-stage approach to SEA/SA (UK)*

environment'. It appears to provide a broad legal mandate that the Council on Environmental Quality (CEQ, 1986) interprets to include policies, plans and programmes. CEQ regulations on NEPA implementation set out procedures that apply generically to all proposed actions (e.g. notably indicating, for example, whether and how to prepare an environmental impact statement or EIS). In addition, specific guidance is given with regard to an EIS that may be prepared for broad federal actions, such as the adoption of new land use plans or sector programmes (e.g. at Section 1052.4(b)).

From an international perspective, programmatic environmental impact statements (PEIS) comprise a long-established and well-developed area of SEA practice (e.g. Sadler and Brooke, 1998; Wood, 1999). Early CEQ annual reports refer to the increased use of, and document experience with, 'programme impact statements' (CEQ, 1975). Most federal departments and major agencies had applied this form of SEA more than 25 years before the EU SEA Directive came into force (Sadler, 2004). Subsequently, CEQ regulations included provisions for focusing this process on actions that are related regionally, or generically by stage of technology development, or which are otherwise connected (e.g. by reference to potential cumulative effects). Federal agencies use this approach for a broad range of strategic activities, applying it in particular to land use and integrated resource management and to the transport, water and waste sectors amongst others (see the US Environmental Protection Agency website: www.epa.gov/).

Table 3.3 *Stages, decisions and outputs of SEA and sustainability appraisal in the UK*

Planning stage	SEA or Sustainability Appraisal stage	The purpose of this stage	What to decide	What to record
Identify the issues and options and prepare for consultation	A. Setting the context and establishing the baseline • identify other relevant plans and programmes; • identify environmental protection objectives, and state their relation to the plan; • propose SEA and sustainability appraisal objectives; • propose indicators; • collect baseline data, including data on likely future trends; • identify environmental and sustainability problems.	• document how the plan is affected by outside factors; • suggest ideas for how any inappropriate constraints can be addressed; • focus on key environmental and sustainability issues; help to identify SEA and sustainability problems, objectives and alternatives; • streamline the subsequent baseline description, prediction and monitoring stages; • provide a base for effects prediction and monitoring.	• what other plans, programmes and environmental protection objectives influence the plan; • what environmental/ sustainability objectives and indicators to test the plan options and policies against; • what data to collect and how to structure them so they can be easily used; • what environmental and sustainability problems to consider during plan-making.	• list of relevant plans, programmes and environmental protection objectives; • list of SEA/SA objectives and indicators; • data on environmental/ sustainability baseline; • list of relevant environmental/ sustainability problems.
Consultation on issues and options	B. Deciding the scope of SEA and developing alternatives • identify alternatives; • choose preferred alternatives; • consult authorities with environmental responsibilities and other bodies concerned with aspects of sustainability.	• clarify baseline, identify problems and alternatives; • ensure that the SEA and sustainability appraisal covers key issues; • help to ensure that the plan is sustainable.	• what alternatives to consider, possibly linked to each problem identified in Stage A; • what to include in the draft report.	• list of alternatives; • results of Stages A– B.
Prepare proposed plan	C. Assessing the effects of the plan • predict the effects of the plan;	• consider all likely effects; • ensure that all relevant effects	• what the effects of specific options, policies and	• effects of the plan options, policies and proposals;

	• evaluate the plan's effects; • propose measures to prevent, reduce or offset adverse environmental effects.	are identified and proposed mitigation measures are considered.	proposals will be; • how any adverse effects of implementing plan policies can be avoided, reduced or offset (mitigated); • the preferred alternatives; • how to present the information.	• list of preferred alternatives and explanation of why these are preferred; • proposed mitigation measures and how they will be implemented; • what methods have been used to analyse data and limitations; draft environmental report.
Full public consultation on proposed plan	*D. Consulting on the draft plan and the Environmental Report* • present the results of the SEA up to this point; • seek inputs from the public and authorities with environmental responsibilities; • take consultation results into account; • show how the results of the environmental report were taken into account in finalizing the plan.	• gather more information on the environmental baseline and problems; • discover the opinions and concerns of the public on environmental and sustainability issues; • show that information and opinions on environmental and sustainability issues have been appropriately considered.	• who to consult (in addition to statutory consultees) and how; • how to analyse to consultation results.	• consultation process.
Monitor plan implementation	*E. Monitoring the significant effects of implementing the plan on the environment* • ensure that plan is well implemented and feeds into the future plans or reviews in the next round of SEA/SA; • ensure that adverse effects can be identified; • provide information for future SEAs.	• how to measure the actual effects of the plan on the environment and sustainability.		• proposed monitoring programme.

Source: ODPM (2003)

In comparison to other types of NEPA application, the contemporary use of PEIS remains limited. It comprises a small proportion of the c500 draft, final and supplemental EISs that are completed each year in the US (Clark and Richards, 1999). As a consequence, the PEIS may be seen as the apex of a broad base of project-specific EIS (which themselves represent a very small proportion of the 50,000 less-detailed environmental assessments completed each year). This approach is reported still to be underutilized, but observers (e.g. Bass and Herson, 1999) comment that it is particularly helpful in considering alternatives and addressing the cumulative effects of subsequent projects and activities. PEIS provides a framework for any further EIA of individual projects, and subsequent requirements for analysis can be 'tiered' to the results of the PEIS. This is acknowledged to save time and resources, particularly where there is a multi-stage sequencing of activities.

PEIS also vary substantially in their strategic focus and in the way that agencies use and adapt the approach. A study of the effectiveness of NEPA after its first 25 years of operation noted that the process was rarely used to formulate specific policies and was often skirted in developing programmes (CEQ, 1997). As with other areas of NEPA implementation, there is a large body of case law relating to the scope and application of the process. NEPA is not triggered unless there is a federal action that has a demonstrable environmental impact. For example, the finding of 'no action' under NEPA was used to exempt the national energy policy, which normally would be assumed to have a wide range of environmental consequences (Clark, reported in Sadler and Brooke, 1998). On the positive side, the same department was commended in the NEPA effectiveness study for its extensive use of programmatic and site-wide analyses in determining how to reconfigure its nuclear weapons complex and address environmental clean-up obligations (CEQ, 1997).

More recently, the use of 'programmatic analyses and tiering' was one of five key themes addressed in the report of the NEPA Task Force (2003). It noted that this approach was used in a variety of ways and decision contexts and summarized the continuum of actions addressed in PEIS or related documents in three main categories (Table 3.4). It also emphasized that there are no clear-cut boundaries and some activities might fit into more than one category. This typology refers to SEA-type applications at the policy level that are not labelled as programmatic and may challenge some of the conventional wisdom about NEPA. One of the examples cited is the EIS of the Bonneville Power Administration Business Plan, summarized in Box 3.25.

The NEPA Task Force (2003) reported that the use of programmatic analyses is increasing at most government levels and coordination of analyses is improving. Most of the federal agencies appear to view these processes positively and they are considered to be particularly valuable in addressing issues at the broad landscape, ecosystem or regional level. Programmatic analyses also allow agencies to address environmental law or policy obligations such as the protection of threatened and endangered species. However, there was also considerable criticism and public concern about aspects of

Table 3.4 *Types of actions addressed in NEPA programme analyses*

Category of action	Description	Examples
Policy or strategy	National or regional analyses that establish programme goals and objectives.	• Tennessee Valley Authority – 'Integration of NEPA into a Comprehensive Environmental Management System'. • Bonneville Power Administration 'Business Plan' – an example of use in 'Longview Energy Development Plan'.
Land use	Integrated planning analyses for a geographical or landscape area – may prescribe general standards and controls and procedures for project implementation.	• White River National Forest Plan and EIS. • APHIS – 'Bison Management Plan for Montana and Yellowstone National Parks'.
Programme	Resource plan or programme – analyses that decide future priorities for development and scheduling and set controls for implementation of site-specific actions.	• Animal and Plant Health Inspection Services – 'Rangeland Grasshopper and Mormon Cricket Suppression Programme'. • Bonneville Power Administration – 'Fish and Wildlife Improvement Plan'.

Source: NEPA Task Force (2003)

programmatic analysis. Some agencies have abandoned the concept of tiering, concluding that it is ineffective and inefficient – another finding that challenges the conventional wisdom on SEA that accords tiering an iconic status. The NEPA Task Force also provide recommendations on how to address these and other issues related to programmatic analyses and tiering.[29]

29　Key recommendations of the NEPA Task Force (2003, Section 3.6) were stated as follows: to promote consistent, clear, cost-effective programmatic NEPA analyses, documents, and tiering that meet agency and stakeholder needs, the Task Force recommends that the CEQ provides guidance to:
- emphasize the importance of collaboration as agencies expand the use and scope of programmatic NEPA analyses;
- include a section in the first-tier document that explains the relationship between the programmatic analysis and document and future tiered analyses and documents, and describes how stakeholders will be involved;
- emphasize that programmatic documents should explain where and when deferred issues that were raised by the public and/or regulatory agencies will be addressed, and describe the proposed temporal and spatial scales that will be used when analysing those issues; and
- develop criteria for agencies to use when evaluating whether a programmatic document has become outdated, and articulate a general life expectancy for the different programmatic documents.

BOX 3.25 BONNEVILLE POWER ADMINISTRATION BUSINESS PLAN EIS

The electric utility market is increasingly competitive and dynamic. To participate successfully in this market and to continue to meet specific public service obligations as a federal agency, the Bonneville Power Administration (BPA) needs adaptive policies to guide marketing efforts and its other obligations such as its energy conservation and fish and wildlife responsibilities. This EIS evaluated six alternatives to meet this need.

(1) *No Action.* BPA would maintain its traditional activities in planning for long-term development of the regional power system, acquiring resources to meet customer loads, sharing costs and risks among its firm power customers and non-federal customers using the federal transmission system, and administering its fish and wildlife function, with the goal of fulfilling the requirements of the Northwest Power Act.

(2) *BPA Exercises Market Influences to Support Regional Goals.* In addition to its own activities to acquire energy resources and enhance fish and wildlife, BPA would exercise its position in regional power markets to promote compliance by its customers with the goals established by the Northwest Power Act.

(3) *Market-driven BPA* (The BPA Proposal). BPA would change its programmes to try to achieve its mission whilst competing in the deregulated electric power market. BPA would be a more active participant in the competitive market for power, transmission, and energy services, and use its success in those markets to ensure the financial strength necessary to fulfil its mandate under the Northwest Power Act.

(4) *Maximize BPA's Financial Return.* BPA would operate like a private, for-profit business. It would focus on limiting costs and investing its money where it could get the best return, whilst continuing to fulfil the requirements of the Northwest Power Act.

(5) *Minimal BPA Marketing.* BPA would not acquire new power sources or plan to serve customers' load growth. Activities would focus on meeting revenue requirements through the long-term allocation of current federal system capability, whilst continuing to fulfil other requirements of the Northwest Power Act.

(6) *Short-term Marketing.* BPA would emphasize short-term (five years or less) marketing of power and transmission power products and services, whilst continuing to fulfil requirements of the Northwest Power Act.

Source: Clark (personal communication), based on Business Plan Final EIS (DOE/EIS-0183)

Recently, there have been some interesting developments in SEA independent of NEPA. The environmental review of trade agreements was first required by a presidential executive order in 1999. It was confirmed by the new administration in 2001 and enacted in the Trade Promotion Authority Act of 2002 (Norton-Miller, 2004). Such reviews address the domestic impacts of trade agreements. In addition, a voluntary SEA has been proposed for a programme of the Immigration and Naturalization Service to enhance immigration points of entry (Case Study 3.3). Whether or not this will be a harbinger of a more widespread non-NEPA use of SEA remains to be seen.

3.3.13 SEA experience in other industrial countries

In this chapter, our primary focus has been to cover the mainstream of national experience in SEA amongst the developed countries and to illustrate aspects and areas of practice that we consider to be of note or wider interest internationally. Obviously, there is a degree of subjectivity in the countries selected for examination. Also, as noted previously, SEA is a rapidly developing field. This is well illustrated by the briefing papers tabled by the countries and international organizations attending the Eighth Intergovernmental Policy Forum on Environmental Assessment, held in Vancouver in association with IAIA 04 (CEAA, 2004). For these reasons, the SEA experience of four other countries (Japan, Korea, Portugal and Spain) is summarized in this section to exemplify different arrangements or elements of approaches.

Japan

A Cabinet Directive in 1972 established a national-level EIA system in Japan and this was given legal recognition in the Basic Environment Law (1993). Article 19 of this Law stipulates that consideration must be given to environmental protection in the formulation and implementation of government policies that are expected to have an impact on the environment. So far, no formal provision has been made for a national system of SEA of policies, plans or programmes that are not subject to the EIA law of 1997. But during the preparation of this latter law, there was discussion of the potential role of SEA and a review of international experience in this field (Omori, 1997, 1999).

Since then, a number of actions and studies have been undertaken to establish a basis for introducing and implementing SEA in the event of a decision in principle by the Government to introduce it. The policy cornerstone for such a decision is laid down in the Cabinet approval of the Basic Environment Plan (2000), which, inter alia, provides a mandate to (Nishikubo, 2004):

- carry out a review of the content and methods for including environmental considerations in decision-making on policies, plans and programmes;
- evaluate the effectiveness and practicability of such measures by reviewing cases and formulating guidelines based on the review; and
- consider the framework for including environmental consideration in decision-making on policies, plans and programmes, if necessary.

The Ministry of the Environment has published several reports on aspects of international experience with SEA and its possible application in Japan at both the national and local government levels. This work began by examining legal and institutional arrangements for SEA established in Organisation for

Economic Co-operation and Development countries (Fuller et al, 1998). The focus has now shifted to SEA effectiveness and methodology (Mitsubishi Research Institute, 2003), which may be of wider international interest. In addition, in 2003, the Ministry of Environment issued a preliminary guideline on SEA in the formulation of municipal waste management plans. The Ministry of Land, Infrastructure and Transport introduced guidelines for promoting public involvement in road, airport and harbour planning and for taking into consideration alternatives in an early stage of the planning process. In addition, several local governments have introduced an SEA component in their environment-related plans and programmes, for example Saitama Prefecture, Hiroshima City and the Tokyo Metropolitan Government (cited in Mitsubishi Research Institute, 2003).

Korea

EIA was adopted in Korea in the late 1970s and an SEA-type process was introduced in 1999. The prior environmental review (PER) or preliminary environmental scan (PES) system was legislated to identify and minimize environmental impacts at an early stage for certain plans and projects that are specified under the Environmental Policy Act. However, this process is applied after the framework decisions for projects have been taken (e.g. site or route), making it difficult to assess the best alternatives. It also overlaps with the EIA system with both in following a similar approach and incorporating a review procedure (see Box 3.26). As a consequence, there has been a recent increase in demands for a new assessment process related to the strategic level of policies, plans and programmes. In response, the focus is now on upgrading and expanding the PES system to incorporate internationally accepted SEA principles (see Box 3.26).

Portugal[30]

At present (pre-transposition), there are few legal requirements bearing on SEA in Portugal. A general requirement for EIA of plans and programmes was included in the National Environmental Law (1987) but regulations to implement this provision were never issued. In addition, recent legislation on the development of mineral exploration plans contains a requirement for an SEA report to be included in the plan but so far there has been no legal definition of the process, methodology and content for SEA. As a member state of the European Union, Portugal is also bound by Council Regulation EEC No 2081/93 regarding proposals for regional development plans and structural funds programmes and now must implement the SEA Directive 2001/42/EC (see Section 3.2).

At the time of writing, the institutional framework for SEA in Portugal is not yet clear. However, it is probable that the main responsibilities will rest with the Ministry of Environment. The local government authorities

---

30 Information in this section was contributed by Maria Partidário, New University of Lisbon.

BOX 3.26 PRELIMINARY ENVIRONMENTAL SCAN (PES) IN KOREA: AN SEA-LIKE SYSTEM

The PES system (also called the prior environmental review system) aims to balance development and conservation by identifying possible environmental impacts of development plans or projects in the early stages of planning. It includes considering ways to carry out development plans whilst harmonizing the built and natural environments in an aesthetically pleasing manner (Korean Ministry of Environment, 2001).

The PES system is applied to:

*   39 *administrative plans* specified under the Basic Environmental Policy Act and other individual laws; and
*   any *development activities* conducted in 20 specified types of conservation and protection areas (e.g. conservation areas for natural environment, wildlife and/or wetland, and protection areas for waterworks and/or groundwater, etc.).

An example of how the PES and EIA systems work together

The following example for housing land illustrates how the PES and EIA systems provide an overall EA process. In order to develop housing land, a PES is required to check the following main concerns:

*   sustainability of the goal;
*   alternatives;
*   environmentally friendly land use plan;
*   conditions of location; and
*   relevance of the project.

When a target site fulfils these requirements, listed above, it is designated as official housing land for development. An EIA is then undertaken with detailed analyses to mitigate the negative environmental effects predicted in specific fields such as air quality, water quality, flora and fauna, geology and noise. Public participation in this process is mandatory and a sound monitoring plan must be prepared.

However, if the development is anticipated to cause critical and severe environmental problems, it can be terminated at the PES stage and no further action is permitted. In 2002, the development plans for several major housing sites were withdrawn after being subject to the PES process.

The Ministry of Environment controls both the PES and EIA systems through consultation processes with development agencies. Research is being undertaken with a view to introducing SEA as early as possible, probably from 2005. One possible option is to upgrade and expand the PES system to incorporate SEA principles.

Further information on PES is available in Korean Ministry of Environment (2001) (see also: www.me.go.kr).

Source: Young-Joon Lee, Korea Environment Institute (http://www.kei.re.kr)

responsible for land use planning and the environment will have the duty of overseeing SEA implementation in their respective regions.

As part of Portugal's moves to comply with the European SEA Directive, the Land Use Planning Department of the Ministry of Environment commissioned the New University of Lisbon to prepare guidance for SEA of land use plans. This guidance has now been released in a formal publication (DGOTDU, 2003). It sets out a technical methodology for strategic impact assessment (SIA) to be used during the planning process as part of the conception, preparation, discussion, approval and implementation of spatial plans in Portugal. It applies to regional, special, inter-municipal, and municipal master plans as defined in the Spatial Planning Act and regulations (Law No 48/98 of 11th August, and Decree-Law No 380/99 of 22 September 1999). The SIA methodology is designed to be used in close articulation with the planning methodology, to fit to the sequence and nature of planning activities and functions that are normally part of a plan development process.

The only known applications of an SEA approach to date in Portugal occurred in 1994 and 2000 in connection with reports prepared as part of the regional development plans and structural funds programmes. Full studies and reports are not publicly available. A summary of the 1994 report shows that the study focused mainly on the requirements of the Council regulations at the time. In general, the approach addressed the individual project components proposed in the programme. Frequent arguments were made that insufficient information was available to enable adequate impact assessment. It is assumed that the 2000 report followed the approach set out in the EC guidance (CEC, 1998) but it is not publicly available.

Spain[31]

Prior to transposition of Directive 2001/42/EC, there was no provision for SEA at the national level in Spain. However, there had been significant development of SEA legislation in different autonomous regions[32] and for different categories of land use and sector plans and programmes. In most cases, this provision is made under the EIA legislation (e.g. in Castilla y León, Valencia and Andalucía). In other cases, SEA is required under a general environmental protection law (e.g. in the Basque Territory and also Andalucía) or integrated in planning procedure (e.g. in Catalunya).

Prominent examples of SEA legal requirements in Spanish regions include the frameworks established by Castilla y León, the Basque Territory and Andalucía (see Appendix 8). In these jurisdictions, the responsibilities for overseeing SEA regulations vary, for example:

---

31 Information in this section was contributed by Maria Partidário, New University of Lisbon.
32 Andalucía, Asturias, Islas Baleares, Canarias, Cantabria, Castilla y León, Castilla-La Mancha, Extremadura, Madrid, Murcia, País Vasco, Valencia, La Rioja, and also in Catalunya.

- Castilla y León – the Junta de Castilla (regional government executive body);
- The Basque Territory – the Environmental Authority of the Autonomous Community; and
- Andalucía – the Environmental Agency of the Autonomous Community.

As in Portugal, experience with SEA practice in Spain has been gained through the preparation of regional development plans and structural funds programmes, which require an SEA equivalent assessment that covers environmental issues in accordance with Council Regulation (EC) No 1260/1999. Examples include:

- SEA of the regional development plans and structural funds programmes for Andalucía;
- SEA of the Operational Programme for Rural Development in Castilla y León;
- SEA of the FEDER (Fonds Européen de Developpement Régional) Operational Programme in Castilla y León; and
- SEA of regional development plans and structural funds programmes: 2000–2006.

In addition, implementation of SEA legislation enacted in the regions has resulted in a growing body of practice.[33] Examples include:

- SEA of urban development plans and the Wind Energy Plan in Castilla y León following the adoption of Legal Decree 1/2000 of 18 May;
- SEA of the Urban Plan (2002) for Puerto de la Cruz, Islas Canarias under Law 11/90 of 23 July;
- SEA of wind energy plans in Valencia and Cataluyña under Valencia Law No 2 1989 of 3 March;
- SEA of territorial plans in the Basque Territory under Law 3/1998 of 27 February; and
- SEA of the Review of the Municipal Plan of Málaga.

---

33 One example at the national level was the SEA of the Hydrologic Plan carried out in 2001–2002 for the Ministry of the Environment, which was widely criticized for its weaknesses including lack of consideration of environmental aspects.

Case Study 3.1

SEA of Parliamentary Bills in Denmark

Source: Elling and Nielsen (1998)

The aim of this review was to draw the lessons from experience gained in the first phase of implementation of the Danish system of SEA of bills and other government proposals sent to Parliament and to develop methods in relation to internationally recognized principles and elements of procedure. In this context, it also addresses the overall requirements and character of SEA as a policy-level instrument. The concept of SEA adopted here is that it:

1 is a tool for integrating environmental considerations into the legislative and policy process;
2 has a different content from EIA of projects and will not replace this level; but also
3 builds on the same fundamental principles, including documentation, procedure, significance, alternatives and the involvement of the public.

THE CONTEXT FOR SEA APPLICATION

The above concept and principles of SEA were tested on two Danish bills with the cooperation of the Ministry of Housing, the agency responsible for drafting them. One bill (L 229 to amend laws on tenancy and relating to arrangements for heating charges and individual water meters etc.) was tested retrospectively. The other (L 105 on private urban renewal) was analysed as part of the drafting process. Both cases followed the procedure set out in the Administrative Order (Circular No 12 of 11 January 1995 issued by the Prime Minister's Office). They are also examples of environmentally oriented legislation generating many small projects with potential cumulative effects when combined. With this type of bill, it is relatively easy to calculate and assess the effects on the environment of individual subsidized or regulated activities. Yet it is the scale of the cumulative effects that is more critical and uncertain since the level of activity may be unpredictable.

The approach taken

For this last reason, the approach was based on two aims:

1 to balance the degree of detail when assessing effects in accordance with the level at which the decision is reached, and primarily in relation to the *direction* rather than the *magnitude* or scale of the impact, and judging significance from that perspective; and
2 to expand the concept of environmental impact to include the *subsequent* course of events in addition to the formal approval, and exploit the opportunities for further amendments. In fact, this is what happens in the legislative process.

A test of the principles of public participation and the assessment of alternatives was also added in both cases. These elements are *not* requirements of the Circular but they are recommended as good practice in Ministry of Environment guidance. In the retrospective analysis (L 229), they were included respectively: (i) through a hearing that the Ministry of Housing held on the environmental impact of the Bill; and (ii) by reviewing the impact assessment in light of potential alternatives and their environmental outcomes. In the prospective example (L 105), public participation and alternatives were incorporated throughout the drafting of the Bill and the assessment of its environmental impact.

SEA in practice

There were marked differences between the assessments carried out as part of this project and those presented by the Ministry of Housing as observations on the Bills L 229 and L 105. In both cases, the Ministry's observations were far more general and less detailed than shown to be necessary by the scope for environmental assessment revealed in the analyses undertaken. For example, the retrospective analysis of Bill L 229 indicated that the environmental effects were calculated for limited areas and on a limited scale compared to what would have been possible (e.g. quantification of savings from revised arrangements for heating bills and from installing individual water meters). With regard to Bill L 105, there was no detailed assessment of the environmental effects of the measures to promote energy and resource savings in private urban renewal schemes through a 'green positive list of subsidies' (e.g. installation of water- and energy-efficient fittings).

A comprehensive objectives-led SEA of this Bill could be undertaken on two different (or complementary) levels:

• SEA of the measures on the 'green positive list' as a starting point to identify their direct and indirect, positive and negative, impacts on the environment, preparatory to tightening up on schemes that can be approved and/or to overhauling the list; and

- SEA of the environmental impact of Danish housing stock as a starting point for a green positive list of subsidies for private urban renewal, which would be oriented towards significant issues (securing energy, water and waste efficiencies).

In the final analysis, the role and influence of SEA in the adoption of Bills L 105 and L 229 was unclear. The commentaries accompanying the Bills stated that their enactment would bring positive environmental effects but this was not substantiated in the documentation. As such, the cases run counter to the intent of SEA to make environmental concerns visible throughout the decision-making process. Members of Parliament did not have a sufficient basis of information on which to take environmental aspects into account and reach decisions about the merits of the Bills. For example, the debate on Bill L 105 centred on whether the green positive list would put a brake on urban renewal, as opposed to clarifying the ecological principles and premises underlying the approach.

Other conclusions and wider implications

The wider implications of the above review centre on the testing of certain internationally recognized elements of SEA (documentation, procedure, significance, alternatives and involvement of the public). Specifically, the last two elements are of interest because they are not formal requirements under the Danish system. Nor are alternatives and public involvement necessarily well addressed elsewhere at the policy level (although they are obligatory under the European SEA Directive and transposed in Denmark as Act 316 of 5 May 2004). A key conclusion of the case studies was that these elements could be applied to parliamentary bills without any major or fundamental difficulties.

However, these aspects may need to be adapted to maintain the flexibility of the legislative process. For example, interest groups already play a defined role in parliamentary procedure and this could be broadened to provide for public comment and input at key stages of scoping and/or to review the completed assessment (building on the Danish parliamentary tradition of public hearings). At both levels, consideration of alternatives will be critical, respectively, to finding a low impact course of action and to clarifying the environmental impact of a bill when it is presented.

In principle, the Danish process for SEA of bills and other government proposals can be implemented in accordance with the internationally accepted elements, as listed above. However, in practice, the retrospective analysis of Bill L 229 indicated that a number of factors can impede this happening, including a lack of time, data, resources and political support. The first three constraints were not present in the case of Bill L 105 but analogous political obstacles may be recognized. Above all, however, the case analyses demonstrate that SEA of the environmental effects of bills and other government proposals is technically feasible and can be done in a meaningful way and in a form that is accessible to non-expert decision-makers and the public.

Some further requirements

Based on the above discussion, there are some immediate opportunities to enhance SEA and the presentation of findings to decision-makers:

- Although 'the public' was confined to organized groups in the cases analysed, the results suggest that it is possible to involve the general public in the SEA procedure. This would strengthen and add transparency to the procedure.
- A role for the general public in scoping and assessment may also prevent the responsible authority that is preparing legislation from attributing importance a priori to certain interested parties and may encourage wider debate.
- Making it obligatory for the responsible authority to consider all inputs would preclude the current practice of overlooking the environmental statement or paragraph in the observations on a bill.
- More explicit specification of the content and scope of SEA would help to get the information on the environmental effects of a bill *presented* to decision-makers.

SOME CHARACTERISTICS OF SEA OF BILLS

The above review also draws attention to the characteristic features of SEA at this level:

- A decision-making process for a bill consists not of one single decision but of a series of decisions and SEA also will be sub-divided into a number of different elements. The elements of SEA at any one stage provide both the basis for and constraints on the elements at the next stage.
- The dynamic nature of strategic decision-making means that no decision is ever definitive. In the case of bills, this implies amending or reforming acts that are not achieving the intended effect or are having unintended impacts, including those on the environment. This can help compensate for the lack of predictability in SEA.
- Law-making is a complex process, influenced by many activities and interests. These features emphasize the importance of matching SEA to the dynamics of decision-making, notably by presenting information in a way that promotes environmental considerations being taken into account and influencing choice.
- Except for construction legislation, the cumulative effects associated with bills are general and not tied to a specific locality or type of physical environment. This makes attribution of significance difficult.
- Other things being equal, the assessment of the impact of a bill on the environment will be more abstract than for a project (or plan) and the negative effects will be correspondingly easier to conceal.
- When assessing the environmental impact of a bill, analysts will often be able only to identify the *direction* of an impact rather than its *degree* of impact.

Case Study 3.2

SEA of The Netherlands National Waste Management Plan 2002

Source: Verheem (2003)

BACKGROUND

In The Netherlands, the policy and planning framework for waste management is highly structured and facilitates a tiered process of SEA and EIA as follows (Sadler and Verheem, 1996):

- *At the national level*: Policy-planning decision(s) are made on the technologies for final waste treatment, for example refuse dumping or incineration and total treatment capacities – SEA addresses alternative technologies and their environmental consequences.
- *At the regional level*: Spatial planning level decision(s) are taken on where treatment sites will be located – SEA addresses location options and their environmental consequences.
- *At the local level*: Project decisions are taken on design and mitigation measures for each of the selected locations – EIA focuses on project and site-specific impacts tiered to earlier strategic assessments.

THE NATIONAL WASTE MANAGEMENT PLAN

The National Waste Management Plan (2002–2006) is a responsibility of the Minister of the Environment. It sets the policy-planning framework for a four-year period and will then be renewed. A major objective of the Plan is to set the so-called 'minimum standard' for environmental performance of techniques that are used to process a number of waste streams. Under the Plan, no licence can be issued for techniques that do not meet the minimum standard. In some cases, this is defined very broadly (e.g. 'incineration with energy retrieval') but, for other waste streams, it is defined as a specific technique. A second component of the Plan is to define the preferred capacity for waste incineration in The Netherlands.

THE SEA AND DECISION-MAKING PROCESS

SEA was mandatory for this Plan in accordance with the then Dutch EIA Decree.[34] It was carried out to set those standards that were to be defined as a specific technique and focused on a comparison of the environmental performance of major alternatives for these standards. It was also meant to establish the environmental foundation for capacity planning for waste incineration, recognizing that appropriate capacity should neither be too little (leading to too much waste dumping) nor too large (removing the incentive for prevention and re-use of waste). Other objectives to be taken into account in this context included optimizing energy generation from incinerating waste and more effectively utilizing existing incineration capacity in The Netherlands.

An eight-step process was followed:

Step 1 – Public notification to explain the Plan and its objectives;
Step 2 – Mandatory public participation in scoping the required content of the SEA and the Plan;
Step 3 – Review and advice on content from state environmental and nature agencies and the independent EIA Commission;
Step 4 – Plan and SEA preparation;
Step 5 – Release of the draft plan and SEA report (the content was legally prescribed and included a requirement to describe the best alternative from an environmental perspective);
Step 6 – Public participation and comment on the quality of the SEA report and draft plan;
Step 7 – Review and advice on quality from environmental and nature agencies and the EIA Commission;
Step 8 – Approval of the Plan by the Cabinet and Parliament and adoption by the Ministry of Environment.

---

34 The first and second ten-year waste management programmes were developed by the Waste Management Council – a non-statutory voluntary body (bringing together the Ministry of Environment and provinces) with no decision-making power. The provinces, again voluntarily, then streamlined their provincial waste plans with the ten-year programme. For this streamlining, a national-level SEA was undertaken, but the provinces did not have to undertake repeat SEAs. At the national level, there was no statutory waste management plan in the past (although objectives were set in the National Environmental Policy Plan). But in 2002, the Dutch waste management planning system was changed and a new formal National Waste Management Plan was introduced. This set minimum standards that the provinces have to follow in their own plans. Because formal decisions were taken in this new national plan, an SEA was mandatory. In summary, SEA for the ten-year programmes was voluntary; SEA for the National Waste Management Plan is mandatory.

Approach and methodology

Information assembly: The SEA was primarily based on existing information including:

- experience with the implementation of previous waste management plans;
- the results of an action programme to fill in knowledge gaps in these previous plans;
- information from EIAs carried out for licensing waste processing facilities;
- monitoring programmes of the Ministry of the Environment; and
- information from a number of research programmes from state institutes.

Development of alternatives for minimum standards: Specific techniques were applied for 26 waste streams (asbestos, batteries, organic, solvents, oil, etc.). For each stream, alternative techniques were described and compared to identify the preferred option from an environmental viewpoint.

Development of alternatives for capacity planning: The SEA compared the environmental effects of four alternative scenarios for the incineration of waste in 2012 from households, industry and construction activities (these three streams account for approximately 80 per cent of total waste incinerated). The scenarios differed in terms of the processing techniques used. A precondition was that techniques had to either be in operation on a commercial scale now or have the potential to be so in the near future).

- *Scenario 1*: First, waste is divided into three components: most combustible (RDF), paper and plastics (PPF) and organic with a high water content (ONF). Then PPF and plastics is separated from RDF and the former is burned as additional fuel in coal-fired power plants or cement ovens. The rest of the RDF is burned in new waste incinerators using the latest technology. The ONF with a high water content is first either digested or composted, and then burned in existing waste incinerators.
- *Scenario 2*: Waste is processed into RDF and then incinerated in new waste incinerators, specifically designed for this purpose (i.e. fluidized bed or grate incinerators with combined heat and electricity generation).
- *Scenario 3*: All waste is integrally incinerated, with low caloric waste in existing incinerators, high caloric waste in new waste incinerators and incineration capacity increased until demand and supply are balanced.
- *Scenario 4*: (status quo): No increase of incineration capacity; waste that cannot be incinerated is land filled.

Impact analysis of minimum standards: For each waste stream, alternative techniques were compared using 'life cycle analysis' (LCA) to identify their environmental effects from production to disposal. It included the effects of re-use of material, which are often positive (e.g. the savings in raw materials).

BOX C3.2.1 WEIGHTING SETS USED IN THE LCA

- all themes are equally important (i.e. climate change, acidification, etc.);
- all sub-themes are equally important (i.e. greenhouse, biodiversity effects, etc.);
- effects that contribute most to achieving policy targets are most important;
- only the greenhouse effect is important (reflecting the importance of reduction of energy use in Dutch policy);
- only the dispersion effects are important; in other words health impacts are most important because this is the main concern of the general public.

LCA described the effect on six standard 'environmental themes' under which 12 'sub-themes' were investigated: climate change (greenhouse and ozone layer effects), acidification, eutrophication (water and land), dispersion (toxics in humans, land and water systems, photochemical oxidants), use of resources (abiotic) and disruption (to life support systems and biodiversity).

The LCA was also carried out from different political perspectives to make the results more useful for decision-making. For this purpose, different weightings were given to specific effects (Box C3.2.1). A 'distance to target' analysis was also carried out to compare alternatives in terms of their contribution to existing policy objectives. In all cases, the total burden on the environment was also given.

In addition, the SEA also investigated the relative contribution of waste processing to overall environmental problems in The Netherlands, to use of space, amount of waste to be land filled, use of energy and use of water.

The SEA included the following information for the LCA of each waste stream:

- characteristic and composition of the waste stream;
- alternative waste processing techniques;
- process descriptions and (LCA) system boundaries;
- mass balance of the process and use of space;
- financial cost of the technique;
- effects of waste transport;
- energy balance;
- means used during waste processing;
- emissions to water, soil and air;
- gaps in knowledge and uncertainties; and
- overview of the environmental effects (use of resources, use of space and emissions).

Impact analysis for capacity planning: The environmental effects of the four alternative scenarios were compared using a simplified form of LCA, in other words only the most relevant environmental aspects were considered: use of space for landfill waste; and emissions of NO_x, CO_2, carbon monoxide (CO), carbon hydroxides, ammonia (NH_3) and dioxins.

On the basis of this limited set of aspects, the six standard environmental themes and effects (as described above) were scored in the LCA together with the four additional themes (use of space, amount of waste to be land filled, use of energy and use of water).

The LCA addressed the environmental effects of the processing techniques, of the residual waste to landfill, and of reduced demand for primary resources and fuels from re-use of waste and from electricity and heat generation from waste processing. In addition, the effects of road transport of waste or primary resources were taken into account (the major such effect).

A sensitivity analysis was carried out using the weightings described in Box C3.2.1. In this analysis, uncertainties were taken into account concerning the amounts of waste that would be processed using the different techniques in each scenario, as well as uncertainties in the environmental effects of these techniques.

Comparison of alternatives for minimum standards: For each alternative technique, quantitative scores were given in the following formats:

- matrix of alternatives and their scores against all LCA sub-themes;
- a bar chart of alternatives with the added scores (without 'weighting') of environmental impact;
- matrix of alternatives and their scores against land use, final waste production, use of energy and use of water;
- matrix of the alternatives with the added scores against each of the five different weighting sets; and
- matrix of techniques illustrating the cost per ton of processed waste.

In addition, the techniques were discussed qualitatively (based on the quantitative scores) and final conclusions drawn.

Comparison of alternatives for capacity planning: The different scenarios for capacity planning were compared in the same way as described above.

Public participation: A distinction was made between the 'organized public' (e.g. NGO's, local political parties) and the general public or individual citizens. The organized public was actively canvassed to send comments at both the scoping and review stages of the SEA process (compared to the more passive right of individual citizens to comment). Major NGOs were invited to two round tables on alternatives and impacts and a selected group was invited to become part of a 'sounding board' that provided feedback throughout the planning process. Other methods were also used for public participation:

- discussion groups in an early stage;
- communication through the media and via an information bulletin;
- technical workshops throughout the process; and
- information meetings for the general public.

There was a high-level of response from NGOs, notably on the alternatives to be examined (environmental NGOs, in particular, focused on options to prevent and re-use waste) and from the organized public (although this focused mainly on local issues and was less useful for the more strategic level of decision-making associated with the waste plan). Very few individual citizens responded.

One concrete result of public participation was the introduction into the planning process of a new alternative – the option to separate waste before incineration. Although it was not possible to include this alternative in the final plan, it will play a significant role in the new round of planning.

Monitoring and follow-up: The results of the current waste management plan will be subject to monitoring and evaluation in preparing the next version of the plan (2006). For that reason, it was considered redundant to establish a specific programme for monitoring and plan evaluation. This also will take place through:

- EIA of the effects of specific waste processing facilities (compared to the minimum standard); and
- annual monitoring of the composition and amount of waste to be processed in The Netherlands (including import/export and development of techniques for waste separation).

OVERVIEW OF WHAT WORKED WELL AND WHY

Uncertainty analysis: The SEA discussed a number of areas of uncertainty including:

- the composition of waste streams is often highly variable (sensitivity analyses were used);
- emissions to soil, because levels of seepage are often not known;
- LCA methodology still has a number of flaws (e.g. in factors used to calculate the environmental effect of emissions);
- costs of processing a ton of waste are often subject to company secrecy;
- *some* techniques are in question or disputed as 'proven' technology; and
- the projection of amounts of waste (suitable for incineration) expected in the future.

Quality review: In its review of the SEA report, the independent EIA Commission argued that an enormous amount of useful information had been generated and this was sufficient for purposes of decision-making. Although the results of the LCA had many uncertainties (above), the Commission found they were robust enough to designate minimum standards and plan future capacities.

RESULTS AND LESSONS

The contribution of the SEA to decision-making on minimum standards: Although it was possible to establish the minimum standard (see above), it proved harder to conclude which techniques were the best from an environmental viewpoint. In all cases, the final score was most influenced by the scores of three environmental effects: use of abiotic resources; the greenhouse effect; and ecotoxicity in land systems (and to a lesser degree acidification and eutrophication of land systems).

The contribution of the SEA to decision-making on capacity planning: The LCA showed that all scenarios had overall positive environmental effects. In all cases, the negative effects of burning and processing the waste were more than compensated for by the positive effects of energy generation and re-use of waste material. Of course, it should be remembered that only a limited set of effects was taken into account.

Overall, Scenarios 1 and 2 were rated as having the most positive effect and scored approximately equally. Scenario 1 scored better on the effects on ozone layer, photochemical smog production, eco-toxicity, toxicity for humans, residual waste to landfill and use of water. Scenario 2 scored better on eutrophication of water systems, use of space and use of energy. Scenario 3 ranked third and scored best on biodiversity and life support. Scenario 4 (the status quo) had the fewest positive effects. In all cases, waste incineration in a coal-fired power plant had better environmental scores than in a cement oven (which generates less energy and more emissions).

The sensitivity analysis confirmed the above ranking and discriminated further between Scenarios 1 and 2. Using the 'distance to target' weighting, Scenario 1 was ranked as best overall. With the other three weighting sets, Scenario 2 was ranked as best overall. Because in all scenarios the final scores were heavily influenced by the positive effects of energy generation, an additional sensitivity analysis was carried out on the assumed efficiency of energy generation associated with waste incineration. It indicated that if waste incinerators could achieve a 10 per cent increase in energy efficiency, then Scenario 3 scored as positively as Scenarios 1 and 2. Although Scenarios 1 and 2 scored best on environmental issues, they did not achieve the objective of using the existing waste incineration capacity optimally since both were based on building new incinerators using new technology.

What actually happened: Minimum standards were set for waste streams in the National Waste Management Plan based on environmental effects and other aspects such as costs, public health, reliability, feasibility, practicability and impact on import/export. Incineration capacity under any scenario was overtaken by rapid changes in the structure of the European waste market as a result of new EC regulations (which effectively preclude capacity planning within one country).

Conclusions for SEA good practice: LCA was a useful approach, although such a comprehensive method did not appear to be necessary in all cases. A number of minimum standards could have been founded with a simpler method.

Public participation played an important role in the SEA process and in plan elaboration. The involvement of NGOs was considered to be positive by the planners. First, because there was wide support for applying an integrated approach to waste management (rather than focusing only on a particular interest or concern); and, secondly, the plan that was finally adopted had wide acceptance.

NGO participation largely comprised technical experts and the most senior representatives were insufficiently involved. For the next round of planning, a 'high-level steering group' should be part of the sounding board as well as technical groups. In contrast, on the environmental side, NGOs focused too little on technological issues and had weak positions in the sounding boards compared to other NGOs. Next time, environmental NGOs should be engaged bilaterally and challenged explicitly to give an opinion on technological issues. Finally, a strategic plan (and the SEA of it) contains many assumptions and preconditions and it is crucial that public participation takes place in the formulation of both. This will help significantly to increase the credibility of the end results and the final plan, itself. It is also important to record and file all of the choices made during the SEA and planning processes in order to reinforce their transparency and justify the alternative(s) selected.

Case Study 3.3

Proposed SEA of Point of Immigration Entry Enhancements, US

Source: Ray Clark (personal communication)

BACKGROUND

As a result of the terrorist attack on the US on 11 September 2002, the Immigration and Naturalization Service (INS) is required by legislation to enhance all points of entry (POEs), for example, with more sophisticated technology such as finger, face or biometric identification. Prior to the start of any proposed actions, the INS, like any other federal agency, is required to comply with the requirements of the National Environmental Policy Act (NEPA) and evaluate their potential effects on the environment. The General Services Agency (GSA) will conduct whatever site-specific analyses are necessary to implement the proposed POEs.

APPROACH

The technology for this POE enhancement programme was not known and not developed; so no actual actions could be proposed. Yet the INS knew that it was going to have to do something at 66 POEs and its environmental staff was put under great pressure to prepare the required EIAs very quickly. The scenario was that once the proposed actions were decided, 66 EIAs would then have to be undertaken and the NEPA process would hold up implementation. Enhanced POEs could have a range of impacts due, for example, to tearing up roads, widening lanes, or placing electronic towers for technology.

The Clark Group (TCG) proposed to the INS that the most appropriate, efficient, and effective approach was to prepare a strategic environmental appraisal (SEA) before any proposal was offered. The SEA is not a NEPA analysis but will provide the INS with vital information to facilitate rapidly the preparation of the required analysis and assist the implementation and completion of POE enhancements. The SEA will be a document from which the INS may reference in subsequent site-specific NEPA analyses. The SEA will be a part of the administrative record for the POE project and will provide a scientifically defensible approach for more focused EIAs. It will support decision-makers in directing the level of NEPA analysis required and the level of detail for the analysis.

The SEA will involve several steps:

* *Develop a 'road map'* to inform agency personnel and others about the objectives of the SEA and provide a clear indication where input will be needed. Rather than look at the impacts of individual POE projects, the SEA is concerned with the 'big picture', dealing with the health and trends of ecosystem resources, and the authorities accountable for them. As the POE technology is being developed, the SEA report will be used by planners to ensure efficient compliance with NEPA.
* *Scoping*: The SEA can be used to ensure the efficiency of the scoping process part of NEPA to ensure that the planners are focused on the significant issues, rather than all issues.
* *Develop current strategy and alternatives.*
* *Conduct the SEA*:
    – An analysis of the actions and activities involved in each alternative, and the development of matrices of impact issues (by resource area) to determine potential problem areas (using a qualitative scale), areas of lesser concerns, and areas where additional information is needed.
    – Identification of areas where the INS/GSA may need to conduct site-specific NEPA analyses.
    – Identification of data needs, suggested levels of significance, mapping/geographical information system requirements and level of NEPA analysis in an attempt to standardize any subsequent NEPA analyses (and thus streamline that portion of the process). TCG will rely on expert approach as a data collection method.
    – Regional workshops (representing US Fish and Wildlife Ecosystems 1, 4, 10 and 24) and interviews will be used to collect information on potential problems, impact areas and areas where no significant impact would be expected. These workshops will rely on regional experts in a variety of technical fields drawn from state and federal agencies, universities and NGOs.
    – The results of the SEA will provide the INS with a scientifically defensible approach (which will be part of the agency's administrative record) for how to conduct NEPA analyses in a more focused manner.
* *Develop a catalogue of mitigation measures* that the INS may then apply to site-specific analyses. Expert input in the previous step will also provide recommended mitigation strategies. These mitigation options will supplement INS strategies of avoidance, minimization and conservation. The catalogue will provide contractors working on environmental assessments for the INS and GSA with an immediate NEPA reference tool for avoiding or minimizing impacts to specific resource areas. Where possible, other sources of mitigation approaches will be identified such as a guide to the Congestion Mitigation and Air Quality Improvement Programme based on the Intermodal Surface Transportation Efficiency Act of 1991.

Chapter 4

SEA Experience in Development Cooperation

Environmental impact assessment (EIA) requirements are now an established component of development cooperation. Recently, multilateral and bilateral donor agencies and other international development organizations have emphasized the use of strategic environmental assessment (SEA) to promote more sustainable and integrated approaches to sectoral and broader development plans, programmes and policies. This emphasis by the donor community has resulted in growing SEA practice in developing countries and has been a vector for the wider introduction and adaptation of SEA for domestic applications. The World Bank is in a leading position in this regard and we describe its activities first. Other multilateral and bilateral donor agencies also have important SEA initiatives underway. These are then described in alphabetic order in Sections 4.1 (multilateral development agencies) and 4.2 (bilateral aid agencies).

In the last few years, poverty reduction strategies have become the most prominent strategic planning processes in development cooperation. Multilateral development banks, bilateral donor agencies, international organizations and many poor countries now see such strategies as the main framework within which to address sustainable development. Poverty alleviation is a driving theme of the United Nations (UN) Millennium Development Goals (MDGs) and the Plan of Implementation of the World Summit on Sustainable Development (WSSD) agreed at Johannesburg in 2002. They both make it clear that an integrated approach is necessary to achieve poverty reduction. MDG 7 (Target 9) sets a key objective to 'integrate the principles of sustainable development into country policies and programmes and reverse the loss of environmental resources' (UNGA, 2001). Endorsed at the World Summit on Sustainable Development, it potentially represents the overriding focus for SEA in the next decade (see Section 4.3).

4.1 SEA IN MULTILATERAL DEVELOPMENT AGENCIES

4.1.1 The World Bank[1]

SEA provision and procedure

World Bank policy and procedures for environmental assessment (EA) have been in place for 15 years and include provision for sectoral- and regional-level environmental assessment. Both forms of SEA were introduced by Operational Directive 4.00 (Annex A, 1989). This was subsequently converted into an Operational Policy/Bank Procedure (OP/BP 4.01, 1999), confirming a requirement for borrowers to conduct sectoral and regional EA, as and where relevant. For example SEA would typically be conducted for sectoral investments and adjustment loans and credits with Bank assistance to ensure the process was relevant and effective in terms of their development impacts.

The introduction of OP/BP 4.01 also coincided with a broadening of environmental and social assessment approaches in Bank operations. EA at the Bank is now part of a set (system) of ten environmental and social safeguard policies that apply to all investment lending (about two-thirds of the new lending during the last years). They receive considerable internal and external attention. In August 2004, the Bank's Board approved a new Development Policy Lending policy (OP/BP 8.60) – a major development that promises to influence the use of SEA in World Bank operations. This new policy significantly updates Operational Directive 8.60 on adjustment lending and requires the Bank to determine if specific country policies supported by the operation are likely to have significant effects on the environment and natural resources of the client country. In such cases, an assessment must be conducted – using existing analytical work – of the borrowers' systems for reducing the adverse effects and enhancing the positive effects of the specific policies being supported. Programme documentation must describe how any significant gaps in the analysis or shortcomings in the borrowers' systems will be addressed before or during programme implementation, as appropriate.

The implementation of EA policy for the fiscal years (FYs) 1996–2000 was examined in the Third Environmental Review of World Bank experience (Green and Raphael, 2002). Like the previous review (covering FYs 1992–1996), it notes the increasing use and acceptance of sectoral EA to address sector-wide issues and programmatic loans covering numerous similar sub-projects, for example roads and irrigation (Box 4.1). Sectoral EA addresses issues early in the process of decision-making, and so helps to eliminate environmentally damaging alternatives and reduce the information requirements for project-level EA. Regional EA is used to take a spatial, area-wide approach to development planning, and is acknowledged to have useful potential for addressing cumulative effects. Currently, the Bank has less experience with regional EA than sectoral EA, but there are some 'good practice' examples (Box 4.2).

---

1 With contributions by Kulsum Ahmed and Jean Roger Mercier, the World Bank.

Box 4.1 SEA of Gujarat State Highways Programme, India

The World Bank financed a programme to improve the Gujarat state highway system. First, a study of strategic options identified 1500km for a detailed feasibility study. On this basis, approximately 800km of roadway were selected for improvement within the available budget and were subjected to an SEA. The SEA covered the following aspects:

- environmental and social impact at a state-wide level (e.g. classifying highway corridors into three levels of environmental sensitivity);
- guidelines and methodology for the conduct of the project-level EIAs;
- early coordination with a large number of administrative and technical agencies;
- mitigation and monitoring plans relating to road construction and operations;
- avoiding impacts through design and routing changes (e.g. keeping the cleared zone to an absolute minimum consistent with safety constraints);
- impact zones included immediate right of way (to 100m) and indirect area of influence (to 10km);
- some relocation of people and plots (various instruments were used including letters of credit);
- recognition of protected areas and sites of heritage and cultural significance (Gujarat has numerous roadside shrines and temples);
- social assessment of state-, district- and local-level impacts (socioeconomic, demographic and community profiles);
- consultation with local stakeholders and interested parties (village meetings and focus group interviews); and
- transportation of hazardous materials, emergency response and environmental health and safety.

Source: Kjørven and Lindhjem (2002)

In recent years, the Bank has made increasing and broader use of SEA. It has employed a more diverse suite of tools as part of its corporate strategy to 'mainstream and upstream the environment' (World Bank, 1999, 2000). Mercier (2001) explains the relationship to OP/BP 4.01 procedure as follows:

> *Regional and sector assessment of Bank-financed developments by borrowing countries now take place alongside and often support what the Bank calls 'targeted environmental interventions', for example to implement national environmental action plans, promote biodiversity conservation and ecosystem planning and build EA and management capacity. In addition, ten environmental and social safeguard policies and instruments have been developed for quality assurance of all Bank-financed operations. SEA is identified as a key means of moving the safeguard policies 'upstream' to ensure compliance of national, regional and sectoral programme.*

Box 4.2 Regional environmental assessment of Argentina's flood protection

A regional environment assessment (REA) was undertaken for an investment programme to protect communities occupying the floodplains of the Paraguay, Parana and Uruguay rivers in Northern Argentina. This region had suffered enormous losses from periodic flooding, but the flooding also sustains ecological systems and many forms of productive activities. So the project adopted a 'living with floods' strategy. Proposed construction works included flood defences in areas of economic importance and with the greatest vulnerability to repeated flooding. Non-structural measures included: strengthening institutional capacity and coordination to deal with periodic flooding; upgrading flood warning, preparedness and shelter in areas not warranting structural defences; and capacity-building and technical assistance to support these activities

The REA was initiated at an early stage of the decision-making process and included:

- description of the interaction of hydroecological and socioeconomic systems of the region;
- screening of potential investments to select sub-projects with clear economic, social and environmental benefits;
- analysis of alternatives for each site using criteria of least possible interference with natural flooding patterns;
- analysis of the cumulative effects of all flood protection projects;
- public consultation aimed at improving the design of all sub-projects;
- design changes to take into account the results of the REA and public consultation;
- identification of mitigation and monitoring measures;
- identification of institutional weaknesses in dealing with the flood problem; and
- recommendation for a regional action plan to address the issues identified.

The REA studied the interactions of natural and man-made systems within the floodplains. These included the ecological functions of the periodic floods and the current state of critical ecosystems such as wetlands and gallery forests. The study found that, to a surprising extent, many ecosystems and human activities depended on the floods. This had a direct impact on the way the project was designed. Criteria for the selection of investments were modified to ensure that flooding would continue, but not threaten human well-being and economic infrastructure.

The study documented the extent to which wetlands, gallery forests and aquatic ecosystems of the tributaries to the three rivers are threatened by human activities. It found that the most disruptive activities were road construction, followed by poorly planned urban expansion and effluent from the meat packing industry. Poor urban sanitation services were directly undermining existing flood protection works. For example, many communities disposed of garbage along protective dykes. This attracted rodents, which weakened the dykes by digging tunnels and making them ineffective against floods.

The REA assisted the design of four key project components to help improve the environmental and economic benefits of the project:

1 strengthening EA procedures in key institutions within the seven provinces;
2 technical assistance for urban environmental management;

---

3   environmental education and awareness programmes in communities benefiting from protection works; and

4   support to protection and management initiatives for wetlands and other ecosystems.

Perhaps the most important outcome of the REA was its direct contribution to screening all potential investments under the project. It helped reduce the number of possible sub-projects from 150 to 51, all with a clear economic, social and environmental justification. Once these sub-projects had been selected, the REA team prepared project-specific EAs for each one. When they were completed, the REA team returned to examine the likely cumulative impacts of all the 51 sub-projects, to ensure that such impacts would be minimized.

Sources: World Bank (1996b); Kjørven and Lindhjem (2002)

SEA diversification at the Bank

In 2001, the Bank approved its first environmental strategy. This commits the Bank to using SEA as a central instrument for helping countries move towards sustainable development (Kjørven and Lindhjem, 2002) (Box 4.3). It broadens the perspective of environmental (and, to some extent, social) assessment and adds a more proactive 'do good' approach to the 'do no harm' principle of mitigating the adverse impacts of development projects. New para-SEA tools are now used across a range of Bank-funded activities. Monitoring of these activities has started and reporting will follow.

Country-level analytical and advisory work is important in defining strategic priorities and influencing development outcomes. So the Bank has introduced a systematic diagnostic analytical tool called *country environmental analysis (CEA)*. This is promoted as a flexible tool with three analytical building blocks: assessment of environmental trends and priorities; policy analysis; and assessment of institutional capacity for managing environmental resources and risks (World Bank, 2002a). It has three main objectives (World Bank, 2003):

- to facilitate mainstreaming by providing systematic guidance on integrating information on, and analysis of, key environment, development and poverty links into the country policy dialogue. The mainstreaming of environmental issues is more likely to happen when the diagnostic work is carried out before preparing poverty reduction strategy papers (PRSPs), country assistance strategies (CAS), and large structural adjustment operations and other programmes;
- to guide environmental assistance and capacity-building supported by the Bank or other development partners through an assessment of capacity issues, especially in relation to specific environmental priorities; and
- to facilitate a strategic approach to environmental safeguard issues by providing information and analysis about environment–development links at the earliest stages of decision-making. This will help shape key lending

---

Box 4.3 The World Bank's environmental strategy

In July 2001, the World Bank approved its first environmental strategy. This emphasizes the need to:

1   integrate environment into poverty reduction and development strategies and actions and explicitly target health, sustainable livelihoods and vulnerability reduction impacts;
2   create conditions for the private sector to become the driver of sustainable economic growth; and
3   help find equitable solutions to regional and global environmental challenges.

The strategy has three objectives:

* *improve the quality of life:*
    - reduce environmental health risks;
    - improve people's livelihoods; and
    - protect against vulnerability to environmental change.
* *improve the quality of growth:*
    - support reforms to improve incentives and encourage efficient use of natural resources;
    - promote environmentally sustainable rural and urban development; and
    - assist clients to strengthen their environmental management capabilities.
* *protect the quality of regional and global commons:*
    - convene stakeholders on collective solutions to transboundary problems;
    - maximize the overlap between local and regional/global benefits; and
    - apply Bank skills and experience as an executing agency under international conventions with specific mandates and funds.

Use of SEA and related tools: The strategy calls for strengthened analytical tools, particularly at the strategic level. SEA is positioned as a means of integrating the environment into sector development planning processes ('mainstreaming') through early identification of issues, evaluation of alternatives, assessment of cumulative impacts, and so on. It is also seen as having potential to address policy-based lending ('upstreaming'), especially to International Development Association (lower income) countries. Examples of related tools for this purpose include country environmental analyses and poverty and social impact analysis, and overlay analysis to relate local and global environmental issues.

Source: World Bank (2002e)

---

and programmatic decisions at the country and sectoral levels and help manage risks at the project level.

CEA provides a framework to systematically link country-level analytical work with strategic planning processes. Like other country-level diagnostic analyses, CEA is linked with a wide range of collaborative work with clients and development partners to guide their development assistance. It contributes to the Bank's policy dialogue with client countries, primarily through the CAS and also helps in developing country strategies and formulating effective lending programmes (World Bank, 2003). Many of the tools and analytical approaches used in CEA approximate to SEA. Their focus is large scale and general. In an individual country, lessons can be drawn from previous SEA applications to provide key inputs to the broader review in the CEA. Conversely, the CEA can identify sectors and policies where a more in-depth analysis through SEA could provide more specific guidance for policy development.

The Bank has reviewed its use of a range of environmental diagnostic methods that might be used in a CEA toolkit (World Bank, 2002b). It has also completed a desk review of Bank experience with CEA to identify the strengths and weaknesses of the existing tools and their applicability in this context (Pillai, 2002). This showed that there has been no systematic, institution-wide approach and led to the introduction of CEA as a key analytical tool. In addition, the Bank recently published a review of international experience with country-level environmental analytical tools, prepared by the Stockholm Environment Institute (Segnestam et al, 2003). CEA pilot studies have been initiated in all regions in the Bank.[2]

Other forms of SEA
The World Bank also uses other forms of SEA.

Energy and environment review (EER) is a specific example of upstream analytical work on environmental issues related to the energy sector. It has been mainly supported by the Energy Sector Management Assistance Programme (ESMAP), but as part of the Bank's country and sector assistance programmes. Three general types of EER have been undertaken:

- full-scale, which looks comprehensively at energy and environment issues in one or more sectors in a country;
- rapid assessments, which are carried out to quickly prioritize key energy–environment issues in a country – based on existing data. This may lead to a full-scale EER; and
- targeted issues, such as fuel quality, sulphur emissions or indoor air quality.

Full-scale EERs are underway or have been completed in Bulgaria, Egypt, Iran, Macedonia, Sri Lanka and Turkey, while rapid and more targeted EERs are underway or completed in Bangladesh, Bolivia, China, Mongolia, Thailand,

---

2   These include studies in Egypt; Tunisia; in the Indian states of Andhra Pradesh, Uttar Pradesh and Karataka; Morocco; Bangladesh; Pakistan; Ghana; Colombia; Dominican Republic and Ethiopia. A study in Serbia and Montenegro has been completed. Pilots are being undertaken in parallel with the development of the CEA methodology and will provide feedback on preliminary lessons (World Bank, 2003).

Vietnam, Eastern Europe and the Central Asia region, and Latin America and the Caribbean region. The Bank is currently reviewing the results and impacts of EERs, and to what extent, and in what ways, they can be a useful tool for influencing energy and environment policies and programmes in client countries. Further information on the EERs supported by ESMAP can be found at: www.esmap.org.

Poverty and social impact analysis (PSIA) has been developed to provide improved support to PRSP and other processes used by the Bank. The approach is set out in a user's guide with a menu of possible economic and social tools and quantitative and qualitative techniques (http://poverty. worldbank.org/files/12685). To supplement the guide, the Bank plans to issue a toolkit with more in-depth guidance on available economic tools, and an intensive learning programme is being organized to provide further guidance on available social tools.

PSIA is not strictly new. It draws from existing methods for the analysis of poverty and for social impact assessment, but it addresses the fact that these methods have been weakly applied to the design of government policy. So PSIA is used to mean 'analysis of the distributional impact of policy reforms on the well-being or welfare of different stakeholder groups, with particular focus on the poor and vulnerable'. In doing so, it aims to address issues of sustainability and risks to policy reform that accompany social impacts of policy changes.

Although the guidance suggests no formal methodology, it identifies various elements (and tools that can be used to address each of them) that make for good PSIA:

- asking the right questions;
- identifying stakeholders;
- understanding transmission channels;
- assessing institutions;
- gathering data and information;
- analysing impacts;
- contemplating design and compensatory schemes;
- assessing risks;
- setting up monitoring and evaluation systems; and
- fostering policy debate and feeding back for policy adjustment.

These elements are entirely consistent with the essential steps to developing and implementing strategies for sustainable development (see OECD/UNDP, 2002).

The guidance acknowledges that there might be a logical sequence to addressing these elements of PSIA. But it cautions against taking this to imply that they need to be undertaken in a strict chronological order or that all the steps will be feasible in all country circumstances. 'Pulling these elements together in a coherent, strategic and integrative fashion is what makes for good

PSIA' (http://poverty.worldbank.org/files/12685). A summary matrix may be a useful tool to aid analysis (e.g. Table 4.1). It can provide a framework for the key aspects of PSIA for a given reform. It can also serve as a template in which some of the results and assumptions underlying the analysis can be made explicit.

Pending developments and future directions
In order to help clients respond to the recently approved policy on development policy lending (DPL), OP/BP 8.60, the Bank expects to focus the SEA programme in the medium term on three main objectives (Ahmed and Mercier, 2004):

- to promote greater use of SEA in conjunction with DPL and programmatic operations (primarily linked to infrastructure sectors);
- to promote capacity-building for client-led SEA through programmatic economic and sector work and other capacity-building tools; and
- to participate with development partners, donors and clients in harmonization efforts on critical elements of SEA good practice.

Specific activities to move forward with these three objectives are part of the World Bank's structured learning programme on SEA. They includes new directions for capacity-building within the Bank and amongst client countries (see: http://www.worldbank.org/sea).

4.1.2 African Development Bank

The African Development Bank (AfDB) formulated its Environment Policy in 1990. Since then, it has issued a number of policy documents oriented to sustainable development (e.g. on energy, forestry and integrated water resources management). These provide staff, regional member countries (RMCs) and the public with guidance and practical advice on policy implementation, and on environmental issues to be considered in project design in order to achieve environmental sustainability.

The effectiveness of implementing the AfDB's environmental policy from 1993 to 1998 has been evaluated by the Bank. It concluded that environmental assessment at the Bank has evolved from a reactive tool for avoiding negative impacts towards a positive, proactive planning tool. It also noted a clear need to move impact assessment 'upstream' into project planning and 'downstream' into supervision of implementation. The use of strategic impact assessment (SIA) has now been recommended to address sustainable development concerns at the policy, plan and programme (PPP) level and draft guidelines have been prepared (Box 4.4).

Table 4.1 A summary matrix for Poverty and Social Impact Analysis of policy change

Reform:

Objective:

Channel	Specific	Stakeholders*		Effect on the poor (or target stakeholder group)			Critical assumptions (including counter-factual)	Institutional changes	Indicators
		Potential winners	Potential losers	Direct short-run	Indirect short-run	Medium-run			
General									
Labour market	Formal Informal								
Prices	Output demand Output supply Input demand Input supply Other								
Access	Private goods and services Public goods and services								
Assets	Physical Financial Human Social Natural								
Transfers and taxes	Private transfers Public transfers and taxes								
Net impact									

Other generally relevant assumptions (e.g. economic growth, political stability, external environment)

Key risks

Information base and analytical methodology

Mitigation or enhancement measures

Summary recommendations

Note: * Stakeholders include those who influence policy and those who are influenced by it
Source: World Bank (2002e)

4.1.3 Asian Development Bank[3]

Since the early 1980s, the Asian Development Bank (ADB) has responded to growing concern about the impact of the region's rapid economic growth on the environment. It has made significant progress in establishing a comprehensive system of environmental safeguards for its operations. The Bank has developed formal EA requirements including review procedures and guidelines, staff instructions, and a management system to monitor the progress of environmental interventions in projects and programmes. These all aim to integrate environmental concerns into the mainstream of the Bank's development activities. It has used various forms of SEA in socioeconomic development programming and planning at all levels – sub-regional, national, sub-national and sectoral. It has also been active in strengthening the capacity of environmental institutions and line agencies in developing member countries (DMCs). As environmental awareness at the ADB and in the DMCs has grown, the environment has been gradually integrated into sector development policies, and this, in turn, has led to a sizeable environmental lending portfolio.

Early on, the ADB recognized that EIA was being used as an add-on to project planning; and, at best, this was only partially effective. Often, EIA results were unable to effect necessary changes in project design because the study was commenced after the design was more or less settled. In addition, the implementation of prescribed mitigation and monitoring requirements documented in EIA reports was not always successful. These requirements were not built into construction contracts or supervised on a day-to-day basis during implementation (ADB, 1994). As a result, the Bank introduced SEA-type approaches into upstream activities such as country programming (e.g. country environmental analysis), sub-regional programming and planning (e.g. the Strategic Environmental Framework for the Greater Mekong Sub-region (GMS)), and environmental-cum-economic (E-c-E) planning for sub-national areas.

New environment policy

In 2002 a new environment policy was introduced. It strengthened the consideration of the environment at the ADB. The policy was prepared through a broad consultation process with governments and civil society within the region and with many major donor countries. It mandates the integration of environmental considerations in all ADB operations at various stages of project and programme cycles, including planning, preparation, implementation and evaluation. The policy requires environmental assessment of all project loans, programme loans, sector loans, sector development programme loans, financial intermediation and private sector investment operations.

---

3   With contributions by Robert Everitt, Environmental and Social Safeguard Division, Regional and Sustainable Development Department; and Dewi Utami, ADB.

Box 4.4 Draft strategic impact assessment guidelines for the African Development Bank

Objective: Guidelines for SIA are being developed by the AfDB with the aim to change attitudes and culture within the Bank and its regional member countries (RMCs). They will be for use by Bank staff and technical experts of RMCs in assessing the impacts of PPP on Bank-financed, policy-based lending, structural and sector adjustment projects and programmes. The guidelines are also aimed at guiding the Bank task managers and proponent RMC governments in applying for loans to assess environmental and social impacts at the PPP level.

Annexes include more detailed criteria and tailored checklists to guide addressing specific SIA issues in various sectors: agriculture, infrastructure, transport, health, education, land development, irrigation, industry, energy, water management, fisheries, forestry, waste management, tourism, telecommunications, spatial planning, land use, trade, nature conservation and modern biotechnology.

Limitation: The guidelines recognize that no single SIA methodology is apt to be applied uniformly to the different tasks in the diversity in PPP; and that approaches need to be adaptive to different agendas, actors, discourses, knowledge requirements and bargaining styles within different policy-making sectors. Consequently, the AfDB guidelines provide only general instructions for assessing impacts.

Roles and responsibilities: The guidelines cater to a number of players in the SIA process. They aim to:

- assist RMCs in carrying out SIA as part of their decision-making process in developing PPP for which they require AfDB lending. As part of applying for policy-based lending, structural and sectoral adjustment loans, RMCs are expected to demonstrate to the AfDB that environmental and social issues have been taken into consideration in the decision-making process, and that the PPP aims to achieve sustainable development goals;
- assist the Bank's country environmentalists in evaluating the quality of SIAs submitted by the RMCs to the Bank. Dialogue between the Bank, the initiating RMC government and civil society is essential during the SIA preparation process;
- provide consultants with a 'how-to' tool when assisting either the RMC in carrying out the SIA or when assisting Bank staff in evaluating the quality of a submitted SIA;
- serve as a guideline to the Poverty Reduction and Sustainable Development Unit (PSDU) when assisting country environmentalists in their evaluation of the SIA report and PPP implementation; and
- facilitate civil society organizations in their role as stakeholders.

When applying for policy-based, structural or sectoral adjustment loans from the Bank, the borrower must demonstrate to the Bank that environmental and social considerations are part of the PPP development process.

The *country environmentalist* is responsible for the practical aspects of SIA implementation – ensuring that environmental and social considerations are integrated into policy-based, structural and sectoral adjustment programmes and plans. The SIA process should be integrated in the cycle of PPP decision-making and implementation.

By comparison, the *task manager* must use the results of the SIA as one of the tools for negotiating the loan agreement between the Bank and the borrower. He/she has the authority and mandate to propose lending instruments to the Board that respond to the Bank's vision; and to engage with the RMCs in the policy dialogue on environmental and social issues.

The *PSDU* should ensure that the Bank's lending approvals comply with the Bank's vision, policies and guidelines, particularly those relating to cross-cutting issues. It is responsible for clearing SIA screening (the decision on whether an SIA is required or not). The Unit also assists the country environmentalists to fulfil their requirements under the SIA guidelines. It gives environmental and social expert advice on missions and audits and provides peer-level advice on SIA studies. In addition, the Unit assists task managers in policy dialogue on environmental and social issues with RMCs.

In preparing the SIA, public *participation* and the involvement of *civil society organizations* are encouraged by the general policies of the Bank. Such dialogue with stakeholders to elicit their concerns are key for any SIA assessment. More constructive inputs from the public are likely when preliminary information is made available to them – this facilitates their understanding of the ramifications of the proposed initiative.

Options: The guidelines urge that the SIA process be introduced at the very early stage of project preparation. They suggest that SIA be used to identify and assess alternative options for the proposed PPP. They should include the status quo or do nothing alternative to provide a benchmark for comparison of other alternatives.

Source: Eugene Shannon (AfDB)

Key aspects introduced by the policy include:

- environmental assessment as an ongoing process throughout the project cycle;
- increased emphasis on environmental management plans to ensure mitigation during project implementation;
- strengthened environmental screening procedures; and
- strengthened disclosure and public consultation requirements.

Country environmental analysis

The ADB has moved EA upstream into the development of a country strategy programme (CSP) in each DMC by requiring a CEA. SEA is a recommended tool to support the sector and policy analyses that are undertaken to prepare programmatic and sector interventions. CEA provides the information necessary for informed decision-making on environmental constraints, needs and opportunities in a DMC, including those that impinge upon poverty partnership agreements. It outlines environmental issues that are most important to DMC development strategy and describes the Bank's role in addressing the environmental constraints on sustainable development. The assessment is directed at the policy, programme and sector levels. It is envisaged as a participatory process that is initiated before the CSP preparation, and it continues throughout this process to assess potential environmental issues associated with the strategy. The ADB is working closely with the World Bank, Inter-American Development Bank (IADB) and other institutions in further developing CEA methodology and coordinating its application in selected countries.

Policy-based and sector lending

SEA is sometimes applied by the ADB to programme loans, to help prepare a matrix of environmental impacts of policy and institutional actions, mitigation measures and the institutional basis for implementing and monitoring them. It is also used to review environmental sustainability objectives of the programme and to propose criteria, targets or indicators for evaluating the effects of the loan. For sector loans, SEA helps with the cumulative impact assessment of all projects envisaged as a part of the loan. It is also used to enhance the efficiency of sub-project-level initial environmental examinations (IEEs) by avoiding the need to redo analyses for issues covered adequately in an SEA for the entire sector. The assessment of sub-projects is then able to concentrate on their site-specific impacts.

E-c-E planning

The ADB recognizes that a piecemeal approach is an overarching deficiency in the integration of economic and environmental management in the Asia and Pacific region. Overcoming this problem requires a nested hierarchy of integrated economic, social and environmental plans (also called sustainable development plans) that covers global, regional, national, sub-national and local levels. The approach recommended by the ADB is E-c-E planning (experience of this approach is detailed in Appendix 7). In practice, this approach has limitations due to the costs of the needed planning studies and the need for strong institutional commitments to develop and implement the plans.

The Bank has carefully reviewed a wide range of integrated environmental and economic plans. It concluded that global, regional and national plans rarely contain sufficient detail for direct implementation. Equally, at the other end of the spectrum, project and local plans are often disconnected from national, regional and global goals. A particular gap in the hierarchy of plans in the Asia and Pacific region is at the sub-national level. Some sub-national plans have been developed for river basins, integrated area development regions, provinces, islands and biosphere reserves. Planning guidelines developed by the ADB have been applied in a small number of integrated plans in Indonesia, Malaysia, the Philippines, China and Thailand (ADB, 1988). An important lesson from these plans is the need to vertically link E-c-E plans at all levels to ensure that they are consistent and compatible. The Bank has funded a limited number of such studies at various levels and anticipates that such a hierarchy of integrated plans will eventually emerge.

Sub-regional – strategic environmental framework (SEF)

A strategic environmental framework (SEF) has been developed to support the GMS Programme,[4] which aims to protect the environment and promote sustainable development. It was initially established to guide investment decisions in the transport and water resources sectors. The ultimate goal of the SEF is to ensure investments in all sectors are environmentally and socially sustainable. This means that environmental and social aspects, as well as cumulative impacts, are considered at an early stage in the planning process for all projects. Various environmental and social databases have been developed within the SEF. The information systems are expected to assist national-level policy-makers, as well as non-governmental organizations (NGOs), the private sector and academic and international institutions in drawing up more sustainable plans and programmes and analysing and assessing their potential impacts.

A key element of the SEF is dedicated to providing accurate environmental information to support decisions about development. Under the auspices of the Working Group on Environment, various activities have been undertaken to expand knowledge and create reliable information. Studies of remote watersheds and important wetlands have not only provided additional information, but have also greatly added to knowledge about existing environmental and social conditions. There are new programmes to develop national and sub-regional environmental performance assessment systems within the SEF. These aim to enable governments and other stakeholders to plan development that optimizes the sustainable use of resources. They will also be able to measure the environmental losses and gains in respect to sub-regional, national and local development initiatives.

4.1.4 Inter-American Development Bank[5]

Over the last decade, there has been significant demand for SEA within the Inter-American Development Bank (IADB). In the early stages, SEA development was characterized by what Milewski (2004) calls the 'wild west syndrome'; i.e. it was anything you wanted it to be as long as it was related to plans, programmes or policies. For some years now, the IADB has used the SEA process flexibly in relation to various types of operations. It is seen as complementing and preceding project-level assessments in defining policies and sectoral programmes, identifying key issues and mainstreaming environmental considerations where they matter most. Key areas include

---

4   The GMS Programme promotes closer economic ties and cooperation amongst the six countries that share the Mekong River: Cambodia, Yunnan Province of the People's Republic of China (PRC), Lao People's Democratic Republic (PDR), Myanmar, Thailand, and Vietnam. Home to some 250 million people, the GMS covers 2.3 million km². Its rich human and natural resources make it a new frontier for economic growth in Asia.

5   With contributions by Joseph Milewski, IADB; and Maria Partidário.

regional-based projects, sectoral loans, investment loans with sectoral or multi-sectoral programmes, and regional development initiatives and policy analysis (see Section 6.4 and Boxes 6.18 and 6.20).

On average, about ten SEAs are conducted annually, but there are significant variations from year to year. For example, 25 assessments were undertaken between 2001 and 2003, many in response to requests from project teams and country counterparts. The demand for SEA is expected to continue as recognized in the Bank's new Environment Strategy:

> *Additional work needs to be done to incorporate environmental concerns at the policy or program level, using methodologies such as Strategic Environmental Assessment (SEA). This effort is important to address up front social and environmental issues related to broad regional development programs and policy loans. The proper application of SEAs coupled with good project level environmental impact assessments are necessary in the development and review of large infrastructure projects, given the complexity of operations, their indirect impacts, the need to establish a constructive dialogue with the affected stakeholders, their bi-national or regional dimensions, and the often-fragmented institutional framework and scant resources available in many cases.* (IADB, 2003, paragraph 3.13)

The Strategy outlines specific actions for the Bank's environmental activities, including:

> *Strengthening environmental quality of Bank operations... The Bank will seek to assure the appropriate application of both upstream environmental assessment (strategic environmental assessment) as well as downstream environmental impact assessment at the specific project level.* (IADB, 2003, paragraph 5.10)

New directives for SEA are included in the IADB Environmental Policy, currently under preparation. It is anticipated that SEA will also be used for country strategies. These are the key programming instrument with which the Bank establishes a dialogue and formal agreement with each country on a specific project 'pipeline'. The Bank places importance on incorporating consideration of environmental issues (seen as cross-cutting) in this phase. The aim is to seek strategic coherence amongst sectors and to enable targeting to define the right priorities. Strategic prioritization is expected to be undertaken in the context of specific studies and assessments at the local, national and regional levels, to set the framework for the Bank's environmental support in each country.

Beyond country strategies and policies, the Bank is starting to undertake SEA for the Conditional Credit Line for Investment Projects (CCLIP) – a new financial instrument that essentially provides a public sector line of credit.

It is expected that the more systematic use of SEA in the Latin America and Caribbean region will address issues early in the decision-making cycle, and help make decisions more cost-effective by:

- avoiding some environmental and social costs by tackling problem areas upfront;
- reducing direct project liabilities;
- reducing uncertainty in decision-making which, in itself, often translates into costly investment delays; and
- reducing some of the additional environmental requirement often added to specific investment projects as a palliative to weak environmental policies and practices.

All of the SEAs undertaken for IADB operations have been carried out without specific guidance, and have varied greatly in scope and objectives. This has enabled creativity, experimentation and flexibility in elaborating the processes and exploring a range of possibilities in a variety of contexts. But, at the same time, project teams have requested the Bank to develop guidance on SEA based on field experience. Draft IADB guidance was issued in September 2004 (www.iaab.org/sds/doc/SEADraftGuidance.pdf). It provides a common framework but is flexible to facilitate application to a variety of operations.

The guidance has three key objectives:

- to provide support to project teams, so that environmental, social and sustainability issues might be mainstreamed early in the decision-making process;
- to improve project-level EIA by 'flagging' and addressing sector-wide issues in anticipation of project-specific investments; and
- to simplify the involvement of stakeholders, including project managers at the IADB, country and regional levels.

The SEA model being adopted by the Bank is outlined in Box 4.5. It provides a framework, adaptable to the nature and timeframe of each initiative – so that SEA is structured as a key process but with flexible implementation and is adapted to the specific needs of each initiative. This generic process, combined with case studies presenting lessons learned from past Bank SEAs, will allow project teams to adapt their processes to specific operational needs.

4.1.5 United Nations Development Programme (UNDP)[6]

In the early 1990s, UNDP introduced the environmental overview (EO) approach as an SEA tool to support programming processes. It was set out in its *Handbook and Guidelines for Environmental Management and Sustainable Development* (UNDP, 1992). The EO is no longer current within UNDP, but it

---

6   With contribution by Linda Ghanime, UNDP.

Box 4.5 The proposed six-step SEA methodology for the IADB

1 **Understand the nature of the proposal**
  – Clarify aims and objectives of the proposal.
  – Understand the context (e.g. policy-making or planning process, legal and institutional framework, sectoral development).
  – Understand expected environmental and social opportunities and potential conflicts.
  – Identify major environmental and social outcomes and/or value-added that justify the need for SEA.

2 **Set the context for SEA**
  – Identify relevant strategic environmental and social goals, objectives and principles, and also sustainable development objectives if adequate.
  – Establish SEA objectives.
  – Define adequate multi-sectoral focus and interrelationship.
  – Design a suitable process for SEA adjusted to the policy-making or planning process and to the institutional context.

3 **Define a participation approach**
  – Identify key stakeholders.
  – Establish a communication plan.
  – Identify adequate participation mechanisms.

4 **Scope major issues and alternatives**
  – Develop an adequate problem-solving approach and refer to key environmental and social issues.
  – Identify possible alternatives to the proposal that meet initial, or revised, aims.
  – Identify the strategic consequences of different alternatives.
  – Interact with the relevant stakeholders.
  – Identify forms of improvement of the proposal (e.g. solving conflicts).

5 **Assess environmental and social outcomes and benefits**
  – Establish adequate assessment criteria.
  – Assemble relevant background studies that enable adequate problem analysis and meeting the assessment criteria.
  – Compare and evaluate alternatives based on their social and environmental implications.
  – Interact with the relevant stakeholders.
  – Elaborate final assessment and requirements.

6 **Establish a scheme for subsequent action**
  – Establish monitoring schemes.
  – Define institutional arrangements for subsequent actions.
  – Assure feedback mechanisms.

Source: Partidário (2004)

is regarded as a sound and effective approach. Box 4.6 describes how the method was trialled. Many UNDP country offices have adopted its underlying principles in their programming practices and these are also captured in the

BOX 4.6 TRIALLING THE ENVIRONMENTAL OVERVIEW APPROACH

In the mid-1990s, the environmental overview (EO) approach was applied by UNDP in the formulation stages of aid programmes. It was trialled extensively in training programmes in developing countries for the assessment of aid projects. EO involves four critical aspects:

- the project/programme must be in its draft formulation stages;
- there must be sequential completion of each of three structured 'questions' of the EO;
- the EO must be undertaken in a participatory way, using a broad mix of specialists and others; and
- the process must include modification of the draft project/programme as an integral part of the EO. The tool should be recognized as a creative process, not just a document.

The tool is flexible. It has been applied to non-geographically based projects and programmes, to sectoral activities and to policies. The EO can be completed with considerable speed, perhaps in a single day, or less. It asks a set of questions, similar to those asked by conventional EIA, but with different emphasis. First, it asks questions concerning the baseline conditions for the project/programme. This is followed by questions concerning the impacts and opportunities and how the draft project/programme can be redrafted in an operational strategy to take these, and the baseline conditions, into account. Additional questions focus on modifications that should be made to the original design. Answering these questions results in a brief document, but it is the interactive process of assembling the EO that is the heart of the process. It is claimed that the EO represents an innovative procedural form of SEA in the development context, and that the characteristics of the EO conform to many of the emerging principles for effective SEA espoused by contemporary writers.

EO was effectively applied to a range of UNDP activities:

- tourism development and management (Cambodia and Tonga);
- planning for the resettlement of tsetse-fly cleared area (Zimbabwe);
- state enterprises reform programme: privatization (Vietnam);
- institutional support to the implementation of the National Shelter Strategy (Indonesia and Namibia);
- essential oils project (Bhutan);
- improvement of land settlement schemes (Mekong Secretariat);
- achieving international competitiveness through technology transfer and development (Philippines);
- technical assistance to the Roads Branch (Swaziland);
- employment generation through development of small, medium and micro enterprises (South Africa);
- regional development policies for a province (Thailand); and
- a set of policies for handling urbanization issues (Africa).

EO has been shown to have potential for capacity-building, for structural adjustment programmes and for feasibility studies for project-based developments. It also works for land use planning policies and on sectoral development problems such as urbanization. It operates at any scale: whether at project level, programme level, or country level. Brown (1997a, b) has advocated using the adapted EO for wider applications as part of the formulation of development projects, programmes and policies.

Source: Brown (1997b)

current version of the UNDP programming manual (available at: www.undp.org/bdp/pm/) and in other guidance described below. UNDP programming is the process of assessment and analysis, objective setting, strategy development, implementation, monitoring and evaluation and allocation of resources in support of national development.

During the mid-1990s, efforts were made to adapt the EO into a proposed strategic overview (SO) described as (UNDP, 2003):

> *An interdisciplinary, in-country, participatory, structured process where a group examines a development programme proposal against a set of environmental and social systems, identifies potential environmental and social opportunities as well as alternatives, options and modifications to enhance the sustainable development outcomes. The process is based on multi-stakeholder, participatory procedures at the earliest stages of policy and programme formulation in order to systematically integrate equity, environmental management and sustainable development considerations into development activities.*

Drawing from the experience in developing the EO and proposed SO, several integrated programming tools were proposed in the late 1990s: an integrated programming and assessment tool (IPAT), revised environmental management guidelines (EMGs) and a good practice handbook on integrating sustainable human development in project design. Updates were also made to the UNDP programming manual incorporating considerations for quality programming. Annex 2F to the programming manual provides a series of questions for quality assurance, which provide reference dimensions for the preparation of country programmes (CPs) (Appendix 12). The essence of these questions is also incorporated in informal UNDP EMGs (not available publicly).

CPs set out UNDP activities for the country concerned, building on the UN Development Assistance Framework (UNDAF) – a strategic framework for the country-level activities of the entire UN system. A common country assessment (CCA) exercise feeds into these approaches. This is undertaken by the UN country team (led by the resident coordinator). It provides a common analysis and understanding of key development issues with a focus on the MDGs and the other commitments, goals and targets of the Millennium Declaration and international conferences, summits, conventions and human rights instruments of the UN system.

Mechanisms for undertaking CCA often involve thematic groups comprising a wide range of development partners. The CCA document includes:

- an assessment and analysis of key development problems and trends, including those addressed by the global conferences and conventions; and
- a set of key issues that provide a focus for advocacy and a basis for providing the UNDAF.

The country programme is the basis of UNDP planned collaboration over a multi-year period. Review committees have an advisory and oversight function and base their reviews, inter alia, on the considerations for quality programming. They are presented in Annex 2F of the programming manual. These same considerations are used in the planning and design of programmes and projects. They include stakeholder participation, contribution to poverty reduction, protection and regeneration of the environment, governance, incorporation of lessons learned and capacity development and sustainability as well as issues of integration and synergies.

UNDP advocates the programming approach where the problem to be addressed cuts across sectors, themes and geographical areas:

> *All UNDP-supported programmes and projects must be environmentally sustainable. Negative impacts need to be avoided or minimized; positive impacts should be strengthened and environmental opportunities seized. The Environmental Management Guidelines are to be used irrespective of the sectors covered by a programme or project.* (UNDP, 2000, 4.1.10)

Most of the EO principles have been incorporated in the programming approach and guidance. But subsequently there appears to have been no further promotion and implementation of SEA, or the strategic overview per se. However, UNDP has renewed its interest in SEA and is now piloting its application to poverty reduction strategies (in Tanzania, Vietnam and possibly Rwanda) with the objective of drawing lessons and experience both for programming and building country capacity.

4.1.6 United Nations Environment Programme (UNEP)

For more than a decade, the Economics and Trade Branch of UNEP has pursued a programme of activities related to EIA and SEA in response to Agenda 21 under a mandate from the UN Conference on Environment and Development in 1992. UNEP'S Governing Council (17th Session, Nairobi, 1992) specifically asked the organization to:

> *[undertake] further development and promotion of the widest possible use of environmental impact assessment, including activities carried out under the auspices of United Nations specialised agencies, and*

> *promote widespread use of environmental impact assessment (EIA) procedures by governments and, where appropriate, international organizations as an essential element in development planning and for assessing the effects of potentially harmful activities on the environment.*

During the 1990s, UNEP developed an EIA training resource manual as a focus for capacity-building. Recently, a second version was issued incorporating a module on SEA (Sadler and McCabe, 2002). This was developed in response to continued requests to UNEP for assistance, information and training in SEA, particularly from developing countries. UNEP intends to work with partner institutions in each developing region to adapt EIA and SEA to the particular situation and circumstances. The UNEP SEA module will provide one of the inputs to another being prepared by the UN Economic Commission for Europe to support implementation of the SEA Protocol to the Espoo Convention (see Chapter 2).

UNEP has also issued guidance on EIA and SEA good practice (Abaza et al, 2004). It is intended as a resource document for those involved in EIA and SEA practice, training and professional development. The guidance emphasizes concepts, procedures and tools in current use or those that are potentially relevant for several purposes: integrated impact assessment; implementing EIA and SEA as tiered systems; and adopting a differentiated approach to SEA of development policies, plans and programmes that recognizes how they differ. Specific reference is made throughout the document to the context and requirements for EIA and SEA application in developing countries and countries in transition.

Integrated assessment of trade-related policies is an approach developed by UNEP (2001) to help policy-makers and practitioners examine the economic, environmental and social effects of trade policy and trade liberalization (Box 4.7). This approach aims to facilitate informed and balanced decision-making in support of sustainable development. It points towards appropriate policy responses to mitigate any harmful impacts of proposed actions and to promote positive effects. For example, trade agreements can be modified prior to or after implementation by the adoption of 'flanking' policies that simultaneously promote economic, environmental and social goals. These policies can be applied at national, regional or global levels.

A four-part framework for an *integrated assessment* is described as follows:

- Step 1: *identifying the purpose* – establishing appropriate parameters for integrated assessment.
- Step 2: *designing an integrated assessment* – key issues to be decided at the beginning of the process: timing of assessment, stakeholder and public participation and appropriate methodology and indicators.
- Step 3: *use of methods and techniques* – selecting those that support the particular priorities of the user.
- Step 4: *integrated policy response* – ranging from the macroeconomic, such as changes in fiscal and monetary policies, to the microeconomic, including environmental and social policy.

Box 4.7 UNEP MANUAL ON INTEGRATED ASSESSMENT OF TRADE-RELATED POLICIES

An integrated assessment considers the economic, environmental and social impacts of trade measures, and the linkages between them. It aims to build upon this analysis by identifying ways in which the negative consequences can be avoided or mitigated, and ways in which positive effects can be enhanced. The tool serves a number of purposes: exploring the linkages between trade, environment and development; informing policy-makers across government departments and international negotiators; developing policy packages to integrate policy objectives on trade, the environment and development; and increasing transparency in policy-making.

An assessment can be undertaken as part of negotiations within national governments to decide approaches to trade policy and liberalization. It can be carried out before, alongside, or following international trade negotiations, to investigate the environmental and social impacts of policies that may be, or have been, introduced. Ex ante assessments can help to plan the nature and timing of trade measures, and the introduction of complementary policies. Ex post assessments provide a retrospective examination of the impacts of a trade policy. They can provide evidence of effects that can be mitigated or encouraged through the introduction of complementary policies designed to promote sustainable development. Both ex ante and ex post assessments can provide lessons and data for future assessment.

UNEP worked with a multidisciplinary, international group of experts and national team members to prepare a manual on integrated assessment of trade-related policies. This is for use in UNEP country projects on trade liberalization and the environment and UNEP–UN Commission on Trade and Development (UNCTAD) capacity-building task force country projects (UNEP, 2001). The approach was introduced to the World Trade Organization (WTO) negotiators at a workshop in 2001.

No single, all-encompassing approach is promoted. Rather the manual presents a range of approaches. They include formal modelling, qualitative analysis and other methods such as cost–benefit analysis, risk assessment, multi-criteria analysis, extended domestic resource cost analysis, life cycle analysis, global commodity chain analysis and scenario building. In effect, this integrated assessment methodology is a conventional toolbox approach where the challenge is to identify what suite of assessment methodologies is appropriate to the task/situation in hand. Meaningful stakeholder participation is posited as a central element of the approach, providing data, insights and information that are not available to the traditional economic policy analyst.

The manual was developed in parallel to another UNEP initiative. Between 1999 and 2001, UNEP worked closely with national institutions in six countries to identify environmental, social and economic effects of trade liberalization. This involved data collection and empirical research by country experts on interactions and linkages between trade, environment and development policies and objectives. The assessment projects covered various sectors: fisheries (Argentina and Senegal), cotton (China), banana (Ecuador), cocoa and rubber (Nigeria), and forestry (Tanzania).

Sources: UNEP (2001, 2002a)

Box 4.8 Steps in integrated coastal area and river basin management

1   **assessment and data/information management**
    - development of an environmental and socioeconomic profile
    - establishment of a computer-based database for environmental and socioeconomic conditions
    - use of remote sensing techniques and a geographical information system (GIS)
    - definition of management scope
2   **Identification of conflicts and opportunities**
    - development of environment development scenarios
    - environmental carrying capacity analysis
3   **Plan and strategy development**
    - identification of management goals and objectives
    - analysis of alternative management strategy
    - establishment of a strategic action plan (SAP)
4   **Implementation of plan and strategy**
    - regulation, control and legislation
    - application of economic instruments
    - development of programmes for public awareness
    - capacity-building and education
    - environmental impact assessment
    - SEA – for the developed SAP
    - economic evaluation of costs and benefits
5   **Monitoring and evaluation**

Source: www1.unep.org/icarm

Another approach promoted by UNEP is integrated coastal area and river basin management (ICARM). In 1999, UNEP's Technical Cooperation Branch and the Priority Actions Programme Activity Centre (PAP/RAC) of the Mediterranean Action Plan jointly developed a conceptual framework and planning guidelines for ICARM (see: www1.unep.org). Several demonstration projects were sponsored for specific river basin–coastal areas.[7] Each aimed to undertake a series of steps that have much in common with the principles of SEA as well as good planning (Box 4.8).

Recently, UNEP has introduced an ambitious project to develop and test a framework for integrated assessment and planning for sustainable development in partnership with a number of developing and transitional countries. It aims to strengthen and improve existing plans and planning processes through a series of pilot or demonstration projects. These will incorporate an integrated assessment of critical issues and linkages of poverty,

---

7   For example, the Krka river basin (Croatia); the watershed area of the Rhone river (France); Penang Island (Malaysia); the Lower Limpopo river basin (Mozambique); the Cetina river basin (Croatia and Bosnia and Herzegovina); the Senegal river basin (Senegal).

Box 4.9 Proposed comprehensive SEA system for multilateral development banks

The primary focus of multilateral development bank (MDB) activity is providing technical assistance (TA) and loans to developing member countries. Generally speaking, more resources are expended on loans than TA. The idea of project administrative or processing 'cycles' is common to all MDBs. The most significant change to current MDB practice proposed by Annandale et al (2001) is a redesign of the CAS process to include new and enhanced SEA inputs so that it is integrated and sustainability-led.

> These consist of a new policy EA process and a new supra-national strategic environmental framework process. Enhanced inputs would include country environmental reviews (CENRs; based on current environmental profiles and environment sector strategies) and strategic assessment of economic and sector work (ESW). These new and enhanced inputs would obviously be combined with all of the other existing, non-environmental, inputs to CAS development. (our emphasis)

A completed draft CAS would include a preliminary lending and granting framework, as it currently tends to. But in this new comprehensive SEA system, the draft would be modified by the SEA inputs mentioned above. At this point, potential loans and grants may be clear enough to enable either sector EA or programme EA to be instituted as ex post assessment, if required.

A final CAS would then provide the framework for country assistance plans (CAPs), as is currently the case. Two environmental assessment steps would remain. First, there would be a need to undertake sector EA and programme EA in the post-CAP phase, if programme loans and sector loans have not been well defined at the draft country operational strategy studies (COSS) stage. Finally, all that would remain for EA would be the residual issues associated with specific projects as defined in CAPs.

The proposed comprehensive SEA system aims to provide linkages for tiering of EA:

> Those environmental issues that do 'flow' through from the draft CAS can be assigned to either sector EA, programme EA, or sub-national E-c-E planning [see Appendix 7] by developing member country governments. In this way, residual environmental issues might be grouped according to whether they should be best dealt with at a sector, programme, or sub-national level. Some issues, of course, will reappear through the tiers and will receive increasingly detailed consideration as they travel down the hierarchy.

trade, environment and sustainable development in selected sectors or regions (UNEP, 2004). This approach is being undertaken as part of the formal planning system of the country concerned using a generic methodological framework and kit of analytical tools. It is expected to reinforce specific policy initiatives and concrete actions being taken to develop and implement sustainable development strategies or equivalent frameworks, consistent with the approach outlined in the WSSD Plan of Implementation. It also aims to provide countries undertaking the pilot studies with the necessary expertise to conduct future integrated assessments in other sectors. UNEP intends to evaluate the lessons of the pilot projects with a view to refining the framework and providing guidance and training on the methodology of integrated assessment and its wide dissemination.

4.1.7 A proposed comprehensive approach for multilateral development banks

Collectively, the multilateral development banks (MDBs) play a major role in introducing and promoting SEA practice in developing countries. Annandale et al (2001) argue that although responsibility for PPP in developing countries is usually divided among departments and jurisdictions, MDBs tend to have more control over the different levels of the PPP hierarchy. As a consequence, the notion of 'tiering' – one of the key tenets of SEA – might be achievable more readily by MDBs, leading to efficiency gains and improved environmental outcomes in recipient countries. They propose an outline for a generic, comprehensive SEA system that could be applied to the lending and granting activities of MDBs, linking SEA with the programming cycle (Box 4.9). Annandale et al (2001) acknowledge that the way that SEA systems are implemented in developing countries themselves is extremely important, yet they do not explore the implications. We would argue that development cooperation agencies should think hard about the process and methods that are being exported and promoted and how best to build capacity for SEA development. This is particularly important in the poorest countries that arguably need SEA the most but are least able to take up this process.

4.2 SEA IN BILATERAL AID AGENCIES

4.2.1 Canadian International Development Agency (CIDA)

CIDA has prepared an SEA handbook to provide guidance on implementing the federal 1999 Cabinet Directive on the Environmental Assessment of Policy, Plan and Programme Proposals[8] (CIDA, 2003). The handbook is intended for those who may be involved in the development of a policy, plan, or programme, in other words Cabinet liaison staff, environmental specialists, programme and project analysts, and policy-makers. Two features of the handbook stand out:

- It includes a set of principles on SEA (based on principles developed in South Africa) that provide general guidance on how to conduct an effective SEA, outline the implications for CIDA and the key actions that need to be taken (Appendix 6). These principles (e.g. flexibility, sustainability, early integration, being participative) allow for a variety of SEA applications depending on the context of the policy, plan or programme.
- It outlines the agency's SEA process. This was developed in consultation with the operational branches to complement existing decision-making structures and approval processes. The principal design criterion was process flexibility so that it can be adapted to the many different types of policies, plans, and programmes that CIDA develops and implements. As a result, the foundation of CIDA's SEA process is a series of questions to be posed throughout the development of an initiative (Box 4.10).

---

8   See Section 3.3.3 on Canada in Chapter 3.

Box 4.10 CIDA process for SEA

CIDA's SEA process involves asking the following series of questions throughout the development of an initiative:

- What is the existing situation (in a particular sector or region)?
- What are the goals and objectives of the policy, plan or programme? How do these support CIDA and Government of Canada policies (particularly those related to the environment and sustainable development)?
- What are the different feasible options for delivering the policy, plan or programme?
- What are the most pronounced environmental issues (positive or negative) associated with each of the preferred options?
- How significant are these environmental effects?
- What can be done to avoid/lessen negative effect issues and to enhance positive ones?
- What is the best feasible policy, plan or programme?
- How do I measure, monitor and report on the environmental effects?

Source: CIDA (2003)

4.2.2 Department for International Development (DFID), UK[9]

As aid delivery mechanisms have moved away from specific projects to strategic assistance, DFID has recognized the need for a concomitant change in environmental assessment methods and procedures. To cater for this change, DFID's mandatory screening procedures for expenditure in excess of £1 million were comprehensively revised in 2003 (Box 4.11). Below this threshold, screening is not mandatory but strongly recommended where potentially significant environmental impacts are identified.

The revision of DFID's procedures took account of previous experiences with SEA-type approaches. For example, in 2000, DFID funded an SEA of Tanzania's draft transport policy, although, in hindsight, this was recognized to be more an expanded EIA.[10] Debate on the transport policy has collapsed but the analysis should be useful if development of the policy resumes. DFID is also working with UNDP to support an SEA of Tanzania's PRSP. It has also experimented with SEA-like approaches in other countries.

---

9   With contributions by Jon Hobbs and John Warburton, DFID.
10 The appendices of the report (WSAtkins, 2002) present detailed framework matrices that address the 31 policy objectives in the national transport policy, assessing, for each of the socioeconomic and environmental elements of the objectives, those aspects that have beneficial effects or adverse implications. For each element, the matrices assess/provide: the potential impacts of the policy, comments/assumptions, a qualitative assessment of effect (positive, neutral or negative), risks to/opportunities for achievement of environmental/social targets, and recommendations. The depth of analysis is limited due to both the SEA being performed late in the process of developing the policy, and to limited time allowed.

BOX 4.11 DFID'S SCREENING GUIDE

In 2003, DFID produced a revised *Environment Guide – A Guide to Screening*. It indicates when and why it is necessary to be used. The guide now focuses on the environmental screening of significant strategic interventions as opposed to the historic focus on infrastructure support. As such it represents a move towards strategic environmental assessment/sustainability appraisal approaches.

The responsibility for undertaking screening rests with the line manager. A step-by-step guide to the completion of an environmental screening note is provided. Specific guidance is included on how to screen poverty reduction strategies and direct budget support initiatives. This indicates what further measures will be necessary and where additional support can be obtained should more detailed investigation be considered prudent. In addition to examples of screening notes, a series of checklists are provided. These cover development themes such as: national development plans, fiscal reform, privatization and reform of state-owned enterprises, trade and direct foreign investment, education policy, tackling corruption, local government reform, humanitarian relief, accession to the WTO, and so on. The screening system provides the opportunity to consider the wider environmental impacts – both negative and positive.

A screening note will still be produced in co-funded proposals and, as a minimum, DFID will comply with developing country partners' environmental legislation and regulations.

Examples of DFID experience include the following:

- In Uganda, DFID has supported SEA-type approaches in development planning, including participatory poverty and environment assessments. These have had a marked influence on integrating environmental and sustainability concerns into the country's Poverty Eradication Action Plan (PEAP) (Box 6.17).
- In Nepal, help was provided to the National Planning Commission to assess the need, demand, opportunities, feasibility and requirements for introducing an SEA to improve future consideration of poverty–environment linkages in the planning process (Box 6.24; Table 6.5).
- In South Africa, DFID worked with the Department of Water Affairs and Forestry to develop and test an approach to SEA of stream flow reduction activities in water management areas (see Case Study 6.5).
- In Ghana, the agency collaborated with the Dutch EIA Commission to fund and support the National Development Planning Commission and Environmental Protection Agency to carry out an SEA of the Ghana poverty reduction strategy (PRS) (Box 6.16).
- In Andhra Pradesh state, India, DFID and the World Bank supported an SEA-type process to help prepare a long-term development strategy that integrates the environment as a key component (Box 4.12).

BOX 4.12 ANDHRA PRADESH: OPERATIONALIZING VISION 2020 ENVIRONMENTAL MANAGEMENT

Background: The Government of Andhra Pradesh collaborated with McKinsey and Company, Inc to prepare a long-term development strategy, published as Vision 2020. It requested World Bank assistance to identify specific steps and measures to achieve the strategic goals in a number of sectors, including the environment.

The Vision 2020 document integrates environmental improvements with the long-term goals for the state. It stresses the need to 'safeguard its environment and make its cities and villages clean, green, and safe to live in'. It sets ambitious targets to increase the area under forest cover from 23–33 per cent, and for universal access to clean drinking water and basic sanitation, as a key public health investment. The document recognizes the critical importance of developing a sound institutional and policy framework to achieve the vision of a 'clean and green' Andhra Pradesh. Specifically, it recommends internalizing environmental considerations in development planning, improving standards setting, strengthening compliance through complementing command and control regulations with market-based incentives, and increasing the role of stakeholders in decision-making and enforcement.

Vision 2020 emphasizes the importance of sound environmental management and provides broad directions. But the document lacks specific analyses and prioritization of environmental problems, as well as recommendations on possible efficient, feasible and enforceable policies and measures.

Programme – includes a number of components including:
* assisting Andhra Pradesh to prepare an *update of the state of the environment* (SOE) report (November 2002 – September 2003); and
* assistance for an in-depth *assessment of environmental priorities and mitigation strategies* in selected sectors/areas (May 2003 – May 2004), identified through the SOE update process. The process of preparing the SOE report and engaging various actors in the environmental management arena helped to identify sectors and/or 'hot spot' areas warranting in-depth follow-up work. An example is SEA of development plans and programmes in these sectors/areas.

The work was targeted at agencies responsible for environmentally sensitive sectors and/or degraded areas, as well as other relevant stakeholders. It aimed to inform them about the main potential environmental impacts of planned developments in a sector or area, and about least-cost strategies to avert or minimize environmental damage that could constrain growth. It was also expected to identify opportunities to enhance positive environmental impacts. The 'buy-in' and demand from sectoral agencies was seen as crucial for the success of this component. In addition to the Department of Environment and Forests and the Pollution Control Board, the likely candidates to be involved in this component were the government departments responsible for energy, urban affairs, industries, mining, rural development, finance, and planning. Key guiding principles for selecting sectors or areas for the SEA included: the probability of significant environmental impacts; and the existence of local champions to take up this work (e.g. demonstrated interest and commitment from the sectoral or local authorities). The scope of this component was developed through further dialogue and the process of developing the SOE.

* The scope of SEA was to be tailored to needs and priorities in specific sectors/areas. But the studies under this component were to comprise three basic elements: (i) formulating development plans for a sector and/or geographical area (preferably more than one scenario); (ii) assessing the environmental consequences of these plans and the cost of mitigation programmes; and (iii) proposing specific actions to integrate environmental considerations in the least-cost manner.

4.2.3 The Netherlands[11]

The Directorate General for International Cooperation (DGIS, a department of the Ministry of Foreign Affairs) and The Netherlands' embassies are responsible for governmental support of development cooperation activities. They do not have mandatory guidelines for the application of SEA, although there are internal guidelines for environmental screening to help in checking for impacts. The DGIS and embassies are responsive to, and also stimulate, requests from environmental and/or planning ministries in developing countries for support in undertaking SEA. This is provided by the Netherlands Commission for EIA. Preference is given to countries with which The Netherlands has a bilateral relationship in international cooperation.

The EIA Commission provides advisory services and related training activities to support the development of SEA in a country as well as advice on the terms of reference for SEA. It reviews the outcome, and gives coaching on SEA processes and the development of SEA systems. When applied, SEA is undertaken in the framework of the national context. Recent Commission activities[12] include: several two-day introductions on SEA in Guatemala, Nicaragua and Costa Rica; introduction and training in SEA for the Tunis International Centre for Environmental Technologies (CITET – an EIA centre for North African and Middle Eastern countries); SEA needs assessments, coaching and system-building in Mozambique (Box 4.13), Bolivia, Southern Caucasus countries and Sri Lanka; and contributions to many workshops. The DGIS and The Netherlands' embassy in Ghana are collaborating with DFID to support the SEA of the Ghana PRS (see Box 6.16). This is being carried out by the National Development Planning Commission and the Environmental Protection Agency, with advisory support provided by the Dutch EIA Commission. Finally, the Dutch EIA Commission is developing an SEA database that will provide a broad array of easily accessible information.

In support of the World Bank Structured Learning Programme for SEA, the DGIS is funding the Dutch EIA Commission to provide technical help to strengthen World Bank staff capacity in SEA and to review SEA good practices in the Bank.

The DGIS has also supported the development of the Strategic Environmental Analysis (SEAN) methodology by AIDEnvironment in cooperation with the Netherlands Development Organisation (SNV) (AIDEnvironment and SNV, 1999; Kessler, 2000). SEAN is designed to help identify relevant environmental sustainability issues and to integrate these into PPP at the earliest possible stages of planning and policy-making at local, regional and national level. The method has several phases of preparation: scoping, detailed analyses, synthesis and monitoring. It involves ten steps (Box 4.14), each with tools and approaches to be implemented in a participatory

---

11 With contributions by Petrie van Gent, and Rob Verheem, Dutch EIA Commission; Rob van den Boom, DGIS; and Jan Joost Kessler, AIDEnvironment.

12 The Dutch EIA Commission is also assisting Turkey and Lithuania in implementing the European SEA Directive.

BOX 4.13 SEA DEVELOPMENT IN MOZAMBIQUE

At the request of the Ministry for Coordination of Environmental Affairs (MICOA) in Mozambique, The Netherlands Commission for EIA provided advice on the environmental assessment of infrastructure for the transport of bulk goods from a titanium smelter in Chibuto, north of Maputo. Several facts were important to the advice given: this infrastructure was planned in a coastal zone reserved for tourism development; other favourable mining concessions had been issued; and the infrastructure could boost development in the region. So it was recommended that a decision on transport infrastructure should be based on an integral assessment of all interests through an SEA.

The SEA process is still underway, and it is too early to draw conclusions on its influence on planning. But it is clear that this SEA has stimulated interest within MICOA in the potential role of assessment tools in development planning. As a result, Mozambique has become one of the pilot countries under the World Bank–Netherlands' Partnership Programme where a needs assessment is being conducted on the use of various assessment tools (e.g. SEA, PSIA) in support of planning. An inventory of the current use of such tools showed that SEA is the most used tool, albeit not very often. Stakeholders (including various ministries) agreed that SEA would be the preferred tool to use in the future and that capacity-building is required. The needs assessment resulted in an action plan, including:

- identification of a number of SEA pilot applications;
- training and technical capacity-building for those involved in the pilots; and
- evaluation of the pilots, leading to recommendations on SEA application and guidelines in Mozambique.

---

manner involving local stakeholders and decision-makers. This process can be applied either over a period of several months or compressed into a workshop of a few days. It focuses on the linkages amongst environmental, social, economic and institutional issues, and, where possible, attempts to integrate them into 'win–win' outcomes and sustainable development policy choices.

SEAN has been applied in various countries, including Cameroon, Nicaragua, Honduras and Benin, to support and strengthen local governments in undertaking strategic and integrated planning and in assessing and improving existing plans and planning processes. It aims to involve public institutions, local governments and NGOs (see Case Study 4.1) and to create a local development vision and strategic plan, raise awareness among decision-makers, strengthen commitment and local ownership and establish a stakeholder platform. Guidance manuals are now available in a number of languages and there is a self-introduction to SEAN on CD-ROM. (for further information see: www.seanplatform.org).

BOX 4.14 STRATEGIC ENVIRONMENTAL ANALYSIS: THE MAIN STEPS

Ten analytical steps create a logical structure and provide guidance to participants in clarifying the complex issues involved. These steps can be implemented as a whole, or a selection can be made based on an assessment of what has already been done and available information.

Steps 1–4: Society–environment context analysis:
1   stakeholder analysis and mapping interests and positions; identification of environmental functions (production, regulation and cultural) with importance defined for different stakeholders;
2   assessment of past and current trends/changes of main environmental functions;
3   assessment of environmental, social and economic consequences of defined environmental trends;
4   defining a sustainability vision and bottom-line norms, standards and thresholds.

Steps 5–6: Environmental problem analysis:
5   definition of the main development problems as defined and perceived by stakeholders;
6   identification of direct and root causes (and responsible actors) of problems in a participatory and integrated manner, using the problem-in-context approach (root causes may be of sociocultural, economic and/or institutional nature).

Steps 7–8: Environmental opportunity analysis:
7   definition of main environmental potentials and development opportunities; identification of win–win options (matching opportunities with causes of problems);
8   sustainability assessment of main opportunities (using priorities and bottom-line standards as existing in national policy documents and/or as defined in Step 4); defining activities and responsibilities to realize opportunities.

Steps 9–10: Strategic planning and monitoring:
9   synthesis of previous steps to define a vision with main strategic orientations for sustainable development; integration with social and economic priorities; institutional analysis and recommendations for relevant institutions to implement the defined strategic orientations;
10 definition of a monitoring system with sustainability indicators to monitor performance and progress of the defined strategy.

Sources: AIDEnvironment and SNV (1999); Kessler (2000)

4.2.4 Organisation for Economic Co-operation and Development (OECD) Development Assistance Committee (DAC)

In 1995, the Working Party on Development Assistance and Environment approved a project to examine SEA as applied to development cooperation. This useful exploratory study reviewed, documented and analysed the collective experience of bilateral donors, multilateral financing institutions and developing countries in applying SEA (CIDA/DGIS, 1997; Box 4.15). It identified 41 cases where such agencies or partner countries had attempted some form of SEA. Most of these had been to evaluate the policies, programmes or planning frameworks of either the donor/lender or the partner government (Types IB/IIB in the typology in Box 4.15). In the majority, the main focus appears to have been on economic development, with environmental analysis considered as a complementary or supportive initiative. Of the 41 cases identified in the OECD study, in only four cases was the SEA process integrated into the partner government's policy, programming or planning framework (Type IIA):

- SEA around Victoria Falls – Governments of Zambia and Zimbabwe, assisted by the World Conservation Union (IUCN), financed by CIDA, 1996 (see Box 6.12);
- Gaza Environmental Profile – The Netherlands/Palestine Environmental Protection Agency, 1995;
- Argentina Flood Protection Project – Government of Argentina, in cooperation with World Bank, 1995 (see Box 4.2); and
- Environmental Management Plan for Dakshina Kannada District, India – Government of India, assisted by Denmark, 1994.

In only one case was the evaluation concerned directly with evaluating the partner government's own policy, programming or planning framework (Type IIB):

- EIA of Bara Forest Management Plan – IUCN/Government of Nepal, 1995 (see Box 6.24).

The study report recommended a promotional strategy to implement more widespread use of SEA/SIA with donor and lending agencies and developing countries (OECD/DAC, 1997). It also recommended that the Working Party encourage greater collaboration in SEA/SIA with the multilateral finance institutions and partner countries. In 2002, the Working Party returned to this challenge and established a task team on SEA. The proposal for a work programme notes that 'to improve and promote the further understanding and application of SEA/SIA it will be necessary to demonstrate the added value of the approach in development cooperation. There is therefore a need for a review of current experiences and examples of best practice' (OECD/DAC, 2002). This book aims to provide such a review. The work programme itself is described in Box 7.1.

BOX 4.15 SEA IN DEVELOPMENT COOPERATION

In 1995–1997, the Working Party on Development Assistance and Environment of the OECD/DAC undertook a project to examine SEA experience in aid agencies. The project report (CIDA/DGIS, 1997) revealed that:

> it is apparent that the concept and general goal of SEA are understood and accepted by most environment professionals in the development assistance community. The concept is not as familiar to managers at the policy and corporate levels of aid agencies, and those that do understand are generally less willing to adopt SEA without further evidence of the resulting costs and benefits.

The review identifies over 40 examples of the application of various forms of strategic assessment in a wide variety of development contexts. The majority of these studies were cooperative efforts between the donor/lender and the partner government. However, substantive joint ventures were not common. There were a number of cases in which developing countries had taken the initiative to request and/or conduct SEAs.

The report categorizes SEAs into:

*   those undertaken primarily as a means to upgrade environmental management capacity and institutional competence within a sector; and
*   those that were designed to address environment/development issues within a regional context.

It points out a significant difference in the approach and outputs associated with these categories. An SEA typology for development cooperation is suggested to clarify the context within which such assessments are undertaken:

*   Type IA: integration into donor's or lender's policy, programming or planning framework;
*   Type IB: evaluation of donor's or lender's policy, programming or planning framework;
*   Type IIA: integration into partner government's policy, programming or planning framework; and
*   Type IIB: evaluation of partner government's policy, programming or planning framework.

The report notes that 'a number of donors and lenders have already incorporated some form of SEA within their policy and operational frameworks and others are seriously considering doing so'.

Source: CIDA/DGIS (1997)

4.2.5 Swedish International Development Cooperation Agency (Sida)[13]

Sida has developed SEA guidelines for strategic environmental and sustainability analysis for use in the preparation of country strategy (available at: www.sida.se/Sida/articles/15300-15399/15361/CountryStrat02[4].pdf). These emphasize key links between poverty, the environment and sustainable development (Sida, 2002b). The guidelines define the objectives as to:

- understanding how environment and sustainability are related to other aspects of development;
- mapping the environmental and sustainability aspects that should be considered when the general scope and focus of development cooperation is decided; and
- developing a basis for decisions on environmentally sustainable interventions.

The guidelines do not prescribe a specific process or set procedures. Rather they cover analytical methods and focus, in particular, on the linkages between environmental and other development issues. Sets of five to ten strategic questions are provided on a range of key themes:

- poverty, poverty reduction and environment;
- economic policies and environment;
- health and environment;
- population change, migration and environment;
- development of capacity and institutions;
- legislation and environment;
- human rights and democratic development;
- equity and environment;
- conflict risk;
- vulnerability and environment;
- state of the environment and sustainable development; and
- a country's work for sustainable development.

Box 4.16 provides an example of questions for the theme 'economic policies and environment'. In addition, five to ten indicators for each theme are suggested – mainly existing indicators monitored by international organizations.

These strategic analyses can be very detailed and extensive in scope, provided that their findings are integrated with the country analysis and that the main conclusions are part of the country strategy document. Typically the reports derived from these analyses cover environmental state, pressures and driving forces, national initiatives and responses, national policy frameworks,

---

13   With contribution by Anders Ekbom, University of Göteborg, Sweden.

BOX 4.16 SIDA'S STRATEGIC QUESTIONS ON ECONOMIC POLICIES AND ENVIRONMENT

Strategic question: What are the connections between the country's economic policies and the environment?
Underlying questions to support the analysis:

- Is the country's economy based on unsustainable resource consumption?
- Are there 'critical' sectors or actors that contribute particularly to environmental degradation?
- Are there subsidies that cause significant emissions or overexploitation of resources?
- Are policy instruments (regulations, taxes) used to contribute to sustainable resource use?
- Do quotas, concessions, and permits contribute to unsustainable resource use?
- Is the country financing its debt service through unsustainable exploitation and export of natural resources?
- How have the structural adjustment and economic reforms affected the environment?
- Are there existing initiatives in the country to analyse and understand these issues?

Source: Sida (2002a)

---

commitments and capacity, existing and planned Swedish cooperation, and strategic recommendations for the future (Segnestam et al, 2003).

With the assistance of an external help desk at Göteborg University (www.handels.gu.se/econ/SEA-helpdesk), a brief strategic environmental policy analysis is produced within each country strategy process (10–15 per year). Occasionally, in-depth strategic 'environmental sustainability' analyses are carried out. Typically, they are commissioned by Sida's country desk officer as part of the country analysis process, and produced by international consultants. Recent examples of country SEAs include China, Vietnam, Ethiopia, Tanzania and the Balkan region.

Sida's country strategy assessments are process-oriented and emphasize dialogue between environmental economists (within and outside Sida) and the other subject-matter specialists involved in the country strategy process. Guidelines have also been produced for such dialogue on SEA with partner countries on sector programmes and include checklists for particular sectors (Sida, 2002b).

The external SEA help desk provides advice and statements pertaining to all draft documents produced during the process. It is also commissioned to assist the country teams with analysis, conduct training in SEA, and ensure that the key environmental sustainability issues are adequately addressed in each country strategy process.

4.2.6 United States Agency for International Development (USAID)

Under the US Foreign Assistance Act, 1961, all USAID strategic plans must include an analysis of the actions needed in host countries to achieve conservation and sustainable management of tropical forests and biodiversity, and of the extent to which the actions proposed for support by USAID meet the needs identified. In response, each USAID country mission conducts an environmental sector analysis prior to making strategy-related decisions. At a minimum, this covers the country's biodiversity and tropical forest resources. Country strategic plans (CSPs) are formulated following guidance that requires a comprehensive environmental threats and opportunities assessment (ETOA) (USAID, 1995). These assessments vary considerably in detail and level of analysis: some are short appendices to the CSPs; others are long reports (150 pages or more) with a detailed review of the state of the environment and key environmental issues. There is a strong emphasis on cross-sectoral linkages with non-environmental USAID programmes and strategic objectives in the country. Box 4.17 provides an example of a regional ETOA for Africa.

Recently, USAID commissioned a report on introducing strategic environmental planning (SEP) into the country strategic planning process (Freeman and Vondal, 2000). The introduction states that:

> USAID's experience in Africa in the past 25 years, and that of other donors, points to the need to think strategically about the environment and natural resources, to take a long-term view (10–20 years), to be flexible, and to develop concrete actions for achieving strategic goals.

BOX 4.17 USAID's REGIONAL ENVIRONMENTAL THREATS AND OPPORTUNITIES ASSESSMENT FOR AFRICA

In May 2000, a comprehensive environmental threats and opportunities assessment (ETOA) was conducted by USAID's Regional Economic Development Services Office (REDSO) for Eastern and Southern Africa as part of the process for preparing a strategic plan. It involved:

- a review of information on environmental threats and opportunities relevant to countries in the region of study;
- environmental review of proposed strategy components to identify critical factors and linkages with other sectors, transboundary issues and areas of opportunity in environmental and other programmatic areas; and
- identification of environmental strategic objectives and opportunities for addressing environmental issues under strategic objectives and activities in other sectors.

Source: Freeman and Vondal (2000)

It defines SEP as:

> *a planning process that recognizes environmental needs and possibilities in all sectors, and undertakes to identify them at the earliest point in USAID program planning.*

The CSP is the indicated context for this work, especially for early definition of topical and geographical priorities, cross-sectoral coordination possibilities, synergies and donor coordination.

The report aims to guide mission planners, analysts and programme implementers through each of the five stages of the CSP development process:

- mission-wide strategic problem analysis, trends and assessments;
- SO-specific assessments;
- SO environmental issues review;
- SO development hypotheses; and
- SO performance monitoring plan.

Drawing on USAID experiences of supporting planning approaches related to SEP and other emerging approaches, the report profiles various tools and information resources that can be employed in SEP. It offers procedures and questions at each stage and provides examples of application from USAID missions in Africa. The report provides a guide to resources that can be employed and suggestions for when it would be most useful and efficient to call on environmental expertise or other skilled professional help. It also proposes both a structured process and procedures for considering environmental issues during mission strategic planning exercises, particularly for CSPs. Three elements are described as necessary for SEP (the planning process, information, and analytical tools – Box 4.18) and a list of important principles is given to guide the process.

4.3 THE ROLE OF SEA IN PRSPs

The first generation of national sustainable development strategies (NSDS) have come and gone. This experience reveals a range of common tasks in the more successful initiatives that provide entry points and leverage opportunities for applying policy-level SEA (see Appendix 14). In this context, SEA can be seen as a tool that can enable better-informed options to be considered and more robust decisions to be reached. SEA is an analytical approach that can operate at key leverage points through the NSDS cycle – provided there is political will to allow this to happen. Typically, this is likely to be easier to apply where there is a formal provision for SEA, for example in legislation, regulations or administrative orders.

So far, however, this approach has been little practised in strategic planning frameworks, including in the preparation of poverty reduction strategies (PRS)

Box 4.18 Elements in strategic environmental planning: Proposed to USAID

A planning process that ensures review of relevant environmental issues

The strategic planning process entails:

- explicit consideration of inter-sectoral environmental linkages and synergies;
- identification of proactive environmental elements;
- consideration of impacts in the formulation of development hypotheses; and
- logical consistency in the chain: problem > hypotheses > intermediate results > illustrative activities > indicators.

The process breaks down the CSP development into its different stages, poses strategic questions at each stage and makes use of information resources and analytical approaches appropriate to the questions.

Environmental information resources to inform the planning effort

A number of information resources can be drawn upon at different stages of the CSP. The ETOA is an information and analytical resource that can be applied to all SOs. Similarly, the required EA of biodiversity and tropical forests can be expanded to capture information on trends in agricultural land quality, urban and town environments and demographic trends related to pressures on land and forest resources. For individual SOs, special planning studies are often commissioned (e.g. evaluations or reviews of problems in the SO sector), and these can be designed to include relevant SO-specific environmental information. For environment/natural resource-specific SOs, numerous background documents have been developed in the recent past, including national environmental action plans (NEAPs). USAID's EA and ETOA will also be helpful, though special studies may be needed to update the mission's knowledge or re-assess priorities.

Data gathering and analysis tools that facilitate the strategic planning process

Models and tools for data gathering and analysis can be used, especially geo-spatial tools such as GIS and remotely sensed images. Many of these are now much cheaper and easier to use than in the past.

Source: Freeman and Vondal (2000)

– the latest addition to the family of strategy approaches. Such strategies are promoted by the World Bank, which also strongly advocates the use of SEA. But the poverty reduction strategy papers (PRSPs) completed to date have paid only weak attention to environmental concerns. PSIA is the main diagnostic tool used (see Section 4.1.1) but this takes little or no account of environmental considerations. In 2002, the World Bank and International Monetary Fund

(IMF) received a report on a *comprehensive review of the PRSP approach* (started in mid-2001). It provides descriptions of good practice for countries and partners, numerous country examples and coverage of sector issues. The key points of the report are set out in Box 4.19. It is notable that the environment receives no mention.

A number of bilateral aid agencies have drawn attention to the 'neglect of the environment' in PRSPs. For example, in a submission to the World Bank in December 2001, DFID noted that:

> *For lasting growth and poverty reduction it is critical that relevant poverty–environment issues are given priority in PRSPs, and that those dealing with the environment in country are actively engaged in the PRS process. Reviews by DFID and the World Bank have revealed a mixed picture. Some countries' PRSPs (e.g. Bolivia, Honduras, Mozambique and Uganda) have given priority to relevant poverty–environment issues, but even these countries have been less successful in identifying how they should be addressed. Very few PRSPs have costed interventions in the policy matrix, especially where action is needed across sector. Only a few PRSPs (e.g. Bolivia, Uganda) include poverty–environment indicators. Crucially, even where the environment is covered in the PRSP, environment agencies and civil society groups are rarely engaged in the process. We therefore urge the Bank to focus on mainstreaming the poverty–environment agenda among staff working on PRS issues.* (www.worldbank.org/poverty)

Until recently, no PRSP process had involved any form of formal EA (either as an input to its development, or as a post hoc audit) that might equate to SEA or 'para-SEA' (Jan Bojo, World Bank environmental economist, personal communication). The Bank's Environment Department undertakes an unofficial review of PRSP documents as they are submitted. A scoring system is used to ascribe ratings for the way in which the PRSP addresses a range of 17 environmental and other variables (0 for no mention to 3 for good practice). Draft reviews are shared for comment with Bank country teams. So far, about 50 such reviews have been completed (a mix of full and interim PRSPs). An example is provided by Vietnam, which achieved an average score of 1.9 (Table 4.2). For comparison, the top score to date was for Mozambique (2.2).

The World Bank has now conducted two reviews of the environmental performance. The second (Bojo and Reddy, 2003b) showed considerable variation across countries (Box 4.20). There was a continuing low average level of mainstreaming, but a stronger tendency for full PRSPs to integrate environmental factors than interim PRSPs. An updated version is due to be released in late 2004.

Building on the World Bank's approach, the Southern African Institute for Environmental Assessment (SAIEA) has developed a framework for the

BOX 4.19 PROGRESS WITH PRSPS: KEY POINTS OF THE COMPREHENSIVE REVIEW BY THE WORLD BANK AND IMF

It is clear that the development of PRSPs is a major challenge for low-income countries, in terms of both analysis and organization. Besides managing a complex policy dialogue with development partners, low-income governments have to put together an integrated medium-term economic and poverty reduction strategy, complete with short- and long-term goals and monitoring systems; these are a set of tasks few industrial countries could systematically do well. And in many countries, these tasks must be managed with limited technical and institutional capacity and in ways that reinforce – rather than undermine – existing national institutions, processes, and governance systems. Thus, there is a need to have realistic expectations about the PRSPs that are being developed.

The central message is that there is broad agreement among low-income countries, civil society organizations and their development partners that the objectives of the PRSP approach remain valid ... and that there have been improvements over time in both process and content... There is widespread agreement on four key achievements of the PRSP approach to date:

- *a growing sense of ownership among most governments of their poverty reduction strategies;*
- *a more open dialogue within governments and with at least some parts of civil society than had previously existed;*
- *a more prominent place for poverty reduction in policy debates; and*
- *an acceptance by the donor community of the principles of the PRSP approach.*

While it is premature to draw any firm conclusions about the development impact of the PRSP approach, there are nonetheless a range of good practices by countries and their development partners. In reality, there are only a few concrete cases where such practices are in place.

Interim PRSPs

The requirements for an I-PRSP were deliberately minimal, although this was evidently not widely understood by all stakeholders. The I-PRSP was to describe the existing situation (with respect to poverty: the existing poverty reduction strategy and macroeconomic and policy framework) and set out a plan for developing the full PRSP (including the participatory processes; plans for identifying and developing appropriate policies, targets and indicators; and a system for monitoring and evaluating implementation). Policy commitments and targets for the outer years were to be revised in the full PRSP.

While the quality of I-PRSPs has varied, their preparation has served a useful purpose by encouraging countries to take stock of existing data and policies, to launch a broader process of rethinking current strategies, and to produce time-

bound roadmaps for the preparation of their first full PRSP. In many cases (e.g. Mongolia and Nicaragua), I-PRSPs were longer than expected, as countries put forward quite comprehensive documents. At the same time, however, the roadmaps were sometimes relatively weak with respect to plans for participatory processes (e.g. Senegal); plans to fill data gaps (e.g. Sierra Leone) and the proposed institutional arrangements for the PRSP (e.g. Moldova and Tajikistan). This appears to have been due to both an unclear understanding about the intended nature of an I-PRSP, coupled with pressures imposed by HIPC and/or PRGF timetables.

Although I-PRSPs were initially viewed as a transitional device, they may still be useful in many of the nearly three dozen low-income countries that will need to prepare PRSPs for access to Bank/Fund concessional lending and/or debt relief.

In order to qualify for debt relief, many countries prepared their I-PRSPs too hastily. In fact, the push by many countries to reach their Decision Point at the earliest possible date came at the expense of the quality of some I-PRSPs roadmaps, for example, participation plans and proposed institutional arrangements.

Full PRSPs

Ten countries ... have now finalized their first full PRSPs. These varied considerably in form and content, reflecting each country's own starting point, capacities and priorities. Each of the documents included the four elements proposed in the joint Bank/Fund paper on PRSPs (Operational Issues, SM/99/290, 12 December 1999):

(1) a description of the participatory process used in preparing the PRSP;
(2) a poverty diagnosis;
(3) targets, indicators and monitoring systems; and
(4) priority public actions.

However, the PRSPs varied considerably in the relative weight given to the treatment of the core elements and to key areas within these elements, and in style and format of presentation. Key points raised about PRSP documents and the approach include:

*   PRSPs have generally built on existing data and analyses and on prior strategies.
*   They reflect considerable improvement in both process and content relative to their corresponding I-PRSPs.
*   They have received attention at the highest political level in almost all countries, and many provide useful information about the institutional arrangements for preparation and implementation.
*   In some cases, documents have clarified the linkages between PRSPs and existing governmental plans and decision-making processes – especially budget formulation.

Participation
*   PRSPs have established a presumption in favour of openness and transparency and broad-based participation – the approach has often led to an improved dialogue

within the various parts of government and between governments and domestic stakeholders, and has brought new participants into the policy dialogue.

- However, some concerns have been expressed about inadequate engagement by certain groups or institutions seen as key to successful poverty reduction efforts.
- Sectoral ministries generally are less fully involved than core ministries, such as the Ministry of Finance or the Ministry of Planning.
- The role of parliaments in the PRSP process has generally been limited, although individual parliamentarians have been involved in some countries.
- In most countries, bringing civil society organizations into the process has improved with time.
- In some cases, there have been constraints to deepening and widening the process to all constituents to meet their expectations.
- There is some evidence that civil society's efforts have affected PRSP content, particularly in drawing attention to problems of social exclusion and the impoverishing effects of bad governance.
- In some countries, there may be a risk of 'participation fatigue'.

Poverty diagnostics
- Despite the significant advances in poverty data and analysis in PRSPs relative to pre-existing government strategies and policy frameworks, analysis of the impact of the policy actions on the lives of the poor appears to have been limited.
- Poverty and social impact analysis of major policies and programmes has typically not been undertaken as part of PRSPs.

Targets, indicators, monitoring and evaluation (M&E)
- Many PRSPs set long-term targets that seem overly ambitious relative to prior achievements and/or likely available resources.
- PRSPs often lack good indicators of intermediate processes that would help track the implementation of public programmes.
- Many PRSPs have detailed plans for improvement of M&E capacities, but the institutional structure for monitoring has not always been clearly defined.

Priority public actions
- PRSPs are generally weak regarding the prioritization and specificity of public actions.
- Some early PRSPs have made progress in identifying pro-poor growth policies.
- There were various shortcomings in the macroeconomic frameworks put forward in the early PRSPs, both in terms of presentation and content. All included ambitious growth targets and could have benefited from a sharper analysis of the likely sources and levels of growth.
- Key cross-cutting issues (e.g. gender, HIV/AIDS, good governance, rural development) have been addressed to varying extents.
- All PRSPs have emphasized access to services as a key concern, with improved access to education a priority.
- In general, the primacy of the private sector for growth is acknowledged.
- Most PRSPs have dealt with issues concerning trade openness in only a limited way.

Source: Based on extracts drawn from the main review report and the separate summary of main findings (available at: www.worldbank.org/poverty/strategies/review).

quantitative analysis of poverty/environment linkages and integration in PRSP (Croal, 2003). It also uses a cumulative index, but for a different set of key questions/issues. These cover the context of the PRSP, the focus issues, causal links, response systems, and the PRSP development process. Each question is scored (0 = issues not mentioned, 1= issues mentioned but not elaborated, 2 = issues elaborated, 3 = best practice on environment/poverty integration) (Table 4.3).

The SAIEA methodology goes further than the World Bank system and suggests indicators to identify if a PRSP has integrated poverty and environment issues, covering:

- assets of the poor;
- opportunities to use assets;
- enabling conditions (barriers and links between assets and opportunities);
- macro environment and potential crises (remedial or preventative; regional, national or international level, leading to potential impact on the poor); and
- expected results.

Following the conclusions in the World Development Report 2000/2001 (World Bank, 2002e), the World Bank Institute has launched a series of workshops on 'mainstreaming environment in poverty reduction strategies' under the name Attacking Poverty. A dedicated website has been established for workshop participants and others interested in PRSP and sustainable development strategies (www.worldbank.org/wbi/sdstrategies/mainstreaming). The workshops aim to promote the exchange of experience and knowledge in linking environment and poverty. But further experimentation in the use of SEA in PRSP preparation is needed. This will require something of a leap of faith on the part of policy-makers and a commitment on the part of SEA practitioners to operate much more holistically, and well beyond their traditional 'environmental' confines. The incentives for developing countries to initiate such an approach remain to be identified.

For any strategy for sustainable development to be effective, its preparation and implementation need to integrate environmental, social and economic dimensions and the potential impacts of policy options and of implementing actions (whether through plans, programmes or other initiatives). This process must be closely linked with research and analysis and with SEA. In this context, the focus might be on the following linkages:

- *strategy processes* that link the main centres of policy debate and decision-making – government, business and civil society – on a continuing basis, which will facilitate assessment of options for and proposals for sustainable development; and
- *the use of SEA* as an instrument that brings together diverse sources of knowledge in an interdisciplinary context, preferably on a continuing basis, which will lead to better strategies.

Table 4.2 *Environmental review of Vietnam PRSP*

Variable	Description	Score	Cumulative score
A Issues in focus			
1 Land use	Degradation, deforestation, erosion, overgrazing, mining, etc.	3	3
2 Water	Drinking water, irrigation, fishery and water pollution	2	5
3 Air	Quality and pollution	1	6
4 Biodiversity	Threats to ecosystem, ecotourism opportunities	1	7
B Causal link assessment			
5 Poverty and natural resource degradation	Resource dependence and inequality	3	10
6 Environmental health	Contagious and vector-borne infections, e.g. diarrhoea, malaria	1	11
7 Vulnerability	Impacts of climate variability (hurricanes, floods, drought)	2	13
8 Property rights	Tenure and natural resource management	2	15
9 Incentives	Prices, subsidies, taxation, trade, debt, exchange rate, income and employment policies	1	16
10 Empowerment	Decentralization and partnerships	2	18
11 Gender	Concerns relating to gender and environment links	1	19
C Response systems			
12 Environmental management	Regulation, legislation, institutions, information, environmental standards and economic instruments like cost recovery, product pricing, private sector participation	3	22
13 Investment in natural capital	Projects and programmes relating to land and water resource management, air quality and pollution abatement	3	25
14 Investment in man-made capital	Projects and programmes relating to water supply, sanitation, urban infrastructure and housing for poor	3	28
15 Monitoring natural resource outcomes	Deforestation, protected area, soil and water conservation, renewable energy use	2	30
16 Monitoring human development	Housing, sanitation, preventative care (life expectancy, infant mortality, etc.)	2	32
D Process and planning			
17 Participatory process	Process of environmental integration into PRSP preparation and implementation	1	33
Average score		**1.9**	

Source: Bojo and Reddy (2003a)

BOX 4.20 VARIANCE IN **PRSP** ENVIRONMENTAL PERFORMANCE

Using the ratings listed in Table 4.2, the World Bank's second review of PRSP environmental performance re-assessed the degree to which integration (mainstreaming) of environmental factors occurs in 50 PRSPs (30 of which are now full PRSPs), joint staff assessments (JSAs), and PRSP progress reports (PRSP-PRs) (Bojo and Reddy, 2003b).

The main findings are:
- High variance. *There is considerable variation in environmental mainstreaming. It ranges from marginal attention (0.3) to consistent mainstreaming across sectors (2.4).*
- Low but improving average. *The average score across the sample is only 1.3 on the 0–3 scale. It is not reasonable to expect all countries to score a '3' across the board, as priorities differ across countries. The average is an improvement over the 2002 assessment, which averaged 0.9.*
- Full PRSPs are better mainstreamed. *In comparison to interim PRSPs, there is a tendency for full PRSPs to better integrate environmental factors. As the sample matures, we expect mainstreaming to further improve.*
- High-scoring countries. *Countries in the high-scoring cluster are Zambia, Ghana, Cambodia, Mozambique, Azerbaijan, Sri Lanka, Yemen, Honduras, Nicaragua and Bolivia.*

A practical approach for doing this is the 'continuous improvement' framework (Figure 4.1), which would integrate SEA and policy actors in a step-by-step learning and adaptation process of change driven by multi-stakeholder groups. There is emerging political consensus that this is the right approach to strategies: for example, in NSDS policy guidelines developed by the OECD and eight developing countries (OECD/DAC, 2001) and guidelines developed by the UN (UNDESA, 2002b). These apply to all forms of strategy aiming at sustainable development including poverty and environmental strategies. In the final analysis, the test lies in their implementation and the evidence is not yet to hand and the jury is still out.

Table 4.3 *SAIEA proposed framework for PRSP assessment*

Does the PRSP:	Score	Comment

(a) PRSP context

Integrate environment as a cross-cutting theme?

Consider environment as a strategic objective?

Consider environment as an integral element of monitoring and evaluation?

Consider environment as a theme that requires risk management?

Evaluate environmental history and resultant situation of the country (cause and effect)?

Integrate poverty environment issues into national development frameworks?

Sub-total

(b) Focus issues

Evaluate land use and resultant environmental problems (desertification, deforestation, erosion, overgrazing etc.)?

Evaluate issues related to loss of species and natural habitats?

Evaluate water use and resultant environmental problems (access to potable water, water use and sustainable management, water quality and quantity, water equity)?

Evaluate air issues and resultant environmental problems (air pollution, ozone depletion, greenhouse gases, dust)?

Respect multilateral environmental agreements to which the country is a party (Ramsar, CBD, CMS, climate change etc.)?

Evaluate natural resource methods of extraction and sustainability limits (including inputs such as energy, other raw materials)?

Sub-total

(c) Causal links

Consider poverty profiles and resultant natural resource degradation (resource dependency and inequality)?

Evaluate environmental vectors and resulting health issues (malaria, gastrointestinal illness etc.) resulting from land, air, water or biomass degradation?

Address environmental degradation and links to HIV/AIDs?

Consider vulnerability of the population to social, economic and health stress due to environmental degradation and events (floods, storms, infertile soil etc.)?

Address property rights and entitlements (land tenure, access, control over management)?

Analyse economic catalysts (price stability, market access, taxation, subsidies, policies, exchange rates, trade etc?) and their relationship to environmental quality

Make foreign investment more pro-poor and pro-environment?

Encourage sustainable consumption and production?

Enhance development cooperation and debt relief?

Consider devolution of land and environmental management to
  local and community authorities (partnerships, co-management,
  decentralization, conservancies, empowerment)?
Consider anti-corruption efforts to protect the environment and
  the poor?
Consider gender equality in environmental management?
Sub-total

(d) Response systems

Consider how the environment can be managed sustainably
  (regulation, legislation, policy, taxation, incentives, voluntary
  environmental standards, co-management, institutional
  development)?
Evaluate how the country's ecosystems have the capacity to
  buffer any serious natural disasters or environmental shocks?
Consider economic valuation of natural capital (including
  commercial and social use functions as well as ecological
  functions)?
Implement pro-poor environmental fiscal reform?
Integrate poverty–environment issues into economic policy
  reforms?
Encourage more private sector involvement in pro-poor
  environmental management?
Address how the environment can be monitored and evaluated
  regularly?
Evaluate how investment in natural resources can be improved
  (land and water resources management and conservation, air
  quality, sustainable extractive industry management)?
Expand access to environmentally sound and locally appropriate
  technology?
Evaluate investment for human needs (health, housing,
  infrastructure, energy, water, education etc.)?
Evaluate human and institutional capacity needs for sustainable
  environmental management?
Sub-total

(e) PRSP development process

Have input from a broad range of environmental specialists,
preferably in country?
Have input from a broad range of policy, technical, social and
scientific experts, preferably in country?
Have input from a range of 'publics' from the country and
elsewhere?
Have input from a range of environmental NGOs, and local
environmental ministries and institutions?
Allow sufficient time for proper consultation and redrafting?
Sub-total

TOTAL   **Out of 120**

Source: Croal (2003)

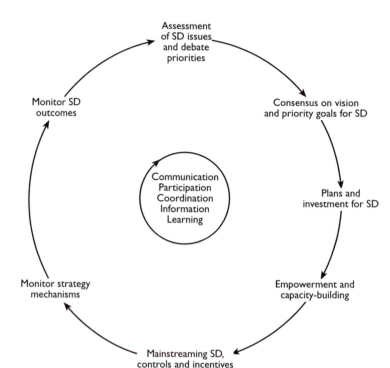

Note: As portrayed, this figure suggests that the overall process involves a rigid sequence of steps. However, in practice, these are ongoing and necessarily overlap. Key features of the central tasks are stakeholder identification, strengthening capacity, collaboration and outreach.
Source: OECD/UNDP (2002)

Figure 4.1 *A continuous improvement approach to sustainable development stategies*

Case Study 4.1

Application of the Strategic Environmental Analysis (SEAN) Methodology in Cameroon, and in Honduras and Nicaragua

Source: Jan Joost Kessler (personal communication)

The SEAN methodology is described in Box 4.14 of this book. Two different applications are described below.

(A) Quick scan SEAN for developing a regional strategy for Northern Cameroon

With funding from the Netherlands Development Organisation (SNV), the SEAN method was used in 2003 to develop a strategic development plan for the northern region of Cameroon. The challenge was to link up to existing plans and make use of existing studies and materials, involve different stakeholders, generate commitment and also execute the analysis in a three-day workshop.

The workshop was structured as follows:

- *Day 1: Analysis of regional development context*, to determine the main problems, opportunities, underlying factors and key actors. Based on that, a vision and strategy were developed for a desirable future of the region (in line with the mission and development themes of the main stakeholders). This was done during the workshop, on the basis of existing knowledge, using SEAN steps in a quick manner.
- *Day 2: Analysis of the institutions and key actors*, to make an inventory and to know strengths and weaknesses of each institution and their plans and policies.
- *Day 3: Analysis of the demands for support* by the institutions and key actors, to be able to realize the vision and strategy.
- *Day 3: Decisions on what support donors will provide*, and what will be provided by the local and regional institutions, and what competencies will then need to be developed.

The approach can be used by any organization to define its development priorities (for building the capacity of local organizations), and then to define its own required competencies, partners, budget and operational plans.

(B) SEAN FOR INTEGRATING ENVIRONMENTAL CARE IN MUNICIPALITY PLANNING IN HONDURAS AND NICARAGUA

This type of application started in 1997. It aims to support local development planning at the municipality level, and show ways to integrate environmental care into local development plans. During a six-month period, with Dutch technical assistance, a local NGO implemented the ten SEAN steps (see Box 4.14). The process included a variety of workshops, mini-workshops, informal meetings, research carried out by university students, detailed work by resource specialists and reporting. The SEAN steps were carried out for the ten main themes/issues in the municipal area (e.g. tobacco cultivation, urban waste management, forest management, sustainable agriculture). Reports were prepared on the outcomes of the SEAN steps for each theme. They covered both solutions to perceived problems and identified opportunities.

At first, some municipal members and institutions in the area were sceptical about this approach, but they all actively made use of the results by integrating relevant issues in their strategic and operational planning. The whole exercise has raised a lot of interest amongst other councils and donors. It is seen as an opportunity to support local councils in their own planning processes. Building on this experience, SNV has now implemented the SEAN method in more than 30 different municipalities in Honduras and Nicaragua. A major aim has been to strengthen local governments to undertake strategic and operational planning with a sustainable development focus, by adopting participatory approaches. The concepts are not new, but putting them in practice by using a practical method is.

CONCLUSIONS

A number of lessons can be drawn from the various experiences of applying the SEAN methodology:

1   The resulting strategic plan is not an environmental plan. Rather it is an integrated (sustainable development) plan. This underlines how the SEAN methodology takes the environmental domain (goods and services provided to human society) as a starting point to find solutions and opportunities in the areas of overlap with the socioeconomic and institutional domains.

2   The planning process is at least as important as the content of the ten methodological steps. A number of factors determine the success of the

planning process: local ownership and clear demand, involving the private sector, high quality facilitation, a minimum of time, local co-funding and consistent application of participatory tools and methods.

3 Even if limited time is available, the process facilitates common views to surface amongst the different actors involved. Participants are satisfied about the method as a logical framework to structure discussions in broad stakeholder 'negotiation platforms'. For many participants, it was the first opportunity to collaborate actively with other disciplines, and for government officers to exchange views and information with NGOs.

4 One of the main differences between the strategic plan resulting from SEAN and existing environmental action plans is the emphasis on priority themes agreed upon by participants at the meso level, as well as some commitment to work on agreed activities.

5 In Latin America and in many African countries, the approach is particularly useful at the meso level, for example to support districts and local councils prepare their development plans as part of a decentralization and capacity-building process. The meso level is the highest level at which local stakeholders can deal with concrete issues concerning the natural resources on which they depend, and at which they can organize themselves. But it is the lowest level at which government departments are well informed and can negotiate with other stakeholders.

6 A challenge is to develop the SEAN method further as a tool for integrated planning, by linking tools from other disciplines. The entire planning process also requires continuous facilitation support (i.e. over a longer period of time, not by being more intensive) to implement, monitor and evaluate the activities that have been agreed upon.

Chapter 5

SEA Experience in Countries in Transition[1]

Countries in transition are commonly understood to be the ex-socialist states of Europe and Central Asia that are in the process of economic restructuring and political reform. They comprise the countries of Central and Eastern Europe (CEE) and the newly independent states (NIS) of the former Soviet Union, which have major differences in their level of development and democratization. In addition, there are notable differences in the CEE region between countries that have now joined the European Union (EU)[2] and the Balkan countries of Southeast Europe,[3] which are undergoing reconstruction following a period of war, conflict and political instability. Countries waiting in the EU accession queue (Bulgaria, Croatia and Romania) are intermediate. By comparison, many NIS[4] are still in the early phase of introducing political and market reforms, although there are significant differences between European countries, some of which have EU membership aspirations, and the Caucasian and Central Asian countries which face fundamental challenges in governance and democracy.

Environmental impact assessment (EIA) systems were first introduced in the region in the mid-1980s. Today, nearly all NIS and CEE countries have

---

1   This chapter has benefited from information and inputs from a number of SEA experts from the Central and Eastern European region. In particular, we acknowledge the extensive review of an initial draft of this chapter by Jiri Dusik of the Regional Environmental Center for Central and Eastern Europe (REC) and for NIS by Aleg Cherp of the Central European University, Budapest, who both provided many valuable corrections and additions. Other valuable contributions came from Ingrid Belãáková, Leyli Bektashi, Ursula Rzezsot and participants at an REC workshop on SEA of National Development Plans, Szentendre, Hungary, 28–30 April 2003.

2   The countries in transition that joined the EU on 1 May 2004 were the Czech Republic, Estonia, Hungary, Latvia, Lithuania, Poland, Slovakia and Slovenia.

3   The Balkan countries comprise Albania, Bosnia and Herzegovina, Croatia, Federal Republic of Yugoslavia (Serbia and Montenegro), Kosovo (UN administered territory) and Macedonia.

4   The newly independent states comprise Armenia, Azerbaijan, Belarus, Georgia, Kazakhstan, Kyrgyzstan, Moldova, Russia, Tajikistan, Turkmenistan, Ukraine and Uzbekistan.

established some type of EIA legislation and many have incorporated provision for strategic environmental assessment (SEA) under these frameworks. Since 1996, in particular, SEA trends and developments in transitional countries have evolved rapidly and certain countries already have considerable practical experience (notably the Czech Republic, Slovakia and Poland).[5] Elsewhere in the region, the use of SEA is evolving rapidly. Many countries in transition (CIT) established legal requirements for SEA before some EU states, such as Austria, Greece and Portugal. Also, NIS have made legal provisions for some form of SEA. But these are not always implemented in the way intended, experience is still limited and processes are not yet aligned with internationally accepted practice (Cherp, 2001).

There are a number of reviews of SEA procedure and practice in CIT. For example, a special issue of the journal *Impact Assessment and Project Appraisal* (vol 22, no 2, 2004) addressed environmental assessment, particularly SEA, in emerging democracies. There are also 'state of the art' articles and volumes on CIT, CEE and NIS experience, respectively (Therivel, 1997; Bellinger et al, 2000; Cherp, 2000a) and status reports on SEA development prepared as part of the Sofia Initiative on EIA (Mikulic et al, 1998; Dusik et al, 2001; Dusik and Sadler, 2004). The Sofia Initiative has provided a flexible, cooperative framework for regional networking and exchange of views and information amongst SEA administrators and professionals (Box 5.1). Most importantly, it established a body of pilot and demonstration projects on SEA practice and their lessons for CEE application and process development. The examples provided concrete guidance on SEA approaches and methods that work in a CIT context, recognizing that these need to be adapted to distinctive arrangements and rules in place in national jurisdictions.

Major changes in SEA systems are underway in CEE countries. The eight CEE member states that have joined the EU are in the process of amending or introducing SEA legislation to conform to the requirements of the EU SEA Directive (2001/42/EC). Other CEE countries with accession agreements with the EU almost certainly will follow a similar course in the next few years. In the longer term, it is also likely that certain Balkan states and possibly some NIS will establish SEA legislation that is harmonized with the SEA Directive. For NIS, however, the SEA Protocol to the Espoo Convention may be the more important international legal instrument. A number of NIS became signatories to the SEA Protocol at Kiev in 2003 and it is likely that much of the work of the parties on SEA process development and capacity-building will focus on this block of countries.

---

5   A review by Therivel (1997) of SEA in the Czech Republic, Hungary, Poland and the Slovak Republic provides a basis of comparison with the situation reported in this chapter (see Appendix 5).

BOX 5.1 SOFIA INITIATIVE ON ENVIRONMENTAL IMPACT ASSESSMENT

Under the Environment for Europe process, substantial progress has been made in implementing the Environmental Action Programme (EAP) for CEE. This recommends that priority environmental problems should be tackled through a mix of policy, institutional and investment measures. Following the Sofia Conference of Ministers of the Environment (1995), the initiative on the application of EIA was jointly implemented by the Ministry of Environment of the Republic of Croatia and the REC and financed by a number of donors. The Sofia Initiative on EIA gave a high priority to the development and use of SEA in CEE countries. It built initially on existing requirements in EIA laws or elements in land use planning laws, and later addressed wider institutional constraints and capacity-building for SEA in the region. In this last respect, from 1996 to 2003, the Sofia Initiative on EIA was an important exercise in regional self-help. It provides a model that might be adapted to wider application internationally. The main lessons are:

- *The establishment of a sound national consultative process appears to be the most important starting point for the development of a sound SEA system in each country.* Donor agencies can assist by making this a prerequisite for their support for SEA capacity-building in particular countries. The benefits of this approach are twofold: it strengthens the national institutional and policy processes; and it provides the basic framework for adjusting capacity-building programmes to the particular needs of each country.
- *A comprehensive capacity-building strategy should be developed before individual programmes begin.* Experience from the CEE region indicates that such a strategy should include the following components:
  - *pilot SEA projects* to test and develop methods and procedures and to highlight good practice;
  - *promotional materials* to explain the rationale for SEA to planners and decision-makers;
  - *practical guidance* to explain the key elements of effective SEA to practitioners;
  - *professional networking* of SEA practitioners to help share lessons and benchmark performance; and
  - *training* to build core professional capacities to undertake SEA.
- *Capacity-building should facilitate comprehensive learning about all relevant international SEA norms and standards.* Donor agencies often promote a particular SEA system or process. It is unrealistic to expect that they will establish a uniform approach to SEA training and capacity-building. But more could and should be done to introduce and compare the advantages and disadvantages of SEA arrangements and practices, recognizing that these vary more than those for project EIA.
- *Regional East–East and South–South networking should replace traditional programmes based on one-way transfer of experience from the North.* The Sofia Initiative on EIA was implemented by CEE institutions for CEE participants who jointly addressed the specific needs of the countries involved. It promoted regional and national policy debates on the introduction of SEA and pilot projects to test new approaches. Much of the value from these exercises came from professional exchange and learning from each other.

Sources: Dusik (2003b): Dusik and Sadler (2004)

5.1 Newly independent states[6]

EIA-type frameworks that include SEA elements are in place in nearly all NIS. Arrangements vary, but they have common features based on the system of state environmental review (SER, also called 'ecological expertise') of all planned actions including strategic proposals. This process was established in the former Soviet Union in the mid-1980s as a largely internalized procedure and was undertaken by the responsible environmental authority or through an appointed committee of experts (Cherp and Lee, 1997). It underwent various reforms before the disintegration of the Soviet Union. Most notably, EIA requirements (called OVOS or 'assessment of environmental impacts') were established alongside the SER procedure.

The SER/OVOS system was inherited more or less intact by the NIS that emerged from the end of the Soviet Union in 1991. Since then, this system has been variously retained or reformed by individual NIS and there are important regional variations in national legislation and procedure. These are described below. In comprehensive form, the SER/OVOS regime comprises two interdependent sub-systems. These are regulated by different acts, implemented by different actors and guided by different objectives (von Ritter and Tsirkunov, 2002). Despite considerable progress, this approach remains firmly anchored on SER foundations with OVOS applied primarily at the project level. Both procedures are insufficiently delineated or applied in relation to strategic proposals. As such, SER/OVOS systems represent an interim step toward SEA as understood internationally. They have elements that can be classified as a para-SEA process under the schema outlined in the introductory chapter, although these are difficult to define unambiguously.

5.1.1 Main features of SER/OVOS systems

The distinctive features of the SER arrangements in most NIS include the following (Cherp, 2001):

- SER is intended to apply to all planned actions, including strategic proposals.
- The environmental authority has a dominant role in the SER process, whereas the developer is responsible for the preparation of an EIA report under the OVOS procedure at the project level.
- In principle, SER applies to all plan or project documents including, where applicable, the OVOS or EIA report and related materials.
- This process addresses the environmental acceptability of the proposed activity as a whole, rather than only identifying the impact on the environment.
- SER resolutions (or conclusions) are legally binding on decision-making. A 'negative' conclusion means that a proposed activity cannot proceed.

---

6   Much of the introductory analysis in this section is based on Cherp (2001).

SER/OVOS systems differ from EIA/SEA frameworks as applied internationally in a number of important procedural respects. These are identified in a recent World Bank review (Klees et al, 2002):

- SER/OVOS processes lack appropriate checks and balances. For example, screening is so broad and indiscriminate that it includes nearly all proposed actions, including minor ones. In turn, the sheer volume of activities reviewed at all levels leads to problems of avoidance, cost and delay. It also results in superficial examination of environmental aspects. Scoping is an 'internal' procedure rather than a mandatory requirement under both the SER and OVOS provisions of most NIS.
- Many NIS have ratified both the Aarhus and Espoo Conventions, but SER/OVOS frameworks lack transparency and do not fully adhere to the principles of public involvement. For example, legal provisions do not clearly define the rights of the public with respect to disclosure and examination of documents. It is reported that only Moldova, and to a lesser extent Georgia and Ukraine, have directly addressed these deficiencies.
- In most NIS, provision is made for the independent organization of 'public environmental expert review' (PER) of information and submission of comments. This is a potentially far-reaching and internationally significant provision, but, usually, there are no procedural stipulations relating to the review or consideration of comments.

5.1.2 Regional trends and variations

During the past decade, the SER/OVOS systems of individual NIS have been reformed in various ways in response to both internal and international trends. But they still fail to address strategic proposals adequately. Cherp (2001) suggests three categories, depicting development and current status of these systems (Table 5.1):

- Five countries (Ukraine, Belarus, Kazakhstan, Turkmenistan and Russia) have retained and reformed the previous SER system through new national legislation. Formally, SER had to be applied to all planned actions (above), but, in practice, many strategic proposals are not subject to this procedure.
- Three countries (Armenia, Georgia and Moldova) have introduced EIA systems that correspond to internationally accepted steps and elements. However, their implementation has proven difficult and proceeded slowly and, in practice, this group still relies on SER-based procedures with relatively limited coverage of strategic actions.
- Four countries (Azerbaijan, Kyrgyzstan, Tajikistan and Uzbekistan) continue to follow the old SER procedure and, in practice, there is little or no application at the strategic level.

Table 5.1 *SER/OVOS systems in NIS*

Countries	Features of SER/OVOS system
Belarus, Kazakhstan, Russia, Turkmenistan, Ukraine	Soviet SER/OVOS systems were strengthened by national EA legislation (1993 onwards). Now substantial experience with implementing these procedures
Armenia, Georgia, Moldova	National EA legislation (1995 onwards) introduced Western elements of EA. Implementation of these procedures still limited
Azerbaijan, Kyrgyzstan, Tajikistan, Uzbekistan	No new national EA legislation introduced and practice, where it exists, follows Soviet-style SER procedure

Source: Cherp (2001)

A somewhat different perspective emerges when NIS legal frameworks are compared with World Bank Operational Policy (OP) 4.01 as a proxy for internationally accepted procedural standards. The Bank used five broad evaluation criteria,[7] to rank SER/OVOS systems on three levels of comparability (Klees et al, 2002):

- *high comparability* – indicating a legal framework and process that includes all internationally accepted elements and requires only minor adjustments (only Ukraine qualified from the NIS block);
- *medium comparability* – indicating evident progress in updating legislation but with issues related to implementation, compliance and enforcement of various provisions and the involvement of the public (Georgia, Moldova, Kazakhstan, Russia, Kyrgyzstan, Uzbekistan, Azerbaijan and Turkmenistan – listed in order of ranking); and
- *low comparability* – indicating limited progress in the development of an EA system (Armenia, Tajikistan and Belarus – in order of ranking). NIS and other countries in this group (mainly from Southeastern Europe) will require significant medium-term assistance to develop EA frameworks and the institutional capacity to deliver them, especially at the strategic level.

---

7   The ranking criteria reflect the provisions of the World Bank, the European Commission and internationally accepted EIA framework and elements, comprising (Klees et al, 2002):
   - firmly established legal basis;
   - transparent screening and well-coordinated scoping process;
   - timely, transparent and meaningful public participation;
   - compliance with all applicable laws and standards; and
   - clarity and modernity of EIA and integrated consideration of social, transboundary and global impacts.

Table 5.2 *OVOS/SER application to strategic proposals*

System	Development plans	National policies	Laws, regulations
OVOS	Armenia, Kazakhstan, Moldova	Armenia, Kazakhstan, Moldova	Armenia, Kazakhstan, Moldova
SER	Belarus, Georgia, Kazakhstan, Kyrgyzstan, Moldova, Russia, Turkmenistan, Ukraine	Belarus, Georgia, Kazakhstan, Kyrgyzstan, Moldova, Russia, Turkmenistan, Ukraine	Belarus, Georgia, Kazakhstan, Kyrgyzstan, Moldova, Russia, Turkmenistan, Ukraine

Source: Klees et al (2002)

5.1.3 Implementation of SER provision and procedure

To date, there are no examples of SEA arrangements in NIS that are comparable to international legal or policy instruments. Nevertheless, SEA requirements and elements have been instituted widely, for example in the Russian Federation, although they may not be called that (Grishin, 1997). In most NIS, strategic actions are addressed under SER rather than OVOS frameworks (these are in place in Armenia, Kazakhstan and Moldova). On the face of it, strategic actions include development plans, national policies and legal acts and regulations (Table 5.2). But, as Cherp (2001) notes, SER procedure for strategic actions is rarely specified or differentiated from that applied at the project level; and there appears to be a mechanical extension of requirements from one to the other. According to Klees et al (2002), OVOS legislation also applies to policies, plans and programmes without specifying the procedure to be followed but, in practice, it is rarely applied at this level.

From an SEA perspective, these concerns raise general questions about the adequacy of the SER legal framework and the consistency of its procedural application at the strategic level. These aspects also might be expected to differ with the regional variations noted above; notably, for example, amongst NIS systems that are rated, respectively, low, medium and high in comparison with internationally accepted standards. Box 5.2 provides a second perspective on the SER/OVOS regime in selected NIS, with reference to these categories. In all cases there seems to be a wide gap between legal frameworks and their implementation. In reality, NIS practice is not well known, particularly at the strategic level, and there are differences of opinion on its extent and effectiveness. This is evident, for example, in recent reviews of SER/OVOS experience in NIS (in general) and in the Russian Federation (in particular), although rapid changes are taking place with new facets of SEA emerging (see Cherp and Golubeva, 2004).

5.1.4 SEA practice in NIS

Cherp (2001) has analysed SER applications in different NIS (e.g. Box 5.3) and draws several conclusions and observations that appear to apply generally, in many cases, to SER of strategic actions:

BOX 5.2 STATE ENVIRONMENTAL REVIEW (SER) IN NIS

In the post-Soviet era, SER procedure (also called 'state ecological expertise') has been retained in the NIS block as the main cornerstone of EIA and SEA-type processes. With the introduction and adoption of OVOS (as an EIA-equivalent), a dual approach has emerged. In this, the scope and quality of the OVOS report are determined by SER requirements. As such, SER remains the predominant procedure, with or without OVOS (and not all NIS have established this latter system). Where it is linked to OVOS, SER combines two functions: evaluation of the environmental acceptability of the proposed development, particularly its compliance with environmental norms and planning standards; and quality control of an EIA, which is conducted by the developer (i.e. OVOS). SER resolutions are legally binding but, in some cases, this provision does not apply to strategic actions. The comparability of SER frameworks with internationally accepted standards varies from low to medium to high (when rated against World Bank OP 4.01). Below, national experience in selected NIS is described for each category, with particular reference to strategic proposals.

Belarus (low comparability with internationally accepted standards)
The Soviet system of SER (introduced in 1989) remained in place in Belarus until superseded by national legislation on Environmental Protection (1992) and on State Environmental Review (1993). The provisions of the latter were further refined in 1995 by the Ministry of Environment in the Instruction on the Order of Conducting SER of Project Documentation. SER is mandatory for 'all economic and other activities' including development plans and programmes. As its full title indicates, the 1995 Instruction defines the SER procedure only in relation to projects. No guidelines are specified for strategic actions and SER at this level is carried out on an ad hoc, case-by-case basis by staff of the Ministry of Natural Resources and Environmental Protection (Cherp, 2000b). There are SEA-related provisions in other legislation. Notably, under planning norms, city master plans are required to include a chapter on the protection of the environment, and these are subject to SER during the planning process. According to Elizarova et al (1998), this process approximates to a legal instrument for SEA as understood internationally. But it does not include key procedural requirements such as consideration of alternatives (see also Box 5.3).

Kazakhstan (medium comparability with internationally accepted standards)
Under Kazakhstan law, SER is mandatory for all projects and certain strategic actions including development plans. The enabling legislation is the Environmental Protection Law (1997, amended 1998, 1999). This mandates SER and PER (Articles 63–65) and certain requirements for and applicable to EIA (Articles 35–42, 46–62). Articles 46 and 63 of the Law refer to SEA. The Ecological Expertise (Review) Law (1997) includes stipulations regarding EIA and SER of policies, plans, programmes and legislation. However, as in other NIS, these are non-specific. According to a World Bank review of the Kazakhstan legal regime (Klees et al, 2002), SEA-related requirements and procedures need to be better defined. There are also some positive procedural steps and elements, particularly at the screening phase. For example, the Ecological Expertise (Review) Law (1997) identifies types of activities and planning, programme and project documentation that are subject to SER. Articles in this legislation and in the Environmental Protection Law (1997 as amended) establish requirements for public participation in OVOS and SER. The World Bank review recommends that the

Government should regulate timely, transparent and meaningful public participation at the national and other levels (Klees et al, 2002). Kazakhstan is a Party to the Aarhus Convention (2001) and has accepted international obligations in this area.

Ukraine (high comparability with internationally accepted standards)
Ukraine operates a reformed version of the former Soviet SER/OVOS system that is relatively well defined in law and practice. The Law on Environmental Protection (1991) provides enabling provisions that require, inter alia, the application of SER to all levels of economic activity (Articles 50, 51 and 59). Article 36 of the Law on Environmental Expertise (1995) sets out detailed provision for SER together with general requirements for OVOS (EIA). SER application is stipulated for listed types of project and strategic actions and these cannot proceed without a positive conclusion from this process. OVOS Regulations and State Construction Norms DBN A.2.2-1-95 (*Structure and Content of Documents on EIA (OVOS) in Designing and Construction of Business, Houses and Buildings: Main Designing Principles*) gives detailed guidance on the form and content of EIA materials. The World Bank review of SER/OVOS legislation in NIS gave Ukraine high marks on basic provision and on screening and scoping procedure. But it also notes that the transposition of obligations under the Espoo Convention (ratified 1999) still needs improvement (Klees et al, 2002). Similar ratings are given for public participation provisions at critical stages in the SER/OVOS process. As with other NIS, Ukraine has ratified the Aarhus Convention (in 1999) and made progress toward transposing its requirements.

Source: Dalal-Clayton and Sadler (1998a) updated from materials cited

- Strategic actions are subject to SER even in more conservative NIS, although the majority are lower-level physical plans or schemes and applications to policy are relatively rare.
- The main focus of SER is on compliance with formal provisions regarding the content of planning documentation and mandatory approvals, and on meeting environmental protection norms and objectives.
- Most SER applications that reach positive conclusions impose environmental conditions, but these refer primarily to subsequent project EIA and there is little evidence that strategic actions are modified other than superficially during their preparation.
- These outcomes reflect the basic features of SER described above, notably the indiscriminate application of the process across a wide range and large number of actions, and the use of relatively simplified, technocratic procedures, which, together, encourage a limited, pro-forma approach.
- SER practitioners must decide the environmental acceptability of a strategic proposal without necessarily having a full understanding of the social and economic effects, or views and information from public consultation (a concern that applies well beyond NIS).
- SEA elements and principles are built into certain strategic planning procedures, particularly land use and urban plans elaborated through the former Soviet process of territorial integrated schemes for nature protection (so-called TerKSOPs; see Section 5.1.5). Recent reforms in land

BOX 5.3 STATUS OF SEA PRACTICE IN BELARUS

Belarus has inherited a Soviet SER/OVOS system that has been modified by the Laws on SER (1993 and 2000) as well as by several ministry-level regulations (see also Box 5.2). New OVOS Regulations (2004) prescribe EIA procedure for projects in great detail and are due to be adopted by the Government. They depart from the previous system and specify a multi-stage procedure. This involves screening, scoping, preparation of an EIS and public consultation procedure in line with the requirements of the Aarhus Convention. The EIS (OVOS report) and all project documentation should undergo an SER procedure to ensure the 'environmental suitability' of the proposed development.

According to the Law, SER is also mandatory for the following strategic documents:

• concepts, programmes (including investment programmes) and schemes for sector and territorial social and economic development;
• schemes of complex use and protection of nature resources; and
• city construction documentation (general plans of cities and settlements, designs and schemes of detailed designs).

However, there is no legally defined or prescribed procedure for SER of strategic documents. As a result, SER at the project level is relatively widespread and practice is effective (3000–4000 cases a year with 5–10 per cent of projects rejected or modified as a result of SER). But SER of strategic activities is very rarely conducted and, when undertaken, is not based on a systematic assessment procedure. Several SERs of urban master plans of larger cities (e.g. Minsk) have been conducted in recent years. It is reported that they have resulted in improved environmental components in the plans. In addition, an SER of a national programme of industrial development was conducted and a non-governmental organization (NGO) prepared an informal SEA of the National Strategy for Sustainable Development in 2003.

At the same time, a large number of programmes have been developed in the field of economic and regional development, transport, tourism, agriculture, forestry, energy, and so on, which have not been subjected to systematic SEA. The Government is currently contemplating signing the UN Economic Commission for Europe (UNECE) Kiev SEA Protocol and this may improve the situation. The UN Development Programme (UNDP) and the REC are planning a set of capacity-building activities to facilitate the development of SEA in Belarus.

Source: Prepared by Aleg Cherp (Central European University, Budapest)

use planning did not incorporate a strong SEA dimension because this did not occur in the SER/OVOS systems, in other words there was internal resistance to intrusion into policy and planning mandates and lack of strong incentive to do so.

• Where reforms are being made to OVOS regulations, as in Belarus in 2004 (Box 5.3), the disparity between SER practice at the project and strategic levels will become even more evident. This might lead to improved SEA procedure, but much will depend on countries adopting the SEA Protocol (to the Espoo Convention) and on the capacity-building activities of international agencies.

5.1.5 Recent developments and issues in the Russian Federation

The World Bank has undertaken an in-depth evaluation of the Russian SER/OVOS system (von Ritter and Tsirkunov, 2002). This was precipitated by the abolition of the State Committee of Environmental Protection (SCEP) and the transfer of SER/OVOS responsibilities to the Ministry of Natural Resources (MNR). From the Bank's perspective, the immediate concern was whether or not implementation of SER/OVOS in the Russian Federation was sufficiently robust to ensure environmental compliance with the terms of project-, programme- and policy-based lending agreements. This new operational regime also became the focus of wider attention, internationally and within Russia, where there were differing interpretations. These ranged from the official view that the SER/OVOS system was intact and functioning to NGO concerns that it had collapsed and was unable to implement basic requirements (Khutoleya, 2002).

Whilst there is considerable information on SER/OVOS arrangements, far less is known about how this process works in practice, or performs against internationally accepted principles of EIA and SEA (Box 5.4). Under the applicable Russian legislation, SER is mandatory (SER, Articles 11, 12) and OVOS may apply to strategic actions, including policies, plans, programmes and draft legislation. However as in other NIS, there are no specific guidelines that apply at this level and implementation of the basic provision depends largely on the interpretation of the competent authority and government. Overall, a World Bank study has rated SER/OVOS implementation and performance in relation to strategic actions as low to medium (between 2 and 3 on the following scale[8]) (von Ritter and Tsirkunov, 2002):

- 1 – SEA provision is rarely applied;
- 3 – SEA is sometimes applied, but practice varies because of lack of clear guidance; and
- 5 – SEA is regularly applied in accordance with procedural framework and regulations.

The World Bank study concluded that, in practice, it was reasonable to assume that only a small fraction of strategic proposals are subject to formal SER procedure. The failure to implement this provision is a systemic weakness that relates both to the procedural deficiencies noted above and to more fundamental structural constraints and consequences of recent legal and regulatory reforms (Box 5.4). However, the Bank evaluation also noted a number of positive aspects and examples that can be built on. Box 5.5 provides a case example of a major city plan that was subject to formal SER procedure and included additional SEA-type elements. Other reviews that could be classified as approximating to SEA were undertaken outside the SER/OVOS

---

8   Note that points 2 and 4 on this scale are not defined. The intervening scores are subjective.

BOX 5.4 SEA APPLICATION IN THE RUSSIAN FEDERATION

Recently, significant modifications have been made to the Russian SER/OVOS regime. Some of these developments are positive, but other aspects have weakened its implementation. In practice, procedures and their application are unclear, particularly at the strategic level. Recent legal and regulatory reforms were initiated without clear direction, interpreted differently and implemented unevenly across the regions (*oblasts*) of the Russian Federation. Since then, ongoing restructuring and downsizing have led to declines in institutional capacity to implement EIA- and SEA-related processes and to effectively apply SER expertise. A recent review by the World Bank probed the effectiveness of the Russian SER/OVOS arrangements and their on-the-ground application (von Ritter and Tsirkunov, 2002).

Adequacy of legislation: The legal foundations of Russia's SER/OVOS system are, prima facie, reasonably strong. They include the Law on Ecological Expertise (SER, 1995), Regulations on the Assessment of Environmental Impacts (OVOS, 2000) and the Law on Environmental Protection (2002). Under the latter, measures have been introduced to integrate the SER and OVOS components or sub-systems, although they still remain separate processes (see below). Certain elements of internationally accepted EIA and SEA processes are present, at least in embryonic form. Over the last ten years, new features have been added. These include enabling language that allows regions to develop screening guidelines to distinguish between complex, medium and simple actions and stronger requirements for public participation and information disclosure. Overall, the legal and regulatory framework is assessed as satisfactory (rating of 4 out of 5), providing a supportive framework for EIA and SEA but requiring refinement and attention to procedural gaps.

Effectiveness of implementation: On closer inspection, the SER/OVOS regime is not implemented coherently or systematically and the two sub-systems are not well coordinated. Despite enabling legislation, only a few SER offices have actually developed screening and scoping guidelines, for example Moscow City has prepared a draft regulation. Regions give different explanations for this situation, but ambiguity and ambivalence in the responsibilities of central and territorial authorities are underlying factors. Without such guidelines, case-by-case decisions are made. This adds to preparation costs and time, and creates uncertainty. In relation to strategic actions, it allows proposals to escape prior SER. Also, only EIA (OVOS) procedures have been developed and, in many cases, these are not designed for SEA application. Some provisions might, potentially, be used to address this concern (e.g. the right of NGOs to organize PER. But these must be seen in the context of structural realities such as de facto state secrecy and control of mass media. Overall, the implementation of the SER/OVOS regime is rated as medium–low. This reflects the fact that requirements are not always followed, opportunities provided by the law to apply the system are missed and there are perverse incentives to circumvent application to strategic proposals.

Source: von Ritter and Tsirkunov (2002)

BOX 5.5 SEA OF THE MOSCOW CITY MASTER PLAN FOR THE PERIOD TO YEAR 2020

Moscow City has a long tradition of urban planning and this process became progressively more systematic in the later part of the 20th century. The Moscow City Master Plan for the Period to Year 2020 was developed in 1997–1999 in accordance with existing Russian planning regulations and subject to SER procedure. Other additional, positive elements of the SEA approach were also integrated within (and reinforced) the planning process.

In this case, the major innovation introduced by the developers (the Moscow City Committee for Architecture and Town Planning) was to make the relevant documentation available to all the stakeholders through a permanent exhibition (opened in late 1998). Various aspects of the Master Plan were the focus of expert and public consultation prior to its approval. These included environmental, socioeconomic, sustainability, health and risk issues. The Master Plan was adjusted to consolidate the most important comments and suggestions, and was amended later to incorporate the results of the SER of the Plan (carried out in March 1999).

These additional elements helped to overcome some of the recognized deficiencies of the SER approach, such as lack of consideration of alternatives and limited public participation. The greater transparency resulted in increased public trust in the mechanisms of planning and decision-making. It led to the commitment of the Government to improve social, economic and environmental conditions of the population. Finally, this example appears to have inspired a number of other regions of the Russian Federation to initiate similar SEA-type approaches (beyond SER procedure) as part of their planning processes.

Sources: Leyli Bektashi (based on SEA research in CIT undertaken at the University of Manchester, UK); Moscow City Government (2001) *Moscow City Master Plan for the Period to Year 2020 and Its Implementation*

---

system as part of other frameworks. Examples are the Regional Environmental Action Plan for Greater Rostov and the Sectoral Environmental Action Plan for the chemical industry.

5.2 CENTRAL AND EASTERN EUROPE[9]

Most of the CEE countries have made provision for some form of SEA, including at the policy level. Recently, the pace of SEA adoption and adaptation in the region has been rapid and impressive. For example, the Czech Republic, Slovakia and Poland have each established relatively advanced legal frameworks and built a solid record of SEA practice. Other CEE countries are in different phases of SEA process development and implementation as described below. These activities have been assisted by a continuing exchange of information and views on aspects and lessons of SEA experience within the

---

9   This section draws heavily on Dusik et al (2001), Dusik (2003b) and Dusik and Sadler (2004).

region under the Sofia Initiative. By many standards, this represents one of the more successful innovations in SEA capacity-building, networking and, above all, self-help by the countries concerned and within the region (Box 5.6).

This section describes SEA trends, issues and practice in the CEE region with reference to:

- the foundations of SEA arrangements in place in CEE countries;
- regional trends and issues in SEA law, process and practice;
- the predominant relationship between SEA and land use planning;
- recent experience with SEA of national and regional development plans under the EU accession process; and
- emerging developments in SEA practice at the policy level.

5.2.1 Origins of SEA in CEE

In the ccommunist era prior to 1989, the majority of CEE countries had well-established and relatively sophisticated planning systems. These included macroeconomic, sector development and spatial planning systems and procedures. From an environmental perspective, land use planning was a particularly important instrument for guiding overall financial allocations to competing activities and providing coordination of other processes at the local and regional levels. For example, it provided a mechanism for negotiating limits on the use of a territory. This role distinguished the planning experience in CEE countries from that in the former Soviet Union, where land use planning played a relatively minor role in state decision-making compared to sector and macroeconomic development plans, and contributed to the differing evolution of SEA in the CEE and NIS regions. The three Baltic countries (Estonia, Latvia and Lithuania), although previously part of the former Soviet Union, have a post-communist history that has far more in common with other CEE countries and are now considered part of this larger regional grouping.

Most CEE countries had similar legal frameworks for land use planning, which included basic rights for citizens to comment on proposed plans and stipulations related to protection of the environment and public health. But, with the exception of the former Yugoslavia, these were only partially implemented. At the regional and local level, for example, environmental analyses were carried out. These included mapping environmental vulnerability and resource potentials and identifying the effects of the land use options on areas of importance for landscape or nature conservation. But these analyses were seldom influential in decision-making on major industrial developments. Despite environmental and public heath standards, centralized state planning under the communist regime left a legacy of severe environmental problems. Examples include high levels of air and water pollution and large areas of contaminated land.

Box 5.6 Examples of legal provision for SEA in CEE countries prior to the transposition of Directive 2001/42/EC

Currently, several CEE countries have legislative provision for SEA. Key developments are summarized here:

- *Bulgaria:* The Bulgarian EIA system is based on Chapter 4 of the Environmental Protection Act (1991). The stipulations of the Act are elaborated and EIA procedures are defined by Regulation No 1 (1993). The application of EIA is related to a final decision-making process, such as the approval of a plan or programme or a specific project. Under the Law, an EIA must be carried out for national development programmes, territorial development and urban development plans, as well as for specific projects.

- *Czech Republic:* The Law on Environmental Impact Assessment (No 244/1992) applied to certain 'development concepts' that are submitted and approved at the level of the central authorities of state administration in the fields of energy, transport, agriculture, waste treatment, mining and processing of minerals, recreation and tourism (Article 14). Under this Law, territorial planning documentation and the General Water Management Plan were also 'concepts'. With the amendment of the Czech EIA Act (100/2001), Article 14 or the SEA component was left as a free-standing EIA of the Concepts Act (254/2001). In 2004, Czech EIA legislation was consolidated and amended as part of the transposition of the SEA Directive.

- *Estonia:* The Law on Environmental Impact Assessment and Environmental Audit was passed in June 2000. In Article 22, SEA is defined as 'an assessment of the potential environmental impact resulting from activities proposed by a plan, national development plan or programme'. The Act requires potential impacts to be assessed in the course of drafting plans. It also requires that the assessment is published together with the plan, pursuant to the requirements of the Planning and Building Act, and that the SEA statement constitutes a separate part of a plan, national development plan or programme.

- *Lithuania:* The Environmental Impact Assessment Law (1996) requires initial EIA of all territorial planning. This Law, together with the Territorial Planning Law of 1995, regulates the EIA process for development. The development process is defined as beginning with planning and continuing to a full EIA on technical projects. In this way, it aims to establish the basis for an integrated approach. Government resolutions 1305 (1996) and 456 (1997) identify, respectively, the requirements for informing the public and activities that shall be subject to a full EIA.

- *Poland:* The Law on Access to Information on the Environment, its Protection and Environmental Impact Assessment (2002) incorporates key requirements of EC EIA Directives 97/11, 85/337 and 90/311, the EU SEA Directive (as then proposed in COM/96/511, COM/99/73) and the UNECE Espoo and Aarhus Conventions. The SEA requirements apply to policies, plans and programmes that are required by law (as opposed to administrative provision). A uniform public participation procedure applies to EIA and SEA and is governed by the provisions of the Aarhus Convention.

- *Slovakia:* The Slovak Law on Environmental Impact Assessment (EIA Act 127/1994, amended 2000) provides for a comprehensive approach to SEA. Part 4 of the EIA Act (Article 35) outlines a brief procedure for EIA. This is obligatory for proposed development policies in the areas of energy supply, mining, industry, transport,

> agriculture, forestry and water management, waste management and tourism, and for legislative proposals that may have an adverse impact on the environment. In addition, EIA is required for territorial planning documentation for regional and residential settlement in selected areas, and for plans of optional location of linear constructions (transport, pipelines).
>
> • *Slovenia*: EIA is required for physical plans under Articles 53 and 54 of the Environmental Protection Act (No 801-01/90-2/107, 1993). Specific regulations for EIA of physical plans have not yet been adopted. But, according to Article 54.2, a comprehensive EIA study must be prepared by the body responsible for the preparation of the physical planning document or sector plan. Under Article 51, planning, programming and designing of activities shall be based on an environmental vulnerability study.
>
> *Source:* Dusik et al (2001); updated by Dusik (personal communication)

5.2.2 Recent developments in SEA arrangements and implementation

The collapse of socialist regimes started a period of democratization, economic restructuring and institutional reforms, including the overhaul and modification of central planning systems and their infrastructure. Land use planning systems were considerably simplified but remained a major decision-making instrument. Many CEE countries introduced EIA requirements within deregulated spatial or land use planning frameworks and integrated them with elements of traditional environmental analyses (e.g. in Bulgaria, the Czech Republic, Lithuania, Poland, Slovakia and Slovenia). In addition, EIA legislation in CEE countries also applies to certain plans and programmes at the sector level. Generally, there is less experience at this level compared to the SEA of spatial plans, although sector applications are increasing rapidly in some countries and others have undertaken pilot studies (Table 5.3).

Some countries have provision for SEA of strategies and policies, as well as plans and programmes, notably the Czech Republic, Slovakia and Poland (see Box 5.6). In the first two cases, SEA applies to 'concepts' that are submitted to national governments for approval. These requirements were not implemented systematically in the early phase of EIA development (from 1992 in the Czech Republic and 1994 in Slovakia) because there was a lack of understanding of what such a process might entail.[10] Consequently, there was little or no procedural guidance. Pilot applications at this level of decision-making began in 1997 when both countries undertook large-scale SEAs of their respective national energy policies. Since then, considerable experience has been gained with SEA of policy, particularly in the Czech Republic. To date, Slovakia remains the only CEE country with provision for SEA of legislative proposals. But there is no specific guidance on this requirement and only a pilot application has been made (SEA of the Slovak Waste Management Act in 2000).

---

10 This illustrates the nature of these early reform processes when legal frameworks were often formulated on an experimental 'trial and error' basis.

Table 5.3 *Overview of the status of SEA provision in CEE countries*

Level of SEA	Legal frameworks	Comments on practical application
Plans and programmes within a framework of spatial planning	Partial environmental analyses in land use planning required in all CEE countries since the 1980s.	Partial environmental analyses still used extensively within land use planning systems in virtually all CEE countries.
	SEA of key spatial planning documents required in Poland (1991), Bulgaria (1992), the Czech Republic (1992), Slovenia (1993) Slovakia (1994) and Lithuania (1996).	SEA in land use planning most extensively applied in Poland (over 300 regional and local land use plans have been subject to SEA since 1991). SEA also applied for land use plans in Bulgaria (over 130 SEAs for local urban plans since 1997) and the Czech Republic (over 25 SEAs for regional land use plans since 1992). But both countries report problems in effective integration of SEA into planning.
	New SEA frameworks to be established by the transposition of the SEA Directive by July 2004.	SEA practice in Slovakia, Slovenia and Lithuania still in early stage of development, partly because of a lack of official guidance.
Sectoral plans, and programmes outside spatial planning framework	Legal provisions for SEA established in the Czech Republic (1992), Slovakia (1994), Poland (2000), Estonia (2000) and Bulgaria (2001).	Practice rapidly emerging in Poland (e.g., over 30 SEAs reported on regional level in 2002–2003).
	New SEA frameworks to be established by the transposition of the SEA Directive by July 2004.	Quite extensively used in the Czech Republic (over 15, mainly national, SEAs up to 2003). Initial practices emerging in Estonia (e.g. five SEAs projects up to 2003).
Programming documents for EU structural funds in all EU accession countries	EC Regulation 1269/99/EC and related EC guidance (EC, 1998) requires applicant countries to carry out thorough ex ante assessment that also covers environmental issues for all development plans and the subsequent operational programme.	SEA applied to nine national plans and programmes for EU structural funds in the Czech Republic between 2000 and 2003. Large-scale pilot SEAs for key programming documents for EU structural funds undertaken with donor assistance in Estonia, Hungary, Poland and Latvia. Smaller-scale pilot projects to test possible SEA application within the programming process for EU structural funds in Slovenia and Bulgaria.
Policies	General legal provisions established in the Czech Republic (1992), Slovakia (1994) and Estonia (2001).	Ten SEAs completed in the Czech Republic and four in Slovakia for national policies up to 2003. First pilot SEA applications for national policies or strategies undertaken in Poland and Estonia.
Legislative proposals	Legally required in Slovakia (1994) and Hungary (1995).	Occasionally applied in Hungary. Practice in Slovakia limited by lack of official guidance.

Source: Dusik and Sadler (2004)

As part of EU accession, most CEE countries have been engaged in a lengthy process of both structural and legal reform. This has included harmonization of their planning and regulatory regime with that of the European Community. In addition to countries improving existing planning frameworks (e.g. for waste or river basin management) and establishing new ones (e.g. for regional development), two other SEA developments in this region are particularly noteworthy:

- First, CEE countries were required to assess their proposed plans and programmes for future use of the EU structural funds in accordance with EC Regulation 1269/99/EC and subsequent guidance. Several countries have now carried out comprehensive SEA-type processes in that regard, including the Czech Republic, Poland, Estonia, Hungary and Latvia.
- Second, since 2001, CEE countries have worked on transposing the SEA Directive into their national legislation. This process was formally completed by July 2004 following the CEE countries joining the EU and the SEA Directive entering into force.

At the time of writing,[11] the new generation of SEA arrangements in CEE countries has still to emerge. In particular, it remains to be seen whether those countries that mandate SEA of policy will retain or remove that provision (it is not required by the SEA Directive and is discretionary under the SEA Protocol). This provision is enshrined in the amended Czech EIA Act (100/2004). This maintains the broad focus of SEA (e.g. covering policies, strategies, plans and programmes) at all levels of government, whilst extending the procedure laid down in earlier legislation and the factors to be considered (Box 5.7). Key requirements relate to early notification of the concept to the affected authorities prior to beginning a strategic planning process, to screening and scoping procedures and to other provisions laid down in Directive 2001/42/EC. Additional specific provisions apply to SEA of a land use plan document. The new Act also extends the scope of SEA to include consideration of the impact of 'concepts' on public health as well as the environment (i.e. consistent with the SEA Protocol).

5.2.3 SEA practice in land use planning

Between 1996 and 2003, the REC and the Sofia Initiative on EIA organized a series of workshops on SEA practice in land use planning in the CEE region. This process was instrumental in benchmarking the development and status of this process:

- Land use planning and SEA procedure have many elements in common. Both require definition of issues, public participation and review of draft documents prior to submission to political decision-making. However, traditional land use planning gives limited consideration to alternatives and assessment of their environmental and social impacts, and CEE countries have looked to strengthen this relationship.

BOX 5.7 SECOND GENERATION OF SEA ARRANGEMENTS IN THE CZECH REPUBLIC

In 2004, Czech EIA legislation was consolidated and amended as part of the transposition of the SEA Directive. The EIA Act (100/2004) includes a new Article 10 that stipulates requirements for SEA of 'concepts' in listed sectors. Concepts cover polices, plans, programmes, strategies or other strategic initiatives that are prepared or adopted by public authorities and set a framework for activities that require EIA or that are co-financed by the EU. When such a concept is proposed, the proponent must notify – before formal initiation – the relevant environmental authority and provide comprehensive information about the nature of the planning process. This information is used in SEA screening and scoping. If an SEA is required, this phase concludes by determining its scope and the manner in which SEA should be undertaken. The SEA report is prepared in accordance with this guidance and, once finalized, is subject to a public hearing and review by relevant authorities, including environmental and health bodies. The SEA's conclusion on the proposed concept is issued by the relevant environmental authority.

Source: Prepared by Jiri Dusik (Regional Environmental Center for Central and Eastern Europe)

- A particular concern was whether SEA should be integrated into the planning process or conducted as a parallel, independent process in light of the realities, opportunities and constraints in different countries. These and related issues were addressed in a number of pilot experiments, and practical applications were undertaken by the agencies responsible (see below).
- Although progress has been made, SEA has yet to be fully integrated into land use planning processes. Appropriate procedural and methodological guidance is lacking. Land use planners in the region are reluctant to modify their procedures to incorporate or replace partial environmental analyses with more thorough assessment of the impact of a proposed plan.
- Other areas and aspects of SEA practice remain superficial. In particular, little or no attention is given to cumulative effects or to health and socioeconomic impacts. However, this situation is beginning to change, particularly in respect of health. The latter is the focus of increasing work as a result of the requirement to address health issues in the SEA Protocol.
- Quality and effectiveness of SEA practice are variable. In many countries they have not yet advanced beyond a basic level. This reflects the lack of resources, procedural controls (checks and balances) and methodological guidance. Public consultation in SEA is widely promoted in CEE countries but, in reality, opportunities are often restricted and methods are inadequate.
- Despite such concerns, the overall trend is positive in CEE countries. It appears to be leading to better SEA of land use plans and related processes. Recent experience indicates that SEA is becoming integrated within land use planning and decision-making processes. But there has been less

progress than was expected at the outset of the Sofia Initiative on EIA, and experience varies amongst CEE countries.

Poland is widely considered to be a regional leader in this area of SEA practice (see Table 5.3). For example, Parol (2003) reports that, since 1991, SEA-type processes have been applied to over 300 regional and local land use plans. Yet formal requirements for SEA were only introduced in 1995 and applied only to the local level. SEA of regional plans has occurred under informal arrangements and pilot schemes that promote procedural integration of the steps of assessment in land use planning (Rzeszot, 1999, 2001). By comparison, in the Czech Republic, about 25 regional land use plans had been subject to SEA by the end of 2003. A relatively separate SEA-type process was used to compare land use options – a compulsory requirement. SEA was based on detailed maps and overlays prepared under the direct supervision of the environmental authority. A similar approach has been followed in Bulgaria, Slovakia and other CEE countries.

Reviews of initial experience with this approach indicate that a number of deficiencies remain to be addressed. In many cases, SEA was undertaken too late in the land use planning process to provide real input into, or to influence, decision-making. Early applications were hampered by a lack of practical guidance and readily available methods. In the interim, however, much has been learned from SEA practice. Examples of SEA of land use plans from Latvia (Box 5.8), Bulgaria (Box 5.9) and Slovakia (Box 5.10) illustrate evolving realities of CEE practice at this level (see also Table 5.3). These cases may be of wider interest when relating SEA and spatial planning in other transitional or start-up situations.

5.2.4 SEA of sector plans and programmes

Several accession countries in the CEE region have made provision for this level of SEA (see Table 5.3). Major sectors of SEA application include transport, energy, waste and tourism. So this experience may be seen as preparation for implementing the SEA Directive in the countries concerned. However, except in the Czech Republic, SEA practice is not extensive. But it may be stronger than 'internally driven' activities suggest (see below). Countries have gained familiarity and experience with sector plan elements from SEA application within spatial planning frameworks. Also, SEA of sector plans and programmes in the CEE region often has a strong spatial dimension. For example, the Slovenia Environmental Protection Act (1993) requires that plans and programmes are based on environmental vulnerability analysis. This methodology also underpins SEA of sector as well as spatial plans, as exemplified in the SEA of the National Transport Plan (Box 5.11).

A more comprehensive approach incorporates analysis of the consistency of policies and plans as well as a qualitative environmental and health risk assessment. This is exemplified by the SEA of the waste management plan (WMP) for the Czech Republic (Box 5.12). In this case, the national-level plan

---

Box 5.8 SEA of the Jurmala Territorial Development Plan, Latvia

Jurmala is located 30km from Riga. It occupies a narrow coastal strip between the Gulf of Riga and the River Lielupe. The administrative territory covers 8937ha and is rich in natural resources. The town itself is well known in Latvia as a health resort and has approximately 60,000 inhabitants.

The Territorial Development Plan is the basis for future land use in Jurmala and district. It is intended to establish the environmental and socioeconomic preconditions for sustainable development. An area-wide assessment was undertaken to clarify resource potentials and optimize land use, with reference to ecological process and to different functions. These included cost-effective public transport and energy use, minimizing impacts of development activities and setting aside natural areas such as wildlife corridors. In drafting the plan and undertaking the assessment, links were made with other policies and actions in neighbouring municipalities and the larger district. This included work on planning for Kemeri National Park where coordination was particularly close.

The Jurmala Plan was developed during a transitional period in the political and planning systems of Latvia. Local officials were unfamiliar with the SEA-type approach, and with incorporating environmental considerations into decision-making. As a result, the assessment and planning components were not synchronized and public consultation and input into the process were minimal. Also, the lack of experience and limited resources restricted the consideration of alternatives (these were accepted largely on technical rather than environmental grounds).

More positively, assessment resulted primarily in the incorporation of mitigation measures into the plan, including:

* zoning terms and conditions;
* allocation of green space (e.g. wildlife corridors); and primarily
* promotion of alternative transport (e.g. bicycles, footpaths).

In these circumstances, integration was totally dependent on how the early stages of the planning and assessment process were carried out and, equally importantly, who was present and from which authority. Essentially, the best results occur through personal contact and communication rather than sending out documents for review and feedback. As far as possible, planners and assessors should carry out their work jointly and with a specific aim of 'learning by doing' from each other. This is important in transitional countries and situations where land use planning has not yet taken on a fully comprehensive environmental dimension and where there is relatively little experience with the conduct of SEA.

Source: Rotbergh (1998)

---

sets a framework for the preparation of regional waste management plans and facility location. Regional waste management plans (also subject to SEA) set binding targets and suggest preferred approaches that should be considered in the elaboration of specific waste management projects (which are subject to EIA).

Box 5.9 SEA of the Varna Municipality Development Plan, Bulgaria

Introduction: The Varna Municipality Development Plan (MDP) was part of a World Bank-financed programme of development of the Bulgarian Black Sea coast. This programme included the preparation of an act for management of the Black Sea coast and the surrounding area, the elaboration of the regional structure for the development of the Black Sea coast and the preparation of development plans for the 14 municipalities of this region. Each plan was subject to a pilot SEA. Collectively, these represented the first practical application of this process in Bulgaria. A number of problems were encountered in carrying out these SEA processes: determining the scope of the SEA; organizing meetings for public discussion of the report; and fulfilling the conditions stipulated in the decisions. The SEA of the Varna MDP exemplifies the advantages and disadvantages of the approach taken.

Background: According to the Varna MDP, the municipality should function as a resort centre with tourism in the littoral zone as a priority development. The area has natural potential (preserved flora and fauna) and elements of cultural and historical heritage. But the quality of air and coastal water in the urban area does not meet required standards. There are concerns regarding the health of the population (a high mortality rate). It is proposed to relocate some industries away from the coastal area, concentrating them in existing industrial zones. Infrastructure (water supply, sewerage, power and transport) and health facilities are well developed.

SEA process: The Bulgarian EIA system applies to national development programmes, territorial development and urban development plans as well as projects. SEA of plans is carried out in accordance with the requirements of the Environmental Protection Act (1991), EIA Regulations (1993, 1995) and the Territorial and Settlement Planning Law (1973) and the Special Regulations. Under this regime, the SEA procedure for plans is determined on a case-by-case basis by the Minister of the Environment and Water and is an obligatory requirement for the approval of a plan. The main purpose of SEA is to integrate environmental conditions into territorial and urban development.

Key elements of this process include:

- use of registered experts to carry out the SEA independently;
- public notification of the procedure and access to documentation;
- mandatory identification of the reasons for the proposal, location, technological alternatives and measures for mitigating adverse consequences;
- preparation of a statement describing the environmental conditions and impacts of the plan (e.g. on air, water, flora, fauna, relief, soils, landscape, cultural heritage);
- obligation on the competent body to hold a public meeting to discuss EIA results; and
- opportunity for a legal appeal against the decision.

Dualities in the approach to planning and SEA: In Bulgaria, as in other CEE countries, spatial planning is based on analysis of environmental conditions and potentials and of socioeconomic infrastructure. SEA focuses on analysis of environmental elements and sensitivities in relation to plan priorities and directions. Inevitably, this duplication of environmental analysis within the planning and assessment frameworks has led to discussion about who should undertake this component (see also below). Similarly, both procedures require public participation when reviewing the final planning and assessment documentation. Potentially, this can lead to two different public participation processes. In reality, the two procedures are implemented by different administrations, which do not always consult each other. In this case, however, practical progress was achieved by the two responsible institutions for planning and assessment holding a joint public meeting to review the results of both processes.

Major issues during the SEA process: As with other SEA pilots, there were problems regarding the scope of assessment and the type of information to be included. A significant issue regarding scope (particularly the description and analysis of the existing environmental situation) was the lack of conformity between the legal provisions for territorial planning and environmental assessment. It is mandatory that spatial planning includes studying the existing environmental conditions in order to establish the development framework. SEA of plans and actions must also examine the existing situation. There was also considerable debate on whether the SEA should be based only on available data or would require further research.

This remains a major question as it applies to SEA of plans and has not been settled yet. In the Varna case, time and resource limitations meant that only currently available data was used, even though there were complex technical issues to be addressed regarding waste management, water supply and energy. Regional waste disposal is advocated in the plan because of limited space within the municipality. But assessment experts preferred a local solution for effective control. Water supply and energy sources lie outside the municipality's territory. So proposals for their future development had to be considered through an area-wide assessment involving three neighbouring municipalities (Varna, Beloslav and Aksakovo).

Results and implications: When canvassed, the main parties involved in the SEA process made several points:

- EIA specialists emphasized the importance of applying the SEA procedure from the earliest phase of plan preparation. They identified a need to address discrepancies in the role, scope and relationship of the two processes – beginning with their respective laws.
- Decision-makers noted that although this was the first practical attempt to apply SEA in Bulgaria, there was little or no public interest during the SEA review. They also identified the lack of correspondence between the Planning Act and the Environmental Protection Act as a major problem.
- Planners perceived that territorial planning and SEA had the same aim to contribute to the sustainable development of territories. They considered that SEA should have a short scope and that compliance with the planning process must be voluntary.
- NGOs supported the SEA procedure as useful input to plans, particularly because it guarantees public access and improves transparency.

As a result of the above findings, the Ministry of the Environment and Water amended the EIA Regulations to clarify the procedure in relation to the planning process.

Key lessons: The effective implementation of SEA of territorial plans depends on:

- better coordination amongst all decision-making authorities;
- early determination of the scope of SEA and the guiding principles of the process;
- application of SEA in parallel with the planning process rather than after the fact;
- opportunity for public involvement in all phases of SEA and planning and not just in the EIS review; and
- taking account of public input in EIS preparation and decision-making.

Source: Grigorova and Metodieva (2001)

Box 5.10 SEA of the Bratislava Land Use Plan, Slovakia

According to Article 35 of the 1994 EIA Act, draft land use plan documents must contain an assessment of the environmental impact and mitigation measures to address the adverse effects. In addition, the plan 'proponent' must discuss the predicted impacts and proposed compensations with the Ministry of Environment. However, there is no official methodology or rules for undertaking SEA in accordance with these and other requirements. But draft guidelines were prepared for SEA of policies (Kozová et al, 1994, 1996, 2000) and landuse plans (Finka et al, 1997; Krumpolcová et al, 1997, 1998). These have not been approved or issued but remain on file in the Ministry of Environment and can be informally consulted.

New methodological principles for SEA in land use planning proposed in the above documents include:

- coordination of different sector policies with respect to sustainable development;
- full consideration of ecological, social and economic issues; and
- SEA as assistance in land use planning procedures towards sustainable development.

A voluntary SEA of the draft Bratislava Land Use Plan was undertaken between October 2000 and March 2001 to verify the above principles. Environmental issues have been considered in land use planning in Slovakia for many years, but the focus has been on describing existing conditions rather than the impacts on the environment of actions set out in plans. SEA provides an opportunity to generate more environmental information, particularly on impacts. It provides both a 'controlling' mechanism and helps to bring greater transparency and democracy into the land use planning process. Related objectives are to increase the quality and acceptance of the plan and to promote citizen involvement in its implementation.

Three 'blueprint' variants of the Bratislava Land Use Plan concept were prepared – each stating a general objective to promote sustainable development. But they specified only alternative costs rather than differences in approach.

The SEA procedure followed a two-tier approach:

- First, a strategic evaluation was undertaken of the goals, aims and aspects of the Plan against sustainability principles and criteria – selected from the international literature. A (rather general and abstract) comparative matrix was constructed as a sustainability test.
- Second, a relatively detailed evaluation was made of the Plan against sustainability criteria and indicators. This used both tables and map graphics, together with cumulative assessment; and both qualitative and quantitative indicators, drawn from relevant case studies in Germany and the UK.

The Slovak Land Use Planning Act requires a public hearing to be held to present and debate draft plans. In this case, some 50 meetings were organized for different stakeholder groups and the general public. They focused on particular aspects of the Plan, e.g. transport, housing and the countryside. All planning documents were open for public review and comment over a four-month period from December 2000 to March 2001 in Bratislava City Hall. Over 20,000 written comments were submitted but it is not clear how these were used in revising the Plan.

The report of the SEA followed a structure similar to that recommended by the EU Directive on SEA. Sections covered:

- comparison of the objectives of the Comprehensive Development Strategy of Bratislava City and those of the three alternative land use plans (using a sustainable development test);
- assessment of environmental quality to identify positive and adverse environmental impacts of individual land use plan policies (e.g. housing, technical and social infrastructure);
- selection of individual plan policies to be evaluated and criteria to be used; and
- identification of mitigation measures (mostly for lower levels in the hierarchy of land use plans and for EIA of projects).

The report was submitted for review to the Ministry of Environment, which provided its comments to Bratislava City Authority (unpublished).

Lessons from experience with this SEA include:

- The SEA was initiated late in the land use plan preparation process; it would have been far more effective if conducted proactively and initiated at the outset of the planning process.
- SEA should be linked (procedurally and methodologically) to a tiered approach at different levels of land use planning.
- The sustainability goals set out in the Bratislava Development Strategy were too general.

Sources: Belčáková (2003a, b); SEA undertaken collaboratively by the EIA Centre, Slovak University of Technology, and the Faculty of Natural Sciences, Commenius University, both in Bratislava

5.2.5 SEA of programming documents for EU structural funds in all EU accession countries

In addition to internally driven processes, EU accession has been an external force for SEA development at the level of national and regional plans and sector programmes in CEE countries. Article 41 of Regulation 1260/1999/EC specifically requires applicant countries to undertake an 'ex ante evaluation' of such initiatives for the use of structural funds for the period 2000–2006. This evaluation includes the potential environmental impact and applicant countries are expected to follow guidance laid down in:

- Vademecum, Plans and Programming Documents for Structural Funds 2000–2006 (DG XI, 1999); and
- Handbook on Environmental Assessment of Regional Development Funds and EU Structural Funds (DG XI, 1998).

Within a relatively short period of time, CEE accession countries have gained considerable experience in SEA-type work under the above EU regime. The

Box 5.11 Methodology and approach to SEA of major transport routes in Slovenia

Introduction: A two-part pilot SEA study was undertaken before adoption of the regulations for SEA of physical planning documents (pursuant to Articles 53 and 54 of the Environment Protection Act, 1993):

* assessment of the proposed changes to the National Physical Plan for Transportation; and
* development of a proposed methodology for similar, location-oriented cases (the main focus below).

Main objectives of the pilot SEA (set in the scoping phase):

* consideration of certain alignment alternatives: proposed corridors for new highways, railways and roads; and proposed alternatives within one corridor for transport modes;
* identification of potential environmental impacts and issues, for example changes in soil, air, water, landscape, habitats, natural resources and cultural heritage;
* delineation of relevant impact zone or study boundaries (i.e. Slovenia in its entirety); and
* selection of approach – vulnerability/sensitivity modelling as the most appropriate methodology, and geographic information system (GIS) as the most appropriate technique.

Assessment methodology: In the impact assessment phase, the proposed changes were assessed by a preliminary vulnerability evaluation of the entire territory of Slovenia, using existing data. A five-stage approach was followed:

1   Three distinctive aspects of environmental protection were defined:
    – naturocentric – originating in the demand for nature conservation;
    – anthropocentric – protection of the human environment for the present; and
    – anthropocentric – conservation of resources for future generations.
2   Vulnerability was defined in terms of areas and/or environmental components with high intrinsic quality or elements, in other words where transport routes and activity cause a significant loss. Examples of criteria used include:
    – degree of wilderness and naturalness (nature protection objective);
    – quality and quantity of drinking water (human health and next generation objective); and
    – high potential for recreation (resource conservation objective).
3   Expert inputs were used to define relevant vulnerability models, their parameters and rules for combining them into particular and composite vulnerability maps. An example is the approach for the water environment which included:
    – hydrology – mapping stream buffer zones, water quality, groundwater recharge areas and flood zones;
    – natural heritage – areas of high value rated for their uniqueness, diversity or aesthetic quality; and
    – erosion and stability – areas that were sensitive, unstable or slow to regenerate.
4   An assessment was undertaken of the impact of all proposed or potential transport alignments and activities on the vulnerable environments of Slovenia, as well as

assessment of each section and activity. Overlays, GIS, workshops and expert groups were amongst the tools and analytical techniques used.

5 Significance of impacts was defined by reference to five categories: (i) negligible impact, (ii) small impact, (iii) moderate impact, (iv) severe impact and (v) inadmissible impact. This fifth category denotes activities within the area of the Triglav National Park. Other categories were defined by proportion of vulnerable and protected areas, prime agricultural land, productive resources, and so on.

Summary of findings: The proposed plan was adopted without major changes. The results of the vulnerability assessment were taken into account at lower planning levels. The evaluation indicated that, at the higher planning levels, the transport routes would have a relatively severe impact in terms of the ratio of vulnerable areas covered. However, the assessors cautioned that this should not be automatically construed as a criticism of the planning. Rather the environmental impact of the national plan was as much a consequence of the spatial qualities and features of the Slovenian territory (rugged relief, narrow valleys, karst landscapes). More rigorous environmental standards need to be incorporated into transport planning and design particularly in high vulnerability areas.

Source: Koblar (1998)

Fourth Regional Workshop of the Sofia EIA Initiative was held in Bratislava (19–21 May 1999). It reviewed the SEA experience in CEE countries to identify basic directions for SEA application and capacity-building in the CEE region (Box 5.13). Some of the workshop conclusions have already been overtaken by the international regime established by the SEA Directive (2001/42/EC). This does not apply to the current phase of structural funding (ending in 2006), but will be in force for the next round. Recently, lessons have been derived from several pilot projects on SEA of large-scale national and regional development plans and programmes.[12] These provide pointers to future good practice with SEA of development plans using EU structural funds. The benefits have been recognized by senior decision-makers involved in the programming process (see Box 5.14).

In three countries (the Czech Republic, Estonia and Hungary), the SEA pilots highlighted the importance of initial review of analytical components of strategic plans and programmes. This can ensure that attention is given to environmental trends and linkages, problems and opportunities in subsequent stages of the planning process. By contrast, in Poland, it was not possible to carry out this task because the domestic planning process began with the identification of proposed activities. It continued with establishing objectives to fit these activities, and concluded with an analysis to justify proposed interventions. In this case, the SEA started by identifying relevant environmental objectives for the National Development Plan and then evaluated the proposed activities and development objectives (see Case Study

12 Large-scale pilots were undertaken in the Czech Republic, Poland, Estonia and Hungary. Smaller-scale pilots were carried out in Slovenia and Bulgaria. Full information can be found in REC (2003).

BOX 5.12 SEA OF THE WASTE MANAGEMENT PLAN OF THE CZECH REPUBLIC

Background – context and issues: The Waste Management Plan (WMP) was prepared in 2002 as a framework document for the period 2003–2012. It sets out objectives and demand-and-supply measures for managing the main types of waste. It will be complemented by regional waste management plans to identify the technology and location for specific facilities. A mandatory component of the WMP is coverage of hazardous, medical and PCB-contaminated waste.

Introduction: The SEA of the WMP was carried out as a separate, parallel process with four main steps:

- scoping (based on an extensive process of public consultation);
- review of the detailed terms of reference for SEA;
- preparation of an SEA report; and
- public review of the SEA report.

Key features of the SEA approach and methods used:

(a) *Consideration of alternatives:* The plan was prepared in two major alternatives:

- an official version of the proposal developed by the proponent (Ministry of Environment); and
- a 'green' alternative developed by a local network of NGO experts, with financial support provided by the proponent.

(b) *Selection and analysis of issues and alternatives:*

- use of a matrix to identify and compare the environmental and health risks of various waste management approaches; this included the collection, separation and transport of waste, use of waste as a source of secondary materials and incineration of waste for production of energy;
- ranking of the waste management options, to provide a basis for general comments on proposed measures;
- evaluation of environmental risks through collective expert judgement (expressed in relative terms such as 'poor', 'good', 'nearly sufficient', etc.);
- use of a matrix to identify potential environmental and health impacts of proposed objectives and measures of the WMP, and of all specific proposals of the plan, through collective expert judgement and a simple rating scale (+ good, 0 neutral, − adverse); and
- review of internal consistency of the plan including whether objectives corresponded with issues raised in the analysis, or if suggested indicators were appropriate measures of the attainment of specific objectives.

Based on this assessment, the SEA team identified numerous inconsistencies amongst plan objectives and measures, issues and indicators. For example, many indicators were considered to be either irrelevant or unrealistic with regard to data gathering. This consistency analysis is strongly reflected in the concluding sections of the SEA report.

(c) *Public participation:* A single process was organized for both the planning and SEA. Information was distributed in various ways including a dedicated website and email address for comments. A network of regional coordinators also facilitated the dissemination of information and organized regional workshops. The main opportunities for public participation were provided by workshops organized for key stages of the process:

- initial review of the draft plan and scoping of issues to be addressed in the SEA (14 regional and two national workshops, attended respectively by between ten and 25, and 50 persons in each case);
- review of the detailed terms of reference for SEA at a national workshop (following comments on the proposed assessment methodology in the scoping phase); and
- the SEA report was reviewed through two national workshops (each attended by approximately 30 persons).

Results and lessons: The SEA showed a number of positive aspects (indicated above). In the final analysis, however, it is difficult to establish the contribution that the SEA made to the WMP process. From an SEA perspective, the planning process was insufficiently structured and lacked transparency. From a planning perspective, the SEA process was overly concerned with methodology and report preparation rather than influencing decision-making at different stages of plan development.

Source: Dusik (2003d)

5.2). A similar approach was followed in the SEA pilots in Slovenia and Bulgaria, where the entire assessment was based on the review of proposed actions against pre-established environmental objectives and criteria. One of the lessons of the pilots was that objectives-led SEA is a necessary but not sufficient key to good practice (Box 5.15).

5.2.6 SEA of policy

To date, SEA of policies and higher-level strategies in the CEE region is limited primarily to the Czech Republic, Slovakia and Poland. All three countries have EIA legislation that applies at this level (see Box 5.5). In the Czech Republic and Slovakia, there is now considerable experience with SEA of policies that generally fall under the category of development 'concepts'. SEA practice and case examples from these countries are notable internationally because the procedures of policy elaboration and SEA application are relatively systematic, involve the public and result in the environmental authority issuing a statement on the proposal. Czech SEA practice is also of interest because it can be implemented through an EIA-derived or an appraisal-based approach, and most assessments comprise a mix of elements.

In both the Czech Republic and Slovakia, large-scale pilot applications of SEA of national policy began with the energy sector and laid the groundwork for process development and practice (Box 5.16, Case Studies 5.1 and 5.3). This was followed in the Czech Republic by application to a range of other

Box 5.13 SEA of national (regional) development plans in CEE

The Fourth Regional EIA Workshop of the Sofia EIA Initiative (Bratislava, 19–21 May 1999) brought together 72 participants from ministries of environment and regional development, together with SEA experts from ten CEE countries. The following key conclusions were reached:

Role of SEA within development planning in the CEE region

- SEA is an important tool for practical implementation of sustainable development. Governments and institutions responsible for policy-making and planning should encourage its application on both a formal and informal basis.
- The preparation of development plans for the use of EU structural funds represents an important opportunity for wider strengthening of SEA systems in the CEE region. It is unclear whether the European Commission will require a systematic SEA procedure within ex ante evaluation of national development plans and related programming documents (rural development plans and investment strategies).
- The Commission should clearly state its position in respect of SEA as a mandatory requirement and the quality standards that should be met. Without such a statement, it is evident that the national development plans of most CEE countries (except the Czech Republic, Estonia and Slovenia) will not be subject to this procedure.

Relatively easy and transparent procedures for the SEA of national development plans and related programming documents should be introduced, tested and broadly disseminated in CEE countries prior to the elaboration of more sophisticated SEA methodologies.

Capacity-building for SEA in the CEE region

- The quality of SEA in the CEE region is dependent on methodological know-how, availability of adequate information and institutional and professional capacities. There is a pressing need for SEA capacity-building amongst policy-makers and practitioners.
- In CEE accession counties, building capacity for SEA to EU standards may be facilitated by improved exchange of information between the CEE countries and member states and between the Commission and EU member states. An important aspect will be the continued exchange of experience amongst CEE countries themselves under the framework of the Sofia Initiative.
- Both EIA and SEA capacity-building needs are particularly acute in the non-accession countries of Southeast Europe. Direct exchange of experience amongst Balkan and other CEE countries should be a matter of priority for the European Commission and other multilateral and bilateral donors. (This recommendation was subsequently taken forward as the regional reconstruction for environment programme.)

BOX 5.14 SEA OF DEVELOPMENT PLANS FROM THE PERSPECTIVE OF DECISION-MAKERS

SEA is not a complicated and theoretical tool. It is a flexible mechanism that gave us feedback from environmental experts. It ran in parallel to the elaboration of the Estonian Single Programming Document and provided operative and practical inputs. It helped us to improve quality of the document and increased awareness among NGOs of the entire planning process.

(Kerli Lorvi, Ministry of Finance, Estonia)

The SEA for the first National Development Plan of **Poland** *provided us with useful recommendations for improved consideration of environmental issues. The SEA has a wider applicability and can also be used in elaboration of other documents. We will be able to use the lessons learned and methodology developed in the future.*

(Piotr Zuber, Ministry of Economy, Labour and Social Policy, Poland)

SEA helped us to improve the quality of the **Hungarian** *Regional Operational Programme. Proponents of this programme often did not take into account natural resources, which form the basis of any economic activity. The SEA team identified the main relevant environmental issues and helped us to consider this information throughout the entire planning process. SEA also facilitated our cooperation with the Ministry of Environment, other sectoral ministries and regional authorities during environmental optimizing of the programme.*

(Ágnes Somfai, Prime Minister's Office, Hungary)

SEA was very useful experience in elaboration of the **Czech** *National Development Plan. It had benefits that went beyond its original purpose of ensuring full consideration of sustainable development during the planning process. SEA helped us to improve openness of the entire programming process and established a 'bridge' between the planning team and the public. This turned out to be very positive feature that we later very much appreciated.*

(Tomas Nejdl, Ministry of Regional Development, the Czech Republic)

Source: Dusik et al (2003)

---

sectors and more than 20 policy concepts have been subject to SEA. For example, the SEA of the National Tourism Policy (2002–2007) was carried out through an interactive process. This was characterized by strong cooperation between the proponent (the Ministry of Regional Development) and the Ministry of Environment. Opportunities for public input and comment were provided through a seminar, public hearings and web-based submissions. The policy document was assessed and altered at key stages of the process in response to public inputs and the SEA findings. In addition, the SEA team initiated changes to the analysis of the situation and the establishment of strategic targets for the sustainable development of tourism.

BOX 5.15 USE OF ENVIRONMENTAL OBJECTIVES IN THE SEA OF PLANS AND PROGRAMMES

The SEA pilots were undertaken in Bulgaria, the Czech Republic, Estonia, Hungary and Poland to assess programming documents for EU structural funds. They demonstrated important practical lessons for the objectives-led approach advocated by Sadler and Verheem (1996). The assessment of proposed development objectives and actions against relevant environmental objectives provided an opportunity for early review of proposed strategies and their relation to sustainable development. However, environmental objectives proved difficult to identify because they were:

- too general (e.g. lacking clear sector- or region-specific objectives);
- mutually inconsistent or overlapping (as well as conflicting with development policies); and/or
- irrelevant as benchmarks for evaluating plans and programmes.

As such, SEA cannot rely only on appraisal of consistency of proposed initiatives with pre-established environmental objectives. Critical review and adjustment are also needed to ensure their relevance and applicability for each strategic proposal. Examples of the approaches taken include:

SEA of the National Development Plan for Estonia – ad hoc objectives were established as part of the evaluation framework. Those in the National Environmental Strategy did not provide clear benchmarks for integration of environmental issues into development planning.

SEA of the National Development Plan for Poland – objectives were selected from more than 250 specific commitments in plans, programmes and policies, national legal acts and international treaties signed by Poland. These criteria were used in initial assessment. They were supplemented by procedural criteria, to evaluate the soundness and consistency of the planning process, and issue-oriented criteria, to evaluate the impact on the environment and resource use.

SEA of the Regional Operational Programme for Hungary – quantitative objectives were selected for the state of the environment. Various impact categories were identified in the National Programme for the Protection of the Environment, National Nature Conservation Plan, National Environmental Health Action Programme, National Regional Development Concept and the National Agro-environmental Programme. In addition, general sustainability criteria were identified to reflect the main social, economic and environmental objectives of the National Development Plan for Hungary.

Source: Dusik and Sadler (2004)

A series of assessments of the Slovak Energy Policy have resulted in its progressive elaboration and updating. This process began in 1995 with an ad hoc environmental review of the Policy and was followed by more detailed assessments of subsequent versions in 1996 and 1997. In 2000, a new national

---

Box 5.16 SEA of energy policy in the Czech and Slovak Republics

SEA of Czech Energy Policy (1997): This identified objectives and measures for the development of the entire sector (electricity, coal and gas) including future privatization and use of economic instruments. It also addressed the future use of nuclear power, including specific project issues:

- whether to stop or proceed with a second nuclear power plant already approved and partly built; and
- whether to change the limits for open-cast coal mining, which would result in the destruction of additional villages in North Bohemia and North Moravia.

The SEA process focused mainly on the elaboration of the report. Extensive scoping included a national public hearing to comment on the draft policy and the proposed assessment methodology. The scoping process initiated the development of three distinct scenarios of energy mixes. These could be achieved by the use of available administrative, and legal and economic instruments to regulate the behaviour of companies and individuals. The scenarios were extensively modelled and assessed against a set of 16 categories of environmental, social and economic impacts. A public review of the draft SEA report was held in the main chamber of the Czech Senate.

SEA of the Slovak Updated Energy Policy (EP 1997): This comprised a number of steps:

- provision of information to the public about preparation of the EP;
- expert review, including presentation of opinions for public discussion;
- public forum on the EP with participation from state and professional bodies, industry, universities and research institutions, NGOs and the media;
- statement by the Ministry of Environment (MoE) on the basis of expert opinion, other comments and public discussion;
- conclusion of the public discussion, with the statements of the MoE and the Ministry of Economics sent to all participants; and
- submission of a new version of the proposed EP to the Slovak Government – subsequently approved.

The SEA process had a number of positive features, notably with regard to public consultation and input. But NGO representatives strongly criticized the shortcomings of EP 1997 and weaknesses in the process. Specifically, it did not provide for all stages of effective procedure. Further guidance is needed on screening, scoping, EIA report review and public participation.

Sources: Dusik (2003e, f)

Energy Policy was subject to a systematic process of SEA. This stands as one of the most intensive and interactive processes of SEA of policy applied anywhere. It included consultation with neighbouring countries on transboundary impacts. Case Study 5.1 describes the SEA of the 2000 Energy Policy in greater detail and summarizes its advantages and disadvantages.

A number of other lessons can be drawn from Czech and Slovak experience. These may have broader applicability to SEA of policy:

- When SEA was carried out at the instigation of the Ministry of Environment rather than the proponent, there was little or no consideration of practical alternatives to the proposed policy. In these circumstances, the SEA process prima facie did not meet widely accepted international standards.
- Yet, the transparent and open SEA processes (incorporated in the assessments of Czech and Slovak energy policies) also compensated to some degree for this omission. Notably they mobilized public awareness and the submission of valuable inputs. In practice, a 'backwards process' was followed in identifying and assessing alternatives. This occurs in other countries more often than is commonly realized.
- In the pilot cases, the quality of assessment was limited by the financial support available for the preparation of the SEA report. Generally this was not considered to be adequate for undertaking quick, yet thorough, assessment processes.
- Key principles for SEA of national policy are the same as those for land use planning:
  - the purpose of the assessment is to inform the decision;
  - screening and scoping are crucial to identify priority issues; and
  - post-SEA monitoring is important to follow through on policy implementation.

5.3 FUTURE DEVELOPMENT OF SEA IN THE NIS AND CEE REGIONS

Recent developments in SEA in the CEE region have been striking, except in Balkan countries where (other than Bulgaria and Croatia) basic approaches have yet to be established. The introduction of this process has built upon a sound basis of technical expertise and a long tradition of formal planning. This is exemplified by the use of preliminary environmental evaluation in the preparation of regional and local land use plans. SEA at this level is now widely established as a formal procedure. But further action is required to make this process more participatory and transparent. It is less developed for sector programmes and policies, although the EIA legislation in certain countries provides for broad coverage. The experience of the Czech and Slovak Republics in undertaking SEA of major policy proposals is particularly notable. Similarly, there has been experimentation with SEA of national development plans in order to access EU structural funds.

Across the CEE region generally, basic principles of SEA have now been verified for application (Box 5.17; see also Chapter 3) and further elaborated as priorities for strengthening SEA systems (Box 5.18). Key directions for improving SEA practice include:

Box 5.17 Recommended principles for SEA application in the CEE region

When supporting the application of SEA in the CEE region, the following baseline principles should apply:

* the agency proposing the programme, plan or policy should undertake the assessment;
* there should be a well-founded basis of SEA requirements;
* the SEA procedures should provide for evaluation of alternatives;
* there should be early and adequate public participation;
* consideration should be given to human health and socioeconomic as well as environmental impacts;
* there should be clear reporting and documentation of the process and of commitments;
* there should be a clear and substantive relationship between the SEA and the decision-making process; and
* the SEA process should have in-built checks and balances, both formal and informal.

Sources: REC (2003) adapted for use in capacity-building from Sadler (2001c)

---

* developing procedural and methodological guidance on SEA, for example to policies and plans in the major sectors such as energy, transport and agriculture;
* gradual development of 'hands-on' skills and competencies through testing and evaluation of pilot SEA applications (particularly in relation to policy); and
* better integration of SEA into planning and policy processes – specific options and measures for achieving this are summarized in Table 5.4.

Looking ahead, major changes are also pending across the region. These are most obvious amongst the CEE countries that are now EU member states, and which must transpose the requirements of the EU SEA Directive into national legislation. At the time of writing,[13] there are two key uncertainties (Dusik and Sadler, 2004):

* Will those SEA systems currently applying to policies (which, therefore, go beyond the scope of the EU SEA Directive) be scaled back to cover only plans and programmes? It is encouraging that this has not happened with the new Czech EIA Act (2004) which retains coverage of concepts or policies.
* Will CEE member states (and accession countries) opt to follow the letter of the Directive or will they try to customize its provisions to their traditional planning (and policy-making) processes, style and culture?

---

13   May 2004.

Box 5.18 Priorities for the development of national SEA systems in the CEE region

1   National SEA systems in CEE countries should provide a flexible framework for the integration of SEA elements into the development of 'strategic actions' (policies, plans and programmes). National framework laws with provision for SEA may need to be complemented by administrative orders/regulations that interpret general SEA requirements for the most important strategic actions (e.g. preparation of national policies, etc.).

2   The SEA process should be initiated at the earliest possible development stage of a strategic action. It should begin at the same time as the preparation of a policy, plan or programme. Preferably, terms of reference for SEA should be adopted at the same time as those for the strategic action.

3   The SEA process should run parallel to the decision-making process and should be fully integrated into the different development stages of strategic action (see Table 5.4 for proposed options).

4   The authority responsible for the strategic action should be responsible for carrying out the SEA. CEE countries should establish systems that ensure the quality of the SEA process. A formal review of SEA findings may be needed where there is no institutional capacity for carrying out SEA.

5   The SEA process should review:
    – environmental/health problems relevant to the sector or region covered by the strategic action;
    – environmental/health (sustainability) goals and targets of the strategic action;
    – key alternatives of the strategic action – attainment appraisal of environmental/health goals (sustainability) and targets;
    – specific environmental/health impacts of proposed implementation measures; and
    – monitoring of environmental/health impacts of the strategic intervention.

6   Consultation with environmental and health authorities and the general public should be organized throughout the SEA process. At least two stages of consultation should be carried out: during scoping (review of the environmental goals and targets of the strategy) and after the completion of the SEA findings. Additional stages of consultation may be organized as required. The SEA process should also enable access to information in accordance with the requirements of the Aarhus Convention.

7   The findings of the SEA should be published to enable external review (by public bodies, national environmental and health authorities, etc.). SEA findings, whether draft or final, should be made publicly accessible and should be communicated to the concerned public in good time and form.

8   Authorities responsible for development and/or approval of strategic action should take due account of SEA findings and of public comments in their decision-making.

9   Public participation provisions and access to justice are important elements in designing SEA systems. Given the importance and difficulty of this subject, further CEE region-wide discussions should be organized.

SEA systems should ensure proper monitoring of the actual effects of strategic action on the environment, human health and/or sustainable development. Monitoring reports should be made publicly accessible and should be communicated to the concerned public.

Source: REC (2001a)

Table 5.4 *Proposed options for incorporating SEA into strategic planning processes in the CEE region*

Authority responsible for strategic action		SEA administration by environmental authorities
Development of strategic action	Role of SEA	
Terms of reference for strategic action	Terms of reference (TOR) for SEA.	Comments on TOR for strategic action and joint preparation of TOR for SEA including specification of public participation procedure.
Analysis of past developments/trends of the area or sector covered by the action	Review of strategic intervention – whether it properly reflects past environmental/health problems in the respective area or sector.	Overall cooperation in strategy development including provision of information and supervision of the SEA process.
Determination of goals and targets to be achieved by the action	Review of goals and targets – how they relate to relevant environmental and health (sustainability) goals and targets for the area or sector.	Overall cooperation in strategy development including provision of information and supervision of the SEA process.
Design of scenarios for the action	Objective-led appraisal of key scenarios – how they relate to relevant environmental/health goals and targets.	Overall cooperation in strategy development including provision of information and supervision of the SEA process.
Design of implementation measures and management and monitoring	Assessment of specific environmental/health impacts of implementation measures for the selected scenario. Identification of proposed environmental monitoring and management system.	Overall cooperation in strategy development including provision of information and supervision of the SEA process.

Source: REC (2001b)

In the NIS block, progress has been more modest. But there is increasing use of elements of the SEA approach within the hybrid EIA/SER system inherited from the former Soviet Union. Still, further structural reforms will be necessary to develop SEA to meet internationally accepted legal standards as defined in the EU SEA Directive and the UNECE SEA Protocol. In that regard, the programme of activities to be carried out under the SEA Protocol could provide an important first step, given that many NIS and Balkan countries have already adopted this instrument. This focus is officially endorsed in the Cavtat Declaration (agreed at the Third Meeting of the Parties to the governing Espoo Convention, June 2004):

> *... Signatories of the Protocol on SEA to develop capacity for the ratification and implementation of the Protocol on the basis of demonstrated need, giving particular support for the countries of Eastern Europe, the Caucasus and Central Asia and, wherever possible, working with regional institutions to make the expertise and resources available as necessary.* (paragraph 14, ECE/ENHS/NONE/2004/14)

Case Study 5.1

SEA of Slovak Energy Policy (EP 2000)

Source: Adapted from Kozová and Szollos (2001)

INTRODUCTION

During the 1990s, several energy policies were adopted in Slovakia. The 1993 Energy Policy for the Slovak Republic to the Year 2005 was the first to be issued following independence. It emphasized energy saving, notably through macroeconomic measures, pricing and modernization of production processes. An Updated Version of the Energy Policy for the Slovak Republic to the Year 2005 (with a perspective up to 2010) was prepared in 1995. It was subjected to a simple SEA in accordance with Article 35 of the EIA Act (1994). Further processes of SEA were applied to a subsequent version of that Policy (1996–1997), and to a new Energy Policy initiated in 1998 by the newly elected Government and accelerated as part of the EU accession process. This last round of policy development was characterized by a high level of public participation and improvements to SEA procedure and implementation.

POLICY CONTEXT AND OBJECTIVES

Earlier versions of the Energy Policy, notably the 1997 document, outlined broad directions and perspectives to 2010. Key objectives included security, safety and stability of supply, energy efficiency and savings, reducing the adverse impact of the energy sector on the environment, and increasing the utilization of renewable energy sources. The responsible authority (the Ministry of Economy) also included 'nuclear' alternatives as part of the policy review.

In comparison, the objectives of the 2000 Energy Policy (EP 2000) were elaborated in more detail and broken down into short-, medium- and long-term criteria. Short-term objectives were stated for individual energy industries (electric energy, supply of heat, oil, natural gas and coal) as well as the means for their achievement. Longer-term strategic goals included meeting international agreements such as the Kyoto Protocol, reducing energy intensity to the level of EU member states, building emergency oil stocks (until 2010) and managing the radioactive fuel cycle in nuclear power plants.

NATURE AND SCOPE OF ISSUES

In the SEA of EP 2000, the circle of issues expanded beyond the 1997 agenda, which itself was relatively broad. On the environmental side, the 1997 review focused on achieving gains through energy demand and conservation measures (e.g. co-generation and improved thermal efficiencies in power plants), as well as through the increased use of renewable energy resources. EP 2000 also specifically addressed issues of sustainable development of the Slovak energy sector. A key concern was to find technically and economically acceptable ways to achieve the Kyoto Protocol goals before 2008. An examples is higher utilization of natural gas to minimize CO_2 emissions and other pollutants.

Other matters considered in EP 2000 included:

- nuclear policy including the close-down of an operating power station and completion of the back-end fuel cycle;
- restructuring and privatization of the energy sector;
- pricing and subsidy policy; and
- preparation for integration into the internal market of the EU.

SEA PROCESS AND PROCEDURE

Article 35 of the EIA Act prescribes the specific duties of the main participants in the SEA process: the Ministry of Economy as the policy proponent or authority responsible for drafting the proposal; and the Ministry of Environment (MoE) as coordinator of the SEA processes. Other expert, administrative and competent bodies (district and regional authorities, the Slovak Environmental Agency, etc.) were involved formally through the statutory bodies. An SEA team was established to work in parallel with, but independently of, the proponent team. In addition, NGOs and others interested in the environment, energy and sustainable development participated in the process. In some cases, they played significant roles in policy development (e.g. as members of a task group) and public review and discussion.

The SEA of EP 2000 comprised five key steps:

1   *Pre-consultation during the initial phase of policy preparation* (January–June 1999). The Ministry of Economy first developed an outline for NGO comment, and then drafted a discussion document for meetings held by the Parliamentary Committee for the Environment and Nature Conservation. NGO representatives made inputs to the SEA schedule and public consultation.

2   *Public information and review of scope* (July–September 1999). This phase started with a notification in the Economic Newspaper and release of the full text of the draft energy policy (available on the internet and at government offices). A two-month period was allowed for public review and submission of comments. The MoE received over 400 comments and an alternative energy policy was submitted by an NGO coalition (Energy 2000). In contrast to the 1997 review, expert opinion was sought only at the end of this phase as a part of consultations to determine the scope of SEA assessment, key issues and impacts and matters of documentation.

3   *Public hearing and statement on Energy Policy 2000* (September–November 1999). The public hearing on EP 2000 was attended by more than 150 participants, including experts and representatives of national bodies from countries bordering the Slovak Republic. Both the official draft of EP 2000 and the alternative proposal were reviewed in accordance with pre-determined rules of procedure (e.g. time limits, discussion moderated by independent facilitators). A transcript of the proceedings was issued and contributed to the statement of the MoE on EP 2000. This was finalized following consultation with the agency responsible for preparing the draft policy (as required by Section 35.2 of the EIA Act).

4   *Policy submission and approval* (November 1999–January 2000). A final version of the proposed Energy Policy took account of SEA conclusions and recommendations. It was submitted by the Ministry of Economy and received government approval in early 2000 (Tables C5.1.1 and C5.1.2). Compared to the original draft, the version finally adopted was substantially different. It incorporated, inter alia, ideas generated through the SEA process and in the statement of the MoE. This is an important measure of SEA effectiveness and is described further below.

5   *Monitoring of policy implementation and SEA terms and conditions* (started January 2000). This is the weakest link of the SEA processes in Slovakia. In this case, the NGO evaluation of the quality of the SEA process for SEA of EP 2000 provides a framework for follow-up to draw lessons from the experience.

RESULTS AND OUTCOMES

The SEA appeared to make a definite contribution to EP 2000 as approved. At a comprehensive level, Table C5.1.1 briefly evaluates the degree of policy acceptance of several broad directions related to sustainable development. Although circumstantial, it conveys a sense of the strategic impact or purchase of the SEA process on energy policy design and decision-making. A follow-up review by Slovak EIA experts indicated that EP 2000 meets several principles of sustainable development. It tested the likelihood of EP 2000 changing the behaviour and attitude of social groups (e.g. towards the environment, the needs of future generations etc.). In addition, a number of specific recommendations were taken up in EP 2000, for example those related to

Table C5.1.1 *Relationship of SEA to policy development*

SEA statement	Adoption in EP 2000			
Selected recommendation	Yes	Part	No	Evaluation of policy acceptance
Promote transition towards sustainable development, abandoning nuclear generation (long-term) and not expanding current operating units.		X		Positive in that EP 2000 addresses the use of renewable sources and energy savings. But no assessment of the social impacts of energy development, risks of nuclear energy or cumulative effects from viewpoint of sustainable development principles.
Include aims of key environmental and sustainability policy documents.		X		Some elements of these documents are incorporated in EP 2000.
Provide international perspective and commitments, e.g. to EU integration.	X			Included detailed analysis of international documents on energy and environment and preparing for integration with single market. But no analysis of Aarhus Convention.
Define main goals, instruments, timelines and relationship to other policies.		X		Mixed. Identifies long-, medium- and short-term goals, but not their relationship to other policies. Key targets are missing, e.g. for the use of renewable energy and non-nuclear alternatives.
Promote energy self-sufficiency for local and regional communities.			X	No evident connection to existing or proposed regional energy concepts.
Overall attention to environmental and social concerns.		X		In contrast to previous versions, major attention is given to environmental concerns, although not all aspects are taken into account and indicators of the impact of energy on the environment are inadequate.
Overall relation to policy-making.		X+		The government resolution on EP 2000 adopted a number of SEA findings on, for example, disposal of spent nuclear fuel, procedures for abandonment of nuclear energy installations and rationalization of fuel and energy consumption.

disposal of nuclear waste. Despite certain omissions (see below), the quality of the SEA statement and the influence on decision-making can be compared favourably with the earlier process (the SEA of EP 1997).

PROCESS EFFECTIVENESS

As indicated above, the SEA process appeared to 'make a difference' to decision-making. It provided information and advice that added value to the content of EP 2000, although the measure of success is relative and open to qualification. Similarly, the particular components of the SEA procedure that supported or facilitated this contribution can be interpreted only broadly, as reflected in the general rating scale below (Table C5.1.2).

Public participation stands out as the single most important success factor. By many standards, this was an open, transparent and interactive process. It was well organized and based on sound information and documentation. Expert and NGO involvement was constructive and, generally, interventions at the public hearing were of high quality. Cooperation between the two key ministries (Economy and Environment) was much improved compared to the SEA of EP 1997 and also played a part. Finally, the credibility of the SEA process was enhanced by making the NGOs' alternative policy available for public discussion.

The scope and depth of assessment of the impact of EP 2000 on ecosystems, health and socioeconomic aspects were considered to be superficial and inadequate, particularly by NGO representatives. Information was missing on certain impacts on the environment (e.g. those arising from the extraction of fuels and waste disposal), on health and social impacts and on the risks of energy development, particularly nuclear power. Slovak EIA experts evaluated the process on this basis. They considered it to be incomplete and to fall short of being thorough (as required by Section 35 of the EIA Act). In contrast, the range of policy alternatives considered in EP 2000 was extensive and complemented by an entirely different draft proposal. The high level of expert opinions, public discussion and inter-agency consultations contributed to the review of alternatives, and also partly compensated for the analytical deficiencies noted above.

Table C5.1.2 *Evaluation of major components of the SEA of EP 2000*

Assessment components	Rating	Evaluation
Consideration of alternatives	2	Broad range of alternatives considered, but only superficial analysis of energy development scenarios.
Impact assessment	1	Inadequate analysis of ecosystem, health and socioeconomic impacts.
Public participation	2–3	Comprehensive provision of information with appropriate opportunities to review and comment.
Procedural compliance	2	Other than monitoring, implementation of checks and balances generally satisfactory.

Note: Rating scale: 0 – non-existent; 1 – low, major deficiencies; 2 – moderate, some problems; 3 – good, functioning well. Evaluation by Slovak EIA experts

IMPLICATIONS AND LESSONS FOR IMPROVING SEA

Implementation of the SEA procedure in the Slovak Republic could be improved through better guidance on good practice. In this case, the draft regulation on SEA (prepared over a long period) was referred to informally, together with draft handbooks on SEA of policies, territorial planning and legislation. A new handbook on SEA was completed at the end of 2000. It incorporated the (then) most up-to-date version of the EU SEA Directive, with case examples including EP 2000. Guidance on SEA procedure and methodology can be advisory or enshrined in regulation. But, ultimately, the effectiveness of SEA depends on the goodwill and willingness of all parties involved to participate cooperatively and constructively (e.g. to realize environmentally friendly options and solutions).

This case reconfirms that public involvement plays a critical role in quality control and assurance in the SEA process. But this is not formalized in the Slovak Republic. Article 35 of the EIA Act (1994, as amended), does not prescribe an arrangement for participation other than for the MoE and the proponent. Article 6 of the EU SEA Directive (2001/42/EC) suggests that, at a minimum, the MoE should establish a list of statutory authorities, administrative bodies, professionals and NGOs that must be consulted. This would include organizations with expertise or interest in the field of environment and sustainable development, and the policy fields listed in the EIA legislation as being subject to concept assessment. Ideally, funding and support should be allocated to support the participation of independent experts, NGO representatives, community groups and the general public.

Case Study 5.2

Framework SEA of the Polish National Development Plan 2004–2006

Prepared by Urszula A. Rzeszot (Institute of Environmental Assessment, Warsaw; urszula.rzeszot@ios.edu.pl)

BACKGROUND

The National Development Plan (NDP) is a programming document prepared by the Ministry of Economy with the aim of improving and strengthening the international competitiveness of the national economy. In addition, it is intended to support continued and balanced economic and social development, in accordance with the principles of sustainability. Once Poland becomes a member of the EU, it will apply for EU structural funds support to implement the plan. Such support requires co-financing from national funds (state, local or private). So the NDP will significantly influence the way in which public money will be spent in the years covered by the Plan, and the type and scale of the developments that will be undertaken.

With the agreement of the Ministry of Economy, a framework SEA of the Polish NDP (2004–2006) was initiated by the Polish Office of the Regional Environmental Center for Central and Eastern Europe (REC). It was undertaken by a team of independent experts.[14] In parallel, similar SEAs were carried out in Hungary and Estonia as part of a larger project coordinated by the REC.

The NDP did not formally require an SEA. According to the regulations governing EU structural funds, environmental issues are included in the ex ante evaluation. Under Polish law, only the plans and policies that are required to be prepared by an act of law are subject to mandatory SEA. Since the NDP is not required by an act, an SEA was not compulsory. Nevertheless the Ministry of Economy granted the SEA team full access to draft documents and helped to

---

14 The team was led by Andrzej Kassenberg, and also included Krzysztof Kacprzyk, Zbigniew Karaczun, Urszula Rzeszot and Bożenna Wójcik. Malgorzta Koziarek, of the Polish REC office acted as project coordinator and expert advice was provided by Jiri Dusik, of REC Head Office.

arrange meetings with the planning teams and coordinators of the NDP. It also took the conclusions of the SEA into account in preparing the final version of the NDP, and included information about SEA in the text of the document.

APPROACH

The assessment was carried out as an 'objective-led appraisal' approach. The main aim was to improve the final NDP document by making it 'greener' and more sustainable, rather than to produce a judgemental opinion on its shortcomings. The team tried not only to assess the environmental consequences of the proposed actions and the significance of environmental issues discussed in the NDP, but also to formulate recommendations to improve the NDP.

The NDP had to be developed within a very limited timeframe in order to be submitted to the European Commission by the end of the year 2002. The SEA project was initiated in Spring 2002 (and completed by October 2002). At that time, a draft version of the NDP was not available. So an SEA was first undertaken on sectoral operational programmes (SOPs) in parallel to the preparation of the NDP.[15] Before starting the SEA, the team produced an 'opinion' on the SEA. This was placed on the REC's website and provided to the team undertaking the ex ante evaluation of the NDP.

The SEA was organized in several key stages: selection of assessment criteria; initial assessment; integration of selected criteria and sustainability criteria; and preparation of the final version of the assessment. Methods were chosen to suit the materials and time available.

Selection of assessment criteria

The NPD document had to meet both EU and Polish standards. So the SEA team decided to draw upon major national and international legislation to define assessment criteria against which proposed actions could be assessed. An initial list of over 100 acts was prepared. Then the 14 acts most relevant to the task were chosen through 'expert scoring'. These were then analysed in detail and an initial set of 250 assessment criteria identified. The criteria were reformulated to obtain a final set of 52 detailed criteria. These covered general issues as well as others addressed by the SOPs. They were organized in two groups:

- *resource management*: general and horizontal issues, transport, energy, agriculture, nature and landscape, forestry, and water management and fisheries; and

---

15 As originally envisaged, the SEA was to cover the NDP, except the Regional Development Programme. The SOPs were excluded due to limited available time and funds. However, as the draft SOPs were available before the draft NDP, the project team decided to carry out an informal assessment of the operational programmes.

- *changes in the environment*: air, noise and radiation, soil and wastes, water, nature, and others.

Initial assessment

The initial assessment used a matrix format to 'map' the actions proposed in the SOPs, which, in turn, would influence the selected detailed criteria. The actions were defined only in general terms, and their potential impacts (positive or negative) depended on the size, number or location of the technical options chosen. A scale of 1–3 was used to score the impact of individual planned activities on achieving each criteria. At this stage, there was no detailed consideration about whether the potential impact was predominantly positive or negative.

The assessment was carried out in close cooperation with the SOP programming teams:

- Representatives of the SEA team met with each of the programming teams to explain the SEA approach.
- Draft assessment matrices were forwarded to the teams and discussed.
- A joint meeting was held to discuss issues where the teams disagreed.
- The final version of the assessment was made available.

Integration of selected criteria and sustainability criteria

The draft NDP was assessed once it became available. The detailed criteria used for the initial assessment of the draft SOPs were considered inappropriate for this purpose so a new set of 23 general criteria was adopted. They were drawn mainly from international and national sustainability criteria and split into two groups: 12 formal criteria and 11 issue-oriented criteria (Box C5.2.1). These criteria were not formally approved by the Ministry of Economy.

The criteria were formulated as questions, in part to make them useful to the NDP planning teams. For each one, both a general and a detailed assessment were undertaken. The general assessment involved a relatively short and direct answer (yes, probably yes, probably no, definitely no, not applicable). The detailed assessment provided a longer commentary on key parts of the text of the NDP, and suggested general or detailed changes and conclusions. The general changes pointed out issues that were lacking or insufficiently addressed in the NDP and that would need to be added or considerably changed. The detailed changes suggested modifications of the existing document to make it 'greener' and more sustainable.

The NDP did not specify types, extent, location and grouping of activities. So, locally, the predicted impacts/effects might by greater or less than assessed by the SEA. In addition, long-term and multi-sectoral effects of activities to be undertaken during implementation of the NDP were not fully considered. This was partly because the draft NDP did not state clearly which other policies were to be implemented in parallel with the NDP. The interdependence of proposed NDP activities was insufficiently clear to allow reliable analysis of cross-sectoral impacts.

Box C5.2.1 Sustainability criteria for assessing the Polish National Development Plan, 2004–2006

Formal/procedural criteria

- Were diagnosis and SWOT (strengths, weaknesses, opportunities and threats) analysis prepared that took into account sustainable development?
- Were environmental aims and goals suggested?
- Are proposed actions in accordance with environmental policy documents?
- Were negative environmental impacts quantified?
- Is publicly accountable EIA envisaged for proposed activities?
- Are sustainability indicators taken into account?
- Is 'green purchasing' promoted?
- Did the document undergo public consultations and were the results taken into account?
- Are sustainability aims in different sectors coherent?
- Are environmental criteria for the choice of project suggested?
- Are diagnosis, aims, proposed activities and monitoring indications coherent and sustainable?
- Is the role of environmental protection authorities made clear?

Issue-oriented criteria

- Will proposed activities result in effective use of resources (production, consumption, management)?
- Will proposed activities result in decreased use of non-renewable resources?
- Is eco-innovation promoted?

Also do proposed activities:

- promote sustainability (including mitigation measures and monitoring)?
- improve the state of the environment?
- take into account nature and landscape protection?
- reduce environment-related health risks?
- maintain cultural values?
- create conditions for fair competition in the use of the environment?
- raise environmental awareness?
- improve spatial management structure?

This assessment was carried out for the general part of the NDP and for each of the parts describing the basis for action to be undertaken in the SOPs.

Preparation of the final version of the assessment

In the final assessment, the findings of both the general and detailed assessments were taken into account, based on sustainability criteria (Box C5.2.1). Over 60 general and detailed recommendations were formulated to make the findings as 'user friendly' as possible for the programming team.

Thus, where the programming teams decided not to make major modifications to the text of the NDP, it was still possible to use the detailed recommendations to improve the existing documents.

Participation

The draft version of the assessment was forwarded to the programming teams, made available for public consultations and put on the REC website. Individual SEA team members alerted their contacts to the draft SEA report to encourage comments but, unfortunately, the NGO network was not notified.

There was no effective public participation in the process and no comments were received from the public. This may be due partly to the restricted time and partly to the effort required. Those commenting would have had to be aware of the contents of both the NDP and SEA as well as the general context of those documents. In addition, when the draft SEA was made available, public consultations were being undertaken on the draft NDP. This is where most organizations probably concentrated their efforts. When asked why they had not commented on the draft SEA, some NGOs replied that it was because they supported its findings. The limited comments received were incorporated into the final SEA document. A summary of the findings of the SEA accompanied the draft NDP during the NDP consultation process. Subsequently, the SEA team carried out a general review of the final version of the NDP document to identify which recommendations has been included.

OUTCOMES

Although not required to do so, the Ministry of Economy took into account some of the changes suggested in the SEA report. During the consultation process, changes were made to the NDP. These included:

- a broader approach to the environment;
- better structure and coherence of the NDP document;
- changes in diagnosis concerning:
    - organic farming – now seen as an opportunity
    - Polish environment – now considered as an asset
    - environmental aspects of competitive economy – now discussed;
- sustainable development (limited) is now promoted as a new 'axis' in the NDP;
- a number of detailed provisions are included for:
    - EIA
    - environmental requirements in project implementation
    - the Environmental Monitoring Sub-committee;
- greater consideration is given to environmental issues by sectors:
    - the opportunity for 'green jobs' is perceived
    - some support for renewable energy sources
    - changes in the flood control approach.

A number of changes suggested in the SEA were not included in the final NDP, including:

- monitoring of implementation against sustainable/sustainability indicators;
- promoting innovation through increasing the effectiveness of resource use and reducing impacts;
- education and staff training to improve understanding of the idea of sustainability;
- incorporating environmental preferences in project criteria (yes to environmental gain; no to environmental impact); and
- subjecting development of transport infrastructure to environmental and economic justification – this is currently lacking in the strong preference for road-building (in particular motorways).

The Ministry of Economy used the SEA assessment criteria and methodology for an internal evaluation and quality control exercise.

LESSONS

For the next programming cycle or indeed future assessment, the main lessons are:

- Try to start early and make sure that the assumptions and aims of both the NDP and SEA are made clear, and that they are mutually understood by the programming and assessment teams.
- Aim to achieve broad consensus on the aims – ideally these should also be subject to public participation.
- Seek better cooperation between the NDP programming and SEA teams.
- Continue assessment for all of the NDP (including SOPs, regional OPs and complementary documents) and all of the programming cycle, including noting lessons for future cycles.

Case Study 5.3

SEA of the Energy Policy of the Czech Republic (EP-CR)

Source: Dusik (2003f)

BACKGROUND: CONTEXT AND ISSUES

The Energy Policy of the Czech Republic (EP-CR) was drafted in 1998. It was the first comprehensive strategic document to set out objectives and measures for developing the entire energy sector (electricity, coal and gas). The SEA addressed four main issues for decision-making:

- whether to enforce limits on coal mining (established in 1992) that lead to the gradual closure of main coal mines in the country;
- whether to proceed with or stop construction (already initiated) of the second nuclear power plant (NPP Dukovany);
- whether more extensive state support should be provided for energy savings and alternative energy sources; and
- what the rate of internalization of external environmental costs in the energy market should be.

THE ROLE OF THE SEA

SEA of the EP-CR was the first pilot SEA in the Czech Republic. It started after the draft policy was prepared by the proponent (the Ministry of Industry). The proposal policy only considered one alternative. The Ministry of Industry only learned about the need to apply SEA when the EP-CR was first submitted to the Czech Government. The SEA was initiated on the basis of the Czech EIA Act (Article 14 dealing with SEA of concepts) at the request of the Ministry of Environment. Subsequently, an external consultant (SEVEn) was hired to carry out the SEA.

The SEA team focused mainly on the preparation of the SEA report and applied the following steps:

- scoping (one national public hearing to comment on the draft plan and on the proposed assessment methodology);
- preparation of the draft SEA report; and
- public review of the draft SEA report (one national public hearing in the main chamber of the Czech Senate).

Two external expert teams were established to help carry out the SEA. Team A comprised 13 multi-stakeholder experts with the task of defining the scope of the SEA, including:

- delineating the main alternatives to the policy;
- determining timeframes for evaluating impacts (e.g. whether only immediate or long-term impacts should be analysed, and over what timeframe(s); and
- establishing the main environmental indicators to compare alternatives.

Team B comprised 19 experts with the task of carrying out the actual assessment. The terms of reference for Team B, inter alia, were to:

- describe, as precisely as possible, each of the main alternatives in terms of their outputs to the environment;
- quantify environmental indicators established by Team A for each alternative;
- evaluate impacts against the quantified environmental indicators; and
- design measures to offset or mitigate negative environmental impacts.

After completing the above assessments, another small expert team was established to carry out a multi-criteria comparison of alternatives. This team organized a survey of 32 representative sample respondents to define the social importance (weight) of each impact category and each indicator used.

APPROACH AND METHODS USED

Development of alternatives

SEA Team A defined three main policy alternatives (described below). Each alternative met the following assumptions:

- Annual gross domestic product (GDP) growth is 2–4 per cent.
- Energy demand of the economy (expressed by an index of primary energy sources per GDP unit) steadily decreases.
- The Czech Republic meets all international obligations, including Kyoto targets.
- All alternatives are fully aligned with EU legislation.

Alternative A proposes development of the energy sector based on locally available sources of fossil fuels (black and brown coal). Previously established limits of coal mining are not enforced and the economic burden of the current energy process does not increase (i.e. there is no further internalizing of external environmental costs, and carbon tax and energy tax are not introduced). The use of primary energy sources will slightly increase. Growth of energy use is higher than growth of primary energy sources. The second nuclear power plant will be finalized by 2004–2005.

Alternative B proposes development of the energy sector based on locally available sources of fossil fuels. Previously established limits of coal mining are enforced. This is compensated for by importing electricity and gas. Energy prices will probably be higher than under Alternative A – triggering changes in the structure of energy sources. There will be more use of energy-saving schemes and alternative energy sources will also increase. Growing use will be made of co-generation units. Use of primary energy sources will not increase. Energy use may slightly increase. The second nuclear power plant will be finalized by 2005.

Alternative C proposes energy-saving schemes (including increased efficiency in energy use) and rapid increase of alternative energy sources. Increased efficiencies are supported by stimulation of business dealing with energy savings and by targeted state actions (e.g. major energy savings in state-owned facilities, and funding and technical assistance programmes for technological changes in private enterprises). The target is to reduce use of primary energy sources by 1.5 per cent annually, in other words by 16 per cent by 2010. Energy use will decrease. The following alternative energy sources will be developed: biomass (by a maximum of 90PJ), small water plants (by 4PJ), wind (up to 5PJ), solar collectors (by 3PJ) and photovoltaic cells (limited use). Energy prices increasingly reflect external environmental costs leading to growing use of co-generation units. The second nuclear power plant will not be finalized. Previously established limits of coal mining are enforced.

Selection of issues and indicators

The set of indicators defined by the SEA Team to analyse the proposed policy are described in Table C5.3.1.

Impact analysis and comparison of alternatives

The main SEA contractor and external consultants defined a set of implementation measures for each alternative. A comprehensive mathematical model (MARKAL) provided data for the majority of indicators. Collective expert judgements were used only for three indicators: 'waste waters', 'radioactive waters' and 'impacts on employment'.

Indicators were estimated for all three alternatives. In order to compare all alternatives mutually, the impacts of Alternatives B and C were compared

Table C5.3.1 *Indicators for analysing the Energy Policy*

Impact category	Weight of category	Impacts and main indicators	Weight of impacts	Weight of indicator
Environmental impacts	*30%*			
		Air emissions	**58%**	
		CO_2 (tons)		12%
		CH_4 (tons)		15%
		SO_2 – total (tons)		21%
		SO_2 – local (tons)		5%
		NO_x – total (tons)		22%
		NO_x – local (tons)		7%
		Particulate matters (tons)		18%
		Water pollution	**21%**	
		Waste waters from mining (m^3)		50%
		Other waste waters (m^3)		50%
		Impacts on soil		18%
		Land occupation by mining (km^2)		30%
		Land occupation by flooding (km^2)		10%
		Land occupation by landfills (km^2)		35%
		Land occupation by new installations (km^2)		25%
		Annual production of waste	**3%**	
		Ash from power plants (tons)		20%
		Unused gypsum (tons)		10%
		Used nuclear fuel (tons)		30%
		Radioactive waste (tons)		40%
Impacts on resources	*20%*			
		Impact on energy sector	**20%**	
		Reduction of primary energy sources (tons)		10%
		Reduction of gypsum sources (tons)		25%
		Share of renewable energy sources in primary energy sources (%)		25%
		Use of primary energy sources per capita (giga joules (GJ)/person)		25%
		Use of primary energy sources per economic unit (GJ/GDP)		15%
Social impacts	*20%*			
		Impact on infrastructure	**20%**	
		Number of people to be reallocated		
		Impact on employment	**80%**	
		Employment changes by energy savings		50%
		Employment changes by energy production		
		Employment changes by changes of mining		50%
Economic impacts	*30%*	**Impact on economy**	–	–
		Investment costs per 1GJ unit	–	–
		Running costs per 1GJ unit	–	–
		Costs of energy-saving schemes	–	–
		Costs of measures to offset and mitigate adverse environmental impacts	–	–

against the baseline situation established by Alternative A. For example, all alternatives were compared using 'CO$_2$ emissions' as an indicator. CO$_2$ emissions for Alternative A were classified as 100 per cent. Alternatives B and C then produced 95 per cent and 87 per cent, respectively, of CO$_2$ emissions compared with Alternative A. Such comparisons were done for all indicators.

After completing this analysis, it was evident that Alternatives C and B score much better Alternative A on almost all indicators. Alternative A scored best only for the economic indicators.

This conclusion did not reflect the social values attributed to each category impact. For this purpose, a multi-criteria comparison of alternatives was carried out. A survey of 32 representative respondents was used to define the social importance (weight) of each impact category and each indicator used.

The multi-criteria analysis (including sensitivity analysis) yielded similar conclusions to the original analysis of alternatives. The assignment of weights to impact categories did not alter the basic finding that Alternatives C and B performed much better then Alternative A on almost all indicators.

This main conclusion was presented to the proponent (Ministry of Industry) in the draft SEA Rreport. It was agreed that the proponent would consider these findings in selecting an optimal alternative. Detailed mitigation measures and a monitoring scheme were to be designed for the alternative finally selected.

Public participation

Identification of stakeholders

A separate public participation process was organized for the SEA. Measures to identify and notify the public included:

- a web page with announcement of the SEA process and background documents for the SEA; and
- a special email address to gather comments.

In addition, NGOs established a network of six regional coordinators to disseminate information about the SEA, organized six regional public workshops and forwarded comments to the SEA team.

Mode(s) of involvement

A highly interactive national public workshop was held to initially review the draft policy and scope out the SEA. Approximately 80 people attended the workshop (mainly EIA experts, energy experts, energy lobbies and NGOs). They worked in small groups to define specific impacts and comment on the proposed alternatives.

A formal, national, public hearing on the draft SEA report was held in the Czech Senate (under the personal auspices of the speaker). Approximately 170 people attended (mainly municipalities, energy lobbies, NGOs, members of the Senate and of the Parliament).

Comments on effectiveness of public participation

Evaluation of responses and comments revealed that participants were generally satisfied with both events. The involvement of the Senate contributed to the prestige and transparency of the entire SEA process.

RESULTS AND LESSONS

Contribution of SEA to decision-making

The SEA process lasted approximately 12 months and the draft report was given to the Ministry of Industry shortly before a change of government. The incoming Government decided to prepare a new Energy Policy – it strongly preferred Alternative A. This was in line with its own priority to maintain energy-intensive industries and develop the second nuclear power plant (NPP Dukovany). The SEA had documented major environmental problems with these proposals, so the Ministry of Industry decided to ignore the findings. It drafted a new Energy Policy and commissioned another SEA. Neither the new policy nor the new SEA was prepared in a publicly transparent manner. They were made publicly available only shortly before submission to the Government. Both documents were heavily criticized. The completion of NPP Dukovany then became the subject of a major diplomatic dispute between the Czech Republic and Austria. The SEA was considered to be of very poor quality and highly biased.

Conclusions for SEA good practice

The earlier SEA process had a number of elements of good practice (e.g. comparison of alternatives, public hearing) and the report was of good quality. But it could have been concluded much more quickly if additional complicated analyses (i.e. multi-criteria analysis) had not been performed. The main environmental issues and trends associated with implementing each alternative were already evident from prior evaluations. If the SEA had been completed in a shorter time, it would have provided an earlier input into decision-making on the policy. However, it is questionable whether this would have made any difference to the incoming Government in terms of it accepting the finalized policy. Most likely, it would have drafted its own new policy anyway.

The main lessons for SEA practice are:

- Always use the simplest technique available to carry out the given task – it will save time and money.
- SEA takes place within the larger context and climate of political decision-making. The report is only a decision-support document that is meant to inform, not bind, choice. It is likely to be ignored when the findings run counter to major priorities of a government.

Key information sources

This project has not yet been reported in international or national literature. Further information on the overall design of the SEA procedure (including public participation) can be obtained from Jiri Dusik (jdusik@rec.org). More information on the SEA report can be obtained from Jiri Zeman (jiri.zeman@svn.cz).

Chapter 6

SEA Experience in Developing Countries

Increasingly, developing countries are experimenting with strategic environmental assessment (SEA) and some have SEA-type approaches and elements in place already. There is also considerable experience with using a variety of strategic planning processes that display many of the characteristics of SEA (para-SEA). We focus first on SEA in Southern Africa where a dedicated regional workshop on SEA was organized to feed into this review (SAIEA, 2003a), followed by sections covering francophone Africa, the rest of Sub-Saharan Africa, Latin America and the Caribbean, Asia and elsewhere. But our survey of this field represents no more than a preliminary reconnaissance.

Selected examples of SEA and para-SEA illustrate some of the indigenous approaches that have been adopted. These are less common than SEAs promoted and funded by development assistance agencies (which are reviewed in Chapter 4). In most cases where formal SEA has been undertaken in developing countries, the basic aim and approach has mirrored that in the North – namely to identify the environmental consequences (and associated social and economic effects) of existing, new or revised policies, plans and programmes (PPP). These represent only a small number of the broad family of SEA approaches. But they are a highly visible sub-set of the larger suite of informal or para-SEAs (that form part of development policy-making, land use planning or resource management).

No strict boundaries can be drawn for this latter area of application. Only the more evident SEA-type elements and approaches are introduced in this chapter. Nevertheless, they indicate the scope and diversity of the extended SEA family in developing countries, where political and economic realities constrain what can be done. In this context, we consider that methodological pluralism is a positive response; the real issue is whether SEA, however structured, informs decision-making and integrates the environment in strategies for poverty reduction and sustainable development in accordance with the Millennium Development Goals. At issue here are larger concerns about the form(s) of SEA that are appropriate to developing countries and their relationship to donor capacity-building and training programmes that promote a particular institutional procedure. We discuss this issue in the concluding chapter and readers may want to have it in mind when reviewing the experience of developing countries.

6.1 SEA IN SOUTHERN AFRICA[1]

EIA is now used extensively in most countries in Southern Africa. However, many of the governments tend to be ad hoc in their planning and, as a result, environmental impact assessment (EIA) is often regarded as an 'add on' process 'that gets done "later on", after the government, board of directors or other body has decided that the intended initiative is viable and thus worthy of detailed planning' (Tarr, 2003). In recent years, there has been rapid progress in the formulation of policies, legislation and guidelines for EIA (SAIEA, 2003b). A number of countries are now considering making SEA a formal requirement. There are a number of existing legislation entry points for SEA (Box 6.1). Discussions underway at the SADC (Southern African Development Community) level on harmonizing such policies, and laws may also encourage further interest in SEA. Increasingly, calls are being made to develop a protocol for environmental assessment in the SADC region, which would cover both EIA and SEA (Chonguiça and Katerere, 2002; SAIEA, 2003a).

BOX 6.1 EXAMPLES OF LEGAL ENTRY POINTS FOR SEA IN SOUTHERN AFRICA

No countries in Southern Africa explicitly require the use of SEA, though South Africa's National Environmental Management Act (No 107 of 1998) makes provision for the development of assessment procedures that aim to ensure that the environmental consequences of PPP are considered (DEAT, 2000). Similarly, Clause 1 of the appendix of Mozambique's EIA Regulations (No 76 of 1998) stipulates a number of programme-level activities that require an 'environmental impact study', and Malawi's Environmental Management Act (No 23 of 1996) includes 'major policy reforms' as an activity requiring an EIA.

Perhaps the most exciting new laws regarding the use of SEA in the region are the draft Environmental Management Bills for Swaziland and Namibia. Both countries have drafted framework acts that explicitly require SEAs for new legislation, regulations, policies, programmes or plans or PPP. Whilst the Swazi Bill was given royal assent in November 2002, the Namibian Government has still not finalized its law, which has been under discussion since 1995. Other countries currently working on new environmental assessment (EA) legislation are Botswana, the Seychelles, Tanzania and Zimbabwe. In the case of Mauritius, the Government is currently in the process of revising its 1991 Environmental Protection Act, which will include clauses that require the use of SEA.

Source: Tarr (2003)

---

1   This section draws heavily from Tarr (2003).

Box 6.2 Socioeconomic and political context for planning and SEA in Southern Africa

Various factors have shaped the difficult socioeconomic and political circumstances that, to a large extent, dictate the way planning is executed in Southern Africa: decades of oppression, resource mining, cultural erosion and poor post-colonial governance.

> Decision-making is theoretically a rational process that strives for the good of the community in the long term (Nilsson and Dalkmann, 2001). However, the pressures (be they external or personal greed) on high level decision-makers in southern Africa are such that planning is often driven by forces and desires that result in extremely short-term time horizons. Similarly, entrepreneurs operating in developing countries with inadequate laws and inefficient bureaucracies are, all too often, driven by quick profits rather than longer-term returns. This is exacerbated by the perception that developing countries tend to be unstable and that their investments are 'unsafe'. Thus, many professional planners regard the decisions of politicians and private sector developers as environmentally and socially unsound and thus unsustainable. Indeed, it could be argued that the fast-growing economies of southern Africa are being built on a platform of unsustainable projects, many of which have been initiated in the absence of policies, plans and programmes.
>
> The situation in southern Africa is perhaps not significantly different from that found elsewhere. Research has shown that rationality in real decision-making processes is usually very limited (Nida-Rümelin, 1997) and decisions are usually driven by values and political considerations. Partidário (2000) and other authors suggest that SEA works best where well-structured, rational planning processes exist. Moreover, Nilsson and Dalkmann (2001) report that there are very few examples of SEA influencing policy level decisions. The latter are typically characterised by non-rational processes.
>
> This is the challenging setting within which to promote concepts such as SEA in southern Africa.

Source: Tarr (2003)

Many countries in the region have committed themselves to sustainable development and have adopted national constitutions that oblige the state to balance economic development with the long-term needs of the people and the sensitivities of the natural environment. However these constitutional foundations still need to be translated into action on the ground. A major constraint remains the lack of institutional capacity and the resources to adequately guide, administer or control EA processes, or to establish and maintain systems to monitor the implementation of EA at any level (IUCN/World Bank, 1997). The political and socioeconomic context and circumstances are quite different from those in the North, as are the rational norms that are assumed to be most conducive to introducing and applying SEA (Box 6.2).

BOX 6.3 EIA[3] IN THE SOUTHERN AFRICAN DEVELOPMENT COMMUNITY (SADC)

The SADC's Strategy for Environment and Sustainable Development (SADC/ELMS, 1996) states (p iii):

> Throughout the SADC region, the largely separate policies and programmes for economic reform, social progress and environmental improvement must be increasingly integrated in a single agenda and strategy for sustainable development. The new agenda needs to be anchored and reinforced by incorporating impact assessments as an integral part of decision-making in at least three key respects:
>
> - assessing the likely environmental impacts of economic policies and activities;
> - assessing the likely economic impacts of environmental policies and measures; and
> - assessing the likely equity impacts of both economic and environmental policies.
>
> Although there are few absolutes in public policy, at least one should prevail in the SADC region. If EIA[3] review of a proposed policy or programme indicates that it will not lead to at least some improvement in the living conditions and prospects of the poor majority, then a sustainable alternative must be found that does.

At the regional level, SADC's Strategy for Environment and Sustainable Development (SADC/ELMS, 1996), approved in 1996, takes a broad approach. It focuses on 'keeping the poor majority of people at the front and centre of the new development agenda for economic growth, poverty alleviation and environmental protection'. To meet this challenge, it identifies the need to undertake environmental, economic and equity impact assessments (EIA[3]) – in all key development policies, plans and decisions as a crucial step in meeting this challenge (Box 6.3). This approach has much in common with the idea of sustainability analysis but has yet to be tested. However, it may find expression in the work of the New Economic Partnership for African Development (NEPAD).

The Secretariat for Eastern African Coastal Area Management (SEACAM), based in Mozambique, is expanding its Environmental Assessment (EA) programme and is trying to tie it more closely to a broader framework of integrated coastal zone management. SEA will build on the ongoing EA programme and address the cumulative effects of a large number of smaller developments that cannot be captured by the 'traditional' project EA. For example, the large number of small tourism developments springing up along the Mozambican coast do not have major environmental and social impacts on their own. However, collectively, they degrade important natural areas and can disrupt local communities. The SEA programme aims to help regional

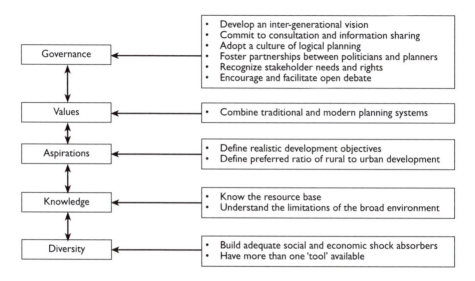

Source: Tarr (2003)

Figure 6.1 *Key requirements for implementing decision-focused SEA in Southern Africa*

planners, non-governmental organizations (NGOs) and EA managers to better understand and proactively manage the environmental impacts of policies, programmes, sector developments and regional plans.

The use of SEA in the region to date has been extremely limited, but there has been considerable experience of national-level strategic planning and more local, integrated, land use and resource management planning that, in the broader sense, can be regarded as para-SEAs. This experience might offer a platform for an SEA approach suited to planning and decision-systems in the region that work. In this regard, Tarr (2003) questions whether SEA in Southern Africa should follow the 'EIA route' or pursue a totally different approach aligned to the actual dynamics of decision-making in the region. He suggests five criteria as key requirements for implementing SEA in the region (Figure 6.1).

In 2002, the World Conservation Union – Regional Office for Southern Africa (IUCN-ROSA) commissioned a desk study review of EA documents produced for three development initiatives taking place in the region (the Lesotho Highlands Water Project, the Lubombo Spatial Development Initiative in South Africa, and the Sugar Cane Irrigation Industry in Swaziland). The study aimed to understand how the EIA processes were applied with respect to transboundary and cumulative implications for natural resources essential to agriculture or for the livelihood of people who depend on agriculture (Chonguiça and Katerere, 2002). It found no evidence that these issues had been accounted for by the individual projects, but did identify the emergence of several initiatives that were attempting integrated development planning across SADC countries: the Kalagadi transfrontier initiative (South Africa–Botswana), the Great Limpopo Transfrontier Park (South Africa–Zimbabwe), and river basin commissions (e.g. the Zambezi River Authority).

Below, we review SEA use in different SADC countries, starting first with South Africa which has the most experience, and then alphabetically. Information has been drawn, inter alia, from Tarr (2003) and from presentations made at a recent workshop on SEA in Southern Africa (SAIEA, 2003a).

6.1.1 South Africa[2]

South Africa has a history of EIA application dating back to the 1970s. The EIA Committee of the Council of the Environment was established in 1983 and initiated research on EIA that led to the introduction of integrated environmental management (IEM). Guideline documents on IEM were published (e.g. Department of Environmental Affairs, 1992) which are still widely used in South Africa and which have provided a basis for several hundred voluntary EIAs.

In principle, IEM included application to policies and plans. It was originally intended that IEM and planning be integrated. However, after the establishment of the first democratic government in 1994, two separate processes and decision-making procedures were developed for planning and IEM. The first legislated EIA requirements came into effect on 1 September 1997 in the form of regulations under the old Environmental Conservation Act (No 73 of 1989). These regulations only made provision for EIA and not monitoring, auditing and environmental management planning. Furthermore, they did not apply to policies and plans. The IEM philosophy (of integrating environmental issues into all stages of policy, planning and the project cycle) was therefore lost.

The EIA regulations emerged separately from the consultative national environmental policy process (CONNEPP) which culminated in the promulgation of a new National Environmental Management Act (NEMA) in 1998. This Act states that any activities (defined as policies, plans, programmes and projects) that may significantly affect the environment must be considered, investigated and assessed, and outlines minimum requirements for assessing impacts, including cumulative effects. But the EIA regulations issued under the old Environmental Conservation Act still remain in force. However, amendments to the NEMA chapter on IEM have been tabled in the Parliament. New regulations to legislate for the mandatory use of environmental assessment tools are currently being prepared in support of NEMA. It is likely that they will ensure the implementation of a greater range of EA tools than just EIA.

In the mid-1990s, changing perceptions led to the emergence of an innovative approach to SEA pioneered by the Council for Scientific and Industrial Research (CSIR) (Wiseman, 1997). This is of particular interest

---

2   With contribution by Nigel Rossouw, CSIR, South Africa.

Table 6.1 *The conceptual differences in understanding and emphasis between EIA and SEA in South Africa*

EIA	SEA
Is reactive to a development proposal.	Is proactive and informs development proposals.
Assesses the effect of a proposed development on the environment.	Assesses the effect of the environment on development needs and opportunities.
Addresses a specific project.	Addresses areas, regions or sectors of development.
Has a well-defined beginning and end.	Is a continuing process aimed at providing information at the right time.
Assesses direct impacts and benefits.	Assesses cumulative impacts and identifies implications and issues for sustainable development.
Focuses on the mitigation of impacts.	Focuses on maintaining a chosen level of environmental quality.
Has a narrow perspective and a high level of detail.	Has a wide perspective and a low level of detail to provide a vision and overall framework.
Focuses on project-specific impacts.	Creates a framework against which impacts and benefits can be measured.

Source: CSIR (1996)

because, in practice, South Africa is a unique amalgam of developed and developing economies and societies. It can draw on and adapt lessons from industrial countries readily, but also must have regard to their portability and use in settings that are comparable to those in many developing countries. As a first step, an SEA primer was published (CSIR, 1996) followed by a draft SEA protocol (CSIR, 1997a). The emphasis was placed on 'assessing the effect of the environment on development needs and opportunities' with a strong focus on assessing cumulative impacts. Table 6.1 presents a frequently referenced comparison by CSIR of the conceptual differences in understanding and emphasis between EIA and the evolving SEA process in South Africa. CSIR highlights these differences to suggest ideal objectives and characteristics to which EIA and SEA should aspire, although they are not always realized. The political and socioeconomic realities under which SEA is practised results in the process responding to context-specific needs.

SEA has not been adopted by national policy-making institutions or for policy-making processes, but has been applied at the plan and programme levels of the project cycle – in two distinct but related ways (CSIR, 1997a):

- *Integrated studies* forming part of the processes of planning and programme design – providing strategic information on the environment, including resource opportunities and constraints, existing activities and processes and the carrying capacity of the environment. The information

---

Box 6.4 Preliminary SEA for the KwaZulu-Natal Trade and Industry Policy, South Africa

In 1996, the Regional Economic Forum (REF) in KwaZulu-Natal embarked on a process to formulate a Trade and Industry Policy for the province. Various investigations were initiated to provide an input to the process, including the preparation of a regional industrial location strategy. The Council for Scientific and Industrial Research (CSIR) was commissioned to undertake an SEA. Given that only a broad framework for the Policy existed, it was not possible to undertake a review-based SEA. Instead a preliminary SEA was carried out which aimed to identify opportunities for and constraints to industrial development in the province.

The intended role of the SEA was, therefore, to guide policy formulation, and the SEA was structured to provide a mechanism whereby the environmental implications of the components of the Policy could be reviewed rapidly. However, it is not clear that a Trade and Industry Policy has yet emerged. So the utility and influence of the SEA is difficult to gauge. It comprised several components:

* *SWOT analysis:* To provide an overview of strengths, weaknesses, opportunities and threats (SWOT) pertaining to the KwaZulu environment. Ten specialist (discipline) studies were commissioned from which SWOT issues were drawn.
* *Industry profiles:* An 'environmental' profile was then drawn up for each of 11 industry types (sugar, textiles, chemicals, etc.). The profile listed resources consumed, and air, water and solid waste generated by the industry type.
* *Environmental assessment matrix:* Designed to link the industry profiles with the SWOT analysis so that the environmental implications of promoting a certain industry would be understood in formulating the Trade and Industry Policy. For example, sulphur dioxide was listed as an air pollution emission for several industry types, and was frequently linked to a major weakness in the sulphur dioxide-carrying capacity of Durban and Richards Bay. The idea proposed was that if other industry types (those not included in the preliminary SEA) were being considered in the Policy, then they could quickly be profiled, added to the EA matrix and assessed.

Source: CSIR (1997a)

---

from these SEAs is intended to inform later stages of the project cycle. Examples include several SEAs: the Port of Cape Town (see Case Study 6.7); the Durban South Industrial Basin; Middleburg Mining; the East London West Bank Industrial Development Zone (IDZ) (see Case Study 6.1); the KwaZulu-Natal Trade and Industry Policy (Box 6.4), and the Mhlathuze municipality (where the aim was to integrate SEA and planning).

* *Large-scale EIA studies* that were labelled as SEA, although questionably in some cases. For example, the 'SEA' of the Coega Harbour and IDZ was undertaken after strategic decisions on the nature of the development and its location had been made. The EIA process for the Harbour occurred in parallel with the SEA process. So the SEA did not link to strategic decision-

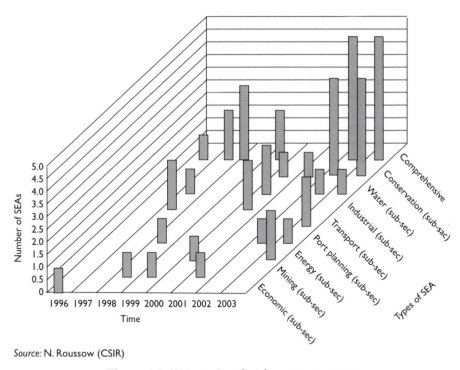

Source: N. Roussow (CSIR)

Figure 6.2 *SEAs in South Africa: 1996–2003*

making processes and was focused solely on answering the question: 'Under what conditions can development proceed?' Another example of such a post hoc regional EIA is the 'SEA' of the Cape Town Olympic bid.

In other cases, there has been a call for cumulative effects analysis following completion of a number of project EIAs with SEA to be undertaken to coordinate the projects and to achieve better regional planning.

Figure 6.2 indicates the types and number of SEA processes conducted in South Africa over the decade. Nine distinct types of SEA approaches are identified illustrating the diverse and customized framework that has emerged with elements possibly influencing experimentation in neighbouring countries. This range of approaches reflects the parallel diversification in SEA provision and systems in South Africa (Box 6.5). In addition to national SEA guidelines (DEAT/CSIR, 2000), various policies and regulations also require SEA as part of planning processes (Box 6.5).

Building on its early research work and practical experience, CSIR prepared SEA guidelines in partnership with the Department of Environmental Affairs and Tourism for application at the planning and programme level as a proactive management instrument (DEAT/CSIR, 2000). The guidelines describe the main benefits of SEA and the contribution that it can make to guide development within sustainable limits. They include principles for SEA

BOX 6.5 PROVISIONS FOR SEA IN SOUTH AFRICA'S POLICIES, LEGISLATION AND PROGRAMMES

National Environmental Management Act (1998) – requires any activity (policy, plan, programme or project) which has 'significant impact' to investigate and assess impacts:

- Land Use Bill (2003) – specifies SEA as a component of the provincial and municipal spatial development frameworks;
- White Paper on National Commercial Ports Policy (2002) – recognizes SEA as a tool for port planning to promote sustainable port development;
- National Water Act (1996) – introduced integrated catchment management agencies and plans using a catchment-wide approach;
- Mineral and Petroleum Resource Development Act (2002) and draft regulations – call for 'big picture' assessment, including cumulative impacts, a long-term social plan, etc.;
- National Forests Act (1998) – requires use of EA in deciding forestry permits;
- Some of the provincial planning ordinances – include provisions for EIA;
- Department of Trade and Industry – calls for strategic spatial planning for strategic development initiatives; and
- The Municipal Planning and Performance Management Regulations (2001) – require SEAs of the municipal spatial development framework.

---

that provide a basis for the development of local SEA processes. These are that SEA:

1 is driven by the concept of sustainability;
2 identifies the opportunities and constraints that the environment places on the development of plans and programmes;
3 sets the criteria of environmental quality or limits of acceptable change;
4 is a flexible tool that is adaptable to the planning and sectoral development cycle;
5 is a strategic process that begins with the conceptualization of the plan or programme;
6 is part of a tiered approach to environmental assessment and management;
7 has a scope defined within the wider context of environmental processes;
8 is a participative process; and
9 is set within the context of alternative scenarios.

The guidelines present SEA as including the concepts of precaution and continuous improvement and the following steps and elements:

- identify broad plan and programme alternatives;
- screening;
- scoping;
- situation assessment;

- formulate sustainability parameters for the development of the plan or programme;
- develop and assess alternative plans and programmes;
- decision-making;
- develop a plan for implementation, monitoring and auditing; and implementation.

Individual and specific SEA elements can either be used to support existing processes for plan and programme formulation, or they can be combined into a separate stand-alone SEA process, depending on what the context requires. Thus SEA is promoted as a tool to complement the planning process, by providing the information necessary to ensure that development maintains and enhances environmental resources. An example of how elements or components of SEA can be used to support local municipal planning processes is illustrated in Figure 6.3. One of the outputs of the municipal planning process illustrated in this figure is municipal spatial development frameworks (SDFs).[3] The primary objective of an SDF is to manage the type, location and quality of future growth and change in a region so that it contributes to sustainable development. Sustainable development embraces consideration of both human and ecosystem well-being, taking into account such aspects as equitable access to resources and opportunities, resilience to change, sustainable livelihoods, poverty reduction, economic efficiency and ecological integrity. An SDF is used to inform a land use management policy, and clarify needs and implementation priorities for the local authority. The preparation of an SDF thus requires a strategic approach.

There are also examples of private sector organizations coming together to commission SEAs to help them assume environmental responsibility in their operational protocols (e.g. for marine diamond mining off the west coast of South Africa – see Case Study 6.9).

6.1.2 Botswana[4]

In Botswana, the Department of Water Affairs has pioneered the application of SEA. It undertook the first documented 'SEA' process in 1991 in developing the National Water Master Plan. This outlined the social, economic and

---

3   An SDF is one strategic component of an integrated development plan (IDP) for local authority areas, required in terms of the Municipal Systems Act (2000); sectoral plans make up the remaining components of the IDP. The IDP/SDF process is based on the principles of sustainable management and use of resources making up the natural and built environment, equality, efficiency, integration, and fair and good governance. The SDF has four specific components: policy for land use and development, guidelines for land use management, a capital expenditure framework, and a strategic environmental assessment (Susie Brownlie, personal communication).

4   With contributions by Kagiso Keatimilwe, CSIR, South Africa; and Bothepa Kgabung, University of Botswana.

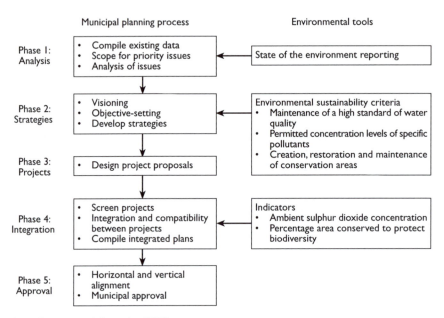

Municipal planning process   Environmental tools

Phase 1: Analysis	• Compile existing data • Scope for priority issues • Analysis of issues

State of the environment reporting

Phase 2: Strategies	• Visioning • Objective-setting • Develop strategies

Environmental sustainability criteria
• Maintenance of a high standard of water quality
• Permitted concentration levels of specific pollutants
• Creation, restoration and maintenance of conservation areas

Phase 3: Projects	• Design project proposals

Phase 4: Integration	• Screen projects • Integration and compatibility between projects • Compile integrated plans

Indicators
• Ambient sulphur dioxide concentration
• Percentage area conserved to protect biodiversity

Phase 5: Approval	• Horizontal and vertical alignment • Municipal approval

Source: Rossouw and Govender (2003)

Figure 6.3 *Example of how SEA elements can be integrated and used to support the municipal development planning process*

environmental implications of various options for providing water to the country. The plan also identified topics that should be included in an environmental assessment of water development projects: hydrology, plant ecology, faunal studies, archaeology, medico-ecological aspects, land use changes, and tourism and recreation.

Other SEA-like processes include the incorporation of environmental issues into the district and national development planning processes, and environmental management plans (EMPs) for protected areas, for example the Okavango Delta Management Plan. The application of SEA principles within the national development planning process was initiated in 1997. The process involved an audit of the seventh National Development Plan – then being implemented – to identify the environmental implications of the proposed development activities to be undertaken by each government ministry. This was an initial step towards ensuring that future development plans would reflect better consideration of environmental issues.

The audit showed that the environmental limitations to development were not considered at the outset. Most ministries did not undertake any environmental assessment of their activities and had no budget to deal with any emergencies resulting from the impact of their activities. A key output of this process was a revised *Planning Officers Manual* (still in draft) which, amongst other things, sets out the need to address environmental issues in the early stages of development planning. The revised manual has not yet been formally approved. But the principles in it have been applied in preparing subsequent development plans, and have helped to address environmental implications more explicitly. The latest development plan (National Development Plan 9) includes a chapter on the environment. It identifies key environmental issues needing to be addressed as well as pointing out the limits that the environment places on development.

Following the national process, a pilot exercise was undertaken in three local authorities (Central District, Selibe-Phikwe, and Gaborone) in 2000 to examine the adequacy of district plans in addressing environmental issues (Figure 6.4). The audit of the three authorities looked at the likely impacts of projects contained in the district plans (e.g. Republic of Botswana, 2001a, b). There were two main outputs: the *Environmental Planning Manual* which provides a detailed process for integrating environmental issues in district planning; and a revised version of the *District Planning Handbook*, which summarizes the key aspects. The documents have been instrumental in shaping the latest local authority plans, although they are still in draft form.

The Okavango River has been subjected to two SEA-type processes: one for the whole river basin (covering Angola, Botswana and Namibia); another for the part of the system in Botswana (the delta). The development of the Strategic Action Plan for the basin (OKACOM, 1999) involved several components: (i) specialist studies on particular issues such as climate, hydrology and land use; (ii) an assessment of characteristics and limits of the various parameters; and (iii) the formulation of development and management options consistent with maintaining the integrity of the delta. The development of a management plan for the Okavango delta (still ongoing; Box 6.6) is the most recent example of an SEA-type process in Botswana. The process will involve the setting of a vision for the delta and the formulation of development options consistent with that vision.

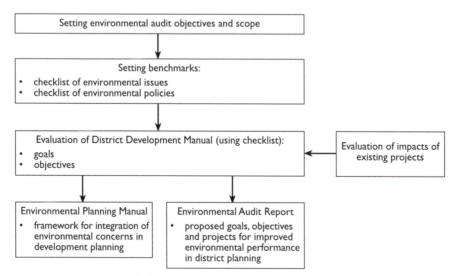

Figure 6.4 *Framework for environmental audit of district development plans, Botswana*

BOX 6.6 OKAVANGO DELTA MANAGEMENT PLAN

The Okavango Delta Management Plan was prepared to:

> integrate resource management for the delta that will ensure its long-term conservation and that will provide benefits for the present and future well being of the people, through sustainable use of its natural resources; and to develop a comprehensive, integrated management plan for the conservation and sustainable use of the delta and surrounding areas.

There have been various proposals for large-scale water off-take and watershed development in the delta area. But there is little climatic and hydrological information to predict the impacts of hydrological changes on the delta's ecology. In the past, planning and decision- making did not consider the overall economic value of an intact delta ecosystem. Key issues in the delta area include: land and resource use conflicts; tourism; settlement; and grazing (zoning for both of the latter two issues is provided in the Plan). The Management Plan aims to:

- provide a long-term vision of the development options and management scenarios for the Okavango Delta;
- serve as an integrated, dynamic management plan, which provides the overarching framework and contextual guidelines for individual area and sector plans;
- determine levels of use in order to ensure sustainability and protection of the natural resources of the Ramsar site;
- set up the institutional framework required for the management of the Ramsar site;
- determine research and monitoring requirements and standards;
- provide data and information requirements and feed development options into the OKACOM (the Okavango River Basin Commission – Botswana, Namibia and Angola) basin management planning exercise; and
- build capacity in the implementing institutions and in communities.

Source: Source: NCSA (2002)

6.1.3 Lesotho[5]

The Environment Act No 15 of 2001 does not specifically refer to SEA, but it is implicit in the provisions under the schedule on types of projects for which an EIA is required:

(a) major changes in land use;
(b) urban and rural development including:
  – re-zoning;
  – declaration of development areas;
(c) national conservation areas which include:
  – formulation or modification of forest management policies;
  – formulation or modification of water catchment management policies;
  – policies for management of ecosystems, especially by use of fire;
  – any government policy on the use of natural resources.

---

5 With contribution by Bore Motsamai, Botswana.

The Act also provides an umbrella safeguard by stipulating that any policy that will lead to projects that are likely to impact on the environment will require an EIA. It still remains to be seen how this will be put into practice. The most appropriate route would be through promulgation of enabling regulations of the Act.

Prior to the Rio Earth Summit on sustainable development, Lesotho developed the first National Environmental Action Plan (NEAP) in Africa in 1989. It was subsequently incorporated into a National Action Plan to Implement Agenda 21 to provide a basis for integrating environment and socioeconomic concerns. These issues are also central in Lesotho's Poverty Reduction Strategy and National Vision (2003).

The feasibility studies for Phase 1A of the Lesotho Highlands Water Project (LHWP)[6] had no EIA but, based on the lessons from this phase, Phase IB involved several baseline studies. These culminated in a comprehensive environmental impact study (undertaken by consultants) and an accompanying environmental action plan aimed at mitigating project impacts. The latest report (2002) on 'Development of a Katse and Mohale Reservoir Zoning Plan' by the Lesotho Highlands Development Authority (LHDA) has a component on SEA. The description of the features of the two areas, Phase 1A (Katse) and 1B (Mohale), was used to define a suite of strategic environmental issues. Criteria for sustainable development were then identified. These were used to guide zoning and management options.

Similarly, under the Maloti–Drakensberg Conservation and Development Project – a transfrontier initiative straddling the borders of Lesotho and South Africa – a resource analysis and strategic environmental assessment will be carried out for development planning under the protected area planning programme.

6.1.4 Malawi

Several legal documents support EA in Malawi: the Malawi Constitution, Vision 2020, the National Environmental Action Plan (1994), the Environmental Management Act (1996), and the National Environmental Policy (1996). Policies were restructured whilst formulating the Decentralisation Act (1998). From the late 1990s, the Danish International Development Agency (DANIDA), the World Bank and other donors funded the Environmental Support Programme and supported the process of decentralization. This included support for the formulation of district environmental action plans (DEAPs). By the time DANIDA funding ceased in

---

6   The LHWP is Africa's largest infrastructure project – a massive, multi-dam scheme built to divert water from Lesotho's Maloti Mountains to South Africa's industrial Gauteng Province. Construction is being undertaken in four phases. The first phases of the World Bank-supported project involve the construction of three large dams which, when completed, will dispossess more than 30,000 rural farmers of assets (including homes, fields, and grazing lands) and deprive many of their livelihoods.

2002, some districts had not fully formulated their DEAPs. As a consequence, some activities stopped whilst others have continued under normal government programmes.

The Environmental Management Act (EMA) mandates the Department of Environmental Affairs to certify projects requiring an EA. The EMA makes EA mandatory for all sectoral projects and requires that all sectoral policies should integrate EA. If other sector policies are in conflict with the EMA, the EMA takes precedence.

6.1.5 Mozambique[7]

EIA has been applied in Mozambique since 1993, but the regulation was only formally approved in December 1998. It includes provisions covering EIA, EMPs and environmental auditing. It also requires that an EIA be undertaken for all development projects and PPP that may have a significant impact on the environment.

The Ministry of Environmental Affairs recognized the need to improve the planning process. In 2002, it engaged in a series of internal discussions with other government bodies and provincial authorities. These led to an SEA being undertaken in Inhambane Province. It was driven by the need to improve planning in a large coastal area with growing tourism to several beaches (Tofo, Barra, Rocha, Tofinho and Rocha Tofo), and to make EIA more efficient and flexible. SEA was used to encourage an holistic approach to environmental management in this area. It also aimed to overcome the need for separate EIAs for the increasing number of tourist lodges being constructed (see Case Study 6.2). Subsequently, several more SEAs have been undertaken (Table 6.2).

One is being undertaken in connection with the exportation of sands rich in heavy minerals. Initially, the idea was to export the sands by rail from the mine through the port of Maputo. Separate EIAs were started for different components of the operation (power line, mine, railway to Maputo). But it was then proposed to construct a new coastal jetty away from Maputo where plans were also being developed for tourism. The new proposal was assessed by the Government, supported by the Southern African Institute for Environmental Assessment (SAIEA) and the Netherlands Commission for EIA. It was recommended that an SEA be undertaken due to the wider potential effects of the proposal. A decision-making group has been established (directors of government departments) as well as a 'platform group' of technical experts and stakeholders where the outcomes will be discussed. The best alternative was selected from six scenarios identified during a platform group workshop assisted by an independent facilitator. The final decision will be taken by the National Council for Sustainable Development (CONDES), co-chaired by the Prime Minister and Minister of Environment.

---

7   With contribution by Felicidade Munguambe.

Other assessments include:

- A para-SEA is being undertaken in support of the Tourism Development Plan for the Limpopo National Park (the Mozambican side of the Great Limpopo Transboundary Park covering Mozambique, South Africa and Zimbabwe). It is considering a variety of issues relating to the movement of wildlife, the erection of fences, tourism and various management issues.
- SEA exercises are being undertaken in the coastal areas of Mozambique, for example the coastal districts of Inhambane Province (700km long), Manhica District and in the lakeshore of Lake Niasa.
- An SEA for an industrial park in Maputo (funded by the World Bank) was initiated under environmental planning for the Natal Free Trade Zone; and a sectoral environmental assessment for the agricultural sector investment programme was required by the Bank.
- The overview and initial EA of the PROAGRI (agricultural sector development programme) corresponds to a sector-based SEA (Chonguiça et al, 1998).

Table 6.2 *Examples of SEAs in Mozambique*

SEA	Type	Scale	Tier	Did SEA provide information before decision?	Did SEA precede EIA?	Was SEA linked to PPP?
1. SEA for Tofo, Barra, Tofinho and Rocha, Inhambane Province	Tourism	Local	Plan	No	No	Yes
2. SEA for corridor sands, Chibuto District	Mines	Regional	Plan	Yes	No	No
3. SEA for zoning planning, Jangamo District	Tourism	Local	Plan	No	No	No
4. SEA of Zoning Plan of Limpopo National Park	Tourism	Local	Plan	No	Yes	No
5. SEA of Zoning Plan of Manhica District	Development plan	Local	Plan	No	–	Yes
6. SEA of Zoning Plan of the Coastal Zone of Lake Niassa	Development plan	Local	Plan	No	–	Yes
7. SEA for Plan of Poverty Alleviation (PRSP)*	Poverty strategy	National	Policy	–	–	–
8. SEA of District Plans of Sanga, Niassa and Nampula provinces	Development plan	Regional	Plan	No	–	Yes

Note: * PRSP = poverty strategy reduction paper

- The Well-being Assessment approach, using the 'barometer of sustainability' method developed by Prescott-Allen (2001a), has been adopted as part of district planning. It combines an Ecosystem Well-being Index (EWI) and human indicators into a Human Well-being Index (HWI).

6.1.6 Namibia[8]

Various SEA-type activities have been undertaken in Namibia. At the highest level, an effort has been made to incorporate environmental and sustainable development issues into Namibia's Second National Development Plan (NDP2), 2001–2006 (see Case Study 6.4). In addition, Vision 2030 aims to help guide the country's five-year development plans from NDP3 through to NDP7, whilst providing direction to government ministries, the private sector, NGOs and local authorities. This exercise embraces the idea of sustainable development and refers to tools such as EIA and SEA.

Like many countries in the region, Namibia has also initiated a number of sector and land use planning processes. These fit some of the criteria for SEA because of the levels of integration achieved, their emphasis on environmentally sustainable development, and the stated need to balance strategic thinking with more detailed project-specific planning. They include the Sperrgebiet Land Use Plan (Case Study 6.8), the Northwest Tourism Master Plan and the Walvis Bay Structure Plan. The 'Every River Has its People' project has assessed the resource use potential and development options of the Okavango River in all three basin countries (Angola, Namibia and Botswana). This study included a comprehensive analysis of socioeconomic and land tenure issues, and is a good example of a basin-wide approach to development planning. Namibia's community-based natural resource management programme has also undertaken SEA-type activities. These include broad-based planning at the conservancy[9] level and more detailed tourism development planning at project level.

Perhaps the most 'classic' SEA in Namibia is a study of the development of the agricultural and fisheries potential of eastern Caprivi (Box 6.7). This began as a project-specific EIA to assess the impacts of a proposed sugar project, but soon shifted to an SEA. This change in status was prompted by an early realization that sugar was probably not the ideal crop for the area. It also became evident that the Ministry of Fisheries was planning to rehabilitate Lake Liambezi – the area originally intended for the sugar project. Whilst the study

---

8   With contribution by Peter Tarr, SAIEA.
9   A conservancy is a defined geographical area for wildlife management. The approach developed in South Africa where groups of adjacent commercial farmers removed fences to allow animals to roam freely. They agreed a constitution, a set of operating rules and criteria for distributing income from wildlife. The idea spread to Namibia and was also taken up in the communal areas of Namibia as a mechanism to provide rights to wildlife. Here a conservancy also occupies a specified area, has a defined membership (of individuals), a legal constitution and a land management plan. Some conservancies are very small; others comprise several villages.

Box 6.7 SEA of Caprivi Sugar Project, Namibia

Background

In 1998, the Namibian Government commissioned a feasibility study to investigate the possibility of developing a 10,000ha sugar plantation and mill in the Lake Liambezi area of the Caprivi Region in northeastern Namibia. The purpose of the project was to create employment in the region, to supply sugar for domestic use and for export to countries within Southern Africa. The study was optimistic about the project. But falling sugar prices, the weakening of the Namibian dollar against international currencies and various other factors prevented it from proceeding.

The Ministry of Agriculture, Water and Rural Development (MAWRD) re-examined the proposal in 2001. It hired a consortium of international and local consultants to undertake a project-level EIA. The scope of the EIA included an assessment of the project's economic viability as well as more conventional biophysical and social impacts. The MAWRD engaged the services of the Southern African Institute for Environmental Assessment (SAIEA) to guide and review the study as an independent broker.

The issues

After a comprehensive scoping exercise which included consultations with all the key stakeholders, both within Namibia and neighbouring countries, the major issues of concern were identified as:

- water use and the impact on the environment and downstream users (450 million m^3 per annum would be pumped out of the Zambezi River, a watercourse shared with Zambia, Botswana, Zimbabwe and Mozambique);
- the control of pests (including elephants, hippos and other wildlife);
- surface and groundwater pollution (mainly from agrochemicals and pesticides);
- land alienation (displacement of villagers in the area);
- conflicts with other land use (e.g. conservation, subsistence fisheries, subsistence crop production, small-scale cattle ranching and tourism); and
- social and health impacts associated with the influx of workers, either foreign or from different tribes.

The study

Initially, the study strictly followed the terms of reference. But concerns over the suitability of soils in the project area and the financial viability of the project soon prompted a rethink of the approach. Both the consultant and SAIEA encouraged the proponent to take a more strategic approach, to consider crops other than sugar, and to examine areas other than Liambezi.

Moreover, it emerged that the Ministry of Fisheries and Marine Resources (MFMR) was also considering a project at Lake Liambezi that would stimulate improved subsistence fish harvesting. The lake can remain dry for years on end, filling only when the nearby River Zambezi is in high flood. With the arrival of the floods, the lake teams with fish and a short period of plenty is enjoyed by the surrounding community. The MFMR project aimed to artificially increase the 'flood times' and thus extend the period when fish would be available, though still allowing the lake to become dry. The dry lake is important for seasonal crop growing and cattle grazing.

> The MAWRD and the MFMR agreed that a more strategic approach was more sensible under the circumstances, and the EIA was transformed into an SEA in 2003. Important aspects are:
>
> *   investigating a variety of high value crops in various areas, especially those that will require less water and that will be less vulnerable to pests and droughts;
> *   examining the possibility of planting crops that can be harvested at different times, (thus providing opportunities for permanent rather than seasonal labour);
> *   reducing opportunity costs between the agriculture and fisheries options; and
> *   integrating existing farmers into the new projects.
>
> The SEA aimed to highlight which projects were likely to be sustainable and how best synergies between the various forms of land use could be obtained.
>
> ### Lessons learned to date
>
> This case illustrates the importance of maintaining flexibility in an EA process and ensuring a healthy dialogue between the proponent, the reviewer and the consultant.
>
> However, it would have been far more sensible to commission an SEA at the start of the process. This would have reduced the need to overcome preconceived ideas and entrenched positions. Nevertheless, the case shows that it is possible to 'upstream' a project-level EIA.
>
> *Source:* Box contributed by Peter Tarr, SAIEA

is not yet complete, it is likely that a 'mixed bag' of crops will replace the original sugar proposal. The SEA will provide detailed guidelines of how each 'crop project' should be implemented and how the development of infrastructure and the provision of labour should be planned.

Another case involved the innovative application of sustainability assessment (SA) to determining the future of the Rössing uranium mine. This followed a number of previous EIAs, which had been completed previously. The SA included strategic aspects and options that focused on far more than the sustainability aspects of mine operations. It compared the consequences of mine closure (scheduled for about 2008) with a scenario of extending mine operations for a further 15 years (Box 6.8). The SA was also participative, guided by a multi-stakeholder steering committee that included government agencies, NGOs, labour and company management.

A less comprehensive 'SEA' was undertaken by Namibia's Ministry of Environment and Tourism in 2000. It assessed the potential for community-based tourism in the proposed Bwabwata National Park. This assessment included government, community and private sector participation. It considered the combined impacts of at least three tourist camps in the Kwando area and the use of the area by three up-market lodges adjacent to the park. The assessment remains the guiding document for the development of the campsites, which have proceeded without individual EIAs.

Box 6.8 Rössing uranium mine sustainability assessment

Rössing Uranium Limited (RUL) has been mining at Arandis in the Erongo Region of Namibia since 1976. Over the past 12 years the company has conducted seven EIAs on the mine and component parts of the mining process. These have all contributed to the development and continuous upgrading of its EMP, which includes a closure plan. The key biophysical issues relating to the mine include water use, groundwater pollution from the tailings, air quality and biodiversity loss as a result of physical disturbance to the environment. Socioeconomic issues include direct and indirect employment, skills development and significant contributions to the local and national economy.

In 2004 RUL was considering expanding the mine and thus extending its life for approximately 15 years beyond the expected closure in about 2008. In addition to technical and financial feasibility investigations, the company has taken into account the environmental, social and economic implications of mine life extension. Towards this end, RUL commissioned an SA rather than simply doing more EIAs for the extension components. The SA was guided by a multi-stakeholder steering committee. This included government agencies, NGOs, labour and RUL management. External consultants and Rio Tinto Zinc (RTZ) experts conducted the SA.

The SA was conducted in two parts for two scenarios:

1 an initial comparative EA of the potential impacts of the expansion of the life of the mine within its footprint area, against the environmental performance of the base case (i.e. operation of the mine until closure in 2008); and
2 a comparative SA of the broader implications of the base case operation against the proposed expansion of the life of the mine, including implications for the town of Arandis and the Erongo Region as well as the broader Namibian economy.

To guide the SA, the first step was the formulation of RUL's vision for sustainable development through discussions with key stakeholders and mine management:

> During its continued operation as well as following closure, RUL activities will have made a positive contribution to the ability of current and future generations in Namibia and more specifically, in Arandis and the Erongo Region, to improve their quality of life.

This vision is also consistent with, and served to translate for local conditions, RTZ's Group Policy for Sustainable Development: 'To ensure that our businesses, operations and products contribute to the global transition to sustainable development.' (Rio Tinto Sustainable Development Working Group, November 2000).

The project team used a cumulative EA approach to identify sustainability indicators. This included considering the compounding (synergies) of several effects: the crowding (additive effects) of potential impacts in the local area surrounding the mine, in the Erongo Region and in Namibia; and the potential for impacts to become manifest after a time lag (as opposed to immediate or short-term effects). In this way, all indirect downstream effects of the two mine development scenarios were analysed for their contribution to achieving, or reducing the ability to achieve, sustainability. The rationale for this approach was that the higher the incidence of, or significance of, cumulative negative impacts, the lower the potential for sustainability. Conversely, the higher the potential for positive cumulative effects, the higher the potential for sustainability.

Each of the two alternative development scenarios was evaluated for its sustainability performance against the agreed sustainability criteria, using the selected sustainability indicators.

The overall aim of the SA was: (i) to create awareness amongst decision-makers about the impacts of the two scenarios on sustainable development; and (ii) to help them establish which scenario would contribute more to maintaining or improving natural, social and economic systems rather than just minimizing environmental impacts.

The SA showed that extension of mine operations will enable RUL to significantly improve its positive legacy through a number of actions: more focused social development programmes; reskilling the workforce and assisting people in finding alternative employment following mine closure; improving the management of mine tailings and downstream water quality monitoring; and finding ways to diversify the economic base of Arandis town.

Following the SA the decision was taken to extend the life of the mine until 2015.

Source: Peter Tarr, personal communication

6.1.7 Swaziland[10]

The Swaziland Environment Authority was established by the Environment Authority Act of 1992. In 2000, the Authority produced the Environmental Audit, Assessment and Review Regulations (with support from the UK Department for International Development, DFID). These Regulations provide for both EIA and SEA, but they could not be enforced due to weaknesses in the legal framework and shortages in human resources and capacity. The Environment Management Act has recently received royal assent but has not yet been fully enacted. It will require SEAs for new legislation, regulations, policies, programmes or plans. Furthermore, it will make the Swaziland Environment Authority a 'parastatal organization'[11] with increases in human resources and skills and budget to help the organization to fulfil its mandate and objectives.

Box 6.9 lists several ongoing SEA-like processes in Swaziland.

6.1.8 Tanzania[12]

There are still no comprehensive legal requirements for either EIA or SEA in mainland Tanzania, although there are specific requirements for EIA in some sectors (e.g. minerals). However, a new Environmental Management Act was passed by parliament in 2004. This sets out the institutional arrangements for environmental management. Regulations for EIA and SEA will now be developed.

---

10 With contribution by Themb'a Mahlaba, University of Swaziland.
11 A semi-autonomous body.
12 With contributions by Raphael Mwalyosi, Institute of Resource Assessment, University of Dar es Salaam; and David Howlett, UNDP, Tanzania.

Box 6.9 Some SEA-like processes in Swaziland

Expressions of interest have been invited to undertake the *Joint Umbeluzi River Basin Study* – covering Swaziland, Mozambique and to a lesser extent South Africa. The primary objective of this study is to quantify the present and future water balance in the Umbeluzi river basin in each of the two co-basin states. It also aims to plan and/or propose future water resource development or management options so as to meet the future water demands as optimally, sustainably and equitably as possible. This nine-month study will also consider opportunities for water utilization, conservation and, basin management, and will include assessment of the social and biophysical environments.

The country's *Biodiversity Strategy and Action Plan* calls for increased protection of representative examples of biodiversity. So a project was initiated in 2001 under the Southern Africa Biodiversity Support Programme to identify areas worthy of protection. Earlier surveys (1972 and 1979) identified over 30 such pristine areas vulnerable to human impacts. In 2001, the information from these surveys was updated through a desktop assessment undertaken by local ecologists. Forty-three areas were identified and visited. Using the World Wide Fund for Nature's rapid assessment technique, land was scored and prioritized according to the following factors:

1   biological importance (species richness, presence of endemic species, etc.);
2   socioeconomic importance (tourist accessibility, development opportunities, local resource dependence etc.); and
3   threats from: alien plants and animals; resource utilization; poaching; settlement; impending land use changes; isolation; pollution; and erosion from cattle, tracks, footpaths, etc.

The *Swaziland Biodiversity Conservation and Participatory Development Project* will develop ecotourism through partnerships with businesses and communities. The heart of the project involves the development (and implementation) of integrated corridor management plans (ICMPs) through an integrated spatial development planning process (ISPP). It represents a land- use planning exercise on a large, landscape scale that takes into account both physical resources and ecological and economic processes. These ICMPs will provide the framework for land use, development and investment within each proposed biodiversity-tourism (B-T) corridor.

The objectives of ICMPs stress the conservation and sustainable use of natural resources (particularly biodiversity), ecological systems and processes, and aesthetic landscapes of the area. The ICMPs will aim to ensure environmental sustainability and positive social and local economic impacts. So they will be based on strategic environmental (including social) assessments, and on economic analysis. The latter will highlight the economic value of the land and natural resource base, and elucidate the short- and long-term trade-offs associated with various development options. Government and stakeholder commitment to these ICMPs is expected to provide an attractive environment for stimulating responsible private sector investment and leveraging other government and donor support.

In practice, the B-T corridors are ecosystem planning areas in which different types of land uses at different sites all contribute in their own way to overall biodiversity conservation and natural resource management objectives. Four main land use categories are envisaged. These are based on their main role in relation to the project objectives: (i) core protected areas (PAs), (ii) tourism development zones, (iii) linkage/connection areas, and (iv) 'support zones'. Core PAs may include both existing formally gazetted PAs and new areas under some form of community-based conservation scheme. Tourism development zones will be based on high potential for attracting tourism investment and contributing to local sustainable development. Linkage/connection areas may serve an ecological function (ensure habitat continuity, migratory pathways, etc.) and/or a tourism function (e.g. creating a suitable circuit that hikers or others can follow between tourism development 'foci').The remaining areas within the corridors will be support areas. Here, neither biodiversity conservation nor tourism development will be priority objectives; but improved natural resource management will be required to support the broader conservation and tourism objectives. Also in these support areas, communities will be able to participate in and benefit from the conservation and tourism initiatives taking place in neighbouring areas, for example by supplying goods and services to tourism facilities. Like the spatial development initiatives (SDIs) pursued by Swaziland and others in the region (e.g. South Africa, Mozambique), the B-T corridors represent a vehicle for promoting coherent economic development within a spatially defined area, on a scale large enough to attract a critical mass of private sector investment.

In 1998, the *Ministry of Economic Planning* initiated a system under which project proponents were required to complete a form quantifying the environmental implications. Following the end of donor funding, the system has not been pursued.

It is anticipated that the new law will include provisions for incorporating EA in national, sectoral, district and community planning processes (although there is extremely limited capacity at the last two levels) as well as requirements to undertake SEA. Formal requirements for EIA have been in place for the island of Zanzibar for several years but do not cover SEA.

Several examples of EAs and planning processes in the wildlife and other sectors in Tanzania correspond to the notion of SEA or para-SEA approaches:. general management plans (GMPs) for national parks and conservation areas; and programmatic environmental assessment for road improvements.

GMPs for national parks and conservation areas

EIA has been extended to cover the GMPs prepared for Tanzanian national parks (e.g. TANAPA Planning Unit, 1993, 1994a, 1994b). More than half of Tanzania's parks have such plans in place. These deal with issues within the parks and do not include external dimensions or all key stakeholders. EIA is also being extended to cover the general management zone plans (MZPs) currently being prepared for each national park (Box 6.10) and the Board of the Tanzania National Parks (TANAPA) has signalled that all GMPs must be subjected to an SEA. Training for park ecologists and planners has been undertaken through the Institute of Resource Assessment, University of Dar es Salaam.

The development of the Ngorongoro Conservation Area General Management Plan was undertaken over a period of almost ten years (1987–1996). The planning involved a wide range of technical studies, field surveys and censuses, assessments, workshops, and community-level meetings – all concerned with the status and management of natural resources, social

BOX 6.10 MANAGEMENT ZONE PLANNING/EIA IN TANZANIAN NATIONAL PARKS

Background

In 1994 Tanzania National Parks (TANAPA) became the first sector organization in the country to develop its own policy and guidelines for EIA in Tanzanian national parks. TANAPA's policy requires the preparation of an EIA for all developments and activities within and adjacent to the national park boundaries (TANAPA Planning Unit, 1994a, b). The policy includes all development activities proposed by TANAPA, as well as other government agencies and private sector proponents. EIA is also being extended to cover the general management zone plans (MZPs) currently being prepared for each national park. To -date, such initiatives have been undertaken for Serengeti, Manyara, Kilimanjaro, Ruaha and Tarangire National Parks.

The MZPs have been undertaken in response to tourism development pressure in the parks, exacerbated by a politically motivated decision to construct tourist facilities in ecologically sensitive areas of the parks. These pressures have emerged in the wake of the implementation of the new national liberalization policy, which encourages tourism and private sector development. The MZPs are intended to guide tourism infrastructure development in the parks.

The MZP/EIA process is an interdisciplinary park planning effort intended to achieve the following objectives:

* establish the park's purpose and significance;
* identify exceptional resource values and management objectives;
* prepare a management zoning scheme that identifies what can and cannot occur, with specific emphasis on development and use;
* determine the limits of acceptable use and development for the overall park and for each zone within the park; and
* assess the environmental impacts of the zoning scheme and limits of acceptance use.

Unfortunately, the above objectives focus primarily on visitor use and development and to a more limited degree on natural resources management. A full range of management objectives, which also address the integration of interests lying outside the park boundary, will be incorporated into the comprehensive general management plans when they are prepared at a later point in time.

The EIA process

This cannot be considered as an EIA, as conventionally viewed. TANAPA has consistently misused the EIA concept as a proxy for environmental review, which is intended to rationalize tourist management within the parks. As a result, the process has not involved scoping, has not determined impact significance and has not identified mitigation measures or prepared a monitoring plan. Finally, the environmental consequences of the plans have been considered in terms of positive gains as opposed to disadvantages or losses that are likely to result if the plans are not implemented. The EIAs can be criticized for several technical inadequacies:

- The planning process has lacked the participation of government and other stakeholder groups.
- Planning has been biased towards tourism development and its related impacts on the viability of national parks. Ideally, it should have also considered other issues, such as those related to wildlife/natural resource management and (baseline) research.
- The planning, zoning and EIA process should have considered both the positive and negative impacts of implementing and not implementing the plan.
- There should have been a more explicit commitment to impact mitigation and monitoring the plan – clarifying the roles of TANAPA-HQ, individual national park management teams and research. Where possible, the costs of mitigation and monitoring should have been estimated.

Because this was an environmental review rather than a conventional EIA, it is difficult and probably too early to appraise its effect on decision-making. However, the adoption of management zone planning and EIA by TANAPA has played a major role in guiding the scale and type of development activities in the country's parks.

Lessons for EIA policy

The EIAs on the MZPs for national parks represent a form of para-SEA in Tanzania. But it would be much better if the planning process involved all the stakeholder groups.

Although MZPs/EIAs are in place in some parks, this does not guarantee their effective implementation and, hence, also not the sustained viability of the parks unless anthropogenic factors emanating from the park surroundings are also addressed and incorporated in the GMP.

Source: Prepared by Raphael B. B. Mwalyosi, Institute of Resource Assessment, University of Dar es Salaam

---

and economic conditions and future development directions. The GMP was subjected to a comprehensive EIA.

Programmatic environmental assessment for road improvements

The programmatic environmental assessment (PEA) for road improvements in Tanzanian national park roads was jointly conceived by the United States Agency for International Development (USAID) and TANAPA and motivated by TANAPA initiative and USAID regulatory requirements (Box 6.11).

In 2003, the Office of the Vice President initiated a study, with the support of the United Nations Development Programme (UNDP), on SEA and its potential for use in Tanzania and linkages to the poverty reduction strategy process. This study is being used in a comprehensive review of Tanzania's poverty reduction strategy (PRS). The new PRS was expected in late 2004 and is likely to address the integration of environment into policy- and plan-making and the potential role of SEA in this.

BOX 6.11 SEA OF ROAD DEVELOPMENT IN NATIONAL PARKS, TANZANIA

USAID is funding equipment for road improvements in several national parks and its regulations required that a PEA be undertaken. TANAPA also had its own procedures and guidelines that required an SEA for this project. So a joint PEA/SEA was undertaken. The National Environmental Management Council (NEMC) became a partner in the SEA to use the case to test the draft Environmental Policy.

The PEA study considered:

- the role of roads in national parks in the future;
- road improvement and TANAPA's efforts to enforce the 'limits of acceptable use' in park zoning with respect to road improvements;
- biodiversity conservation;
- contribution to revenues; and
- tourism development.

The process was undertaken in 2001 and began with an intensive, month-long scoping exercise to identify the significant issues to be addressed in the full assessment. This involved full consultation with all affected parties and review of the draft report. The scoping report underscored that the PEA should contribute to sounder design, construction, operation and decommissioning of roads in national parks and other protected areas; and thereby reduce potentially adverse environmental impacts and avoid the cost of correcting serious problems after the fact.

The PEA team was then selected with a mix of required skills to address the key issues: engineering, planning, ecology, EIA, and so on. Due to limited time and financial resources, the full PEA study sampled physical and ecological conditions in five representative parks on the 'northern circuit'. Over four weeks, the team assessed the impacts of 2200km of different road types (using TANAPA's road classification system) in a range of geological, soil, meteorological, topographic and ecological conditions. The 'no roads' options were also considered.

Issues were addressed under four broad categories: physical resources, ecological systems, landscape issues and socioeconomics. Matrices were developed to analyse and rank road activities against environmental and social impacts (both adverse and beneficial) during the road planning and design, construction, operation and decommissioning stages. Consideration was also given to indirect, induced and cumulative impacts. Each team member was polled in a group session to obtain a ranking from high, medium or low adverse or beneficial impact for each road activity. The team members reached a consensus as a group on the rankings for each category of impact. The results of the exercise were compared with the priority issues identified by stakeholders. Mitigation measures were also developed through such consultative discussions and joint review of drafts.

Outputs of the study have included:

- a set of recommended environmental procedures to (i) screen categories of road improvements, and (ii) for the environmental review of the construction, rehabilitation, realignment, operation and maintenance, and decommissioning of roads over which TANAPA has responsibility;
- a template identifying impacts and mitigation measures;
- suggestions for alternative road design and maintenance;
- recommendations for the minimum number of members for a multidisciplinary team;
- comments on institutional considerations; and
- preferred action recommendations.

Source: Raphael Mwalyosi (presentation at SEA workshop, Windhoek, Namibia, 15–16 May 2003)

6.1.9 Zambia[13]

In 1997, Statutory Instrument No 28 established a framework for management of EIA in Zambia. The Environmental Council of Zambia (ECZ) is the focal point for management of the EIA Regulations. It has a mandate for three main functions: EIA quality control conducted within country; supervision and guidance during the EA process; and ensuring adherence to standards and regulations during the implementation and operation of projects.

There is now a fairly well-developed regulatory system, which is well recognized by major stakeholders such as the mining industry and other developers. However, there is still a need to increase awareness of EIA and its role and benefits in other development sectors such as roads, tourism and industry. As a consequence, the ECZ faces an enforcement problem due to limited financial and staff resources in relation to the growing number of development projects – many of which go unnoticed with no EIA.

The ECZ was established in 1992 under the Environmental Protection and Pollution Control Act (1990), cap 204. EIA regulations were introduced in 1997 and the ECZ is developing sector guidelines for EIA reviews. There is no specific provision for SEA in the regulations although the Act states (Section 6, sub-section (j)) that:

> *the Council shall identify projects or types of projects, plans and policies for which environmental impact assessments are necessary and undertake or request others to undertake such assessments for consideration by the Council.*

Under the law, this provision can only be effected by establishing guidelines through regulations to implement it. The absence of such regulations means that SEA is not formally enforced and the mode of operation is little understood.

One initiative that approximates to an SEA is the Copperbelt Environmental Assessment. It was prepared for Zambia Consolidated Copper Mines (ZCCM) Investment Holdings Limited in February 2002 as part of an assessment of the Copperbelt Environmental Project (CEP). The overall objective of the CEP is to address historical, environmental and social liabilities arising from copper mining operations in Zambia and also to strengthen the environmental regulatory framework. The CEP was categorized as an 'A' project under World Bank guidelines and thus required a full EA to be completed and disclosed prior to project appraisal. The EA identified potential impacts but did not quantify them (e.g. the footprint of a tailing dam failure and the downstream impacts on numbers of people and property areis not determined). It is anticipated that the detailed impacts will be addressed during the preparation of individual or consolidated EMPs.

---

13   With contributions by Edward Zulu, Environmental Council of Zambia; and Mushimbeyi Muliya, Department of Roads, Zambia.

Several SEA-like processes have been conducted in the tourism sector. Examples are the design of management plans for national parks (e.g. Lower Zambezi National Park, Kafue National Park, South and North Luangwa National Parks). The management plans aimed to ensure efficiency in the management of wildlife resources and development and management of tourism enterprises. They included EAs combining aspects of land use planning and principles of project-specific EAs. The studies identified various land use zones as a basis for park planning and set out goals (visions) with timeframes. In addition, plans prepared for many game management areas (GMAs) surrounding national parks (where development activities may have an effect on the sustainability of parks) can be regarded as a form of para-SEA (e.g. for GMAs surrounding the Lower Zambezi National Park and Mosi-o-Tunya National Park).

Various sectoral programmes have been subjected to EA:

- The Zambia Social Investment Programme (ZAMSIF) comprises several sub-projects that are now being considered for EIA;
- An integrated approach is being applied to the Water Resources Action Plan (WRAP) in which environmental and social concerns are being integrated in developing the plan. This is expected to be implemented in association with communities at catchment levels.
- A number of action plans have been prepared for the management of shared water bodies such as the Zambezi River Basin. The process has outlined strategic visions and goals to allow for efficient and fair management of, and access to, the use of water by member countries (mostly SADC) in the river basin.

6.1.10 Zimbabwe

The Ministry of Mines, Environment and Tourism published an EIA policy in 1994, but there are no formal requirements for SEA. However, this approach has been applied on an ad hoc basis, for example as a result of concern about the cumulative effects of expanding tourism in the area around the Victoria Falls (a designated UN Educational, Scientific and Cultural Organization – UNESCO – World Heritage Site). This issue prompted the Governments of Zambia and Zimbabwe to conduct an SEA (completed in 1996), using a scenario approach, as part of efforts to prepare a master plan for the area (Box 6.12).

An SEA of safari and cultural tourism in and around Hwange National Park was undertaken by Spenceley (1997) as a research project. The approach relied heavily on the use of semi-structured interviews and questionnaire surveys with selected stakeholder target groups. Subsequently, the findings of the SEA were incorporated into the new master plans for the area prepared under the Town and Country Planning Act. Such master plans are prepared for sensitive areas where there is conflict over land use.

BOX 6.12 SEA OF DEVELOPMENT AROUND VICTORIA FALLS, 1996

The Victoria Falls area was designated a UNESCO World Heritage Site in 1989. In response to this, and to the need to deal with the cumulative impacts of expanding tourism in the area, an SEA was commissioned by the Governments of Zambia and Zimbabwe and financed by the Canadian International Development Agency (CIDA). The IUCN Regional Office for Southern Africa (IUCN-ROSA) provided technical assistance. The objectiive was to provide information for the development of a master plan for the Victoria Falls area, and to prepare an outline management plan with policies, management measures, zoning, monitoring and institutional arrangements.

The focus and framework for the SEA was set by a scoping workshop attended by 50 representatives of key stakeholders. Overall guidance was provided by a steering committee comprising representatives of the National Heritage Conservation Committee (Zambia), the Department of the Environment (Zimbabwe), local authorities and IUCN-ROSA. The study team involved 20 experts from both countries. A comprehensive public consultation programme was organized, involving opinion surveys, workshops, 'open houses' and media publicity. One hundred and fifty stakeholders were involved in reviewing and commenting on the draft report and recommendations.

The SEA focused within a 30km radius of the Falls and looked at a ten-year time horizon. Using a scenario approach, the SEA attempted to forecast the environmental (particularly cumulative) impacts from four different levels of growth in tourism (low growth to super growth). For each scenario, the methodology involved estimating adverse and beneficial impacts, calculating carrying capacities and limits to use, developing 'problem trees' to show linkages between issues and concerns, charting cumulative effects, and estimating the potential loss in tourism revenue. Analysis suggested that the sustainable limits to growth lie between the low and medium growth scenarios, in other words 500,000–800,000 tourists per year.

Source: IUCN-ROSA (1996)

The Ministry of Environment and Tourism is currently examining policies and programmes to determine how to incorporate consideration of environmental issues. The Ministry is also implementing the District Environmental Action Programme, which requires all districts to examine environmental opportunities and constraints.

6.2 SEA IN FRANCOPHONE francophone AFRICA[14]

The legal provisions for SEA in developing francophone countries with some examples of practice are described in the following sections and compared in Table 6.3.

6.2.1 Bénin

A number of elements of environmental legislation in Bénin make reference to SEA. For example, several articles in the Outline Law on the Environment (Articles 3, 6, 21, 54, 59, 87 and 88 of Law No 98-030 of 12 February 1999) provide for environmental assessment of policies, sectoral strategies, plans and programmes, either implicitly or explicitly.

The Bénin Environment Agency (Agence Béninoise pour l'Environnement – ABE) is responsible for ensuring that environmental considerations are included in sectoral policies and/or strategies. The Outline Law on the Environment provides for the establishment of environmental cells (administrative units) in the various ministries and in each prefecture and *département*, to act as an interface between the ABE and public and private promoters who carry out development programmes and projects. Their purpose is 'to ensure that environmental dimensions are included in development policies and programmes in the ministerial sector or *département* concerned'.

But it is not clear whether any SEAs have actually been undertaken under these laws and whether the environment cells are functioning.

Some SEAs were undertaken in Bénin prior to this legislation, conducted as part of programmes funded by donor agencies. They took the form of strategic environmental analyses (*analyses stratégique de l'environnement* – ASE) or sectoral environmental assessments: for example:

- an ASE of several *départements* in the humid region in the southwest of the country; and
- sectoral environmental assessments of tourism development, and the management and conservation of national parks and protected areas.

Also, a number of studies, analyses and diagnoses were conducted as part of the preparation of national plans, which often took environmental issues into account.

---

14 With contribution by Koassi d'Almeida, Université du Québec à Montréal (UQAM).

Table 6.3 SEA in developing francophone countries

Legal texts relating to environmental assessment	Explicit or implicit references to strategic environmental assessment (SEA)					National SEA procedure	Examples of SEAs or other studies, analyses or diagnoses, carried out beforehand with the help of aid donors
	Draft laws, decrees, ministerial orders or circulars	Policies	Strategies	Plans	Programmes		
Bénin							
Outline Law on the Environment No 98-030, 12 February 1999				Articles 3, 6, 59, 21, 54, 87 88,			Strategic environmental analysis of the humid area in southwest Bénin. Sectoral environmental assessment of tourism development, and the management and conservation of national parks and protected areas. Prospective studies and analyses carried out in the context of national plans
Decree No 95-47, 20 February 1995		Article 2					
Burkina Faso							
Environment Code, Law No 005/97/ADP, 30 January 1977						—	Environmental assessment of the village land management programme, Phase II Environmental and social impact assessment of the national natural ecosystems management programme Sectoral assessments of the detailed draft of the EIA downstream of the Ziga dam
Decree No 2001-342/ PRES/PM/MEE, 17 July 2001					Article 2		
Decree No 2002-542 PRES/PM/MECV, 27 November 2002	Article 2						

Cameroon	Outline Law No 96/12, 8 August 1996, relating to management of the environment	–	Article 14	
Côte d'Ivoire	Environment Code, Law No 96-766, 3 October 1996	Article 35	Article 35 –	Strategic environmental assessment of the coastal management programme.
Djibouti	Outline Law on the Environment, Law No 106/AN/00/4e L	Articles 52, 53		–
Guinea–Conakry	Environment Code, Order No 045/PRG/87/SGG, 28 May 1987 Decree No 199/PRG/SGG/89, 8 November 1989, codifying EIAs			– Strategic environmental assessment of the transport sector.
Madagascar	Law No 90.033, 21 December 1990 (Environment Charter) Decree No 99-945 (MECIE), 15 December 1999.	Annexe 1	Annexe 1	– Environmental assessment of the transport sector. Environmental assessment of the development plan for areas set aside for tourism and ecotourism. Regional environmental assessment (REA) of the Anosy region.
Mali	Law No 91-04/ AN-RM, 23 February 1991, relating to protection of the environment and living conditions Decree No. 99-189, 5 July 1999			One of the objectives of the Decree

	Legal texts relating to environmental assessment	Explicit or implicit references to strategic environmental assessment (SEA)					National SEA procedure	Examples of SEAs or other studies, analyses or diagnoses, carried out beforehand with the help of aid donors
		Draft laws, decrees, ministerial orders or circulars	Policies	Strategies	Plans	Programmes		
Mali (cont.)	Order No. 98-027/P-RM, 25 August 1998		Article 2		Article 2			
Morocco	Law on environmental protection							Sectoral environmental assessment of agriculture
Niger	Law No 98-56, 29 December 1998 (outline law governing management of the environment)					Article 31		Assessments of the national poverty alleviation strategy and the community action plan (*plan d'action communautaire/PAC*)
	Order of 10 January 1997, institutionalizing EIAs.					Article 4		
Sénégal	Law No. 2001-01, 15 January 2001 (the Environment Code)		Article 48		Article 48			
Togo	Law No. 88-14, 3 November 1988 (Environment Code)	Article 4						
Tunisia	Decree No 91-362, 13 March 1991, relating to EIAs Law No 88-91, 2 August 1988, creating a National Environmental Protection Agency Law No 88-20, 13 April 1988, revising the Forestry Code							

Source: d'Almeida (2003)

6.2.2 Burkina Faso

Provisions for EIA in Burkina Faso are set out in Article 17 of Law No 005/97/ADP, 30 January 1997, which instituted the Environmental Code. References to EAs of policies and programmes are made in different pieces of legislation: Decree No 2001-342 PRES/PM/MEE, 17 July 2001; and Article 2 of Decree No 2002-542 PRES/PM/MECV, 27 November 2002.

The institutional and regulatory framework for EA in Burkina Faso is not yet fully operational, but some SEAs have been undertaken in the context of programmes funded by aid donors:

- an environmental assessment of the national village land management programme (*programme national de gestion des terroirs*), Phase II;
- an environmental and social impact assessment of the national natural ecosystems management programme (*programme national de gestion des écosystèmes naturels*);
- sectoral assessments of the detailed preliminary draft of the EIA of the area downstream of the Ziga dam;
- programme to rehabilitate small dams on the central plateau;
- sectoral support programme for transport (phase II); and
- decennial plan for basic education.

6.2.3 Côte d'Ivoire

Article 35 of Law No 96-766, 3 October 1996, instituted the Environment Code and states that any major project, programme or plan likely to have an impact on the environment must be subject to a prior impact assessment (Djeri-Allassani, 2001).

No precise framework for implementing SEA has yet been established, but a procedure for carrying out an SEA for the coastal management programme has proposed (Box 6.13).

BOX 6.13 PROPOSED PROCEDURE FOR AN SEA OF THE COASTAL MANAGEMENT PROGRAMME, CÔTE D'IVOIRE

- Prepare environmental profile of the coastal area.
- Determine main development options.
- Identify environmental issues associated with development programmes.
- Identify all concerned stakeholders in the coastal area.
- Develop an environmental protection strategy.
- Include strategic analysis in the policy document for the development of the coastal area.

Source: N'dah Etien (2002)

6.2.4 Madagascar

Regulatory provisions for SEA are contained in Law No 90.033, 21 December 1990 (the Environmental Charter), which sets out the general framework for implementing environmental policy in Madagascar. The Charter was amended and added to in 1997.

Decree No 99-945, 15 December 1999, was intended to ensure compatibility between investment and the environment (*Mise en Comptabilité des Investissements avec l'Environnement* – MECIE). In effect, it implements Article 10 of the Environmental Charter. Annex 1 of the MECIE Decree states that:

> *any PPP likely to modify the natural environment or the use of natural resources and/or the quality of the human environment in the urban and/or rural setting shall be subject to an environmental impact assessment.*

Table 6.4 *SEAs carried out in Madagascar*

	Transport sector	Tourism sector	Mining sector	REA
Subject	The whole sector	Area of interest: ecotourism	Study area: pilot studies	Regional development scheme
Approaches	1 diagnosis of the sector 2 general impacts 3 environmental management plan	EIA of the development plan of the Isalo ecotourism interest area)	1 basic study 2 environmental audits 3 social/economic impacts	1 integration of rural development scheme and REA 2 Ilmenite project
Results	1 institution 2 legislation 3 training 4 physical projects	In progress	General and global measures	In progress: scenarios
Aid donors	World Bank	Ministry for Tourism/USAID	Mining sector reform project/ World Bank	World Bank/ USAID/Qit Madagascar Minerals
Special issues	Coordination of sectors	EIA of ecotourism projects	1 methodology 2 reform of the sector and environmental actors	1 methodology 2 regional/ local scales 3 harmonization of information and observation units

Source: Andrianaivomahefa (2001)

Prior to this Decree, some sectoral and regional environmental assessments had already been conducted with the support of aid donors (see Table 6.4). For example:

- EA of the transport sector, carried out in accordance with the World Bank's Operational Directive 4.01;
- EA of the development plan for areas set aside for tourism and ecotourism – an initiative of the Ministry for Tourism and supported by USAID;
- EA of the mining sector, carried out with support from the World Bank;
- REA of the Anosy area, with support from the World Bank, USAID and Qit Madagascar Minerals;
- evaluation of the current environment programme, supported by the World Bank;
- evaluation of the energy sector, supported by the World Bank; and
- evaluation of the rural development support programme.

6.2.5 Morocco

There are no legal provisions covering SEA, but a number of such assessments have been carried out. An example is the sectoral environmental assessment for agriculture undertaken by the Moroccan Government and the World Bank in relation to an irrigation project. The aim of this study was to include environmental issues in the development of the whole of the irrigation sector (Box 6.14).

BOX 6.14 SECTORAL ENVIRONMENTAL ASSESSMENT OF MOROCCAN AGRICULTURE

Procedure:
- Assessment of the long-term implications of investment for the whole sector (from the point of view of operations and maintenance, as well as the institutional, legal and regulatory factors).
- Proposal for a management framework based on the development of environmental units covering irrigation at national and district levels.

Result:
- The various actors involved were made more aware of the diversity and complexity of the environmental issues in this sector.

Recommendation:
- Creation of new institutions with responsibility for formulating policy and strategies, environmental monitoring and training, and preparing new legislation to improve overall management and performance in the sector.

Source: André et al (2003)

Box 6.15 EA of the Second Transport Sector Programme (PST II), Sénégal

As part of the long- and medium-term structural adjustment programme for Sénégal, donors and the Government have agreed on the need to implement appropriate measures to enable the transport infrastructure sector to support production. As a foundation, a transport sector policy document has been prepared. In anticipation of implementing the Second Transport Sector Project (PST II), the Government commissioned a diagnostic study to define new orientations for transport in May 1997.

This study was conducted by a group of national experts and an international consultant. It aimed to provide a framework for project implementation as well as guidance for the four sub-sectors of the PST II (roads, fluvio-maritime, rail and air), complying with the quality security and environmental protection standards. The study also aimed to guide the assessment of environmental impacts. Its main objectives were to:

*   evaluate the Government's environmental policy;
*   define the regulatory, legal and organizational frameworks through which the EA should be conducted;
*   systematically assess the different ecological, economic and socioeconomic impacts of transport infrastructure, and the mitigation or cost of identified impacts; and
*   propose an environmental monitoring plan and a strategy for implementing the EIA in the transport sector.

An extensive review was undertaken of survey documents prepared for the transport sectoral adjustment programme. Interviews and discussions were held with the partners, the public and different transport user groups. These led to the preparation of proposals for an overall environmental and social management programme for the transport infrastructure sector.

The study was expected to:

*   provide information and raise awareness of the principles and role of EA amongst decision-makers, partners and transport users;
*   enable the efficient enforcement of legislation and operational guidelines; and
*   promote the systematic implementation of EIA for all transport activities and infrastructure that are likely to have adverse environmental impacts.

Source: Contributed by Abdoulaye Sene, Dakar

6.2.6 Sénégal

Article 48 of Law No 2001-01, 15 January 2001 (the Environment Code) covers the use of EA and stipulates it that shall also apply to PPP, and to regional and sectoral studies.

A preliminary environmental impact assessment (PEIA) was undertaken for the programme of revitalization of 'fossilized' valleys in Northern Sénégal. The programme encompassed 3000km of six watercourses experiencing drought, salinization and/or burial under eroded materials. The PEIA was primarily used to identify the notification, compensation and monitoring measures necessary to implement the programme rather than to review options (Bitondo et al, 1997).

Box 6.15 describes EA work undertaken for Sénégal's transport sector.

6.2.7 Other countries

A number of other countries have limited experience of SEA; and some have outline environmental legislation that provides for the use of EA at the level of PPP. But the extent of implementation is unclear.

Cameroon – the Environment Department is required to ensure that that environmental considerations are taken into account in all economic, energy-related, land tenure and other plans and programmes (Djeri-Allassani, 2001).

Djibouti – SEA is required in two circumstances: (i) planning in relation to a sector or industry; and (ii) whenever a large-scale project is likely to affect important aspects of the environmental balance – water resources, desertification, natural resources, population, etc.

Guinea–Conakry – there is no provision for SEA in the environmental legislation of Guinea. However, an SEA has been performed in the transport sector and, in 2002, an SEA was undertaken of the 1992 forest management plan for Sangareya Bay – an area dominated by mangroves. The latter involved a review of the existing situation; observations and enquiries in a case study site; stakeholder consultations; and analysis and discussion of the outcomes of the plan (Samoura et al, 2003).

Mali – has no specific reference to SEA, but the legislation states that one of the objectives of EIA is to 'assess and guard against the environmental risks associated with development projects and programmes' (Keita, 2001). The National Office for the Restoration and Control of Pollution and Environmental Damage (*Direction Nationale de l'Assainissement et du Contrôle des Pollutions et des Nuisances*) has responsibility 'to monitor and ensure that sectoral policies and development plans and programmes take into account environmental issues and the implementation of measures [to protect the environment]'.

Niger – no precise SEA framework, but several SEAs have been undertaken, for example, assessments of the national poverty alleviation strategy and the community action plan (*plan d'action communautaire* / PAC).

Togo – no operational SEA framework, but there is legal provision for a process of EA of draft laws, decrees, ministerial orders or circulars of a regulatory nature which have to do, directly or indirectly, with the general interests declared by the Environmental Code. The Code declares the following areas to be of general interest (Djeri-Allassani, 2001):

- conservation of the environment;
- maintenance or restoration of the natural resources supporting human life;
- prevention or limitation of activities likely to degrade the environment and prejudice people's health or property; and
- reparation or compensation for environment damage.

6.3 SEA IN THE REST OF SUB-SAHARAN AFRICA

6.3.1 Nile Basin

Under the Nile Basin Initiative, launched in 1999, a transboundary environmental assessment (TEA) was undertaken by riparian countries. It addressed basin-wide environmental trends, threats and priorities and outlined the elements for a long-term agenda for environmental action for the Nile basin (NBI, 2001; see Case Study 6.6). The TEA also mapped the spatial extent and relative severity of major threats, linking them to immediate, proximate and underlying causes. From an SEA perspective, it may be represented as a large-scale regional assessment undertaken as part of cooperative river basin management in support of sustainable development.

6.3.2 Cape Verde

The EIA legislation in force in Cape Verde includes requirements for the EA of plans and programmes. However, SEA is still lacking specific regulations and no practical experience has yet been developed, although initial training courses have been conducted under the initiative of the Ministry of Environment.

6.3.3 Ghana

In 1997, SEA was applied to a US$800 million village infrastructure project (Amoyaw-Osei, 1997) encompassing rural water, transport, and post-harvest infrastructure, as well as institutional strengthening. The SEA was undertaken by a Ghanaian consultant with assistance from the Ghanaian Environmental Protection Agency. Recently, Ghana has initiated an SEA on its Poverty Reduction Strategy with assistance from The Netherlands and the UK's DFID (Box 6.16). This is one of the first SEAs of such a strategy and promises to yield valuable methodological lessons.

6.3.4 Uganda

In Uganda, SEA-type approaches are beginning to be used in development planning and policy-making. A notable example is in the processes to revise the Poverty Eradication Action Plan (Box 6.17).

BOX 6.16 SEA OF THE GHANA POVERTY REDUCTION STRATEGY

The Ghana Poverty Reduction Strategy (GPRS) was published by the Government in February 2002. It covers the period 2002–2004 during which it was subject to review and monitoring.

The GPRS identifies environmental degradation as a contributory cause of poverty. It also refers to the need for EIAs and audits to ensure that growth arising from the GPRS is environmentally sustainable. However, overall, the GPRS treats the environment as a sectoral or 'add on' matter rather than a cross-cutting issue. Consequently the environmental impacts of the policies and strategies for delivering growth and poverty reduction highlighted in the GPRS are not considered or are poorly understood. This is problematic since many of the policies will have significant environmental impacts. In some instances, lack of focus on environmental management issues will affect the efficacy of the GPRS to deliver sustainable economic growth and poverty reduction.

In many instances, poor environmental quality and management is an important but often neglected factor contributing to poverty. By ignoring the poverty–environment linkage, the poverty reduction goal of the GPRS could be significantly hampered.

The Ministry of Environment and Science, therefore, decided to carry out an SEA so that the GPRS could be adjusted. The SEA aimed to assess the environmental risks and opportunities represented by the policies encompassed by the GPRS, and to identify appropriate management/mitigation measures to ensure that sound environmental management contributes towards pro-poor sustainable growth and poverty reduction in Ghana.

The SEA was led by the National Development Planning Commission and Environmental Protection Agency (EPA) and undertaken in collaboration with DFID and the Royal Netherlands Embassy in Accra. The first phase was to raise awareness and generate buy-in at senior level from key ministries. The SEA was initiated in June 2002 when a scoping exercise was undertaken by the Dutch EIA Commission on behalf of the EPA. The following stepped approach was recommended:

- *Step 1*: Screen the policy lines and interventions stated in the GPRS for their impacts on the environment functions poor people depend on, either directly or indirectly.
- *Step 2*: Analyse the scope offered by the environment for new policy, or the 'environmental space'. Identify which threshold values must not be exceeded, because this would lead to irreversible impacts on poor people; and what opportunities environmental measures present for reducing poverty.
- *Step 3*: Place the proposed policy within this 'environmental space'. Seek 'environmentally friendly and poverty-reducing alternatives' where critical thresholds are exceeded. If any opportunities remain, see whether these can still be included in the strategy.
- *Step 4*: Attempt to secure as much commitment to the SEA as possible from all the actors concerned by jointly identifying the relations between the environment and poverty reduction.

A pilot study of the GPRS was undertaken from February to April 2003, and the full SEA commenced on 1 May 2003. In addition to reviewing the GPRS through national sector studies, active participation of stakeholders has led to greater emphasis on the role of

SEA in improving the processes whereby the policies themselves are translated into budgets, programmes and activities. This is where the failure to address environmental, social, cultural and microeconomic shortcomings of policies is thought to be most acute. The SEA team initiated sustainability appraisals of all 110 district assembly medium-term development plans – the principal vehicles for implementing the GPRS. Findings of the district plan appraisals were to be combined with the results of the national-level policy review to expose gaps and inconsistencies and develop improved procedures for ensuring that funds reach their intended targets; the poor, vulnerable and excluded.

Sources: Jean Paul Penrose (DFID, personal communication); Netherlands CEIA (2003); Nelson (2003)

BOX 6.17 USE OF SEA-TYPE APPROACHES TO INFORM THE DEVELOPMENT OF THE POVERTY ERADICATION ACTION PLAN, UGANDA

There has been a gradual introduction of SEA-type approaches during the development of the Poverty Eradication Action Plan (PEAP) in Uganda. The first PEAP was developed in 1996 when it became clear that poor people themselves had not been involved. A short consultation with the poor people resulted in a major shift of approach and the development of the Uganda Participatory Poverty Assessment Project (UPPAP), funded by DFID and the World Bank. The project was undertaken over a two-year period under the auspices of the Ministry of Finance Planning and Economic Development (MFPED). It involved a series of participatory poverty assessments (PPAs) in 36 sites in nine districts.

The PEAP was officially launched in 1997. A first revision was prepared in 1999 and was informed substantially by the founding of UPPAP and other initiatives such as the Plan for Modernization of Agriculture (PMA). One of the major impacts of UPPAP was the shift in the definition of poverty – from a purely income-based one, to being based on characteristics defined by poor people themselves, including their relationship with the environment.

As a result, it was recognized that environmental issues had to be better reflected in the revised PEAP. DFID funded national and international consultants to assist the Ugandan National Environment Management Authority (NEMA) to strengthen its engagement in the drafting process. This involved articulating poverty–environment linkages and lobbying those leading the process. The aim was to strengthen integration into the PEAP of environmental and long-term sustainability considerations, and to improve the achievement and sustainability of the intended outcomes. This marked a major shift in the Government's approach. It was the first time that environmental issues had been addressed and integrated in the planning and development phases of national policy.

In late 1999, the PMA also began to take shape. A national consultant made recommendations on how environmental concerns could be reflected better in the development of this programme.

In early 2001, a second set of national participatory poverty assessments (PPA2) was designed under the UPPAP-2 project. This included specific case studies to examine, in greater depth, a number of key areas that had emerged and had remained unexplored from the first set of assessments. One of these areas was the environment; and DFID supported a specific participatory poverty and environment assessment (PPEA) case study. It was carried out in three phases:

Phase 1: A desk-based *literature review* of the nine district reports from PPA1 to identify unexplored environmental issues. It was seen as critical for the researchers to undertake *consultations with key policy-makers* across government at this early stage, to further identify knowledge gaps concerning environment–poverty links. A specific environment-focused *field manual* was developed, drawing from the desk research and experience of the researchers. Key to its design was ensuring that all aspects of the environment were captured (including provision of environmental services such as water and sanitation, energy, waste management) and not just natural resource sub-sectors.

Phase 2: Collection of *primary data* using participatory tools and methodologies. A *field guide* was developed for collecting information and exploring environmental change issues through tailored participatory approaches. The aim of this approach was to establish from the perspective of poor people themselves how they perceived their environment to be changing, how they interacted with their environment and how, if at all, it impacted on their well-being. The findings were then analysed and a range of reports produced: individual case studies, consolidated policy analysis and specific sector briefing papers.

Phase 3: Assimilating and crystallizing the findings of the PPEA into clear *sector-specific policy* briefs – essential for targeting specific audiences and ensuring that key policy-makers were not overwhelmed with unnecessary information.

A second revision of the PEAP is currently underway. It is informed substantially by the outcomes of UPPAP-2 (including the PPEA). Much emphasis has been placed on the design of the revision process in order to ensure wide participation of all key stakeholders as well as the effective inclusion of cross-cutting issues (CCI) in the revised PEAP. This has meant the establishment of CCI teams comprising environment, gender, HIV and poverty specialists to sit on each of the pillar revision teams (there are currently four pillar teams).

CCI teams are expected to play a key role in assessing the wider impact of proposed policies on other government strategies and programmes. This approach is expected to have several outcomes:

*   better recognition of the positive returns (in terms of economic growth and poverty reduction) on government investments in the environment;
*   minimization of the negative environmental impacts of the proposed PEAP; and
*   general integration of environmental sustainability into all PEAP objectives.

Source: Based on an internal report prepared by Claire Ireland, DFID, UK

6.4 SEA IN LATIN AMERICA AND THE CARIBBEAN

Most of the Latin American and Caribbean countries have legal and administrative systems to deal with EIA, some of them dating from the mid-1970s. A study undertaken by the Inter-American Development Bank (IADB) covering 26 countries in the region indicates that almost all include environmental criteria for project review and authorization, and over three-quarters have enacted regulations regarding EA (Brito and Verocai, 2002). But these regulations are only weakly enforced due to lack of resources and government attention being focused on other matters (e.g. pressing social problems). All countries (except the Bahamas and Surinam) have now implemented some form of EIA system and, in a few countries, these are decentralized to regional and local levels (e.g. Argentina, Brazil, Chile, Colombia and Bolivia). But overall, the quality of EA studies is poor (Alzina and Spinosa, 2001).

There has been very limited domestic application of SEA to date in the region. Most SEAs have been led by international organizations operating in the region (e.g. the IADB and World Bank – Box 6.18), with the outstanding exceptions of the Avança Brasil case in Brazil, the urban territorial plans in Chile and the telephone network in Guatemala (see the country descriptions below).

However, SEA-type assessments have been undertaken as part of integrated planning. For example, with support from the UN Environment Programme (UNEP) and the Organization of American States, an EA was undertaken in 1995–1996. It was part of preparations for an environmental management initiative under the Binational Master Plan for Integral Development of the Lake Titicaca, Desaguedero River, Poopó, Coipasa Salt Marsh (TDPS) System drawn up by the Governments of Bolivia and Peru. This study covered a broad array of issues from climate, water use and pollution to ecosystems, soils and development considerations (e.g. agriculture, fisheries, tourism).

Sanchez-Triana and Quintero (2003) note that SEA is beginning to be used as an administrative procedure within environmental policy instruments in the region: command and control instruments (e.g. standards); economic instruments (e.g. fees and pollution taxes); legal mechanisms; and mediation (e.g. of conflicts). They also cite various positive outcomes from the application of SEA in the region:

- improvements in environmental regulations (Argentina, Colombia, Panama, the Dominican Republic);
- improvements in EIA systems (Brazil, Colombia, Ecuador);
- clarification of environmental responsibilities for private sector participation (Colombia, Argentina);
- promoted preparation of government sectoral environmental guidelines (Colombia, Bolivia, Argentina, Brazil and others);
- institutional strengthening; and
- establishment of government task forces for SEAs (Brazil, Chile, Colombia).

Box 6.18 Examples of SEAs in Latin America and the Caribbean led by the Inter-American Development Bank and World Bank

IADB

- Bolivia: Corredor de Integracion Santa Cruz–Porto Suarez, first phase (see Box 6.19)
- Brazil: Programa de Transporte Urbano de Forzaeiza
- Peru: Renovación Urbana del Cenro de Lima
- Colombia: Programa de Vivienda Social
- Trinidad and Tobago: National Settlements Programme, second stage
- Ecuador: Programa del Desarrollo Sostenible de la Frontera Amazonica Norta de Ecuador
- regional: Programa de Apoyo al Plan de Ación para la Integración de la Infrastructura Regional en América
- Brazil: Tourism Development Programme in Northeastern Brazil, second stage (PRODETUR/NE-II)
- Brazil: Programa vial de Santa Catarina, Cuarta stapa
- Brazil: Desarrollo Sostenible de Acra.

World Bank

- water sector modernization: Colombia, Argentina, Mexico (ongoing), Brazil
- power sector: Colombia, El Salvador, Ecuador, Brazil (planned as part of private sector adjustment loan (PSAL))
- transport: Bolivia, Guatemala (rural roads), Colombia (transportation corridor and low-income regional roads)
- water resources: Brazil (Ceara, Bahia)
- flood protection: Argentina
- gas sector: Bolivia–Brazil gas pipeline: SEA of gas exploration/exploitation
- regulations and legislative bills: Dominican Republic, Ecuador
- development plans: Panama Metropolitan Plan, Bogota's Land Use Plan
- sectoral programmes: e.g. IADB and International Bank for Reconstruction and Development (IBRD)
- sectoral/regional EAs: Dominican Republic's tourism centres
- cumulative impact assessments: Cartagena water, sewerage and environmental management project.

Process components

Most SEAs covered the same range of components: scoping; baseline studies; regulatory framework; identification of impacts and cumulative effects; environmental externalities; analysis of alternatives; description of alternative PPP; impact mitigation plans; strengthening of environmental institutions; promotion of public participation; and monitoring and follow-up.

Source: Sanchez-Triana and Quintero (2003)

6.4.1 Bolivia

There are no specific legal requirements or institutional framework for SEA. But several SEAs have been undertaken as initiatives of the IADB:

- Bolivia–Brazil gas pipeline project;
- Santa Cruz–Porto Suarez Road – looks at development opportunities and produced a management plan covering a vast area (Box 6.19); and
- Corridor La Paz–Guayaramerín–Conija – currently at the initiation stage.

In the 1990s, the World Bank collaborated with the National Secretary for the Environment to sponsor a sectoral EA for mining to assist institutional strengthening.

BOX 6.19 SEA OF THE SANTA CRUZ–PORTO SUAREZ ROAD, BOLIVIA

The SEA of the Santa Cruz–Porto Suarez Road has evolved to address the development of a major regional plan covering the whole area (where impacts can be expected as a consequence of the construction of this highway). The impacts of the proposed road were analysed in relation to a set of alternative regional development scenarios (setting out development opportunities, but dominated by an economic perspective). One of the main outcomes was a management plan covering the whole area and providing for the monitoring and minimization of the expected impacts.

Source: Maria Partidário (personal communication)

6.4.2 Brazil[15]

SEA has not yet been introduced formally in Brazilian federal legislation, but a bill has been presented by a deputy. Some practitioners believe that mandatory SEA will only lead to an overload of SEA reports (Paulo Eglar, personal communication). A decree requiring SEA of plans and programmes was issued in the state of São Paulo in 1986, but is not implemented.

Recently, the IADB requested an SEA (effectively a large-scale EIA) for the natural gas pipeline between Brazil and Bolivia. The assessment covered both countries and focused primarily on the cumulative and long-term impacts of the associated projects that will be fostered by the availability of natural gas in the region.

At the moment, most SEA initiatives in Brazil are led either by the national government (the Ministries of the Environment, Planning, Transport and Energy), by the National Development Bank (BNDES) and the National Oil Agency; at state level by the state environment agencies in São Paulo and Rio

---

15 With contribution by Paulo Egler, Brazilian Academy of Sciences.

de Janeiro; and also by universities and private companies such as Petrobrás and Electrobrás.

During the last five years, SEA has been undertaken as a requirement of international development banks such as the IADB and the World Bank. Examples include SEAs for sectoral programmes such as the Water and Sanitation Programme (1997) and the Transportation Programme for the Southern Corridor of Brazil (1996). The IADB is currently leading an SEA of the Catchment Area Plan of the Tocantins and the Araguaia rivers. It has also indicated that an SEA will be required for a loan in support of a tourism development plan in the Northeast Region of Brazil. Another SEA initiative, undertaken with the support of the IADB, is connected to the Programme for the Rehabilitation of Downtown São Paulo, executed by the Municipal Company of Urbanism (Box 6.20).

There are several notable initiatives at state level:

- the LIMA/COPPE–Federal University of Rio de Janeiro SEA of the Development Plans for the Production, Transport and Utilization of Oil and Natural Gas in the southern coastal area of Bahia State (in progress);
- the SEA of the Indicative Plan of the Expansion of the Electric Sector – a research project developed by the Centre of Research for Electric Energy (CEPEL) which proposed an approach to SEA (concluded in 2000);
- SEA of the natural gas infrastructure (PhD study, concluded in 2001, State University of Mato Grosso do Sul); and

---

BOX 6.20 SEA OF THE PROGRAMME FOR THE REHABILITATION OF DOWNTOWN SÃO PAULO, BRAZIL

The SEA is an integral part of the development of the Programme and aims to provide for its 'greening'. It addresses four key areas:

- the programme's global environmental sustainability (related to urban environmental policies);
- the sustainability of individual projects;
- the environmental viability of individual projects; and
- the sustainability of the Programme's environmental procedures (linked to environmental management systems).

Key elements in the strategic approach adopted by the Programme and the SEA process include:

- a vision on the development of São Paulo;
- engagement of three local players (private sector, community and public sector);
- identification of common global and sectoral issues; and
- establishment of an environmental policy and strategy for the municipality (including strategic objectives and the establishment of development scenarios).

Source: Information provided by Arcindo dos Santos, Social Programmes Division SO1, IADB

- the São Paulo Municipality EIA of the bus urban track programme – an integrated project assessment approach was adopted.

6.4.3 Chile

Although there is no legal requirement for SEA, there is growing interest in its potential, stimulated by realization of the limitations of current EIA practice and methods when applied to strategic initiatives. Some examples of SEA application and the potential and challenges to introducing SEA in Chile are discussed in Box 6.21.

6.4.4 Dominican Republic

The General Law on Environment and Natural Resources (No 64-00), 2000, established the Department of Environment and Natural Resources (DENR). Article 38 introduces strategic environmental evaluation as an available assessment instrument, and Article 39 stipulates that PPP of public administration be evaluated in terms of the environmental effects and that the alternative of least negative impact must be selected. The DENR will issue directives for evaluations and approve/supervise compliance with their recommendations. It is not clear if any such applications have been undertaken.

6.4.5 Guatemala

Guatemala has adopted new Regulations on Environmental Assessment, Control and Follow-up (Acuerdo Gubernativo No 23-2003 of 27 January, in force after April 2003). These cover the use of a range of tools: SEA, initial environmental assessment, EIA, risk assessment, social impact assessment and cumulative effects assessment. They set the scope of SEA: it applies to policies, national and governmental plans, and projects of transnational relevance that imply the generation of economic and social development patterns with potential environmental impacts.

According to Sanchez-Triana and Quintero (2003), since 1997 proponents have undertaken 15 EIAs for different projects in the telephone sector (including for transmission towers, cells, telephone cabins, operational centre, etc.) that appear to have included elements of SEA by using an integrated project approach.

BOX 6.21 CHALLENGES TO INTRODUCING SEA IN CHILE

EA legislation

EA in Chile is regulated by the General Environment Framework Law of 1994 (Ley 19.300), and by the EIA System Regulation of 1997. Section 3(h) of Ley 19.300 requires that certain land use planning instruments (*instrumentos de planificación territorial* – IPTs) be subject to the EIA system (CONAMA, undated) – in particular regional plans for urban development and inter-district, district zoning and sectional plans. As a result, since 1997, almost 200 plans have been subject to EIA.

Potential moves towards SEA

In recent years there have been attempts to improve the integration of environmental concerns into planning instruments. Examples include coastal zone management plans, IPTs, river basin plans and sustainability planning, all of which can contribute to the foundations of SEA in Chile.

A notable example of the application of strategic assessment in Chile is that of the forthcoming trade agreement with the European Union (Blanco, in press). The Ministry of Public Works, Transport and Telecommunications has been studying potential applications of SEA. It has undertaken pilot studies on water management plans together with other government agencies. It is also exploring SEA methods for the transport plan of Santiago de Chile. Like other Latin American countries, Chile is also influenced by the requests and the guidance of international funding agencies. In the late 1990s the World Bank began negotiations for a river basin management programme (DGA, 1998) and requested that sectoral and regional EAs be applied (DGA/MOPTT/World Bank, 2002).

Challenges

These initial experiences, together with the application of EIA to urban plans, have also raised important questions about existing policy-making and planning mechanisms. As in many other countries, the normative and hierarchical ideal of 'PPP' (policies, plans and programmes) is rarely encountered in Chile. More often, implicit strategic decisions appear to be taken and mega-projects initiated that do not conform with existing strategies or policies; and their implications for development, and sustainability in particular, can be far reaching and long term. Hence, it will be crucial to identify the most important, and urgent, types of initiatives that will benefit from SEA.

There is debate on the role of SEA and testing of approaches. But this is hampered by slow progress in key sectoral institutions in integrating environmental considerations in their work and decisions. This is particularly important since the main environmental institution, the Comisión Nacional del Medio Ambiente (CONAMA), delegates responsibilities for environmental management to sectoral agencies. There is a particular need to emphasize the development of policies for natural resource management and to strengthen public participation.

In 1998, the environmental policy for sustainable development was approved (CONAMA, 1998). It calls for the production of 'environmentally sustainable policies', and the harmonization of environmental, economic and social policies; and for the strengthening of environmental institutions, including the responsibility of all public organizations to integrate environmental sustainability principles in their respective sectors.

A document posted on CONAMA's website draws a link between the above requirements, its own coordination role and the purpose of SEA (CONAMA, undated). It describes SEA as an 'appropriate instrument' for the 'definition and implementation of procedures which can strengthen the establishment of environmentally sustainable sectoral policies'. It also recognizes the 'preventive' nature of SEA, and considers this of growing importance in the pursuit of sustainable development. The existence of different approaches to SEA is recognized. But it is stressed that Chile 'must create its own instrument of SEA' and that, although attention should be given to international experience, 'there is the liberty to shape an instrument that is appropriate for our reality'.

Progress in applying a new SEA instrument will depend on overcoming the prevailing culture of using EIA in a mechanistic and technocratic way.

Source: Olivia Bina, University of Cambridge, UK; personal communication

6.5 SEA IN ASIA

Most Asian countries have established EIA processes and some now have considerable experience with EIA. The early focus was on controlling pollution and restricting industrial development that was clearly detrimental to human health and the natural environment. Increasingly EIAs are examining a broader range of environmental, social, economic and cultural issues and reportedly are becoming more participatory processes.

According to Naim (2002), most countries in South and Southeast Asia have the infrastructure in place to make SEA work:

> *In fact, many SEA 'look alike' activities have already taken place, for example, as part of Nepal's forest plan, Pakistan's water and drainage programmes, Sri Lanka's city and tourism plans, and National Conservation Strategy development in many countries. Some countries would like to try out SEA in energy, water and forest sector planning, but no follow-up has occurred because of lack of funds. Most recently, the Vietnamese Transport Ministry has proposed to use SEA on a pilot scale for three provinces.*

On a regional level, the Environment Programme of the Mekong River Commission (MRC)[16] is focusing on aspects of EA systems, including related areas such as SEA, cumulative environmental assessment (CEA) and EIA. It is examining how transboundary impacts can be accounted for and incorporated into the various EA processes. Cambodia, Lao People's Democratic Republic (PDR), Thailand and Vietnam already have standard EIA procedures and

---

16 The MRC is an intergovernmental agency of the four countries of the Lower Mekong Basin: Cambodia, Lao PDR, Thailand and Vietnam. The MRC replaced the Mekong Committee (1957–1976) and the Interim Mekong Committee (1978–1992), and was formed with the signing of the 1995 Agreement on Cooperation for the Sustainable Development of the Mekong River Basin.

legislation in place, but none yet have procedures to deal with transboundary impacts. Several sets of issues need to be addressed on a regional basis, including how to establish mechanisms that allow environmental impact investigations to be carried out across national borders.

The MRC has commissioned consultants (ERM UK) to work with the national Mekong committees to develop guidelines and suggest potential procedures and protocols that may be adopted by the four national governments as mechanisms to incorporate transboundary impacts into their environmental impact procedures.

In a recent report, Öjendal et al (2002) note that:

> *SEA is being increasingly discussed and promoted in the Lower Mekong Basin. Several projects and initiatives have been initiated by the Asian Development Bank and the MRC, including the ADB Reta 5783: Strategic Environmental Framework (SEF) for the Greater Mekong Region (ADB, 2000) and a project to develop guidelines for SEA by the MRC. Although riparians have reportedly responded positively, these are, however, isolated initiatives and SEA is so far rarely used for mainstream development planning*

Under the SEF project, the Stockholm Environment Institute was commissioned by the Asian Development Bank (ADB) to assist the development of a strategic framework for guiding decision-making in the transport, water resources and environment sectors in the Greater Mekong Sub-region (see Section 4.1.3).

Another regional initiative, the Asia-Pacific Environmental Innovation Strategy (APEIS) project was launched in 2001 under the framework of the Environment Congress for Asia and the Pacific (ECO ASIA). The project aims to establish scientific infrastructure on environment and development, and to provide policy-makers with knowledge-based tools and innovative policy options that can support their informed decision-making for sustainable development in the Asia-Pacific region. APEIS consists of three scientific sub-projects:

- satellite- and ground-based integrated environmental management (IEM);
- assessments using environment–economy integrated models (integrated environmental assessment); and
- research on innovative and strategic policy options (RISPO), in collaboration with multiple research organizations in the region.

6.5.1 China

The Environmental Protection Law (1979) included broad elements requiring EIA, particularly construction projects. Subsequently, the Environmental Protection Management Ordinance for Construction Projects (1998) introduced regional environmental assessment. This extended EIA beyond the project to higher levels (i.e. regional development).

For the past decade, regional development environmental impact assessments (RDEIAs) have been undertaken in response to the accelerated economic growth now taking place in special investment zones. For example, these have been applied to the Pudong Economic Development Zone in Shanghai, the Donghu Technological Zone in Wuhan, the Yalong Bay Tourism Development Zone in Hainan, and transformation of old industry areas in Lianong (Qi and Wang, 1993).

Until recently, there was no legal requirement for SEA in China. But since 1995 a small, but growing, number of SEAs have been conducted. These have been undertaken partly because of the inherent limitations of conventional EIA (e.g. failure to suggest alternative projects and sites), and partly because the Government has recognized the significance and utility of SEA as a tool for sustainable development (Che et al, 2002). Examples include SEAs of:

- the *Coal and Electricity Strategy in Shanxi Province*, undertaken by the Institute of Environmental Science, Beijing Normal University (Wang et al, 1997);
- China's Automobile Industry Development Policy;
- the *East Coastal Zone Development Plan for Xiamen Province*, conducted by Xiamen Planning and Design Institute (funded by CIDA); and
- the *Air Pollution Prevention and Control Act* – for the revision process, undertaken by the Environmental and Economic Policy Research Centre of the National Environmental Protection Department (Huang, 2002).

So far in China, SEA has faced numerous methodological and procedural limitations, which also restrict public participation. Policies and strategies have been kept secret from the public.

The Environmental and Resources Protection Committee of the National People's Congress spent four years preparing a new Environmental Impact Assessment Law. This was adopted on 28 October 2002 and became effective on 1 September 2003 (Box 6.22).

6.5.2 Hong Kong

In Hong Kong, the EIA system was initially established on an administrative pursuant to a policy address by the then Governor in 1992. It applies to PPP proposals submitted to the Executive Council. A statutory basis was provided by the EIA Ordinance (1998). During the past five years, over 20 plans have been assessed under this Ordinance, whilst major policies and planning strategies have been reviewed under the SEA system. This was established pursuant to the then Governor's Policy Address (1992) and applies to policy, plan and programme proposals submitted to the Executive Council. A series of major initiatives have been subject to SEA including the following:[17]

---

17 For more information, contact: Environmental Assessment and Noise Division, Environmental Protection Department, 27/F Southorn Centre, 130 Hennessy Road, Wanchai, Hong Kong.

BOX 6.22 THE NEW EIA LAW IN CHINA

The new EIA Law is a supplement to the 1979 legislation but is much more focused and incorporates the concept of SEA. In the early stages of its development, the aim was that it should cover three areas of focus: area (local) planning, strategic planning, and policy. The latter focus was subsequently dropped. The new Law now provides for EIAs of long-term (i.e. five to ten years) strategic plans at national, provincial and sector levels; and short-term (i.e. less than five years) project plans at local levels:

> *EIA as used in this Law refers to the methodology and system of performing analysis, projection and evaluation on potential environmental impacts resulting from implementation of a plan or a construction project, proposing counter measures to prevent or alleviate adverse impacts, and carrying out tracing monitoring.*

EIA for plans

1   The Law requires relevant departments under the State Council, and local governments at or above the level of municipality with districts and relevant departments under them, to:
    – organize an EIA and prepare chapters or descriptions of environmental impacts of draft land use plans and construction projects and exploitation plans of regions, river basins and sea areas; and
    – prepare EIAs and submit an environmental impact statement (EIS) for draft sectoral plans concerning: land use; agriculture; livestock breeding; forestry; natural resources; cities; industries; energy; transportation; tourism and other specific plans.
2   Project proponents must consult with the 'interested' public (holding expert meetings and public hearings or other means) to solicit comments and suggestions on the draft EIS from relevant government agencies, experts and the public; and the EIS must provide an account of the participation process and indicate what comments/suggestions have been adopted.
3   The EIS must state how monitoring will be implemented, state what mitigation measures will be established and how they will be applied.
4   The EIA study must be rigorous and undertaken in a realistic and scientific manner.
5   The EIA report must be prepared by qualified professionals, who must sign it and assume legal responsibility for its accuracy.
6   The submitted EIS will be examined by a review group selected randomly from an experts database.

Sources: Interview with Professor Chen Fu, Former Director, Chinese Research Academy of Environmental Sciences People Republic of China, Hong Kong, 12 December 2002; National Peoples Congress (2002)

- Port and Airport Development Strategy, 1989;
- Tseung Kwan o New Town Feasibility Study of Opportunities for Further Development, 1989;
- North Landau Development Plan, 1992;
- Railway Development Study, 1993;
- North West New Territories (Yuen Long District) Development Statement Study, 1994;

BOX 6.23 SEA OF THE TERRITORIAL DEVELOPMENT STRATEGY, MEDIUM-TERM OPTIONS, HONG KONG

The primary objective of the review of the Territorial Development Strategy (TDS) was to formulate a long-term development strategy for Hong Kong. The aim was to keep apace with regional development and maintain Hong Kong's position as a leader within the region. Several rounds of detailed multidisciplinary evaluations, studies and screening processes were undertaken. Individual components of the industrial, residential, commercial, transport, recreational, land use and port development strategies were considered in detail.

The TDS review provided two basic development strategies reflecting different growth characteristics. They had two different time horizons: a long-term strategy to year 2011; and a medium-term strategy with forecasts for the year 2006. The TDS also considered two development scenarios for the major economic hinterland for Hong Kong in the next few years: the Pearl River delta (the 'low-growth' scenario) and the neighbouring Guangdong Province in China.

Due to time constraints, the SEA undertook a comparative and qualitative review of three medium-term development options:

* harbour-based reclamation;
* land-based developments in the New Territories (NT); and
* balancing the development needs of the Metro Area and North West NT.

The SEA drew on a range of assessment criteria/performance measures in several categories (used for an earlier SEA of the TDS preferred options in 1995): water quality; air quality (traffic and industry); noise (rail traffic, major road links); waste; potentially hazardous installations; ecology; planning guidelines compliance; and sustainability of development proposals.

The analysis suggested that a number of environmental problems will emerge before 2006. An action plan is proposed to mitigate the impacts of three issues of particularly serious concern:

* air quality deterioration linked to predicted increases in diesel-engined goods vehicle traffic;
* overloading of environmental infrastructure, including especially the NT sewerage systems and the strategic landfills; and
* increases in impacts from traffic noise.

Sources: CD-ROM of Hong Kong experience of SEA, Environmental Protection Department, Hong Kong; Au (1998)

---

* Freight Transport Study, 1994;
* Territorial Development Strategy Review, 1996 (Box 6.23);
* Third Comprehensive Transport Study, 1999;
* Second Railway Development Study (ongoing); and
* Future Strategic Growth Areas – North Western New Territories, North Eastern New Territories, and Hong Kong Island South and Lamma (ongoing).

Hong Kong Special Administrative Region (SAR) is not a developing country. But the extent of SEA practice and experience is of particular interest in light of its status in China, and the emerging number of transboundary environmental issues with the neighbouring province of Guangdong, especially in the Pearl River delta. The Hong Kong Environmental Protection Department has been active in documenting the lessons of experience gained in the past ten years. It has used CD-ROMs and websites to disseminate these materials (http://www.epd.gov.hk/eia/english). An interim SEA manual summarizes practice as applied to plans, strategies and certain policy proposals and draws on several regional and international conferences on SEA held in Hong Kong (Au, 2004).

6.5.3 Indonesia

The EIA approach in Indonesia (*analisis mengenai dampak lingkungan* – abbreviated as AMDAL) is based on the Canadian Environmental Assessment Review Process. Under the Environmental Management Act 1982 an EIA is required for 'every plan which is considered likely to have a significant impact on the environment'.

6.5.4 Nepal

The environmental assessment of the Bara Forest Management Plan demonstrates the use of a generic EIA approach to the level of plan assessment (Box 6.24). The focus is on an evaluation of plan formulation rather than integration of environmental concerns into the ongoing process of decision-making.

In 2002, with support from DFID, the NPC began a study to consider links in the draft Tenth Plan/Poverty Reduction Strategy Paper (PRSP) between the Government's strategic goal of poverty alleviation and Nepal's environmental assets and constraints (Box 6.25; Table 6.5).

6.5.5 Pakistan

An SEA training programme was initiated in 1997 by the World Conservation Union (IUCN) for staff of government Planning and Development Departments. This has led to increased awareness and demand for SEA in Pakistan. IUCN-Pakistan has undertaken an independent SEA of Thermal Power Generation Policy in Pakistan and presented this to government (Box 6.26). It led to a series of discussions within the Planning and Development Department which is now beginning to request that SEAs be undertaken for major national and provincial-level initiatives at the policy level.

An SEA training programme was initiated in 1997 by the IUCN for staff of government planning and development departments. This has led to increased awareness and demand for SEA in Pakistan. IUCN-Pakistan has undertaken an independent SEA of thermal power generation policy in Pakistan and presented this to government (Box 6.26). It led to a series of

---

Box 6.24 Bara Forest Management Plan, Nepal

The National Planning Commission (NPC), in collaboration with the IUCN, has established a national EIA system in the country. Following the publication of national EIA guidelines in 1992, sectoral guidelines were formulated. Those for the forest sector require a mandatory EIA for the preparation of forest management plans. The Bara Forest Management Plan aims to shift the emphasis from protection-oriented management of Sal (*Shorea robusta*) forests to sustainable production-oriented management of the species. The proposed plan includes activities that will have both positive and negative environmental, economic and social effects.

This SEA considered the major impacts arising from two alternatives: (i) the do-nothing option (existing impacts continue) and (ii) implementation of the proposed plan. Over 150 possible impacts of varying significance were determined and arranged into 19 main issues of concern. Each issue was examined by a team of professionals to determine and rank the magnitude, extent and duration of the positive and negative impacts associated with each alternative. The results of this analysis formed the basis for recommendations to change the proposed management plan.

It was determined that the plan had considerable merit and should be implemented with some changes. The recommendations covered such topics as:

- the plan should cover all aspects of forest use;
- the development of necessary baseline data;
- the adoption of the required policy, legislative authority and institutional frameworks;
- working cooperatively with the people affected by the plan; and
- the development of sound silvicultural and harvesting practices.

Sources: IUCN Nepal (1995); CIDA/DGIS (1997)

---

discussions within the Planning and Development Department, which is now beginning to request that SEAs be undertaken for major national and provincial-level initiatives at the policy level.

6.5.6 Thailand

EIA is required in Thailand for a range of project categories under the Improvement and Conservation of the National Environmental Quality Act (1975).

An independent SEA of shrimp farming was undertaken in 2001 to assist the Swedish International Development Agency (Sida) decide whether to support this industry (Lindberg and Nylander, 2001). The aim was to assess the situation of the coastal shrimp farming industry in the southeast of Thailand. The SEA compared the most common shrimp farming method (semi-closed intensive) with two alternative systems (closed recirculated, and sludge removal). The study was conducted in five provinces and included interviews with shrimp farmers as well as experts in government departments, universities and environmental organizations. The report compares the environmental and socioeconomic impacts of the different shrimp farming systems (based on a 'back-casting' assessment of existing shrimp farms).

BOX 6.25 ASSESSING THE POTENTIAL TO INTRODUCE SEA IN NEPAL

The project was undertaken with support from consultants funded by DFID. It aimed to stimulate debate amongst various sector ministries about poverty–environment links in the planning process. It involved:

- examining the extent to which the links between poverty and environment are currently considered during development planning in Nepal;
- organizing an informal Policy Forum, during which participants from the NPC, sector ministries/departments (agriculture, forestry, industry, local development, physical planning, roads and environment) and donor observers discussed the opportunities to strengthen the consideration of poverty–environment links during the Tenth Plan process; and
- assessing the need, demand, opportunities, feasibility and requirements of introducing SEA in Nepal to improve future consideration of poverty–environment linkages in the planning process.

This assessment of SEA was limited to a few discussions with NPC and sector ministry staff and to debate arising during the Policy Forum. Nevertheless, it led to several conclusions:

- There is clear support for SEA in Nepal within central government and academia.
- There are several possible entry points for SEA within the existing planning process: during the selection and prioritization of programmes and projects; during mid-term evaluation of the Tenth Plan; and during the preparation and evaluation of future plans.
- Various stakeholders could have a role in developing and using SEA, for example the NPC, sector ministries and local government planning teams, the Ministry of Population and Environment (MoPE) and public stakeholders such as NGOs.
- SEA would need to be integrated within wider efforts aimed at making planning activities more focused on meeting strategic development objectives.
- In addition to SEA, it would also be useful to monitor the extent to which development plans, programmes and activities are responding to poverty–environment issues.

The assessment concluded that the effective application of SEA in Nepal would depend on:

- sufficient demand for SEA in a wider context. The value of SEA needs to be recognized more widely within the NPC, sector ministries, local government and public stakeholders;
- sufficient capacity (both staff numbers and competencies) existing within relevant agencies to develop and apply an SEA tool;
- the development of an SEA toolkit;
- SEA being given sufficient support and recognition to enable it to become an integral tool within the planning process; and for its results to effectively feed into the decision-making process. In other words, consideration of environment is fully integrated within the approach to planning.

It was recommended that:

- Wider consultations should be undertaken to determine the extent of wider demand for SEA – possibly through a pilot study.
- An examination of how SEA and poverty–environment monitoring could feed into ongoing and/or planned initiatives to improve the planning process in Nepal. Where possible, the development of SEA should build on existing efforts to make planning more sustainable, for example linking with the efforts of the Sustainable Development Agenda for Nepal (SDAN) and Sustainable Community Development Programme (SCDP).
- The capacity needs necessary for the development and application of SEA (and poverty–environment indicators) should be clearly identified – leading to a suitable capacity-building programme.
- A draft SEA toolkit (including methods, guidelines, criteria, poverty–environment indicators and poverty–environment profile) should be developed – preferably through a broad stakeholder process. This should be simple, straightforward, quick to use, not require excessive knowledge or data, and be based, as far as possible, on existing approaches and methods.

The draft SEA tool (and draft poverty–environment indicators) should then be piloted – possibly by a small number of authorities (e.g. the Ministries of Agriculture and Forestry) and local government administrations. This would provide the basis for training and capacity-building and to help improve the tool and enable the experience to be disseminated to a wider audience.

Since this assessment was undertaken, the level of conflict in Nepal has worsened and it has not been possible to take these ideas forward.

Source: ERM (2002)

6.6 SEA ELSEWHERE

Most countries in the *Middle East and North Africa* region have enacted some form of EIA legislation but few have established provision for SEA or consideration of transboundary impacts.

6.6.1 Lebanon[18]

Recent regulatory developments have paved the way for the development and application of SEA in the Lebanon: a Framework Law for Environmental Protection (Law 444, adopted in 2002), and a draft Decree on EIA (under consideration at the Council of Ministers). The Framework Law highlights the principle of EIA as a tool for planning and management (Article 4). It stipulates that private and public proponents must undertake an environmental assessment for all projects that are likely to affect the environment due to their sizes, nature, impacts or activities (Article 21), including study or programme or investment or planning proposals that concern a complete area or sector of activity (Article 22).

18 With contribution by Alissar Chaker, Project Manager, Ministry of Environment, Lebanon.

Table 6.5 *Possible roles for the development and use of SEA in Nepal*

Stakeholder	Remit	Opportunities to have a role in SEA	Possible role in the development and/or use of SEA
NPC	Directs planning process, how planning is undertaken and how programmes and projects are carried out	• influential role and strong links with sector ministries • has a department and a member responsible for environment	• leads development and introduction of SEA • encourages sector ministries to use SEA
MoPE	Responsible for: • environmental management • disseminating information • monitoring and evaluation • developing capacity	• based on its remit, MoPE has an important role in development and implementation of SEA • has persons trained in environmental management	Supporting NPC to: • develop SEA toolkit • select criteria and indicators • manage preparation of poverty–environment profile • manage SEA of periodic plans against this profile • disseminate information on SEA • carry out pilot introduction of SEA and disseminate results • provide technical support and guidance for SEA activities • review quality of SEA outputs • monitor its effectiveness
Sector ministries	• plan and carry out development activities within their sectoral areas • prepare sectoral submissions for periodic plans • select and prioritize programmes and projects for implementation	Ministries relevant to poverty–environment: Agriculture, Forestry, Water Resources (includes energy), Physical Planning, Local Development, Industry and Tourism Each ministry has a unit responsible for planning and one for environment	• applying SEA to the selection of programmes and projects • monitoring poverty–environment indicators relevant to their sector

Stakeholder	Remit	Opportunities to have a role in SEA	Possible role in the development and/or use of SEA
Local government	• same as sector ministries but focused on local level	• planning becoming increasingly decentralized • their role is therefore increasing • better placed to recognize local poverty–environment linkages • good links with public stakeholders – can therefore encourage their involvement	• informing the development of the SEA tool, e.g. during selection of criteria and indicators and supporting preparation of poverty–environment profile • piloting a draft SEA tool • using SEA to select and prioritize development programmes and projects • monitoring contribution of development activities to poverty-alleviation at local level • disseminating experience
Public stakeholders (e.g. NGOs, community organizations, academics etc.)		• increasingly being engaged in planning and sustainable development activities • represent poor people and recognize their opportunities and constraints • existing activities (SDAN, SCDP) could be used as a vehicle to encourage participation in SEA	• informing debate on SEA – whether it is useful, what form it could take, what criteria and indicators to use etc. • reviewing relevance of tool, criteria, indicators and impact of SEA

Source: ERM (2002)

BOX 6.26 SEA OF THERMAL POWER GENERATION POLICY, PAKISTAN

In a race to attract foreign investment, the Government of Pakistan has provided unprecedented incentives that guarantee high profit to investors in thermal power generation. In return, the country stood to receive clear short-term economic gains. In pursuit of this goal, the Government set up a Private Power and Infrastructure Board, based in Islamabad, with a mandate to facilitate the establishment of power stations throughout Pakistan. It entered into over 30 agreements for independent power plants (IPPs).

The National Conservation Strategy (1992) recommends the location of highly polluting units away from populated and ecologically sensitive areas. According to the National Environmental Quality Standards (NEQS), 1993, oil-fired thermal power stations need to substantially reduce emissions, if installed in an already polluted environment. In 1994, with support from CIDA, a National Power Plan was developed. However, the Government did not take this into account in negotiating agreements for foreign funding.

Government policy on thermal power generation gave investors the freedom to choose the site, the technology and the fuel. Contracts required investors in such projects to submit an EIA to the Government. Yet these EIAs had little influence on project location and design, and much less on the actual need for such projects.

In 1994, IUCN-Pakistan undertook a study of a plan to meet the electricity needs of Karachi – an already highly polluted city. This proposed several new oil-fired thermal power stations to meet projected power demand. The study found that, individually, each of the proposed stations was well within the NEQS maximum allowed limit of 500 tons of SO_2 emission per day. But cumulatively, these stations would emit an additional 1000 tons of SO_2 plus one ton of toxic metals daily.

Favourable terms were offered to foreign investors and soon led to an increase in electricity prices. As a consequence, many local industrialists pooled their resources and established their own power generation plants for their own use (captive units). This reduced the load on the National Grid System. But many of these plants were installed with little or no pollution control devices. Other industrial consumers signed agreements with the private power companies. Due to public pressure, lobbying and a strong role by the media, several of the proposed plants (IPPs) were relocated. Use of SEA at an early stage would have avoided these problems. To mitigate similar problems, training workshops on SEA were organized in Pakistan by IUCN.

The Ministry of Environment wrote to IUCN-Pakistan giving an assurance that 'because of the requirement for EIAs and the existence of the NEQS, the new IPPs would not pollute the environment'. This prompted IUCN-Pakistan to undertaken an SEA of the thermal power generation policy. It involved a desk exercise to develop scenarios for a range of conditions. These drew from past experience of power plant developments, particularly the preferences and tendencies of entrepreneurs in selecting sites (e.g. in or close to Karachi, or in remote areas close to water for cooling) and the problems of transporting oil to remote plants and connecting them to the national electricity grid.

A working document set out the environmental consequences under these scenarios. It was presented to staff of the Planning and Development Department – senior officers from sections dealing with agriculture, industry, irrigation, population welfare, the power sector, etc. They had experience of dealing with thermal power plant issues and other large development projects. Subsequent discussion focused on the cumulative impacts on both a local and country-wide scale.

> The SEA revealed that whilst the Government was fully aware of the environmental dimensions associated with thermal power generation, assessment was based only on EIA.
>
> The SEA made it clear to the policy-makers that EIA alone was not sufficient to guarantee sustainable development. EIA was used as a downstream decision-making tool applicable to individual projects, especially after deciding the site, technology and fuel. So its scope was very limited and missed the big picture. As a consequence, many thermal power stations using high-sulphur furnace oil became clustered in one city and added to the already polluted air. Alternatively, they were developed in a scattered way in remote places. This made it difficult to supply them with furnace oil and to connect them with the National Grid System.
>
> This SEA was used as a case study to illustrate the need for an SEA as an upstream decision-making tool, and to minimize all the foreseeable problems at the policy formulation stage. Following a training programme, the Planning and Development Department is beginning to request that SEAs are undertaken for major national and provincial-level initiatives at the policy level.
>
> *Sources:* Naim (1997, 1998, personal communication 1998)

So far, there has been only limited strategic planning, particularly with respect to assessing environmental impacts and linkages amongst potentially damaging public actions and undertakings. This has prompted the Ministry of Environment, in collaboration with UNDP, to implement a project on SEA and land use planning. Funding has been provided by the European Commission through its LIFE Third Countries Programme (Box 6.27).

6.6.2 Pacific Islands[19]

In this region, EIA is still in its infancy. Since 1991, the South Pacific Regional Environment Programme (SPREP) has promoted the use of project EIA in Pacific Island Countries (PICs) focusing on awareness-raising, training and technical assistance. This Programme aimed to influence the integration of EA principles and economic development planning and the enactment of environmental legislation and revision of EA guidelines. But, following a review of progress in 2001, McIntyre (2003) reports on the slow uptake of EIA laws, the marginalization of EIA processes and continued spasmodic EIA application in development processes. The wider array of EA, planning and design management techniques, including SEA approaches for PPP and large area assessments of development initiatives, have not been targeted.

The focus has now shifted to SEA methods, techniques and tools (Onorio, 2002). National reports have been prepared for the Review of the Implementation of the Barbados Programme of Action[20] (BPOA+10) (in Mauritius in January 2005). These call for integrated planning systems

---

19 With contribution by Matt McIntyre, South Pacific Regional Environment Programme, Samoa.

20 An international programme adopted in 1994 at a global conference on the sustainable development of small island developing states (SIDS), held in Barbados.

BOX 6.27 SEA AND THE LAND USE PLANNING PROJECT IN LEBANON

Aim of the project

The project started in January 2002. Its overall aim is to integrate environmental considerations into policies, strategies, programmes and plans at the national level in order to alleviate major problems facing the national sustainable development agenda in the country. Three objectives were set:

- Develop a framework for SEA for Lebanon.
- Build relevant institutional capacities at the Ministry of Environment and the Directorate General of Urban Planning, as well as in other concerned line ministries and stakeholders.
- Apply the proposed SEA framework for the development of environmental guidelines to be applied to land use planning at the national level.

Main interventions

Policy aspects:
- Develop a framework for SEA suitable to the Lebanese context, including institutional and procedural arrangements.
- Develop environmental guidelines for land use planning.

Capacity-building:
- Train concerned public institutions on mainstreaming:
  - SEA application, monitoring and evaluation in their planning and decision-making processes; and
  - environmental guidelines in urban planning and land use management procedures.
- Train private sector consultants on:
  - scope and significance of the SEA process; and
  - mainstreaming proposed environmental guidelines in land use planning studies.

Institutional strengthening:
- Develop a national strategy for the application and monitoring of the SEA process in priority sectors.
- Develop a national strategy for incorporating and monitoring the application of environmental guidelines in urban planning and land use management procedures.

Dissemination and general awareness:
- Prepare a guiding manual on the SEA process and application procedures.
- Draft a guidebook on the application of environmental guidelines in land use planning.
- Develop a general advocacy brochure for strategic decision-makers.
- Organize regional meetings to disseminate SEA to NGOs and local authorities.

Demonstration activity:
- Apply SEA procedures and environmental guidelines for land use planning in a pilot project and publish a good practice case study for future reference.

A demonstration activity will be undertaken for land use planning. In the Lebanon, poor land use planning is one of the major problems leading to environmental degradation, and threatening natural and cultural resources. Approximately 80 per cent of the country remains unclassified and is often subject to haphazard development. This is an important fact given that land use planning plays a critical role in shaping and regulating economic trends in real estate and tourism markets – two of the major economic sectors in the country. Major stakeholders in this sector include the Directorate General of Urban Planning, the Higher Council for Urban Planning, the Council for Development and Reconstruction (CDR), and municipalities.

This project complements the national land use planning initiative being executed by the CDR in collaboration with the Directorate General of Urban Planning for the preparation of a National Land Use Plan.

A participatory approach

Partners and stakeholders represented on the project steering committee include:

- Ministry of Environment
- Directorate General of Urban Planning
- CDR
- Parliamentary Committee for the Environment
- Other concerned public institutions
- Municipalities
- NGOs
- Private consultants
- Academia and research centres.

Source: Contributed by Alissar Chaker, UNDP-Lebanon

(environmental/resource use). In response, the SPREP Secretariat is pursuing a long-term programme to help PICs develop and use appropriate tools for integrating environment and development decision-making, for example SEA, environmental economics and planning guidelines (Box 6.28). A regional Environmental Assessment Facilitation Office is planned to provide advisory services to PICs and assist with capacity development.

The first SEA in the region was undertaken in 1996. There has been an increase in assessments in the smaller island states related to integrated coastal management that includes consideration of socioeconomic development, fresh water management, coastal protection and climate change considerations. For example, an SEA case study of the Fiji Islands Tourism Development Plan (TDP) is being sponsored by the Asian Development Bank in partnership with SPREP and the World Wide Fund for Nature – South Pacific Programme (WWF-SPP)[21] (Box 6.29)

---

21 A regional NGO working in the PICs.

BOX 6.28 PROMOTING SEA IN PACIFIC ISLAND COUNTRIES

In *Samoa*, the Planning and Urban Management Act (PUMA) (and Authority), 2003, promotes environmental planning that incorporates EIA, strategic planning, and infrastructure coordination, and provides for SEA of area-wide plans. It is unclear if the Act enables SEA of national policies and programmes.

In *Niue*, the Resource Use Planning Project, completed in 2000, provided the Government with a contemporary integrated planning system. It culminated in a draft Integrated Environmental Planning and Management Bill. This incorporates SEA principles, objectives and legal provisions. The explanatory notes describe Part 3 of this Bill (Environmental Instruments) as instituting the overarching aim of the legislation: 'to bring together multi-sector and cross sector policy documents and give them power under a consistent legislative platform. Over time even their contents, styles and designs will have some consistency allowing easier governance.'

In *Vanuatu*, a unique catchment case study dealt with vertical and horizontal government linkages, land and access tenure disputes, conflict over land use, slum developments and catchment–coast degradation issues. The study explored the use of sub-national environmental planning approaches to mainstreaming the environment and produced a road map towards integrated platforms over time. The road map included the nomination of projects that could assist the country strive quickly towards the integrative approaches.

BOX 6.29 SEA OF THE FIJI ISLANDS TOURISM DEVELOPMENT PLAN

The ADB in cooperation with the Government of New Zealand (NZAID) is formulating the Pacific Region Environmental Strategy. To help achieve this, case studies are being conducted to develop and test, in cooperation with partners in the Pacific, tools and approaches such as SEA and methodologies for policy integration. One of these was an SEA of Fiji's TDP (1985–2005) undertaken by WWF-SPP from March–April 2003. Tourism is the country's fastest growing industry and has the greatest capacity to generate wage and salary employment for the country.

The objectives of the study were to:

- inform the mid-term review of TDP in 2003 by assessing the environmental and sustainable development impacts of the current plan; and
- test the usefulness of SEA as a tool for improving the sustainability of strategies and plans in the Asia-Pacific region.

WWF-SPP formed a team comprising a team leader and SEA expert, a socioeconomist and a tourism specialist, supported by university and technical experts from the region. The team compiled relevant data and information, conducted public meetings and prepared the SEA reports.

In a memorandum of understanding between WWF-SPP and the Ministry of Tourism, it was agreed that the SEA would provide the environmental and social components of the TDP mid-term review. Furthermore, the SEA results would be integrated into the TDP and other national and sector policies, plans and programmes.

The process was guided by an advisory group representing a range of stakeholder interests (tourism industry; Ministry of Tourism; Ministry of Local Government, Housing and Environment; University of the South Pacific; Fiji Visitors' Bureau). It met three times during the assessment. A consultation strategy was devised to ensure full stakeholder participation.

Methodology

The SEA compared the current environmental, social and economic baseline and likely trends under the TDP against sustainability objectives. The approach adopted was based on the EU SEA Directive and the methodology followed is summarized in Table 6.6.

Results

The study found that, whilst tourism is providing considerable economic benefits to Fiji, a significant percentage of tourism income leaks back out of the country, and the country is becoming highly dependent on this sector. There are many areas where tourism is causing serious environmental degradation (e.g. to coral reefs). Much of the policy, legislation and regulations to ensure good tourism practice are in place but they are not enacted, implemented or enforced. Thus, the 'step-change' growth in tourism (proposed in the TDP to replace 'bumbling along') is likely to increase tensions between tourist developers, landowners and local communities. Therefore, a precautionary approach to future tourism development is suggested and various directions are recommended. In addition, full implementation of institutional and regulatory frameworks for environmental assessment and management are recommended as necessary for sustainable tourism expansion.

The SEA has led to a number of tangible outcomes:

- The SEA recommendations have been adopted by the National Tourism Council (NTC), accepted by the Permanent Secretaries Meeting and endorsed by Cabinet.
- The Ministry of Tourism and WWF are exploring the possibility of recruiting a policy officer to work on the SEA recommendations with all stakeholders.
- A work plan has been developed at a stakeholders consultation workshop (attended by 50 members of the NTC and government departments) to implement key recommendations; and WWF and local stakeholders have developed action plans to guide and implement the recommendations.
- Key stakeholders such as resource owners and the tourism industry have begun to discuss closer collaboration on sustainable tourism issues.
- The Tourism Department of Fiji's university is exploring how to include SEA as a tool in its sustainable tourism course, and is planning a one-week workshop on SEA to build awareness and capacity in the region.
- WWF and partners have developed a global environment facility (GEF) proposal to examine funding implementation of the recommendations.
- The ADB has added a biodiversity component to a proposed loan to the Fijian Government for sustainable tourism and outer-island infrastructure. Central to this are the links between sustainable tourism and environment.

Source: Levett and McNally (2003)

Table 6.6 *Summary of process for SEA of Fiji's TDP*

SEA/SA stage	What to decide		What to record
A Identify relevant plans and programmes and their relation to the plan	What other plans and programmes influence the plan in question		List of relevant plans and programmes and their requirements
B Devise draft SEA objectives; indicators and targets; collect baseline data, including data on likely future trends; issues and constraints	What are the sustainability objectives, targets and/or indicators to test the plan options and policies against; what sustainability issues and constraints to consider during plan-making	In the scoping report (linked to issues and options report)	List of SEA objectives, and indicators and targets where relevant; data on baseline environment; list of relevant sustainability issues and constraints
C Identify (more sustainable) options for dealing with the plan issues	What options to consider for each issue identified		List of options for each plan issue
D Prepare scoping report; consult	What to include in the scoping report		Results of Stages A–C; agreed written statement of how to proceed with Stages E–H
E Assess the plan options' effects on the SEA objectives, and their consistency with relevant other plans and programmes; choose preferred options; propose mitigation measures	What are the preferred (mitigated) options from Stage C, using the objectives, indicators and targets developed in Stage B	In the environmental report (linked to draft plan)	List of preferred (mitigated) options; explanation of why these are preferred; effects of these options; mitigation measures proposed
F Screen the plan policies and proposals; assess their effect on the SEA objectives; propose mitigation measures including links to EIA	What policies and proposals to assess; what the effects of those proposals are on the sustainability; how effects can be minimized/enhanced		Summary of effects of plan policies and proposals; mitigation measures proposed, including links to EIA and lower-level plans and programmes
G Propose SEA monitoring	How to measure actual effects of the plan on sustainability		Proposed monitoring measures
H Prepare the environmental report to accompany the draft plan; consult	How to present the data from stages A–G; how to consult the environmental and other authorities and the public		Prepare the environmental report; amend if necessary in response to consultation
I Take consultation results into accoount	How to respond to consultation results		How consultation results were addressed

Source: Adapted from Levett and McNally (2003)

Case Study 6.1

SEA for the Proposed East London Industrial Development Zone, South Africa

Source: CSIR (1997b)

An industrial development zone (IDZ) – 'an optimal area for the location of intentionally competitive industries' – was proposed for the West Bank area (west of the Buffalo River) of East London in the Eastern Cape. The IDZ was part of the Government's Spatial Development Initiatives (SDIs) programme. Possible modifications to the existing East London harbour or, alternatively, a new harbour at Fullers Bay on the West Bank were associated with the proposed development. The Border Metropolitan Development Corporation (BOMEDCO) is a non-profit company. It comprises provincial and local government representatives in the Eastern Cape, together with companies having an interest in development of the area for industry. BOMEDCO commissioned an SEA as part of a feasibility study for the IDZ. The SEA was initiated during the earliest stages of the feasibility studies for the proposed IDZ and harbour. It aimed to inform decision-making by BOMEDCO members on whether, and under what conditions, an IDZ could proceed in the area concerned. As far as can be judged from the SEA report, no specific industrial developments were identified or proposed by BOMEDCO for possible location within the proposed IDZ. Neither were any restrictions suggested for the type of industrial developments that might be sited there. So it would have been difficult to assess specific impacts on the environment.

The SEA was undertaken by the CSIR. It followed the approach that it has pioneered in South Africa (see Section 6.1.1 for details). This approach differs from most other SEA methodologies. The focus is not so much on impacts of the development on the environment, but on the opportunities and constraints that the environment presents for development. The stated objectives of the SEA were to:

- assess the environmental opportunities (resources and potential benefits) and constraints (sensitive environments and potential costs) that could affect the development of the proposed IDZ;

- assess the possible direct, secondary and cumulative impacts and benefits that could result from the proposed IDZ; and
- evaluate the strategic benefits and impacts that must be considered by relevant authorities and decision-makers.

Current land uses in the area include: residential (formal and informal), agricultural, business, existing industry, railways and harbour facilities, recreational, conservation, quarries, and open spaces (both passive and active). East London has a high unemployment rate and economic growth rates are below the average for South Africa. Current industrial development in the area is limited. The city has not succeeded in attracting tourism as a major income source.

The SEA was conducted over a relatively restricted timeframe during 1997 (initiated February, preliminary report by 31 March, feasibility studies by 31 July, draft report by 8 August). The process is shown in Figure C6.1.1. The draft SEA report was circulated widely for public comment and was also independently reviewed.

The draft SEA has eight chapters which:

- introduce the study;
- set out the approach and methods used;
- describe the proposed IDZ area;
- discuss how the environment affects potential development in the area;
- consider potential cumulative effects and 'sustainability' indicators;
- present proposed development principles and guidelines for the West Bank area (to be adhered to if the project proceeds to the next stage of detailed planning) – including criteria for project EIA and guidelines for the environmental quality of air, water and other resources;
- describe the 'public participation' process followed; and
- make conclusions and recommendations – including for environmental management.

The public participation was managed initially by the Institute for Democracy in South Africa (IDASA) and subsequently by the Independent Mediation Services of South Africa (IMSSA). It involved:

- public meetings;
- a review workshop involving specialists, authorities and decision-makers;
- focus group meetings;
- distribution of information sheets at regular intervals (faxed, posted and available at meetings);
- an authority review (to obtain feedback from the authorities on the scope of the SEA, the preliminary issues identified, and to confirm roles and responsibilities with respect to the IDZ);
- public open days to present the finding of the SEA; and

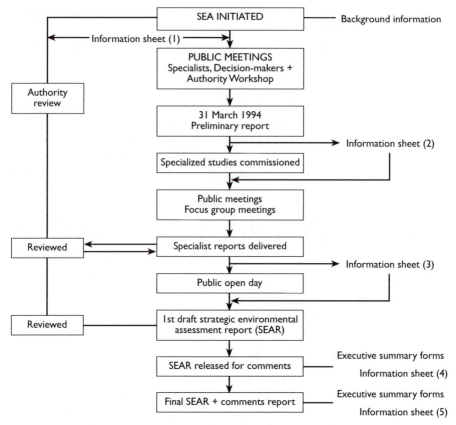

Figure C6.1.1 *Process for SEA of East London IDZ*

- comments submitted to the IDASA and IMSSA (telephonically and by fax), and passed to the CSIR.

Various *specialized studies* were also commissioned (marine environment, terrestrial ecology, air quality, visual assessment, near shore processes and coastal dynamics, and social and economic issues).

The SEA examined the no-go options. It concluded that if the IDZ were not to proceed, the risk of a negative impact on tourism opportunities would be removed, and there would be real potential for critically needed increased housing (both higher and lower income), recreational facilities and conservation areas.

The report tabulated findings on potential strategic benefits and costs for a range of issues. These covered:

- the natural environment (marine environment; terrestrial ecosystems; and air quality);
- infrastructure (water resources and supply; disposal of solid, liquid and hazardous wastes; transportation networks);

- socioeconomic issues (displacement of communities; housing; demands on health, education and other services; jobs creation and economic growth; and other economic opportunities); and
- planning and management (environmental management system; conservation, tourism, agriculture, marine and recreational resources; regional assessment of site options; and financial and environmental costs and benefits).

The SEA report discusses conditions under which further planning of the proposed IDZ could proceed. It sets out a proposed approach to develop a strategic EMP to facilitate development within the West Bank area.

The overall conclusion of the SEA was that 'there are no environmental reasons prohibiting further planning of the proposed development' provided 'that the principles provided in the SEA are applied in the further planning and development of the IDZ and harbour'. Nevertheless, the report did list significant environmental constraints that needed to be considered in decision-making and detailed planning. These included:

- existing residential areas and informal settlements;
- existing recreational areas;
- existing poor marine water quality;
- wave-driven long shore drift sediment movement;
- vegetation of high conservation importance;
- areas of high sensitivity;
- key terrestrial processes;
- historical sites;
- a car manufacturing plant;
- existing land zoning (with respect to ambient air quality guidelines that would be required for industries siting in close proximity to residential areas); and
- fresh water supply.

The SEA also identified potential cumulative effects from the proposed IDZ and suggested 'sustainability indicators' (in practice a range of environmental, social and economic indicators) against which cumulative effects could be tracked and examined at a later stage.

The SEA focused narrowly on the immediate West Bank area. Issues not covered by the study include an assessment of alternative sites for the proposed IDZ, and possible 'upstream and downstream' effects (environmental, social or economic) in the hinterland of the IDZ and wider afield.

There was considerable media interest when the SEA was published. But, subsequently, there has been very little progress with the IDZ. Politicians have been considering the enormous investment that will be required to establish a new deep-water port and/or IDZ in a climate when national economic growth has been below predicted levels.

Case Study 6.2

SEA of the Tofo, Barra, Tofinho and Rocha Beaches area, Mozambique

Source: Gove (2003)

INTRODUCTION

Following the end of civil war, there was rapid occupation of coastal land in Southern Mozambique with the aim of constructing tourism infrastructure. This has resulted in several problems:

- unorganized occupation, for example installation of hotels in the crests and slopes of fore-dunes;
- illegal occupation and selling of land (by Mozambican law, land belongs to the state and can not be sold);
- illegal tourism activities; and
- conflicts between investors, and between investors and local communities.

As a consequence, the Provincial Government of Inhambane requested the assistance of the Centre for Sustainable Development for Coastal Zones (CDS-ZC) – an advisory institution attached to the Ministry for Coordination of Environmental Affairs (MICOA) – in conducting an SEA. This would be an input to the preparation of the Macro-zoning Plan for the Tofo, Barra, Tofinho and Rocha (TBT) Beaches area. It was foreseen that the plan might result in significant environmental impacts in the region that could be reduced by submitting it to an SEA by:

- establishing a framework requiring an EIA – in accordance with existing legislation – for various types of project (e.g. the implementation of new tourism facilities, the redesign of existing facilities, the development of new tourism activities such as diving and fishing, and the development of livestock and agriculture); and
- the development of infrastructure including roads, cattle dips, and waste water treatment systems that could have impacts on the environment.

During 2001, a series of presentations on SEA were organized by CDS-ZC. These were held within MICOA (at central and provincial levels), with line ministries, and with the Governments of Gaza and Inhambane Provinces. The presentations were made by an external advisor, supported by the Integrated Coastal Zone Management Project (Phase II) and financed by DANIDA.

Following these, in 2002, CDS-ZC applied a trial SEA procedure in the TBT Beaches area. This was undertaken together with the Provincial Directorate for Coordination of Environmental Affairs of Inhambane (DPCA-I) and the Provincial Technical Team (ETP – comprising several provincial directorates and representing sectoral ministries at provincial level).

The TBT Beaches area covers 88km^2 (46 per cent of the total area of Inhambane municipality) and is one of the main tourism destinations in Mozambique, used mainly by South African tourists.

STEPS IN THE SEA PROCESS

The steps in this process are summarized in Box C6.2.1. The SEA involved several standard elements:

- *scoping* of environmental objectives;
- *evaluation* of environmental indicators (e.g. beach cleanliness, area occupied by natural dune vegetation, fish catches, quantity/quality of aquifers);
- *defining and gathering* required baseline environmental and socioeconomic information – to forecast the magnitude of impacts of activities envisaged in the Macro-zoning Plan;
- *assessment of potential impacts* – based on expert judgement and through two (costly) workshops – one for national and provincial technical government staff; the second involving stakeholder participation;
- *consideration of alternatives* to mitigate negative impacts – including general alternatives such as prohibiting or restricting particular practices/activities, and/or separating certain activities geographically to avoid cumulative impacts; as well as specific alternatives (Table C6.2.1); and
- *application of SEA results to TBT Beaches area Macro-zoning Plan* – in two ways:
  - identifying community protection zones and a community reforestation zone; and
  - integrating recommended alternatives into the Plan as obligatory conditions to be met in the seven different identified zones for approval of development proposals.

Box C6.2.1 Steps in SEA in the Tofu, Barra, Tofinho and Rocha Beaches area, Mozambique

1 *Presentation of the SEA procedure* to the Provincial Government of Inhambane – to sensitize decision-makers and obtain their approval and endorsement.

2 *Planning of SEA activities* for the Tofu, Barra, Tofinho and Rocha (TBT) Beaches area between CDS-ZC and DPCA-I, for all to be at provincial level (coordinated by the DPCA), and with the involvement of all relevant provincial and municipality authorities as well as local communities, private sector and national environmental institutions.

3 *Creation of the ETP* composed of the DPCA-I, Municipal Council of Inhambane City, Provincial Directorate of Public Works and Habitation, Provincial Services for Geography and Cadastre, and Provincial Services of Fisheries. Other Provincial Directorates (Tourism and Agriculture and Rural Development) were contacted, but were unable to participate.

4 *Collation and processing of biophysical, socioeconomic, legal and institutional information.* This work was done slowly to enable local communities, fishermen and tourism operators to understand it and gain confidence with the ETP; and so they could participate actively in the SEA process. Information was collated by the ETP together with secretaries of the TBT Beaches area neighbourhoods.

5 *First workshop*, with the participation of technical staff from provincial and national institutions. Provincial authorities included the members of the ETP. National institutions included the National Directorate for Environmental Management (Department of Coastal Zone Management) and the National Directorate for Territorial Planning.

6 *Feedback* of the results of the first workshop to local communities and tourism operators for information, critical comments, suggestions and corrections. Separate meetings were held between the ETP and the tourism operators of Barra and Tofo Beaches, the local communities of all the neighbourhoods of the TBT Beaches area and the local fishermen of Barra, Tofo and Rocha Beaches.

7 *Preparation for participation* of local communities and tourism operators in the second workshop – through separate meetings. The different groups chose their representatives in a transparent way and to represent all the neighbourhoods within the TBT Beaches area and activities in the region (agriculture, livestock, fisheries and tourism).

8 *Second workshop*, with the participation of local communities, tourism operators, government institutions and tourism associations. Beside ETP members, the government institutions included the Provincial Directorates of Agriculture and Rural Development, Tourism, Planning and Finance, the Maritime Authorities, and National Directorates for Environmental Management (Department of Environmental Management), Territorial Planning, and EIA.

9 *Feedback* of information to local communities and tourism operators for information, critical comments, suggestions and corrections. Separate meetings were held between the ETP and the tourism operators of Barra and Tofo Beaches, the local communities of all the neighbourhoods of the TBT Beaches area and the local fishermen of Barra, Tofo and Rocha Beaches.

10 *Elaboration of preliminary SEA.*

11 *Presentation to the Provincial Government for approval.* This meeting included the National Directors of Tourism Planning (in Ministry of Tourism) and Territorial Planning, the Director for Environmental Affairs of Maputo Province, and a consultancy company (KPMG).

12 *Production of final version of SEA report.*

13 *Inclusion of alternatives* in the Macro-zoning Plan – taking account of the potential impacts identified during the SEA procedure, setting requirements for the design of macro-zones and the elaboration of matrices for each of the identified macro-zones, with permitted and forbidden activities and norms for permitted activities.

Table C6.2.1 *TBT Beaches area SEA: specific alternatives*

Potential impact	Alternatives	Approach
Proliferation of litter.	• Permanent environmental awareness campaigns to tourists during the peak seasons. • Creation of permanent conditions for accommodation of litter on beaches and its rapid removal.	Campaigns in partnership with private sector, NGOs and civil society.
Increase in beach erosion.	• Prohibition of installation of tourism facilities on primary dunes.	Application of the law in force.
Reduction, depletion and/or contamination of aquifers.	• The installation of tourism facilities, beach houses and campsites should be done in accordance to the capacity of aquifers in providing sufficient water (determination of carrying capacity of the aquifers). • Consider forms of reutilization of residual water. • Implementation of proper treatments of liquid and solid residues as a way of avoiding contamination of aquifers. • The use of fertilizers and pesticides for the improvement of agricultural activities should be done in such a form as to minimize the contamination of aquifers. • The construction and functioning of cattle-dips should be done in such a manner as to minimize the contamination of aquifers.	Elaboration of EIA that highlights these alternatives.
Increase in Inhamua mangrove deforestation.	• Prohibition on the use of mangrove poles for building and maintenance, and as fuel wood for tourist facilities.	Elaboration of norms.
Dune erosion.	• Restriction of the movement of motorized vehicles on the beaches and dunes. This action includes the opening of access routes from behind the primary dunes (longitudinal paths, along the coast), where there should be some transverse paths to facilitate the access of tourists and local communities onto beaches for launching boats, swimming, recreational fishing, collection of invertebrates, etc. • Prohibition of installation of tourist facilities on the primary dunes (the fore-dunes between the former Combinado Pesqueiro and Lighthouse should not be used for any infrastructure, due to their bad condition. They should be reforested). Some exceptions, however, should be considered based on the use of environmentally friendly technology.	Application of the law in force and elaboration of norms.

Potential impact	Alternatives	Approach
	• Restriction on cutting of wood and poles and production of charcoal for tourism facilities and local communities. In this case there is a need to protect vulnerable areas, where none of these activities is to be permitted. Also, there is a need to create areas for the production of fire-wood (intensive reforestation zones) for use in the tourism industry and local communities, which does not promote environmental degradation and represents an income for local communities. This last point could minimize community conflict whilst maximizing the protection of vulnerable areas.	
	• Prohibition of agriculture in the primary dune areas, including the practice of burning. There is potential for the promotion of this activity in areas of major agricultural potential, such as swamps, where the environmental impacts can be mitigated. This includes the control of the opening of drainage ditches for the passage of rainwater, and the effective application of fertilizers and pesticides, to reduce the chances of saltwater intrusion and contamination of aquifers.	
	• Limitation on the quantity of goats per family in sensitive areas, in order to regenerate the natural vegetation. It is also necessary to control the access and opening of pathways in dunes leading to the beaches, to minimize the occurrence of soil erosion. The opening of planned pathways to the beach could help to minimize this issue.	
Negative impacts on the biological communities (crustaceans, turtles, etc.) found on the beaches.	• Restriction of the movement of motorized vehicles on the beaches and dunes. This action includes the opening of access routes from behind the primary dunes (longitudinal paths, along the coast), where there should be some transverse paths to facilitate the access of tourists and local communities onto beaches for launching boats, swimming, recreational fishing, collection of invertebrates, etc.	Application of the law in force and elaboration of norms.
Noise pollution.	• The movement of motorized vehicles (4x4s, etc.) through the villages, should be done within the pathways and only during daylight.	Elaboration of norms.

Potential impact	Alternatives	Approach
Negative impacts on juveniles and reproduction of fish and crustaceans.	• Prohibition of trawl fishing on Barra Beach, at least, during the main reproductive season. • The installation of fish traps in the Inhamua mangrove should not be done across the channels in a mode that prevents the free circulation of marine organisms into the mangrove and vice versa.	Elaboration of norms.
Negative impacts on the corals.	• Prohibition of any type of fishing and collection of invertebrates in the reef areas. • Determination of the number of diving centres in the TBT Beaches area, their capacity and the establishment of a code of conduct that needs to be complied with by all divers.	Elaboration of norms.
Overexploitation of fish and sedentary crustaceans.	• Establishment of fishing quota, per tourist, per day, including the prohibition of the sale of the catches by tourists.	Application of the law in force.
Increment of exploitation of invertebrates.	• Prohibition of the use of invertebrates as a building material.	Elaboration of norms.
Saltwater intrusion in certain swamps.	• Prohibition of indiscriminate opening of drainage ditches for rainwater in the swamps. Ditches should be opened allowing for the uni-directional movement of water to the sea.	Elaboration of norms.

CONCLUSIONS

Some aspects of this SEA can be highlighted:

- High commitment, since the start of the process, from the Provincial Government and the municipality to adopt and use SEA inputs in the Macro-zoning Plan. New land concessions were stopped until the finalization of these processes.
- Full involvement of all relevant stakeholders and decision-makers for the TBT Beaches area throughout the SEA process. This allowed the early resolution of conflicts and the achievement of consensus, except concerning the mandates of the municipality and provincial authorities to license land use.
- The preparation of the Macro-zoning Plan and the SEA were undertaken simultaneously, maximizing the integration of environmental aspects into strategic decision-making.
- The different government departments with environmental responsibilities were deeply involved both in the preparation of the Macro-zoning Plan and in the SEA. This inhibited the revision of the SEA report by an

independent environmental authority as envisaged when the SEA was designed.

• The monitoring of environmental, economic and social aspects raised in the SEA report and in the Macro-zoning Plan will de undertaken by a Commission, proposed by the Provincial Government. It includes the Provincial Directorate for Support and Control and the Provincial Directorate for Environmental Affairs and the CDS-ZC in order to guarantee the correction of implementation aspects.

Case Study 6.3

SEA of the Great Western Development Strategy, China

By Haakon Vennemo (hve@econ.no) and Sam Bartlett (srb@econ.no) (both at the ECON Centre for Economic Analysis, Oslo, Norway)

A number of regions in Eastern and Central China have undergone rapid economic development in the last decade, but China's western region remains relatively poor and underdeveloped. In response, the Chinese Government's Great Western Development (GWD) Strategy provides a strategic framework linking over 20 national policies and a range of key construction projects. The SEA of the GWD Strategy (the GWD SEA) was commissioned by the State Environmental Protection Administration (SEPA). The aim was to examine environmental consequences and risks, and investigate possible modifications to specific elements of the Strategy.

CHINA'S WESTERN REGION

China's western region includes 12 provinces, autonomous regions and municipalities: Shaanxi, Qinghai, Ningxia, Xinjiang, Gansu, Sichuan, Chongqing, Yunnan, Guizhou, Tibet, Inner Mongolia and Guangxi. The region hosts a diverse range of ecosystems, communities and economic activities. It covers 6.6 million km^2 (68 per cent of the country's land area) and has a population of 355 million people (27.4 per cent of the total population of the nation) including a large proportion of China's minority cultures.[22]

A number of regions in Eastern and Central China have achieved rapid economic development in the last decade. This transition has had a profound impact on these communities, increasing job opportunities and access to new technologies, and contributing to significant advances in education and healthcare. It has also had significant social and environmental impacts, including ongoing challenges relating to pollution, environmental degradation and access to natural resources. In contrast, China's western region remains

---

22 Chinese Academy of Environmental Planning (2002, p2).

relatively poor and underdeveloped, with significantly higher incidence of poverty (per capita gross domestic product for the region is 50–75 per cent of the national average). Low soil fertility, highly variable rainfall and severe wind erosion present significant challenges in many areas. However, the region also has considerable untapped human and natural resources. It is said that more than half of the country's identified natural resources are in the western region. Sustainable economic development of these resources has the potential to significantly reduce underdevelopment and poverty. However, a range of social and environmental impacts and risks require considered examination.

THE GWD STRATEGY

The goal of enhancing sustainable economic development in the western region has attracted significant interest in recent years. In 1999, the Chinese Government announced its official plan to develop Western China. Its goal is to try to achieve a satisfactory level of economic development in the western part of the country in a five- to ten-year timeframe and to establish a 'new Western China' by the middle of the 21st century.

In October 2000, the Fifth Plenary Session of the Central Committee of the Communist Party of China (CPC) agreed that 'the distributions of productive forces should be rationally readjusted for the benefit of the strategy of developing China's western areas' and that 'efforts must be intensified to improve infrastructure, protect the environment and strengthen control of population growth and resources so as to maintain sustainable development'.[23] Chinese Premier Zhu Rongji is quoted as saying that 'western development is of great economic and political significance and needs several generations' persevered efforts; we should seek every opportunity to implement the western development strategy to achieve a coordinated development among different regions of the country'.[24]

The GWD Strategy includes a range of public policy instruments – with links to over 20 national policies and a range of construction projects. At the most 'strategic' level, a range of policies address issues such as foreign investment, infrastructure development, natural resource management, energy, telecommunications, education and urbanization. Major projects currently envisaged include: a south-to-north water diversion, a west-to-east natural gas transfer, a west-to-east power transmission and the construction of a Qinghai–Tibet railway. These massive infrastructure projects have generated great concern amongst some observers within China and, perhaps more vocally, outside the country, about the potential impacts on the environment and minority cultures.

The Chinese Government is in the initial stages of implementing policies and projects in accordance with the GWD Strategy. Additional policies and

---

23 *China Daily*, 12 October 2000, p1 cited in MA (2002, p3).
24 *China Daily*, 12 October 2000, p4 cited in MA (2002, p3).

initiatives are being formulated, and there is significant potential to influence the development and execution of the strategy over the coming years.

THE PURPOSE OF THE GWD SEA

The Chinese Government has listed 'strengthening eco-environmental protection and construction' as one key work area in its agenda. A feature of this commitment is the application of EIA and SEA. In October 2002, China passed an EIA Law requiring SEAs of plans and programmes in several sectors including the energy sector and transportation (see Box 6.22).

The GWD SEA was commissioned by SEPA – the 'Ministry of Environment' in China. SEPA is interested in examining the environmental consequences and risks of the GWD Strategy in order to suggest modifications to the concrete elements of the Strategy. With its extremely long-term perspective and broad scope, the implementation of the GWD Strategy can accommodate modifications if, for instance, harmful environmental consequences are pointed out. This is one reason why SEPA wishes to bring the environmental consequences of the GWD Strategy to the negotiating table with other line ministries. Another important concern for SEPA is to prepare environmental impact mitigation measures for certain aspects of the GWD Strategy.

The project team, supported by the World Bank, consisted of researchers from the Chinese Academy for Environmental Planning, and Beijing Normal University. The Norwegian Centre for Economic Analysis (ECON) provided scientific advice to the team. The GWD interim SEA report 'analyses in detail some factors of environmental impacts from GWD, briefly analyses the environmental impacts of certain specific policies, and proposes necessary counter measures to be adopted to alleviate the environmental impacts'. It also includes a case study of the Guizhou Province. More broadly, the GWD SEA makes a contribution to the development of SEA capacity in China.

SEA METHODOLOGY

The SEA applied a relatively simple methodology involving coordinated analysis of the possible impacts associated with the implementation of the GWD Strategy. This analysis focused on a broad range of environmental media. The interim report includes chapters on water, air and biodiversity, land resources, and social impacts.

The project team used expert panels (the Delphi method) to examine both 'direct' (predominantly intended) and 'indirect' (predominantly unintended) impacts of the Strategy. They also explored alternative impact mitigation options.

Sector-based studies also applied a range of additional techniques. In the case of water resources, the analysis was supported by a demand gap analysis, projecting the likely gap between water demand and available water supply as the region develops and demand grows.

Significantly, the case for increasing public participation and stakeholder dialogue was briefly explored in the report. But there were no references to any formal mechanisms for public participation within the SEA process. It is therefore unclear to what extent the SEA report addresses specific concerns highlighted by some key stakeholders.

INTERIM RESULTS

As noted, the interim report explores a range of direct and indirect impacts arising from activities proposed in accordance with the GWD Strategy. The matrix of possible direct and indirect environmental impacts is very complex and involves a large number of factors. Nevertheless, a simple message emerges from the analysis: the environmental situation in China's western provinces is already serious, and aspects of the GWD Strategy tend to exacerbate some crucial environmental risks. For instance, the increased water demand that follows from the GWD Strategy will increase the pressure on scarce groundwater resources. Water pollution is also projected to increase, putting pressure on water quality. Biological diversity faces pressure from large infrastructure projects as well as from urbanization in general.

The prognosis for emissions to air is slightly more optimistic on the basis that technological development could substantially reduce emissions. On the other hand, various forms of economic development and industrialization have the capacity to significantly increase emissions.

Each chapter of the interim report explores a range of mitigation measures that authorities could apply to alleviate these pressures. But additional work is required to quantify the effectiveness of these measures. The case study of the Guizhou Province focuses on some of these issues and responses in detail, although further work is required in order to strengthen the analysis in this chapter.

CONCLUSIONS

Arguably the ultimate test of the effectiveness of the GWD SEA study will be its capacity to influence audiences and institutions involved in the development, implementation and monitoring of the GWD Strategy. At this stage it is difficult to ascertain whether the SEA process has increased awareness and appreciation of environmental impacts associated with the GWD Strategy proposals. The breadth and scale of the GWD Strategy has made it difficult to isolate specific proposals for detailed investigation. Further work on the draft report is required if it is to effectively articulate the case for a stronger focus on environmental threats and opportunities.

At this stage it is unclear whether the GWD SEA process will move into a second phase. As noted, there is an imminent need to strengthen SEA capacity in China. One option being explored is to organize training courses for SEA practitioners, drawing on experience with several recent SEA initiatives.[25] The lessons learned in preparing the GWD SEA will provide an important source of experience and expertise in this regard.

---

25 For more examples and a review of the Chinese SEA experience to date see Che et al (2002).

Case Study 6.4

SEA for the Second National Development Plan, Namibia

Based on reports by Brian Jones (2001 a, b)[26]

The process to develop Namibia's Second National Development Plan (NDP2) was supported by a project to integrate sustainable development concerns. The approach followed used elements that can be regarded as equivalent to an SEA.

BACKGROUND

Namibia gained its independence from South Africa in 1990. But the legacy of apartheid and colonial rule is still evident in the wide gap between rich and poor, unequal access to land and natural resources, poor education, health and housing for the rural majority. Development is constrained by the semi-arid to arid climatic conditions. The lack of water and often-fragile environment makes strategic planning for sustainable development particularly important. Attempts to link environment and sustainability to national planning processes reflect a growing awareness of the environmental constraints to development in Namibia.

In 1991, the then Ministry of Wildlife, Conservation and Tourism launched a process to develop a Green Plan for Namibia (Brown, 1992). This set out a cross-sectoral and multidisciplinary approach to environmental management. It was the first attempt to initiate processes and actions linking environmental issues and sustainable development.[27] About the same time, the Government launched the First National Development Plan (NDP1) setting out the country's development objectives and strategies for the first five years after independence. But the NDP1 did not address environmental and

---

26 Brian Jones, PO Box 9455, Eros, Windhoek, Namibia. Tel: +264 61 237101; email: Bjones@mweb.com.na.

27 The Green Plan set out key issues and strategies for ensuring environmental health, sustaining renewable natural resources, protecting biodiversity and ecosystems, and contributing to global environmental security. It also focused strongly on the promotion of environmentally responsible decision-making; and addressed overall national development issues such as poverty and its links to environmental problems as a major threat to sustainable development (Brown, 1992).

sustainable development issues. These two strategic frameworks were not linked and were developed in parallel.

In designing the process to develop the NDP2, the Government decided to integrate environmental and sustainable development issues into the national planning process – thereby bringing the issues, concerns and recommendations contained in the Green Plan into mainstream economic and development thinking. The NDP2 was due to become effective on 1 May 2001.

SECOND NATIONAL DEVELOPMENT PLAN PROCESS

The NDP1 was almost entirely written by foreign experts. Development of the NDP2 was initiated in mid-1999. It was coordinated by the National Planning Commission Secretariat (NPCS). Draft chapters on sector development plans and cross-cutting concerns were contributed by line ministries, regional and local government authorities and other government bodies. The line ministries established sectoral planning committees to prepare action work plans for drafting their respective chapters.

The methodology developed for working groups to review and screen clusters or related chapters involved:

- discussion of the sector mission statements of all chapters in the cluster and checking these for consistency with the framework chapters (national development objectives and strategies);
- review of each chapter's objectives, targets, strategies and private sector investment programme (PSIP) to analyse:
  - whether the objectives related to the overall NDP2 objectives
  - whether the targets covered/related to all the objectives
  - whether the strategies were appropriately designed to achieve the objectives, and
  - whether the PSIP fully captured the objectives, targets and strategies;
- particular attention to special concerns such as poverty reduction, employment creation, environmental and sustainable development aspects.

In practice, there was insufficient time to follow this approach adequately. However, a range of useful comments was made and further key issues and links between sectors were identified.

INTEGRATION OF SUSTAINABILITY ISSUES IN NDP2

The Ministry of Environment and Tourism (MET) and the NPCS initiated a joint project in 2000 to strengthen the national development planning process by integrating sustainable development concerns in NDP2. The Danish Development Agency (DANCED) supported the project and interacted at key stages of the NDP2 process.

The project promoted multi-stakeholder processes that generated strategic contributions to the NDP2. The aim was to ensure that the cross-cutting aspects and sector-specific aspects of sustainable development priorities and targets were fully incorporated into the NDP2. The approach involved several phases (Table C6.4.1).

Table C6.4.1 *Phases in NDP2 support project, Namibia*

Phase	Activities
Phase 1: Audit of the Green Plan and NDP1 (by consultants).	• An assessment of the incorporation of Green Plan principles/actions/initiatives into NDP1, and the achievement of the two plans against their objectives and contribution to sustainable development. • Identification and analysis of the ten main threats to sustainable development in Namibia, their root causes, and responses to them.
Phase 2: Development of a shared vision of sustainable development for NDP2.	• Eighteen sector issues/options papers prepared identifying key sustainable development and cross-cutting issues. • Papers used to inform a series of multi-stakeholder cluster (related sectors) workshops: natural resources; social; trade and industry; infrastructure and institutions. • Workshops developed cross-cutting issues and vision statements. • Inter-cluster workshop to consolidate cross-cutting issues and develop sustainable development vision for Namibia.
Phase 3: Support to drafting of four chapters for NDP2 for MET.	• MET decided to draft chapters itself, except for cross-cutting issues.
Phase 4: Screening draft NDP2 chapters (written by line ministries) against sustainable development priorities and targets.	• Consultants reviewed draft chapters, using crossing-cutting issues and vision statements identified by cluster workshops, and looked for gaps (issues not covered).
Phase 5: Assistance to NPCS to consolidate draft NDP2.	• Technical assistance to NPCS on incorporating consultants' review comments. • Support to dialogues, round tables, consultations on draft NDP2; and focused discussions with key officials in NPCS on specific issues and sectors. • Identification of capacity constraints to natural resource management under NDP2 framework; and recommendation of remedial interventions.

Cluster workshops

A central feature of the project was the organization and facilitation of workshops for four clusters of related sectors:

- *natural resources* (agriculture, water, land, wildlife, tourism, fisheries and forestry);
- *social* (health, education, labour and social services);
- *trade and industry cluster* (energy, industry, financial services, mining, and trade); and
- *infrastructure and institutions* (communications, housing, regional administration, and transport).

These workshops were multi-stakeholder events, each attended by representatives from a broad range of private sector companies, NGOs and government agencies (including some of the focal persons for drafting NDP2 chapters from line ministries, and the National Development Planning Commission (NDPC) planners). They served to generate a common understanding of sustainable development. An inter-cluster workshop was organized to consolidate the identification of cross-cutting issues identified by the individual workshops. It also agreed on a national vision for sustainable development: 'sustainable and equitable improvement in the quality of life of all the people in Namibia'.

Chapter screening

Consultants all used a common gap-consistency-conflict analysis approach to screen the draft chapters of NDP2. Each chapter was analysed in terms of:

- compliance of draft chapters with guidelines for preparing sector chapters;
- technical soundness;
- consistency between sectoral and national policies; and
- comments made on chapters by NPCS planners and other experts (e.g. the DANCED project reviewers);

and was assessed for:

- consistent and coherent coverage of relevant cross-cutting issues (as identified during the cluster workshops) in the chapter's objectives and priorities; and
- inconsistencies or areas where sectoral approaches (within clusters of related chapters) conflicted, failed to address major threats to sustainable development, or ran counter to the national vision (as agreed by the inter-cluster workshop).

The screening process was hindered by slow and 'last minute' submission of chapters by line ministries.

Consultants reviewed the results of the screening process. They incorporated revisions and new material into the chapters and discussed these changes with line ministries and NPCS planners in order to reach agreement. Cross-cutting and sustainable development issues were then incorporated and a draft NDP2 was circulated for broad comment.

A national workshop and regional consultations were organized to review the draft document. The national workshop was attended by government officials (particularly those responsible for drafting chapters), consultants advising ministries, and representatives of NGOs and community-based organizations (CBOs). It involved both plenary and facilitated working group sessions to discuss clusters of chapters.

A final revised draft was submitted to Cabinet and approved by Parliament in 2002.

MAIN OUTCOMES

A number of positive aspects of the support project can be identified:

- The alliance between the MET and the NPCS proved a useful mechanism for including environment and sustainable development issues in NDP2. The MET had a strong agenda reflected in the original Green Plan. But it was unable to implement this agenda effectively (apart from activities within its own remit) because of its relatively low status in the government hierarchy. Working closely with the NPCS gave the MET an opportunity to directly influence mainstream development planning.
- The use of consultants to carry out much of the work enabled much to be achieved within a relatively short period of time, and filled a capacity gap within the Department of Environmental Affairs (DEA).
- The project ensured continuous liaison between the DEA and NPCS.
- The sector issues and options papers provided useful background material. They were used by the sectors to identify major cross-cutting issues affecting sustainable development and provided initial discussion points in the cluster workshops.
- The cluster workshops proved to be effective mechanisms for (i) exposing a broad range of stakeholders to the concept of sustainable development and key cross-cutting issues; (ii) helping the different sectors to recognize the inter-relatedness of their activities with other sectors; and (iii) stimulating ideas about how better cooperation and integration could be achieved.
- Some line ministries were receptive to review comments on their chapters; others were defensive and less willing to make suggested changes to incorporate environmental and sustainable development concerns.

The approach appears to have made some impacts on sustainability thinking within the NPCS. There has been a noticeable increase in awareness of sustainable development and cross-sectoral issues amongst the NPCS planners that attended the various cluster and inter-cluster workshops. Some of them were enthusiastic participants in the workshop processes. They appear to have a better understanding of the broad complexity of sustainable development and were more able to incorporate sustainable development issues into the overall national planning processes.

The NPCS indicated that it was keen to use the sector cluster approach and emphasis on cross-cutting issues as a foundation for future planning and monitoring activities, and that it would extend this to the preparation of the national budget.

A number of outcomes are evident regarding the NDP2:

- The vision of sustainable development developed through the cluster workshop process was adopted as the Vision of NDP2.
- The President's foreword to NDP2 highlights 'promoting environment and ecological sustainability' as one of the six key strategies of the Plan. The enhancement of environmental and ecological sustainability is included as one of the Plan's nine national development objectives.
- NDP2 makes clear links between the four pillars of sustainable development: environment, economic development, social development and institutional development.
- The need to address development issues in an integrated way has begun to be accepted by officials in line ministries and other stakeholders.
- Sustainable development has been adopted as a key national development objective. Strategies to achieve sustainable development contained in NDP2 include efforts to explore the potential of alternative energy forms and community-based approaches to natural resource management.
- The importance of land reform and redistribution as well as wise land management is also recognized.

Case Study 6.5

SEA for Water Use, South Africa

*Sources: Paper available on the DWAF website:
www.dwaf.pwv.gov.za/sfra; and personal communications from
Mike Warren and Gavin Quibell (DWAF)*

SEA has had considerable influence on planning water allocations in South Africa. The National Water Act (NWA, No 36 of 1998) abolished the concept of 'private water'. It requires that catchment resources be allocated first and foremost to meet primary or basic human needs, the environmental reserve and international obligations. The Act established 19 water management areas (WMAs), each to be managed by a catchment management agency (CMA). In addition, it empowers the Minister of Water Affairs to declare stream flow reduction activities (SFRAs). These can be any land-based activities (including cultivation of any particular crop or other vegetation) that significantly impact on the flow of a river or stream. At present, only forestry is declared an SFRA. Other activities that might be viewed as SFRAs in the future include: dry land agricultural cropping, *veld*[28] improvement, alien invasives, and, possibly, stock watering dams and small farm dams. Impoundments (storage) are already viewed as a 'water use' by the NWA – an alternative would be to change the minimum size required for licensing storage to include smaller farm and stock watering dams. This can also be done on a specific catchment basis. The Catchment Management and Poverty Alleviation (CAMP) programme (funded by DFID) has, however, suggested that dry land agriculture actually actually increases stream flow over natural *veld*.

In 1994, the Department of Water Affairs and Forestry (DWAF) first committed itself to undertake work on SEA in the Eastern Cape. In 1997, it embarked on an 'SEA for forestry' initiative. Its principal objective was to provide a framework for decision-making to take into account national and regional needs as well as to consider the cumulative impacts of forestry development. There was concern within the forestry industry about perceived discrimination. This led to a widening of the scope of the project to include other SFRAs. The purpose of the SEA for SFRAs is to provide an effective, transparent and equitable 'negotiation and decision support system' for the sustainable development of SFRAs that acknowledges other water uses.

---

28 *Veld*: a South African term meaning open, unforested or thinly forested grass country.

The process evolved further with inputs from DANCED – now incorporated within DANIDA – and through widespread consultation with stakeholders. Two large provincial *indabas* (participative gatherings) were held in KwaZulu-Natal and the Eastern Cape, respectively. In late 1998, DFID agreed to fund a two-year first phase of an SEA for SFRAs. The DWAF organized a workshop on the SEA with the focus on forestry. This brought together some 50 role-players with an interest in the use of the SEA process for forestry and possible other land uses. One outcome was that SEA should include all possible SFRAs – not just forestry. A third *indaba* was held in Mpumalanga in 1999 with a focus beyond forestry.

After protracted debate, the project team finalized a logical framework analysis (LFA) for the process. Each team member assumed responsibility for at least one output and its associated activities and tasks. The technical work was to be supported by a geographical information system (GIS).

The main aim of the SEA was to provide an information base and decision-making framework to ensure that relevant sections of the NWA were implemented with regard to SFRAs. The SEA would not, itself, make decisions, or plan what should happen in a catchment. Its role was to provide information and ideas, which could then be used to guide those plans and decisions.

A key component of the process was to establish a framework for negotiation. The SEA had several aims:

- to contribute to the development of the National Water Resource Strategy;
- to provide support for the development of catchment management strategies and plans at provincial and water management area levels – by new CMAs supported by advisory committees; and
- to assist the licensing of applications for SFRAs in local areas.

The SEA was, therefore, designed to be tiered and nested. The function of the SEA and the type of information provided and required varied for four distinct levels:

- the broad national picture;
- provincial/WMAs;
- focus areas/catchments (sub-divisions of WMAs); and
- local areas (relating to water use licensing).

Some of the key outputs from this process are listed in Table C6.5.1
The main steps in the SEA process can be summarized as:

- *policy appraisal* – analysis of the requirements of the various existing laws that have a direct or indirect impact on SFRA development;
- *establishing a work programme* – discussion of the goals and objectives of the process, tasks to be addressed, budget, timetable and products, staffing plan, and cooperating agencies;

Table C6.5.1 *Key elements of the SEA process for SFRAs*

Component of the NWA	SEA activity/product
National level	
• Interference with other areas of government policy and national standards. • Declaration of SFRAs (NWA, Chapter 4, Part 4). • National Water Balance Model (NWBM). • National Water Resource Strategy (NWRS; S5). • Setting water resource and water quality objectives – resource quality objectives. • Determining the reserve (basic human needs and ecological reserve). • Prevention of pollution. • Licensing and regulation of water use; pricing strategy.	• National policy review. • Definition of SFRAs. • National-level screening. • Analysis of national/regional significance of SFRAs as a contribution to the NWBM. • Contributing to understanding of the relationships between SFRAs and other forms of water use. • Making recommendations on appropriate measures for dealing with SFRAs at national level.
Provincial/regional/local levels	
• WMAs and CMAs.	• Providing an overview of the impact of SFRAs within each WMA/CMA area and the constraints/opportunities for meeting NWRS aims and objectives. • Exploring the interface between SFRAs and regional plans and policies being developed by other institutions. • Developing a framework for public participation, consultation and communication.
Catchment level and local	
• Catchment management strategies (CMS). • Developing water allocation plans.	• Giving guidance on how CMAs should take SFRAs into account in developing CMS. • Producing a framework for negotiation and decision-making on individual SFRA applications for permits/licences. • Providing a detailed database on biophysical, social and economic indices for priority focus areas.

- *definition of the scope of the SEA* – physical limits, impacts addressed, and alternatives;
- *establishing a framework for public participation and consultation* – workshops, distribution of information through the printed and electronic media;
- *setting up a database* – establishing data requirements, collection of baseline data, managing database;

- *manipulating and analysing data* – establishing criteria and weightings, identifying costs and benefits, queries;
- *impact synthesis and evaluation* – weighing of costs and benefits, creating scenarios, testing sensitivity of options;
- *empowering relevant organizations and individuals to use the negotiation and decision support system* (NDSS) – including DWAF regional offices, CMAs, advisory committees, and other relevant organizations;
- *establishing a monitoring and auditing strategy* – appointing a steering committee, project review committee, and specialist review group; and
- *publishing the results.*

One of the tasks of the SEA project team was to elicit the principles used in determining SFRAs and then to assess the scope of candidate activities in terms of their possible declaration as SFRAs.

The DWAF has now fully embraced the concept of SEA as a tool for use in catchment planning and management, and as a support to the NWA (No 36 of 1998), with the following specific objectives:

- to ensure best use of water in an integrated way to most benefit society and the economy without degrading the environment (i.e. the beneficial use of water in the public interest[29]);
- to encourage people to become involved in catchment affairs and to link users with decision-makers;
- to assess and analyse data from the catchment; and
- to provide decision-makers with reliable data from the catchments for more-informed decisions.

National-level screening (NLS) was undertaken to identify how both existing and potential SFRAs related to the most heavily stressed parts of the country (in terms of the balance of water availability and demand). NLS aims to become an iterative process. An initial review was undertaken between December 1998 and March 1999. It identified priority regions for investigation through the SEA process, and indicated that forestry, sugar cane, maize and fibre crops were the key land and water uses that needed to be considered. The water requirements for these crops were assessed and related to information on soil types, relief, climate, rainfall and evaporation. Maps were then produced showing the distribution of forestry SFRAs (the only existing ones) and potential SFRAs. The national screening also produced a range of other maps of the country: identifying views or visions for the future – for SFRAs and for supply and demand of resources (e.g. water); indicating where development is likely to be constrained; and indicating where development is most needed. A database was compiled and a document produced setting the values and context for each sector. Based on this analysis, the SEA team

---

29 The NWA is founded on promoting the beneficial, efficient and sustainable use of water in the public interest.

recommended that attention be focused on four provinces: Northern, Mpumalanga, KwaZulu-Natal and the Eastern Cape.

It was then decided to select a specific secondary catchment where a pilot project SEA could provide more in-depth screening through involving stakeholders and role-players. So, an SEA for Water Use Study was first undertaken in the Mhlathuze Catchment in KwaZulu-Natal. A controversial report on this SEA was released in 2000 which noted that:

- The catchment was under water stress and there was no surplus for allocation to new users (current thinking is that this stress is only on paper!).
- Local communities were not represented at decision-making forums and committees; and there was a need to get people to debate their different needs, demands and visions face-to-face.
- There was an historical inequity in allocating water resources between established commercial sectors and the community.

Many of the findings and lessons arising from the SEA were 'absorbed' by various divisions within the DWAF, notably the Water Resources Planning Group, the Directorate Catchment Management and the Forestry Development Team. The latter has been examining the utility of SEA.

As a follow-up, a proposal was made for an SEA at the much larger WMA level. Here, SFRA developments are likely to have significant impact on water resources, and possibly on other developments (and vice versa). During this process, the provincial context, legislation and political views would be taken into consideration. The next step therefore was an SEA of the Usutu to Mhlathuze WMA (Figure C6.5.1), funded by the DWAF and DFID. This SEA commenced in October 2000, for completion in 2004. One of the aims was to determine the most effective level or scale of SEA and to provide a template for further SEAs in other WMAs.

Research studies were commissioned under the SEA on hydrological, social, hydroeconomic and biophysical issues that were important in the Usutu to Mhlathuze WMA.

Social component: aimed to evaluate water-related and non-water-related issues and to ensure stakeholder participation. Public participation workshops were organized in various areas to identify more about water-related and other issues; and to enable local communities to engage in the SEA and decision-making processes.

The SEA identified several major stakeholder groups:

- DWAF national and regional offices;
- private sector: forestry, mining, agriculture including sugar;
- government/public sector: national and provincial government departments, provincial and local government institutions (metro, district councils and municipalities), traditional authorities; and
- parastatals: water and irrigation boards, water users' associations.

Biophysical component: aimed to accurately describe the potential of the physical environment and biodiversity. This involved developing a Biobase (map overlays identifying important areas for conservation and endangered/rare species) for the WMA and creating biophysical land use potential maps using GIS.

Hydroeconomic component: aimed to provide information to allow decision-makers to weight hydrological and economic impacts using the decision support system (DSS).

A range of sub-reports on these studies are available on the DWAF website: www.dwaf.pwv.gov.za/sfra.

The DWAF has adopted SEA to support decision-making on further afforestation in the Eastern Cape Province. A tender has been issued for such a project and an SEA study is planned. A complementary Biobase may also be launched together with the provincial Environment Department (if not existing). There is a renewed thrust to see at least 100,000ha of land, largely communally held, afforested over the next few years. Significant efforts in this regard were made in the late 1990s, but little has actually happened due to environmental objections and uncertainties concerning social impacts. The SEA in the Usutu to Mhlathuze WMA has shown that decision-making about specific land parcels requires a very fine scale of resolution. The current approach is to focus on specific areas that appear to be suited to forestry (10,000–20,000ha) but within a research process setting the context at the scale of the WMA.

Figure C6.5.1 *Usutu to Mhlathuze WMA: Location*

Case Study 6.6

Transboundary Environmental Assessment of the Nile Basin

Sources: www.nilebasin.org/overview (executive summary);,NBI (2001); and edits provided by Gedion Asfaw (Project Manager of the Nile Transboundary Environmental Action Project) and Astrid Hillers (World Bank, AFTSD, Nile Team)

The Nile Basin covers 3 million km^2 – 10 per cent of Africa, and is shared by ten countries: Burundi, the Democratic Republic of Congo, Egypt, Ethiopia, Eritrea, Kenya, Rwanda, Sudan, Tanzania and Uganda. The total population is 300 million people, with 160 million in the basin itself (2000 figures). Despite its natural endowments, the region faces severe challenges: poverty, instability, rapid population growth and environmental degradation. Yet the Nile holds opportunities for cooperative management and development that could serve as a catalyst for greater regional integration. Recognizing this, in February 1999, the Nile riparian countries established the *Nile Basin Initiative* (NBI) to fight poverty and promote socioeconomic development in the region. The initiative is guided by a Shared Vision 'to achieve sustainable socio development through the equitable utilisation of, and benefit from, the common Nile Basin water resources'.

The initiative provides a unique forum for the countries of the Nile to move forward in a cooperative process to realize tangible benefits in the basin and build a solid foundation of trust and confidence. The NBI Commission (Nile-COM) serves as the highest decision-making body of the NBI. Chairmanship of the Nile-COM rotates annually. The Nile-COM is supported by the NBI Technical Advisory Committee (Nile-TAC) comprising two senior officials from each member country. Since 1999, the NBI Secretariat (Nile-SEC) has operated from Entebbe, Uganda.

The Nile countries seek to realize their Shared Vision through a basin-wide Strategic Action Programme. This comprises two complementary programmes:

- the basin-wide Shared Vision Programme (SVP) – to create an enabling environment for cooperative action through building trust and confidence; and

- subsidiary action programmes – to plan and implement investments and activities on the ground at the lowest appropriate level. These take into account the benefits from, and impacts of, collaborative action, exchange of experience and capacity-building in all riparian countries.

The SVP comprises eight basin-wide projects:

- Nile Transboundary Environmental Action:
  - to provide a strategic framework for environmentally sustainable development of the Nile River Basin; and support basin-wide environmental action linked to transboundary issues in the context of the NBI Strategic Action Programme;
- Nile Basin Regional Power Trade;
- Efficient Water Use for Agricultural Production;
- Water Resources Planning and Management;
- Confidence-Building and Stakeholder Involvement;
- Applied training;
- Socio-Economic Development and Benefit-Sharing; and
- SVP coordination.

The preparation of the projects within the SVP project portfolio was driven by the institutions of the NBI. It involved the active participation of more than 70 technical experts (including eight technical specialists from each of the nine countries) in a range of water-related sectors from across the basin. For many, it was the first time that they had discussed common concerns and potential opportunities with their colleagues from neighbouring and co-riparian countries.

Between February 1999 and March 2001, the SVP evolved from four thematic areas, or pillars (as described in the *NBI policy guidelines*) to a coordinated basin-wide programme. The process was executed and coordinated by the Nile-SEC. It involved the active participation of, and guidance from, the Nile-TAC, and received formal endorsement by the Nile-COM at critical milestones.

An International Consortium for Cooperation on the Nile (ICCON) was established to provide a long-term partnership forum between the Nile Basin States and the international community. It first met in June 2001 in Geneva. At this first ICCON meeting, funding was pledged to support the projects of the SVP.

THE TRANSBOUNDARY ENVIRONMENTAL ASSESSMENT

Under the SVP, a transboundary environmental assessment (TEA) has been carried out by the Nile riparians (NBI, 2001). It includes a collective synthesis of basin-wide environmental trends, threats and priorities, and outlines the elements for a long-term agenda for environmental action for the Nile Basin.

The TEA aims to be both a catalyst and a valuable resource to the Nile riparians and their international partners.

The TEA was initiated in December 1999 within the NBI's SVP. It was undertaken in cooperation with UNDP and World Bank, with additional funding from the Global Environment Facility (GEF). The main objective was to help translate existing national environmental commitments and interest into basin-wide analytical frameworks and, eventually, basin-wide actions. The emphasis was on stakeholder awareness and involvement, water and environmental management, training and education, capacity-building, information-sharing and institutional development.

Priority issues to be addressed at basin-wide, national and local levels were identified and analysed. The synthesis provided the basis to formulate the elements of an agenda for environmental action with complementary preventive and curative actions to address current and emerging issues in the Nile Basin. The agenda aimed for collaborative implementation over the next decade or more in coordination with other development activities. Finally, the TEA outlined transboundary activities to be addressed collaboratively in the initial implementation phase of the agenda for environmental action in the form of a proposed project.

Several key transboundary environmental threats were identified:

- land degradation (deforestation, erosion, and downstream sedimentation, mining impacts);
- loss of wetlands and biodiversity (including loss of habitats, and poaching) and lake degradation;
- water quality degradation (including pollution, sanitation concerns, eutrophication, water weed infestation, and siltation); and
- lack of disaster preparedness and remediation (floods and droughts, refugee problems, climatic variability and uncertain impacts of climate change, navigation risks and aids).

The root causes of the threats identified by the analysis fell into various main groups:

- poverty; macro and sectoral policies;
- governance, institutional and capacity constraints;
- regulatory environment and lack of adequate land use planning;
- unclear tenure and inadequate access to resources for local stakeholders;
- insufficient environmental education and awareness;
- limited access to environmental knowledge and information (including relevant scientific data);
- population growth;
- rapid urbanization; and
- climatic variability.

Two related sets of activities informed the report:

1 Broad and participatory national consultations led by a national expert in each of the nine participating Nile countries, with findings and recommendations documented in national reports. These national consultations were carried out in parallel to assessments of priority needs in other sectors included in the SVP. They were all under the guidance of national Nile-TAC representatives with coordination by an international lead consultant. The national experts consulted with key stakeholders in national and local government agencies, NGOs, and research organizations, as well as people working on related projects and programmes. At least one workshop was held in each country to which a variety of stakeholders were invited. These consultations built on existing national environmental planning processes within the countries as well as sectoral master plans, many of which were themselves based on broad consultative processes. The national experiences and reports were consolidated in the basin-wide analysis, through three basin-wide meetings. These were attended by the 15 drafting group members (consultants and technical experts from Nile government environmental agencies, donors and international organizations) as well as Nile-TAC members.

2 Supported by USAID, a scoping study was undertaken for a multi-country technical background paper. This was based on readily accessible and public domain information supplemented by selected country visits. The latter were organized in cooperation with the national experts referred to above. Key findings from the scoping study were reflected in the TEA report.

Chapters in the final report cover:

• background and process;
• overview of key environmental resources and their uses;
• environmental threats;
• opportunities and an agenda for action;
• resource mobilization and initial actions; and
• concluding comments.

And there are various annexes:

• basin-wide environmental threats;
• threats – ranked by priority and country;
• TEA: common concerns by sub-region;
• environmental priority actions by country;
• stakeholders consulted during national processes;
• protected areas with transboundary significance;
• commitment to international conventions;

- environmental working group and Nile-TAC members;
- stakeholder involvement and participation;
- NBI;
- NBI glossary; and
- background documents and selected studies.

TRANSBOUNDARY ENVIRONMENTAL ACTION PROJECT

The TEA process prioritized transboundary environmental threats. These guided the formulation of a first basin-wide project for environmental action within the SVP. This Transboundary Environmental Action Project has been designed to encourage more effective basin-wide stakeholder cooperation on transboundary environmental issues in selected priority areas.

The expected outputs of the Nile Transboundary Environmental Action Project are:

- enhanced regional cooperation on transboundary environmental and natural resource management issues. Elements include the development and application of a river basin model as part of a decision support system, knowledge management, and linkage of macro and sectoral policies and the environment;
- enhanced capacity and support for local-level action on land, forest and water conservation, and establishment of a micro-grant fund to support community-level initiatives at pilot sites;
- increased environmental awareness of civil society through environmental education programmes and networking of universities and research institutions;
- enhanced regional capacity for sustainable management of wetlands and establishment of wetlands management programme at pilot sites; and
- establishment of standard basin-wide analytical methods for water quality measurements and initiation of monitoring of relevant transboundary hot spots. Enhanced capacity for monitoring efforts and pollution prevention.

Case Study 6.7

SEA in the South African National Ports System

By Stuart Heather-Clark (Project Manager and Researcher, CSIR, South Africa; shclark@csir.co.za)

INTEGRATING SUSTAINABILITY AND SEA INTO THE SOUTH AFRICAN NATIONAL COMMERCIAL PORTS POLICY

Background

Transnet Limited is a public company with the South African Government as its sole shareholder. It is the holding company behind South Africa's largest transport businesses. Portnet was one of its nine business units with responsibility for the management and operation of South Africa's seven commercial ports. In line with the country's restructuring strategy of state-owned enterprises, Portnet has been temporarily divided into two main entities: the National Ports Authority (NPA) and South African Port Operations (SAPO). In due course, once the reorganization of Transnet is finalized, the NPA will report directly to the Department of Transport as a new state-owned corporate entity. The NPA will act as the landlord of the ports. The role of the Ministry and Department of Transport with respect to commercial ports is to ensure that efficient and effective, seamless inter-modal transportation is achieved in the national interests of South Africa. To provide the policy framework within which the NPA will operate, a White Paper on National Commercial Ports Policy was drafted and circulated for public comment in October 2001.

The CSIR[30] recognized the need for and importance of integrating sustainability aspects so that the Ports Policy would better facilitate sustainable port development, and provided comments in this regard. Figure C6.7.1 illustrates the policy-making process and key interactions during the process. The latter are discussed below.

---

30 The Council for Scientific and Industrial Research with a mandate to support government.

CSIR INTERACTIONS   POLICY PROCESS

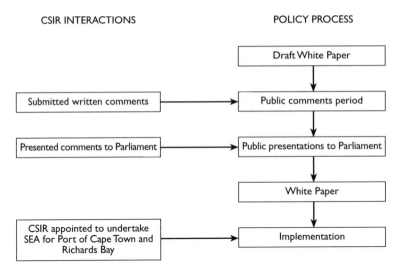

Figure C6.7.1 *Policy process and CSIR's interaction with the process*

The CSIR identified the ports as a key target sector in which to promote planning for sustainable development. It undertook a programme of research on sustainable port development between 1997 and 2002. Numerous papers and discussion documents were presented at South African and international conferences. These were circulated amongst the planning, environment and engineering departments of the NPA. Some conference papers were written in collaboration with NPA staff. The use of environmental assessment and management tools such as EIA and SEA were promoted to ports staff as tools that could facilitate sustainable port development and operation. This research and interaction contributed to the NPA accepting the need to address sustainability issues in planning the development of ports, and identifying SEA as useful for this purpose.

Research conducted by the CSIR over the past five years (Heather-Clark et al, 1998; Heather-Clark, 1999, 2000, 2002) shows that, for South African ports to move toward sustainable development, they need to make improvements in a number of areas:

- port–city relationships and cooperative decision-making;
- individual port relationships with stakeholders including port users, environmental stakeholders and the surrounding local communities;
- environmental management and data collection within the ports, so that it can be used proactively during the port planning process and to inform future operations through the development of well-informed environmental management intervention strategies;
- understanding of how ports impact on the livelihoods and quality of life of local communities;
- economic data collection and analysis (local, provincial, national and regional) for consideration during port planning processes, and

- reporting on 'triple bottom line' performance (i.e. how environmental, social and economic concerns have been addressed).

Commenting on the draft White Paper on the National Commercial Ports Policy

The policy was assessed and recommendations made on improving sustainability issues. These included:

- the need to integrate biophysical, social and economic aspects at all levels of decision-making within the port development cycle, in other words policy, planning, design, construction and operation; and
- the use of various environmental assessment and management tools, including environmental management systems (for port operation), EIA (port design) and SEA (port policy and planning).

The CSIR's comments were also presented (in writing and verbally) to the Parliamentary Portfolio Committee on Transport – responsible for reviewing the policy and comments before the final draft was submitted to the Minister and then to Cabinet for approval. This allowed the CSIR to lobby for its comments to be taken seriously and included in the policy.

More than 80 per cent of the CSIR's comments on including sustainability and the use of various tools to achieve this were included in the final White Paper. For example, it now states that 'SEA should be used for the proactive integration of biophysical issues with social and economic issues at the policy and planning level' (National Department of Transport, 2002). The NPA also committed to undertaking SEAs for all South Africa's major commercial ports.

SEA PORT OF CAPE TOWN – SOUTH AFRICA

Background

The Port of Cape Town is one of South Africa's largest commercial ports and plays a critical role in the development of the economy of the Western Cape and South Africa. It is particularly known for exporting deciduous fruit and other frozen products, core components of the Western Cape economy. Other core businesses include container handling, ship repair, fishing and bulk oil activities. Some of the port's secondary business includes hosting local and foreign fishing fleets operating in the South Atlantic and South Indian Oceans, fuel bunker supply, and providing a logistical base for various countries with bases in Antarctica.

The Port of Cape Town is surrounded by a complex social and built environment and is situated in a sensitive marine environment. The City of Cape Town envelops the port and is experiencing rapid growth, for example the Victoria and Alfred Water Front Development, the Cape Town Convention

Centre, various hotels and other tourist-related developments. The majority of these developments are taking place in close proximity to the port and, in many cases, adjacent to the port boundaries. The city attracts more than 770,000 overseas tourists per year. These are an important component of the economies of both the city and the Western Cape. The marine environment is sensitive in terms of the marine ecosystems and specific threatened marine birds that it supports. The physical marine processes (e.g. sediment dynamics) are sensitive to port and city developments and beach erosion is evident. There has been pressure on the NPA to employ responsible corporate governance and respond to social needs, with the added need to report on its 'triple bottom line' performance.

SEA process

The NPA commissioned the CSIR and SAKAZA Communications to undertake an SEA for the Port of Cape Town to provide a framework for long-term sustainable port development and operation. The SEA process (Figure C6.7.2) broadly followed that defined in the South African SEA Guidelines (DEAT, 2000) and comprised three distinct phases:

- Phase 1: scoping phase;
- Phase 2: strategic assessment (specialist studies); and
- Phase 3: sustainability framework (integration).

Phase 1: scoping

A critical part of this phase was the participation of key stakeholders through workshops to:

- define a vision for sustainable port development (Box C6.7.1) to drive the implementation of the sustainability framework (see Figure C6.7.1). It was developed through key stakeholder consultation and by reviewing the NPA's vision and mission statements and its environmental policy; and
- identify strategic issues for detailed investigation (Box C6.7.2). Such issues were those that, if not addressed by the SEA, would prevent the port from achieving the vision for sustainable port development.

General stakeholders were kept informed of the SEA process through the distribution of information sheets, press notices and access to a website. The port–city issues are important and are highly relevant to sustainable port development (see the section on strategic issues: port–city planning, access, sediment dynamics, etc.). So the City of Cape Town Municipality was identified as the most important key stakeholder and was included in a number of additional meetings and workshops. Information obtained from the key stakeholders was analysed and the draft scoping report was made available to both key and general stakeholders for comment. The final scoping report was submitted to the NPA (it is available at: www.csir.co.za/portofcapetownSEA). It contains draft terms of reference to address the strategic issues.

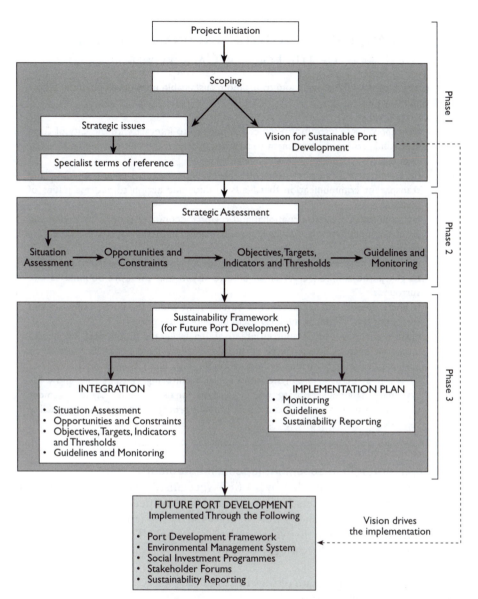

Figure C6.7.2 *SEA process for the Port of Cape Town*

BOX C6.7.1 VISION FOR THE SUSTAINABLE DEVELOPMENT OF THE PORT OF CAPE TOWN

In support of the NPA's vision and to promote sustainable port development, the Port of Cape Town will:

- have appropriate institutional structures in place to interact with the City of Cape Town and provincial government to facilitate informed and efficient decision-making with regards to port–city developments;
- have well-structured port user and stakeholder forums to ensure effective and transparent communication that leads to informed action to address issues of concern;
- facilitate local, provincial, national and regional economic growth by having and sustaining port systems that facilitate and enable competitiveness in a world-class port system;
- ensure the protection of important ecosystems, habitats and biophysical processes to guarantee the conservation of biodiversity within the port boundaries and surrounds;
- facilitate appropriate socioeconomic development within the port boundaries and surrounds that enhances the local social benefits of the port;
- ensure effective use of appropriate tools to integrate biophysical, social and economic aspects into all levels of decision-making, from policy formulation to planning, design, construction and operation (i.e. SEA, EIA, ISO 14001 etc); and
- have well-structured biophysical and social monitoring systems that allow for systematic data collection, storage, and analysis, for use in day-to-day management decisions, as well as future strategic port planning processes and annual sustainability reporting.

Phase 2: strategic assessment (specialist studies)

The SEA process was guided by an SEA specialist, whilst separate subject specialists assessed strategic issues that were identified during the scoping process. Specialist workshops were held to clarify the terms of reference and to facilitate integration between specialist studies. The generic terms of reference for the specialists were:

- discuss the existing state of the environment;
- identify any apparent trends in the environment;
- identify sustainability objectives, targets, thresholds and indicators that will assist with future decision-making and tracking progress towards sustainable development;
- identify opportunities and constraints that the surrounding environment may place on future port development (i.e. the impact of environment on development);
- recommend guidelines to overcome constraints and enhance opportunities; and
- recommend a monitoring programme to monitor indicators.

Box C6.7.2 Strategic issues for detailed investigation during the SEA

1   *Maintenance of marine ecosystem functions and habitats*
    Present and future port operations and future port development will have an impact on the marine environment of Table Bay, thereby constraining the port from achieving its vision of sustainable port development.

2   *Maintenance of shoreline stability*
    The future physical expansion of the port into Table Bay and possible sourcing of fill material from the bay to support such development, may have an impact on the shoreline stability of Table Bay. If this potential impact is significant, in other words if it could result in substantial amounts of erosion of the coastline, the future long-term development of the port could be constrained.

3   *Disturbance of marine archaeology*
    The location of shipwrecks within the area of future port expansion (physical expansion, source of fill material, dredge spoil dumpsite) may pose a constraint to future port development. Under the National Heritage Resources Act No 25 of 1999, shipwrecks older than 50 years are classified as national heritage sites and a full archaeological investigation may be required before the site can be disturbed.

4   *Access corridors to the port*
    The restricted access to the port via city, regional and national road and rail routes may prevent the port from achieving its future economic and efficiency goals and therefore pose a constraint to meeting the long-term sustainable vision for the port.

5   *Port–city land use planning issues*
    The development of non-port-related activities adjacent to the port may place unrealistic operational constraints on port activities and constrain the port from future physical expansion.

6   *Institutional arrangements*
    The limited formal communication between the higher levels of decision-makers within the city and port may result in a continued mismatch of the needs and expectations of the port and the city. This could constrain future sustainable port–city development, as a result of delays in decision-making and unnecessary conflict.

7   *Consideration of local, provincial and national policies, economic data and trends for port planning*
    Future port development and infrastructure investment must be informed by regular assessments of local, provincial, national and regional economic growth scenarios of key sectors.

8   *Socioeconomic impact of port development and operations*
    The Port of Cape Town plays a vital role in the socioeconomic development of the region as well as the City of Cape Town. The socioeconomic impact of the port needs to be maximized through proactive policies.

A core task was to identify specific, monitorable indicators to track the port's progress to sustainable development and to assist with decision-making about future port expansion, in other words by using this information in project-specific EIAs.

A number of strategic issues were assessed (for each, existing date and literature were reviewed and expert opinion obtained and, in some cases, additional activities were undertaken – as indicated):

- maintenance of marine ecosystems and habitats;
- marine archaeology;
- shoreline stability (plus the use of computer shoreline modelling and expert opinion);
- access to the port (plus the use of computer traffic modelling and expert opinion);
- port–city spatial planning;
- socioeconomics;
- economics; and
- institutional arrangements (plus meetings with key stakeholders and expert opinion).

Each specialist provided a detailed analysis of the existing state of the environment concerning 'their' strategic issue, and used this information to identify sustainability objectives and targets. Guidelines to promote sustainable port planning and development were then drafted for use by port planners and environmental managers in future port planning initiatives. Sustainability indicators (together with detailed monitoring programmes) were identified to assist the port with tracking its progress towards achieving the objectives and targets, in other words sustainable port development. Recommendations were made on reporting against the indicators to track progress towards sustainable port development, in other words triple bottom line reporting.

Phase 3: sustainability framework
The SEA specialist was also responsible for compiling the specialist studies and preparing the final output – an integrated report or 'sustainability framework' (available at: www.csir.co.za/portofcapetownSEA) and for presenting this to the client and the stakeholders in July 2003. This framework includes the following for each strategic issue:

- a brief description of the state of the environment;
- opportunities and constraints;
- guidelines for future sustainable port development; and
- a monitoring programme for key sustainability indicators.

Various departments within the Port of Cape Town will be responsible for implementing the actions required to ensure sustainable port development. Some departments within the City of Cape Town will also play a critical role in addressing port–city issues in collaboration with their counterpart port departments. The sustainability framework is also available at: www.csir.co.za/portofcapetownSEA.

A key outcome of the SEA process was the building of port–city institutional linkages which, ultimately, should facilitate cooperative decision-making about port–city issues. The intended outcome of the SEA process is that recommended sustainability objectives, targets and indicators will influence future port planning and environmental management processes by ensuring the integration of social, biophysical and economic aspects early on in the port planning phase.

Some learning points

- It is critically important to obtain commitment to the process and the outcomes of the process right from the start.
- Engaging stakeholders in defining a vision and identifying strategic issues is challenging and requires structured facilitation and sufficient background information.
- Specialists require additional coaching to move away from the impact assessment approach (i.e. the impact of development on the environment) to the SEA approach of looking at the opportunities and constraints to future development (i.e. the impact of the environment on development).
- Identifying appropriate indicators and thresholds requires a sound understanding of the surrounding environment.

Case Study 6.8

The Sperrgebiet Land Use Plan, Namibia

By Bryony Walmsley; based on Walmsley Environmental Consultants (2001)

BACKGROUND

The Sperrgebiet is a desert area stretching some 300km north to south and 100km inland from the coast. It is the 'Forbidden Territory' comprising an area also known as Diamond Area 1 in the southwest of Namibia (Figure C6.8.1), and it has been closed off to the general public for nearly a century. The area came to prominence in 1908 when the first diamond was found in the desert near Lüderitz, sparking a major diamond rush. Conditions on the diamond fields were chaotic and the German Government (then the colonial power in Namibia) was concerned about illegal mining and the security of the diamonds. In an effort to control these problems, the Sperrgebiet was proclaimed as a prohibited area in 1908. Although sole prospecting and mining rights were granted over the entire 30,000km^2 area, diamond mining was confined to those areas where diamonds occurred: a narrow strip along the coast and along the banks of the Orange River. However, the exclusive licence was retained so that the intervening 100km could act as a security buffer. This has meant that the Sperrgebiet has effectively been preserved as a pristine wilderness throughout much of its extent. The irony is that, whilst the area has benefited from de facto preservation, the same restrictions on access have meant that very few scientific investigations have been carried out. However, whilst the detail of its biodiversity may not be known, it is recognized that the Sperrgebiet falls within one of the world's top 25 biodiversity hot spots. In addition, the area is rich in archaeological sites, has a remarkable geology, a fascinating history and a breathtaking landscape and seascape.

In 1994, the exclusive prospecting and mining licences of the non-diamondiferous areas were relinquished. There is considerable interest in the area for a variety of conflicting uses. So the Government of Namibia, in consultation with Namdeb (the mining licence holder) and NGOs, agreed that a well-thought-out land use plan (LUP) should be formulated before the area could be opened up. The plan will guide the sustainable development of this fragile area. A steering committee was established with representatives from four line ministries: Environment and Tourism; Lands, Resettlement and Rehabilitation; Mines and Energy; and Fisheries and Marine Resources – a unique collaboration in Namibia. DANCED funded the project.

The long-term objective is to proclaim the Sperrgebiet as a formal conservation area and, ultimately, to incorporate it within a transfrontier conservation area involving Angola, Namibia and South Africa. But the main development objective of the first phase of the process, the LUP, was stated to be 'that the long-term sustainable economic and ecological potential is ensured in the Sperrgebiet'.

In order to achieve this objective, the steering committee set out a number of additional goals:

- to establish an overall management and development vision for the area;
- to use the LUP as a guideline for the sustainable use and development of the area, as other possible land uses emerge;
- to improve the quality and standard of living of the sparse local population around the Sperrgebiet, by guiding the use of resources in a sustainable direction;
- to provide a guide for the decision-makers of Namibia and the Karas and Hardap Regions to plan and implement sustainable developments in the area; and
- to guide existing and potential future operations in the Sperrgebiet ... in the formulation of acceptable and appropriate environmental management practices and rehabilitation.

The land use planning process (Figure C6.8.2) can be considered a para-SEA. It was used to *develop* the plan, rather than as the tool to assess an existing plan. It is also noteworthy that the objectives of the LUP pre date, but are compatible with, some of the recommendations of the World Summit on Sustainable Development Plan of Implementation, for example to:

> *38 (b) develop and implement integrated land management ...*
> *plans that are based on sustainable use of natural resources*

Furthermore, all ten principles of SEA developed by the CSIR in South Africa (see Section 6.1.1) and set out in a guideline document (DEAT, 2000) were adopted in the LUP process, making this study an SEA in all but name.

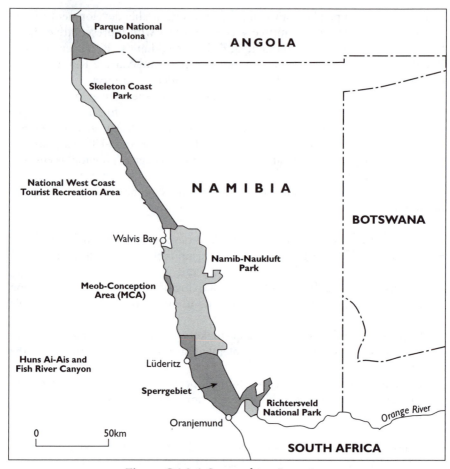

Figure C6.8.1 *Sperrgebiet: Location*

METHODOLOGY

The study involved the following steps:

1   A particularly contentious point in the study was whether a meaningful LUP could be drawn up on the basis of so little information. The team undertook a thorough *literature review* using as much of the existing information as possible. Then, by extrapolation and through extensive consultation with specialists, gaps were filled as much as possible. The precautionary principle was adopted in developing the zoning plan to ensure that areas of suspected, but not known, biodiversity were afforded the highest level of protection until such time as further research indicates otherwise.

2   A *field trip* with conservation officials and a wilderness expert.

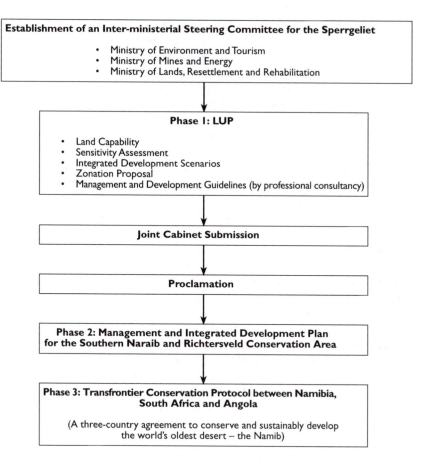

Figure C6.8.2 *Process for planning the sustainable development of the Sperrgebiet*

3   A *description of the biophysical and archaeological environments* and a description of current land use in and adjacent to the Sperrgebiet. Each environmental component was assessed in terms of its opportunities and constraints for various land use activities.

4   Development of a series of *sensitivity maps* for various biophysical and archaeological parameters. Social issues were not ignored, but since the only people living in the Sperrgebiet are Namdeb company employees in the private and closed mining village of Oranjemund, there is no social profile for the study area. The sensitivity maps were drawn up based on the available literature and consultation with specialists.

5   An extensive *public consultation programme*. This involved four public meetings, the production of information documents and feedback forms, land use questionnaires and a technical workshop with the steering committee and selected specialists. The public meetings took the form of

workshops after the main presentations. The public were asked to identify those land uses that would be suitable and/or which they would deem to be desirable. The consultation programme enabled a list of possible land use options for the area to be drawn up.

6   *Evaluation of land use options.* Each land use option was considered in terms of the environmental opportunities and constraints for such a development. For example, the presence of the Orange River would suggest an opportunity for irrigation agriculture. However, such a land use would be constrained by factors such as saline soils, strong winds, sand abrasion, distance to markets and so on, and therefore the only crops that could be considered would be high value crops and, even then, such endeavour would be marginal.

7   *Formulation of a vision.* An assessment of all the inputs and an evaluation of the land use options led to a decision that the entire Sperrgebiet should be declared a protected area under the forthcoming Namibian Parks and Wildlife Act. The proposed Act was still in draft form at the time of the study, but it was considered likely that it would adopt the IUCN Guidelines for Protected Areas Management. However, the study team was of the opinion that simply designating an area as protected does not ensure its preservation or allow for sustainable utilization. Thus a zoning plan was developed.

8   *Development of a zoning plan.* This was based on public input, IUCN wilderness guidelines, IUCN management categories for land use, carrying capacities, available scientific information and, where such information was absent, the precautionary principle was applied. It was recognized that this plan was a 'first attempt' and that, as more information becomes available, the zoned areas would be refined. However, it has provided a framework to guide immediate decisions regarding land use in the area. For example, subsequent prospecting operations have complied with the requirements of the LUP, even though the plan has not yet been ratified by the Namibian Cabinet.

9   A *technical workshop* was held involving members of the steering committee and specialists to discuss and refine the draft zoning plan.

10 A *preliminary economic analysis* was conducted of the main land use options for the Sperrgebiet. This indicated the relative income generation from diamond mining, base metal mining and ecotourism, in terms of the local, regional and national economies. The main aim of this exercise was to show that ecotourism by itself would not be financially sustainable due to the low carrying capacities of the Sperrgebiet, and that multiple land uses would have to be considered. The model was based on the premise that any mining operations in the Sperrgebiet would have to pay some sort of royalty to the national park. This would help to subsidize the development of the national park for the benefit of all Namibians and in the interests of global biodiversity.

11 The LUP also presented an *administrative framework.* This outlined the legal processes required for proclamation of the land, the formation of a

management advisory committee (MAC) and definition of its role, ecotourism models, zoning, future access control and integration into the surrounding political and economic structures. For each potential land use, guidelines were prepared outlining what needs to be included in a project-specific EIA and EMP.

Outcomes

The Land Use Plan was finalized in April 2001. It was then presented to the three ministers involved in the project, as well as to the cabinet secretaries. At a Cabinet meeting on 6 April 2004, the proclamation of the Sperrgebiet as a national park was approved but its name remains to be finalized. The recommendations of the LUP have been accepted in toto.

Conclusions

It is somewhat unusual for three line ministries to collaborate as equal partners in compiling an LUP. Similarly, in Namibia it is rare for such a process to be highly interactive and consultative, ensuring that decisions on the future use of the land are based on a truly shared vision. This collaborative approach came 100 years after the Sperrgebiet was closed to the citizens of Namibia with scant regard for their views, opinions and needs. Lessons appear to have been learned from the mistakes of the past.

This para-SEA could allow the value of the Sperrgebiet to be unlocked through an integrated, holistic planning process that properly considers the costs and benefits of various types of land use. The challenge for the Government is to reconcile the short-term benefits of mining with the longer-term benefits of biodiversity conservation and low-impact tourism. This land use planning process provided a unique opportunity to consider all the options and to propose the Sperrgebiet as a national park, so that it can be managed in perpetuity for the nation and future generations of Namibians. Now that proclamation has been achieved, the next step will be to conserve the Namib, the world's oldest desert, in a unique, three-nation transfrontier conservation area.

Case Study 6.9

Sectoral SEA: Generic Environmental Management Programme for Marine Diamond Mining off the West Coast of South Africa

Prepared by Sue Lane (Sue Lane & Associates, Professional Services in Environmental Planning and Management, Cape Town, South Africa; sue@suelane.co.za) and Robin Carter (Specialist Consultant, Applied Marine Sciences, Cape Town, South Africa; robinc@ibox.co.za) (1999)

ISSUE, PROBLEM, BACKGROUND (WHY THE SEA WAS DONE)

Diamonds are mined economically on the continental shelf of the west coast of South Africa (and adjoining Namibia). Onshore mining began in the early 1900s and, since the 1960s, has extended into the surf zone and shallow subtidal areas of the sea. In the mid-1980s, the South African Government recognized the potential to mine commercially viable quantities of diamonds in deeper waters. It established formal concession areas covering 100,000km^2 of the continental shelf off the west coast of South Africa.

Most of the concessions have been allocated for prospecting. Current mining effort is limited as techniques for efficient mining outside of safe diving depths have only recently been developed, and prospecting in a large proportion of the concessions has not yet been completed.

Mining law governs the environmental management aspects of marine diamond mining. Environmental assessments and management programmes have to be compiled and implemented for each mining operation. Compliance is monitored by the Department of Minerals and Energy. Mining authorizations and permits are contingent on satisfactory performance. Guidance largely comes from two sources:

- The central themes of the Minerals and Mining Policy for South Africa focus on ensuring the sustainability of the natural environment and management of socioeconomic impacts.
- The White Paper for Sustainable Coastal Development in South Africa focuses on:
  - recognizing the value of the coast;
  - facilitating sustainable coastal development;
  - promoting coordinated and integrated coastal management; and
  - introducing a new facilitatory style of management.

The response to these policies by South Africa's marine diamond mining industry has been to adopt environmental responsibility into their operational protocols and to see that the required environmental standards are met. However, they realized that there is commonality in the environmental problems they face and in the mitigation and environmental management actions required. In addition, there were no standardized/prescribed compliance monitoring standards or management methodologies.

Therefore, a consortium of members of the Marine Diamond Mines Association (MDMA) commissioned a generic environmental management programme (GEMP) for their operations in South African waters. This approach was justified by three facts:

- Broadly similar mining technologies and processes are employed.
- Physical disturbances between mines differ mainly in scale and not in character.
- The socioeconomic aspects of potential conflicts with other marine and coastal resource users are common across the individual mines.

The challenge was to develop a uniform approach to environmental assessment to overcome duplication of effort and expense and to provide a standardized monitoring programme that was both pragmatic and scientifically valuable. This was to contribute to the sustainable use of living resources and development of the west coast region.

The GEMP was to address all of the activities encompassed in current marine diamond mining practices, as well as those related to expected developments in technology over the ensuing three years. It was to include all the proclaimed marine diamond prospecting concessions on the South African west coast. The concessions extend from the high water mark through the surf zone to the 500m depth contour.

WHO COMMISSIONED/INITIATED THE ASSESSMENT?

Nine marine diamond mining companies, members of the South African private sector's MDMA, initiated and commissioned the generic assessment and management programme.

WHO WAS INVOLVED/PARTICIPATED?

Private enterprise, research specialists, NGOs and government agencies from national to local levels with jurisdiction over activities in the coastal and marine environment were consulted iteratively throughout the compilation of the GEMP. Sectors included mining (diamonds, oil and gas), fishing, shipping, recreation, nature conservation, farming and archaeology. The neighbouring Namibian diamond, fishing and environmental conservation sectors were also consulted.

APPROACH/METHODS
(HOW THE ASSESSMENT WAS DONE)

The consultants employed to compile the GEMP were experienced in undertaking EAs, EMPs and related studies for marine diamond mining and oil and gas exploration/exploitation projects in Namibia and South Africa. They drew on international experience in marine placer deposit mining and local and international dredging projects. Environmental objectives were drawn from South Africa's policies for mining and for coastal development.

The process comprised:

- consultation with the mining industry to identify all activities associated with marine diamond mining in different areas of the sea;
- identification of threats and opportunities caused by mining to all marine users and administrators, and coastal communities, by consulting them;
- description of the biophysical and socioeconomic baseline environment, and trends in components where relevant;
- assessment of cumulative impacts of disturbances caused by mining and estimation of limits (rate, extent and nature) of disturbance the system could potentially withstand; and
- preparation of guidelines for management of mining activities within the different marine zones extending from the outer edge of the continental shelf through mid and shallow water zones, surf and inter-tidal zones, to the immediately adjoining land.

The GEMP is currently being tested and refined through use by the industry in compiling project-specific EAs and EMPs, and is being adjusted in response to the needs of the permitting authorities. Further revisions will be needed owing to advances in mining technology that could result in significantly different impacts on the natural system. So the GEMP should be modified to be consistent with the theme of constant improvement through application.

OUTCOMES (IMPACTS OF THE SEA, DECISIONS INFLUENCED)

The GEMP process has helped to inform decision-making by establishing a framework through which mining (and ideally other marine activities) can be managed at strategic and at project-specific levels. The framework can be used to promote sustainable development on the west coast of South Africa (and potentially in Southern Namibia too). The GEMP has demonstrated that an agreed and standardized approach is useful to mining companies, government authorities and other interested parties alike.

Over and above cost savings to the mining companies, the Government benefits by having a uniform set of environmental management standards or guidelines. Monitoring requirements are clearly given. Required management actions target clearly defined objectives, methods and reporting procedures and allow auditing. Applicant miners are able to make adequate financial provisions for environmental management, and the Government is able to put the required infrastructure in place to audit the EMPs.

The GEMP has enabled mining companies to compile project-specific management programmes that consider the bigger picture. These programmes promote environmentally responsible operations as they adequately address the concerns of co-users of the area, neighbours and other interest groups, and enable self-regulation. They have also facilitated auditing of company performance by government agencies, and allowed miners and regulatory authorities to take informed decisions about adjusting strategies or targets to continually improve industry-wide environmental performance.

More specifically the GEMP:

- informs the industry about policy and legal requirements of all relevant government sectors, and gives an explanation of how mining activities do and could affect the environment;
- provides management objectives, appropriate actions and their legal and/or scientific justification for industry to comply with;
- establishes forums for resolution of conflict between industries and other users;
- promotes joint management of resources, by government and industry, and promotes 'partnerships' between larger companies and small-scale mining;
- guides mining to contribute to knowledge about ecosystem functioning; this is paid for directly by mining and the results are widely applicable to marine resource management by the Government and others (e.g. on geology, climate, marine life, shipping observations etc.); and
- encourages the South African and Namibian Governments to establish joint policies and management strategies, with standardized monitoring and reporting procedures particularly to determine cumulative effects and thresholds of disturbance, and to share skills and information.

Chapter 7

Retrospect and Prospect

7.1 POINTS OF DEPARTURE

Over the past decade, there has been rapid development of strategic environmental assessment (SEA) processes and practice and a corresponding explosion of literature covering this field. Recognizing this, our aim has been to undertake a broad-based empirical review of SEA practice, taking stock of trends and issues in developing and transitional countries and amongst international lending and aid agencies. From that perspective, we have extended our consideration of the scope of SEA processes and elements beyond formal systems – whether instituted separately, under environmental impact assessment (EIA) systems, or based on approximate processes of policy and plan appraisal – and we have termed these systems 'para-SEA'. As a reminder, this term includes those processes and elements that have some, but not all, of the characteristics of formal SEA procedure.

In retrospect, our reasons for taking this approach are worth revisiting. The prevailing view of SEA is as a formal instrument instituted through legal or administrative arrangements established by developed countries. Many normative definitions in the SEA literature are derived from this paradigm and elaborated in terms of procedural features and characteristics. This model also appears to be promoted internationally through SEA capacity-building and training. But often there is no critical perspective on the pros and cons of its application in developing countries where elements of this approach may be reflected partially or incompletely in policy- or plan-making. Our concern is that this thrust may need to be reconsidered and possibly replaced in developing countries by a more pragmatic, needs-driven strategy that builds on and improves existing policy and planning processes. After all, a key principle of SEA is that it should be fit for purpose, adapted to the context and circumstances of countries and their political culture and institutional arrangements.

In order to provide a basis for an informed interpretation and commentary on the above issues, it is important to take stock of and understand what is happening in SEA in different parts of the world. This is the focus of the preceding chapters. In this chapter, we attempt to pull together the many threads of international experience in SEA and identify future directions of this field.

Our conclusions require two caveats that arise from the basic characteristics of SEA. First, and most importantly, SEA is a fast-moving and still-diversifying field, especially if its boundaries are defined broadly as in this review. Second, in many parts of the world, it is too early to come to a definitive view of the status and effectiveness of SEA application. What follows should, therefore, be regarded as preliminary conclusions regarding the main aspects and lessons of international experience with SEA and with particular reference to its uptake in the South.

7.2 CONCLUSIONS AND RECOMMENDATIONS

In the following sections, we draw some conclusions from our survey of SEA processes and practice. They are summarized as a series of 'headlines' of the story to date. They are organized in approximate order from global and generic developments to regionally or methodologically oriented features. We hope that it will provide an aide-mémoire on the SEA agenda that is emerging internationally and the trends and issues that require attention and discussion.

7.2.1 SEA revisited and reconsidered

In the three observations-cum-propositions below, we represent our reinterpretation of the nature and scope of the field of SEA. But these views are not necessarily widely or fully accepted by other commentators.

- The development and implementation of SEA systems and elements represent the most striking trend in impact assessment during the past decade although its dimensions may not be fully appreciated.

A key feature of SEA is the scale and rapidity of its adoption and adaptation in different countries and regions following the early precedent established by US federal and state experience at the level of plans and programmes. It was only in the 1990s that a new generation of SEA systems was introduced and taken up by an increasing number of developed and transitional countries. Recently, there has been increased interest in, and greater use of, SEA procedures and methods by international aid and lending agencies. This is driving new applications in the developing world where the SEA agenda is becoming refocused on poverty and related issues. Despite the flood of literature on SEA, much of the rich experience associated with these trends in developing and transitional countries appears to have been overlooked and possibly may not be widely understood. From that perspective, it can be argued that SEA practice has run ahead of theory. The gap may be just as difficult to bridge as that between theory and practice because it runs against the grain of conventional wisdom on the field.

- SEA comprises a family of processes and tools that, individually and collectively, are being applied to new aspects and areas, leading to continued extensions of the field that have procedural and methodological implications.

The concept of SEA as a family of approaches with proliferating applications is widely accepted. A new, more encompassing paradigm of SEA is emerging. It is one characterized by procedural and methodological pluralism that extends well beyond the common definitions found in the literature. In our view, SEA is an umbrella concept that accommodates a broad range of processes for assessing the environmental and sustainability effects of options and proposals at the policy and planning level. The area covered by this frame of reference is elaborated in the typology of approaches outlined in Chapter 1 and exemplified in subsequent chapters. EIA-based systems stand out as the main cornerstone on which SEA is founded, and undoubtedly this approach will continue to be important or predominant in the case of the European Union (EU) and the United Nations Economic Commission for Europe (UNECE) region (see below). Internationally, near-equivalent processes operated by certain lending and aid agencies (see Chapter 4) are more prevalent together with an array of domestic, individualized, para-SEA processes and elements in many developing countries. At this end of the spectrum, the boundaries of SEA are fluid and ill defined. We recognize that impact assessment theorists will not be the only ones to find this ambiguity unsatisfactory. For the time being, we are content to live with a relatively open-ended map that is inclusive of a number of routes to the same end, rather than marking only an EIA-recommended highway – particularly for developing countries.

- The emergence of SEA symbolizes and forms part of a more fundamental and potentially far-reaching change in approach – one that integrates the environment into the policy and planning mainstream in support of sustainable development.

This larger transition is widely promoted in international law and policy. Most recently, it was a major theme threaded throughout the World Summit on Sustainable Development (WSSD) agenda and *Plan of Implementation*. In this context, SEA is one of the tools available for taking a more integrated, strategic and cross-sectoral approach to incorporating environmental (and social) considerations into development decision-making. Although not yet well defined, such an approach is understood as addressing the root causes of environmental problems and their structural linkages. Many of these are beyond the traction of conventional impact management and mitigation measures. In practice, with few exceptions, SEA still largely approximates to this latter focus of policy analysis and action, and the same goes for many other tools and measures. Nevertheless, there are a number of entry points for using SEA and related processes to gain a firmer perspective on the environmental sustainability of proposed initiatives. For example, many countries already have policy frameworks that can be used for this purpose, notably strategies for sustainable development, biodiversity conservation and climate change. Furthermore, new opportunities are opening up for linking SEA with economic and social appraisal tools to gain a greater measure of sustainability assurance and there is growing interest in the next generation of integrative approaches. A number of issues remain outstanding in that regard and are discussed further below.

7.2.2 Key trends in SEA process development

- The initial phase of SEA development has been characterized by diversified arrangements, increasing adoption by countries and international agencies, and a steady extension in coverage of levels and types of decisions.

Prior to the EU SEA Directive coming into force, it is estimated that approximately 25 countries and international agencies had operating SEA systems, in other words with identifiable arrangements and practices. Others were in the process of introducing SEA, or had done so, but had not moved to implementation. Within this larger group, SEA frameworks vary with respect to their legal and non-statutory basis, their arrangements for implementation, their scope of application to policy, legislation, plans, programmes and other proposals, and their relationship to decision-making. So far, few, if any, countries could be said to have SEA systems that are comprehensive in their coverage, in other words that apply to all strategic proposals with potentially important environmental effects. As a general rule, SEA is more commonplace and better developed at the level of plans and programmes than for policy and legislation. Yet, SEA of policies and legislation is no longer exceptional as often claimed in the literature. On the contrary, a number of countries apply SEA at this level; some under a dedicated system using a minimum, flexible procedure (e.g. Denmark, the Netherlands' E-test) and others using the same procedure that is applied to plans and programmes (e.g. Canada).

- A second phase of SEA development is underway, driven by supra-national and multilateral legal instruments.

The transposition and implementation of the EU SEA Directive by the 25 member states of the EU will increase the number of countries with formal SEA systems. It will eventually lead towards the consolidation and standardization of approach at the level of plans and programmes. At the time of writing, member states are at different stages in their transposition of the new Directive into national legislation and in preparing guidance materials. If experience with the EIA Directive is any guide, significant variations can be expected in the manner and effectiveness of implementation of the SEA Directive in the newly enlarged EU. Further ahead lies the even larger challenge of implementing the SEA Protocol to the Espoo Convention across an even larger, more diverse group of 35 signatories that eventually may include non-UNECE member countries. Recently, a work programme was adopted by the Parties to the Convention to prepare countries for implementation of the Protocol. This promises to play an important role in SEA capacity-building, particularly among the newly independent states (NIS) and the Balkan Stability Pact group of countries, much as the earlier round of EIA capacity-building under the Espoo Convention was important in raising standards among Central and Eastern Europe (CEE) countries.

- Currently, a new, third phase of SEA development in developing countries is being opened through the activities of international assistance and lending agencies.

A major change has taken place in international development and cooperation policy. Increasingly, the focus of lending and aid is shifting towards the macro level (e.g. direct budgetary support) and away from funding individual projects, with a corresponding growing interest in the use of strategic assessment approaches. This transition is perhaps most evident at the World Bank, where SEA of sector and financial intermediary lending has been in place for more than a decade and is now undertaken in accordance with environmental and social safeguard compliance policies. Recently, the Bank has also promoted greater use of SEA for policy-based lending. Other multilateral financial institutions and bilateral aid agencies have endorsed similar approaches in support of strategies that deliver on WSSD undertakings and the Millennium Development Goals (MDGs).

Looking ahead, the work of the Organisation for Economic Co-operation and Development's Development Assistance Committee (OECD/DAC) ENVIRONET Task Team on SEA is expected to shed further light on the nature and scope of these activities and on the effectiveness of different models (Box 7.1). Such an evaluation will be important for a number of reasons, not least because the use of SEA by international development agencies has a strong capacity-building component. Currently, there is a high demand from developing countries for SEA training. This activity has become something of a growth industry that is likely to influence the models of SEA that are introduced in developing countries. In that light, the area of training and capacity-building itself warrants closer scrutiny from SEA practitioners and others than it has received to date.

7.2.3 Status of SEA and experience in different parts of the world

- Most developed countries now have SEA arrangements in place but many have yet to implement them. Only a relatively small number have in-depth experience in this area. The quality and effectiveness of much SEA practice remain questionable and increasing attention is being given to this area, although much more needs to be done.

BOX 7.1 WORK PROGRAMME OF THE OECD/DAC TASK TEAM ON SEA

The objectives of the Task Team include developing and promoting the practical use of SEA in the formulation and assessment of development policies, plans, programmes and 'mega-projects' and to help ensure that:

- environmental considerations are effectively incorporated into strategic decision-making at the formative stage;
- the linkages between environmental, social and economic factors are better understood and addressed; and thus
- the outcomes of policies, plans and programmes have better prospects to contribute to sustainable development.

To this end, the Task Team has developed a ten-point programme that aims to:

- improve understanding of SEA based on reviewing international experience and practice, particularly through case studies;
- establish and evaluate the relationship of SEA to other approaches to policy formulation, assessment and implementation used in development cooperation (such as poverty and social impact assessment and country environmental analysis); develop any potential synergies between these approaches; and consider how the transaction costs of these similar approaches can be reduced;
- identify, develop and promote SEA 'methodologies' based on agreed principles;
- promote transparency, stakeholder participation, accountability and other prerequisites of effective SEA, as a contribution to good governance;
- contribute to harmonized approaches in the application of SEA (as part of general environmental assessment harmonization) to development policies, plans and programmes formulation, assessment and implementation;
- encourage the alignment of SEA approaches applied by development cooperation agencies with the priorities and processes of developing countries;
- provide a forum for further dialogue on the development of SEA;
- promote the value of SEA to decision-makers and others engaged in formulating, assessing and implementing development policies, plans and programmes;
- provide practical guidance for both decision-makers and practitioners on:
  - how SEA can be effectively applied in development cooperation processes, and to which types of actions; and
  - how to plan, design, undertake and monitor an effective SEA in development policy, plan and programme formulation, assessment and implementation; and
- launch the DAC SEA Guidance at the International Association for Impact Assessment (IAIA) Global Conference on SEA in Prague in September 2005.

Source: OECD/DAC (2004)

Whatever its pros and cons, there is no doubt that the EU SEA Directive has changed the SEA landscape. It has increased the number of countries with provision for SEA and imposed minimum procedural requirements on 25 member states that collectively represent a significant proportion of the developed world. Prima facie, there are grounds for concern with the casting of the SEA Directive in the narrow mould of the EIA Directive, given the diversity of arrangements and approaches in other developed countries (see Chapter 3). However, these arguments are now moot and, increasingly, attention will turn to issues of compliance and implementation. But problems related to implementation should not be underestimated given the SEA experience of other countries.

Weaknesses in SEA practice have been reported generally and for individual countries, for example Canada, where process audits have been undertaken by the Commissioner of the Environment and Sustainable Development. Areas of concern include the appropriateness of SEA approaches at the policy level compared to the planning level, the transparency of SEA processes and their openness to public input, and the lack of monitoring and follow-up. In addition, there has been a ground swell of interest in SEA principles and guidance on good practice, drawing primarily on experience in leading countries (see Appendix 11). There is much more that could and should be done in these areas. In particular, greater attention should be paid to the value added by the SEA process to policy development and plan-making and the measures for quality assurance and control that can ensure better outcomes (see Section 7.3.1).

- There is a strong planning tradition in countries in transition that has typically incorporated SEA elements and provided a sound basis for their further development, including the establishment of a new generation of SEA systems. There are significant variations between the systems in NIS and CEE countries. In the latter, in some cases, advances in SEA legislation and practice have been impressive, even by international standards.

The evolution of SEA in NIS and CEE countries reflects certain features of the planning systems of the ex-socialist regime of the USSR and the different modalities of internally and externally driven reforms. On the breakdown of the former USSR, all NIS (and the Baltic states) inherited the then-current process of state environmental review (SER) or expertise. With limited modifications, this framework continues in force in all NIS and applies in principle to strategic proposals. However, other than on an ad hoc basis, it does not appear to be implemented at this level and SER systems are perhaps best represented as an interim, para-SEA process.

The status of SEA is quite different in CEE (now including Baltic) countries driven by a combination of internally and externally imposed reforms – first towards closer alignment with internationally accepted practice and now, in the case of new EU member states, towards compliance under the SEA Directive. In the interim, some of these countries enacted and implemented progressive SEA legislation. They have considerable practical experience, particularly at the level of land use plans. This experience deserves to be much better known, not least because regional networks for professional exchange and pilot applications have served to catalyse change that was uniquely adapted to the prevailing political and planning culture. It points towards further opportunities for 'East–East' networking and capacity-building. CEE experts could support such initiatives in NIS and Balkan Stability Pact countries. Here such an approach was used successfully but now may be replaced by EU-driven arrangements.

The wider message is that it really is time to move beyond the traditional North–South relationship and provide new, creative frameworks for self-help and mutual support. In Southern Africa, for example, the work of the Southern African Institute for Environmental Assessment (SAIEA) focuses on using local expertise in undertaking and building capacity for EIA and in promoting SEA training and capacity building. SAIEA is the Southern African node under the Capacity Learning for EIA in Africa (CLEIAA) initiative – a network that links together a number of such regional centres and associations across Africa. Finally there are larger inter-regional linkages that could be productive in terms of SEA capacity-building. For example, the Regional Environmental Center for Central and Eastern Europe (REC) and the South African Council for Scientific and Industrial Research (CSIR) have recently been collaborating to share experiences and organize exchange visits as part of a broader, more generic notion of transitional countries. In this context, transitional countries include both post-industrial CEE and certain African, Asian and Latin American states that are characterized by significant levels of socioeconomic development and underdevelopment. Table 7.1 suggests some important elements for SEA capacity-building.

Table 7.1 *Elements of SEA capacity and their development*

Elements of SEA capacity development	Components of effective SEA systems
Supporting conditions and 'infrastructure' for SEA	• political stability; • sound governance; • clear role for non-governmental organizations and civic groups; • environmental awareness of local communities.
Designing and strengthening institutional arrangements	• clear framework of law, regulation and policy; • transparent procedure; • guidance on implementation; • defined agency roles and responsibilities; • mechanisms for compliance and follow-up, etc.
Improving professional competencies and skills	• ability of practitioners to implement the SEA process, apply appropriate tools and perform the main activities to an acceptable level of competence and professionalism.

Source: Adapted from Sadler (2003c)

- Much is happening at the level of international agencies, but SEA at the domestic level in developing countries is best described as mixed and difficult to interpret. Only a small number of developing countries have established recognizable SEA-type processes or elements, although many more have considerable experience of para-SEA processes.

Multilateral development agencies have been promoting and using SEA approaches in the context of their investment projects in developing countries. For example, the World Bank has used sectoral and regional environmental assessment since 1989 and has recently developed a broad family of SEA-like diagnostic and assessment tools, for example country environmental assessment, energy and environment reviews and poverty and social impact analysis (see Section 4.1). The Bank is now committed to using SEA to help borrower countries to move towards sustainable development, in part through a structured learning programme. Key aims of this programme are (Ahmed and Mercier, 2004):

> *to define better how SEA can add value to World Bank operations; to establish what forms of SEA can be identified as most useful to staff and clients; and to help build capacity within the World Bank staff to provide better assistance to countries on SEA.*

Bilateral development agencies have only more recently begun to experiment with SEA in the context of their activities. But they are keen to examine how best to adopt and use the tool, as evidenced through their collective work through the OECD/DAC (see Box 7.1). In this work, it will be important to explain, clearly and simply, the aims and potentials of SEA to senior decision-takers so that they 'buy in' to the process. Furthermore, SEA might best be promoted within development cooperation, at least initially, by concentrating on its application to the emerging key areas of donor focus: direct budgetary support; major strategic policies and action plans (e.g. poverty reduction strategies); key sectors; and mega-regional projects (e.g. transnational pipelines).

The SEA procedures and methods that are applied by the multilateral financial institutions and the main bilateral assistance agencies have been instrumental in introducing SEA into developing countries, particularly the poorer low-income countries. Most indications are that this will continue for the foreseeable future. Indeed, Peter Croal argues persuasively that the use of SEA in developed countries, and by their development agencies, can provide an important lever to promote SEA in developing countries (Box 7.2). If that interpretation is correct, then the various agencies need to make a much more concerted effort to coordinate their requirements and activities.

The multilateral development banks are perhaps ideally suited to help with the development of SEA, for example, along the lines of a multi-level comprehensive approach as proposed by Annandale et al (2001) (see Section 4.1.7). They acknowledge that the way that SEA systems are implemented in

BOX 7.2 THE LEVERAGE OF DONORS: A PERSONAL REFLECTION

Peter Croal, CIDA

It is imperative that developing countries embrace the practice and benefits of SEA to ensure that higher level decision-making commences with a more sustainable foundation. Opportunities and support for leveraging the application of SEA in developing countries can come from developed countries where there is an existing formal requirement for SEA. For example, in Canada, the 1999 Federal Cabinet Directive on SEA requires that SEA be applied to policies, plans and programmes that need to be submitted to a Minister or the Cabinet for approval. This provides a 'default' mechanism to trigger SEA in developing countries. Thus, if Canada were to approve an education programme for a developing country, it would be necessary to apply SEA to the programme; but it would make sense for the developing country to undertake an SEA for the more discrete and detailed aspects of the programme as they become identified and prepared. Both applications of SEA would be mutually supporting and would ensure better development outcomes in the long term. Requirements to apply SEA could also become an element of a memorandum of understanding between a donor and a developing country.

Donors can play an important role in promoting the application of SEA and sector-wide approaches (SWAPs) to development in developing countries, much as they did 10–15 years ago when EIA was a condition of many bilateral development agreements.

developing countries themselves is extremely important, but do not explore the issue. We would argue that development cooperation agencies should think hard about the process and methods that are being 'exported' and promoted, and how best to build capacity for SEA development. This is particularly important in the poorest countries that arguably need SEA the most but are least able to take up this process.

Clearly, there is growing interest and demand to learn about and use SEA in developing countries. But, at present, most of the examples of SEA application in developing countries are, in practice, connected to and driven by projects funded by multilateral development banks and, to a lesser extent, bilateral aid agencies. There are fewer examples of domestically driven applications. Only perhaps in South Africa (an atypical developing country) have we seen the emergence of a 'home-grown' approach to SEA (see Section 6.1.1). Yet there is a far richer experience of para-SEA approaches in developing countries, geared increasingly towards addressing broader sustainability concerns and embedded in an array of land use and strategic planning processes. The evidence from SEA workshops in developing countries is that there is reluctance to promote SEA as an additional formal assessment requirement, and a preference to incorporate the principles and best practices of SEA in order to improve existing policy-making, planning and decision-taking processes.

7.3 FUTURE DIRECTIONS AND WAYS FORWARD

Looking ahead, we see three main, interrelated avenues for the further development of SEA:

- *environmental focus* – strengthening existing SEA arrangements and approaches as mechanisms for environmental sustainability assessment and assurance;
- *sustainability focus* – utilizing SEA as a component or means of integrated assessment of the effects of policy and planning proposals in relation to the environmental, social and economic objectives of sustainable development; and
- *convergence focus* – promoting the convergence of SEA within integrated assessment and planning systems for sustainable development.

Some common threads run through all three lines of approach, notably environmental integration, although the relative emphasis shifts in moving from the existing SEA approach to sustainability appraisal or integrated assessment and planning. These routes can be seen as sequential, progressive steps, securing one base before progressing to the next; and the process will take time. In doing so, it will be essential to maintain the integrity of assessing the environmental effects of proposals in order to ensure these are sufficient to protect the environment. At present, we have serious reservations that SEA as a separate process, and as now applied, provides sufficient environmental safeguards; and also about moving towards more integrated approaches until that issue is resolved.

With that reservation in mind, below, we discuss these three alternative directions for SEA development separately. But, in practice, it is more likely that progress will be simultaneously incremental in all three. Such is the nature of experimentation and learning. Furthermore, each alternative is likely to be driven by different (often competing) needs, agendas, proponents and groups of practitioners.

7.3.1 Improving SEA quality and effectiveness

The quality and effectiveness of SEA are becoming subjects of increasing concern and attention for process administrators and practitioners. This is evidenced by the discussion at the Eighth Intergovernmental Policy Forum on Environmental Assessment, held in association with IAIA 2004 (in Vancouver) (CEAA, 2004). Recent evaluations of SEA implementation, including work reported in this volume, have helped to clarify these concerns and identify ways and means of improving SEA procedure and practice.

In summary, there are three main building blocks for improving SEA quality and effectiveness (see also Table 7.2):

- First, strengthen the institutional arrangements that serve as quality 'controls'. At a minimum, these include procedural requirements and guidance to ensure compliance and consistency of implementation, 'basics' that are lacking even in some well-established SEA systems (see Section 7.2.3). The main steps and elements of the SEA process themselves provide means of quality assurance, particularly scoping, review of report quality, public comment, and monitoring and follow-up (which is widely recognized as lacking).
- Second, undertake reviews of SEA effectiveness and performance, using a systematic framework and criteria to evaluate the lessons of practical experience (learning by doing). This should apply both to the micro level of the SEA of an individual policy or plan proposal and to the macro level of the implementing SEA systems. In both cases, the focus should be on the contribution of SEA to decision-making and, as far as possible, on the results achieved. Ultimately, the outcomes of the SEA process define how well it works and whether it meets its fundamental purpose(s).
- Third, promote SEA good practice through benchmarking standards and measures for carrying out the process and the main activities and elements. A start to this has been made already, notably through IAIA activities in specifying principles (see Box 2.4) and performance criteria (see Box 2.5).

Table 7.2 *Elements of review of SEA quality and effectiveness*

Main element	Primary function	Components
Policy or plan monitoring and environmental management	Implementation and intervention	• tracking plan or policy implementation against objectives; • monitoring environmental effects and measures; • management actions as necessary.
Effectiveness and performance review	Learning and process improvement	• evaluating the contribution of SEA in policy or plan preparation; • review of quality of SEA information; • audit of SEA process and procedure; • identifying environmental outcomes of policy and plan implementation.
Benchmarking and reporting EIA good practice	Setting and improving standards	• drawing lessons of experience; • identifying the elements of good practice; • SEA principles, performance criteria and step-by-step guidance.

Source: Adapted from Sadler (2004)

In our view, this work now should be extended beyond the procedural and focus on environmental safeguards and required outcomes, in other words substantive performance – at the end of the day, this is the one that really matters.

7.3.2 Towards a sustainability approach

Our original intention was to explore emerging experience and the future for sustainability appraisal or assessment in this concluding chapter, believing it still to be a 'frontier' challenge. But in exploring the field, we were quickly struck by the sheer volume of experimentation and initiatives being undertaken (in this area) under its umbrella term. It was clear that we could not do justice to this subject within the confines of a final chapter. Therefore, a second volume devoted to sustainability appraisal is in preparation.

SEA provides an initial entry point to sustainability appraisal. It already has features and characteristics of an integrated, sustainability-oriented approach – notably when considering social, health and economic effects either directly or using specialized forms of impact assessment. These include social impact assessment (SIA) and health impact assessment (HIA), as well as longer-established economic appraisal tools. When used in combination, these procedures approximate to integrated assessment or sustainability appraisal. Much has been written in the SEA literature on this transition. But, far more importantly, a number of countries and international organizations are beginning to experiment with, and implement, sustainability appraisal. Examples include the approach to sustainability impact assessment of trade policy used by the EC and new UK planning regulations that require a process of sustainability appraisal (which, inter alia, will need to be integrated with the requirements of the EU SEA Directive).

If the promise of this approach is to be fully realized, a number of institutional and methodological issues need to be addressed. These include the appropriate provision and arrangements for implementing sustainability appraisal within policy-making and planning processes. In this respect, perhaps the most critical issues are '*how* environmental, social and economic information is analyzed, integrated and presented to decision-makers' (Buselich, 2002, our emphasis) and, above all, within what framework of sustainability objectives and measures (Sadler, 1999). For present purposes, we define sustainability appraisal as an integrated assessment of the environmental, social and economic effects of proposed actions at all levels of decision-making, from policy to projects, which is undertaken against a national or international framework of sustainability principles, indicators or strategies. With important exceptions, we consider that the discussion of these issues in the impact assessment literature lacks a cutting edge and is predominantly theoretical and methodological. To date, there have been few surveys of the larger field of sustainability appraisal or what is happening in practice. We hope our forthcoming volume on sustainability appraisal (Dalal-Clayton and Sadler, 2004) will help shed further light on this field.

By any standards, sustainability appraisal will be difficult to implement, particularly for many developing countries where capacity is limited and institutional preconditions are missing. The approach may be best introduced incrementally, for example by modifying the EIA and SEA process to address key questions. But it is also clear that further progress on this front is related to the extent to which different levels of integration are in place (Lee, 2002), for example:

- *vertical integration of assessments*, which are undertaken at different stages in the policy, planning and project cycle ('tiering');
- *horizontal integration of assessments*, in other words bringing together different types of impacts – environmental, economic and social – into a single overall assessment, at one or more stages in the planning cycle (others have called this *substantive integration*); and
- *integration of assessments into decision-making*, in other words integrating assessment findings into decision-making at different stages in the planning cycle (sometimes called *process integration*).

7.3.3 Promoting integrated assessment and planning

The development of an integrated assessment and planning or policy-making process perhaps represents the final stage of structural convergence. We envisage this stage as one where sustainability appraisal of the environmental, economic and social effects of proposed actions is an integral part of the planning and policy-making rather than applied as a separate or arms-length procedure.

The WSSD *Plan of Implementation*, agreed at Johannesburg, emphasizes the importance of taking a 'holistic and inter-sector approach' to implement sustainable development, in general, and to deliver on the Millennium Development Goals, in particular. Work undertaken by the United Nations Environment Programme (UNEP, 2001) and other international organizations has underlined the importance of integrated assessment and planning, particularly for addressing the root causes of sustainability issues and taking account of the linkages amongst environmental, economic and social factors. This is particularly important at the strategic level in the context of international development.

Currently, a major shift is taking place in the development assistance strategies of the multilateral lending agencies and bilateral donors. This realignment is focused on new pro-poor policies that combine a range of actions previously taken separately; for example to alleviate hunger, improve public health and provide basic infrastructure. It also involves a shift from the micro to the macro or strategic level, with much greater emphasis given to direct budget support, policy-based lending and support, and sector programme development rather than funding individual projects and capacity-building. A major issue, especially in lower-income countries, is how the rural poor can achieve sustainable livelihoods whilst maintaining environmental sustainability (one of the seven Millennium Development Goals).

In turn, this underlines our earlier emphasis on the importance of ensuring that the integrity of environmental assessment is maintained, whether in an expanded process of sustainability appraisal or as part of the larger structure of integrated assessment and planning. Many people are concerned that the environmental dimension will be watered down in moving from SEA toward convergence with other appraisal and planning processes. It is also not clear if there are processes that approximate to integrated assessment and planning and, if so, what their pros and cons are. Currently we are surveying this field in support of a major initiative by UNEP (2003b) to undertake a number of demonstration projects on integrated assessment and planning (which will be coordinated with the OECD/DAC initiative on SEA (see Box 7.1).

7.4 CHALLENGES TO REAL PROGRESS?

In the preceding chapters, we have set out evidence of the rapid uptake of SEA around the world and illustrated the breadth of applications. Clearly, there is much overlap and sometimes contradiction in terminology and considerable variation in emphasis and approach. But this is also a healthy reflection of both the demand for an assessment tool upstream of projects (EIA is accepted to be unsatisfactory at this level) and the enthusiasm to apply SEA and related approaches to further the aims of sustainable development. As we have seen, this eagerness to 'get on and do it' has driven SEA practice well ahead of theory.

It is also evident that much thought and energy is being devoted to how and when to best apply SEA approaches. The real challenges to achieving both the aims and potential of SEA are not methodological. Rather they lie in the institutional and political arena. Further progress will be dependent on:

- explaining more clearly what SEA is – particularly to those who need to be convinced to request its application (politicians, policy-makers, planners, decision-takers, senior bureaucrats, etc.);
- clarifying to those same audiences what SEA can achieve (why it is important, what benefits it can provide), and when and how it can be applied. It will be important to position SEA more as an aid to existing planning and decision-making processes, and less as a new formal requirement;
- working to secure political commitment so that SEA is 'enabled', in other words that it is able to be applied at the appropriate stages in policy- and decision-making cycles (not at the end when major decisions and commitments have already been taken – a problem still suffered by EIA); and
- ensure that its role is understood and welcomed so that outputs/results are expected and have a place in the processes SEA seeks to support (i.e. a genuine seat at the decision-making table).

SEA has evolved a great deal over the past decade and there is now a need to take stock and consolidate before moving forward, particularly in developing countries. We hope this volume helps in that regard, both generally and specifically in supporting the work of UNEP and establishing a baseline for the OECD/DAC Environment Task Team described above. Looking ahead, the DAC initiative should be particularly useful in clarifying terms, confirming principles, assembling best-practice case studies and developing guidance that is designed for and relevant to developing countries. It will complement the activities that will be undertaken to implement the SEA Directive in the European Union and subsequently the SEA Protocol to the Espoo Convention on a pan-European basis.

Appendices

Appendix 1

SEA Legal and Policy Benchmarks

1970 US *National Environmental Policy Act* (NEPA; 1969) – requires 'proposals for legislation and other major federal actions significantly affecting the ... environment' to include a 'detailed statement ... on the environmental impact' (Section 102 (2) (c)).
California Environmental Quality Act – modelled after NEPA and applies to activities proposed or approved by state agencies, including programmes, plans and staged projects (Guidelines Section 15165–15168).

Mid-1970s Public inquiries and environmental reviews of major proposals – consideration of policy issues (e.g. Mackenzie Valley Pipeline Inquiry, Canada, 1974–1977, Ranger Uranium Environmental Inquiry, Australia, 1975–1977).

1978 NEPA *Regulations* issued by Council on Environmental Quality – specify actions subject to programmatic environmental impact statements (EIS) as those that can be grouped generically, geographically or by technology (Section 1052.4 (b)).

1987 Netherlands *EIA Act* (amended 1994) applies to specified national plans and programmes, including all those fixing the locations of projects for which an environmental impact assessment (EIA) is mandatory.

1989 Australia *Resource Assessment Commission Act* – established independent inquiry body on resource policy issues (Commission disbanded in 1993, legislation retained).
World Bank *Operational Directive 4.00* (amended 1991, 1999) – refers to preparation of sectoral and regional environmental assessment (EA) (Annex A 6–8).
UNECE (Espoo) Convention on EIA in a Transboundary Context (came into force 1997) states that Parties 'to the extent appropriate ... shall endeavour to apply' the principles of EIA to policies, plans and programmes (PPP) (Article 2(7)).

1990 Canada *Environmental Assessment Process for Policy and Programme Proposals* by Order in Council (amended 1999) – applies to proposals submitted to Cabinet.

1991   New Zealand *Resource Management Act* – landmark sustainability law combining policy, planning and regulatory functions into omnibus regime.

UK Guide on *Policy Appraisal and the Environment* – advice for central government agencies (updated by good practice guidance, 1994; amended 1997).

1992   UNECE pilot study of EIA of PPP recommends its application by member countries.

Hong Kong *Environmental Implications of Policy Papers* by decision of the then Governor – applies to proposals to Executive Council (later development plans).

1993   Denmark *Strategic Environmental Assessment of Government Bills and Other Proposals* by Prime Minister's Office (PMO) circular (amended 1995, 1998 when it became legally binding) – applies to draft legislation to Parliament and to strategic proposals on which Parliament must be consulted.

European Commission *Environmental Assessment of Legislative Programme* by internal communication – applies to legislative proposals and other actions by the Commission.

1994   UK Guide on *Environmental Appraisal of Development Plans* – advice to local authorities on how to carry out their responsibilities under planning legislation (updated 1998).

Norway *Assessment of White Papers and Government Proposals* by administrative order contains provisions relevant to environment but applies primarily to economic and administrative consequences.

Slovakia *EIA Act* – contains requirement to assess basic development policies, territorial plans in selected areas and any legislative proposal that may have an adverse impact on the environment (Article 35).

1995   Netherlands *Environmental Test* by cabinet directive – applies to draft legislation, part of comprehensive review of enforceability, feasibility and impact on business.

1996   *Proposal* by European Commission for a directive on the assessment of the effects of certain plans and programmes (COM (96) 511, amended by COM (99) 73), hereafter SEA Directive finalized in 2001.

1998   Finland *Guidelines on the Environmental Impact Assessment of Legislative Proposals* by decision-in-principle – apply to law drafting, also decrees, resolutions and decisions.

UNECE (Aarhus) *Convention on Access to Information, Public Participation in Decision Making and Access to Justice in Environmental Matters* – provisions for public participation in Articles 7 and 8, respectively, refer to PPP and to laws and regulations relating to environment.

Declaration by the environment ministers of the UNECE region on strategic environmental assessment (ECE/CEP/56) – inviting countries and international finance institutions to introduce and/or carry out SEA 'as a matter of priority'.

1999   Australia *Environment Protection and Biodiversity Conservation Act* – introduces provisions enabling SEA of PPP.

Finland *Act on Environmental Impact Assessment Procedure* applies to policy, plans and programmes.

UK *Proposals for a Good Practice Guide on Sustainability Appraisal of Regional Planning Guidance.*

World Bank *Operational Policy/Bank Procedure (OP/BP 4.01, 1999)* confirming a requirement for borrowers to conduct sectoral and regional EA, as and where relevant.

2000   Canada *Guidelines on Implementing the Cabinet Directive on SEA.*

2001   European SEA Directive (2001/42/EC) adopted; all member states to be in compliance by 21 July 2004.

Decision to negotiate an SEA Protocol by the Parties to the Espoo Convention for possible adoption at Fifth Ministerial Conference 'Environment for Europe', Kiev (2003).

2002   World Summit on Sustainable Development *Plan of Implementation* calls for more integrated and strategic approach to implement sustainable development (no explicit reference to SEA).

2003   SEA Protocol to the Espoo Convention adopted on 23 May 2003 at 5th Ministerial Conference 'Environment for Europe', Kiev.

2004   World Bank Board *Development Policy Lending Policy (OP/BP 8.60)* – requires the Bank to determine if specific country policies supported by the operation are likely to have significant effects on the environment and natural resources of the client country.

Appendix 2

Some Key Questions for Assessing the Utility of SEA in Developing Countries

Given the interest in promoting the use of SEA in developing countries, some countries might find it useful to undertake a preliminary stock-take to capture current experience, identify opportunities and constraints to SEA, and draw lessons. This could take the form of a two-part approach:

- a 'survey' component to gather some basic information about SEA (and parallel) experience and the institutional and other conditions within which it applies or might apply; and
- a less rigid component which could be based on one-to-one discussions, interviews, meetings, round tables and other appropriate mechanisms to generate a (critical) analytical perspective on SEA and on its utility and appropriateness in the country.

Direct experience of SEA at the level of plans, projects and policies should be covered, as well as experience in undertaking EAs at these levels that may not have been actually called SEA, but which nevertheless conform to the general concept of SEA.

In some cases, there may have been little or no such direct experience of SEA or of processes akin to SEA, but different approaches may have been followed. Thus, it would be useful to examine experience of those in parallel areas that are close to the SEA concept, or to look at others that could lend practical experience which could inform the direction that SEA might usefully take in developing countries. Such parallel areas could include environmental action plans (national, district and local levels), regional plans, sector plans and assessments, spatial planning, environmental overviews, state of the environment reporting, and so on.

Analysis of both direct experience of SEA and related or different experience in other areas will be key to considering the utility of the SEA approach.

Below, we set out some suggested questions and issues that could be explored as part of such an exercise to examine the context in which SEA is applied, or could usefully be applied, in any country.

1 SETTING FOR SEA IN THE COUNTRY/REGION

Consider:

- any formal provisions for SEA, noting that the term 'SEA' may not be used, and that other terms may be used, for example environmental appraisal, policy appraisal, sustainability analysis, EIA of PPP and EIA of activities (to include PPP);
- if there is a legal/administrative basis for this provision (or proposed provision) for SEA in the country, for example separate law, part of EIA law, included under other regulations, policy directive/decree, or required by donor or funding agencies;
- if there are institutions with actual or potential responsibility for SEA, and with competence to undertake SEA;
- if there is compliance with the process – mandatory, or voluntary, and if the main objectives and/or key principles of SEA are stated in the legal/administrative provision(s) for SEA (e.g. 'the proper integration of environmental considerations into the plans and programmes which are adopted within the country');
- if SEA provisions apply to: policies, programmes, plans, plans and programmes (if these are differentiated); all sectors with environmental effects; or only particular sectors, for example energy, tourism, which activities/sectors SEA has been applied to (or is proposed to be applied to), for example all cabinet decisions, land use plans, transport infrastructure programmes, etc.);
- the stages in the PPP formulation process in the countries concerned (illustrated, for example, by a simple flow diagram) and where in this process SEA is or could be applied, and how;
- whether the findings of SEAs are provided in writing and, if so, whether the contents of reports are specified in any provisions for SEA (when there is formal provision for SEA), what factors an SEA is required to address, for example environmental, social, economic, cumulative effects, global effects, sustainability, and so on;
- where any formal SEA provisions exist, who is responsible for: conducting the SEA, administering the process, and decision-making;
- what SEA steps are followed. The main steps in an SEA process usually include: scoping, comparison of alternatives, impact identification and analysis, mitigation, public involvement, review, and reporting for decision-making. For each of these steps, it might be helpful to consider which aspects are: (i) required by any formal provision for SEA and (ii) undertaken in practice. It could also be helpful to consider which parties are: (iii) responsible for, and which are (iv) involved in the various aspects of the SEA process (e.g. environmental agency, policy formulating body, the public, local government, nature conservation agencies);
- is any (i) procedural and (ii) methodological guidance provided by government, agencies or others for SEA processes or for any stage of such processes, for example guidelines, checklists, matrices, criteria, and so on?

- whether there is no guidance, if it is limited or extensive; and whether it is clear and provides explicit directions on the steps/approaches to be followed;
- for these forms of guidance, what status do they have? For example, statutory/formal, non-statutory/non-formal (i.e. widely accepted and adopted), or discretionary.

2 SEA IN PRACTICE

It will be helpful to capture actual experience of undertaking SEAs in the country (whether called SEAs or known by some other name, or near-equivalents to SEA). Consider the approaches adopted and their effectiveness and influence on outcomes, for example policies, plans, decisions, securing inputs across sectors and from different institutions, and so on. If known, it could be useful to secure some of the following in formation:

- the total number of SEAs that have been undertaken in each country, and how many per year;
- the main sectors addressed by these SEAs (e.g. waste, transport, wildlife, national budget);
- the times (months) taken to conduct SEAs;
- the costs of undertaking SEAs;
- PPP or other provisions changed as a result of SEAs (indicating whether often, sometimes, occasionally or never);
- whether such changes have been recorded or notified; and
- whether voluntary SEAs have been undertaken by government agencies or other organizations.

3 SEA CASE STUDY PROFILES

Detailed SEA case study profiles could be developed. For each, the following information is likely to be useful:

- the name of the SEA (or equivalent process);
- the name of the sponsoring/commissioning agency;
- an indication of who conducted the SEA;
- a description of the background (location, problem concerned, when undertaken, etc.);
- a discussion of the methodology or approach used;
- a description (if known) of who participated and how – in other words who the stakeholders were and which of them were involved;
- an indication (if known) – or a 'best judgement' estimate – of what the purpose and role of the SEA was (was it an end in itself or did it actually inform or influence PPP or decision-making?); and
- a description of the main problems and successes of the SEA process.

4 UTILITY OF SEA, OPPORTUNITIES AND CONSTRAINTS

Whilst the 'survey' information will be important, mere information-gathering will not be adequate to assess the potential utility of SEA. It will be important to address critically and objectively the opportunities that are being met by SEA or equivalent or parallel processes, or that SEA could potentially provide in the country. It will also be useful to consider the constraints that might be attached to adopting an SEA approach. For example, there may be no existing EIA regime or no official EIA procedures, or those that exist may not function well or effectively. In such circumstances, would SEA provide an alternative approach that might overcome such problems? Would SEA, by being undertaken at a higher level (e.g. PPP level) – and thus upstream of potential projects – obviate or reduce the need for EIAs? Or would the introduction of SEA merely add to existing burdens such as insufficient operational budgets, limited capacity or skills, institutional bureaucratic intertia, and so on. And what efforts (including external assistance) might be needed to overcome the constraints or to promote uptake of SEA? In some cases, for example for transboundary river basins, further complications are introduced by competing political or transfrontier considerations or by the lack of institutional coordination.

Consideration should be given to:

- the main strengths and weaknesses (actual or potential) of SEA application: procedurally, methodologically, and with particular reference to public involvement; and
- the features/aspects of SEA that are the most and least valuable, and the needs and priorities for introducing and/or improving SEA performance, for example capacity-building, institutional strengthening, training, professional exchange, research and development, and so on.

Methodological approach

A variety of different approaches might be used to address the issue of the utility of SEA and the associated opportunities and constraints. It will be important to use the approach(es) that best suit the context and/or circumstances of the country/region concerned. Some possible approaches are:

- meetings with a range of key players or groups to discuss SEA experience, awareness, opportunities and constraints;
- semi-structured interviews with key individuals; and
- one or more round table meetings to discuss these issues, and to surface the different perspectives held by different players and stakeholders. Participants could include representatives from different government departments and agencies, different sectors, business and industrial communities, non-governmental organizations (NGOs), academics, and other potential stakeholders. They might include people who have been

involved in EIA/SEA, those who have (or might have) formal responsibilities for EIA/SEA and others with an interest or potential interest in SEA.

In most cases, a combination of such approaches might be the most appropriate. It might also be possible to 'piggy-back' such interviews, meetings and round tables on some other workshop or event.

Appendix 3

The Situation Regarding SEA in Countries in Transition Prior to 1997

SEA trends and developments in transitional countries have evolved rapidly since 1996. Research by Riki Therivel provides a basis of comparison between the situation prior to 1996 and that discussed in Chapter 5.

Therivel (1997) reviewed how SEA is conducted in the Czech Republic, Hungary, Poland and the Slovak Republic. Three case studies are presented: for an express motorway network in Hungary; agricultural ownership transformation in Poland; and drinking water policy in East Slovakia. Examples of SEAs carried out to date in these countries are listed in Table A3.1.

POLAND

In Poland, formal EIA regulations were adopted in 1990, but the only formal regulation of an SEA type is the requirement for EA of land use plans[1] introduced in the 1994 Land-Use Management Act (Rzeszot, 1997). The Act was implemented in 1995 by an executive order of the Minister of Environmental Protection, Natural Resources and Forestry. This states that such an SEA should:

- evaluate and assess the environmental consequences of the proposed action;
- consider previous land uses;
- describe the baseline environment (including total environmental capacity);
- consider the maintenance of biodiversity and the potential environmental effects of the proposed activity; and
- propose alternatives if the proposed activity is unsatisfactory.

Therivel notes that:

> a range of (not formally agreed) methodological guidelines has been published [in Poland], which has been to a large extent inspired by the British guidelines on development plan appraisal.

---

1   Poland has a well-established system of national, provincial (*voivoidship*) and local land use plans.

They suggest that the SEA results should be summarised in a matrix form ... and include provisions for public consultation. Unfortunately, local authorities are given no direction regarding when an SEA is needed, so even minor modifications to plans have been subject to SEA: to date, several dozen have been carried out for new plans and plan modifications. The average length of these SEAs is about ten pages.

Therival records that various voluntary forms of EA of different plans and policies have been carried out in the country, for example:

• the application of EIA methods for the selection of a physical planning strategy in the case of the Green Lungs of Poland area;
• the assessment of a number of government and national policies by various authors, on behalf of NGOs; and
• an overall study of the impact of the motorway network on the natural environment in Poland.

Therivel also points to a problem in Central European countries in carrying out SEAs that is also common in many developing countries – the lack of relevant baseline information:

Although SEAs, especially those that compare alternative PPPs, can be carried out with little environmental information, it is impossible to set environmental targets, limits or carrying capacities without such data, nor is it possible to identify particularly problematic issues (such as whether the PPP will exacerbate the loss of an already scarce habitat type).

SLOVENIA

An SEA of major transport routes has been undertaken as a pilot project. The environmental effects of proposed changes to the National Physical Plan to accommodate new road and rail transport links were assessed, including alternative locations to and within the project. However, the Plan was adopted without change by Parliament (Koblar, 1998). The methodology used to assess regional-scale impacts may be of wider interest (see Koblar, 1998, Part II, Case 7).

LATVIA

EIA is a voluntary process in Latvia. It is used informally, including SEA-type approaches, for example to both review and develop land use plans. Although experience is limited, it appears that incorporating SEA into the planning process is likely to achieve better results than the separate or parallel application (Rotbergh, 1998).

Table A3.1 *SEA examples in Central Europe*

Country	SEA examples	Date	Type, scale and tier of PPP*	Proponent
Czech Republic	Landscape protected area, Zelezne Hory (Iron Mountains)	1996	a, r, plan	Min. of Environment
	Landscape protected area, Moravsky Kras (Moravian Karst)	1996	a, r, plan	Min. of Environment
	Litomericko region	1996	a, r, plan	Min. of Environment
	Landscape protected area, Jizerské Hory (Isere Mountains)	ongoing	a, r, plan	Min. of Environment
Hungary	Express motorway network	1993	a, r, plan	UVATERV Engineering Consultants
Poland	Green Lungs management+	1992	a, r, plan	Inst. for Sustainable Devel.
	Privatization of industry+	1993	s, n, policy	Inst. for Sustainable Devel.
	Privatization of agriculture+	1995	s, n, policy	Inst. for Sustainable Devel.
	Privatization of energy+	ongoing	s, n, policy	Inst. for Sustainable Devel.
	National transport policy+	1996	s, n, policy	Inst. for Sustainable Devel.
	National motorway network+	ongoing	s, n, programme	National Fund for Envir. Protection PHARE*
Slovak Republic	Bogdanka coalfield area	1996	a, l, plan	Bogdanka Coal Mine
	New local plans and plan modifictaion (20–30/year)	1992–present	a, l, plan	Local authorities
	Territorial development policy	1994	a, n, plan	Min. of Environment
	Water management policy	1994	s, n, policy	Min. of Environment
	Drinking water policy for Eastern Slovakia	1995	s, r, policy	Water Mgmt. State Co.
	Actualization of energy policy 1995–2010	1995	s, n, policy	Min. of Economy
	Spatial planning strategy: Zahorsha Bystica, Bratislava, Zilina, Lucenec	ongoing	a, l, plan	Min. of Environment

Notes: Type: a = area-wide PPP which applies to all activities in the area. s = sectoral PPP which applies to a specific sector
Scale: l = local; r = regional; n = national
Tier: policy, plan or programme
+ Carried out separately from the decision-making process
* PHARE is an EU programme for accession countries, originally created in 1989 to assist Poland and Hungary. It now covers ten new member states: the Czech Republic, Estonia, Hungary, Latvia, Lithuania, Poland, Slovakia and Slovenia, as well as Bulgaria and Romania, assisting them in a period of massive economic restructuring and political change.
Source: Therivel (1997)

SLOVAKIA

The EIA Act (1994) provides the basis for the application of SEA. A draft SEA Regulation is under preparation pursuant to Article 35 of the Act. Recently, a simplified form of SEA was applied to the updated version of the national Energy Policy (see Case Study 5.1). On the basis of this experience, it is clear that the draft SEA Regulation will be insufficient to secure an effective process (Kozová, 1998).

Appendix 4

Millennium Ecosystem Assessment

Source: www.millenniumassessment.org

SCOPE AND PURPOSE

The Millennium Ecosystem Assessment (MA) is a four-year international work programme designed to meet the needs of decision-makers and the public for scientific information concerning the consequences of ecosystem changes for human well-being and options for responding to those changes.

The MA focuses on how changes in ecosystem 'goods and services' (food, timber, water purification, flood protection, biodiversity, etc.) have affected human well-being (health security, livelihood security, cultural security, etc.), how ecosystem changes may affect people in future decades and what types of responses can be adopted at local, national, or global scales to improve human well-being and contribute to poverty alleviation.

Leading scientists from more than 100 nations are conducting the Assessment. Oversight is provided by a board with representatives of international conventions, United Nations (UN) agencies, scientific organizations and leaders from the private sector, civil society and indigenous groups. The MA is designed to meet some of the assessment needs of several Conventions (Biological Diversity, Combating Desertification, and Wetlands) as well as the needs of other users in the private sector and civil society. It was launched by UN Secretary-General Kofi Annan in June 2001. The first products were released in 2003, and the main products followed in 2004. It is anticipated that the MA will be repeated every 5–10 years. The specific aims of the MA are listed in Box A4.1.

A purpose of the MA is to provide the scientific underpinning to a wide range of national and international efforts to address environment and development challenges. These environmental challenges are interwoven, and so an integrative assessment process is needed (Box A4.2) to highlight for decision-makers the linkages amongst climate, biodiversity, fresh water, marine and forest issues.

BOX A4.1 AIMS OF THE MILLENNIUM ECOSYSTEM ASSESSMENT

- Significantly increase understanding of the linkage between ecosystems and the goods and services they provide.
- Build human capacity and the capacity of global, regional, national and local institutions to undertake integrated ecosystem assessments and act on their findings.
- Strengthen international environmental agreements and improve environment-related decisions of national governments by improving access to the best scientific information.
- Support regional, national, and local integrated assessments that will directly contribute to planning and capacity-building needs.
- Enhance civil society efforts to promote sustainable development by enabling ready access to peer-reviewed data and information.
- Increase the incentives and information available to guide change in private sector actions.
- Develop methodologies to undertake cross-sectoral assessments and to effectively integrate information across scales.
- Identify important areas of scientific uncertainty and data gaps that hinder decision-making and deserve greater research support.

BOX A4.2 INTEGRATED ECOSYSTEM ASSESSMENT

An integrated ecosystem assessment (IEA) is an analysis of the capacity of an ecosystem to provide goods and services important for human development. Such goods and services are the entire array of products ranging from food to clean water, not a single product such as a crop. An IEA includes both ecological and economic analysis and it considers both the current state of the ecosystem and its future potential. It should be both place-based (i.e. focus on a particular area or location) and multi-sectoral. A benefit of an IEA is that it provides the information necessary to weigh trade-offs amongst various goods and services and to identify opportunities to increase the aggregate development benefits obtained from ecosystem goods and services. Sectoral assessments for water, food production, carbon sequestration, timber and so on do not provide decision-makers with the information needed to identify 'win–win' opportunities or to avoid potential negative trade-offs.

Ecosystem assessment is not entirely new. Many features are evident in a number of existing approaches, for example community resource assessments and national environmental assessments, which address a wide range of factors influencing ecosystems and a wide range of products of those ecosystems. By contrast, national assessments for biodiversity, forests and agriculture have tended to have a sectoral focus.

A major difficulty is that the information needed to conduct an IEA is often lacking. The most readily available ecosystem 'indicators' (those that have shaped our current understanding of ecosystems) are far from complete and give us only a partial description of the 'big picture'.

MULTIPLE-SCALE APPROACH

In addition to its distinct focus on ecosystems and human well-being, the MA includes another pioneering aspect that distinguishes it from past 'global' assessments. It is being conducted as a 'multi-scale' assessment with integral assessment components being undertaken at local community, watershed, national and regional scales, as well as at the global scale. Each of the assessments at sub-global scales contributes to decision-making in the regions and communities where they are being undertaken, and each will be strengthened by the information and perspectives gained from each other and from the global assessment. Assessments at sub-global scales are needed because ecosystems are highly differentiated in space and time, and because sound management requires careful local planning and action. Local assessments alone are insufficient, however, because some processes are global, and because local goods, services, matter and energy are often transferred across regions. The sub-global assessments will directly meet the needs of decision-makers at the scale at which they are undertaken, strengthen the global findings with on-the-ground reality and strengthen the local findings with global perspectives, data and models.

The global scenarios assessment

The MA will present a range of plausible scenarios for how the quantity and quality of ecosystem goods and services may change in coming decades in different regions of the world and how this will affect human health and economic development. It will assess the trade-offs amongst various goods and services. The Scenarios Working Group will assess the findings of previous global scenario analyses concerning goods and services and develop a set of scenarios providing quantitative estimates of the consequences of various plausible changes in primary driving forces on proximate forces, ecosystem goods and services (including biodiversity) and human well-being. The working group will seek to illustrate the connection of global changes in ecosystem services (ES) at every scale (global to local) and the connection of ES to human well-being. The Working Group will seek to: highlight major trade-offs amongst ES; evaluate the effectiveness of policy to provide ES whilst maintaining the capacity to provide ES in the future (sustainability); and fulfil the objectives of the users of the MA findings.

Sub-global assessments

The sub-global assessments have been designed to foster and build capacity for widespread adoption of integrated assessment approaches in other regions and nations. These sub-global assessments aim to directly meet the needs of decision-makers at the scale at which they are undertaken, strengthen the global findings with on-the-ground reality, and strengthen the local findings with global perspectives, data and models. Sub-global assessments approved by or linked to the MA include:

- the Arafura and Timor Seas
- the Argentine Pampas
- the Northern Floodplains of Australia
- São Paulo, Brazil
- Coastal British Columbia, Canada
- the Caribbean Sea
- the mountains of Central Asia
- Salar de Atacama, Chile
- Western China
- Colombia
- Chirripo river basin, Costa Rica
- Sinai Peninsula, Egypt
- the Hindu Kush-Himalayas
- several regions within India
- Indonesia
- small islands of Papua New Guinea
- Vilcanota Region, Peru
- Laguna Lake Basin, the Philippines
- Portugal
- Altai-Sayan ecoregion, Russia
- Saudi Arabia
- Southern Africa (including Mozambique, South Africa, Zambia, and Zimbabwe)
- Sweden
- Trinidad and Tobago
- Northern Wisconsin, US
- Mekong wetlands
- Vietnam
- the tropical forest sites of the Consultative Group of International Agriculture Centres (CGIAR) Alternatives to Slash and Burn Project.

In addition, a pilot assessment has been completed in Norway. Additional sub-global assessments can join the MA through a process described on the MA website (www.ma.org).

The global responses assessment

The MA will identify policy, institutional, legislative or technological changes that could improve the management of ecosystems, thereby increasing their contributions to development and maintaining their long-term sustainability. The Response Options Working Group will assess the effectiveness of various types of response options, both historical and current. A series of case studies will be used to assess the effectiveness of response options to deal with particular issues concerning the intrinsic value of biodiversity, ES and the consequences of changes in ecosystems on human well-being. The group will use the case studies to develop a methodology that could be used by policy-makers to evaluate response options in a way that will reveal opportunities for 'linked' responses that address multiple goods and services or multiple user needs.

AUDIENCE

A primary audience for the global findings of the MA will be the parties to the ecosystem-related conventions. The MA will synthesize information of particular relevance to each of the conventions. A Summary for Policymakers has been prepared for these conventions, approved by the MA board, and then submitted to the conventions' scientific bodies. Parties to the conventions will then determine which findings will be formally accepted into the individual convention process, based on their specific information needs.

Other important audiences include national governments, NGOs, civil society, business, indigenous peoples and the media. Representatives of the conventions and other audiences have been actively engaged in determining the specific focus and products of the MA through their representation on the board and participation in the design process. An advisory group of some 90 individuals from 35 countries has been established and the MA has also established links to the national focal points for the ecosystem-related conventions in all nations.

A RESPONSE TO NEEDS

The global assessment and each of the sub-global assessments aim to respond to decision-makers' needs by:

1 *Providing information requested by decision-makers.* More specifically, by assessing:
    – the condition, pressures, trends and change in ecosystems and the current economic and public health consequences of those changes;
    – the state of scientific knowledge;
    – the ecosystem (and consequent economic and public health) impacts of plausible future scenarios of change in 'driving forces', such as population, consumption, climate, technology and economic growth; and
    – the strengths and weaknesses of various policy, legislative, technological or other actions that have been taken or proposed to improve the management of ecosystems.
2 *Building human and institutional capacity.* The specific capacity needs were identified during the first year of the MA, but capacity-building has been addressed through at least the following basic approaches:
    – increasing skills and expertise of the individuals and institutions involved in all scales of the MA;

- increasing access to technical tools and scientific models for undertaking integrated assessments;
- increasing access to data and indicators for use in local and national assessments;
- developing and disseminating new approaches for linking local level expertise and assessments with national, regional and global expertise and assessments;
- increasing experience with the design of assessments that fully involve 'stakeholders' at the local, national and regional scales; and
- increasing international stature and access to international sources of support.

ASSESSMENT PROCESS

A 13-member assessment panel of leading social and natural scientists has overseen the technical work of the assessment supported by a secretariat with offices in Europe, North America, Asia and Africa and coordinated by the UN Environment Programme (UNEP).

Technical experts. More than 500 authors have been involved in four expert working groups preparing the global assessment and hundreds more are undertaking more than a dozen sub-regional assessments.

The working groups have focused on conditions, scenarios and response options. Each has been co-chaired by leading natural and social scientists from industrialized and developing countries. The working groups comprised a geographically balanced group of experts from universities, the private sector, government and civil society.

Design and methods. In its first year, the MA focused on the development of an internally consistent set of methodologies for conducting the assessment at local, national, regional and global scales. The methodology for the MA (2003) defined the information to be produced, questions to be answered and capacity needs to be filled. The methodology presented common design elements to be applied at all scales and features unique to different scales.

Peer review. All of the assessment findings are subjected to extensive peer review. Reviewers from all countries are nominated by scientists, governments, business and civil society. The review process has been developed and overseen by the MA board and an independent review body. The review process has been tailored to the unique characteristics of the different scales of the assessment, thereby enabling incorporation of unpublished local expertise and knowledge.

Linkages with research and assessment activities. The MA has been closely coordinated with other global assessments, including the UNEP Global

Environmental Outlook, the Global International Waters Assessment, and the Intergovernmental Panel on Climate Change. It has been designed to strengthen planned and ongoing assessment activities and sustainable development planning activities at regional and national levels. The MA has included new analyses, but was not designed as a research project. Instead, it has been a mechanism to bring the findings of research and monitoring to bear on decision-makers' needs. The MA has worked closely with research programmes such as the International Geosphere Biosphere Programme (IGBP) and the International Human Dimensions Programme on Global Environmental Change (IHDP), and also with monitoring activities, including the Long Term Ecological Research Network and the Global Observing System.

PRODUCTS

The first product (MA, 2003) set out the conceptual framework and methodology for undertaking the MA. It described the rationale for the goods and services approach used in the MA and provides users with a useful methodological tool. The technical assessment reports produced by each of the four MA working groups have entered the peer review stage and were due to be published in early 2005. Five synthesis reports distilling the MA findings will be prepared for specific audiences. Each of the MA sub-global assessments will produce additional reports to meet the needs of their own audiences. All printed materials will be complemented by the information- and data-rich MA website, capacity-building activities and briefings and workshops designed to help communicate the findings, tools and methods to users at multiple scales.

INSTITUTIONAL ARRANGEMENTS

MA secretariat staff have been housed (in a 'distributed' manner) by a range of institutions:

- Food and Agriculture Organization of the United Nations (FAO), Italy
- Institute of Economic Growth, India
- Meridian Institute, US
- National Institute for Public Health and the Environment (RIVM), The Netherlands
- Scientific Committee on Problems of the Environment (SCOPE), France
- Stanford University, US
- The Cropper Foundation, Trinidad and Tobago
- UNEP-World Conservation Monitoring Centre (UNEP-WCMC), UK
- University of Pretoria, The Centre for Environmental Economics and Policy in Africa (CEEPA), South Africa
- University of Wisconsin-Madison, US

- World Resources Institute, US
- World Fish Center, Malaysia.

Appendix 5

Recommendations for SEA of Regional Development Plans in Central and Eastern Europe (CEE) Countries

Source: Conclusions of the Fourth Regional Workshop of the Sofia Initiative on EIA, Bratislava, 19–21 May 1999

In CEE, regional development plans and related programming documents (i.e. rural development plans) are drafted under considerable financial and time constraints. Relatively easy and transparent SEA approaches should be used in order to effectively carry out SEA during the preparation of these plans. Within these simplified SEA procedures, the following principles should apply (it is understood that SEA quality is largely pre-determined by the capacities of the participating stakeholders).

General principles for SEA of CEE regional and rural development plans (RDPs):

1   SEA should be carried out by a multidisciplinary and multi-stakeholder team of experts. The SEA team should be provided with a mandate that is sufficient to access information on materials generated by the elaboration of RDPs and for the proposing of changes in their formulation.
2   The SEA team should be formed as soon as possible in the elaboration of RDPs. It should work in parallel, and in continuous interaction with, the planning team. Its goal is to provide an independent environmental review of all documents leading to the elaboration of RDPs.
3   SEA should be based on thorough public participation – in accordance with the requirements of the Aarhus Convention.

SEA focus:

4   SEA should focus mainly on impacts that have been identified as priority concerns by the affected public administration and concerned public (i.e. NGOs, academics, citizens).

5   SEA should address both national and transboundary/global issues.

Impact assessments:

6   Given the lack of resources, time and information available for the elaboration of complex prognostic models, SEA should use collective expert judgements undertaken by qualified multidisciplinary and multi-stakeholder teams (see Principle 1 above).
7   Impacts should be evaluated on the basis of:
    – their conformity with formally adopted governmental goals in environmental and health protection (e.g. national strategies in the fields of environment and health, global conventions, transboundary issues and European Union (EU) standards)
    – the degree of public concern associated with the forecast impact.

SEA outcomes:

8   SEA should suggest environmentally friendly modifications of RDPs. This information can be most effectively used during the elaboration of RDPs. So SEA should be undertaken, where possible, in parallel with the elaboration of these development plans (see Principle 2 above).
9   Assessment findings should be documented in an SEA report, which should be made available to the public. The SEA report can be used effectively for monitoring the actual environmental impacts of development plans and for the elaboration of further programming documents.

Appendix 6

Principles, Their Implications for the Canadian International Development Agency (CIDA) and Key Factors for SEA

Source: CIDA, November 2003; adapted from DEAT (2000)

Principle	Implications	Action
(a) Substantive/content principles		
1 SEA is driven by the concept of sustainability.	The focus of SEA is on integrating the concept of sustainability into the objectives and outcomes of PPP.	Ensure the concept of sustainability is integrated into different levels of decision-making, within the spatial context of the PPP.
	Sustainability objectives are applicable to the level, scale and sector of the PPP as well as to the environmental resources to be sustained. The sustainability objectives should be developed with the participation of interested and affected parties.	
	Targets and measurement tools are defined to guide development towards sustainability.	
2 SEA identifies the opportunities and constraints that the environment places on the development of the PPP.	The environmental resources (e.g. potable water, forests, fertile soil) needed to achieve the sustainability objectives are identified. These resources are maintained and enhanced through the PPP. The resources are prioritized through effective participation procedures.	Identify environmental resources that should be maintained and/or enhanced in the PPP.

Principle	Implications	Action
	The environmental resources form the basis for the identification of opportunities and constraints, which guide the formulation of the PPP.	
3 SEA sets the criteria for levels of environmental quality or limits of acceptable change within an ecosystem (e.g. maintain 'x'ha of rainforest).	The levels of acceptable change of the environmental resources are determined. This process reflects public views and scientific information.	Identify level of acceptable change for environmental resources.
	The PPP is developed in such a way as to maintain and enhance the quantity and quality of environmental resources. This includes an iterative process of developing alternatives and predicting whether the resources will be maintained and enhanced.	
	Management programmes are developed to respond to potential negative environmental effects. These should be implemented if the limits of acceptable change to environmental resources are, or are threatened to be, exceeded.	
4 Sea is a flexible process that is adaptable to the PPP or development cycle.	SEA is integrated into existing processes for PPP formulation and implementation.	Integrate sustainability objectives into existing context-specific processes for PPP.
	There is no single SEA process for all contexts, but different processes for various contexts and strategic tasks.	
	The focus is on understanding the context-specific, decision-making and PPP formulation procedure. The objectives of sustainability are then integrated into this process at key decision points, throughout the various levels and scale of PPP development. The SEA consistently interacts with the PPP procedure in an iterative way.	

(b) Procedural principles

Principle	Implications	Action
5 SEA is a strategic process, which begins with the conceptualization of the PPP.	SEA introduces sustainability objectives at the earliest stage in the PPP process; from conceptualization through to the many stages of decision-making.	Integrate sustainability objectives into the PPP, starting from the stage of conceptualization.

6 SEA is part of a tiered approach to environmental assessment and management.	SEA addresses higher levels of decision-making in order to provide the context for lower levels. Linkages are established between the various levels of decision-making.	Identify PPP which influence the maintenance and enhancement of the environmental resources identified.
7 The scope of an SEA is defined within the wider context of environmental process. SEA needs to encompass local, regional and national considerations.	SEA is not limited to a particular site, but considers significant local, regional, national and international linkages.	What are the political, socioeconomic, and biophysical processes influencing the maintenance and enhancement of the environmental resources identified?
8 SEA is a participative process.	Participation processes are adapted to the specific socio-political context of the PPP. The public participation process should inform and enhance the entire SEA process, in particular the scope and sustainability objectives of the SEA.	Identify the level and type of participation to enable role-players to engage in the process at a level that is appropriate to their needs and resources.
9 SEA is set within the context of alternative scenarios using the concept of cost–benefit analysis.	Scenarios, visions and alternative PPP options are developed in a participatory way. Alternative PPP are evaluated in terms of their ability to maintain and enhance the environmental resources identified.	Identify PPP alternatives that will most effectively maintain and enhance the environmental resources identified.
10 SEA includes the concepts of precaution and continuous improvement.	A risk-averse and cautious approach is applied, which recognizes the limitations of current knowledge about the consequences of decision-making. This approach should be linked to a commitment to continuous learning and improvement. This link contributes to increasing understanding of sustainability for a region or sector. SEA must lead to a process for: • monitoring and continuous improvement; and • improvement of baseline information; and understanding of sustainability objectives.	Identify SEA risk analysis mechanism, as well as SEA monitoring and evaluation protocols.

Appendix 7

Sub-national Economic-cum-environmental (E-c-E) Planning in Asia

In the early 1980s, the Asian Development Bank started working on ways to integrate environmental concerns into decision-making. It began to promote economic-cum-environmental (E-c-E) planning, particularly at sub-national levels, building on a model developed by the Organization of American States (OAS) (Box A7.1). E-c-E planning integrates sociocultural, economic, natural resource and environmental objectives. It incorporates stakeholder participation and develops an integrated package of PPP to achieve those objectives in a sustainable manner. So it has much in common with sustainable development strategy approaches.

King et al (2000) compare case studies of sub-national E-c-E planning in Asia against the OAS model to determine key success factors and constraints:

- Songkla Lake Basin Planning Study, Thailand
- Klang River Valley, Malaysia
- Hainan Island, South China Sea
- Haihe River Basin, China
- Coastal Environmental Management and Planning Project, Indonesia.

They found that reforms are needed before a cohesive, integrated E-c-E planning approach can be uniformly applied at the sub-national level in the Asian region. However, experience is starting to emerge that can provide the basis for an integrated economic and environmental planning system involving improved planning at all levels. Recommendations to improve the E-c-E planning process at the sub-national level included a mix of administrative process and technical content reforms:

- *Administrative process improvements* include:
  - establishing political support for E-c-E planning;
  - boosting stakeholder participation;
  - securing cross-agency involvement;
  - obtaining commitments from governments to fund implementation projects;

BOX A7.1 REFINED SUB-NATIONAL E-C-E PLANNING MODEL USED BY THE ASIAN DEVELOPMENT BANK

Analysis of the existing system

The boundaries of the planning area may be a river basin, an island or group of islands, sea or lake region, an administrative region, an ecosystem or biosphere reserve, or some other ecologically defined 'bio-region'.

Ideally, the study region should be defined as one of a series of plans that together would cover the entire nation. The planning study generally starts with a comprehensive description of the existing social, cultural, economic, natural resources and environmental systems, in sufficient detail to gain a thorough understanding of how all these dimensions interact. This description provides a synthesis of all previous investigations in the study area. The description is based on generally available data. It may include some mathematical models, which can be used for subsequent projections or predictions. The description of the study area includes an inventory of projects that have been planned, approved or are waiting in the pipeline of sectoral agencies.

Policy framework

The next step is to document all relevant policies in the study area, both explicit and implicit. These policies are analysed to highlight any overlaps or conflicts between policies applied to different sectors. Generally, the multidisciplinary study team must stick to broad dimensions of the policy debate, as detailed refinements may take much longer to resolve than the study period. Policy instruments are also documented, for example legislation, regulations, planning guidelines and standards. To the extent possible, decision-making processes in the study area are investigated and reported, including political systems and influences.

Scenario formulation

Once the study area is well understood and the policy framework is clear, then alternative development scenarios are constructed. Three or four scenarios are formulated to provide an envelope around realistic development options, rather than representing unachievable extremes. The scenarios are projections from the baseline derived in the description of existing conditions. They cover social, economic, natural resource and environmental dimensions. The social, economic and environmental implications of each scenario are then presented in terms that decision-makers can understand. In consultation with the government and stakeholders, a preferred development scenario is chosen as a consensus vision for the long-term future of the study area. Revised projections are then made for various key aspects of the preferred scenario, such as economic growth rates, population growth, employment generation, natural resource depletion rates, pollutant loads and so on.

Plan formulation

The study team then prepares detailed plans consistent with the preferred scenario: a socioeconomic development plan, natural resources development plan and an environmental management plan. The interactions between the plans are documented to illustrate the integrated approach that is needed to attain the vision encompassed by the preferred development pathway.

Spatial and sector strategies

The spatial context of the preferred scenario is presented so that the impact on specific locations or groups of beneficiaries can be identified. Similarly, for each sector (agriculture, mining, forestry, etc.), the various plan components are amalgamated to give a comprehensive sectoral view. For example, an agriculture sector plan will contain social, economic and environmental strategies consistent with the preferred scenario. At this stage, refinement of the strategies and plans may be desirable following consideration of separate sector studies and presentations to sectoral agencies and interest groups.

Selection of priority projects

During preparation of the scenarios, a range of project ideas is discussed. To be included in the ultimate development plan, each project concept must pass through a screening mechanism that assesses economic viability, resource demands, social and environmental impacts. Along with economic evaluation at the pre-feasibility study level, preliminary environmental impact assessments (EIAs) and social impact assessments (SIAs) are undertaken for all selected projects. Terms of reference are drawn up for full SIAs and EIAs for socially or environmentally sensitive projects included in the action plan. These SIAs and EIAs are undertaken as part of the feasibility studies for these projects in Phase II of the planning process.

Action plan and implementation arrangements

The various plan components are amalgamated and presented as a synthesis development plan, covering the goals, objectives, strategies and vision for the future. To enable the vision to be attained, an action plan of all priority projects and programmes is presented as a consolidated public investment plan. The action plan demonstrates the scale and phasing of investment required over the plan period. The administrative arrangements and responsibilities are documented and linkages to the national and local levels are established. The synthesis development plan is presented in draft form for public comment and consultation. Seminars and workshops may be needed for specific sector groups or groups of stakeholders affected by the plan.

Maintaining momentum

There is a constant battle in any integrated planning effort to avoid the tendency for carefully integrated project packages to fall apart, often due to the intervention of special interest groups after the plan is finalized. Short-term 'do-able' projects (that can proceed even before the plan is finally accepted) help to maintain the momentum. Arrangements are made for the feasibility studies and detailed design in Phase II. Consideration may also be given to strengthening the regional and local implementation agencies. Arrangements for monitoring implementation progress and plan revision are made so that the plan remains a process, rather than a static exercise with a defined end point. Additional effort may be needed to present the plan in a format that facilitates its incorporation into national economic development plans and/or local plans.

Expected outputs

A synthesis development plan for the study region is made up of a socioeconomic development plan, natural resources development plan and environmental management plan, all of which are linked. These, in turn, are presented as a consolidated action plan, divided into short-term, medium-term and long-term phases. At this stage, the selected short-term priority projects of the action plan go forward into detailed feasibility studies in Phase II. To maintain momentum, funding must be arranged for the Phase II feasibility studies.

Source: King et al (2000)

- training for government staff in E-c-E planning; and
- a phasing of the planning process.

• *Technical content improvements* include:
  - more extensive baseline data to enable better description of existing social, economic and ecological systems;
  - more reliable models that link environmental and economic parameters and that generate results that can be monitored and verified, or fed back into further refinement of the models;
  - more effective use of the scenario approach so that decision-makers and stakeholders can easily envision alternative futures;
  - increased use of environmental economics and SIA in project screening;
  - further development of cumulative environmental assessment and strategic environmental assessment;
  - implementation of short-term projects to assist in maintaining momentum; and
  - development of sound monitoring systems.

Appendix 8

Legal Requirements for SEA in Selected Spanish Regions

Castilla y León – Legislative Decree 1/2000 of 18 May

Environmental Impact Assessment and Environmental Audits of Castilla y León.
Scope:
- environmental impact assessments
- strategic assessments of plans and programmes
- environmental audits in the Autonomous Community of Castilla y León.

Article 1 – the Junta de Castilla y León is responsible for strategic assessment:
- before the environmental impacts of regional development plans and programmes;
- before their approval; and
- specifically of those that have a sector-based content and are applied to determined geographic areas, having in view to prevent potential environmental effects along the several sectors and to study the proper alternatives.

Article 19 – details the sectors considered (e.g. related to forestry, tourism, agriculture, industry).

Article 20 – establishes the content of strategic assessments of plans and programmes:
- description of the plan or programme and its main objectives;
- explanation of how the plan or programme objectives take into account the environmental impacts;
- description of the main alternatives;
- description of the environmental characteristics and, if possible, of the area that could be affected, including a description of sensitive areas;
- description of significant direct and indirect effects on the environment, and especially on ecologically sensitive areas, that the plan could give rise to and their principal alternatives;
- description of the compatibility of the selected alternative with suitable environmental legislation;
- description of monitoring measures of the activity's effects on the environment;
- outline of the difficulties found by the responsible authority during the information search; and
- non-technical summary.

Basque Territory – Law 3/1998 of 27 February

Environmental Protection of Basque Territory. Determines the rights and duties of physical and legal entities to:
* guarantee sustainable development
* preserve biodiversity
* improve life quality
* protect the environment
* minimize environmental impacts
* promote research in the environmental area
* promote environmental education.

Title 3 – regulates the management of activities impacting on the environment.

Chapter 2 – environmental impact assessment:
* establishes a system to estimate the potential effects on the environment of implementing plans and projects established in Attachment 1;
* presents an administrative procedure for EIA of plans (before their approval) that appraises the possible alternatives and estimates accumulated impacts of projects included in the plans. It does not establish the content of assessment.

Attachment 1 – lists the plans that have to be submitted to EIA. All are territorial and include guidelines, norms, urban development plans and special plans.

Andalucía – Law 7/1994 of 18 May

Environmental Protection. Aims:
* set measures to prevent, minimize and correct or, when necessary, stop the effects that some public or private activities can have on the environment and life quality
* define the legal scope and activity of the Autonomous Community of Andalucía, in terms of atmospheric protection, waste in general and water quality, to improve environmental quality through applying prevention, correction and monitoring techniques.

Article 3 – this law is applied to:
* plans, programmes and construction projects, or installations of public or private works included in Attachments 1, 2 and 3;
* industries and any infrastructure or activity that could cause atmospheric contamination; and
* urban solid waste produced by several activities listed in Article 3.

Title 2 – environmental protection.

Chapter 2s – EIA.

Article 13 – requires EIA of plans and programmes to address global effects and consequences of the strategic options.

Section 2 – establishes EIA procedure.

Attachment 1 – includes general urban plans, complementary rules of planning and their revisions and modifications.

Andalucía – Law 7/1994 of 18 May

Decree 292/1995 of 12 December

Regulation of EIA of the Autonomous Community of Andalucía: Executive Law 7/1994 of 18 May, as far as it is concerned with EIA.

Article 2 – EIA is applied to all public or private activities that involve plans, programmes, construction projects, installations and works included in Attachment 1 of Law 7/1994 of 18 May. EIA must also be undertaken for their extensions or modifications.

Chapter 2 – covers EIA.

Article 8 – requires EIA of plans and programmes to appraise their global effects and consequences of their strategic options.

Chapter 3 – covers environmental impact studies.

Article 11 – presents the detailed content of environmental impact studies of projects.

Article 12 – describes the content of environmental impact studies of urban plans:
- schematic description of structural determinations;
- environmental study and analysis of affected territory;
- impacts identification and evaluation; and
- corrective measures, monitoring and environmental planning.

Article 13 – describes the content of environmental impact studies of physical infrastructure plans and programmes:
- general description of the plan or programme;
- overall territorial and environmental analysis of plan or programme development;
- environmental analysis of strategic options, addressing the information obtained in previous groups;
- monitoring criteria of the development of the plan or programme to facilitate the control of environmental factors; and
- synthesis document.

The environmental impact study of plans or programmes is simpler than the EIS of projects.

Chapter 5 – describes general EIA procedure.

Appendix 9

Sustainability Impact Assessment of World Trade Organization (WTO) Multilateral Trade Negotiations

Sources: Documents and reports for this initiative are available for review and comment on the project website (http://idpm.man.ac.uk/sia-trade). Additional information provided by Clive George, University of Manchester, UK.

Phase 1 (July–September 1999)
Literature review of potential methodologies, evaluation of specific trade policies and agreements; and development of SIA methodology.

Phase 2 (September–November 1999)
(a) Broad, qualitative, preliminary appraisal of a specified range of trade-related measures to identify where these might have potentially significant sustainability impacts to be taken into consideration when formulating and finalizing the agenda for the Seattle inter-ministerial meeting in December 1999; and development of proposals for further measures to enhance the impact of the New Round Agenda outcomes on sustainable development. The preliminary appraisal involved the stages described below.

Information checklists to assist in applying the methodology:

- possible measures for negotiation that may be included in the New Round Agenda;
- possible scenarios to be analysed for each measure;
- groupings of countries for which appraisals are to be undertaken;
- sustainability impact indicators and significance criteria to be used in the appraisals; and
- methods, consultation procedures and information sources to be used in the appraisals.

Main stages:

- *screening*: to determine which of the measures, listed in (a) above, require SIA;
- *scoping*: to establish the appropriate coverage of each SIA;
- *preliminary sustainability assessment*: to identify potentially significant effects, positive and negative, on sustainable development; and
- *mitigation and enhancement analysis*: to suggest types of improvements that may enhance the overall impact on sustainable development of New Round Agenda measures.

(b) Development and refinement of the SIA methodology for Phase 3 – building on the findings of the first phase – through an open dialogue (continued through the project) with interested stakeholders via an email address (chk@man.ac.uk). The SIA methodology being used in Phase 3 aims to assist negotiators and other interested parties in the post-Doha WTO trade negotiations; and to help those involved in identifying the likely economic, social and environmental consequences for their region or country, of one negotiated set of outcomes compared to another.

Phase 3 (commenced April 2002)
A preliminary overview assessment has been undertaken of the Doha Development Agenda (DDA) to identify major impacts on the sustainability of proposed measures:

- *existing negotiation mandate*: agriculture; market access for non-agricultural products; services; trade and environment; dispute settlement; trade-related aspects of intellectual property rights (TRIPS); WTO rules (anti-dumping and subsidies; regional trade agreements); implementation issues in developing countries
- *measures introduced at the 1996 Singapore Ministerial Conference*: trade and investment; competition policy; trade facilitation; transparency of government procurement
- *measures subject to discussions under the DDA*: electronic commerce; small economies; trade, debt and finance; technology transfer; technical cooperation and capacity-building; least-developed countries; special and differential treatment

taking into account potential impacts associated with inter-sectoral linkages, and identifying those areas where more detailed assessments should be carried out at the next stage in the process.

In parallel, three sectoral SIA studies have been completed:

1   market access (with special emphasis on pharmaceuticals, non-ferrous metals, textiles);

2   environmental services (with special emphasis on water and waste treatment); and
3   competition policy.

A further three sectoral SIA studies were selected on completion of the overview study and are in progress:
4   agriculture;
5   forestry; and
6   distribution services.

The final report on the overview assessment (George and Kirkpatrick, 2003) presents a review of international trade, sets out the SIA methodology used, provides preliminary sectoral findings and recommendations for further sectoral SIA studies, and proposes refinements to the SIA methodology framework for these detailed studies and for completing the overall SIA of the DDA.

METHODOLOGY FOR PRELIMINARY OVERVIEW SIA OF THE DDA

The assessment was undertaken within a broad screening and scoping update of the earlier preliminary SIA study of the pre-Seattle broad agenda. It involved screening the DDA as a whole, including cross-sectoral linkages and cumulative impacts likely to result from the implementation of the DDA measures. The components included:

- specification of the content and scope of the *trade measures*;
- elaboration of *negotiation scenarios* – a *base scenario* (full implementation of existing agreements); and a *further liberalization scenario* (representing the strongest probable implementation of the negotiations agreed at the Fourth Ministerial Conference in Doha);
- focus on *country characteristics* that influence potential impacts. The subsequent detailed SIAs will assess impacts in four *country groupings* (EU, non-EU developed countries, developing countries, least-developed countries);
- assessment methods – based on *causal chain analysis* using information from econometric modelling and case studies where appropriate:
  - identification of the effects of market incentives and opportunities resulting from negotiated change to a trade agreement
  - assessment of significance of linkages (from effects – long- and short-term – on production relationships to sustainability impacts)
  - evaluation of cumulative effects of trade measures on sustainable development processes and outcomes;
- assessment of the *significance of impacts*;

- use of core *sustainability indicators* (complemented by second-tier and process indicators for detailed SIA studies):
  - *economic*: real income, fixed capital formation, employment
  - *social*: poverty, health and education, equity
  - *environmental*: biodiversity, environmental quality, natural resource stocks
  - *process*: sustainable development principles, sustainable development strategies;
- assessment of *cross-cutting issues* (classified in five broad groups: scale, technology, structural, location and regulatory) and *overall impact*;
- preliminary indication of *mitigation and enhancement measures*, for example trade-related measures that might be built into WTO agreements, side or parallel agreements, collaborative agreements, international and regional agreements and measures by national governments; and
- *consultation process* (dialogue with stakeholders, comments by network of experts, published reports on dedicated website with facilities for comment, civil society meetings).

The preliminary overview SIA involved only limited analysis, with detail added in the individual sectoral SIAs. These aim to inform and assist negotiations up to their conclusion – originally targeted for January 2005, but delayed following the 2003 WTO Inter-Ministerial Conference in Cancun.

Appendix 10

Examples of Integration Mechanisms and Role of Environmental Assessment from Selected EU Member States

Sheate et al (2001)

Status of SEA (at the time of the adoption of the SEA Directive 2001/42/EC in 2001)	Examples of integration mechanisms	Commentary: extent of integration and role of EA
Austria *SEA not a legal requirement.* Progress towards strategic environmental assessment, e.g. the right of the environmental ombudsman in the province of Styria to comment on all laws that are likely to have environmental effects and to propose alternatives.	• Austrian National Environment Plan (NEP, 1995) contains clearly defined objectives and proposes more than 300 measures to achieve them. • Federal Ministry of Agriculture, Forestry, Environment and Water Management and the provincial ministries for the environment deal with the task of integrating the environment in strategic decision-making. Provincial level: re comprehensive environmental programmes with a high degree of integration, using environmental quality targets and corresponding indicators. But only a few provide for monitoring or auditing issues (e.g. Local Agenda 21 Graz). • Sustainability round tables and other communication tools as well as awareness-raising methods are in place, but there is a weakness concerning guidance and training both for SEA and integration of the environment.	Though not yet formal SEA, there is reasonably strong integration of environmental issues into decision-making through a comprehensive system of environmental reporting and environmental communication (e.g. 'sustainability round tables', councils on climate change, sustainable development (SD), and public participation procedures, e.g. in spatial planning legislation). The NEP (1995) acts as a comprehensive framework for Austria's environmental policy; parallel to the federal-level environmental programmes for provinces or municipalities (often in a Local Agenda 21 context). The differentiated and detailed environmental legislation, eco-labelling, voluntary agreements and many other tools contribute to the fact that there is a high degree of environmental awareness.
Belgium *SEA not a legal requirement.* Main progress towards SEA being carried out in region of Flanders; proposals to introduce EA of plans and programmes into present EIA Decree.	• Three regions each with its own framework for integration, for example the regional governments of Flanders and Wallonia have adopted regional laws as frameworks for integration. Also, each region has several bodies responsible for the environment. • The overall law relating to SD was adopted in 1997 (law on coordination of federal policy on sustainable development) at the federal level. Annual reporting on Local Agenda 21 issues. • Development of SD indicators; environmental indicators required for regional environmental reports.	Each region provides its own framework for environmental integration particularly with regard to EIA, environmental management, SD and Local Agenda 21. Both SD and Local Agenda 21 have in recent years become priority areas in each region. A number of bodies are responsible for the implementation of SD at policy level whilst municipal authorities work at local level, implementing Local Agenda 21. There is no mandatory SEA in Belgium; but there is voluntary SEA of the transport plan, and voluntary SEAs in Wallonia.

- At the federal level an interdepartmental commission for SD is responsible for formulating the federal plan and promoting SD. There is inter-regional coordination amongst environment ministers for development of SD indicators.

Denmark

SEA *a legal requirement for*: bills and government proposals. Ministerial guidelines on SEA in place since 1995. No public participation in assessment procedure although chance to participate in preparation of bill during customary consultation process under Danish legislation. State budget proposals are assessed for environmental impacts in selected areas.

- Sector action programmes on SD.
- Danish Nature and Environment Policy presented to Parliament every four years.
- Danish environmental legislation lays down organizational and procedural rules requiring communication between different authorities and stakeholders.
- After elections the Minister for Environment and Energy reports to Parliament on national land use planning, and produces state of the environment reports.
- The National Protection Board of Appeal and Environmental Protection Board of Appeal – monitoring of environmental framework laws.
- The main environmental framework laws have SD as a stated objective in the preamble of the laws.

Sector action programmes on SD define quantitative and qualitative objectives and list initiatives to be carried out. Various systems allowing the integration of environment into decision-making at different levels of government; degree of decentralization is high. The Spatial Planning Department under the Ministry of the Environment cooperates with the National Association of Local Authorities and the Association of County Councils in Denmark in encouraging counties and municipalities to undertake Local Agenda 21. Voluntary SEA of National Land Use Plan carried out. Also research and voluntary SEA of county and municipal plans. Environmental indicators are being developed as parts of SEA systems within the fields of national and regional land use planning.

Finland

SEA *a legal requirement for*: state action plans and economic strategies; policies on taxation and subsidies; plans and programmes for energy, environment, transport, industry, forestry and agriculture; committee reports; government proposals. Guidelines in place since 1999.

- Finnish Action for Sustainable Development (1995), includes measures that vary from sectoral programmes of different ministries and governmental bodies to information campaigns of NGOs.
- National Commission on Sustainable Development.
- Sectoral programmes on SD.
- Annual Ministry of Finance regulation requiring the investigation of environmental effects of state budget and proposed action plans.

An Action Plan on Sustainable Development: strategy document with short-term definitions and proposals and long-term scenarios. Environmental impacts investigated and assessed to a sufficient degree when an authority is preparing policies on taxation, payment and subsidies and when plans and programmes related to the environment, energy, transport, industry, forestry and agriculture are prepared. Environmental impacts assessed in

Status of SEA (at the time of the adoption of the SEA Directive 2001/42/EC in 2001)	Examples of integration mechanisms	Commentary: extent of integration and role of EA
	• Land Use and Building Act of January 2000 emphasizes a more open and interactive approach to planning and local authorities are given more power in decision-making.	preparation of policies as well as plans and programmes related to environment, energy, transport, industry, forestry and agriculture. National Commission makes recommendations on preparation of sectoral programmes on SD.
France SEA *a legal requirement at policy level for proposed laws and also for plans.* Voluntary SEAs have taken place since the 1980s in area of land use planning. SEA methodology recently developed for transport infrastructure and applied to plans and programmes at regional level.	• Environmental integration responsibility of the Ministry of Environment (MoE). • MoE to integrate environmental policy into socioeconomic planning. • Several other bodies with responsibility for promotion and implementation of Agenda 21 with some working directly with the MoE to help increase inclusion of environmental considerations in development programmes and decision-making. • Environmental integration occurs through a number of different laws (mainly related to EIA) and an SD strategy exists with Local Agenda 21 being implemented. Requirement during the development of urban zoning plans for the provision of state of the environment reports.	France was the first country to introduce EIA in Europe. The environment is integrated to a fair use planning and the environmental appraisal of programmes. EIA, environmental regulations, planning documents, zoning plans and SIA all contribute to environmental integration. Environmental assessment takes place at policy level for those laws deemed to have an impact on the environment. Also, proposed laws must demonstrate that they are environmental and sustainable. SD and Local Agenda 21 are also priority areas and an SD strategy exists. Since 1990, SIA has been mandatory at policy level for proposed laws, but voluntary SIAs have taken place since the 1980s. There is also evidence that SIA is being applied to plans and programmes at a regional level.
Germany SEA *not a legal requirement.* Spatial and sectoral planning procedures have made provision towards SEA particularly with regard to landscape planning and zoning/building planning.	• Federal Ministry of Environment, Nature Protection and Nuclear Safety responsible for environmental integration. • National SD strategy and national climate protection programme (comprehensive framework with clear objectives and measures to reach these) exist, both support the integration of the environment on different decision-making levels and serve as coordinated strategies.	Germany is a federal country with 16 Länder and has detailed, comprehensive and differentiated environmental legislation, although, as yet there is no mandatory SEA. But a mandatory requirement for plan- and programme-making activities of public authorities requires all relevant concerns (including the environmental ones) to be considered and weighed against each other. A large number of

commissions and councils deal with the integration of environmental concerns into strategic decision-making, especially at local level. Considerable experience with Local Agenda 21: environmental reporting (including environmental data), the development of environmental indicators, tiered decision-making systems, e.g. within spatial and landscape planning, and other measures support the task of integrating environmental issues into policy-making. Due to a high degree of environmental consciousness and awareness NGOs often play a key role by strengthening environmental integration.

Long history of environmental planning; the 1980s saw the introduction of planning strategies and environmental policy plans including EIA regulations and strategic-level EIA. The environment is integrated to a strong extent. A tiered system of planning is in place with the environment being integrated throughout. National environmental policies are the main systems for integrating the environment into government policies, and for laying the foundation for environmental regulations and SD. All government policies are subject to a review process to assess their level of contribution to SD. SEA is mandatory in The Netherlands and takes the form of an E-test (introduced in 1995) for proposed legislation. A number of government ministries are responsible for environmental policy with a quality control system in place for the strategic assessment process. At the regional level, environmental integration takes place through a series of planning and environmental projects and involves a number of bodies including municipal authorities and environmental groups.

- Environmental ministries of the *Länder*.
- Environmental quality goals are in place, e.g. in many cities, often connected with Local Agenda 21 plans.
- Various environmental concerns are integrated in numerous laws; proposal for a homogeneous National Environmental Code with the intention to summarize, adjust and harmonize the environmental legislation. Different reporting (e.g. certain Enquete Commissions for the Parliament), coordination (e.g. regular conferences of all environmental ministers of the *Länder*) and awareness-raising measures exist and are able to support the integration of the environment.

Netherlands

SEA a legal requirement.
Environmental tests (E-tests) applied to existing and proposed legislation, policy plans and regulations. Recent assessments include an inventory of policy areas at national level and an E-test of the Fifth National Spatial Plan. Strategic-level EIA applied to decisions relating to spatial planning. Voluntary SEA methodology for application at most strategic levels developed in 1995 (Strategic Environmental ANalysis – SEAN).

- National environmental policy plans (NEPPs) are largely responsible for environmental integration into government policies.
- Four government ministries responsible for environmental policy, with the Ministry of Housing, Spatial Planning and Environment being the lead body, which is also responsible for coordination.
- The Netherlands has a tiered system of planning and there is a requirement that the environment be incorporated into each level.
- Commission on EIA for the provision of advice to local authorities and the assessment of the adequacy of environmental information.

Status of SEA (at the time of the adoption of the SEA Directive 2001/42/EC in 2001)	Examples of integration mechanisms	Commentary: extent of integration and role of EA
Spain SEA a legal requirement at regional level in the communities of Castilla-La Mancha, Castilla y León and the Basque Country. Other regions include certain PPP within the list of activities that require EIA. Environmental assessments occur during the preparation of regional development plans under EU structural fund regulations.	• Integration occurs mainly through consultative bodies at national and regional levels. At national level, the Ministry of Environment is responsible for developing national environmental plans and strategies. • Regional level is of primary importance for integration in Spain • SEA occurs at national level only through the Regional Development Plan (as required by the EC) for Objective 1 regions, and in those regions where SEA legislation has been passed (Castilla y León, Castilla-La Mancha and the Basque Country). • Otherwise, integration only takes place through consultative bodies (at national and regional level) and through the (unofficial) efforts of the National Network of Environmental Authorities. The Network is also the only body to issue guidance on integration. • At regional level, consultative bodies (regional environmental assessment councils) exist.	Spain has a pseudo-federal structure with 17 autonomous communities that have wide competencies in environmental policy development and implementation. At national level integration is very limited, mainly through a consultative body (which has been widely criticized and boycotted by NGOs). The other mechanism is the informal Network of Environmental Authorities, with inter-sectoral representation, and that has played a role mainly in establishing SEA guidance for the regional development plans, falling under the EC structural funds regulations. Three regions have passed SEA legislation (Castilla y León, Castilla-La Mancha and the Basque Country). At local level many municipalities have established Local Agenda 21s.
Sweden SEA a legal requirement. EIAs included in government bills and other proposals of comprehensive decision-making. Progress underway to include EIAs at early stage of political process under the Planning and Building Act. Research project also taking place on SEA case studies.	• National environmental quality goals for development in Sweden are elaborated within various areas and sectors and have been adopted by Parliament. National boards are responsible for formulation and implementation of action programmes for achieving the goals. • The overall legislative framework for implementation of goals and action programmes is the Environmental Code from 1999. The guiding principles on implementation of the Environmental Code are applicable to all sectors.	The Government has formulated national environmental quality goals for development in Sweden within various areas and sectors. National boards are responsible for formulation and implementation of action programmes for achieving the goals. The overall legislative framework for implementation of goals and action programmes is the Environmental Code from 1999. The Code, which is a result of a major review of environmental

- National and local-level Agenda 21.
- Environmental Protection Agency presents annual report on environmental policy work in Sweden to Parliament.

UK

SEA not a legal requirement. Environmental appraisals of development plans required under an administrative procedure. Government guidance on sustainability appraisal being extended to the regional planning level. Guidance on environmental appraisal of polices has also been published. Voluntary forms of SEA are also carried out on water resources strategies and multi-modal studies.

legislation, brings many specific laws together in one code. The Swedish Government has for a long time put SD very high on the political agenda and adopted a National Agenda 21. The Environmental Protection Agency supports Local Agenda 21 activities and local governments employ Local Agenda 21 coordinators.

- 'Greening Government' is a ten-year-old government strategy to integrate environmental considerations into government decision-making. A Cabinet-level committee on the environment (ENV) and the presence of a 'green minister' (GM) appointed in each government department are responsible for providing leadership and coordination to the strategy.
- The parliamentary Environmental Audit Committee (EAC) has been set up to audit national policy; and four statutory environmental agencies are responsible for monitoring pollution, biodiversity, national heritage and the landscape change on the ground.
- The Sustainable Development Unit (SDU) provides civil servant support and coordination to GMs and the ENV. The GMs are responsible for producing yearly departmental reports and the GM committee publishes an annual report to the ENV and the EAC.
- The Sustainable Development Commission provides a platform for key stakeholders (business and NGOs) to engage with the Government.
- Fifteen headline indicators as part of its National Sustainable Development Strategy, monitored annually.

As part of the Greening Government strategy a weak form of policy SEA was introduced in 1991 known as Policy Appraisal and the Environment (PAE). Other mechanisms within Greening Government have included setting up cross-departmental bodies at the highest level, identifying individuals with responsibilities for Greening Government and setting up institutions and strategies with an environmental or SD remit, including Local Agenda 21 in local authorities. Despite the institutions and mechanisms of Greening Government having been running for a decade it has not been particularly effective. Moreover PAE has been the least-used mechanism. The SDU has published guidance on the role of GMs and on undertaking SEAs of government policy. SEA-type processes have been introduced within regional planning (sustainability appraisal), local planning (environmental appraisal), water resources planning (SEA) and multi-modal transport planning. Generally SEA has been introduced through a mechanism of disseminating best practice guidance rather than specific regulations.

Appendix 11

Step-by-step Guidance on Application and Use of Procedures and Methods in SEA Good Practice

Source: Sadler (2001a)

Proposal:

Establish the need for and objectives of the proposed action

Before SEA is initiated, the responsible agency defines the basis for a proposed policy, bill, plan or programme. A preliminary statement should be made of the need, purpose and objectives to be achieved. These aims are not subject to review by an SEA, but the justification of a proposal is conditional on its environmental impact. The SEA process itself must be objectives-led in order to fully evaluate the environmental impacts of a proposal. Preparatory methods of identifying environmental objectives include policy and legal review (e.g. goals, standards and targets outlined in government strategy, obligations under international environmental agreements).

Screening:

Determine if an SEA is required and at what level of detail

Formal screening procedures can be divided into two types. Listed proposals subject to SEA are specified in legislation or guidelines. Case-by-case screening applies to all proposals to determine which ones have potentially significant environmental effects and warrant full assessment. Screening criteria and checklists from EIA can be readily adapted to this purpose, supplemented, as necessary, by policy tree diagrams and stakeholder consultation. Use of these methods also helps to indicate the type of approach and level of detail required for an SEA (e.g. policy appraisal versus impact assessment). For certain proposals, timing and tiering are important considerations in SEA screening decisions (e.g. at which level is SEA best carried out, how to relate it to any successive SEA and/or EIA process).

Scoping:

Identify the important issues and impacts that need to examined

EIA scoping procedure can be adapted to the different types of proposal subject to SEA. An early, transparent and systematic process should be followed to focus on the impacts that matter for decision-making and set terms of reference for further study. Modified EIA methods, such as matrices, overlays, and case comparisons can be used to scope the environmental dimensions of specific plans and programmes, e.g. to identify inconsistencies in their objectives, issues that require attention and/or the potential impact of implementing the proposal. Where environmental considerations are generalized and less immediate (e.g. proposed immigration, fiscal or trade policies), appraisal methods can be used, such as environmental scanning to clarify the implications, and/or issue tracking to a stage when key impacts become clarified (e.g. immigration projections linked to housing demand, nationally or regionally).

Information:

Assemble environmental information

The general content of information to be gathered in an SEA can be specified in legislation or procedure. The data that need to be gathered for a specific proposal will be clarified during screening and scoping. SEA is carried out against a baseline or profile, typically a description or characterization of the affected environment or media (e.g. air or water quality). Useful sources of background information include state of the environment reports and country environmental profiles. For plans and programmes with a spatial dimension, the baseline can be recorded as environmental stock and critical natural assets. Key indicators are used to measure change in terms of global sustainability, natural resource management and local environmental quality. Appropriate indicators for sector-specific proposals will depend on the key environmental impacts (e.g. emissions-based air quality indicators for energy, transport strategies).

Consideration of alternatives:

Identify and compare the range of alternatives, including a best practicable environmental option (BPEO)

Formulation of alternatives in the SEA process is central to integrating environment considerations into sector policy and plan-making. A first step is to identify the range of alternatives that meet the objectives of the proposal, and summarize their economic, social and environmental aspects. The alternatives should include a 'do nothing' alternative and BPEO. Where a large number of alternatives are potentially open, methods used to systematically compare them include environmental cost–benefit analysis and multi-criteria evaluation (e.g. formulation of national energy or water policy). The BPEO helps clarify the environmental trade-offs that are at stake, and the basis for choice. Objectives-led SEA is critical for this purpose, and also can empower risk and benefit negotiation (e.g. to reduce NO emissions as part of transport strategy).

Impact analysis:

Identify, predict and evaluate the effects of the proposal and the main alternatives

Usually, there is greater uncertainty to contend with in SEA of projects than in EIA. Often, the relationship of policy-level proposals to environmental effects is indirect or difficult to locate in time or space, mediated by intervening factors. Indicator-based methods can show 'direction of movement' for an impact, e.g. increase in habitat loss, reduction in volume of hazardous waste. Projection methods that are used to deal with uncertainty include trend extrapolation and scenario development. For plans and programmes that initiate projects, environmental impacts are more readily identified and predicted. EIA methods that are used with varying modification include impact matrices, geographical information systems (GIS) and comparative risk assessment. No single method is likely to be sufficient to cover the range of impacts in such cases.

Significance:

Determine the importance of the residual impacts and, if appropriate, relate these to other benefits and costs

To determine significance, predicted and residual impacts (that cannot be mitigated) are evaluated against selected environmental criteria and objectives. As in EIA, this test gives decision-makers a key proxy of the environmental acceptability of a proposal. If appropriate, a balance sheet of gains and losses from a proposal also can be drawn up, e.g. in monetary or descriptive terms, to show their distribution amongst groups, and/or to illustrate the range of uncertainty (worst/best case). If major policy options or critical outcomes are at stake, sensitivity analysis can be used to test the effect of changed assumptions and the robustness of assessment. Alternatively, this test can be based on expert judgement and case comparison with similar actions.

Mitigation:

Identify measures to avoid, reduce and offset the main impacts identified

The EIA mitigation hierarchy should be followed in SEA but with an eye to the greater opportunities for its creative application. So, first avoid, then reduce, and next offset, adverse impacts – using specific measures and actions that are appropriate to their significance and specificity. A precautionary approach should be taken when information is incomplete but analysis indicates the risk or possibility of large-scale, serious or irreversible environmental change. This may entail not going ahead with certain proposals or replacing them with 'no regrets' alternatives. For low-threat situations, standard mitigation measures can be used to minimize an impact to 'as low as reasonably practicable' (ALARP level), e.g. using 'best available technology not entailing excessive cost' (BATNEEC) or contingency policies and plans to cope with low probability but highly damaging risks.

Reporting:

Describe the environmental impacts of the proposal and how they are to be addressed

Typically, a separate SEA report or statement must be prepared and made available to the public. Other than certain prescribed information content, there is no common format. Depending on the context, a report can be an environmental paragraph in a policy memorandum, a *section or chapter* in a plan or strategy, or a separate document or annex ranging from a few to several hundred pages. The proposal itself should contain or be accompanied by a brief explanation of the SEA process and a summary of findings, e.g. key impacts, preferred alternative, mitigation measures and outstanding issues. Use of impact display and trade-off matrices help to focus decision-making. Change already made to a proposal as a result of an SEA should be noted on a policy record sheet.

Decision-making:

Approve, reject or modify the proposal, with reasons for decision

On submission to the final decision-making body, a proposal can be approved, rejected or modified (e.g. as a result of condition-setting). When doing so, the decision-making body has a duty or obligation to take account of the results of an SEA, including public consultation. Despite adverse environmental impact, a policy, bill or plan often will be accepted because the economic and social benefits are considered to outweigh the impact. Reasons for the decision should be issued, specifying the terms of approval and any follow-up requirements.

Monitoring:

Check to see implementation is environmentally sound and in accordance with approvals

Monitoring the implementation of a policy, bill or plan can be a simple check to see if environmental objectives are being met, or a systematic programme to measure its impact. Information tracking systems can be used to monitor issues and progress, and to focus and streamline any subsequent SEA or EIA process. Cumulative effects monitoring may be appropriate for plans and programmes that will initiate regional-scale change in environmental stock or critical natural assets. Methods and indicators for this purpose are not well developed.

Appendix 12

Considerations for UN Development Programme (UNDP) Quality Programming

Source: UNDP (2000)

The following considerations alert the manual user to quality dimensions in programming and are generic to all phases of the programming process. They serve as a reference in the preparation of cooperation frameworks, in programme and project design, in appraisals and in monitoring and evaluating actual performance.

1 Relevance
(a) How relevant are the programme or project objectives in relation to national priorities, the Poverty Reduction Strategy, Millennium Development Goals, and to the Country Programme, UN Development Assistance Framework, and Common Country Assessment?
(b) How relevant are the programme or project objectives to UN conference agreements and to the goals of the global and regional conventions to which the country is a signatory ?
(c) How relevant are the objectives in relation to the aspirations and needs of the target groups and the UNDP mission to promote sustainable human development?
(d) Has the programme or project context with its social, economic, political and environmental dimensions, and the problems and their root causes, been properly understood?

2 Stakeholder participation and partnership-building
(a) Have all the relevant stakeholders been identified, including government and civil society organizations, local communities, beneficiaries, donors and private sector?
(b) To what extent did the main stakeholders of the programme or project participate in the identification and design stages?
(c) Is the situation conducive to participation by all relevant stakeholders, and could the participation mechanisms be improved?

3 Contribution to poverty reduction

(a) Have poor people been identified and does the programme contribute to poverty reduction and, at a minimum, not make poor people worse off than before?

(b) Does the programme address the multidimensional nature of poverty at three fundamental levels: (i) macroeconomic policy; (ii) institutional change; (iii) micro-level interventions?

(c) Is the intervention creating an enabling environment for pro-poor economic growth?

(d) Are employment opportunities and jobs being created?

(e) Does the programme or project build on the assets and strengths of the target population and contribute to strengthening their livelihoods through access to productive assets?

4 Gender equality and the advancement of women

(a) Has all relevant gender information – with gender-disaggregated background data – been identified and have gender issues relevant to impact and anticipated outcomes been systematically identified and pursued?

(b) Is the participation of gender specialists or representatives from women's stakeholder groups ensured in all steps of the programme cycle?

(c) Has the proportion of target for resources assignment from the core (TRAC) and other resources allocated to the advancement of women been clearly indicated?

(d) Have all possible steps been taken to ensure gender equity in the recruitment of project staff and consultants?

5 Protection and regeneration of the environment

(a) Does the programme build on an adequate understanding of the biophysical dimensions, ecosystems and existing environment-related issues in the programme area?

(b) Is the management of land, forest, water and biological resources being improved in ways that ensure their protection and sustainable use?

(c) Does the programme improve the physical, social and economic access to food, water and energy services by impoverished people in rural and urban areas?

(d) Have the Environment Management Guidelines been applied, and is the proposed intervention environmentally sustainable?

(e) Does the programme have implications for the global environmental areas of climate change, loss of biodiversity, pollution of international waters, land degradation or ozone depletion?

6 Governance

(a) Does the programme or project take into account the policy environment and the necessary interrelationships between the government, civil society and the private sector, which underpin sustainability and achievement of objectives?

(b) Are governing institutions being strengthened for people-centred development?
(c) Is decentralization being promoted to support local governance and empower communities and local institutions?
(d) Is an efficient and accountable public sector being promoted that serves all citizens?

7 Most promising strategy

(a) Have a variety of potential strategies been identified and considered?
(b) Does the chosen operational strategy represent the most promising approach to addressing the development problem?
(c) Have the following issues been addressed?
  - social and environmental impacts and opportunities
  - risks and external factors
  - opportunities for synergies with other programmes
  - opportunity costs and trade-offs between various sustainable human development (SHD) dimensions.

8 Incorporation of lessons learned

(a) Has a review of relevant experiences of other development institutions within and outside the programme country been undertaken?
(b) Does the programme or project, in design and implementation, build upon lessons learned from experience?

9 Capacity development and sustainability

(a) Does the intervention contribute to capacity development, by which individuals, groups, organizations and communities develop their abilities to perform functions, solve problems, and set and reach objectives?
(b) Have the different dimensions of capacity at the systems, entity and individual levels been examined in defining the most promising operational strategy? (See the capacity assessment guidelines at: www.undp.org (Democratic Governance) Technical Advisory Paper No 3.)
(c) Have the management capacities been reviewed, and can capacity-building measures for management be improved?
(d) Do elements crucial to ensuring the sustainability of the programme or project results exist? For example:
  - enabling policies
  - financial support and mechanisms
  - individual and institutional capacities to carry on
  - sustainable resource management.
(e) Does the project, programme or country programme document (CPD) build national capacity to follow up UN conference agreements?

10 Feasibility and technical soundness

(a) Is there a logical relationship amongst the different programme or project elements, in other words objectives, outputs, activities, inputs and related indicators?

(b) Does the programme or project build on correct assumptions?

(c) Have risks and other external factors been identified and necessary safeguards incorporated into the design?

(d) Have risks been properly identified, including the potential for economic crisis, natural disasters, conflict and civil strive?

(e) Does the intervention allow adequate flexibility for redefinition and improvement of programme or project components to respond to complex and changing realities?

11 Management arrangements

(a) How effective are the proposed management arrangements?

(b) If national institutions or NGOs are designated to carry out certain activities without competitive bidding, has the justification for waiving competitive bidding been documented?

(c) If a management support unit is to be set up, has its cost-effectiveness as well as its impact on sustainability and capacity-building been documented?

(d) Where country office support is proposed, have cost-effectiveness, capacity-building measures and an exit strategy been documented?

(e) Are the implementation arrangements adequate and prior obligations and respective responsibilities clearly defined?

12 Integration, synergies, complementarity

(a) Does the intervention use the programme approach to the degree possible?

(b) Have linkages (poverty, gender, environment, governance, etc.) with other projects and programmes been identified and pursued?

(c) Does the programme support the mobilization of additional resources for development?

(d) Have opportunities for aid coordination been explored?

(e) Does the intervention provide added value whilst complementing the work of other development partners?

13 Results orientation

(a) Are adequate baseline data available to allow monitoring of progress and results?

(b) Are adequate indicators, benchmarks and means of verification identified to measure results, including the efforts on participation and partnership-building, gender, environment and so on?

(c) Have adequate mechanisms for monitoring and evaluation been established?

(d) Are the objectives clear, precise and measurable?

(e) Is it clear who is responsible for achieving the different results and undertaking the activities?

14 Resources and inputs

(a) Does the envisaged benefit justify the resources to be spent?

(b) Does the budget adequately cover the envisaged activities and are the respective inputs by the government, UNDP and other partners defined?
(c) Does the programme support document (PSD) or project document raise any policy issues concerning inputs?
(d) If the programme or project is to be partly or wholly funded by a contribution from the private sector, have adequate steps been taken to ensure that the association of UNDP with the private entity will be legal and beneficial?
(e) Have the procedures for financial management and reporting been described in the PSD or project document?

Appendix 13

Analytical Strategic Environmental Assessment (ANSEA)

Sources: FEEM (2002) and materials at:
www.taugroup.com/ansea

ANSEA was funded by the EU's Fifth Framework Research Programme and was an ambitious attempt to establish a framework for assisting the implementation of the SEA Directive. It identified, inter alia, a number of procedural steps and a methodological basis for a decision-centred approach. An important dimension from the perspective of the previous discussion is an evaluation of the extent to which environmental integration has been achieved. However, the influence of this project on the implementation of the SEA Directive in member states remains unclear, at best, and, at worst, it is likely to be of academic rather than practical interest

A consortium of eight institutions was established in 1999 to develop the initial ideas and concepts for ANSEA, established by TAU Consultora Ambiental (Spain). It was a two-year project (2000–2002), with the overall objective to provide a framework for assisting in the implementation of the European Directive on SEA (2001/42/EC) and also national directives and procedural requirements in this area. The project had three main objectives:

- development of a sound theoretical basis for SEA as a discussion platform for ANSEA;
- validation of the approach by testing its applicability in diverse institutional and decision-making contexts across Europe – through nine case studies from five countries in Europe and a review of SEA experiences in two additional countries; and
- dissemination activities to reach both the scientific audience and the main users in public administrations: books on the theoretical concepts and generic guidelines for applying the ANSEA framework; a public symposium; and a dedicated website (www.taugroup.com/ansea).

The objective of the ANSEA method is to provide a decision-centred approach to the SEA process. It seeks to provide tools to analyse and assess the decision-making process of PPP – either in an ex ante or an ex post (assessment or audit)

ASSESSMENT PROCESS STEPS   AVAILABLE TOOLS

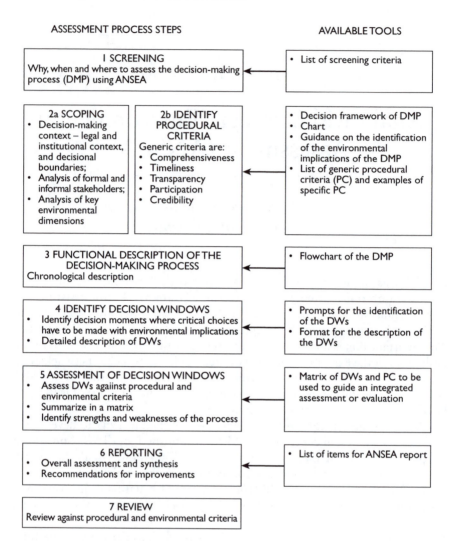

Note: Decision windows (DW) of opportunity = moments in the decision-making process where critical choices are made that have environmental implications. They consist of three components: inputs, analysis and outcomes (IAO framework). Inputs refer to data and information such as values and opinions. In the Analysis, the inputs are considered either formally (e.g. cost–benefit analysis modelling) or informally (e.g. expert judgement and group discussion). The outcomes can be both formal and informal, and will act as inputs in subsequent decision windows.

Procedural criteria = prescriptions on how a decision should be taken in a particular DW in terms of inputs, analysis and outcomes – based on principles of good decision-making and should represent values commonly accepted and held by society.

Source: FEEM (2002)

Figure A13.1 *Procedural steps for the ANSEA framework*

way, focusing on the decisions that are most critical to the environmental impact of PPP. The ANSEA method is designed to be used either as an objective and transparent approach to ensure that environmental considerations are taken into account, or as an evaluation of how far environmental integration has been achieved in decision-making processes. It is designed to be flexible for many types of application and to be undertaken either by the proponents of the PPP or by independent assessors. There is also the option for independent review and wide stakeholder participation is encouraged. The procedural steps are shown in Figure A13.1.

A final project symposium was organized in Milan in February 2002 to enable debate in integrated approaches to SEA in the light of the new EC SEA Directive. The ANSEA approach and outcomes of the project were presented to high-level representatives of European institutions, environment ministries and agencies, and EU researchers. It is unclear what the influence of this project will be on the implementation of the EC Directive in EU member states.

Appendix 14

Steps for Starting, Managing and Improving a Sustainable Development Strategy

Source: Modified from OECD/DAC (2001)

The following steps apply in full to strategy development tasks, that is those needed to scope out and establish the strategy by building on existing mechanisms, and/or initiating new mechanisms if necessary. But the same or similar tasks are then iterative during strategy coordination and continuous improvement.

A useful first step is to undertake an initial *scoping exercise* to identify stakeholders' views on priority issues that need to be addressed, and to estimate the benefits that might derive from developing and implementing a strategy. Such an exercise would involve a preliminary examination of the opportunities for, and challenges of, undertaking the steps suggested below.

It should not be assumed that the subsequent steps should be undertaken as a rigid sequence. In practice, many of them will need to be pursued in parallel and some might best make use of opportunities as they arise.

(a) Establish or strengthen *a secretariat or coordinating body* acceptable to stakeholders, with sufficient authority and resources to coordinate the steps outlined, and the continuing strategy mechanisms.

(b) Establish or strengthen a *steering committee or equivalent multi-stakeholder forum* (e.g. the National Council for Sustainable Development) with a broad balance of representation from government, the private sector and civil society acceptable to stakeholders.

(c) Seek or improve *political commitment* to the strategy preparation and implementation process from the highest levels as well as all other levels.

(d) Secure or confirm a *mandate* for the strategy. The more this represents domestic public demand with high-level support, rather than external mandates, the better.

(e) *Identify the stakeholders* that will own the preparation and implementation of an integrated sustainable development strategy, and encourage discussion of their (potential) roles.

(f) Ensure *broad-based ownership* by key ministries and agencies, civil society and the private sector.

(g) Mobilize the *required resources*. Identify, secure and allocate, in a timely and accountable manner, the required:
- skills, and sources of knowledge and learning
- management, legal and institutional support
- financial resources.

(h) Define and seek agreement on the *roles of stakeholders* (i.e. their rights, responsibilities, rewards, and relations) – private sector, civil society (e.g. NGOs, local communities), donors, national and local government, the secretariat, and so on.

(i) *Map out the strategy process*, taking stock of *existing processes and mechanisms*:
- catalogue the range of existing strategies related to sustainable development
- identify the issues covered, vision, goals and responsibilities
- identify mechanisms and processes used by existing strategies
- review achievements of these mechanisms in terms of synergies, clashes and gaps, and their outcomes
- determine the existence/extent of sectoral policy conflicts and inconsistencies, and the work necessary to resolve them
- identify what is required to improve synergies and plug gaps.

(j) Develop or improve *coherence and coordination* between strategy frameworks at all levels from international to local; and between and within sectors.

(k) Establish or improve the *ground rules* governing the strategy process:
- debate and agree how all decisions will be made and agreed, and uncertainty dealt with
- coordinate means for negotiation of trade-offs and conflict management.

(l) Establish and promote a *schedule or broad calendar* for the strategy process – determine activities, responsibilities, capabilities and resources needed, and their timing.

(m) *Promote the strategy* as a unified concept. Possibly publish a *prospectus* for the strategy outlining all the above.

(n) Establish or improve provisions for *regular analysis, debate, communication, planning, implementation, monitoring and review*; to ensure that all stakeholders are best able to play their part in the strategy. These processes are the 'heart' of the strategy and are discussed in detail in separate chapters. They will involve establishing or improving:
- *means for analysing* sustainability, stakeholders, mechanisms and processes, and scenarios
- *regular stakeholder forums and other means for participation* (thematic, national, decentralized and local) to reach and improve consensus on the basic vision, goals, principles, system components, pilot activities, targets and responsibilities, and to review progress

- *communication and information systems* to ensure regular flows of information concerning both the strategy and sustainable development between stakeholders and between forums. This will include development of key information products to improve awareness and stimulate action, and the establishment of knowledge management systems to ensure sharing of experience and facilitate collective learning
- *major decision-making arrangements*, notably: structures and roles; handling global and local values and risk; means of delivering consensus and handling negotiations; and ways of linking those involved
- *implementation services and control mechanisms* – means for selecting policy implementation instruments (regulations, incentives and voluntary mechanisms) and applying them
- *means for planning investments* – tasks involved in making the case to different investment sources, and the criteria that should be used
- *monitoring and accountability mechanisms* to assess both strategy processes and their results. These will include: developing and reviewing sustainability indicators, baselines, standards and codes of practice; identifying and encouraging innovative processes to promote the culture of action-learning; independent monitoring; and feedback to decision-making.

References

Abaza H., Bisset R. and Sadler B. (2004) *Environmental Impact Assessment and Strategic Environmental Assessment: Towards an Integrated Approach*. Economics and Trade Branch, UNEP, Geneva, Switzerland

ADB (1988) *Guidelines for Integrated Regional Economic-cum-environmental Development Planning*. Volumes I and II, Asian Development Bank, Manila, Philippines

ADB (1994) *Evaluation Study of the Bank's Experience in the Preparation and Review of Environmental Assessment Reports*. Asian Development Bank, Manila, Philippines

ADB (2000) *Asian Development Outlook*. Asian Development Bank, Manila, Philippines

Adhikari A. P. and Khadka R. B. (eds) (1998) *Strategic Environmental Assessment: Proceedings of the South and Southeast Asian Regional Training Workshop on Strategic Environmental Assessment*. Jointly organized by AREAP, IUCN Nepal and the Netherlands Commission for EIA, 18–20 September 1997, Kathmandu, Nepal, Asian Regional Environmental Assessment Program, IUCN, Nepal

Ahmed K. and Mercier J. R. (2004) 'Strategic Environment Assessment at the World Bank'. In CEAA (ed) *Status of Progress and Emerging Challenges in EIA and SEA: Ten Years after the Quebec Summit*, proceedings of the 8th Intergovernmental Policy Forum on Environmental Assessment, 25 April 2004, Vancouver, BC, Canadian Environmental Assessment Agency, Ottawa

AIDEnvironment and SNV (1999) *Strategic Environmental Analysis Toolbox*. SNV, The Hague, The Netherlands

Alcamo J. (2002) *Scenarios as Tools for International Environmental Assessments*. Experts Corner Report, Prospects and Scenarios No 5, European Environment Agency, Copenhagen

Allen Consulting Group Pty Ltd (2003) *Proposed Access to Barrow Island for Gas Development: Advice on Social, Economic and Strategic Considerations*. A report to the Western Australia Department of Industry and Resources, The Allen Consulting Group Pty Ltd, Perth, Western Australia

Alzina V. and Spinosa G. (eds) (2001) *Revisión de la Evaluación de Impacto Ambiental en Países de America Latina y el Caribe – Methodologica, Resultados y Tendnecias*. Inter-American Development Bank and Centro de Estudios para el Desarollo (CEED), Santiago de Chile

Amoyaw-Osei Y. (1997) *Developing Strategic EA Capacity in a Developing Country: The Ghana Experience*. Paper presented to the 17th Annual Meeting of the International Association for Impact Assessment, New Orleans, USA

André P., Delisle C. E. and Revéret J. P. (2003) *L'Évaluation des Impacts sur L'environnement, Processus, Acteurs et Pratiques pour un Développement Durable* (evaluation of environmental impacts – Processes, actors and practices for sustainable development). Presses Internationales Polytechniques, Montreal

André P., Delisle C. E. and Revéret J. P. (2004) *Environmental Assessment for Sustainable Development: Processes, Actors and Practice.* Presses Internationales Polytechnique, Montreal

Andrianaivomahefa P. (2001) *L'Évaluation Environnementale Stratégique à Madagascar: Un État de la Situation* (Strategic Environmental Assessment in Madagascar: Taking Stock of the Situation). Presentation to the 5th international colloquium of francophone specialists in impact assessment, on the topic 'strategic environmental assessments', Paris, 22–24 May 2000

Annandale D., Bailey J., Ouano E., Evans W. and King P. (2001) 'The Potential Role of Strategic Environmental Assessment in the Activities of Multi-lateral Development Banks'. *Environmental Impact Assessment Review*, 21, 407–429

Arbter K., Bass R., Therivel R. and Rakos Ch. (2000) *Handbook on Strategic Environmental Assessment – Environmental Assessment of Policies, Plans and Programmes.* Institute of Technology Assessment, Austrian Academy of Sciences, Vienna (available only in German)

Aschemann R. (2004) 'Lessons Learned from Austrian SEAs'. *European Environment*, 14 (3), 165–174

Ashe J. (2001) *The Australian Regional Forest Agreement Process: A Case Study in Integrated Assessment and Decision Making.* Paper presented to the Annual Meeting of the International Association for Impact Assessment (IAIA'01), Cartagena, Colombia

Ashe J. (2002) 'The Australian Regional Forest Agreement Process: A Case Study in Strategic Natural Resource Assessment'. In Marsden S. and Dovers S. (eds) *Strategic Environmental Assessment in Australia*, The Federation Press, Leichhardt, NSW, pp156–181

Au E. (1998) 'Analysis of Environmental Sustainability of Hong Kong's Territorial Development Strategy Review: Lessons and Experiences. *Environmental Assessment*, 6

Au E. (2004) 'EIA and SEA in Hong Kong Special Administrative Region'. In CEAA (ed) *Status of Progress and Emerging Challenges in EIA and SEA: Ten Years after the Quebec Summit*, proceedings of the 8th Intergovernmental Policy Forum on Environmental Assessment, 25 April 2004, Vancouver BC, Canadian Environmental Assessment Agency, Ottawa

Auckland Regional Growth Forum (1999a) *A Vision for Managing Growth in the Auckland Region: Auckland Regional Growth Strategy, 2050.* Auckland Regional Council, Auckland

Auckland Regional Growth Forum (1999b) *The Auckland Regional Growth Strategy 2050.* Auckland Regional Growth Forum, Auckland

Bailey J. and Dixon J. (1999) 'Policy Environmental Assessment'. In Petts J. (ed) *Handbook of Environmental Impact Assessment*, Volume 1, Blackwell Scientific Ltd, Oxford, UK, pp251–272

Bailey J. and Rention S. (1997) 'Redesigning EIA to Fit the Future: SEA and the Policy Process'. *Impact Assessment*, 15 (4), 319–334

Bass R. and Herson A. (1999) 'Environmental Impact Assessment of Land Use Plans: Experience under the National Environmental Policy Act and the California Environmental Quality Act'. In Petts J. (ed) *Handbook of Environmental Impact Assessment*, Volume 2, Blackwell Scientific Ltd, Oxford, UK, pp273–299

Bass S. M. J., Dalal-Clayton D. B. and Pretty J. (1995) *Participation in Strategies for Sustainable Development.* Environmental Planning Issues No 7, International Institute for Environment and Development, London

Belčáková I. (2003a) *Strategic Environmental Assessment Experience in Land-use Planning in the Slovak Republic*. Paper presented at the International Workshop on Environmental Impact Assessment, Teplý Vrch, Slovakia, 2003

Belčáková I. (2003b) *SEA of Bratislava Land Use Plan*. Presentation at the Workshop on SEA in Selected EU Accession Countries, Regional Environmental Center for Central and Eastern Europe, Szentendre, Hungary, 28–29 April 2003

Bellinger, E. et al (eds) (2000) *Environmental Assessment in Countries in Transition*, Wiley, Chichester, UK

Bertrand F. (2001) *L'Évaluation Environnementale Stratégique de Programmes de Planification Régionale: Analyse du Cadre Réglementaire Français et Européen* (Strategic Environmental Assessment of Regional Planning: Analysis of the French and European Regulatory Framework). Paper presented to the 5th international colloquium of francophone specialists in impact assessment, on the topic 'strategic environmental assessments', Paris, 22–24 May 2000

Bertrand G., Michalski A. and Pench L. (1999) *Scenarios Europe 2010: Five Possible Futures for Europe*. Working Paper, European Commission Forward Studies Unit (available at: http://europa.int/comm/cdp/scenario/resume/index_en.htl)

Bina O. (1999) *SEA to Date, Recent Advances and Current Priorities for Development*. Paper presented at the OECD/ECMT Conference on Strategic Environmental Assessment for Transport, 14–15 October 1999, Warsaw, Poland (available at: www.oecd.org/cem/topics/env/SEA99.htm)

Bina O. (2003) *Re-conceptualising Strategic Environmental Assessment: Theoretical Overview and Case Study from Chile*. PhD thesis, University of Cambridge, UK

Bitondo D., Bomba C. and Huh Abazoa A. (1997) *Preliminary Environmental Impact Assessment of the Programme of Revitalisation of Fossilised Valleys of Senegal*. Paper presented to the 17th Annual Meeting of the International Association for Impact Assessment, New Orleans, USA

Blanco H. (in press) 'Evaluación de la Sustentabiidad de Acuerdos Comerciales y su Aplicación en el Contexto Latinoamericano y del ALCA'. In Murillo C., Araya M. and Blanco H. (eds) *ALCA y Medio Ambiente: Ideas desde Lationoamérica*, Centro de Investigación y Planificación del Medio Ambiente (CIPMA), Santiago de Chile

Bockemuehl L. (2003) *Strategische Umweltprüfung im Landesstraßenbedarfsplan des Brandenburger Landesentwicklungsplans*. Straßenverkehrstechnik 5/2003

Bojo J. and Reddy R.C. (2003a) *Environmental Review of PRSPs: Vietnam*. Environment Department, World Bank, Washington DC (May 2003)

Bojo J. and Reddy R.C. (2003b) *Status and Evolution of Environmental Priorities in the Poverty Reduction Strategies: An Assessment of Fifty Poverty Reduction Strategy Papers*. Paper 93, Environmental Economics Series, Environment Department, World Bank, Washington DC (November 2003)

Bregha F. et al (1990) *The Integration of Environmental Factors in Government Policy-making*. Canadian Environmental Assessment Research Council, Ottawa

Brito E. and Verocai I. (2002) 'Latin America and the Caribbean'. In *Environmental Assessment Yearbook 2002*, Institute of Environmental Management and Assessment, Lincoln, UK, and EIA Centre, University of Manchester, UK

Bromley D. W. (1995) *Natural Resource Issues in Environmental Policy in South Africa*. Land and Agriculture Policy Centre, Witwatersrand, South Africa

Brook C. and Sadler B. (1998) *Strategic Environmental Appraisal*. Department of the Environment, Transport and the Regions, London

Brown C. J. (ed) (1992) *Namibia's Green Plan*. Ministry of Environment and Tourism, Windhoek, Namibia

Brown A. L. (1997a) 'The Environmental Overview in Development Assistance Project Formulation'. *Impact Assessment*, 15, 73–88

Brown A. L. (1997b) *Further SEA Experience in Development Assistance Using the Environmental Overview*. Paper delivered at the IAIA'97 Conference, New Orleans, US, 28–30 May 1997

Brown A. L. and Therivel R. (2000) 'Principles to Guide the Development of Strategic Environmental Assessment Methodology'. *Impact Assessment and Project Appraisal*, 18 (3), 183–190

Buselich K. (2002) *An Outline of Current Thinking on Sustainability Assessment*. Background paper prepared for the Western Australian State Sustainability Strategy, Institute for Sustainability and Technology Policy, Murdoch University, Western Australia

Caldwell L. K. (1998) 'Implementing Policy through Procedure: Impact Assessment and the National Environmental Policy Act'. In Porter A. and Fittipaldi J. (eds) *Environmental Methods Review: Retooling Impact Assessment for the New Century*. International Association for Impact Assessment, Fargo, US, pp8–14

Carew-Reid J., Prescott-Allen R., Bass S. and Dalal-Clayton D. B. (1994) *Strategies for National Sustainable Development: A Handbook for their Planning and Implementation*. International Institute for Environment and Development (IIED), London and World Conservation Union (IUCN), Gland, Switzerland in association with Earthscan, London

CEAA (1999) *Cabinet Directive on the Environmental Assessment of Policy, Plan and Program Proposals*. Canadian Environmental Assessment Agency, Government of Canada, Ottawa

CEAA (2000) *Guidelines for Implementing the Cabinet Directive on SEA*. Canadian Environmental Assessment Agency, Ottawa (available on the Agency's website at: www.ceaa.acee.gc.ca/0011/0002/dir_e.htm#guidelines)

CEAA (ed) (2004) *Status of Progress and Emerging Challenges in EIA and SEA: Ten Years after the Quebec Summit*. Proceedings of the 8th Intergovernmental Policy Forum on Environmental Assessment, 25 April 2004, Vancouver BC, Canadian Environmental Assessment Agency, Ottawa

CEC (1998) *Handbook on Environmental Assessment of Regional Development Plans and EU Structural Funds*. DG-Environment, Commission of the European Communities, Brussels (http://europa.eu.int/comm./environment/eia/)

CEC (2001) *A Sustainable Europe for a Better World – A European Strategy for Sustainable Development*. COM (2001) 264 final, Commission of the European Community, Brussels

CEC (2002) *Communication from the Commission to the European Parliament, the Council, The Economic and Social Committee and the Committee of the Regions: Towards a Global Partnership for Sustainable Development*. COM (2002), Commission of the European Communities, Brussels

CEQ (1975) *Environmental Quality*. The Sixth Annual Report of the (US) Council on Environmental Quality, US Government Printing Office, Washington DC

CEQ (1986) *Regulations for Implementing the Procedural Provisions of the National Environmental Policy Act*. Reprint 40 CFR Parts 1500–1508, Council on Environmental Quality, US Government Printing Office, Washington DC

CEQ (1997) *The National Environmental Policy Act – A Study of its Effectiveness after Twenty-five Years*, Council on Environmental Quality, Washington DC

Che Xiuzchen, Shang Jincheng and Wang Jinhu (2002) 'Strategic Environmental Assessment and its Development in China'. *Environmental Impact Assessment Review*, 22, 101–109

Cherp A. (2000a) 'Integrating Environmental Appraisals of Planned Developments into Decision-making in Countries in Transition'. In Lee N. and Kirkpatrick C. (eds) *Sustainable Development and Integrated Appraisal in a Developing World*, Edward Elgar, Cheltenham, UK

Cherp A. (2000b) 'Environmental Impact Assessment in Belarus'. In Bellinger E. et al (eds) *Environmental Assessment in Countries in Transition*, John Wiley and Sons, Chichester, UK

Cherp A. (2001) 'SEA in Newly Independent States'. In Dusik J. (ed) *Proceedings of International Workshop on Public Participation and Health Aspects in Strategic Environmental Assessment*, Regional Environmental Center for Central and Eastern Europe, Szentendre, Hungary

Cherp A. (2002) 'The Newly Independent States'. In *Environmental Assessment Yearbook 2002*, Institute of Environmental Management and Assessment, Lincoln, UK, and EIA Centre, University of Manchester, UK, pp106–108

Cherp A. and Golubeva S. (2004) 'Environmental Assessment in the Russian Federation'. *Impact Assessment and Project Appraisal*, 22, 121–130

Cherp A. and Lee N. (1997) 'Evolution of SER and OVOS in the Soviet Union and Russia (1985–1996)'. *EIA Review*, 17, 177–204

ChevronTexaco Australia Pty Ltd (2003) *Environmental, Social and Economic Review of the Gorgon Gas Development on Barrow Island*. ChevronTexaco Australia Pty Ltd, Perth, Western Australia (available at: www.gorgon.com.au/readour_submenu.htm)

Chinese Academy of Environmental Planning (2002) *Strategic Environmental Impact Assessment of the Great Western Development Strategy in China – Interim Report* (November 2002)

Chonguiça E. and Katerere Y. (2002) *Assessing the Need for a Regional Approach to Assessing Cumulative and Trans-boundary Impacts of Development Investment in Southern Africa*. Paper presented to the IUCN/SADC-ELMS regional conference on the need for a regional approach to EIA in Southern Africa, 27–31 May, Maputo, Mozambique

Chonguiça E. et al (1998) *Overview and Initial Environmental Assessment of the PROAGRI [Agricultural Sector Development Programme] – Phase 1*. Prepared by IUCN-Mozambique for the PROAGRI Executive Secretariat, Ministry of Agriculture and Fisheries, Maputo, Mozambique

CIDA (2003) *Strategic Environmental Assessment (SEA) Handbook*. Draft, Canadian International Development Agency, Hull, Quebec

CIDA/DGIS (1997) *Strategic Environmental Assessment in Development Cooperation: State-of-the-Art Review. Final Report*. Submitted by a Steering Committee Composed of Canada (CIDA) and the Netherlands (DGIS) to the OECD/DAC Working Party on Development Assistance and Environment (September 1997), DAC, Paris

Clark R. and Richards D. (1999) 'EIA in North America'. In Petts J. (ed) *Handbook of Environmental Impact Assessment*, Volume 2, Blackwell Scientific Ltd, Oxford, UK, pp203–222

Commissioner of the Environment and Sustainable Development (1998) *Report of the Commissioner of the Environment and Sustainable Development*. Chapter 8: 'Environmental Assessment – A Critical Tool for Sustainable Development', Government of Canada, Ottawa

Commissioner of the Environment and Sustainable Development (1999) *Report of the Commissioner of the Environment and Sustainable Development*. Chapter 9:

'Greening Policies and Programs – Supporting Sustainable Development Decisions', Government of Canada, Ottawa

CONAMA (undated) *La Evaluación Ambiental Estratégica Un Instrumento de Gestión Ambiental para ser Aplicado en el País*, Comisión Nacional del Medio Ambiente.

CONAMA (1998) *Una Política Ambiental para el Desarrollo Sustentable*, aprobado por el Consejo Directivo de Ministros de la Comisión Nacional del Medio Ambiente, en la Sesión del 9 de enero de 1998, Chile

Connelly R. (2004) 'Environmental Assessment in Canada: Past Successes and Future Challenges'. Briefing paper in CEAA (ed) *Status of Progress and Emerging Challenges in EIA and SEA: Ten Years after the Quebec Summit*, proceedings of the 8th Intergovernmental Policy Forum on Environmental Assessment, 25 April 2004, Vancouver BC, Canadian Environmental Assessment Agency, Ottawa

Conservation Commission of Western Australia (2003) *Biodiversity Conservation Values on Barrow Island Nature Reserve and the Gorgon Gas Development: Advice to Government from the Conservation Commission of Western Australia*. Conservation Commission of Western Australia, Crawley, Western Australia

Council of the European Communities (1997) 'Proposal for a Council Directive on the Assessment of the Effects of Certain Plans and Programmes on the Environment'. *Official Journal of the European Communities*, European Commission, Brussels, C1997/129/08, 14–18,

Counsell D. and Haughton G. (2002) 'Sustainability Appraisal – Delivering More Sustainable Regional Planning Guidance?'. *Town and Country Planning*, 25, 411–433

Croal P. (2003) *Quantitative Analysis of Poverty Reduction Strategy Papers (PRSPs) for Poverty/Environment Linkages and Integration*. Draft discussion methodology, Southern African Institute for Environmental Assessment, Windhoek, Namibia

CSIR (1996) *Strategic Environmental Assessment: A Primer*. Council for Scientific and Industrial Research, Stellenbosch, South Africa

CSIR (1997a) *A Protocol for Strategic Environmental Assessment in South Africa*. Draft discussion document, 21 August 1997, Council for Scientific and Industrial Research, Stellenbosch, South Africa

CSIR (1997b) *Feasibility Study. Strategic Environmental Assessment for the Proposed East London Industrial Development Zone*. Draft, Council for Scientific and Industrial Research, Division of Water, Environment and Forestry Technology, Durban, South Africa (8 August 1997)

CSIR (2002) *Strategic Environmental Assessment (SEA) Resource Document. Introduction to the Process, Principle and Application of SEA Version 1*. CSIR Report ENV-S-C-2002-073, Stellenbosch, South Africa (August 2002)

Cupei J. (1994) *Vermeidung von Wettbewerbsverzerrungen – Eine Vergleichende Analyse der Umsetzung der UVP-Richtlinie in Frankreich, Großbritannien und den Niederlanden*. Nomos Verlagsgesellschaft, Baden-Baden, Germany

Dalal-Clayton D. B. (1993) *Modified EIA and Indicators of Sustainability: First Steps Towards Sustainability Analysis*. Environmental Planning Issues No 1, International Institute for Environment and Development, London

Dalal-Clayton D. B. (1996) *Getting to Grips with Green Plans: A Review of Recent Experience in Industrial Countries*. Earthscan, London

Dalal-Clayton D. B. (1997) *Southern Africa Beyond the Millenium: Environmental Trends and Scenarios to 2015*. Environmental Planning Issues No 13, International Institute for Environment and Development, London

Dalal-Clayton D. B. and Bass S. (2002) *Sustainable Development Strategies: A Resource Book*. Organisation for Economic Co-operation and Development, Paris, and United

Nations Development Programme, New York, in association with Earthscan, London

Dalal-Clayton D. B. and Dent D. L. (2002) *Knowledge of the Land: Land Resources Information and its Use in Rural Development.* Oxford University Press, Oxford, UK

Dalal-Clayton D. B. and Sadler B. (1995) *Strategic Environmental Assessment. A Briefing Paper.* International Institute for Environment and Development, London

Dalal-Clayton D. B. and Sadler B. (1998a) *The Application of Strategic Environmental Assessment in Developing Countries: Recent Experience and Future Prospects, including its Role in Sustainable Development Strategies.* Unpublished manuscript, International Institute for Environment and Development, London

Dalal-Clayton D. B. and Sadler B. (1998b) 'Strategic Environmental Assessment: A Rapidly Evolving Approach'. In Donnelly A., Dalal-Clayton D. B. and Hughes R. (eds) *A Directory of Impact Assessment Guidelines (Second Edition)*, International Institute for Environment and Development, London, pp31–42

Dalal-Clayton D. B. and Sadler B. (2004) *Sustainability Appraisal: A Review of Experience and Practice.* Draft, International Institute for Environment and Development, London (available at: www.iied.org)

Dalal-Clayton D. B., Dent D. and Dubois O. (2003) *Rural Planning in Developing Countries.* Earthscan, London

Dalal-Clayton D. B., Swiderska K. and Bass S. (2002) *Stakeholder Dialogues on Sustainable Development Strategies: Lessons, Opportunities and Developing Country Case Studies.* Environmental Planning Issues No 26, International Institute for Environment and Development, London

Dalal-Clayton D. B., Bass S., Sadler B., Thomson K., Sandbrook R., Robins N. and Hughes R. (1994) *National Sustainable Development Strategies: Experience and Dilemmas.* Environmental Planning Issues No 6, International Institute for Environment and Development, London

Dalkmann H. and Bongardt D. (2004) 'Case Study – The German Federal Transport Infrastructure Plan (FTIP)'. In Caratti P., Dalkmann H. and Jiliberto R. (eds) *Analysing Strategic Environmental Assessment. Towards Better Decision Making,* FEEM, Edward Elgar, Cheltenham, UK

d'Almeida K. (2003) *Cadre Institutionnel Législatif et Réglementaire de l'Évaluation Environnementale dans les Pays Francophones d'Afrique et de l'Océan Indien: Les Indicateurs de Fonctionnalité, les Écarts Fondamentaux et les Besoins Prioritaires* (The Legislative and Regulatory Institutional Framework for Environmental Assessment in the Francophone Countries of Africa and the Indian Ocean: Indicators of Functionality, Fundamental Discrepancies and Priority Needs). Essay on typology, Institute for Energy and the Environment in Francophone Countries, and Francophone Secretariat of the International Association for Impact Assessment (AIEI/IAIA), Montreal

Dalziel A. and Ward M. (2004) 'EIA and SEA in New Zealand'. In CEAA (ed) *Status of Progress and Emerging Challenges in EIA and SEA: Ten Years after the Quebec Summit,* proceedings of the 8th Intergovernmental Policy Forum on Environmental Assessment, 25 April 2004, Vancouver BC, Canadian Environmental Assessment Agency, Ottawa

DEAT (2000) *Strategic Environmental Assessment in South Africa, Guideline Document.* ISBN 0-621-29925-1, Department of Environmental Affairs and Tourism, Pretoria, South Africa

DEAT/CSIR (2000) *Strategic Environmental Assessment in South Africa: Guideline Document.* Department of Environmental Affairs and Tourism and Council for Scientific and Industrial Research, Pretoria, South Africa

de Boer J. J. and Sadler B. (eds) (1996) *Environmental Assessment of Policies: Briefing Papers on Experience in Selected Countries*, Ministry of Housing, Spatial Planning and the Environment, Report No 54, The Hague

de Jong D. and Noteboom S. (2001) 'Verdwaten we in een Woud van Beleidstoetsen?' (Getting Lost Among the Policy Tests). In *Openbaar Bestur* (Public Management), DHV Netherlands, Amersfoort, The Netherlands

Department of Environmental Affairs (1992) *Integrated Environmental Management Procedure*. Guideline Document No 1, Integrated Environmental Management Guideline Series, Department of Environmental Affairs, Pretoria, South Africa

Department of Prime Minister and Cabinet (2003) *Sustainable Development for New Zealand: Programme of Action*. Department of Prime Minister and Cabinet, Wellington, New Zealand

DETR (1997) *Experience with the 'Policy Appraisal and the Environment' Initiative*. Report from KPMG Consultants, Department of Environment, Transport and the Regions, London (July 1997)

DETR (1998) *Policy Appraisal and the Environment: Policy Guidance*. The Stationery Office, London

DETR (1999a) *Good Practice Guide on Sustainability Appraisal of Regional Planning Guidelines*. Department of Environment, Transport and the Regions, HMSO, London

DETR (1999b) *Planning Policy Guidance Note 12: Development Plans*. The Stationery Office, London

DETR (2000) 'Sustainability Appraisal of Regional Planning Guidance: Good Practice Guide' [online] available at: www.odpm.gov.uk/stellent/groups/odpm_planning/documents/page/odpm_plan_606126.hcsp

de Vries Y. (1996) 'The Netherlands Experience'. In de Boer J. and Sadler B. (eds) *Environmental Assessment of Policies*, Report No 54, Netherlands Ministry of Housing, Spatial Planning and the Environment, The Hague, The Netherlands

de Vries Y. (1998) 'SEA of Government Policies in The Netherlands'. *EIA Newsletter*, 16, 7–8

de Vries Y. and Tonk J. (1997) 'Assessing Draft Regulations – The Dutch Experience'. *Environmental Assessment*, 5 (3), 37–38 (special issue on Strategic Environmental Assessment, September 1997)

DFAIT (2001) *Framework for Conducting Environmental Assessments of Trade Negotiations*. Department of Foreign Affairs and International Trade, Ottawa

DGA (1998) *Plan Director para la Gestión de los Recursos hídricos en la Cuenca del Río San José*. Volume 1, Informe Final Junio de 1998, Ministerio de Obras Públicas, Dirección General de Aguas, Santiago de Chile

DGA/MOPTT/World Bank (2002) *Evaluación Ambiental Regional de la Cuenca del Río Elqui*. Dirección General de Aguas/MOPTT/World Bank, Santiago de Chile (July 2002)

DGOTDU (2003) *Guia para Avaliação Estrategica de Impactes em Ordenamento do Territorio, Coordenação*. Direcção-Geral do Ordenamento do Território e Desenvolvimento Urbano (Directorate-General for Spatial Planning and Urban Development, Ministry of Environment), Lisbon, Portugal

DHV (1996) *Strategic Environmental Assessment Study of Transport Policy. Environmental Issues Associated with Transport Planning in the Republic of Slovenia, Final Report*. Report prepared for the Ministry of Environmental Protection and Physical Planning, Ministry of Transport and Communications, Slovenia, and European Union/PHARE, DHV Consultants BV, Amersfoort, The Netherlands (May 1996)

Dixon J. (1994) *Strategic Environmental Assessment in New Zealand: A Progress Report*. Paper presented to the Annual Meeting of the International Association for Impact Assessment, Quebec City, Canada

Dixon J. (2002) 'All at Sea with SEA'. In Marsden S. and Dovers S. (eds) *Strategic Environmental Assessment in Australia*, The Federation Press, Leichhardt, NSW, pp195–210

Djeri-Allassani K. B. (2001) *La Législation Environnementale Face à la Montée des Évaluations Environnementales Stratégiques* (Environmental Legislation Faced with the Rise of Strategic Environmental Assessments). Presentation to the 5th international colloquium of francophone specialists in impact assessment, on the topic 'strategic environmental assessments', Paris, 22–24 May 2000

DMEE (1995a) *Guidance on Procedures for Environmental Assessment of Bills and Other Proposals*. Danish Ministry of Energy and Environment, Copenhagen (first published in Danish, 1993)

DMEE (1995b) *Strategic Environmental Assessment of Bills and Other Proposals: Examples and Experience*. Danish Ministry of Energy and Environment, Copenhagen (first published in Danish, 1994)

Doberstein B. (2003) 'Environmental Capacity-building in a Transitional Economy: The Emergence of EIA Capacity in Vietnam'. *Impact Assessment and Project Appraisal*, 21 (1), 25–42

DoE (1990) *This Common Inheritance*. The Stationery Office, London

DoE (1991) *Policy Appraisal and the Environment*. The Stationery Office, London

DoE (1992) *Planning Policy Guidance Note 12: Development Plans and Regional Guidance*. The Stationery Office, London

DoE (1993) *Environmental Appraisal of Development Plans: A Good Practice Guide*. The Stationery Office, London

DoE (1994) *Environmental Appraisal in Government Departments*. The Stationery Office, London

DTI (2001) 'Strategic Environmental Assessment of the Former White Zone Volume 1 – An Overview of SEA Process, Key Issues and Findings'. Final issue [online] available at: www.offshore-sea.org.uk/sea/dev/html_file/library_sea1.php

Dusik J. (ed) (2001) *Proceedings of International Workshop on Public Participation and Health Aspects in Strategic Environmental Assessment*. Regional Environmental Center for Central and Eastern Europe, Szentendre, Hungary

Dusik J. (2003a) *Evolution of SEA in CEE*. Unpublished draft, Regional Environmental Center for Central and Eastern Europe, Szentendre, Hungary

Dusik J. (2003b) 'EIA and SEA Capacity Building in Central and Eastern Europe: Lessons from the Sofia EIA Initiative'. In *Environmental Assessment Yearbook 2003*, Institute of Environmental Management and Assessment, Lincoln, UK, and EIA Centre, University of Manchester, UK

Dusik J. (2003c) Case study prepared for the Japan Ministry of Environment and Mitsubshi Research Corporation, and presented at the SEA workshop, Tokyo, 15–17 February 2003

Dusik J. (2003d) 'SEA of Waste Management Plan of the Czech Republic'. In *Effective SEA System and Case Studies*, Mitsubishi Research Institute for the Ministry of the Environment, Government of Japan, Tokyo, pp128–133 (Japanese version first published in 2002)

Dusik J. (2003e) 'SEA of the Energy Policies of the Slovak Republic' In *Effective SEA System and Case Studies*, Mitsubishi Research Institute for the Ministry of the Environment, Government of Japan, Tokyo, pp101–110 (Japanese version first published in 2002)

Dusik J. (2003f) 'SEA of Energy Policy of the Czech Republic', in *Effective SEA System and Case Studies*, Mitsubishi Research Institute for the Ministry of the Environment, Government of Japan, Tokyo, pp95–100 (Japanese version first published in 2002)

Dusik J. and Sadler B. (2004) 'Reforming Strategic Environmental Assessment Systems: Lessons from Central and Eastern Europe'. *Impact Assessment and Project Appraisal*, 22, 89–97

Dusik J., Fisher T. and Sadler B. (2003) *Benefits of SEA*. Briefing paper for UNDP and the Regional Environmental Center for Central and Eastern Europe, Szentendre, Hungary (May 2003)

Dusik J., Sadler B. and Mikulic N. (2001) 'Recent Developments in SEA in Central and Eastern Europe'. In Dusik J. (ed) *Proceedings of International Workshop on Public Participation and Health Aspects in Strategic Environmental Assessment*, Regional Environmental Center for Central and Eastern Europe, Szentendre, Hungary

Early G. (2004) 'Australia's EIA Regime'. In CEAA (ed) *Status of Progress and Emerging Challenges in EIA and SEA: Ten Years after the Quebec Summit*, proceedings of the 8th Intergovernmental Policy Forum on Environmental Assessment, 25 April 2004, Vancouver BC, Canadian Environmental Assessment Agency, Ottawa

EC (1992) 'Council Directive 92/43/EC on the Conservation of Natural Habitats and of Wild Fauna and Flora' (The Habitats Directive). *Official Journal of the European Communities*, European Commission, Brussels, L 206, 22.7.1992, pp7–50

EC (1997) *Vision 2020: Summary and Recommendations* (XI/121/97). European Commission, Brussels

EC (1998) *A Handbook on Environmental Assessment of Regional Development Plans and EU Structural Funds Programmes*. EC, DGXI, Environment, Nuclear Safety and Civil Protection, Brussels, Belgium, http://europa.eu.int/comm/environment/eia/sea-guidelines/handbook.htm

EC (2000) *A Council Directive on Assessment of the Effects of Certain Plans and Programmes (2001/42/EC)*. European Commission, Brussels

EC (2002) *Trans-European Transport Network – TEN-T Priority Projects*. European Commission, Brussels (available at: europa.eu.int/comm/ten/transport/revision/doc/2002_brochure_ten_t_en.pdf)

EEA (1998) *A Checklist for State of the Environment Reporting*. Technical Report 15, European Environment Agency, Copenhagen

EEA (1999) *Environment in European Union at Turn of the Century*. Environmental Assessment Report No 2. European Environment Agency, Copenhagen

Elizarova L., Bykadorov A. and Cherp A. (1998) 'Environmental Assessment of Minsk and Vitebsk Master Plans'. In Mikulic N., Dusik J., Sadler B. and Casey-Lefkowitz S. (eds) (1998) *Strategic Environmental Assessment in Transitional Countries: Emerging Practices*, Regional Environmental Center for Central and Eastern Europe, Szentendre, Hungary, pp13–17

Elling B. (1996) 'The Danish Experience'. In de Boer J. and Sadler B. (eds) *Environmental Assessment of Policies*, Report No 54, Ministry of Housing, Spatial Planning and the Environment, The Hague, The Netherlands, pp39–46

Elling B. (1997) 'Strategic Environmental Assessment of National Policies: The Danish Experience of a Full Concept Assessment'. *Project Appraisal*, 12, 161–172

Elling B. (1998a) 'Environmental Assessment in Denmark'. *EIA Newsletter*, 17, 11–12

Elling B. (1998b) *Strategic Environmental Assessment in Regional Planning*. TemaNord 1998:519, Nordic Ministerial Council, Copenhagen (in Danish with English summary)

Elling B. (1999) *Miljøvurdering i Regionplanlægningen – Evaluering af Nordjyllandsprojektet, Miljø og Energiministeriet, Landsplansafdelingen* (Report of the Evaluation of the Northern Jutland Study on SEA in Regional Planning). Ministry of Environment and Energy, Copenhagen

Elling B. (2000a) 'Integration of SEA into Regional Spatial Planning'. *Impact Assessment and Project Appraisal*, 18 (3), 233–243

Elling B. (2000b) *Erfaringerne med miljøvurderinger af lovforslag* (Experiences with SEA of Bills). Ministry of Environment and Energy, Copenhagen (July 2000)

Elling B. and Neilsen J. (1996) *Environmental Assessment of Regional Plans.* TemaNord 1996:602, Nordic Ministerial Council, Copenhagen (in Danish with English summary)

Elling B. and Neilsen J. (1998) *Strategic Environmental Assessment of Policies in Denmark.* European Commission, Luxembourg

Environment Australia (1997) 'Strategic Environmental Assessment'. Final report of the International Study of the Effectiveness of Environmental Assessment [online] available at www.erin.gov.au

Environmental Protection Authority (2003) *Environmental Advice on the Principle of Locating a Gas Processing Complex on Barrow Island Nature Reserve: Section 16 Report and Recommendations of the Environmental Protection Authority.* Environmental Protection Authority, Perth, Western Australia

EPD (1996) *Gaza Land Resources: Land Use Planning and Resources Protection.* Focus on Environment in Palestine No 2, Environmental Planning Directorate, Ministry of Planning and International Cooperation, The Palestinian Authority, Gaza (December 1996)

EPE (1994) *Towards Shared Responsibility.* European Partners for the Environment, Brussels

Ericksen N., Crawford J., Berke P. and Dixon J. (2001) *Resource Management, Plan Quality and Governance.* Report to government, International Global Change Institute, University of Waikato, New Zealand

ERM (2002) *Linking Environment to Poverty Planning in Nepal.* Report prepared for the National Planning Commission, Nepal, with support from the UK Department for International Development (DFID-Nepal) (July 2002)

Ervasti K., Tala J. and Castrén E. (2000) *Lainvalmistelun Laatu ja Eduskunnan Valiokuntatyö* (The Quality of the Preparation of Legislation and Work of the Parliamentary Committees). Publication 172, National Research Institute of Legal Policy, Helsinki (in Finnish)

Ezekial H. (1975) *Second India Study: Overview.* Macmillan, Delhi, India

Falque M. (1995) 'Environmental Assessment in France'. *EIA Newsletter*, 10, p8.

FEARO (1993) *The Environmental Assessment Process for Policy and Programme Proposals* (the 'Blue Book'). Federal Environmental Assessment Review Office, Ottawa

FEEM (2002) 'Towards an Analytical Strategic Environmental Assessment: The ANSEA Network'. *Nota di Lavoro* 28.2002, Fondazione Eni Enrico Mattei, Milan

Feldmann L., Vanderhaegen M. and Pirotte C. (2001) 'The EU's SEA Directive; Status and Links to Integration and Sustainable Development'. *EIA Review*, 21, 3, 203–222

Ferrary C. (1997) 'SEA – What Are the Prospects?' *Environmental Assessment*, 5 (3), 20–21 (special issue on Strategic Environmental Assessment, September 1997)

Finka M., Belčáková I. et al (1997) *Návrh zásad vykonávacej vyhlášky pre implementáciu časti č §35 Zákona NR SR č. 127/1994 Z.z. o posudzovani vplyvov*

(Proposal of Executive Regulation Principles for §35 of EIA §35 Act). Centrum EIA Slovakia, Bratislava

Finnish Ministry of the Environment (1998a) *Guidelines for the Environmental Assessment of Plans, Programmes and Policies in Finland*. Helsinki (in Finnish) (available at: www.vyh.fi/eng/orginfo/publica/electro/eia/planprog.pdf)

Finnish Ministry of the Environment (1998b) *Guidelines on the Environmental Impact Assessment of Legislative Proposals*. Helsinki (English version issued in 2000, original issued in Finnish by Council of State)

Fischer T. B. (1999) 'Benefits from SEA Application, a Comparative Review of North West England, Noord-Holland and Brandenburg-Berlin'. *EIA-Review*, 19 (2), 143–173

Fischer T. B. (2002) *Strategic Environmental Assessment in Transport and Land Use Planning*. Earthscan, London

Fookes T. (2000) 'Environmental Assessment under the Resource Management Act 1991'. In Memon A. and Perkins H. (eds) *Environmental Planning and Management in New Zealand*, Dunmore Press, Palmerston North, New Zealand

Fookes T. (2002) *Auckland's Regional Growth Strategy 2050: An Application of Strategic Environmental Assessment*. Department of Planning Working Paper Series No 02–1, University of Auckland

Freeman P. and Vondall P. J. (2000) *Strategic Environmental Planning in the Development of Country Strategic Plan: A Proposal*. Report for the Africa Bureau, US Agency for International Development Africa Bureau, Washington DC

Fuller K., Rendall S. and Sadler B. (1998) *The Status and Practice of Strategic Environmental Assessment*. Report to the Japan Environment Agency, Institute of Environmental Assessment, Lincoln

Gallopin G., Hammond A., Raskin P. and Swart R. (1997) *Branch Points: Global Scenarios and Human Choice*. PoleStar Series Report No 76, Global Scenario Group, Stockholm Environment Institute, Stockholm, Sweden

Gascoigne N. (2001) 'The Australia Environmental Protection and Biodiversity Conservation Act, 1999'. In *Environmental Assessment Yearbook 2001*, Institute of Environmental Management and Assessment, Lincoln, UK, and EIA Centre, University of Manchester, UK

George C. and Kirkpatrick C. (2003) *Sustainability Impact Assessment of World Trade Negotiations: Current Practice and Lessons for Further Development*. Institute of Development Policy and Management, University of Manchester, Manchester, UK

Gibson R. B. (2002) *Sustainability Assessment as a Means of Integrating Sustainability-based Decision Making within the Canadian International Development Agency (CIDA)*. Consultation Paper (revised, short version) 1 prepared for the Environmental Assessment and Compliance Division, Policy Branch, Canadian International Development Agency, Hull, Quebec (26 July 2002)

Gibson R. B. (2004) *Sustainability Assessment: Basic Components of a Practical Approach*. Paper presented at the annual conference of the International Association for Impact Assessment, 24–30 April 2004, Vancouver BC

Glasson J. and Gosling J. (2001) 'SEA and Regional Planning – Overcoming the Institutional Constraints: Some Lessons from the EU'. *European Environment*, 11, 89–102

Goodland R. (1997) 'The Strategic Environmental Assessment Family'. *Environmental Assessment*, 5 (3), 17–20 (special issue on Strategic Environmental Assessment, September 1997)

Gove D. Z. (2003) *Strategic Environmental Assessment in Mozambique*. Centre for Sustainable Development for Coastal Zones (CDS-ZC), Ministry for Coordination of Environmental Affairs, Maputo, Mozambique

Government of Canada (1999) *Cabinet Directive on the Environmental Assessment of Policy, Plan and Program Proposals*. In CEAA *Guidelines for Implementing the Cabinet Directive on SEA*, Canadian Environmental Assessment Agency, Ottawa (available on the Agency's website at: www.ceaa.acee.gc.ca/0011/0002/dir_e.htm#guidelines)

Government of Western Australia (2003) *Consideration of Access to Barrow Island for Gas Development: Advice of Government's Environmental, Social, Economic and Strategic Deliberations; Overview*. Government of Western Australia, Perth

Gow L. (1996) 'The New Zealand Experience'. In de Boer J. and Sadler B. (eds) *Environmental Assessment of Policies*, Report No 54, Netherlands Ministry of Housing, Spatial Planning and the Environment, The Hague, The Netherlands, pp75–85

Gow L. (1998) *New Zealand's Approach to Strategic Environmental Assessment*. Paper to international seminar on strategic environmental appraisal, Lincoln, UK

Green K. and Raphael A. (2002) *Third Environmental Assessment Review (FY 92-00)*, The World Bank, Washington DC

Greeuw S. C. H., van Asselt M. B. A., Grosskurth J., Storms C. A. M. H., Rijkens-Klomp N., Rothman D. S. and Rotmans J. (2000) *Cloudy Crystal Balls. An Assessment of Recent European and Global Scenario Studies and Models*. Environmental Issues Report No 17 prepared by staff of the International Centre for Integrative Studies (ICIS), European Environment Agency, Copenhagen

Grigorova V. and Metodieva J. (2001) 'Strategic Environmental Assessment of the Varna Municipality Development Plan'. In Dusik J. (ed) *Proceedings of International Workshop on Public Participation and Health Aspects in Strategic Environmental Assessment*, Regional Environmental Center for Central and Eastern Europe, Szentendre, Hungary

Grishin N. (1997) *Public and Environment*. Ecological Project Centre, Moscow

Hanrahan D. (2003) *SEA at the World Bank – Structured Learning*. Presentation to the OECD/DAC workshop on SEA, Paris, 23–24 January

Harel F. (2003) 'SEA for Transport in France'. *SEA and Transport Planning*, 5, 35–36 (newsletter published by the Transport Research Laboratory, UK)

Harel F., Bourcier A. and Skriabine P. (2003) 'A French Methodological and Exploratory Study of SEA at the Regional Scale'. *SEA and Transport Planning*, 5, 34–35 (newsletter published by the Transport Research Laboratory, UK)

Harvey N. (2002) 'Linkages Between Project-based EIA and the Use of "ad hoc" SEA for Australian Coastal Development'. In Marsden S. and Dovers S. (eds) *Strategic Environmental Assessment in Australia*, The Federation Press, Leichhardt, NSW, pp114–140

Heather-Clark S. (1999) *Integrating Environmental Opportunities and Constraints into Port Planning, Development and Operation*. 5th International Conference on Coastal and Port Engineering in Developing Countries, Cape Town, 19–23 April 1999

Heather-Clark S. (2000) *Sustainable Port Development*. Report on the preparatory seminar for Africa, presented at the International Association for Cities and Ports, 7th International Conference, Marseilles, France, 6–9 November 2000

Heather-Clark S. (2002) *Strategic Integrated Port Planning: Moving from EIA to SEA*. Kuwait Conference, Kuwait, 18–22 March 2002

Heather-Clark S., Wiseman K. and Phelp D. (1998) *Strategic Approach to Integrated Port Planning: The South African Context*. The 29th Permanent International Association of Navigation Congress (PIANC), The Hague, The Netherlands, presented by Hans Moes

Hildén M. (2003a) 'Proposal for SEA Legislation Submitted'. Professional News section, *IAIA Newsletter*, 15 (1), International Association for Impact Assessment, Fargo, North Dakota (July 2003)

Hildén M (2003b) *Finnish Experience and Key Issues in Strategic Environmental Assessment*. Paper prepared for the proceedings of a workshop on SEA systems and applications to policy and legislation, Ministry of Housing, Spatial Planning and Development (VROM), The Hague, The Netherlands

Hildén M. and Jalonen P. (2003) 'Key Issues in Strategic Environmental Impact Assessment'. In Hilding-Rydevik T. (ed) *Environmental Assessment of Plans and Programmes*, Nordregio R2003/4, pp41–73

Hildén M. and Jalonen P. (2004) *Implementing SEA in Finland: Further Development of Existing Practice*. Manuscript

Hildén M., Primmer E., Kuuluvaienen J., Olikainen M. and Pelkonen P. (2000) *Environmental Impact Assessment of Finland's National Forest Programme*. Paper presented at a meeting of the International Association for Impact Assessment, Hong Kong

Hilding-Rydevik T. (ed) *Environmental Assessment of Plans and Programmes*, Nordregio R2003/4a

HMSO (1994) *Sustainable Development: The UK Strategy*. Cm 2426, Her Majesty's Stationery Office, London

Hodek J. and Kleinschmidt V. (1998) 'Strategic Environmental Impact Assessment in Germany with a Focus on the State of Brandenburg'. In Klinschmidt V. and Wagner D. (eds) *SEA in Europe*, Kluwer Academic Publishers, Dordrecht, The Netherlands

Huang J. (2002) 'Strategic Environmental Assessment Begins. Application in the Field of Decision-making and Legislation'. *China Environment Daily*, 26 August 2002

Huntley B., Siegfried R. and Sunter C. (1989) *South African Environments into the 21st Century*. Human & Rouseau Tafelberg, Cape Town

Husmann C. (2004) 'EIA and SEA in The Netherlands: Perspective of the Ministry of Housing, Spatial Planning and the Environment'. Briefing paper in CEAA (ed) *Status of Progress and Emerging Challenges in EIA and SEA: Ten Years after the Quebec Summit*, proceedings of the 8th Intergovernmental Policy Forum on Environmental Assessment, 25 April 2004, Vancouver BC, Canadian Environmental Assessment Agency, Ottawa

Hvidtfelt H. and Kørnøv L. (2001) *Strategisk Miljøvurderinger af Kommuneplaner II, – om Bæredygtige Mål i Kommuneplanlægningen* (Strategic Environmental Assessment of Municipal Plans II – On Sustainable Objectives in Municipal Planning). By- og Landsplanserien nr 12, 2001, Skov & Landskab (FSL), Frederiksberg, Denmark

Hvidtfelt H. and Kørnøv L. (2003) *Strategisk Miljøvurderinger af Kommuneplaner III, – om Metoder, Proces og Organisation* (Strategic Environmental Assessment of Municipal Plans III – On Methods, Process and Organisation). By- og Landsplanserien nr 22, 2003, Skov & Landskab (FSL), Frederiksberg, Denmark

IADB (2003) *Environment Strategy*. Inter-American Development Bank, Washington DC

IAIA (2002) 'Strategic Environmental Assessment: Performance Criteria'. Special Publication Series No 1, International Association for Impact Assessment [online]

available at www.iaia.org/Non_Members/Pubs_Ref_Material/pubs_ref_material_index.htm

IEA (1997) 'Strategic Environmental Assessment'. *Environmental Assessment*, 5 (3) (special issue, September 1997)

IIED (1996) *Towards a Sustainable Paper Cycle*. International Institute for Environment and Development, London

IIED/WBCSD (2002) *Breaking New Ground*. The Report of the Mining, Minerals and Sustainable Development (MMSD) Project, International Institute for Environment and Development and World Business Council for Sustainable Development, in association with Earthscan, London

IPCC (1995) *Climate Change 1994 – Radiative Forcing of Climate Change and an Evaluation of the IPPC IS92 Emission Scenarios*. International Panel on Climate Change, Cambridge University Press, Cambridge, UK

IPIECA (1996) *Long-range Scenarios for Climate Change Policy Analysis*. Report of a workshop held in Brighton, 8–10 January 1996, International Petroleum Industry Environmental Conservation Association, London

IUCN Nepal (1995) *EIA of the Bara Forest Management Plan*. World Conservation Union, Kathmandu, Nepal

IUCN-ROSA (1996) *Strategic Environmental Assessment of Development around Victoria Falls*. World Conservation Union, Regional Office for Southern Africa (IUCN-ROSA), Harare, Zimbabwe

IUCN/World Bank (1997) *Expanding Environmental Assessment Capacity in Sub-Saharan Africa: Issues and Options*. Discussion Paper distributed by the World Conservation Union (IUCN) and the World Bank, Gland, Switzerland

Jacobs P. and Sadler B. (eds) (1989) *Sustainable Development and Environmental Assessment: Perspectives on Planning for a Common Future*. Canadian Environmental Assessment Research Council, Ottawa

Jansson A. (2000) 'Strategic Environmental Assessment for Transport in Four Nordic Countries'. In Bjarnadóttir H. (ed) *Environmental Assessment in the Nordic Countries – Experience and Prospects*, Nordregio R2000/3, pp81–96

Johansen G. (1996) 'The Danish Experience: Perspective of the Ministry of Environment'. In de Boer J. and Sadler B. (eds) *Environmental Assessment of Policies*, Report No 54, Ministry of Housing, Spatial Planning and the Environment, The Hague, The Netherlands, pp47–50

Jones B. T. T. (2001a) *Integrating Environment and Sustainability Issues into the Development of Namibia's National Development Plan 2. A Participatory Process for Developing a Sustainable Development Strategy*. Paper prepared for the OECD/DAC project on Donor-developing Country Dialogues on National Strategies for Sustainable Development (January 2001) (available at: www.nssd.net)

Jones B. T. T. (2001b) *Integrating Environment and Sustainability Issues into the Development of Namibia's National Development Plan 2. A Methodology for Carrying Out a Gap–Consistency–Conflict Analysis of Key Chapters*. Paper prepared for the OECD/DAC project on Donor-developing Country Dialogues on National Strategies for Sustainable Development (January 2001) (available at: www.nssd.net)

Kaljonen M. (2000) 'The Role of SEA in Planning and Decision-making: The Case of the Helsinki Metropolitan Area Transport System Plan, 1998'. In Bjarnadóttir H. (ed) *Environmental Assessment in the Nordic Countries – Experience and Prospects*, Nordregio R2000/3, pp107–116

Keita S. (2001) *Évaluation Environnementale Stratégique et suivi des Impacts dans le Cas de la Mine d'Or de Sadiola au Mali* (Strategic Environmental Assessment and Impact Monitoring in the Case of the Sadiola Gold Mine in Mali). Presentation to the 5th international colloquium of francophone specialists in impact assessment, on the topic 'strategic environmental assessments', Paris, 22–24 May

Kennedy W. and Haumer A. (1999) *SEA and the European Bank for Reconstruction and Development*. Paper presented at the OECD/ECMT Conference on Strategic Environmental Assessment for Transport, 14–15 October 1999, Warsaw, Poland (available at: www.oecd.org/cem/topics/env/SEA99.htm)

Kessler J. J. (2000) 'Strategic Environmental Analysis (SEAN): A Framework to Support Analysis and Planning of Sustainable Development'. *Impact Assessment and Project Appraisal*, 18 (4), 295–307

Khutoleva M. (2002) 'Background Analysis for World Bank Review of Russian Federation EIA'. In von Ritter K. and Tsirkunov V. (2002) *How Well is Environmental Assessment Doing in Russia*, pilot study for the World Bank, Washington DC

King P., Annandale D. and Bailey J. (2000) 'Integrated Economic and Environmental Planning at the Subnational Level in Asia'. *Journal of Environmental Assessment Policy and Management*, 2, 317–338

Kirkpatrick C. and Lee N. (1997) *Sustainable Development in a Developing World: Integrating Socio-economic Appraisal and Environmental Assessment*. Edward Elgar, Cheltenham, UK

Kjørven O. and Lindhjem H. (2002) *Strategic Environmental Assessment in World Bank Operations: Experience to Date – Future Potential*. Environment Strategy Papers No 4, the World Bank, Washington DC

Klassen P. (2002) *The Environmental Test in The Netherlands*. Powerpoint presentation to the Workshop on Sustainability Impact Assessment, British Embassy, Brussels, 23 April 2002

Klees R. Capcelea A. and Barannik A. (2002) *Environmental Impact Assessment (EIA) Systems in Europe and Central Asia Countries*. The World Bank, Washington DC

Kleinschmidt V.and Wagner D. (1996) 'Wind Farms in the Soest District'. In Therivel R. and Partidario M. (eds) *The Practice of Strategic Environmental Assessment*, Earthscan, London

Koblar J. (1998) *Strategic Environmental Impact Assessment of Major Transport Routes in Slovenia*. Paper presented to the Sofia Initiative EIA Workshop, Prague

Korean Ministry of Environment (2001) *Green Korea 2001*. Ministry of Environment, Seoul (available at: www.me.go.kr)

Kozová, M (1998) 'Environmental Assessment of Slovak Energy Policy'. In Mikulic N., Dusik J., Sadler B. and Casey-Lefkowitz S. (eds) *Strategic Environmental Assessment in Transitional Countries: Emerging Practices*, Regional Environmental Center for Central and Eastern Europe, Szentendre, Hungary

Kozová M. and Szollos J. (2001) 'Strategic Environmental Assessment in Slovak Energy Policies'. In Dusik J. (ed) *Proceedings of International Workshop on Public Participation and Health Aspects in Strategic Environmental Assessment*, Regional Environmental Center for Central and Eastern Europe, Szentendre, Hungary, pp87–104

Kozová M., Finka M., Belčáková I. and Petríková D. (2000) *Metodická príručka – Metodická zásady pre výkon vyhlášky η §35 zákona NR SR č. 127/1994 Z.z. o posudãzovani vplyvov na životné prostredie v zneni neskorší neskorších predpisov* (Methodological Principles – for Execution of Regulation to §35 of the EIA Act Nr 127/1994). PRIF UK and FA STU, Bratislava

Kozová M., Spáãilová R., Huba M. et al (1994) *Metodická prírucka k hodnoteniu návrhov rozvojových koncepcií z hladiska ich vplyvov na životné prostredie (zákon NR SR č. 127/1994 Z.z. §35)* (Methodological Introductory Guidelines for Environmental Assessment of Policies, Programmes and Plans (Slovak EIA Act Nr 127/1994 Z.z. §35)). MèP SR, Bratislava

Kozová M., Úradniãek Š., Huba M. Butkovská K., Antalová S., Ira V. et al (1996) *Strategické environmentálne hodnotenie (SEA) ako jeden z nástrojov environmentálnej politiky a stratégie trvaloudržateľného rozvoja, 1.,2.,3 časť a prilohová časť* (Strategic Environmental Assessment (SEA) as One of the Instruments of Environmental Policy and Strategy of Sustainable Development Implementation, 1,2,3, Part and Annexes). EIA Centre at KKE PRIF UK, MèP SR, Bratislava

Krumpolcová M., Krumpolec Krumpolcová M. V. and Krumpolcová M. (1998) *Upresnenie metodických postupov pre environmentálne hodnotenie územnoplánovacej dokumentácie v zmysle §35 Zákona NR SR č. 127/1994 Z.z. o posudzovani vplyvov na P pre sidelný útvar* (Precision of Methodological Procedures for Environmental Assessment of Planning Documentation for Settlements with Regard to §35 of the EIA Act Nr 127/1994). MèP SR, Bratislava

Krumpolcová M., Kalinová Z., Kozová M., Úradniãek Š., Butkovská K., Králik J. and Vaškovič P. (1997) *Dalšie overovanie a upresÀovanie metodických postupov pre environmentálne hodnotenie územnoplánovacej dokumentácie na regionálnej a sidelnej úrovni v zmysle §35 Zákona NR SR č. 127/1994 Z.z. o posudzovani vplyvov na P* (Further Examination and Precision for Environmental Assessment of Planning Documentation at the Regional and Local Levels with Regard to §35 of the EIA Act Nr 127/1994). MèP SR, Bratislava

Lane C. (1996) *Ngorongoro Voices: Indigenous Maasai Residents of the Ngorongoro Conservation Area in Tanzania Give their Views on the Proposed General Management Plan*. Forest, Trees and People Programme, UN Food and Agriculture Organization, Swedish University of Agricultural Sciences, Uppsala, Sweden

Larrue C. (1999) *Évaluation Environnementale Préalable des Contrats de Plan État–Région et Documents Uniques de Programmation 2000–2006*. Ministère de l'Aménagement du Territoire et de l'Environnement, Paris, France

Larrue C. and Lerond M. (1998) *Suivi et Évaluation Environnementale des Contrats de Plan État–Région*. Ministère de l'Aménagement du Territoire et de l'Environnement, France

LeBlanc P. and Fischer K. (1996) 'The Canadian Federal Experience'. In de Boer J. and Sadler B. (eds) *Environmental Assessment of Policies*, Report No 54, Netherlands Ministry of Housing, Spatial Planning and the Environment, The Hague, The Netherlands, pp27–37

Lee N. (2002) 'Bridging the Gap Between Theory and Practice in Integrated Assessment', University of Manchester, UK, www.art.man.ac.uk/PLANNING/cure/workshop/plenary

Lee N. and Hughes J. (1995) *Strategic Environmental Assessment, Legislation and Procedures in the Community*. Final report, EIA Centre, University of Manchester, UK

Lee N. and Walsh F. (1992) 'Strategic Environmental Assessment: An Overview'. *Project Appraisal*, 7 (3), 126–136

Lee N. and Wood C. (1978) 'EIA – A European Perspective'. *Built Environment*, 4 (2), 101–110

Lerond M., Larrue C., Michel P., Roudier B. and Sanson C. (2003) *L'Évaluation Environnementale des Politiques, Plans et Programmes. Objectifs, Méthodologies et Cas Pratiques*. Éd. Tec & Doc, Paris

Levett R. and McNally R. (2003) *A Strategic Environmental Assessment of Fiji's Tourism Development Plan*. Report prepared by the South Pacific Programme, World Wide Fund for Nature, Godalming, UK

Levett-Therivel/Alta (2002) *Guidance on Strategic Environmental Assessment*. Prepared for the Planning Agency of Iceland by Levett Therivel Sustainability Consultants, Oxford, and Alta, Iceland, www.alta.is

Lindberg T. and Nylander A. (2001) *Strategic Environmental Assessment on Shrimp Farms in Southeast Thailand*. Minor Field Studies No 176, Swedish University of Agricultural Sciences, Uppsala, Sweden

MA (2002) 'Integrated Ecosystem Assessment of Western China' [online] available at: www.millenniumassessment.org/en/assessments/a.china.htm

MA (2003) *Ecosystems and Human Well-being: A Framework for Assessment*. Millennium Ecosystem Assessment, Island Press, Washington, DC, USA

McIntyre M. (2003) *Status of Environmental Impact Assessment in Pacific Island Countries (PICs)*. South Pacific Regional Environment Programme (SPREP), Samoa

Malcolm J. (2002) 'Strategic Environmental Assessment: Legislative Developments in Western Australia'. In Marsden S. and Dovers S. (eds) *Strategic Environmental Assessment in Australia*, The Federation Press, Leichhardt, NSW, pp71–83

Marsden S. (2002) 'Strategic Environmental Assessment and Fisheries Management in Australia: How Effective is the Commonwealth Legal Framework?' In Marsden S. and Dovers S. (eds) *Strategic Environmental Assessment in Australia*, The Federation Press, Leichhardt, NSW, pp47–70

Marsden S. and Dovers S. (2002) 'Conclusions: Prospects for SEA'. In Marsden S. and Dovers S. (eds) *Strategic Environmental Assessment in Australia*, The Federation Press, Leichhardt, NSW, pp211–218

Mercier J.-R. (2001) 'Environmental Assessment at the World Bank: New Developments and Strategic Directions (OP 4.01)'. In *Environmental Assessment Yearbook 2001*, Institute of Environmental Management and Assessment, Lincoln, UK, and EIA Centre, University of Manchester, UK, pp63–65

Mercier J. and Ahmed K. (2004) *EIA and SEA at the World Bank*. Paper presented to Proceedings of the 8th Intergovernmental Policy Forum on Environmental Assessment, in association with the Annual Meeting of the International Association for Impact Assessment (IAIA), Vancouver, Canada

Michel P. and Monier T. (2001) *Strategic Environmental Assessment of Plans and Programmes in the Transport Sector in France: A Guidance Document*. Ministry for Management of Land and Environment, Paris (original in French, executive summary in English)

Mikulic N., Dusik J., Sadler B. and Casey-Lefkowitz S. (eds) (1998) *Strategic Environmental Assessment in Transitional Countries: Emerging Practices*. Regional Environmental Center for Central and Eastern Europe, Szentendre, Hungary

Milewski J. (2004) 'Environmental Assessment at the Inter-American Development Bank'. In CEAA (ed) *Status of Progress and Emerging Challenges in EIA and SEA: Ten Years after the Quebec Summit*, proceedings of the 8th Intergovernmental Policy Forum on Environmental Assessment, 25 April 2004, Vancouver BC, Canadian Environmental Assessment Agency, Ottawa

Ministry of Defence (2000) 'Strategic Environmental Appraisal (SEA) of the Strategic Defence Review (SDR)' [online] available at: www.mod.uk/issues/sdr/environment/contents.htm (accessed 19 July 2004)

Mitsubishi Research Institute (2003) *Effective SEA System and Case Studies*. Prepared for the Japanese Ministry of the Environment, Mitsubishi Research Institute, Tokyo (Japanese version published in 2002)

MUNR (1995) *Bauleitplanung und Landschaftsplanung*. Gemeinsames Ministerialblatt für das Land Brandenburg Nr 84, Ministerium für Umwelt, Naturschutz und Raumordnung (MUNR), Potsdam

Mwalyosi R. and Hughes R. (1998) *The Performance of EIA in Tanzania: An Assessment*. Environmental Planning Issues No 14, International Institute for Environment and Development, London

MWSVLSA (1995) *Verkehrsuntersuchung Nordost*. Ministerium für Wohnungswesen, Städtebau und Verkehr des Landes Sachsen-Anhalt, Magdeburg

Nafti R. and George C. (2003) *Working Together to Manage the Environment, Strengthening EIA Systems in the Mediterranean Region*. CITET, METAP, Tunisia (June 2003)

Naim P. (1997) *Thermal Power Generation Policy: A Strategic Analysis*. Lecture at the National Institute of Public Administration, Karachi. November 29, 1997. IUCN-NIPA. IUCN Pakistan Office, Karachi

Naim P. (1998) 'Karachi's Electricity Plan: Need for a Strategic Assessment'. In Adhikari A. P. and Khadka R. B. (eds) *Strategic Environmental Assessment: Proceedings of the South and Southeast Asian Regional Training Workshop on Strategic Environmental Assessment*, jointly organized by AREAP, IUCN Nepal and the Netherlands Commission for EIA, 18–20 September 1997, Kathmandu, Nepal, Asian Regional Environmental Assessment Program, IUCN, Nepal

Naim P. (2002) 'South and South East Asia'. In *Environmental Assessment Yearbook 2002*, Institute of Environmental Management and Assessment, Lincoln, UK, and EIA Centre, University of Manchester, UK, pp90–93

Naim P. and Saeed A. (1997a) *EIA/SEA Workshop for Sindh Planning and Development Department*. 22–28 January 1997, Karachi, IUCN-SDC, IUCN-Pakistan Office, Karachi

Naim P. and Saeed A. (1997b) *SEA Workshop for North West Frontier Province Planning and Development Department*. 3–4 December 1997, Peshawar, IUCN-SPCS, IUCN-Pakistan Office, Karachi

National Assembly for Wales (2002) 'Sustainability Appraisal of Unitary Development Plans in Wales: A Good Practice Guide' [online] available at: www.wales.gov.uk/subiplanning/content/devplans/udp-acs-e.pdf

National Department of Transport (2002) *Draft White Paper on National Commercial Ports Policy*. Department of Transport, Pretoria, South Africa (March 2002)

National Peoples Congress (2002) *Environmental Impact Assessment Law of the People's Republic of China*. Adopted at the 30th meeting of the Standing Committee of the 9th National People's Congress, 28 October 2002, by Order No 77 of the President of the People's Republic of China (effective 1 September 2003) (English translation)

NATO (1996) *Methodology, Focalization, Evaluation and Scope of Environmental Assessment. Fourth Report. Strategic Environmental Assessment: Theory Versus Practice*. Report No 212, NATO Committee on the Challenges of Modern Society, Brussels, Belgium

Natural Resources Canada (2004) *Federal Public Review of the British Columbia Offshore Oil and Gas Moratorium*. Natural Resources Canada, Ottawa (www.moratoriumpublicreview.ca)

NBI (2001) *Nile River Basin – Transboundary Environmental Assessment, Nile Basin Initiative: Shared Vision Programme, May 2001*. Nile Basin Initiative, Global Environmental Facility, UNDP and World Bank, Washington DC

NCSA (2002) *Okavango Delta Management Plan – Project Proposal*. National Conservation Strategy Agency, Gaborone, Botswana

N'dah Etien (2002) *Évaluation Environnementale et Programme de Développement de la Zone Côtière (Côte d'Ivoire)* (Environmental Assessment and the Coastal Development Programme (Côte d'Ivoire)). Presentation to the 6th international colloquium of francophone specialists in impact assessment, on the topic 'energy choices: from evaluation of impacts to strategic environmental assessment', Cotonou, Bénin, 23–27 April 2001

Nelson P. J. (2001) *Sustainability Appraisals on Different Methods of Providing Water to Isolated Rural Communities in Ghana.* Land Use Consultants, Bristol, UK

Nelson P. J. (2003) *Building Capacity in SEA in Sub-Saharan Africa.* Paper presented at the 23rd Annual Meeting of the International Association for Impact Assessment (IAIA'03), Marrakech, Morocco

NEPA Task Force (2003) *Modernizing NEPA Implementation: Report of the NEPA Task Force.* Council on Environmental Quality, Washington DC

Netherlands CEIA (2003) *Annual Report 2002.* Commission for Environmental Impact Assessment, The Hague, The Netherlands

New Zealand Ministry for the Environment (2000) *A Guide to Using Section 32 of the RMA: What Are the Options?* Wellington, New Zealand

Nida-Rümelin J. (1997) *Economic Rationality and Practical Reason.* Kluwer Academic Publishers, Dordrecht, The Netherlands

Nilsson M. A. and Dalkmann H. (2001) 'Decision Making and Strategic Environmental Assessment'. *Journal of Environmental Assessment Policy and Management,* 3 (3) (September 2001)

Nishikubo H. (2004) 'EIA and SEA in Japan'. In CEAA (ed) *Status of Progress and Emerging Challenges in EIA and SEA: Ten Years after the Quebec Summit,* proceedings of the 8th Intergovernmental Policy Forum on Environmental Assessment, 25 April 2004, Vancouver BC, Canadian Environmental Assessment Agency, Ottawa

Norton-Miller A. (2004) 'EIA and SEA in the United States'. In CEAA (ed) *Status of Progress and Emerging Challenges in EIA and SEA: Ten Years after the Quebec Summit,* proceedings of the 8th Intergovernmental Policy Forum on Environmental Assessment, 25 April 2004, Vancouver BC, Canadian Environmental Assessment Agency, Ottawa

NPA (2002) *NPA Development Framework – Cape Town.* Draft, National Ports Authority, Cape Town (January 2002)

ODPM (2002) *Draft Guidance on the Strategic Environmental Assessment Directive: Proposals for Practical Guidance on Applying Directive 2001/42/EC 'on the Assessment of the Effects of Certain Plans and Programmes on the Environment' to Land Use and Spatial Plans in England.* Office of the Deputy Prime Minister, London (23 October 2002)

ODPM (2003) 'The Strategic Environmental Assessment Directive: Guidance for Planning Authorities'. Practical guidance on applying European Directive 2001/42/EC 'on the assessment of the effects of certain plans and programmes on the environment' to land use and spatial plans in England, Office of the Deputy Prime Minister, London [online] available at: www.odpm.gov.uk/stellent/groups/odpm_planning/documents/page/odpm_plan_026670.pdf (October 2003)

ODPM (2004) 'A Draft Practical Guide to the Strategic Environmental Assessment Directive'. Proposals by the ODPM, the Scottish Executive, the Welsh Assembly Government and the Northern Ireland Department of the Environment for practical guidance on applying European Directive 2001/42/EC 'on the assessment of the effects of certain plans and programmes on the environment', Office of the Deputy

Prime Minister, London [online] available at: www.planning.odpm.gov.uk (July 2004)

OECD/DAC (2001) *The DAC Guidelines: Strategies for Sustainable Development: Guidance for Development Cooperation*. Development Assistance Committee, Organisation for Economic Co-operation and Development, Paris (available at: http://new.sourceoecd.org)

OECD/DAC (2002) *Proposal for Future Work Programme on Strategic Environmental Assessment/Strategic Impact Assessment (SEA/SIA)*. Document DCD/DAC/ENV(2002)11, note by the Delegation of the United Kingdom, meeting of the OECD DAC Working Party on Development Cooperation and Environment, 12–13 October 2002, Organisation for Economic Co-operation and Development, Paris

OECD/DAC (2004) *Task Team on Strategic Environmental Assessment/Sustainability Appraisal Status Report and Work Update: 2004–2005*. Document DCD/DAC/ENV(2004)2, 16 June 2004, DAC Network on Environment and Development Cooperation, Development Co-operation Directorate/Development Assistance Committee, Organisation for Economic Co-operation and Development, Paris

OECD/UNDP (2002) *Sustainable Development Strategies: A Resource Book*. Organisation for Economic Co-operation and Development and United Nations Development Programme in association with Earthscan, London

Öjendal J., Mathur V. and Sithirith M. (2002) *Environmental Governance in the Mekong: Hydropower Site Selection Processes in the Se San and Sre Pok Basins*. SEI/REPSI Report Series No 4, Stockholm Environment Institute, Stockholm, Sweden

OKACOM (1999) *Transboundary Diagnostic Analysis*. Final draft, Permanent Okavango River Basin Commission, Luanda

Omori K. (1997) 'International Symposium on EIA held in Tokyo'. *IAIA Newsletter*, 8 (3), 2

Omori K. (1999) 'A Report on the International Workshop on Strategic Environmental Assessment'. *IAIA Newsletter*, 10 (4), 2

Onorio K. (2002) 'Pacific Island Countries'. In *Environmental Assessment Yearbook 2002*, Institute of Environmental Management and Assessment, Lincoln, UK, and EIA Centre, University of Manchester, UK, pp112–113

O'Riordan T. and Sewell W. R. D. (1981) *Project Appraisal and Policy Review*. John Wiley and Sons, Chichester, UK

Parliamentary Commissioner for the Environment (2002) *Creating our Future – Sustainable Development for New Zealand*. Wellington, New Zealand

Parol A. (2003) 'Land Use Planning and SEA – Polish experience'. In REC *Strategic Environmental Assessment in EU Accession Countries*, report of the 6th regional workshop of the Sofia EIA Initiative, April 2003, Regional Environmental Center for Central and Eastern Europe, Szentendre, Hungary

Partidário M. (1996) 'Strategic Environmental Assessment: Key Issues Emerging from Recent Practice'. *Environmental Impact Assessment Review*, 16, 31–55

Partidário M. (2000) 'Elements of an SEA Framework: Improving the Added Value of SEA'. *Environmental Impact Assessment Review*, 20, 647–633

Partidário M. (2004) 'Draft Guidance for SEA'. Inter-American Development Bank (TC-03-03-045-RS 2 September 2004), www.iadb.org/sds/doc/SEADraftGuidance.pdf

Partidário M. and Clark R. (1999) *Perspectives on Strategic Environmental Assessment*. Lewis Publishers, Boca Raton, Florida

Petts, J. (ed) (1999) *Handbook of Environmental Impact Assessment*, Volumes 1 and 2, Blackwell Scientific Ltd, Oxford, UK

Pillai P. (2002) *World Bank Experience with Country-level Environmental Diagnostic Tools: Review and Lessons Learned*. Draft, Environment Department, the World Bank, Washington DC

Pinfield G. (1992) 'SEA and Land-use Planning'. *Project Appraisal*, 7 (3) 157–163

Pope J., Morrison-Saunders A. and Annandale D. (submitted) 'Applying Sustainability Assessment Models'. *Impact Assessment and Project Appraisal*

Pope J., Annandale D. and Morrison-Saunders A. (2004) 'Conceptualising Sustainability Assessment'. *Environmental Impact Assessment Review*, 24 (6), 595–616

Prescott-Allen R. (2001a) 'Well-being Assessment' [online] available at www.altarum.org/SST/

Prescott-Allen R. (2001b) *The Well-being of Nations: A Country-by-country Index of Quality of Life and the Environment*. Island Press, Washington DC, and International Development Research Centre, Ottawa

Project Appraisal (1992) Special issue on SEA. *Project Appraisal*, 7 (3) (September 1992)

Public Health Advisory Committee (2003) *A Guide to Health Impact Assessment: A Policy Tool for New Zealand*. National Advisory Committee on Health and Disability, Wellington, New Zealand

Qi Zhong and Wang Huadong (1993) 'Regional Development Environmental Impact Assessment (RDEIA) in China – Taking Madao Economic Development Zone as a Case'. In Wang Huadong (ed) *Research on Regional Environment and Development*, China Environmental Sciences Press, Beijing

REC (1998) *Policy Recommendations on the Use of Strategic Environmental Assessment in Central and Eastern Europe and in Newly Independent States*. Background Document No 17 to the Fourth Ministerial Conference, Environment for Europe, Aarhus, Regional Environmental Center for Central and Eastern Europe, Szentendre, Hungary

REC (2001a) *Key Elements of SEA: Priorities in Countries of Central and Eastern Europe*. Report of a sub-regional workshop under the UNECE Espoo Convention, Regional Environmental Center for Central and Eastern Europe, Szentendre, Hungary, and Ministry of Environment, Poland

REC (2001b) *Approaches to SEA in Central and Eastern Europe*. Report of the 5th regional workshop of the Sofia EIA Initiative, Regional Environmental Center for Central and Eastern Europe, Szentendre, Hungary

REC (2003) *Strategic Environmental Assessment in EU Accession Countries*. Report of the 6th regional workshop of the Sofia EIA Initiative, Regional Environmental Center for Central and Eastern Europe, Szentendre, Hungary

Repetto R. (1994) *The 'Second India' Revisited: Population, Poverty, and Environmental Stress over Two Decades*. World Resources Institute, Washington DC

Republic of Botswana. (2001a) *Environmental Audit of the DDP 5 for Central District*. Workshop proceedings, Environmental Planning Programme, Technical Report No 13, Ministry of Finance and Development Planning, Gaborone, Botswana

Republic of Botswana. (2001b) *Report of the Environmental Audit of District Development 5 of the Central District*. Environmental Planning Programme, Technical Report No 20, Ministry of Finance and Development Planning, Gaborone, Botswana

RIVM (1988) *Concern for Tomorrow*. National Institute for Public Health and Environmental Protection (RIVM), Bilthoven, The Netherlands

RIVM (1991a) *National Environmental Outlook 2: 1990–2010*. National Institute for Public Health and Environmental Protection (RIVM), Bilthoven, The Netherlands

RIVM (1991b) *Zorgen voor Morgen: Nationale Milieuverkenning 1985–2010* (Caring for Tomorrow, National Environmental Outlook 1985–2010). National Institute for Public Health and Environmental Protection (RIVM), Alphen aan de Rijn, Samson HD Tjeenk Willink

RIVM (2001) *Environmental Balance 2001*. National Institute for Public Health and Environmental Protection (RIVM), Bilthoven, The Netherlands

RIVM (2002) *Environmental Balance 2002: Accounting for the Dutch Environment*. National Institute for Public Health and Environmental Protection (RIVM), Bilthoven, The Netherlands

Robins N., Trisoglio A. and Van Dijk F. (1996) *Vision 2020: Scenarios for a Sustainable Europe*. SustainAbility and International Institute for Environment and Development, London

Rossouw N. and Govender K. (2003) 'SEA and Development Planning in South Africa'. In *EIA Yearbook*, Institute of Environmental Management and Assessment, Lincoln, UK, and EIA Centre, University of Manchester, UK

Rossouw N., Audouin M., Lochner P., Heather-Clark S. and Wiseman K. (2000) 'The Development of Strategic Environmental Assessment in South Africa'. *Impact Assessment and Project Appraisal*, 18 (3) (September 2000)

Rotbergh B. (1998) 'Environmental Assessment of the Jurmala Town Development Plan'. In Mikulic N., Dusik J., Sadler B. and Casey-Lefkowitz S. (eds) *Strategic Environmental Assessment in Transitional Countries: Emerging Practices*, Regional Environmental Center for Central and Eastern Europe, Szentendre, Hungary, pp31–34

Rump P. (1996) *State of the Environment Reporting: Source Book of Methods and Approaches*. Division of Environment Information and Assessment, United Nations Environment Programme, Nairobi

Russell S. (1997) *Sustainability Appraisal: Integrating Planning and Local Agenda 21*. Report of a research workshop held at Coventry City Council, 15 September 1997, EIA Unit, University of Wales, Aberystwyth, UK

Russell S. (1999) 'Environmental Appraisal of Development Plans'. *Town Planning Review*, 70 (4), 529–546

Rzeszot U. (1997) 'Strategic Environmental Assessment in Poland'. *Environmental Assessment*, 5 (3), 31–33 (special issue on Strategic Environmental Assessment, September 1997)

Rzeszot U. (1999) 'Environmental Impact Assessment in Central and Eastern Europe'. In Petts J. (ed) *Handbook of Environmental Impact Assessment*, Volume 2, Blackwell Scientific Ltd, Oxford, UK, pp123–142

Rzeszot U. (2001) 'SEA of Regional Land-use Plans: Lessons from Poland'. In Dusik J. (ed) *Proceedings of International Workshop on Public Participation and Health Aspects in Strategic Environmental Assessment*, Regional Environmental Center for Central and Eastern Europe, Szentendre, Hungary

Rzeszot U. (2003) *Framework SEA of the Polish National Development Plan 2004–2006*. Presentation to the Workshop on Strategic Environmental Assessment in Selected CEE Countries, 28–30 April 2003, Regional Environmental Center for Central and Eastern Europe, Szentendre, Hungary

SADC/ELMS (1996) *Policy and Strategy for Environment and Sustainable Development*. Southern African Development Community, Environment and Land Management Sector Coordination Unit, Maseru, Lesotho (first proposed in 1994)

Sadler B. (1977) *Recent Progress in Strategic Environmental Assessment*. Unpublished manuscript

Sadler B. (1986) 'Impact Assessment in Transition: A Framework for Redeployment'. In Lang R. (ed) *Integrated Approaches to Resource Planning and Management*, University of Calgary Press, pp99–129

Sadler B. (1993) 'National Sustainable Development Strategies and Environmental Impact Assessment: Post-Rio Perspectives'. *Environmental Assessment*, 1 (2), pp29–31

Sadler B. (1994) 'Environmental Assessment and Development Policymaking'. In Goodland R. and Edmundson V. (eds) *Environmental Assessment and Development*, the World Bank, Washington DC, pp3–19

Sadler B. (1996) *Environmental Assessment in a Changing World: Evaluating Practice to Improve Performance*. Final report, International Study of the Effectiveness of Environmental Assessment, Canadian Environmental Assessment Agency, Canada

Sadler B. (1998a) 'Recent Progress in Strategic Environmental Assessment'. *Environmental Protection Bulletin*, 55, 1–10

Sadler B. (1998b) *Institutional Requirements for Strategic Environmental Assessment*. Paper to the Intergovernmental Forum, organized by the Ministry for the Environment, 25 April 1998, Christchurch, New Zealand

Sadler B. (1999) 'A Framework for Environmental Sustainability Assessment and Assurance'. In Petts, J. (ed) *Handbook of Environmental Impact Assessment*, Volume 1, Blackwell Scientific Ltd, Oxford, UK, pp12–32

Sadler B. (2001a) 'A Framework Approach to Strategic Environmental Assessment: Aims, Principles and Elements of Good Practice'. In Dusik J (ed) *Proceeedings of International Workshop on Public Participation and Health Aspects in Strategic Environmental Assessment*, Regional Environmental Center for Central and Eastern Europe, Szentendre, Hungary

Sadler B. (2001b) 'Environmental Impact Assessment: An International Perspective with Comparisons to New Zealand Experience'. In Lumsden J. (ed) *Assessment of Environmental Effects: Information, Evaluation and Outcomes*, Centre for Advanced Engineering, Christchurch, New Zealand

Sadler B (2001c) 'Strategic Environmental Assessment: An Aide Memoir to Drafting a SEA Protocol to the Espoo Convention'. In Dusik J. (ed) *Proceedings of International Workshop on Public Participation and Health Aspects in Strategic Environmental Assessment*. Regional Environmental Center for Central and Eastern Europe, Szentendre, Hungary, pp25–34 (November 2001)

Sadler B. (2003a) *Recent Progress with Strategic Environmental Assessment at the Policy Level, in SEA Systems with Particular Application to Policy and Legal Acts*. Update of Publication No 54, Netherlands Ministry of Housing, Spatial Planning and the Environment, The Hague, The Netherlands

Sadler B. (2003b) *SEA at the Policy Level*. Proceedings of a Workshop on SEA Systems and Applications to Policy and Legislation, Ministry of Housing, Spatial Planning and Development (VROM), The Hague, The Netherlands

Sadler B. (2003c) 'Taking Stock of EA Capacity Development'. In *Environmental Assessment Outlook*, Institute of Environmental Management and Assessment, Lincoln, UK, EIA Centre, University of Manchester, UK and the International Association for Impact Assessment

Sadler B. (2004) 'On Evaluating the Success of EIA and SEA'. Chapter 11 in Morrison-Saunders A. and J. Arts (eds) *Assessing Impact: Handbook of EIA and SEA Follow-up*, James & James (Science Publishers) Ltd/Earthscan, London

Sadler B. and Baxter M. (1997) 'Taking Stock of SEA'. *Environmental Assessment*, 5 (3), 14–16 (special issue on Strategic Environmental Assessment, September 1997)

Sadler B. and Brookes, C. (1998) *Strategic Environment Appraisal*, Department of Environment, Transport and the Regions, London

Sadler B. and McCabe M. (eds) (2002) *Environmental Impact Assessment. Training Resource Manual*. Economics and Trade Branch, UNEP, Geneva

Sadler B. and Verheem R. (1996) *Strategic Environmental Assessment 53: Status, Challenges and Future Directions*. Ministry of Housing, Spatial Planning and the Environment, The Netherlands, and the International Study of Effectiveness of Environmental Assessment

Sadler B., Ward M. and Wilson J. (2004) *Strategic Environmental Assessment: Application to Transport Planning in New Zealand*. Research report, Transfund New Zealand, Wellington, New Zealand

SAIEA (2003a) *Improving the Effectiveness of Environmental Impact Assessment and Strategic Environmental Assessment in Southern Africa*. Proceedings of a workshop held from 13–16 May 2003, Windhoek, Namibia, Southern African Institute for Environmental Assessment, Windhoek, Namibia

SAIEA (2003b) *Environmental Impact Assessment in Southern Africa*. Southern African Institute for Environmental Assessment, Windhoek, Namibia

Samoura K., Diakite S. and Keita S. M. (2003) *Évaluation Environnementale Strategique du Plan d'Amenagement Forestier de la Baie de Sangareya, Guinea Conakry*. Presentation at the meeting of the International Association for Impact Assessment, 17–20 June 2003, Marrakech, Morocco

Sanchez-Triana E. and Quintero J. D. (2003) *Strategic Environmental Assessment: Good Practices for World Bank Countries: Case Studies in Latin America*. Presentation at the World Bank Workshop: Tools for Sustainable Development Assessment, 14 June 2003, Marrakech, Morocco

Schaefer C., Bongardt D. and Dalkmann H. (2003) *Neue Wege für das Land. Strategische Umweltpruefung für eine Zukunftsfaehige Bundesverkehrswegeplanung*. Bundesministerium für Verkehr, Bau- und Wohnungswesen, Bundesverkehrswegeplan, Berlin

Scottish Executive (2003) 'Environmental Assessment of Plans. Interim Planning Advice'. Prepared by David Tydesley and Associates, August 2003, Planning Department, Scottish Executive, Edinburgh (available at: www.scotland.gov.uk/library5/planning/eadp-1.asp)

Scottish Labour Party and Scottish Liberal Democrats (undated) 'A Partnership for a Better Scotland: Partnership Agreement' [online] available at: www.scotland.gov.uk/library5/government/pfbs.pdf

Segnestam L., Persson A., Nilsson M., Arvidsson A. and Ijjasz E. (2003) *Country-level Environmental Analysis: A Review of International Experience*. Environment Strategy Papers No 8, the World Bank, Washington DC

Sheate W. (1995) 'Transport Policy: A Critical Role for SEA'. *World Transport Policy and Practice*, 1 (4), 17–24

Sheate W. R. (2003) 'Changing Conceptions and Potential for Conflict in Environmental Assessment: Environmental Integration in Sustainable Development in the EU'. *Environmental Policy and Law*, 33 (5), 219–230

Sheate W. R., Byron H. J. and Smith S. P. (2004) 'Implementing the SEA Directive: Sectoral Challenges and Opportunities for the UK and EU'. *European Environment*, 14, 73–93

Sheate W. R., Dagg S., Richardson J., Aschemann R., Palerm J. and Steen U. (2001) *SEA and Integration of the Environment into Strategic Decision-making.* Volumes 1–3, final report to the European Commission, DG XI, Contract No B4-3040/99/136634/MAR/B4, Office for Official Publications of the European Communities, Luxembourg (available at: http://europa.eu.int/comm/environment/eia/sea-support.htm#int)

Shell International (1996) *Global Scenarios: 1995–2020.* Shell International, London

Short M., Baker M., Carter J., Jones C. and Wood C. (2003) *The Use of Appraisal in English Land Use Planning.* Paper presented at the 23rd Annual Meeting of the International Association for Impact Assessment (IAIA'03), Marrakech, Morocco

Short M., Jones C., Carter J., Baker M. and Wood C. (2004) 'Current Practice in the Strategic Environmental Assessment of Development Plans in England'. *Regional Studies*, 38 (2), 177–190

Sida (2002a) *The Country Strategies: Guidelines for Strategic Environmental and Sustainability Analysis.* Swedish International Development Agency, Stockholm

Sida (2002b) *Sector Programmes: Guidelines for the Dialogue on Strategic Environmental Assessment (SEA).* Swedish International Development Agency, Stockholm, Sweden

Siemoneit D. and Fischer T. B. (2002) *Die Strategische Umweltprüfung – das Beispiel des Regionalplans Lausitz-Spreewald in Brandenburg* (SEA for the Regional Plan Lausitz-Spreewald). UVP Report, 2001/5, pp253–258

Spenceley A. (1997) *Strategic Environmental Assessment of Tourism at Hwange National Park, Zimbabwe, Incorporating Photographic Safari Tourism and Cultural Tourism.* MSc Thesis. Centre for Environmental Technology, Imperial College for Science, Technology and Medicine, London, UK

Stationery Office (1999) *A Better Quality of Life: A Strategy for Sustainable Development for the UK.* Cm 4345, The Stationery Office, London (May 1999)

Stec S. and Casey-Lefkowitz S. (2000) *The Aarhus Convention: An Implementation Guide.* United Nations, New York and Geneva

Strachan J. (1997) *The Potential for Strategic Environmental Assessment in Samoa.* Draft MSc dissertation, London School of Economics and Political Science (September 1997)

Studsholt A. B. (2001) *Spatial Planning and Environmental Impact Assessment in Denmark.* Europejskie Centrum Proekologiczne, Warsaw, Poland

Sunter C. (1992) *The New Century: Quest for the High Road.* Human & Rouseau Tafelberg, Cape Town

TANAPA Planning Unit (1993) *Kilimanjaro National Park: General Management Plan.* Planning Unit, Tanzania National Parks, Arusha, Tanzania

TANAPA Planning Unit (1994a) *Management Zone Plan: Tarangire National Park.* Prepared for Tanzania National Parks, Arusha, Tanzania

TANAPA Planning Unit (1994b) *Management Zone Plan: Ruaha National Park.* Prepared for Tanzania National Parks, Arusha, Tanzania

Tarr P. (2003) *Strategic Environmental Assessment in Southern Africa: An Initial Overview of Current Policies and Practice*, first draft Southern African Institute of Environmental Assessment, Windhoek

ten Holder V. and Verheem R. (1996) 'Strategic EIA in the Netherlands'. In *EIA in the Netherlands – Experiences and Views Presented by and to the Commission for EIA*, EIA Commission (2003), The Hague, The Netherlands

ten Holder V. and Verheem R. (1997) 'Strategic EIA in the Netherlands – Ten Years of Experience'. *Environmental Assessment*, 5 (3), 34–36 (special issue on Strategic Environmental Assessment, September 1997)

Therivel R. (1993) 'Systems of Strategic Environmental Assessment'. *Environmental Impact Assessment*, 13 (3), 145–168

Therivel R. (1997) 'Strategic Environmental Assessment in Central Europe'. *Project Appraisal*, 12 (3), 151–160

Therivel R. (1998) 'Strategic Environmental Assessment of Development Plans in Great Britain'. *Environmental Impact Assessment Review*, 18, 39–57

Therivel R. and Partidário M. R. (eds) (1996) *The Practice of Strategic Environmental Assessment*. Earthscan, London

Therivel R., Wilson E., Thompson S., Heaney D. and Pritchard D. (1992) *Strategic Environmental Assessment*, Earthscan, London

Thissen W. A. (ed) (2000) Special issue of *Impact Assessment and Project Appraisal*, 18, 3

Thompson D. M. (ed) (1997) *Multiple Land-use: The Experience of the Ngorongoro Conservation Area, Tanzania*. World Conservation Union (IUCN), Gland, Switzerland and Cambridge, UK

Tonk J. and Verheem R. (1998) *Integrating the Environment in Strategic Decision-making – One Concept, Multiple Forms*, Paper presented at the annual meeting of the International Association for Impact Assessment, Christchurch, New Zealand

Transport Canada (2001) *SEA at Transport Canada: Policy Statement*. Transport Canada, Ottawa

UBA (2003) *Requirements of the SEA-Directive on the German Federal Transport Infrastructure Plan and on the Procedure of Transport Development Plans of the Federal States*. Federal Environmental Agency (UBA), Berlin

UK Government (1999) *Modernising Government*. White Paper [online] available at: www.archive.official-documents.co.uk/document/cm43/4310/4310-00.htm (accessed 19 July 2004)

UNCED (1992) *Agenda 21*. United Nations Conference on Environment and Development, United Nations General Assembly, New York

UNDESA (2002a) *Report of an Expert Forum on National Strategies for Sustainable Development*. Meeting held in Accra, Ghana, 7–9 November 2001, Department of Economic and Social Affairs, United Nations, New York (available at: www.johannesburgsummit.org)

UNDESA (2002b) *Guidance in Preparing a National Sustainable Development Strategy: Managing Sustainable Development in the New Millennium*. Background Paper No13, DESA/DSD/PC2/BP13, submitted by the Division for Sustainable Development, Department of Economic and Social Affairs, United Nations to the Commission on Sustainable Development acting as the preparatory committee for the World Summit on Sustainable Development, second preparatory session, 28 January – 8 February 2002, New York. (available at: www.johannesburg summit.org)

UNDP (1992) *Handbook and Guidelines for Environmental Management and Sustainable Development*. United Nations Development Programme, New York

UNDP (2000) 'UNDP Programming Manual'. Annex 2F, December 2000 [online] available at: www.undp.org/bdp/pm/chapters/progm2.pdf

UNDP (2003) *Implementing Strategic Environmental Assessment/Sustainability Impact Assessment in UNDP*. Draft paper, United Nations Development Programme, New York

UNDP/REC (2003) *Benefits of a Strategic Environmental Assessment*. Briefing paper to Ministerial Conference on Environment for Europe, Kiev

UNECE (1992) *Application of Environmental Impact Assessment Principles to Policies, Plans and Programmes*. Environmental Series No 5, United Nations Economic Commission for Europe, Geneva

UNECE (2000a) *Decision 11/9: Strategic Environmental Assessment*. Draft decision to be taken at the Second Meeting of the Parties, United Nations Economic Commission for Europe, Geneva

UNECE (2000b) *Strategic Environmental Assessment*. Note by the Secretariat, United Nations Economic Commission for Europe, Geneva

UNEP (1999) *Global Environment Outlook 2000*, United Nations Environment Programme, in association with Earthscan, London

UNEP (2000) *UNEP Environmental Impact Assessment Training Resource Manual*. United Nations Environment Programme, Geneva

UNEP (2001) *Reference Manual for the Integrated Assessment of Trade-related Policies*. United Nations Environment Programme, Geneva

UNEP (2002a) *Integrated Assessment of Trade Liberalisation and Trade-related Policies, UNEP Country Projects, Round II*. Information Bulletin, Issue No 7, Economics and Trade Branch, United Nations Environment Programme, Geneva

UNEP (2002b) *Global Environmental Outlook 3*. United Nations Environment Programme, Geneva and Earthscan, London

UNEP (2003a) *Desk Study on the Environment in the Occupied Palestinian Territories*. Report No UNEP/GC.22/INF/31 presented to the 22nd session of the United Nations Environment Programme Governing Council and the Global Ministerial Forum, 3–7 February 2003, Nairobi

UNEP (2003b) *UNEP Initiative on Capacity Building for Integrated Assessment and Planning for Sustainable Development*. Briefing paper distributed by the Economics and Trade Unit, United Nations Environment Programme, Geneva

UNEP (2004) *Integrated Assessment and Planning for Sustainable Development: Guidelines for Pilot Projects*. United Nations Environment Programme, Economics and Trade Branch, Geneva

UNEP/GRID-Arendal (1998) *Cookbook: State of the Environment Reporting on the Internet*. United Nations Environment Programme/Global Resource Information Database, Arendal, Norway

UNEP/RIVM (2003) *Four Scenarios for Europe, Based on UNEP's Third Global Environmental Outlook*. United Nations Environment Programme, Nairobi and National Institute of Public Health and the Environment (RIVM), Bilthoven, The Netherlands

UNGA (2001) *Report of the Secretary General: Road Map towards the Implementation of the United Nations Millennium Declaration*. A/56/326, United Nations General Assembly, New York (6 September 2001)

USAID (1995) *Guidelines for Strategic Plans*. US Agency for International Development, Washington DC

UVP (2003) *Report 2/2003*. Special Edition on SEA in Germany, UVP Verein, Hamm (main German language EA journal)

Valve H. and Hildén M. (1994) *Strategic Decisions and Environmental Assessment – The Case of Finnish Agricultural Policy*. Paper tabled at the SEA workshop, The Hague, The Netherlands, 15–16 December 1994, organized by the Dutch Ministry of Housing, Spatial Planning and the Environment van Dreumel M. (2003) 'Netherlands' Experience with the Environmental Test'. In *SEA Systems and Applications to Policy and Legislation*, proceedings of the SEA workshop, held in The Hague (2002), Ministry of Housing, Spatial Planning and the Environment, The Hague, The Netherlands

Veart S. (1997) *Emerging Trends, Issues and some Innovative Approaches* (Challenges for EIA – New Zealand Status Report). Report of the Tripartite Workshop, Canberra, 21–24 March 1994, Department of Environment, Sport and the Territories, for the International Study of the Effectiveness of Environmental Assessment, Canberra

Verheem R. (2003) 'The National Waste Management Plan'. In *Effective SEA System and Case Studies*, Mitsubishi Research Institute for the Ministry of the Environment, Government of Japan, Tokyo, pp68–79 (Japanese version first published in 2002)

Verheem R. (2004) 'EIA and SEA in The Netherlands: Perspective of the EIA Commission'. Briefing paper in CEAA (ed) *Status of Progress and Emerging Challenges in EIA and SEA: Ten Years after the Quebec Summit*, proceedings of the 8th Intergovernmental Policy Forum on Environmental Assessment, 25 April 2004, Vancouver BC, Canadian Environmental Assessment Agency, Ottawa

Verheem R. A. A. and Tonk J. A. M. N. (1998) *Present Status of SEA in The Netherlands*. Background paper for the International Workshop on SEA, Japan (available at: http://assess.eic.or.jp/sea/ws/wssiryou/s-48.pdf)

Verheem R. and Tonk J. (2000) 'Strategic Environmental Assessment: One Concept, Multiple Forms'. *Impact Assessment and Project Appraisal*, 18 (3), 177–182

von Ritter K. and Tsirkunov V. (2002) *How Well is Environmental Assessment Doing in Russia?* Pilot study for the World Bank, Washington DC

VROM (1989) *National Environmental Policy Plan*. Department for Information and International Relations, Ministry of Housing, Spatial Planning and the Environment (VROM), The Hague, The Netherlands

VROM (1993) *National Planning for Sustainable Development: The Netherlands Experience*. Doc No VROM 93523/h/10-93, Directorate for Strategic Planning, Ministry of Housing, Spatial Planning and the Environment (VROM), The Hague, The Netherlands

VROM (1996) *Environmental Test*. VROM 14349/175, Ministry of Housing, Spatial Planning and the Environment (VROM), The Hague, The Netherlands (Dutch version first issued in 1995)

VROM (2001) *Where There's a Will There's a World. Working on Sustainability. 4th National Environmental Policy Plan. English Summary*. Directorate for Strategic Planning, Ministry of Housing, Spatial Planning and the Environment (VROM), The Hague, The Netherlands

Walmsley Environmental Consultants (2001) *The Sperrgebiet Land Use Plan*. Report No W309, Volumes 1–3, unpublished report for the Ministry of Environment and Tourism, the Ministry of Lands Resettlement and Rehabilitation and the Ministry of Mines and Energy, Windhoek, Namibia

Wang H., Li W., Li Z. and Weng S. (1997) 'Study on Regional Strategic Environmental Impact Assessment: Coal and Electricity Resource Strategy in Shanxi Province'. *Energy Environ*, 14 (2), 1–4

Wang Tao (2002) *Sustainability and Environmental Impact Assessment Legislations in China*. Presentation by the Vice Chairman of the Environmental and Resources Protection Committee, National People's Congress of China, at the Conference on Reshaping Environmental Assessment Tools for Sustainability, 9 December 2002, Chinese University of Hong Kong

Ward M., Wilkie R. and Dalziel A. (2002) *Strategic Environmental Assessment in New Zealand: Past Experience and Future Opportunities.* Paper to The Hague workshop on SEA (also included in: *SEA Systems with Particular Application to Policy and Legal Acts* (2003), report updating publication No 54 and incorporating the proceedings of The Hague workshop on SEA, Ministry of Housing, Spatial Planning and the Environment, The Hague, The Netherlands)

Wathern P. (ed) (1988) *Environmental Impact Assessment: Theory and Practice.* Unwin Hyman, London

WCD (2000) *Dams and Development: A New Framework for Decision-making.* The Report of the World Commission on Dams. Earthscan, London

WCED (1987) *Our Common Future.* Report of the World Commission on Environment and Development, Oxford University Press, Oxford, UK

Weik T. (2004) 'Schlanker Plan mit Integrierter Umweltprüfung – Das Beispiel Westpfalz'. In: UVP + SUP in der Planungspraxis, *UVP Spezial* 19

Wende W., Hanusch M., Gassner E., Guennewig D., Koeppel J., Lambrecht H., Langenheld A., Peters W. and Roethke-Habeck P. (2004) 'Requirements of the SEA Directive and the German Federal Transport Infrastructure Plan'. *European Environment* 14 (2) (special issue on Progress towards Meeting the Requirements of the European SEA Directive, edited by T.B. Fischer)

Wiseman K. (1997) *Environmental Assessment and Planning in South Africa: The SEA Connection.* Paper presented to the 17th Annual Meeting of the International Association for Impact Assessment, New Orleans, USA

Wood C. (1996) 'EIA in The Netherlands: A Comparative Assessment'. In *Environmental Impact Assessment: Experiences and Views Presented by and to the Commission for EIA,* Netherlands Commission for Environmental Impact Assessment, Utrecht, pp3–16

Wood C. (1997) 'SEA – The Way Forward'. *Environmental Assessment,* 5 (3), 5 (special issue on Strategic Environmental Assessment, September 1997)

Wood C. (1999) 'Comparative Evaluation of EIA Systems'. In Petts J. (ed) *Handbook of Environmental Impact Assessment,* Volume 2, Blackwell Scientific Ltd, Oxford, UK, pp10–34

Wood C. and Djeddour M. (1989) *Environmental Assessment of Policies, Plans and Programmes.* Interim report to the Commission of the European Communities, EIA Centre, University of Manchester, UK (final report submitted 1990, Contract No B6617-571-572-89)

Wood C. and Djeddour M. (1990) *Environmental Assessment of Policies, Plans and Programmes.* Paper presented at IAIA'90, conference of the International Association for Impact Assessment, Ecole Polytechnique Federale de Lausanne (251–253)

Wood C. and Djeddour M. (1992) 'Strategic Environmental Assessment: EA of Policies, Plans and Programmes'. *Impact Assessment Bulletin,* 10 (1), 3–22

World Bank (1993) 'Sectoral Environmental Assessment'. *Environmental Assessment Sourcebook Update,* Environment Department, the World Bank, Washington DC (October 1993)

World Bank (1996a) *The Impact of Environmental Assessment: Second Environmental Assessment Review.* Environment Department, the World Bank, Washington DC

World Bank (1996b) 'Regional Environmental Assessment'. *Environmental Assessment Sourcebook Update,* No 15, Environment Department, the World Bank, Washington DC

World Bank (1999) *Environmental Matters*. World Bank, Washington, DC

World Bank (2000) *Environmental Matters*, World Bank, Washington DC

World Bank (2001) *Making Sustainable Commitments: An Environmental Strategy for the World Bank*. The World Bank, Washington DC

World Bank (2002a) *A User's Guide to Poverty and Social Impact Analysis*. Draft for comment prepared by the Poverty Reduction Group and Social Development Department, the World Bank, Washington DC (www.worldbank.org/poverty)

World Bank (2002b) *Making Sustainable Commitments: An Environment Strategy for the World Bank – Summary*. Complete volume on CD-ROM, Environment Department, the World Bank, Washington DC

World Bank (2002c) *Package of 'Safeguard Policies' – Ten Environmental, Social and Legal Policies and Procedures*. The World Bank, Washington DC (see: http://wbln0018.worldbank.org/essd/essd.nsf/Safeguard/Homepage)

World Bank (2002d) 'New Information Disclosure Policy (Effective January 1, 2002) Facilitates Implementation of the Safeguard Policies' [online] available at: www1.worldbank.org/operations/disclosure/

World Bank (2002e) *Environmental Matters*. World Bank, Washington, DC

World Bank (2003) *Country Environmental Analysis (CEA): Briefing Book*. Environment Department, the World Bank, Washington DC

WRI/IIED/IUCN (1996) *World Directory of Country Environment Studies*. World Resources Institute (WRI), International Institute for Environment and Development (IIED), and World Conservation Union (IUCN), WRI, Washington DC

WRI/IIED/IUCN (2000) *The World Resources Report*. World Resources Institute, Washington, DC

WSAtkins (2002) *SEA of Tanzania's Draft Transport Policy*. Report to Department for International Development, London, UK

Index